D1060093

Texas

Algebra 2

TIMOTHY D. KANOLD

EDWARD B. BURGER

JULI K. DIXON

MATTHEW R. LARSON

STEVEN J. LEINWAND

© Houghton Mifflin Harcourt Publishing Company • Cover/Title Page Image Credits: (Capitol Building in Austin) ©LMPphoto/Shutterstock; (Dallas) ©John Walker/Shutterstock.

Printed in the U.S.A.

ISBN 978-0-544-36265-9

1 2 3 4 5 6 7 8 9 10   0918   22 21 20 19 18 17 16 15 14

4500484694   A B C D E F G

Authors

Timothy D. Kanold, Ph.D., is an award-winning international educator, author, and consultant. He is a former superintendent and director of mathematics and science at Adlai E. Stevenson High School District 125 in Lincolnshire, Illinois. He is a past president of the National Council of Supervisors of Mathematics (NCSM) and the Council for the Presidential Awardees of Mathematics (CPAM). He  has served on several writing and leadership commissions for NCTM during the past decade. He presents motivational professional development seminars with a focus on developing professional learning communities (PLC's) to improve the teaching, assessing, and learning of students. He has recently authored nationally recognized articles, books, and textbooks for mathematics education and school leadership, including *What Every Principal Needs to Know about the Teaching and Learning of Mathematics.*

Edward B. Burger, Ph.D., is the President of Southwestern University, a former Francis Christopher Oakley Third Century Professor of Mathematics at Williams College, and a former vice provost at Baylor University. He has authored or coauthored more than sixty-five articles, books, and video series; delivered over five hundred addresses and workshops throughout the world; and made more than fifty radio and  television appearances. He is a Fellow of the American Mathematical Society as well as having earned many national honors, including the Robert Foster Cherry Award for Great Teaching in 2010. In 2012, Microsoft Education named him a "Global Hero in Education."

Juli K. Dixon, Ph.D., is a Professor of Mathematics Education at the University of Central Florida. She has taught mathematics in urban schools at the elementary, middle, secondary, and post-secondary levels. She is an active researcher and speaker with numerous publications and conference presentations. Key areas of focus are deepening teachers' content knowledge and communicating and justifying  mathematical ideas. She is a past chair of the NCTM Student Explorations in Mathematics Editorial Panel and member of the Board of Directors for the Association of Mathematics Teacher Educators.

Matthew R. Larson, Ph.D., is the K-12 mathematics curriculum specialist for the Lincoln Public Schools and served on the Board of Directors for the National Council of Teachers of Mathematics from 2010 to 2013. He is a past chair of NCTM's Research Committee and was a member of NCTM's Task Force on Linking Research and Practice. He is the author of several books on implementing the Common Core Standards for Mathematics. He has taught mathematics at the secondary and college levels and held an appointment as an honorary visiting associate professor at Teachers College, Columbia University.

Steven J. Leinwand is a Principal Research Analyst at the American Institutes for Research (AIR) in Washington, D.C., and has over 30 years in leadership positions in mathematics education. He is past president of the National Council of Supervisors of Mathematics and served on the NCTM Board of Directors. He is the author of numerous articles, books, and textbooks and has made countless presentations with topics including student achievement, reasoning, effective assessment, and successful implementation of standards.

Consulting Author

Robert Kaplinsky
Teacher Specialist, Mathematics
Downey Unified School District
Downey, California

STEM Consultants
Science, Technology, Engineering, and Mathematics

Michael A. DiSpezio
Global Educator
North Falmouth, Massachusetts

Michael R. Heithaus
Executive Director, School of Environment, Arts,
and Society
Professor, Department of Biological Sciences
Florida International University
North Miami, Florida

Texas Reviewers

Ashley Alford
Flower Mound High School
Flower Mound, Texas

Sydney Bentz
Flower Mound High School
Flower Mound, Texas

David Surdovel
Manor ISD
Manor, Texas

Matthew J. Waldmann, M.S.,
Educator
Arlington High School
Arlington, Texas

Megan A. Uken
Flower Mound High School
Flower Mound, Texas

Functions

MODULE 1

Analyzing Functions

TEKS

MODULE 2

Absolute Value Functions, Equations, and Inequalities

TEKS

UNIT 2

Volume 1

Quadratic Functions, Equations, and Relations

MODULE 3 Quadratic Functions

MODULE 4 Quadratic Equations

MODULE 5
Quadratic Relations and Systems of Equations and Inequalities

TEKS

Polynomial Functions, Expressions, and Equations

MODULE 6 ## Polynomial Functions

MODULE 7 ## Polynomials

MODULE 8 — Polynomial Equations

TEKS

© Houghton Mifflin Harcourt Publishing Company • Image Credit: ©Matt Jeppson/Shutterstock

UNIT 4
Volume 2

Rational Functions, Expressions, and Equations

MODULE 9 · Rational Functions

MODULE 10 · Rational Expressions and Equations

Radical Functions, Expressions, and Equations

MODULE 11 Radical Functions

TEKS

MODULE 12 Radical Expressions and Equations

TEKS

UNIT 6

Exponential and Logarithmic Functions and Equations

Volume 2

MODULE 13 — Exponential Functions

TEKS

MODULE 14 — Modeling with Exponential and Other Functions

TEKS

MODULE **15** Logarithmic Functions

MODULE **16** Logarithmic Properties and Exponential and Logarithmic Equations

Correlation for Algebra 2

Standard	Descriptor	Lesson Citations
A2.1 Mathematical process standards. The student uses mathematical processes to acquire and demonstrate mathematical understanding. The student is expected to:		*The process standards are integrated throughout the book. See, for example, the citations below.*
A2.1.A	apply mathematics to problems arising in everyday life, society, and the workplace;	SE: 2.1, 2.3, 3.1, 5.1, 13.1
A2.1.B	use a problem-solving model that incorporates analyzing given information, formulating a plan or strategy, determining a solution, justifying the solution, and evaluating the problem-solving process and the reasonableness of the solution;	SE: 2.1, 2.3, 5.4, 8.1, 10.3, 11.3
A2.1.C	select tools, including real objects, manipulatives, paper and pencil, and technology as appropriate, and techniques, including mental math, estimation, and number sense as appropriate, to solve problems;	SE: 2.1, 3.1, 8.1, 11.1, 11.3, 13.2
A2.1.D	communicate mathematical ideas, reasoning, and their implications using multiple representations, including symbols, diagrams, graphs, and language as appropriate;	SE: 2.2, 5.1, 8.2, 11.2, 11.3, 13.2
A2.1.E	create and use representations to organize, record, and communicate mathematical ideas;	SE: 5.4, 11.1, 11.2, 13.3
A2.1.F	analyze mathematical relationships to connect and communicate mathematical ideas; and	SE: 2.1, 2.3, 3.1, 5.1, 8.1, 11.1, 13.1
A2.1.G	display, explain, or justify mathematical ideas and arguments using precise mathematical language in written or oral communication.	SE: 2.2, 3.2, 5.1, 8.1, 11.1, 11.4, 13.1

Standard	Descriptor	Taught	Reinforced
A2.2 Attributes of functions and their inverses. The student applies mathematical processes to understand that functions have distinct key attributes and understand the relationship between a function and its inverse. The student is expected to:			
A2.2.A	graph the functions $f(x) = \sqrt{\sqrt{x}}$, $f(x) = 1/x$, $f(x) = x^3$, $f(x) = \sqrt[3]{x}$, $f(x) = b^x$, $f(x) = |x|$, and $f(x) = \log_b(x)$ where b is 2, 10, and e, and, when applicable, analyze the key attributes such as domain, range, intercepts, symmetries, asymptotic behavior, and maximum and minimum given an interval;	SE: 2.1, 6.1, 9.2, 11.2, 11.4, 13.2, 13.4, 15.1, 15.2	SE: 2.1, 6.1, 9.2, 11.2, 13.2, 15.1, 15.2
A2.2.B	graph and write the inverse of a function using notation such as $f^{-1}(x)$;	SE: 1.4, 11.1, 15.1	SE: 1.4, 11.1, 15.1
A2.2.C	describe and analyze the relationship between a function and its inverse (quadratic and square root, logarithmic and exponential), including the restriction(s) on domain, which will restrict its range; and	SE: 11.1, 11.3, 15.1	SE: 11.1, 11.3, 15.1
A2.2.D	use the composition of two functions, including the necessary restrictions on the domain, to determine if the functions are inverses of each other.	SE: 1.4, 11.1	SE: 1.4, 11.1
A2.3 Systems of equations and inequalities. The student applies mathematical processes to formulate systems of equations and inequalities, use a variety of methods to solve, and analyze reasonableness of solutions. The student is expected to:			
A2.3.A	formulate systems of equations, including systems consisting of three linear equations in three variables and systems consisting of two equations, the first linear and the second quadratic;	SE: 5.2, 5.3	SE: 5.2, 5.3
A2.3.B	solve systems of three linear equations in three variables by using Gaussian elimination, technology with matrices, and substitution;	SE: 5.3	SE: 5.3
A2.3.C	solve, algebraically, systems of two equations in two variables consisting of a linear equation and a quadratic equation;	SE: 5.2	SE: 5.2
A2.3.D	determine the reasonableness of solutions to systems of a linear equation and a quadratic equation in two variables;	SE: 5.2	SE: 5.2
A2.3.E	formulate systems of at least two linear inequalities in two variables;	SE: 5.4	SE: 5.4
A2.3.F	solve systems of two or more linear inequalities in two variables; and	SE: 5.4	SE: 5.4
A2.3.G	determine possible solutions in the solution set of systems of two or more linear inequalities in two variables.	SE: 5.4	SE: 5.4

Standard	Descriptor	Taught	Reinforced
A2.4 Quadratic and square root functions, equations, and inequalities. The student applies the mathematical process standards to formulate statistical relationships and evaluate their reasonableness based on real-world data. The student is expected to:			
A2.4.A	write the quadratic function given three specified points in the plane;	SE: 5.3	SE: 5.3
A2.4.B	write the equation of a parabola using given attributes, including vertex, focus, directrix, axis of symmetry, and direction of opening;	SE: 3.2, 5.1	SE: 3.2, 5.1
A2.4.C	determine the effect on the graph of $f(x) = \sqrt{x}$ when $f(x)$ is replaced by $af(x)$, $f(x) + d$, $f(bx)$, and $f(x - c)$ for specific positive and negative values of a, b, c, and d;	SE: 11.2	SE: 11.2
A2.4.D	transform a quadratic function $f(x) = ax^2 + bx + c$ to the form $f(x) = a(x - h)^2 + k$ to identify the different attributes of $f(x)$;	SE: 3.1	SE: 3.1
A2.4.E	formulate quadratic and square root equations using technology given a table of data;	SE: 3.3, 11.3	SE: 3.3, 11.3
A2.4.F	solve quadratic and square root equations;	SE: 4.1, 4.3, 12.3	SE: 4.1, 4.3, 12.3
A2.4.G	identify extraneous solutions of square root equations; and	SE: 12.3	SE: 12.3
A2.4.H	solve quadratic inequalities.	SE: 4.4	SE: 4.4
A2.5 Exponential and logarithmic functions and equations. The student applies mathematical processes to understand that exponential and logarithmic functions can be used to model situations and solve problems. The student is expected to:			
A2.5.A	determine the effects on the key attributes on the graphs of $f(x) = b^x$ and $f(x) = \log_b(x)$ where b is 2, 10, and e when $f(x)$ is replaced by $af(x)$, $f(x) + d$, and $f(x - c)$ for specific positive and negative real values of a, c, and d;	SE: 13.2, 13.4, 15.2	SE: 13.2, 13.4, 15.2
A2.5.B	formulate exponential and logarithmic equations that model real-world situations, including exponential relationships written in recursive notation;	SE: 13.1, 13.2, 13.3, 15.1, 15.2, 16.1	SE: 13.1, 13.2, 13.3, 15.1, 15.2, 16.1
A2.5.C	rewrite exponential equations as their corresponding logarithmic equations and logarithmic equations as their corresponding exponential equations;	SE: 15.1, 16.1	SE: 15.1, 16.1
A2.5.D	solve exponential equations of the form $y = ab^x$ where a is a nonzero real number and b is greater than zero and not equal to one and single logarithmic equations having real solutions; and	SE: 13.1, 13.2, 13.3, 13.4, 16.3	SE: 13.1, 13.2, 13.3, 13.4, 16.3
A2.5.E	determine the reasonableness of a solution to a logarithmic equation.	SE: 16.3	SE: 16.3

Standard	Descriptor	Taught	Reinforced
A2.6 Cubic, cube root, absolute value and rational functions, equations, and inequalities. The student applies mathematical processes to understand that cubic, cube root, absolute value and rational functions, equations, and inequalities can be used to model situations, solve problems, and make predictions. The student is expected to:			
A2.6.A	analyze the effect on the graphs of $f(x) = x^3$ and $f(x) = \sqrt[3]{x}$ when $f(x)$ is replaced by $af(x)$, $f(bx)$, $f(x - c)$, and $f(x) + d$ for specific positive and negative real values of a, b, c, and d;	SE: 6.1, 11.4	SE: 6.1, 11.4
A2.6.B	solve cube root equations that have real roots;	SE: 12.3	SE: 12.3
A2.6.C	analyze the effect on the graphs of $f(x) = |x|$ when $f(x)$ is replaced by $af(x)$, $f(bx)$, $f(x - c)$, and $f(x) + d$ for specific positive and negative real values of a, b, c, and d;	SE: 2.1	SE: 2.1
A2.6.D	formulate absolute value linear equations;	SE: 2.2	SE: 2.2
A2.6.E	solve absolute value linear equations;	SE: 2.2	SE: 2.2
A2.6.F	solve absolute value linear inequalities;	SE: 2.3	SE: 2.3
A2.6.G	analyze the effect on the graphs of $f(x) = 1/x$ when $f(x)$ is replaced by $af(x)$, $f(bx)$, $f(x - c)$, and $f(x) + d$ for specific positive and negative real values of a, b, c, and d;	SE: 9.2	SE: 9.2
A2.6.H	formulate rational equations that model real-world situations;	SE: 10.3	SE: 10.3
A2.6.I	solve rational equations that have real solutions;	SE: 10.3	SE: 10.3
A2.6.J	determine the reasonableness of a solution to a rational equation;	SE: 10.3	SE: 10.3
A2.6.K	determine the asymptotic restrictions on the domain of a rational function and represent domain and range using interval notation, inequalities, and set notation; and	SE: 9.2, 9.3	SE: 9.2, 9.3
A2.6.L	formulate and solve equations involving inverse variation.	SE: 9.1	SE: 9.1

Texas English Language Proficiency Standards

Standard	Descriptor	Taught	Reinforced
A2.7 Number and algebraic methods. The student applies mathematical processes to simplify and perform operations on expressions and to solve equations. The student is expected to:			
A2.7.A	add, subtract, and multiply complex numbers;	SE: 4.2	SE: 4.2
A2.7.B	add, subtract, and multiply polynomials;	SE: 7.1, 7.2, 7.4, 8.1, 8.2	SE: 7.1, 7.2, 7.4, 8.1, 8.2
A2.7.C	determine the quotient of a polynomial of degree three and of degree four when divided by a polynomial of degree one and of degree two;	SE: 7.4	SE: 7.4
A2.7.D	determine the linear factors of a polynomial function of degree three and of degree four using algebraic methods;	SE: 7.4, 8.1, 8.2	SE: 7.4, 8.1, 8.2
A2.7.E	determine linear and quadratic factors of a polynomial expression of degree three and of degree four, including factoring the sum and difference of two cubes and factoring by grouping;	SE: 7.3, 8.2	SE: 7.3, 8.2
A2.7.F	determine the sum, difference, product, and quotient of rational expressions with integral exponents of degree one and of degree two;	SE: 10.1, 10.2	SE: 10.1, 10.2
A2.7.G	rewrite radical expressions that contain variables to equivalent forms;	SE: 12.1, 12.2	SE: 12.1, 12.2
A2.7.H	solve equations involving rational exponents; and	SE: 12.3	SE: 12.3
A2.7.I	write the domain and range of a function in interval notation, inequalities, and set notation.	SE: 1.1, 6.2, 9.2, 9.3, 11.1, 11.2, 11.3, 13.4, 15.2	SE: 1.1, 6.2, 9.2, 9.3, 11.1, 11.2, 11.3, 13.4, 15.2
A2.8 Data. The student applies mathematical processes to analyze data, select appropriate models, write corresponding functions, and make predictions. The student is expected to:			
A2.8.A	analyze data to select the appropriate model from among linear, quadratic, and exponential models;	SE: 14.2	SE: 14.2
A2.8.B	use regression methods available through technology to write a linear function, a quadratic function, and an exponential function from a given set of data; and	SE: 1.2, 3.3, 14.1, 14.2	SE: 1.2, 3.3, 14.1, 14.2
A2.8.C	predict and make decisions and critical judgments from a given set of data using linear, quadratic, and exponential models.	SE: 1.2, 3.3, 14.1, 14.2	SE: 1.2, 3.3, 14.1, 14.2

Texas English Language Proficiency Standards (ELPS)

HMH Texas Algebra 2 supports English language learners at all proficiency levels.

Beginning – Students at a Beginning level are supported by Success for Every Learner and modified Practice A worksheet in *Differentiated Instruction* and the *Multilingual Glossary*.

Intermediate – Students at the Intermediate level may also use Reading Strategies in *Differentiated Instruction*.

Advanced and Advanced High – Students at the Advanced and Advanced High levels will be successful as the *Student Edition* promotes vocabulary development through visual and context clues.

ELPS	Citations
c.1.A use prior knowledge and experiences to understand meanings in English	This standard is met in: Reading Startup in each unit—Examples: 2, 84, 222
c.1.D speak using learning strategies such as requesting assistance, employing non-verbal cues, and using synonyms and circumlocution (conveying ideas by defining or describing when exact English words are not known)	This standard is met in: Discussion questions in most lessons—Examples: 6, 14, 27, 36, 55
c.2.C learn new language structures, expressions, and basic and academic vocabulary heard during classroom instruction and interactions	This standard is met in: Discussion questions in most lessons—Examples: 6, 14, 27, 36, 55 Reflect questions in most lessons—Examples: 6, 7, 10, 15, 17, 24
c.2.D monitor understanding of spoken language during classroom instruction and interactions and seek clarification as needed	This standard is met in: Discussion questions in most lessons—Examples: 6, 14, 27, 36, 55 Reflect questions in most lessons—Examples: 6, 7, 10, 15, 17, 24
c.2.E use visual, contextual, and linguistic support to enhance and confirm understanding of increasingly complex and elaborated spoken language	This standard is met in: Visualize Vocabulary in each unit—Examples: 2, 84, 222
c.2.I demonstrate listening comprehension of increasingly complex spoken English by following directions, retelling or summarizing spoken messages, responding to questions and requests, collaborating with peers, and taking notes commensurate with content and grade-level needs	This standard is met in: Discussion questions in most lessons—Examples: 6, 14, 27, 36, 55 Reflect questions in most lessons— Examples: 6, 7, 10, 15, 17, 24

ELPS	Citations
c.3.B expand and internalize initial English vocabulary by learning and using high-frequency English words necessary for identifying and describing people, places, and objects, by retelling simple stories and basic information represented or supported by pictures, and by learning and using routine language needed for classroom communication	This standard is met in: Active Reading in each unit—Examples: 2, 84, 222 Reflect questions in most lessons—Examples: 6, 7, 10, 15, 17, 24 Explore Activities in many lessons—Examples: 13, 23, 26, 35, 67, 205
c.3.C speak using a variety of grammatical structures, sentence lengths, sentence types, and connecting words with increasing accuracy and ease as more English is acquired	This standard is met in: Discussion questions in most lessons—Examples: 6, 14, 27, 36, 55
c.3.D speak using grade-level content area vocabulary in context to internalize new English words and build academic language proficiency	This standard is met in: Reading Startup in each unit—Examples: 2, 84, 222
c.3.E share information in cooperative learning interactions	This standard is met in: Discussion questions in most lessons—Examples: 6, 14, 27, 36, 55 Explore Activities in many lessons—Examples: 13, 23, 26, 35, 67, 205
c.3.F ask and give information ranging from using a very limited bank of high-frequency, high-need, concrete vocabulary, including key words and expressions needed for basic communication in academic and social contexts, to using abstract and content-based vocabulary during extended speaking assignments	This standard is met in: Discussion questions in most lessons—Examples: 6, 14, 27, 36, 55 Explore Activities in many lessons—Examples: 13, 23, 26, 35, 67, 205
c.3.H narrate, describe, and explain with increasing specificity and detail as more English is acquired	This standard is met in: Discussion questions in most lessons—Examples: 6, 14, 27, 36, 55 Reflect questions in most lessons—Examples: 6, 7, 10, 15, 17, 24 Elaborate questions in most lessons—Examples: 10, 17, 31, 39, 55 Evaluate exercises in most lessons—Examples: 10, 18, 31, 40, 55
C.4.C develop basic sight vocabulary, derive meaning of environmental print, and comprehend English vocabulary and language structures used routinely in written classroom materials	This standard is met in: Reading Startup in each unit—Examples: 2, 84, 222 Highlighted vocabulary at point of use in instruction: 5, 13, 23, 26, 35

ELPS	Citations
c.4.D use prereading supports such as graphic organizers, illustrations, and pretaught topic-related vocabulary and other prereading activities to enhance comprehension of written text	This standard is met in: Reading Startup in each unit—Examples: 2, 84, 222
c.4.F use visual and contextual support and support from peers and teachers to read grade-appropriate content area text, enhance and confirm understanding, and develop vocabulary, grasp of language structures, and background knowledge needed to comprehend increasingly challenging language	This standard is met through photographs, illustrations, and diagrams throughout instruction—Examples: 9, 20, 21, 38, 54, 62
c.4.G demonstrate comprehension of increasingly complex English by participating in shared reading, retelling or summarizing material, responding to questions, and taking notes commensurate with content area and grade level needs	This standard is met in: Discussion questions in most lessons—Examples: 6, 14, 27, 36, 55 Reflect questions in most lessons—Examples: 6, 7, 10, 15, 17, 24 Essential Question Check-In exercises in each lesson—Examples: 10, 17, 31, 39, 55 H.O.T. exercises in each lesson—Examples: 12, 21, 33, 42, 57

Texas English Language Proficiency Standards

Succeeding with HMH Texas Algebra 2

HMH Texas Algebra 2 is built on the 5E instructional model--Engage, Explore, Explain, Elaborate, Evaluate--to develop strong conceptual understanding and mastery of TEKS.

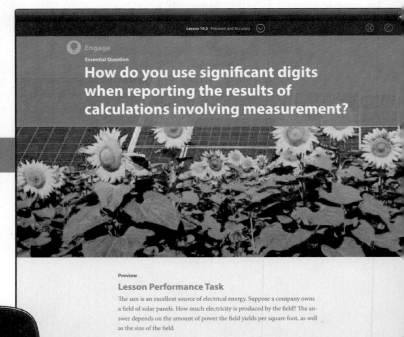

ENGAGE

Preview the Lesson Performance Task in the Interactive Student Edition.

Engage

Essential Question

How do you use significant digits when reporting the results of calculations involving measurement?

Preview

Lesson Performance Task

The sun is an excellent source of electrical energy. Suppose a company owns a field of solar panels. How much electricity is produced by the field? The answer depends on the amount of power the field yields per square foot, as well as the size of the field.

Comparing Precision of Measurements

Eric is a technician in a pharmaceutical lab. Every week, he needs to test the scales in the lab to make sure that they are. He uses a that is exactly 12.000 g and gets the following results:

Scale	Mass
Scale 1	12.03 g
Scale 2	12.029 g
Scale 3	11.98 g

Definition of Precision: The level of detail of a, determined by **the smallest** unit or fraction of a unit that can be reasonably measured.

Definition of Accuracy: The closeness of a given of value to the actual measurement or value.

Which measuring tool is the most precise?

Which scale is the most accurate?

Reflect

EXPLORE

Explore and interact with new concepts to develop a deeper understanding of mathematics in your book and the Interactive Student Edition.

Scan the QR code to access engaging videos, activities, and more in the Resource Locker for each lesson.

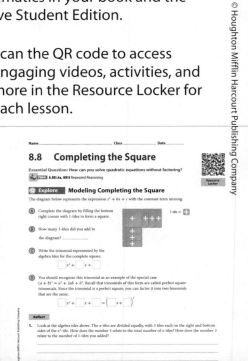

Name _____ Class _____ Date _____

8.8 Completing the Square

Essential Question: How can you solve quadratic equations without factoring?

A.REI.4a, MP.8 Repeated Reasoning

Explore   Modeling Completing the Square

The diagram below represents the expression $x^2 + 6x + c$ with the constant term missing.

Ⓐ Complete the diagram by filling the bottom right corner with 1-tiles to form a square.

Ⓑ How many 1-tiles did you add to the diagram? _____

Ⓒ Write the trinomial represented by the algebra tiles for the complete square.

$$x^2 + \boxed{}x + \boxed{}$$

Ⓓ You should recognize this trinomial as an example of the special case $(a + b)^2 = a^2 + 2ab + b^2$. Recall that trinomials of this form are called perfect square trinomials. Since the trinomial is a perfect square, you can factor it into two binomials that are the same.

$$x^2 + \boxed{}x + \boxed{} = \left(x + \boxed{}\right)^2$$

Reflect

1. Look at the algebra tiles above. The x-tiles are divided equally, with 3 tiles each on the right and bottom sides of the x^2-tile. How does the number 3 relate to the total number of x-tiles? How does the number 3 relate to the number of 1-tiles you added?

Explain Concept 2

Determining Precision

As you have seen, measurements are given to a certain precision. Therefore, the value reported does not necessarily represent the actual value of the measurement. For example, a measurement of 5 centimeters, which is given to the nearest whole unit, can actually range from 0.5 units below the reported value, 4.5 centimeters, up to, but not including, 0.5 units above it, 5.5 centimeters. The actual length, l, is within a range of possible values: centimeters. Similarly, a length given to the nearest tenth can actually range from 0.05 units below the reported value up to, but not including, 0.05 units above it. So a length reported as 4.5 cm could actually be as low as 4.45 cm or as high as nearly 4.55 cm.

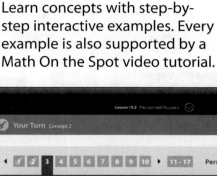

EXPLAIN

Learn concepts with step-by-step interactive examples. Every example is also supported by a Math On the Spot video tutorial.

Your Turn Concept 2

| 1 | 2 | **3** | 4 | 5 | 6 | 7 | 8 | 9 | 10 | ▶ | **11 – 17** | | Personal Math Trainer |

Question 3 of 17   View Step by Step   ▶ Video Tutor   Textbook   X² Animated Math

Solve the quadratic equation by factoring.

$7x + 44x = 7x - 10$

$x = \boxed{}, \boxed{}$

Check

Save & Close   ❓ ⚠   Turn It In

‹ 🔧 Explain   Elaborate ›

Check your understanding of new concepts and skills with Your Turn exercises in your book or online with Personal Math Trainer.

Personal Math Trainer

Explain 1 Completing the Square with Expressions

Finding the value of c needed to make an expression such as $x^2 + 6x + c$ into a perfect square trinomial is called **completing the square**.

Using algebra tiles, half of the x-tiles are placed along the right and bottom sides of the x^2-tile. The number of 1-tiles added is the square of the number of x-tiles on either side of the x^2-tile.

To complete the square for the expression $x^2 + bx + c$, replace c with $\left(\frac{b}{2}\right)^2$. The perfect square trinomial is $x^2 + bx + \left(\frac{b}{2}\right)^2$ and factors as $\left(x + \frac{b}{2}\right)^2$.

Example 1 Complete the square to form a perfect trinomial.
Then factor the trinomial.

Ⓐ $x^2 + 12x + c$

Identify b. $b = 12$

Find c. $c = \left(\frac{b}{2}\right)^2 = \left(\frac{12}{2}\right)^2 = 36$

Write the trinomial. $x^2 + 12x + 36$

Factor the trinomial. $x^2 + 12x + 36 = (x + 6)^2$

Ⓑ $z^2 - 26z + c$

Identify b. $b = \boxed{}$

Find c. $c = \left(\frac{b}{2}\right)^2 = \left(\dfrac{\boxed{}}{2}\right)^2 = \boxed{}$

Write the trinomial. $z^2 + \boxed{}z + \boxed{}\left(\boxed{}\right)^2$

Factor the trinomial. $z^2 + \boxed{}z + \boxed{} = \boxed{}$

Reflect

Complete the square to form a perfect square trinomial. Then factor the trinomial.

3. $a^2 + 18a + \boxed{}$ 4. $p^2 - 5p + \boxed{}$

Your Turn

5.   In Part A, b is positive and in Part B, b is negative. Does this affect the sign of c? Why or why not?

ELABORATE

Show your understanding and reasoning with Reflect and Elaborate questions.

Your Turn

10.   The calculator screen shows the graph of $f(x) = 4x^2 - 8x - 5$. Explain how the graph supports the solution in Part B.

Elaborate

11.   When solving a quadratic equation in the form $x^2 + bx + c = 0$ by completing the square, what is the purpose of moving the constant to the other side of the equation?

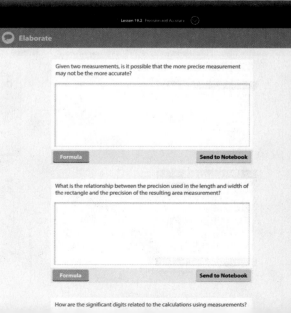

Elaborate

Given two measurements, is it possible that the more precise measurement may not be the more accurate?

Formula   Send to Notebook

What is the relationship between the precision used in the length and width of the rectangle and the precision of the resulting area measurement?

Formula   Send to Notebook

How are the significant digits related to the calculations using measurements?

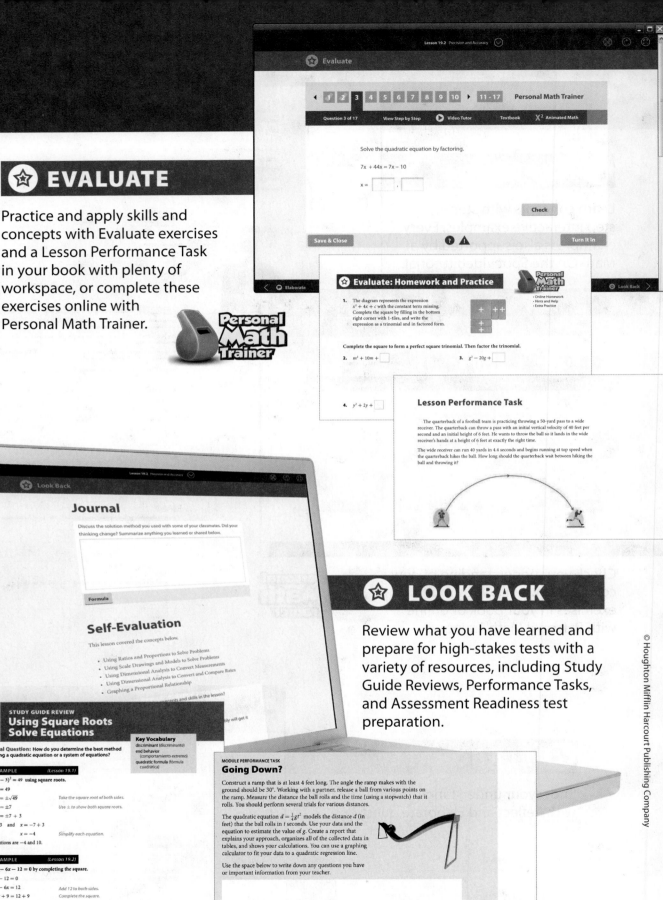

EVALUATE

Practice and apply skills and concepts with Evaluate exercises and a Lesson Performance Task in your book with plenty of workspace, or complete these exercises online with Personal Math Trainer.

Personal Math Trainer

Evaluate

| 1 | 2 | 3 | 4 | 5 | 6 | 7 | 8 | 9 | 10 | 11 - 17 | **Personal Math Trainer** |

Question 3 of 17   View Step by Step   ▶ Video Tutor   Textbook   X² Animated Math

Solve the quadratic equation by factoring.

$7x + 44x = 7x - 10$

x = [ ] , [ ]

Check

Save & Close   Turn It In

Evaluate: Homework and Practice

Personal Math Trainer
- Online Homework
- Hints and Help
- Extra Practice

1. The diagram represents the expression $x^2 + 4x + c$ with the constant term missing. Complete the square by filling in the bottom right corner with 1-tiles, and write the expression as a trinomial and in factored form.

Complete the square to form a perfect square trinomial. Then factor the trinomial.

2. $m^2 + 10m +$ [ ]

3. $g^2 - 20g +$ [ ]

4. $y^2 + 2y +$ [ ]

Lesson Performance Task

The quarterback of a football team is practicing throwing a 50-yard pass to a wide receiver. The quarterback can throw a pass with an initial vertical velocity of 40 feet per second and an initial height of 6 feet. He wants to throw the ball so it lands in the wide receiver's hands at a height of 6 feet at exactly the right time.

The wide receiver can run 40 yards in 4.4 seconds and begins running at top speed when the quarterback hikes the ball. How long should the quarterback wait between hiking the ball and throwing it?

Journal

Discuss the solution method you used with some of your classmates. Did your thinking change? Summarize anything you learned or shared below.

Formula

Self-Evaluation

This lesson covered the concepts below.

- Using Ratios and Proportions to Solve Problems
- Using Scale Drawings and Models to Solve Problems
- Using Dimensional Analysis to Convert Measurements
- Using Dimensional Analysis to Convert and Compare Rates
- Graphing a Proportional Relationship

concepts and skills in the lesson?

LOOK BACK

Review what you have learned and prepare for high-stakes tests with a variety of resources, including Study Guide Reviews, Performance Tasks, and Assessment Readiness test preparation.

MODULE 19
STUDY GUIDE REVIEW
Using Square Roots Solve Equations

Essential Question: How do you determine the best method for solving a quadratic equation or a system of equations?

Key Vocabulary
discriminant (discriminante)
end behavior (comportamiento extremo)
quadratic formula (fórmula cuadrática)

KEY EXAMPLE (Lesson 19.1)

Solve $(x - 3)^2 = 49$ using square roots.

$(x - 3)^2 = 49$

$x - 3 = \pm\sqrt{49}$ Take the square root of both sides.

$x - 3 = \pm 7$ Use ± to show both square roots.

$x = \pm 7 + 3$

$x = 7 + 3$ and $x = -7 + 3$

$x = 10$ $x = -4$ Simplify each equation.

The solutions are −4 and 10.

KEY EXAMPLE (Lesson 19.2)

Solve $x^2 - 6x - 12 = 0$ by completing the square.

$x^2 - 6x - 12 = 0$

$x^2 - 6x = 12$ Add 12 to both sides.

$x^2 - 6x + 9 = 12 + 9$ Complete the square.

$(x - 3)^2 = 21$ Factor left side.

$x - 3 = \pm\sqrt{21}$ Take square roots.

$x = 3 \pm \sqrt{21}$ Solve for x.

$x = 3 + \sqrt{21}$ or $x = 3 - \sqrt{21}$

KEY EXAMPLE (Lesson 19.3)

Solve $3x^2 - 5x - 4 = 0$ by using the quadratic formula.

$3x^2 - 5x - 4 = 0$

$a = 3, b = -5, c = -4$ Find a, b, c.

$x = \frac{-(-5) \pm \sqrt{(-5)^2 - 4(3)(-4)}}{2(3)}$ Use quadratic formula.

MODULE PERFORMANCE TASK
Going Down?

Construct a ramp that is at least 4 feet long. The angle the ramp makes with the ground should be 30°. Working with a partner, release a ball from various points on the ramp. Measure the distance the ball rolls and the time (using a stopwatch) that it rolls. You should perform several trials for various distances.

The quadratic equation $d = \frac{1}{4}gt^2$ models the distance d (in feet) that the ball rolls in t seconds. Use your data and the equation to estimate the value of g. Create a report that explains your approach, organizes all of the collected data in tables, and shows your calculations. You can use a graphing calculator to fit your data to a quadratic regression line.

Use the space below to write down any questions you have or important information from your teacher.

Module 19   3   Study Guide Review

 UNIT 1

Functions

MATH IN CAREERS

Community Theater Owner
A community theater owner uses math to determine revenue, profit, and expenses related to operating the theater. Probability and statistical methods are useful for determining the types of performances that will appeal to the public and attract patrons. Community theater owners should also understand the geometry of stage sets, and algebraic formulas for stage lighting, including those used to calculate light beam spread, throw distance, angle, and overall length.

If you are interested in a career as a community theater owner, you should study these mathematical subjects:

- Algebra
- Geometry
- Trigonometry
- Business Math
- Probability
- Statistics

Research other careers that require determining revenue, profit, and expenses. Check out the career activity at the end of the unit to find out how **Community Theater Owners** use math.

Reading Start-Up

Vocabulary

Review Words
✔ coefficient *(coeficiente)*
✔ domain *(dominio)*
✔ function *(función)*
✔ inequality *(desigualdad)*
✔ interval *(intervalo)*
✔ quadratic function *(función cuadrática)*
✔ range *(rango)*
✔ transformation *(transformación)*

Preview Words
conjunction *(conjunción)*
disjunction *(disyunción)*
even function *(función par)*
inverse function *(función inversa)*
odd function *(función impar)*
parameter *(parámetro)*

Visualize Vocabulary

Use the ✔ words to complete the graphic. You can put more than one word on each spoke of the information wheel.

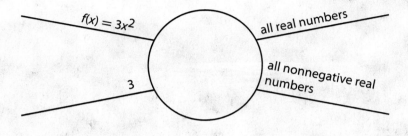

Understand Vocabulary

To become familiar with some of the vocabulary terms in the module, consider the following. You may refer to the module, the glossary, or a dictionary.

1. A __?__ is a constant in the equation of a curve that yields a family of similar curves as it changes.

2. A function $f(x)$ such that $f(x) = f(-x)$ is an __?__ .

3. A compound statement that uses the word *or* is a __?__ .

Active Reading

Three-Panel Flip Chart Before beginning each lesson, create a three-panel flip chart to help you summarize important aspects of the lesson. As you study each lesson, record algebraic examples of functions on the first flap, their graphs on the second flap, and analyses of the functions on the third flap. Add to flip charts from previous lessons by extending the analyses of the functions when possible. For equations and inequalities, record an example on the first flap, a worked out solution on the second flap, and a graph on the third flap.

Analyzing Functions

Essential Question: How can you analyze functions to solve real-world problems?

REAL WORLD VIDEO
Pole vaulting is just one of many track-and-field events that feature a person or object flying through the air. The path of a pole vaulter or of a shot put can be modeled using a quadratic function.

MODULE PERFORMANCE TASK PREVIEW
How High Does a Pole Vaulter Go?

In pole vaulting, a person jumps over a horizontal bar with the assistance of a long fiberglass or carbon-fiber pole. The flexible pole makes it possible for vaulters to achieve much greater heights than jumping without a pole. The goal is to clear the bar without knocking it down. How can mathematics be used to compare the heights of a pole vaulter for two different vaults? Let's jump in and find out!

Are (YOU) Ready?

Complete these exercises to review skills you will need for this module.

Algebraic Representations of Transformations

Example 1   Rotate $A(-6,3)$ 90° clockwise.
$(-6(-1), 3) = (6, 3)$ Multiply.
$A(-6, 3) \rightarrow A'(3, 6)$ Switch.

Translate $B(4,7)$ 5 units down. $(4, 7-5) = (4, 2)$
Subtract. $B(4, 7) \rightarrow B'(4,2)$

• Online Homework
• Hints and Help
• Extra Practice

Find the location of A' given that A is $(1, 5)$.

1. Rotate 90° clockwise.

2. Translate 1 unit left.

3. Reflect across the x-axis.

Linear Functions

Example 2   Name the x- and y-intercepts for $y = -2x + 1$.

x-intercept: $0 = -2x + 1$, so $x = 0.5$. y-intercept: $y = -2(0) + 1 = 1$

Find the x- and y-intercepts for each equation.

4. $y = 8x - 4$

5. $y = -x + 12$

6. $y = 1.2x + 4.8$

Properties of Translations, Reflections, and Rotations

Example 3   The point $P(1, -8)$ is reflected across the y-axis.
Name the quadrant that image, P', is in.
$P(1, -8) \rightarrow P'(-1, -8)$, so P' is in Quadrant III.

Name the quadrant that $R(7,3)$ is in after the transformation.

7. reflection across the x-axis

8. translation 8 units down

9. rotation 270° clockwise

Rate of Change and Slope

Example 4   Two points on a line are $(-3, 3)$ and $(4, 1)$. Find the slope.
$\dfrac{y_1 - y_2}{x_1 - x_2} = \dfrac{3 - 1}{-3 - 4} = -\dfrac{2}{7}$ The slope is $-\dfrac{2}{7}$.

Find the slope represented by the two points.

10. $(0, 5)$ and $(-9, -4)$

11. $(6, -2)$ and $(1, -1)$

12. $(-7, 3)$ and $(-4, -12)$

1.1 Domain, Range, and End Behavior

Essential Question: How can you determine the domain, range, and end behavior of a function?

 A2.7.I Write the domain and range of a function in interval notation, inequalities, and set notation.

Explore   Representing an Interval on a Number Line

An **interval** is a part of a number line without any breaks. A *finite interval* has two endpoints, which may or may not be included in the interval. An *infinite interval* is unbounded at one or both ends.

Suppose an interval consists of all real numbers greater than or equal to 1. You can use the inequality $x \geq 1$ to represent the interval. You can also use *set notation* and *interval notation*, as shown in the table.

Description of Interval	Type of Interval	Inequality	Set Notation	Interval notation
All real numbers from a to b, including a and b	Finite	$a \leq x \leq b$	$\{x \mid a \leq x \leq b\}$	$[a, b]$
All real numbers greater than a	Infinite	$x > a$	$\{x \mid x > a\}$	$(a, +\infty)$
All real numbers less than or equal to a	Infinite	$x \leq a$	$\{x \mid x \leq a\}$	$(-\infty, a]$

For set notation, the vertical bar means "such that," so you read $\{x \mid x \geq 1\}$ as "the set of real numbers x such that x is greater than or equal to 1."

For interval notation, do the following:

- Use a square bracket to indicate that an interval includes an endpoint and a parenthesis to indicate that an interval doesn't include an endpoint.

- For an interval that is unbounded at its positive end, use the symbol for positive infinity, $+\infty$. For an interval that unbounded at its negative end, use the symbol for negative infinity, $-\infty$. Always use a parenthesis with positive or negative infinity.

So, you can write the interval $x \geq 1$ as $[1, +\infty)$.

(A)   Copy and complete the table. Write the finite interval shown on each number line as an inequality, using set notation, and using interval notation.

Finite Interval	←—┼—┼—●—┼—┼—┼—┼—┼—●—┼—┼—→ −5 −4 −3 −2 −1 0 1 2 3 4 5	←—┼—┼—○—┼—┼—┼—┼—┼—┼—┼—┼—→ −5 −4 −3 −2 −1 0 1 2 3 4 5
Inequality	▮	▮
Set Notation	▮	▮
Interval Notation	▮	▮

(B) Copy and complete the table. Write the infinite interval shown on each number line as an inequality, using set notation, and using interval notation.

Infinite Interval	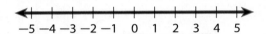 −5 −4 −3 −2 −1 0 1 2 3 4 5		−5 −4 −3 −2 −1 0 1 2 3 4 5	
Inequality		▪		▪
Set Notation		▪		▪
Interval Notation		▪		▪

Reflect

1. Consider the interval shown on the number line.

   −5 −4 −3 −2 −1 0 1 2 3 4 5

   a. Represent the interval using interval notation.

   b. What numbers are in this interval?

2. What do the intervals [0, 5], [0, 5), and (0, 5) have in common? What makes them different?

3. **Discussion** The symbol ∪ represents the *union* of two sets. What do you think the notation $(-\infty, 0) \cup (0, +\infty)$ represents?

⏺ Explain 1 Identifying a Function's Domain, Range and End Behavior from its Graph

Recall that the *domain* of a function *f* is the set of input values *x*, and the *range* is the set of output values *f(x)*. The **end behavior** of a function describes what happens to the *f(x)*-values as the *x*-values either increase without bound (approach positive infinity) or decrease without bound (approach negative infinity). For instance, consider the graph of a linear function shown. From the graph, you can make the following observations.

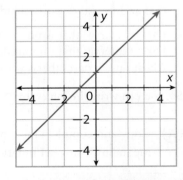

Statement of End Behavior	Symbolic Form of Statement
As the *x*-values increase without bound, the *f(x)*-values also increase without bound.	As $x \rightarrow +\infty$, $f(x) \rightarrow +\infty$.
As the *x*-values decrease without bound, the *f(x)*-values also decrease without bound.	As $x \rightarrow -\infty$, $f(x) \rightarrow -\infty$.

Example 1 Write the domain and the range of the function as an inequality, using set notation, and using interval notation. Also describe the end behavior of the function.

(A) The graph of the quadratic function $f(x) = x^2$ is shown.

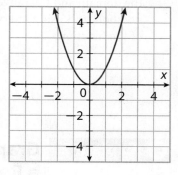

Domain:

Inequality: $-\infty < x < +\infty$

Set notation: $\{x| -\infty < x < +\infty\}$

Interval notation: $(-\infty, +\infty)$

Range: End behavior:

Inequality: $y \geq 0$ As $x \to +\infty, f(x) \to +\infty$.

Set notation: $\{y|y \geq 0\}$ As $x \to -\infty, f(x) \to +\infty$.

Interval notation: $[0, +\infty)$

(B) The graph of the exponential function $f(x) = 2^x$ is shown.

Domain:

Inequality: $-\infty < x < +\infty$

Set notation: $\{x| -\infty < x < +\infty\}$

Interval notation: $(-\infty, +\infty)$

Range:

Inequality: $y > 0$

Set notation: $\{y|y > 0\}$

Interval notation: $(0, +\infty)$

End behavior:

As $x \to +\infty, f(x) \to +\infty$.

As $x \to +\infty, f(x) \to 0$.

Reflect

4. Why is the end behavior of a quadratic function different from the end behavior of a linear function?

5. In Part B, the $f(x)$-values decrease as the x-values decrease. So, why can't you say that $f(x) \to -\infty$ as $x \to -\infty$?

6. The graph of the quadratic function $f(x) = -x^2$ is shown. Write the domain and the range of the function as an inequality, using set notation, and using interval notation. Also describe the end behavior of the function.

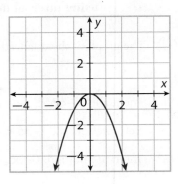

Explain 2 Graphing a Linear Function on a Restricted Domain

Unless otherwise stated, a function is assumed to have a domain consisting of all real numbers for which the function is defined. Many functions—such as linear, quadratic, and exponential functions—are defined for all real numbers, so their domain, when written in interval notation, is $(-\infty, +\infty)$. Another way to write the set of real numbers is $\mathbb{R}$.

Sometimes a function may have a restricted domain. If the rule for a function and its restricted domain are given, you can draw its graph and then identify its range.

Example 2 For the given function and domain, draw the graph and identify the range using the same notation as the domain.

Ⓐ $f(x) = \frac{3}{4}x + 2$ with domain $[-4, 4]$

Since $f(x) = \frac{3}{4}x + 2$ is a linear function, the graph is a line segment with endpoints at $(-4, f(-4))$, or $(-4, -1)$, and $(4, f(4))$, or $(4, 5)$. The endpoints are included in the graph.

The range is $[-1, 5]$.

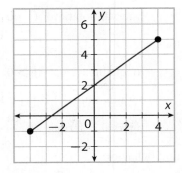

Ⓑ $f(x) = -x - 2$ with domain $\{x | x > -3\}$

Since $f(x) = -x - 2$ is a linear function, the graph is a ray with its endpoint at $(-3, f(-3))$, or $(-3, 1)$. The endpoint is not included in the graph.

The range is $\{y | y < 1\}$.

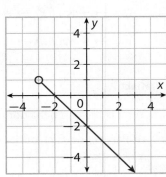

Reflect

7. In Part A, how does the graph change if the domain is $(-4, 4)$ instead of $[-4, 4]$?

8. In Part B, what is the end behavior as x increases without bound? Why can't you talk about the end behavior as x decreases without bound?

Your Turn

For the given function and domain, draw the graph and identify the range using the same notation as the domain.

9. $f(x) = -\frac{1}{2}x + 2$ with domain $-6 \leq x < 2$ **10.** $f(x) = \frac{2}{3}x - 1$ with domain $(-\infty, 3]$

🎸 Explain 3   Modeling with a Linear Function

Recall that when a real-world situation involves a constant rate of change, a linear function is a reasonable model for the situation. The situation may require restricting the function's domain.

Example 3   Write a function that models the given situation. Determine a domain from the situation, graph the function using that domain, and identify the range.

Ⓐ   Joyce jogs at a rate of 1 mile every 10 minutes for a total of 40 minutes. (Use inequalities for the domain and range of the function that models this situation.)

Joyce's jogging rate is 0.1 mi/min. Her jogging distance d (in miles) at any time t (in minutes) is modeled by $d(t) = 0.1t$. Since she jogs for 40 minutes, the domain is restricted to the interval $0 \leq t \leq 40$.

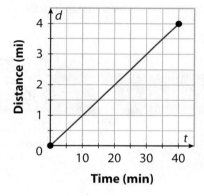

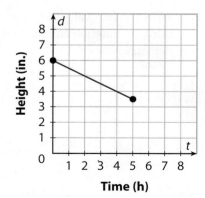

The range is $0 \leq d \leq 4$.

Ⓑ   A candle 6 inches high burns at a rate of 1 inch every 2 hours for 5 hours. (Use interval notation for the domain and range of the function that models this situation.)

The candle's burning rate is -0.5 in./h. The candle's height h (in inches) at any time t (in hours) is modeled by $h(t) = 6 - 0.5t$. Since the candle burns for 5 hours, the domain is restricted to the interval $\left[0, \boxed{5}\right]$.

The range is $[3.5, 6]$.

11. In Part A, suppose Joyce jogs for only 30 minutes.

    A. How does the domain change?

    B. How does the graph change?

    C. How does the range change?

Your Turn

12. While standing on a moving walkway at an airport, you are carried forward 25 feet every 15 seconds for 1 minute. Write a function that models this situation. Determine a domain from the situation, graph the function, and identify the range. Use set notation for the domain and range.

💬 Elaborate

13. If a and b are real numbers such that $a < b$, use interval notation to write four different intervals having a and b as endpoints. Describe what numbers each interval includes.

14. What impact does restricting the domain of a linear function have on the graph of the function?

15. **Essential Question Check-In** How does slope determine the end behavior of a linear function with an unrestricted domain?

✪ Evaluate: Homework and Practice

- Online Homework
- Hints and Help
- Extra Practice

1. Write the interval shown on the number line as an inequality, using set notation, and using interval notation.

    3 4 5 6 7 8

2. Write the interval (5, 100] as an inequality and using set notation.

3. Write the interval $-25 \leq x < 30$ using set notation and interval notation.

4. Write the interval $\{x \mid -3 < x < 5\}$ as an inequality and using interval notation.

Write the domain and the range of the function as an inequality, using set notation, and using interval notation. Also describe the end behavior of the function or explain why there is no end behavior.

5. The graph of the quadratic function $f(x) = x^2 + 2$ is shown.

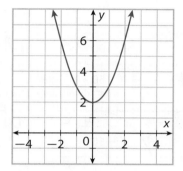

6. The graph of the exponential function $f(x) = 3^x$ is shown.

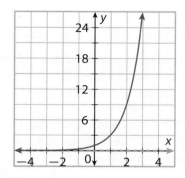

7. The graph of the linear function $g(x) = 2x - 2$ is shown.

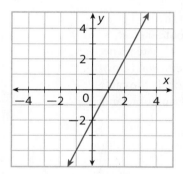

8. The graph of a function is shown.

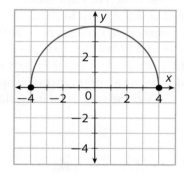

For the given function and domain, draw the graph and identify the range using the same notation as the domain.

9. $f(x) = -x + 5$ with domain $[-3, 2]$

10. $f(x) = \frac{3}{2}x + 1$ with domain $\{x \,|\, x > -2\}$

Write a function that models the given situation. Determine a domain from the situation, graph the function using that domain, and identify the range.

11. A bicyclist travels at a constant speed of 12 miles per hour for a total of 45 minutes. (Use set notation for the domain and range of the function that models this situation.)

12. An elevator in a tall building starts at a floor of the building that is 90 meters above the ground. The elevator descends 2 meters every 0.5 second for 6 seconds. (Use an inequality for the domain and range of the function that models this situation.)

13. **Explain the Error** Cameron sells tickets at a movie theater. On Friday night, she worked from 4 p.m. to 10 p.m. and sold about 25 tickets every hour. Cameron says that the number of tickets, n, she has sold at any time t (in hours) can be modeled by the function $n(t) = 25t$, where the domain is $0 \le t \le 1$ and the range is $0 \le n \le 25$. Is Cameron's function, along with the domain and range, correct? Explain.

14. **Multi-Step** The graph of the cubic function $f(x) = x^3$ is shown.

    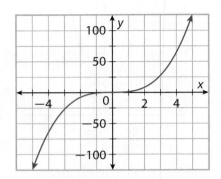

    a. What are the domain, range, and end behavior of the function? (Write the domain and range as an inequality, using set notation, and using interval notation.)

    b. How is the range of the function affected if the domain is restricted to $[-4, 4]$? (Write the range as an inequality, using set notation, and using interval notation.)

    c. Graph the function with the restricted domain.

15. **Represent Real-World Situations** The John James Audubon Bridge is a cable-stayed bridge in Louisiana that opened in 2011. The height from the bridge deck to the top of the tower where a particular cable is anchored is about 500 feet, and the length of that cable is about 1200 feet. Draw the cable on a coordinate plane, letting the x-axis represent the bridge deck and the y-axis represent the tower. (Only use positive values of x and y.) Write a linear function whose graph models the cable. Identify the domain and range, writing each as an inequality, using set notation, and using interval notation.

Lesson Performance Task

The fuel efficiency for a 2007 passenger car was 31.2 mi/gal. For the same model of car, the fuel efficiency increased to 35.6 mi/gal in 2012. The gas tank for this car holds 16 gallons of gas.

    a. Write and graph a linear function that models the distance that each car can travel for a given amount of gas (up to one tankful).

    b. Write the domain and range of each function using interval notation.

    c. Write and simplify a function $f(g)$ that represents the *difference* in the distance that the 2012 car can travel and the distance that the 2007 car can travel on the same amount of gas. Interpret this function using the graphs of the functions from part a. Also find and interpret $f(16)$.

    d. Write the domain and range of the difference function using set notation.

1.2 Characteristics of Function Graphs

Resource Locker

Essential Question: What are some of the attributes of a function, and how are they related to the function's graph?

 TEKS **A2.2.A** Write the domain and range of a function in interval notation, inequalities, and set notation. Also A2.7.I, A2.8.B, TX.A2.8.C

Explore Identifying Attributes of a Function from Its Graph

You can identify several attributes of a function by analyzing its graph. For instance, for the graph shown, you can see that the function's domain is $\{x|0 \le x \le 11\}$ and its range is $\{y| -1 \le y \le 1\}$. Use the graph to explore the function's other attributes.

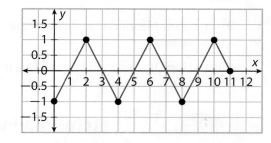

(A) Are the values of the function on the interval $\{x|1 < x < 3\}$ positive or negative?

(B) Are the values of the function on the interval $\{x|8 < x < 9\}$ are positive or negative?

A function is **increasing** on an interval if $f(x_1) < f(x_2)$ when $x_1 < x_2$ for any x-values x_1 and x_2 from the interval. The graph of a function that is increasing on an interval rises from left to right on that interval. Similarly, a function is **decreasing** on an interval if $f(x_1) > f(x_2)$ when $x_1 < x_2$ for any x-values x_1 and x_2 from the interval. The graph of a function that is decreasing on an interval falls from left to right on that interval.

(C) Is the given function increasing or decreasing on the interval $\{x|2 < x < 4\}$?

(D) Is the given function increasing or decreasing on the interval $\{x|4 < x < 6\}$?

For the two points $(x_1, f(x_1))$ and $(x_2, f(x_2))$ on the graph of a function, the **average rate of change** of a function is the ratio of the change in the function values, $f(x_2) - f(x_1)$, to the change in the x-values, $x_2 - x_1$. For a linear function, the rate of change is constant and represents the slope of the function's graph.

(E) What is the given function's average rate of change on the interval $\{x|0 \le x \le 2\}$?

A function may change from increasing to decreasing or from decreasing to increasing at *turning points*. The value of $f(x)$ at a point where a function changes from increasing to decreasing is a **maximum value**. A maximum value occurs at a point that appears higher than all nearby points on the graph of the function. Similarly, the value of $f(x)$ at a point where a function changes from decreasing to increasing is a **minimum value**. A minimum value occurs at a point that appears lower than all nearby points on the graph of the function.

(F) At how many points does the given function change from increasing to decreasing?

(G) What is the function's maximum value at these points?

(H) At how many points does the given function change from decreasing to increasing?

(I) What is the function's minimum value at these points?

A **zero** of a function is a value of x for which $f(x) = 0$. On a graph of the function, the zeros are the x-intercepts.

(J) How many x-intercepts does the given function's graph have?

(K) Identify the zeros of the function.

Reflect

1. **Discussion** Identify three different intervals that have the same average rate of change, and state what the rate of change is.

2. **Discussion** If a function is increasing on an interval $\{x | a \leq x \leq b\}$, what can you say about its average rate of change on the interval? Explain.

🔧 Explain 1 Sketching a Function's Graph from a Verbal Description

By understanding the attributes of a function, you can sketch a graph from a verbal description.

Example 1 Sketch a graph of the following verbal descriptions.

(A) Lyme disease is a bacterial infection transmitted to humans by ticks. When an infected tick bites a human, the probability of transmission is a function of the time since the tick attached itself to the skin. During the first 24 hours, the probability is 0%. During the next three 24-hour periods, the rate of change in the probability is always positive, but it is much greater for the middle period than the other two periods. After 96 hours, the probability is almost 100%. Sketch a graph of the function for the probability of transmission.

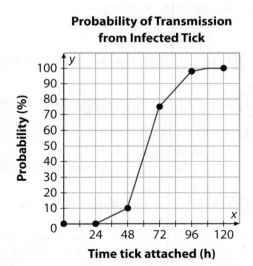

Probability of Transmission from Infected Tick

Identify the axes and scales.

The x-axis will be time (in hours) and will run from 0 to at least 96. The y-axis will be the probability of infection (as a percent) from 0 to 100.

Identify key intervals.

The intervals are in increments of 24 hours: 0 to 24, 24 to 48, 48 to 96, and 96 to 120.

Sketch the graph of the function.

Draw a horizontal segment at $y = 0$ for the first 24-hour interval. The function increases over the next three 24-hour intervals with the middle one having the greatest increase (the steepest slope). After 96 hours, the graph is nearly horizontal at 100%.

Ⓑ The incidence of a disease is the rate at which a disease occurs in a population. It is calculated by dividing the number of new cases of a disease in a given time period (typically a year) by the size of the population. **To avoid small decimal numbers, the rate is often expressed in terms of a large number of people rather than a single person.** For instance, the incidence of measles in the United States in 1974 was about 10 cases per 100,000 people.

From 1974 to 1980, there were drastic fluctuations in the incidence of measles in the United States. In 1975, there was a slight increase in incidence from 1974. The next two years saw a substantial increase in the incidence, which reached a maximum in 1977 of about 26 cases per 100,000 people. From 1977 to 1979, the incidence fell to about 5 cases per 100,000 people. The incidence fell much faster from 1977 to 1978 than from 1978 to 1979. Finally, from 1979 to 1980, the incidence stayed about the same. **Sketch a graph the function for the incidence of measles.**

Identify the axes and scales.

The x-axis will represent time given by years and will run from 0 to 6. The y-axis will represent incidence of measles, measured in cases per 100,000 people, and will run from 0 to 30.

Identify key intervals.

The intervals are one-year increments from 0 to 6.

Sketch the graph of the function.

The first point on the graph is (0, 10). The graph slightly ▓▓ from $x = 0$ to $x = 1$. From $x = 1$ to $x = 3$, the graph ▓▓ to a maximum y-value of 26. The graph ▓▓ steeply from $x = 3$ to $x = 4$ and then ▓▓ less steeply from $x = 4$ to $x = 5$. The graph is horizontal from $x = 5$ to $x = 6$.

Incidence of Measles in the U.S.

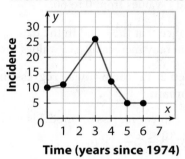

Time (years since 1974)

Reflect

3. In Part B, the graph is horizontal from 1979 to 1980. What can you say about the rate of change for the function on this interval?

Your Turn

4. A grocery store stocks shelves with 100 cartons of strawberries before the store opens. For the first 3 hours the store is open, the store sells 20 cartons per hour. Over the next 2 hours, no cartons of strawberries are sold. The store then restocks 10 cartons each hour for the next 2 hours. In the final hour that the store is open, 30 cartons are sold. Sketch a graph of the function.

⚙ Explain 2 **Modeling with a Linear Function**

When given a set of paired data, you can use a scatter plot to see whether the data show a linear trend. If so, you can use a graphing calculator to perform linear regression and obtain a linear function that models the data. You should treat the least and greatest x-values of the data as the domain of the linear model.

When you perform linear regression, a graphing calculator will report the value of the *correlation coefficient r*. This variable can have a value from -1 to 1. It measures the direction and strength of the relationship between the variables x and y. If the value of r is negative, the y-values tend to decrease as the x-values increase. If the value of r is positive, the y-values tend to increase as the x-values increase. The more linear the relationship between x and y is, the closer that the value of r is to -1 or 1 (or the closer that the value of r^2 is to 1).

You can use the linear model to make predictions and decisions based on the data. Making a prediction within the domain of the linear model is called *interpolation*. Making a prediction outside the domain is called *extrapolation*.

Example 2 **Perform a linear regression for the given situation and make predictions.**

 A photographer hiked through the Grand Canyon. Each day she stored photos on a memory card for her digital camera. When she returned from the trip, she deleted some photos from each memory card, saving only the best. The table shows the number of photos she kept from all those stored on each memory card. Use a graphing calculator to create a scatter plot of the data, find a linear regression model, and graph the model. Then use the model to predict the number of photos the photographer will keep if she takes 150 photos.

Grand Canyon Photos	
Photos Taken	**Photos Kept**
117	25
128	31
140	39
157	52
110	21
188	45
170	42

Step 1: Create a scatter plot of the data.

Let x represent the number of photos taken, and let y represent the number of photos kept. Use a viewing window that shows x-values from 100 to 200 and y-values from 0 to 60.

Notice that the trend in the data appears to be roughly linear, with y-values generally increasing as x-values increase.

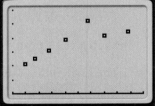

Step 2: Perform linear regression. Write the linear model and its domain.

The linear regression model is $y = 0.33x - 11.33$. Its domain is $\{x | 110 \leq x \leq 188\}$.

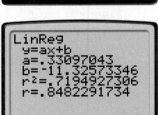

Step 3: Graph the model along with the data to obtain a visual check on the goodness of fit.

Notice that one of the data points is much farther from the line than the other data points are. The value of the correlation coefficient r would be closer to 1 without this data point.

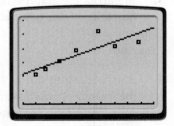

Step 4: Predict the number of photos this photographer will keep if she takes 150 photos.

Evaluate the linear function when $x = 150$: $y = 0.33(150) - 11.33 \approx 38$. So, she will keep about 38 photos if she takes 150 photos.

 As a science project, Shelley is studying the relationship of car mileage (in miles per gallon) and speed (in miles per hour). The table shows the data Shelley gathered using her family's vehicle. Use a graphing calculator to create a scatter plot of the data, find a linear regression model, and graph the model. Then use the model to predict the gas mileage of the car at a speed of 20 miles per hour.

Speed (mi/h)	30	40	50	60	70
Mileage (mi/gal)	34.0	33.5	31.5	29.0	27.5

Step 1: Create a scatter plot of the data.

What do x and y represent?

Let x represent the car's speed, and let y represent the car's gas mileage.

What viewing window will you use?

Use a window that shows x-values from 0 to 80 and y-values from 0 to 40.

What trend do you observe?

The trend in the data appears to be quite linear, with y-values generally decreasing as x-values increase.

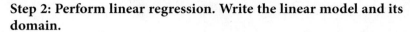

Step 2: Perform linear regression. Write the linear model and its domain.

The linear regression model is $y = -0.175x + 39.85$. Its domain is $\{x \mid 30 \leq x \leq 70\}$.

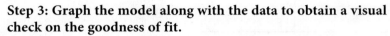

Step 3: Graph the model along with the data to obtain a visual check on the goodness of fit.

What can you say about the goodness of fit?

As expected from the fact that the value of r from Step 2 is very close to -1, the line passes through or comes close to passing through all the data points.

Step 4: Predict the gas mileage of the car at a speed of 20 miles per hour.

Evaluate the linear function when $x = 20$: $y = -0.175(20) + 39.85 \approx 36.4$. So, the car's gas mileage should be about 36.4 mi/gal at a speed of 20 mi/h.

Reflect

5. Identify whether each prediction in Parts A and B is an interpolation or an extrapolation.

Your Turn

6. Vern created a website for his school's sports teams. He has a hit counter on his site that lets him know how many people have visited the site. The table shows the number of hits the site received each day for the first two weeks. Use a graphing calculator to find the linear regression model. Then predict how many hits there will be on day 15.

Day	1	2	3	4	5	6	7	8	9	10	11	12	13	14
Hits	5	10	21	24	28	36	33	21	27	40	46	50	31	38

💬 Elaborate

7. How are the attributes of increasing and decreasing related to average rate of change? How are the attributes of maximum and minimum values related to the attributes of increasing and decreasing?

8. How can line segments be used to sketch graphs of functions that model real-world situations?

9. When making predictions based on a linear model, would you expect interpolated or extrapolated values to be more accurate? Justify your answer.

10. **Essential Question Check-In** What are some of the attributes of a function?

The graph shows a function that models the value V (in millions of dollars of a stock portfolio as a function of time t (in months) over an 18-month period.

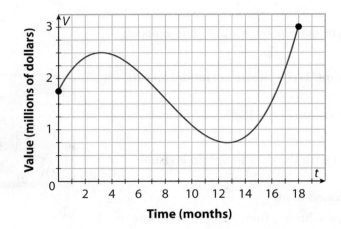

1. On what intervals is the function increasing?
On what intervals is the function decreasing?

2. Identify any maximum values and minimum values.

3. What are the function's domain and range?

The table of values gives the probability $P(n)$ for getting all 5's when rolling a number cube n times.

n	1	2	3	4	5
P(n)	$\frac{1}{6}$	$\frac{1}{36}$	$\frac{1}{216}$	$\frac{1}{1296}$	$\frac{1}{7776}$

4. Is $P(n)$ increasing or decreasing? Explain the significance of this.

5. What is the end behavior of $P(n)$? Explain the significance of this.

6. The table shows some values of a function. On which intervals is the function's average rate of change positive? Select all that apply.

x	0	1	2	3
f(x)	50	75	40	65

a. From $x = 0$ to $x = 1$ **c.** From $x = 0$ to $x = 3$ **e.** From $x = 1$ to $x = 3$

b. From $x = 0$ to $x = 2$ **d.** From $x = 1$ to $x = 2$ **f.** From $x = 2$ to $x = 3$

Use the graph of the function $f(x)$ to identify the function's specified attributes.

7. Find the function's average rate of change over each interval.

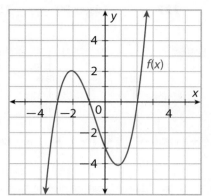

   a. From $x = -3$ to $x = -2$ **b.** From $x = -2$ to $x = 1$

   c. From $x = 0$ to $x = 1$ **d.** From $x = 1$ to $x = 2$

   e. From $x = -1$ to $x = 0$ **f.** From $x = -1$ to $x = 2$

8. On what intervals are the function's values positive?

9. On what intervals are the function's values negative?

10. What zeros does the function have?

11. The following describes the United States nuclear stockpile from 1944 to 1974. From 1944 to 1958, there was a gradual increase in the number of warheads from 0 to about 5000. From 1958 to 1966, there was a rapid increase in the number of warheads to a maximum of about 32,000. From 1968 to 1970, there was a decrease in the number of warheads to about 26,000. Finally, from 1970 to 1974, there was a small increase to about 28,000 warheads. Sketch a graph of the function.

12. The following describes the unemployment rate in the United States from 2003 to 2013. In 2003, the unemployment rate was at 6.3%. The unemployment rate began to fall over the years and reached a minimum of about 4.4% in 2007. A recession that began in 2007 caused the unemployment rate to increase over a two-year period and reach a maximum of about 10% in 2009. The unemployment rate then decreased over the next four years to about 7.0% in 2013. Sketch a graph of the function.

13. The following describes the incidence of mumps in the United States from 1984 to 2004. From 1984 to 1985, there was no change in the incidence of mumps, staying at about 1 case per 100,000 people. Then there was a spike in the incidence of mumps, which reached a peak of about 5.5 cases per 100,000 in 1987. Over the next year, there was a sharp decline in the incidence of mumps, to about 2 cases per 100,000 people in 1988. Then, from 1988 to 1989, there was a small increase to about 2.5 cases per 100,000 people. This was followed by a gradual decline, which reached a minimum of about 0.1 case per 100,000 in 1999. For the next five years, there was no change in the incidence of mumps. Sketch a graph of the function.

14. Aviation The table gives the lengths and wingspans of airplanes in an airline's fleet.

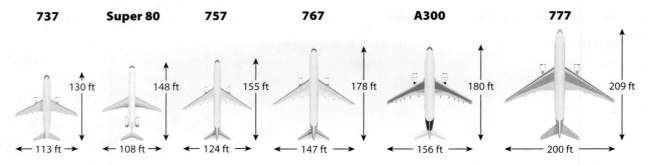

737	Super 80	757	767	A300	777

| 130 ft | 148 ft | 155 ft | 178 ft | 180 ft | 209 ft |
| ← 113 ft → | ← 108 ft → | ← 124 ft → | ← 147 ft → | ← 156 ft → | ← 200 ft → |

   a. Make a scatter plot of the data with *x* representing length and *y* representing wingspan.

   b. Sketch a line of fit.

   c. Use the line of fit to predict the wingspan of an airplane with a length of 220 feet.

15. Golf The table shows the height (in feet) of a golf ball at various times (in seconds) after a golfer hits the ball into the air.

Time (s)	0	0.5	1	1.5	2	2.5	3	3.5	4
Height (ft)	0	28	48	60	64	60	48	28	0

   a. Graph the data in the table. Then draw a smooth curve through the data points. (Because the golf ball is a projectile, its height *h* at time *t* can be modeled by a quadratic function whose graph is a parabola.)

   b. What is the maximum height that the golf ball reaches?

   c. On what interval is the golf ball's height increasing?

   d. On what interval is the golf ball's height decreasing?

16. The model $a = 0.25t + 29$ represents the median age *a* of females in the United States as a function of time *t* (in years since 1970).

   a. Predict the median age of females in 1995.

   b. Predict the median age of females in 2015 to the nearest tenth.

17. Make a Prediction Anthropologists who study skeletal remains can predict a woman's height just from length of her humerus, the bone between the elbow and the shoulder. The table gives data for humerus length and overall height for various women.

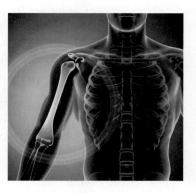

Humerus Length (cm)	35	27	30	33	25	39	27	31
Height (cm)	167	146	154	165	140	180	149	155

Using a graphing calculator, find the linear regression model and state its domain. Then predict a woman's height from a humerus that is 32 cm long, and tell whether the prediction is an interpolation or an extrapolation.

18. Make a Prediction Hummingbird wing beat rates are much higher than those in other birds. The table gives data about the mass and the frequency of wing beats for various species of hummingbirds.

Mass (g)	3.1	2.0	3.2	4.0	3.7	1.9	4.5
Frequency of Wing Beats (beats per second)	60	85	50	45	55	90	40

a. Using a graphing calculator, find the linear regression model and state its domain.

b. Predict the frequency of wing beats for a Giant Hummingbird with a mass of 19 grams.

c. Comment on the reasonableness of the prediction and what, if anything, is wrong with the model.

19. Explain the Error A student calculates a function's average rate of change on an interval and finds that it is 0. The student concludes that the function is constant on the interval. Explain the student's error, and give an example to support your explanation.

20. Communicate Mathematical Ideas Describe a way to obtain a linear model for a set of data without using a graphing calculator.

Lesson Performance Task

Since 1980 scientists have used data from satellite sensors to calculate a daily measure of Arctic sea ice extent. Sea ice extent is calculated as the sum of the areas of sea ice covering the ocean where the ice concentration is greater than 15%. The graph here shows seasonal variations in sea ice extent for 2012, 2013, and the average values for the 1980s.

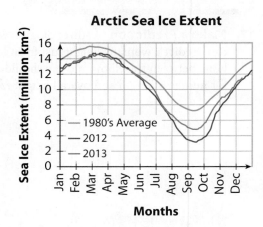

Arctic Sea Ice Extent

a. According to the graph, during which month does sea ice extent usually reach its maximum? During which month does the minimum extent generally occur? What can you infer about the reason for this pattern?

b. Sea ice extent reached its lowest level to date in 2012. About how much less was the minimum extent in 2012 compared with the average minimum for the 1980s? About what percentage of the 1980s average minimum was the 2012 minimum?

c. How does the maximum extent in 2012 compare with the average maximum for the 1980s? About what percentage of the 1980s average maximum was the 2012 maximum?

d. What do the patterns in the maximum and minimum values suggest about how climate change may be affecting sea ice extent?

e. How do the 2013 maximum and minimum values compare with those for 2012? What possible explanation can you suggest for the differences?

1.3 Transformations of Function Graphs

Essential Question: What are the ways you can transform the graph of the function $f(x)$?

 TEKS **A2.6.C** Analyze the effect on the graphs of $f(x) = |x|$ when $f(x)$ is replaced by a $f(x)$, $f(bx)$, $f(x - c)$, and $f(x) + d$ for specific positive and negative real values of a, b, c, and d.

⊘ Explore 1 Investigating Translations of Function Graphs

You can transform the graph of a function in various ways. You can translate the graph horizontally or vertically, you can stretch or compress the graph horizontally or vertically, and you can reflect the graph across the x-axis or the y-axis. How the graph of a given function is transformed is determined by the way certain numbers, called **parameters**, are introduced in the function.

(A) Copy the graph of $f(x)$ shown. Then graph $g(x) = f(x) + k$ where k is the parameter. Let $k = 4$ so that $g(x) = f(x) + 4$. Copy and complete the input-output table and then graph $g(x)$ on the same grid. In general, how is the graph of $g(x) = f(x) + k$ related to the graph of $f(x)$ when k is a positive number?

x	f(x)	f(x) + 4
−1	−2	2
1	2	6
3	−2	
5	2	

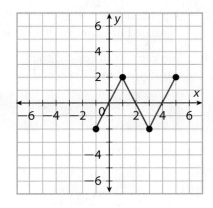

(B) Now try a negative value of k in $g(x) = f(x) + k$. Let $k = -3$ so that $g(x) = f(x) - 3$. Copy and complete the input-output table and then graph $g(x)$ on the same grid. In general, how is the graph of $g(x) = f(x) + k$ related to the graph of $f(x)$ when k is a negative number?

x	f(x)	f(x) − 3
−1	−2	−5
1	2	−1
1	−2	
5	2	

(C) Make another copy of the graph of $f(x)$. Then graph $g(x) = f(x - h)$ where h is the parameter. Let $h = 2$ so that $g(x) = f(x - 2)$. Copy and complete the mapping diagram and then graph $g(x)$ on the same grid. (To complete the mapping diagram, you need to find the inputs for g that produce the inputs for f after you subtract 2. Work backward from the inputs for f to the inputs for g by adding 2.) In general, how is the graph of $g(x) = f(x - h)$ related to the graph of $f(x)$ when h is a positive number?

Input for g	Input for f	Output for f	Output for g

(D) **Make a Conjecture** How would you expect the graph of $g(x) = f(x - h)$ to be related to the graph of $f(x)$ when h is a negative number?

Reflect

1. Suppose a function $f(x)$ has a domain of $\left[x_1, x_2\right]$ and a range of $\left[y_1, y_2\right]$. When the graph of $f(x)$ is translated vertically k units where k is either positive or negative, how do the domain and range change?

2. Suppose a function $f(x)$ has a domain of $\left[x_1, x_2\right]$ and a range of $\left[y_1, y_2\right]$. When the graph of $f(x)$ is translated horizontally h units where h is either positive or negative, how do the domain and range change?

3. You can transform the graph of $f(x)$ to obtain the graph of $g(x) = f(x - h) + k$ by combining transformations. Copy and complete the table to give your prediction for the transformation.

Sign of h	Sign of k	Transformations of the Graph of f(x)
+	+	Translate right h units and up k units.
+	−	▮
−	+	▮
−	−	▮

(⊘) Explore 2   Investigating Stretches and Compressions of Function Graphs

In this activity, you will consider what happens when you multiply by a positive parameter inside or outside a function. Throughout, you will use the same function $f(x)$ that you used in the previous activity.

© Houghton Mifflin Harcourt Publishing Company

(A) Make another copy of the graph of $f(x)$. Then graph $g(x) = a \cdot f(x)$ where a is the parameter. Let $a = 2$ so that $g(x) = 2f(x)$. Copy and complete the input-output table and then graph $g(x)$ on the same grid. In general, how is the graph of $g(x) = a \cdot f(x)$ related to the graph of $f(x)$ when a is greater than 1?

x	f(x)	2f(x)
−1	−2	−4
1	2	4
3	−2	
5	2	

(B) Make another copy of the graph of $f(x)$. Then try a value of a between 0 and 1 in $g(x) = a \cdot f(x)$. Let $a = \frac{1}{2}$ so that $g(x) = \frac{1}{2}f(x)$. Copy and complete the input-output table and then graph $g(x)$ on the same grid. In general, how is the graph of $g(x) = a \cdot f(x)$ related to the graph of $f(x)$ when a is a number between 0 and 1?

x	f(x)	$\frac{1}{2}f(x)$
−1	−2	−1
1	2	1
3	−2	
5	2	

(C) Make another copy of the graph of $f(x)$. Then graph $g(x) = f\left(\frac{1}{b} \cdot x\right)$ where b is the parameter. Let $b = 2$ so that $g(x) = f\left(\frac{1}{2}x\right)$. Copy and complete the mapping diagram and then graph $g(x)$ on the same grid. (To complete the mapping diagram, you need to find the inputs for g that produce the inputs for f after you multiply by $\frac{1}{2}$. Work backward from the inputs for f to the inputs for g by multiplying by 2.) In general, how is the graph of $g(x) = f\left(\frac{1}{2}x\right)$ related to the graph of $f(x)$ when b is a number greater than 1?

(D) **Make a Conjecture** How would you expect the graph of $g(x) = f\left(\frac{1}{b} \cdot x\right)$ to be related to the graph of $f(x)$ when b is a number between 0 and 1?

4. Suppose a function $f(x)$ has a domain of $[x_1, x_2]$ and a range of $[y_1, y_2]$. When the graph of $f(x)$ is stretched or compressed vertically by a factor of a, how do the domain and range change?

5. You can transform the graph of $f(x)$ to obtain the graph of $g(x) = a \cdot f(x-h) + k$ by combining transformations. Copy and complete the table to give your prediction for the transformation.

Value of a	Transformations of the Graph of $f(x)$
$a > 1$	Stretch vertically by a factor of a, and translate h units horizontally and k units vertically.
$0 < a < 1$	

6. You can transform the graph of $f(x)$ to obtain the graph of $g(x) = f\left(\frac{1}{b}(x - h)\right) + k$ by combining transformations. Copy and complete the table to give your prediction for the transformation.

Value of b	Transformations of the Graph of $f(x)$
$b > 1$	Stretch horizontally by a factor of b, and translate h units horizontally and k units vertically.
$0 < b < 1$	

⊘ Explore 3 Investigating Reflections of Function Graphs

When the parameter in a stretch or compression is negative, another transformation called a *reflection* is introduced. Examining reflections will also tell you whether a function is an *even function* or an *odd function*. An **even function** is one for which $f(-x) = f(x)$ for all x in the domain of the function, while an **odd function** is one for which $f(-x) = -f(x)$ for all x in the domain of the function. A function is not necessarily even or odd; it can be neither.

(A) Copy the graph shown. Then graph $g(x) = a \cdot f(x)$ where $a = -1$. Copy and complete the input-output table and then graph $g(x) = -f(x)$ on the same grid. In general, how is the graph of $g(x) = -f(x)$ related to the graph of $f(x)$?

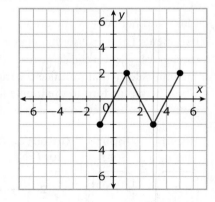

x	$f(x)$	$-f(x)$
-1	-2	2
1	2	-2
3	-2	
5	2	

(B) Make another copy of the graph of $f(x)$. Then graph $g(x) = f\left(\frac{1}{b} \cdot x\right)$ where $b = -1$. Copy and complete the input-output table and then graph $g(x) = f(-x)$ on the same grid. In general, how is the graph of $g(x) = f(-x)$ related to the graph of $f(x)$?

Input for g		Input for f		Output for f		Output for g
1	· (−1)	−1		−2		−2
−1		1		2		2
▢		3		−2		−2
▢		5		2		2

Reflect

7. **Discussion** Suppose a function $f(x)$ has a domain of $\left[x_1, x_2\right]$ and a range of $\left[x_1, x_2\right]$. When the graph of $f(x)$ is reflected across the x-axis, how do the domain and range change?

8. For a function $f(x)$, suppose the graph of $f(-x)$, which you know is a reflection of the graph of $f(x)$ across the y-axis, is identical to the graph of $f(x)$. What does this tell you about $f(x)$? Explain.

9. Is the function whose graph you reflected across the axes in Steps A and B an even function, an odd function, or neither? Explain.

🔧 Explain 1 Transforming the Graph of the Parent Quadratic Function

You can use transformations of the graph of a basic function, called a *parent function*, to obtain the graph of a related function. To do so, focus on how the transformations affect reference points on the graph of the parent function.

For instance, the parent quadratic function is $f(x) = x^2$. The graph of this function is a U-shaped curve called a *parabola* with a turning point, called a *vertex*, at $(0, 0)$. The vertex is a useful reference point, as are the points $(-1, 1)$ and $(1, 1)$.

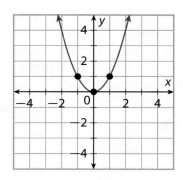

Example 1 Describe how to transform the graph of $f(x) = x^2$ to obtain the graph of the related function $g(x)$. Then draw the graph of $g(x)$.

(A) $g(x) = -3f(x - 2) - 4$

Parameter and Its Value	Effect on the Parent Graph
$a = -3$	vertical stretch of the graph of $f(x)$ by a factor of 3 and a reflection across the x-axis
$b = 1$	Since $b = 1$, there is no horizontal stretch or compression.
$h = 2$	horizontal translation of the graph of $f(x)$ to the right 2 units
$k = -4$	vertical translation of the graph of $f(x)$ down 4 units

Applying these transformations to a point (x, y) on the parent graph results in the point $(x + 2, -3y - 4)$. The table shows what happens to the three reference points on the graph of $f(x)$.

Point on the Graph of $f(x)$	Corresponding Point on $g(x)$
$(-1, 1)$	$(-1 + 2, -3(1) - 4) = (1, -7)$
$(0, 0)$	$(0 + 2, -3(0) - 4) = (2, -4)$
$(1, 1)$	$(1 + 2, -3(1) - 4) = (3, -7)$

Use the transformed reference points to graph $g(x)$.

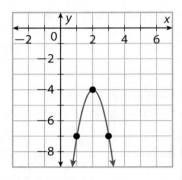

Ⓑ $g(x) = f\left(\frac{1}{2}(x + 5)\right) + 2$

Parameter and Its Value	Effect on the Parent Graph
$a = \boxed{1}$	The parent graph is unaffected.
$b = \boxed{2}$	The parent graph is stretched horizontally by a factor of 2. There is no reflection across the y-axis.
$h = \boxed{-5}$	The parent graph is translated -5 units horizontally.
$k = \boxed{2}$	The parent graph is translated 2 units vertically.

Applying these transformations to a point on the parent graph results in the point $(2x - 5, y + 2)$. The table shows what happens to the three reference points on the graph of $f(x)$.

Point on the Graph of $f(x)$	Corresponding Point on the Graph of $g(x)$
$(-1, 1)$	$(2(-1) - 5, 1 + 2) = \left(\boxed{-7}, \boxed{3}\right)$
$(0, 0)$	$(2(0) - 5, 0 + 2) = \left(\boxed{-5}, \boxed{2}\right)$
$(1, 1)$	$(2(1) - 5, 1 + 2) = \left(\boxed{-3}, \boxed{3}\right)$

Use the transformed reference points to graph $g(x)$.

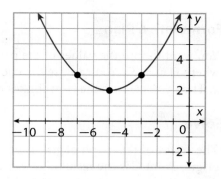

10. Is the function $f(x) = x^2$ an even function, an odd function, or neither? Explain.

11. The graph of the parent quadratic function $f(x) = x^2$ has the vertical line $x = 0$ as its axis of symmetry. Identify the axis of symmetry for each of the graphs of $g(x)$ in Parts A and B. Which transformation(s) affect the location of the axis of symmetry?

Your Turn

12. Describe how to transform the graph of $f(x) = x^2$ to obtain the graph of the related function $g(x) = f\big(-4(x - 3)\big) + 1$. Then draw the graph of $g(x)$.

🔑 Explain 2   Modeling with a Quadratic Function

You can model real-world objects that have a parabolic shape using a quadratic function. In order to fit the function's graph to the shape of the object, you will need to determine the values of the parameters in the function $g(x) = a \cdot f\left(\frac{1}{b}(x - h)\right) + k$ where $f(x) = x^2$. Note that because $f(x)$ is simply a squaring function, it's possible to pull the parameter b outside the function and combine it with the parameter a. Doing so allows you to model real-objects using $g(x) = a \cdot f(x - h) + k$, which has only three parameters.

When modeling real-world objects, remember to restrict the domain of $g(x) = a \cdot f(x - h) + k$ to values of x that are based on the object's dimensions.

Example 2

An old stone bridge over a river uses a parabolic arch for support. In the illustration shown, the unit of measurement for both axes is feet, and the vertex of the arch is point C. Find a quadratic function that models the arch, and state the function's domain.

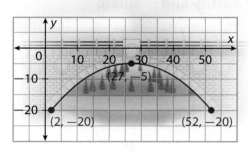

🧩 Analyze Information

Identify the important information.

- The shape of the arch is a parabola.

- The vertex of the parabola is $C(27, -5)$.

- Two other points on the parabola are $A(2, -20)$ and $B(52, -20)$.

Formulate a Plan

You want to find the values of the parameters a, h, and k in $g(x) = a \cdot f(x - h) + k$ where $f(x) = x^2$. You can use the coordinates of point C to find the values of h and k. Then you can use the coordinates of one of the other points to find the value of a.

Solve

The vertex of the graph of $g(x)$ is point C, and the vertex of the graph of $f(x)$ is the origin. Point C is the result of translating the origin 27 units to the right and 5 units down. This means that $h = 27$ and $k = -5$. Substituting these values into $g(x)$ gives $g(x) = a \cdot f(x - 27) - 5$. Now substitute the coordinates of point B into $g(x)$ and solve for a.

$g(x) = a \cdot f(x - 27) - 5$ Write the general function.

$g\left(\boxed{52}\right) = a \cdot f(52 - 27) - 5$ Substitute 52 for x.

$g(52) = a \cdot f\left(\boxed{25}\right) - 5$ Simplify.

$-20 = a \cdot f\left(\boxed{25}\right) - 5$ Replace $g(52)$ with -20, the y-value of B.

$-20 = a(625) - 5$ Evaluate $f(25)$.

$a = \boxed{-\dfrac{3}{125}}$ Simplify.

Substitute the value of a into $g(x)$.

$g(x) = -\dfrac{3}{125} f(x - 27) - 5$

The arch exists only between points A and B, so the domain of $g(x)$ is $\{x \mid 2 \leq x \leq 52\}$.

Justify and Evaluate

To justify the answer, verify that $g(2) = -20$.

$g(x) = -\dfrac{3}{125} f(x - 27) - 5$ Write the function.

$g\left(\boxed{2}\right) = -\dfrac{3}{125} f(\boxed{2} - 27) - 5$ Substitute 2 for x.

$= -\dfrac{3}{125} f\left(\boxed{-2}\right) - 5$ Subtract.

$= -\dfrac{3}{125} \cdot \left(\boxed{625}\right) - 5$ Evaluate $f(-25)$.

$= -20$ ✓

Simplify.

Your Turn

13. The netting of an empty hammock hangs between its supports along a curve that can be modeled by a parabola. In the illustration shown, the unit of measurement for both axes is feet, and the vertex of the curve is point C. Find a quadratic function that models the hammock's netting, and state the function's domain.

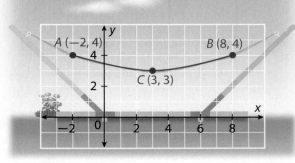

14. What is the general procedure to follow when graphing a function of the form $g(x) = a \cdot f(x - h) + k$ given the graph of $f(x)$?

15. What are the general steps to follow when determining the values of the parameters a, h, and k in $f(x) = a(x - h)^2 + k$ when modeling a parabolic real-world object?

16. **Essential Question Check-In** How can the graph of a function $f(x)$ be transformed?

⭐ Evaluate: Homework and Practice

- Online Homework
- Hints and Help
- Extra Practice

Write $g(x)$ in terms of $f(x)$ after performing the given transformation of the graph of $f(x)$.

1. Translate the graph of $f(x)$ to the left 3 units.

2. Translate the graph of $f(x)$ up 2 units.

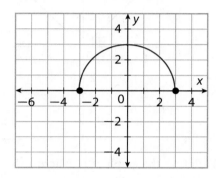

3. Translate the graph of $f(x)$ to the right 4 units.

4. Translate the graph of $f(x)$ down 3 units.

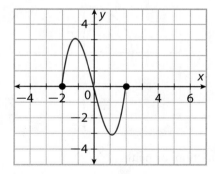

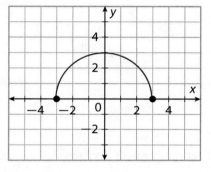

5. Stretch the graph of $f(x)$ horizontally by a factor of 3.

6. Stretch the graph of $f(x)$ vertically by a factor of 2.

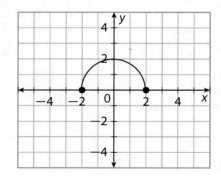

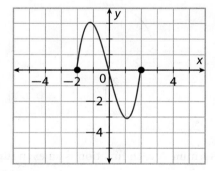

7. Compress the graph of $f(x)$ horizontally by a factor of 3.

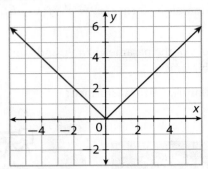

8. Compress the graph of $f(x)$ vertically by a factor of 2.

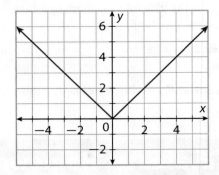

9. Reflect the graph of $f(x)$ across the y-axis.

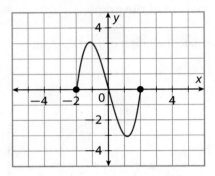

10. Reflect the graph of $f(x)$ across the x-axis.

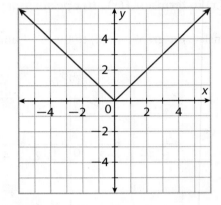

11. Reflect the graph of $f(x)$ across the y-axis.

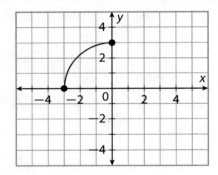

12. Reflect the graph of $f(x)$ across the x-axis.

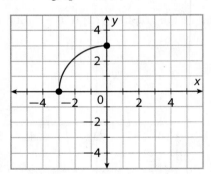

13. Determine if each function is an even function, an odd function, or neither

a. 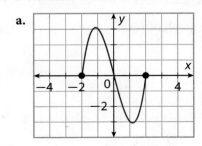 b. 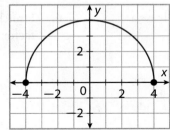 c.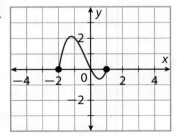

14. Determine whether each quadratic function is an even function. Answer *yes* or *no*.

a. $f(x) = 5x^2$

b. $f(x) = (x - 2)^2$

c. $f(x) = \left(\dfrac{x}{3}\right)^2$

d. $f(x) = x^2 + 6$

Describe how to transform the graph of $f(x) = x^2$ to obtain the graph of the related function $g(x)$. Then draw the graph of $g(x)$.

15. $g(x) = -\dfrac{f(x+4)}{3}$

16. $g(x) = f(2x) + 2$

17. Architecture Flying buttresses were used in the construction of cathedrals and other large stone buildings before the advent of more modern construction materials to prevent the walls of large, high-ceilinged rooms from collapsing.

The design of a flying buttress includes an arch. In the illustration shown, the unit of measurement for both axes is feet, and the vertex of the arch is point C. Find a quadratic function that models the arch, and state the function's domain.

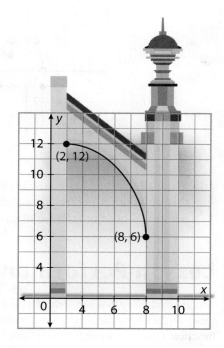

18. A red velvet rope hangs between two stanchions and forms a curve that can be modeled by a parabola. In the illustration shown, the unit of measurement for both axes is feet, and the vertex of the curve is point C. Find a quadratic function that models the rope, and state the function's domain.

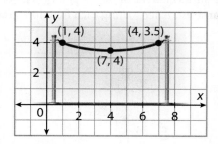

19. Multiple Representations The graph of the function $g(x) = \left(\frac{1}{2}x + 2\right)^2$ is shown.

Use the graph to identify the transformations of the graph of $f(x) = x^2$ needed to produce the graph of $g(x)$. (If a stretch or compression is involved, give it in terms of a horizontal stretch or compression rather than a vertical one.) Use your list of transformations to write $g(x)$ in the form $g(x) = f\left(\frac{1}{b}(x - h)\right) + k$. Then show why the new form of $g(x)$ is algebraically equivalent to the given form.

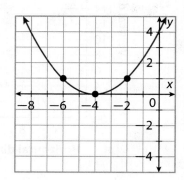

20. Represent Real-World Situations The graph of the ceiling function, $f(x) = \lceil x \rceil$, is shown. This function accepts any real number x as input and delivers the least integer greater than or equal to x as output. For instance, $f(1.3) = 2$ because 2 is the least integer greater than or equal to 1.3. The ceiling function is a type of *step function*, so named because its graph looks like a set of steps.

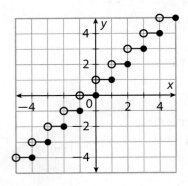

Write a function $g(x)$ whose graph is a transformation of the graph of $f(x)$ based on this situation: A parking garage charges \$4 for the first hour or less and \$2 for every additional hour or fraction of an hour. Then graph $g(x)$.

Lesson Performance Task

You are designing two versions of a chair, one without armrests and one with armrests. The diagrams show side views of the chair. Rather than use traditional straight legs for your chair, you decide to use parabolic legs. Given the function $f(x) = x^2$, write two functions, $g(x)$ and $h(x)$, whose graphs represent the legs of the two chairs and involve transformations of the graph of $f(x)$. For the chair without armrests, the graph of $g(x)$ must touch the bottom of the armrest. After writing each function, graph it.

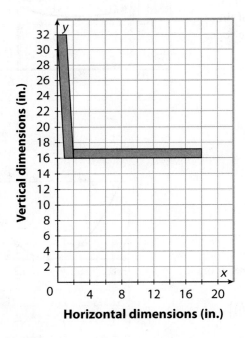

Horizontal dimensions (in.)

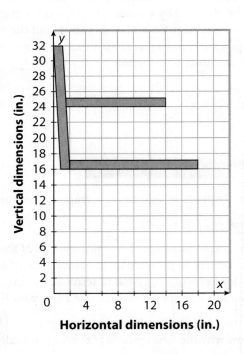

Horizontal dimensions (in.)

1.4 Inverses of Functions

Essential Question: What is an inverse function, and how do you know it's an inverse function?

 TEKS A2.2.B, A2.2.D, A2.7.I Graph and write the inverse of a function using notation such as $f^{-1}(x)$. Also A2.2.D, A2.7.I

Resource Locker

Explore   Understanding Inverses of Functions

Recall that a *relation* is any pairing of the elements of one set (the domain) with the elements of a second set (the range). The elements of the domain are called inputs, while the elements of the range are called outputs. A function is a special type of relation that pairs every input with exactly one output. In a *one-to-one function*, no output is ever used more than once in the function's pairings. In a *many-to-one function*, at least one output is used more than once.

An **inverse relation** reverses the pairings of a relation. If a relation pairs an input x with an output y, then the inverse relation pairs an input y with an output x. The inverse of a function may or may not be another function. If the inverse of a function $f(x)$ is also a function, it is called the **inverse function** and is written $f^{-1}(x)$. If the inverse of a function is not a function, then it is simply an inverse relation.

(A) The mapping diagrams show a function and its inverse. Copy and complete the diagram for the inverse of the function.

Is the function one-to-one or many-to-one? Explain.

Is the inverse of the function also a function? Explain.

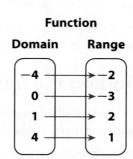
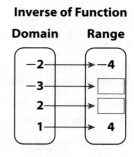

(B) The mapping diagrams show a function and its inverse. Copy and complete the diagram for the inverse of the function.

Is the function one-to-one or many-to-one? Explain.

Is the inverse of the function also a function? Explain.

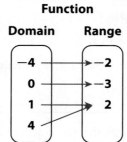
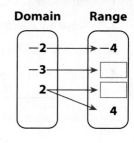

(C) The graph of the original function in Step A is shown. Copy the graph. Note that the graph includes the dashed line $y = x$. Write the inverse of the function as a set of ordered pairs and graph them on the same grid.

Function: $\{(-4, -2), (0, -3), (1, 2), (4, 1)\}$

Inverse of function:

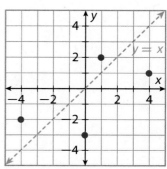

What do you observe about the graphs of the function and its inverse in relationship to the line $y = x$? Why does this make sense?

© Houghton Mifflin Harcourt Publishing Company

Ⓓ The **composition of two functions** $f(x)$ and $g(x)$, written $f(g(x))$ and read as "f of g of x," is a new function that uses the output of $g(x)$ as the input of $f(x)$. For example, consider the functions f and g with the following rules.

f: Add 1 to an input. g: Double an input.

Notice that $g(1) = 2(1) = 2$. So, $f(g(1)) = f(2) = 2 + 1 = 3$.

You can also find $g(f(x))$. Notice that $f(1) = 1 + 1 = 2$. So, $g(f(1)) = g(2) = 2(2) = 4$.

For these two functions, you can see that $f(g(1)) \neq g(f(1))$.

You can compose a function and its inverse. For instance, the mapping diagram shown illustrates $f^{-1}(f(x))$ where $f(x)$ is the original function from Step A and $f^{-1}(x)$ is its inverse. Notice that the range of $f(x)$ serves as the domain of $f^{-1}(x)$. Complete the diagram. What do you notice about the outputs of of $f^{-1}(f(x))$? Explain why this makes sense.

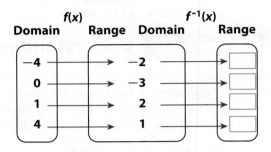

Reflect

1. What is the relationship between the domain and range of a relation and its inverse?

2. **Discussion** In Step D, you saw that for inverse functions, $f^{-1}(f(x)) = x$. What do you expect $f(f^{-1}(x))$ to equal? Explain.

🔑 Explain 1   Finding the Inverse of a Linear Function

Every linear function $f(x) = mx + b$ where $m \neq 0$ is a one-to-one function. So, its inverse is also a function. To find the equation of the inverse function, use the fact that inverse functions undo each other's pairings.

To find the inverse of a function $f(x)$:
1. Substitute y for $f(x)$.
2. Solve for x in terms of y.
3. Switch x and y (since the inverse switches inputs and outputs).
4. Replace y with $f^{-1}(x)$.

To check your work and verify that the functions are inverses, show that $f(f^{-1}(x)) = x$ and that $f^{-1}(f(x)) = x$.

Example 1 Find the inverse function $f^{-1}(x)$ for the given function $f(x)$. Use composition to verify that the functions are inverses. Then graph the function and its inverse.

(A) $f(x) = 3x + 4$

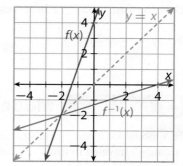

Replace $f(x)$ with y. $\qquad y = 3x + 4$

Solve for x. $\qquad y - 4 = 3x$

$$\frac{y - 4}{3} = x$$

Switch x and y. $\qquad y = \dfrac{x - 4}{3}$

Replace y with $f^{-1}(x)$. $\qquad f^{-1}(x) = \dfrac{x - 4}{3}$

Check: Verify that $f^{-1}(f(x)) = x$ and $f(f^{-1}(x)) = x$.

$$f^{-1}(f(x)) = f^{-1}(3x + 4) = \frac{(3x + 4) - 4}{3} = \frac{3x}{3} = x$$

$$f(f^{-1}(x)) = f\left(\frac{x - 4}{3}\right) = 3\left(\frac{x - 4}{3}\right) + 4 = (x - 4) + 4 = x$$

(B) $f(x) = 2x - 2$

Replace $f(x)$ with y. $\qquad y = \boxed{2x - 2}$

Solve for x. $\qquad y \boxed{+2} = 2x$

$$\frac{y + 2}{2} = x$$

Switch x and y. $\qquad y = \boxed{\dfrac{x + 2}{2}}$

Replace y with $f^{-1}(x)$. $\qquad \boxed{f^{-1}(x)} = \dfrac{x + 2}{2}$

Check: Verify that $f^{-1}(f(x)) = x$ and $f(f^{-1}(x)) = x$.

$$f^{-1}(f(x)) = f^{-1}\left(\boxed{2x - 2}\right) = \frac{(2x - 2) + \boxed{2}}{\boxed{2}} = \frac{\boxed{2x}}{2} = \boxed{x}$$

$$f(f^{-1}(x)) = f\left(\boxed{\frac{x + 2}{2}}\right) = \boxed{2}\left(\frac{x + 2}{2}\right) - \boxed{2} = \left(\boxed{x + 2}\right) - 2 = \boxed{x}$$

Reflect

3. What is the significance of the point where the graph of a linear function and its inverse intersect?

4. The graph of a constant function $f(x) = c$ for any constant c is a horizontal line through the point $(0, c)$. Does a constant function have an inverse? Does it have an inverse function? Explain.

Your Turn

Find the inverse function $f^{-1}(x)$ for the given function $f(x)$. Use composition to verify that the functions are inverses. Then graph the function and its inverse.

5. $f(x) = -2x + 3$

⚙ Explain 2 Modeling with the Inverse of a Linear Function

In a model for a real-world situation, the variables have specific real-world meanings. For example, the distance d (in miles) traveled in time t (in hours) at a constant speed of 60 miles per hour is $d = 60t$. Writing this in function notation as $d(t) = 60t$ emphasizes that this equation describes distance as a function of time.

You can find the inverse function for $d = 60t$ by solving for the independent variable t in terms of the dependent variable d. This gives the equation $t = \frac{d}{60}$. Writing this in function notation as $t(d) = \frac{d}{60}$ emphasizes that this equation describes time as a function of distance. Because the meanings of the variables can't be interchanged, you do not switch them at the end as you would switch x and y when working with purely mathematical functions. As you work with real-world models, you may have to restrict the domain and range.

Example 2 For the given function, state the domain of the inverse function using set notation. Then find an equation for the inverse function, and graph it. Interpret the meaning of the inverse function.

Ⓐ The equation $C = 3.5g$ gives the cost C (in dollars) as a function of the number of gallons of gasoline g when the price is $3.50 per gallon.

The domain of the function $C = 3.5g$ is restricted to nonnegative numbers to make real-world sense, so the range of the function also consists of non negative numbers. This means that the

domain of the inverse function is $\{C \mid C \geq 0\}$

Solve the given equation for g to find the inverse function.

Write the equation. $C = 3.5g$

Divide both sides by 3.5. $\frac{C}{3.5} = g$

So, the inverse function is $g = \frac{C}{3.5}$.

Graph the inverse function.

The inverse function gives the number of gallons of gasoline as a function of the cost (in dollars) when the price of gas is $3.50 per gallon.

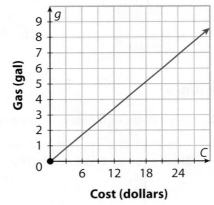

Graph axis: Gas (gal) on vertical axis (0–9), Cost (dollars) on horizontal axis (6, 12, 18, 24)

Ⓑ A car's gas tank, which can hold 14 gallons of gas, contains 4 gallons of gas when the driver stops at a gas station to fill the tank. The gas pump dispenses gas at a rate of 5 gallons per minute. The equation $g = 5t + 4$ gives the number of gallons of gasoline g in the tank as a function of the pumping time t(in minutes).

The range of the function $g = 5t + 4$ is the number of gallons

of gas in the tank, which varies from 4 gallons to 4 gallons. So, the

domain of the inverse function is $\left\{ g \,\middle|\, \boxed{4} \le g \le \boxed{14} \right\}$.

Solve the given equation for g to find the inverse function.

Write the equation. $g = \boxed{5}\, t + \boxed{4}$

Simplify. $\dfrac{\boxed{g - 4}}{5} = t$

So, the inverse function is $t = \boxed{\dfrac{g - 4}{5}}$.

Graph the inverse function.

The inverse function gives the pumping time (in minutes) as a function of the amount of gas in the tank (in gallons).

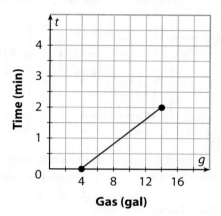

Your Turn

For the given function, determine the domain of the inverse function. Then find an equation for the inverse function, and graph it. Interpret the meaning of the inverse function.

6. A municipal swimming pool containing 600,000 gallons of water is drained. The amount of water w (in thousands of gallons) remaining in the pool at time t (in hours) after the draining begins is $w = 600 - 2t$.

💬 **Elaborate**

7. What must be true about a function for its inverse to be a function?

8. A function rule indicates the operations to perform on an input to produce an output. What is the relationship between these operations and the operations indicated by the inverse function?

9. How can you use composition to verify that two functions $f(x)$ and $g(x)$ are inverse functions?

10. Describe a real-world situation modeled by a linear function for which it makes sense to find an inverse function. Give an example of how the inverse function might also be useful.

11. **Essential Question Check-In** What is an inverse relation?

• Online Homework
• Hints and Help
• Extra Practice

The mapping diagrams show a function and its inverse. Copy and complete the diagram for the inverse of the function. Then tell whether the inverse is a function, and explain your reasoning.

1.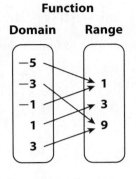

2.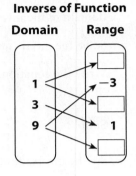

Write the inverse of the given function as a set of ordered pairs and then graph the function and its inverse on the coordinate plane.

3. Function:

{(−4, −3), (−2, −4), (0, −2), (1, 0), (2, 3)}

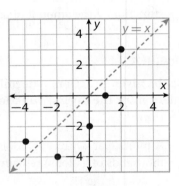

4. Function:

{(−3, −4), (−2, −3), (−1, 2), (1, 2), (2, 4), (3, 4)}

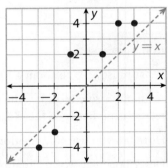

Find the inverse function $f^{-1}(x)$ for the given function $f(x)$.

5. $f(x) = 4x - 8$

6. $f(x) = \dfrac{x}{3}$

7. $f(x) = \dfrac{x + 1}{6}$

8. $f(x) = -0.75x$

Find the inverse function $f^{-1}(x)$ for the given function $f(x)$. Use composition to verify that the functions are inverses. Then graph the function and its inverse.

9. $f(x) = -3x + 3$

10. $f(x) = \frac{2}{5}x - 2$

For the given function, determine the domain of the inverse function. Then find an equation for the inverse function, and graph it. Interpret the meaning of the inverse function.

11. Geometry The equation $A = \frac{1}{2}(20)h$ gives the area A (in square inches) of a triangle with a base of 20 inches as a function of its height h (in inches).

12. The label on a gallon of paint says that it will cover from 250 square feet to 450 square feet depending on the surface that is being painted. A painter has 12 gallons of paint on hand. The equation $A = 12c$ gives the area A (in square feet) that the 12 gallons of paint will cover if applied at a coverage rate c (in square feet per gallon).

The graph of a function is given. Tell whether the function's inverse is a function, and explain your reasoning. If the inverse is not a function, tell how can you restrict the domain of the function so that its inverse is a function.

13.

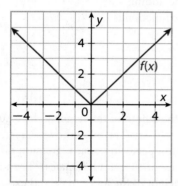

14.

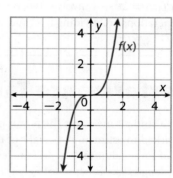

15. **Multiple Response** Identify the domain intervals over which the inverse of the graphed function is also a function. Select all that apply.

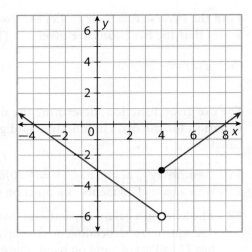

A. $[4, +\infty)$

D. $(-\infty, +\infty)$

G. $(4, 8)$

B. $(0, +\infty)$

E. $(-\infty, 4]$

H. $(8, +\infty)$

C. $[-4, +\infty)$

F. $(-\infty, 4)$

I. $(0, 8]$

16. **Draw Conclusions** Identify all linear functions that are their own inverse.

17. **Make a Conjecture** Among linear functions (excluding constant functions), quadratic functions, absolute value functions, and exponential functions, which types of function do you have to restrict the domain for the inverse to be a function? Explain.

18. **Find the Error** A student was asked to find the inverse of $f(x) = 2x + 1$. The student's work is shown. Explain why the student is incorrect and what the student should have done to get the correct answer.

> The function $f(x) = 2x + 1$ involves two operations: multiplying by 2 and adding 1.
> The inverse operations are dividing by 2 and subtracting 1. So, the inverse function is
> $f^{-1}(x) = \frac{x}{2} - 1$.

Lesson Performance Task

In an anatomy class, a student measures the femur of an adult male and finds the length of the femur to be 50.0 cm. The student is then asked to estimate the height of the male that the femur came from. The table shows the femur lengths and heights of some adult males and females. Using a graphing calculator, perform linear regression on the data to obtain femur length as a function of height (one function for adult males, one for adult females). Then find the inverse of each function. Use the appropriate inverse function to find the height of the adult male and explain how the inverse functions would be helpful to a forensic scientist.

Femur Length (cm)	30	38	46	54	62
Male Height (cm)	138	153	168	183	198
Female Height (cm)	132	147	163	179	194

Analyzing Functions

MODULE

1

Essential Question: How can you analyze functions to solve real-world problems?

Key Vocabulary

finite interval *(intervalo finito)*

infinite interval *(intervalo infinito)*

domain *(dominio)*

range *(rango)*

end behavior *(comportamiento final)*

KEY EXAMPLE   *(Lesson 1.1)*

Write the domain and range of $f(x) = 3^x$ as an inequality, using set notation, and using interval notation. Then describe the end behavior of the function.

	Domain	Range
Inequality	$-\infty < x < +\infty$	$y > 0$
Set notation	$\{x \mid -\infty < x < +\infty\}$	$y \mid y > 0$
Interval notation	$(-\infty + \infty)$	$(0, +\infty)$

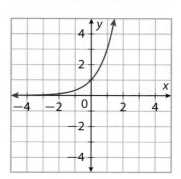

End behavior   As $x \to +\infty$, $f(x) \to +\infty$, and as $x \to +\infty$, $f(x) \to 0$.

KEY EXAMPLE   *(Lesson 1.3)*

Describe how to transform the graph of $f(x) = x^2$ to obtain the graph of the related function $g(x) = 2f(x - 1) + 3$.

Parameter	Effect on the parent graph
$a = 2$	vertical stretch of the graph of $f(x)$ by a factor of 2
$h = 1$	translation of the graph of $f(x)$ to the right 1 unit
$k = 3$	translation of the graph of $f(x)$ up 3 units

A point (x, y) on the graph of $f(x) = x^2$ becomes the point $(x + 1, 2y + 3)$.

KEY EXAMPLE   *(Lesson 1.4)*

Find the inverse function $f^{-1}(x)$ for $f(x) = -2x + 3$.

Replace $f(x)$ with y. $y = -2x + 3$ Replace y with $f^{-1}(x)$.

Solve for x. $\dfrac{y - 3}{-2} = x$

Switch x and y. $y = \dfrac{x - 3}{-2}$

                          $f^{-1}(x) = \dfrac{x - 3}{-2}$

EXERCISES

Write the domain and range of the function as an inequality, using set notation, and using interval notation. *(Lesson 1.1)*

1.

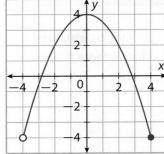

2.

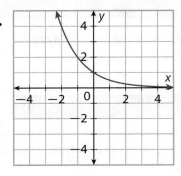

Find the inverse function $f^{-1}(x)$ for the given function $f(x)$. *(Lesson 1.4)*

3. $f(x) = \dfrac{x+3}{5}$

4. $f(x) = 2x + 6$

5. Explain how to transform the graph of the function $f(x) = x^2$ to obtain the graph of the related function $g(x) = -2f(x+1) - 3$. *(Lessons 1.3)*

© Houghton Mifflin Harcourt Publishing Company

MODULE PERFORMANCE TASK

How High Does a Pole Vaulter Go?

A pole vaulter performs two vaults, which can be modeled using the functions $h_1(t) = 9.8t - 4.9t^2$ and $h_2(t) = 8.82t - 4.9t^2$ where h is the height in meters at time t in seconds. How do the two jumps compare graphically in terms of the vertexes and intercepts, and what do these represent? Which was the higher jump? How do you know?

Use your own paper to complete the task. Be sure to write down all your data and assumptions. Then use graphs, numbers, words, or algebra to explain how you reached your conclusions.

1.1–1.4 Analyzing Functions

- Online Homework
- Hints and Help
- Extra Practice

Copy and complete the table. Write the domain and range of the function $g(x) = 3x^2 - 4$ as an inequality, using set notation, and using interval notation. Then, compare the function to $f(x) = x^2$ and describe the transformations. *(Lessons 1.1, 1.3)*

1.	Domain	Range	Transformations
Inequality	▩	▩	
Set notation	▩	▩	▩
Interval notation	▩	▩	

Find the inverse for each linear function. *(Lesson 1.4)*

2. $f(x) = -2x + 4$

3. $g(x) = \dfrac{x}{4} - 3$

4. $h(x) = \dfrac{3}{4}x + 1$

5. $j(x) = 5x - 6$

ESSENTIAL QUESTION

6. What are two ways the graphed function could be used to solve real-world problems? *(Lesson 1.2)*

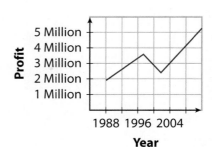

Assessment Readiness

1. What happens to $y = -3^x$ as $x \rightarrow -\infty$?

   A. $y \rightarrow -\infty$

   B. $y \rightarrow \infty$

   C. $y \rightarrow 0$

   D. $y \rightarrow -3$

2. The function $f(x)$ is translated left 3 units, down 2 units, and is reflected across the x-axis to make the new function $g(x)$. Which best represents $g(x)$?

   A. $g(x) = -f(x + 3) - 2$

   B. $g(x) = f(x + 3) - 2$

   C. $g(x) = -f(x - 3) - 2$

   D. $g(x) = f(x - 3) - 2$

3. The formula to convert degrees Fahrenheit F to degrees Celsius C is $C = \dfrac{5(F - 32)}{9}$. What is the inverse of this formula?

   A. $F = \dfrac{9C + 32}{5}$

   B. $F = \dfrac{9}{5}C + 32$

   C. $F = 9C + 32$

   D. $F = 9C + \dfrac{32}{5}$

4. A bike rider starts at a fast pace and rides 40 miles in 2 hours. He gets tired, and slows down, traveling only 20 miles in the next 3 hours. He takes a rest for an hour, then rides back to where he started at a steady pace without stopping for 4 hours. Draw a graph to match the real world situation. Explain your choices.

Absolute Value Functions, Equations, and Inequalities

Essential Question: How can you use absolute value functions to solve real-world problems?

REAL WORLD VIDEO
Gold jewelry is sold with a rating for purity. For instance, 18-karat gold is 75% pure by weight. The purity level has to meet tolerances that can be expressed using absolute value inequalities.

MODULE PERFORMANCE TASK PREVIEW
What Is the Purity of Gold?

Because gold is such a soft metal, it is usually mixed with another metal such as copper or silver. Pure gold is 24 karat, and 18 karat indicates a mixture of 18 parts gold and 6 parts of another metal or metals. Imagine someone wants to sell you a ring and claims it is 18 karat. How can you use math to be sure the gold is indeed 18 karat? Let's find out!

Are (YOU) Ready?

Complete these exercises to review skills you will need for this module.

- Online Homework
- Hints and Help
- Extra Practice

One-Step Equations

Example 1   Solve $x - 6.8 = 2$ for x.

$x - 6.8 + 6.8 = 2 + 6.8$ *Add.*

$x = 8.8$ *Combine like terms.*

Solve each equation.

1. $r + 9 = 7$

2. $\dfrac{w}{4} = -3$

3. $10b = 14$

Slope and Slope-Intercept Form

Example 2   Find the slope and y-intercept of $3x - y = 24$.

$-3x + 3x - y = -3x + 6$ *Write the equation in $y = mx + b$ form.*

$-y(-1) = (-3x + 6)(-1)$

$y = 3x - 6$ *The slope is 3 and the y-intercept is -6.*

Find the slope and y-intercept for each equation.

4. $y - 8 = 2x + 9$

5. $3y = 2(x - 3)$

6. $2y + 8x = 1$

Linear Inequalities in Two Variables

Example 3   Graph $y < 2x - 3$.

Graph the y-intercept of $(0, -3)$.

Use the slope of 2 to plot a second point, and draw a line connecting the points. Shade below the line.

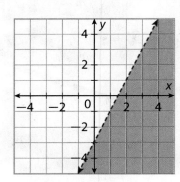

Graph and label each inequality.

7. $y \geq -x + 2$

8. $y < x - 1$

2.1 Graphing Absolute Value Functions

Resource Locker

Essential Question: How can you identify the features of the graph of an absolute value function?

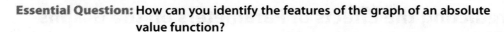 **TEKS** **A2.2.A** Graph the functions… $f(x) = |x|$ …and, when applicable, analyze the key attributes such as domain, range, intercepts, symmetries, …and maximum and minimum given an interval. Also A2.6.C

Explore 1 Graphing and Analyzing the Parent Absolute Value Function

Absolute value, written as $|x|$, represents the distance between x and 0 on a number line. As a distance, absolute value is always positive. For every point on a number line, there is another point on the opposite side of 0 that is the same distance from 0. For example, both 5 and −5 are five units away from 0. Thus, $|-5| = 5$ and $|5| = 5$.

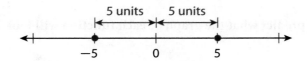

The absolute value function $|x|$, can be defined piecewise as $|x| = \begin{cases} x & x \geq 0 \\ -x & x < 0 \end{cases}$. When x is nonnegative,

the function simply returns the number. When x is negative, the function returns the opposite of x.

(A) Copy and complete the input-output table for $f(x)$.

$$f(x) = |x| = \begin{cases} x & x \geq 0 \\ -x & x < 0 \end{cases}$$

x	f(x)
−8	
−4	
0	
4	
8	

(B) Plot the points you found on a coordinate grid. Use the points to complete the graph of the function.

(C) Now, examine your graph of $f(x) = |x|$ and complete the following statements about the function.

$f(x) = |x|$ is symmetric about the [ ] and therefore is a(n) [ ] function.

The domain of $f(x) = |x|$ is [ ].

The range of $f(x) = |x|$ is [ ].

1. Use the definition of the absolute value function to show that $f(x) = |x|$ is an even function.

⊘ Explore 2 Predicting the Effects of Parameters on the Graphs of Absolute Value Functions

Previously, you examined transformations of various functions using the general transformation function

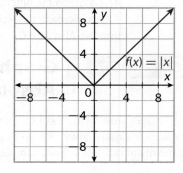

$g(x) = af\left(\frac{1}{b}(x - h)\right) + k$. Now you will learn how to use that knowledge to predict the effects of changing parameters in $g(x) = a\left|\frac{1}{b}(x - h)\right| + k$ on an individual basis. Confirm your predictions using a graphing calculator.

The graph of $f(x) = |x|$ is shown.

Copy the graph of $f(x)$. Then predict what the graph of each function will look like, and then sketch the graph of each function.

Ⓐ The graph of $g_1(x) = |x| + 6$ will be the graph of $f(x) = |x|$ translated ▢.

The graph of $g_2(x) = |x| - 4$ will be the graph of $f(x) = |x|$ translated ▢.

Ⓑ The graph of $g_1(x) = |x - 3|$ will be the graph of $f(x) = |x|$ translated ▢.

The graph of $g_2(x) = |x + 5|$ will be the graph of $f(x) = |x|$ translated ▢.

Ⓒ The graph of $g_1(x) = 6|x|$ will be the graph of $f(x) = |x|$ stretched ▢.

The graph of $g_2(x) = -3|x|$ will be the graph of $f(x) = |x|$ stretched ▢ and reflected ▢.

Ⓓ The graph of $g_1(x) = \left|-\frac{1}{4}x\right|$ will be the graph of $f(x) = |x|$ compressed ▢ and reflected ▢.

The graph of $g_2(x) = 4|x|$ will be the graph of $f(x) = |x|$ stretched ▢.

2. From the graphs, a horizontal stretch by a factor of b appears to be equivalent to a vertical compression by a factor of a. This implies that $a = \frac{1}{b}$. Are there any values for which this relationship doesn't work? Write an equation for the relationship between a and b.

✏ Explain 1 Graphing Absolute Value Functions

The Explore showed the effects of individual parameters on the graph of $f(x) = |x|$. Now let's examine the effects of varying more than one parameter. (To avoid confusion, assume either only a or only b varies.) Consider each function a transformation of the parent function. By examining what happens to the vertex and one point on each side of the vertex, under the transformation, you can easily sketch the resulting graph.

Example 1 Given the function $g(x) = a\left|\frac{1}{b}(x - h)\right| + k$, find the vertex of the function. Use the vertex and two other points to help you graph $g(x)$.

Ⓐ $g(x) = 4|x - 5| - 2$

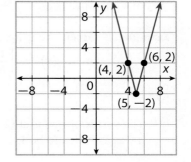

The vertex of the parent absolute value function is at $(0, 0)$.

The vertex of $g(x)$ will be the point to which $(0, 0)$ is mapped to by $g(x)$.

$g(x)$ involves a translation of $f(x)$ 5 units to the right and 2 units down.

The vertex of $g(x)$ will therefore be at $(5, -2)$.

Next, determine the location to which each of the points $(1, 1)$ and $(-1, 1)$ on $f(x)$ will be mapped.

Since $a > 1$ then $g(x)$, in addition to a translation, is also a vertical stretch of $f(x)$ by a factor of 4. The x-coordinate of each point will be shifted 5 units to the right while the y-coordinate will be stretched by a factor of 4 and then moved down 2 units. So, $(1, 1)$ moves to $(1 + 5, 4 \cdot |1| - 2) = (6, 2)$, and $(-1, 1)$ moves to $(-1 + 5, 4 \cdot |1| - 2) = (4, 2)$. Now plot the three points and graph $g(x)$.

Ⓑ $g(x) = \left|-\frac{1}{2}(x + 3)\right| + 1$

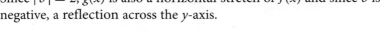

The vertex of the parent absolute value function is at $(0, 0)$.

$g(x)$ is a translation of $f(x)$ 3 units to the left and 1 unit up.

The vertex of $g(x)$ will therefore be at $\left(\boxed{-3}, \boxed{1}\right)$.

Next, determine to where the points $(2, 2)$ and $(-2, 2)$ on $f(x)$ will be mapped.

Since $|b| = 2$, $g(x)$ is also a horizontal stretch of $f(x)$ and since b is negative, a reflection across the y-axis.

The x-coordinate will move 3 units to the left and then stretch by a factor of 2.

The y-coordinate will move up 1 unit.

So, $(2, 2)$ becomes $\left(\boxed{2 - 3}, \left|\boxed{-\frac{1}{2} \cdot 2}\right| + 1\right) = \left(\boxed{-1}, \boxed{2}\right)$, and $(-2, 2)$ becomes $\left(\boxed{-5}, \boxed{2}\right)$.

Now plot the three points and use them to sketch $g(x)$.

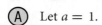
3. Given $g(x) = -\frac{1}{5}\left|(x+6)\right| + 4$, find the vertex and two other points and use them to help you graph $g(x)$.

⚙ Explain 2 Writing Absolute Value Functions from a Graph

If an absolute value equation in the form $g(x) = a\left|\frac{1}{b}(x-h)\right| + k$ has values other than 1 for both a and b, you can rewrite that equation so that the value of at least one of a or b is 1.

When a and b are positive: $a\left|\frac{1}{b}(x-h)\right| = \left|\frac{a}{b}(x-h)\right| = \frac{a}{b}\left|(x-h)\right|$.

When a is negative and b is positive, you can move the opposite of a inside the absolute value expression. This leaves -1 outside the absolute value symbol: $-2\left|\frac{1}{b}\right| = -1(2)\left|\frac{1}{b}\right| = -1\left|\frac{2}{b}\right|$.

When b is negative, you can rewrite the equation without a negative sign, because of the properties of absolute value: $a\left|\frac{1}{b}(x-h)\right| = a\left|\frac{1}{-b}(x-h)\right|$. This case has now been reduced to one of the other two cases.

Example 2 Given the graph of an absolute value function, write the function in the form $g(x) = a\left|\frac{1}{b}(x-h)\right| + k$.

Ⓐ Let $a = 1$.

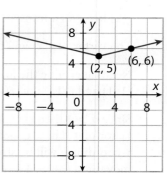

The vertex of $g(x)$ is at $(2, 5)$. This means that $h = 2$ and $k = 5$, and a was assumed to be 1.

Substitute these values into $g(x)$, giving $g(x) = \left|\frac{1}{b}(x-2)\right| + 5$.

Choose a point on $g(x)$ like $(6, 6)$, Substitute these values into $g(x)$, and solve for b.

Substitute. $6 = \left|\frac{1}{b}(6-2)\right| + 5$

Simplify. $6 = \left|\frac{1}{b}(4)\right| + 5$

Subtract 5 from each side. $1 = \left|\frac{4}{b}\right|$

Rewrite the absolute value as two equations. $1 = \frac{4}{b}$ or $1 = -\frac{4}{b}$

Solve for b. $b = 4$ or $b = -4$

Based on the problem conditions, only consider $b = 4$. Substitute into $g(x)$ to find the equation for the graph.

$g(x) = \left|\frac{1}{4}(x-2)\right| + 5$

Ⓑ Let $b = 1$.

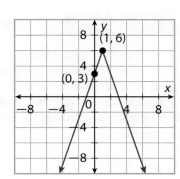

The vertex of $g(x)$ is at (1, 6). This means that $h = \boxed{1}$ and

$k = \boxed{6}$, and b was assumed to be 1.

Substitute these values into $g(x)$, giving $g(x) = a\left|x - \boxed{1}\right| = \boxed{6}$.

Now, choose a point on $g(x)$ with integer coordinates, $\left(0, \boxed{3}\right)$.

Substitute these values into $g(x)$ and solve for a.

$$g(x) = a\left|x - \boxed{1}\right| + \boxed{6}$$

Substitute. $\boxed{3} = a|0 - 1| + 6$

Simplify. $\boxed{3} = a|-1| + 6$

Solve for a. $\boxed{-3} = a$

Therefore $g(x) = \boxed{-3|x-1| + 6}$.

Your Turn

4. Given the graph of an absolute value function, write the function in the form $g(x) = a\left|\frac{1}{b}(x - h)\right| + k$.

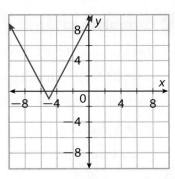

⚙ Explain 3 Modeling with Absolute Value Functions

Light travels in a straight line and can be modeled by a linear function. When light is reflected off a mirror, it travels in a straight line in a different direction. From physics, the angle at which the light ray comes in is equal to the angle at which it is reflected away: the angle of incidence is equal to the angle of reflection. You can use an absolute value function to model this situation.

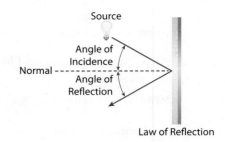

Law of Reflection

Example 3 Solve the problem by modeling the situation with an absolute value function.

At a science museum exhibit, a beam of light originates at a point 10 feet off the floor. It is reflected off a mirror on the floor that is 15 feet from the wall the light originates from. How high off the floor on the opposite wall does the light hit if the other wall is 8.5 feet from the mirror?

🧩 Analyze Information

Identify the important information.

- The model will be of the form $g(x) = a\left|\frac{1}{b}(x - h)\right| + k$.

- The vertex of $g(x)$ is $(15, 0)$.

- Another point on $g(x)$ is $(0, 10)$.

- The opposite wall is 23.5 feet from the first wall.

🧩 Formulate a Plan

Let the base of the first wall be the origin. You want to find the value of $g(x)$ at $x =$ 23.5 , which will give the height of the beam on the opposite wall. To do so, find the value of the parameters in the transformation of the parent function.

In this situation, let $b = 1$. The vertex of $g(x)$ will give you the values of h and k. Use a second point to solve for a. Evaluate $g\left(\boxed{23.5}\right)$.

🧩 Solve

The vertex of $g(x)$ is at $\left(\boxed{15}, 0\right)$. Substitute, giving $g(x) = a\left|x - \boxed{15}\right| + \boxed{0}$.

Evaluate $g(x)$ at 0,10 and solve for a.

Substitute.	$10 = a\left\|\boxed{0} - 15\right\| + \boxed{0}$
Simplify.	$\boxed{10} = a\left\|\boxed{-15}\right\|$
Simplify.	$10 = \boxed{15}\ a$
Solve for a.	$a = \boxed{\dfrac{2}{3}}$

Therefore $g(x) = \frac{2}{3}|(x - 15)|$. Find $g\left(\boxed{23.5}\right)$. $g(23.5) = \boxed{\dfrac{17}{3}} \approx 5.67$

The answer of 5.67 makes sense because function is symmetric with respect to the line $x = 15$. This represents a distance that is a little more than twice as far from the beam's origin as it is from the spot where the beam hits the second wall. Since the beam originates at a height of 10 feet, it should hit the second wall at a height of a little over 5 feet.

Your Turn

5. Two students are passing a ball back and forth, allowing it to bounce once between them. If one student bounce-passes the ball from a height of 1.4 m and it bounces 3 m away from the student, where should the second student stand to catch the ball at a height of 1.2 m? Assume the path of the ball is linear over this short distance.

💬 Elaborate

6. In the general form of the absolute value function, what does each parameter represent?

7. **Discussion** Explain why the vertex of $f(x) = |x|$ remains the same when $f(x)$ is stretched or compressed but not when it is translated.

8. **Essential Question Check-In** What are the features of the graph of an absolute value function?

⭐ Evaluate: Homework and Practice

Predict what the graph of each given function will look like. Verify your prediction using a graphing calculator. Then sketch the graph of the function.

- Online Homework
- Hints and Help
- Extra Practice

1. $g(x) = 6|x - 3|$

2. $g(x) = -4|x + 2| + 5$

3. $g(x) = \left| \frac{7}{5}(x - 6) \right| + 4$

4. $g(x) = \left| \frac{3}{7}(x - 4) \right| + 2$

5. $g(x) = \frac{7}{4}|(x - 2)| - 3$

Graph the given function and identify the domain and range.

6. $g(x) = |x|$

7. $g(x) = \frac{4}{3}|(x - 5)| + 7$

8. $g(x) = -\frac{7}{6}|(x - 2)|$

9. $g(x) = \left| \frac{3}{4}(x - 2) \right| - 7$

10. $g(x) = \left| \frac{5}{7}(x - 4) \right|$

11. $g(x) = \left| -\frac{7}{3}(x + 5) \right| - 4$

Write the absolute value function in standard form for the given graph. Use *a* or *b* as directed, *b* > 0.

12. Let $a = 1$.

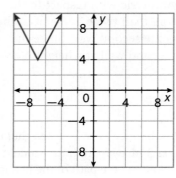

13. Let $b = 1$.

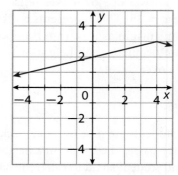

14. A rainstorm begins as a drizzle, builds up to a heavy rain, and then drops back to a drizzle. The rate *r* (in inches per hour) at which it rains is given by the function $r = -0.5|t - 1| + 0.5$, where *t* is the time (in hours). Graph the function. Determine for how long it rains and when it rains the hardest.

15. While playing pool, a player tries to shoot the eight ball into the corner pocket as shown. Imagine that a coordinate plane is placed over the pool table. The eight ball is at $\left(5, \frac{5}{4}\right)$ and the pocket they are aiming for is at (10, 5). The player is going to bank the ball off the side at (6, 0).

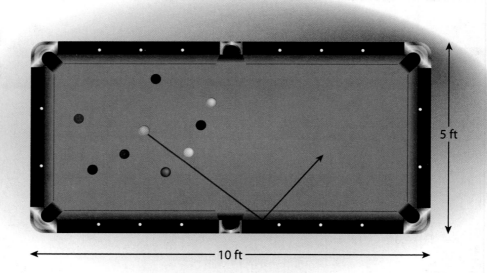

5 ft

10 ft

a. Write an equation for the path of the ball.

b. Did the player make the shot? How do you know?

16. Sam is sitting in a boat on a lake. She can get sunburnt from the sunlight that hits her directly and from sunlight that reflects off the water. Sunlight reflects off the water at the point (2, 0) and hits Sam at the point (3.5, 3). Write and graph the function that shows the path of the sunlight.

17. The Transamerica Pyramid is an office building in San Francisco. It stands 853 feet tall and is 145 feet wide at its base. Imagine that a coordinate plane is placed over a side of the building. In the coordinate plane, each unit represents one foot. Write an absolute value function whose graph is the V-shaped outline of the sides of the building, ignoring the "shoulders" of the building.

18. Match each graph with its function.

A. $y = |x + 6| - 4$

B. $y = |x - 6| - 4$

C. $y = |x - 6| + 4$

a.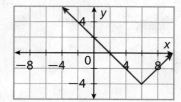

b.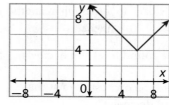

c.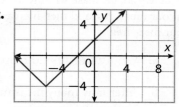

H.O.T. Focus on Higher Order Thinking

19. Explain the Error Explain why the graph shown is not the graph of $y = |x + 3| + 2$. What is the correct equation shown in the graph?

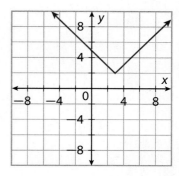

20. Multi-Step A golf player is trying to make a hole-in-one on the miniature golf green shown. Imagine that a coordinate plane is placed over the golf green. The golf ball is at (2.5, 2) and the hole is at (9.5, 2). The player is going to bank the ball off the side wall of the green at (6, 8).

a. Write an equation for the path of the ball.

b. Use the equation in part a to determine if the player makes the shot.

Lesson Performance Task

Suppose a musical piece calls for an orchestra to start at *fortissimo* (about 90 decibels), decrease steadily in loudness to *pianissimo* (about 50 decibels) in four measures, and then increase steadily back to *fortissimo* in another four measures.

a. Write a function to represent the sound level *s* in decibels

b. After how many measures should the orchestra be at the loudness of *mezzo forte* (about 70 decibels)?

c. Describe what the graph of this function would look like.

2.2 Solving Absolute Value Equations

Essential Question: How can you solve an absolute value equation?

 TEKS **A2.6.E** Solve absolute value linear equations. Also A2.6.D

⊘ Explore Solving Absolute Value Equations Graphically

Absolute value equations differ from linear equations in that they may have two solutions. This is indicated with a **disjunction**, a mathematical statement created by a connecting two other statements with the word "or." To see why there can be two solutions, you can solve an absolute value equation using graphs.

(A) Solve the equation $2|x - 5| - 4 = 2$.

Plot the function $f(x) = 2|x - 5| - 4$ on a coordinate grid. Then plot the function $g(x) = 2$ as a horizontal line on the same grid, and mark the points where the plots intersect.

(B) Write the solution to this equation as a disjunction:

$x =$ ⬜ or $x =$ ⬜

Reflect

1. Why might you expect most absolute value equations to have two solutions? Why not three or four?

2. Is it possible for an absolute value equation to have no solutions? one solution? If so, what would each look like graphically?

🔑 Explain 1 Solving Absolute Value Equations Algebraically

To solve absolute value equations algebraically, first isolate the absolute value on one side of the equation the same way you would isolate a variable. Then use the rule:

If $|x| = a$ (where a is a positive number), then $x = a$ OR $x = -a$.

Notice the use of a **disjunction** here in the rule for values of x. You cannot know from the original equation whether the expression inside the absolute value is positive or negative, so you must work through both possibilities to finish isolating x.

Example 1 Solve each absolute value equation algebraically. Graph the solutions on a number line.

Ⓐ $|3x| + 2 = 8$

Subtract 2 from both sides. $\qquad$ $|3x| = 6$

Rewrite as two equations. $\qquad$ $3x = 6$ or $3x = -6$

Solve for x. $\qquad$ $x = 2$ or $x = -2$

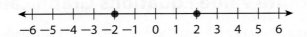

Ⓑ $3|4x - 5| - 2 = 19$

Add 2 to both sides. $\quad$ $3|4x - 5| = \boxed{21}$

Divide both sides by 3. $\quad$ $|4x - 5| = \boxed{7}$

Rewrite as two equations. $\quad$ $4x - 5 = \boxed{7}$ or $4x - 5 = \boxed{-7}$

Add 5 to all four sides. $\quad$ $4x = \boxed{12}$ or $4x = \boxed{-2}$

Solve for x. $\qquad$ $x = \boxed{3}$ or $x = -\dfrac{\boxed{1}}{\boxed{2}}$

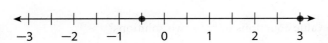

Your Turn

Solve each absolute value equation algebraically. Graph the solutions on a number line.

3. $\dfrac{1}{2}|x + 2| = 10$

4. $-2|3x - 6| + 5 = 1$

Explain 2   Absolute Value Equations with Fewer than Two Solutions

You have seen that absolute value equations have two solutions when the isolated absolute value is equal to a positive number. When the absolute value is equal to zero, there is a single solution because zero is its own opposite. When the absolute value is equal to a negative number, there is no solution because absolute value is never negative.

Example 2   Isolate the absolute value in each equation to determine if the equation can be solved. If so, finish the solution. If not, write "no solution."

Ⓐ $-5|x + 1| + 2 = 12$

Subtract 2 from both sides.	$-5|x + 1| = 10$
Divide both sides by -5.	$|x + 1| = -2$
Absolute values are never negative.	No Solution

Ⓑ $\frac{3}{5}|2x - 4| - 3 = -3$

Add 3 to both sides.	$\frac{3}{5}|2x - 4| =$ $\boxed{0}$
Multiply both sides by $\frac{5}{3}$.	$|2x - 4| =$ $\boxed{0}$
Rewrite as one equation.	$2x - 4 =$ $\boxed{0}$
Add 4 to both sides.	$2x =$ $\boxed{4}$
Divide both sides by 2.	$x =$ $\boxed{2}$

Your Turn

Isolate the absolute value in each equation to determine if the equation can be solved. If so, finish the solution. If not, write "no solution."

5. $3\left|\frac{1}{2}x + 5\right| + 7 = 5$ **6.** $9\left|\frac{4}{3}x - 2\right| + 7 = 7$

Explain 3   Solving a Real-world Problem with Absolute Value Equations

Absolute value functions can be used to model real-world situations involving distances from a point, reflections, and V-shaped paths. While the algebraic process often suggests two solutions, additional knowledge of the problem can reduce the solution to a single answer. For example, you might find an impossible variable value like a negative length, or a solution outside the limited domain implied by the model.

Example 2 Model the real-world situations with an absolute value function to answer the questions asked. Eliminate solutions that are outside the domain of the model function.

(A) Alice, Brian, and Charley are playing the game *keep away*, with Brian between Alice and Charley. Brian is 4 feet from Alice, and 6 feet from Charley. Alice throws the ball over Brian's head to Charley at $t = 0$ with a horizontal velocity of 20 feet per second. Suppose you are looking down at the game from directly overhead. At what time(s) will the ball be 2 feet away from Brian?

The horizontal distance of the ball from Alice is given by the velocity times the time or $20t$. The distance from Brian, as viewed from overhead, is given by the function $d(t) = |20t - 4|$.

To find the time when the ball is 2 feet away, set $d(t) = 2$ and solve the absolute value equation:

$|20t - 4| = 2$

$20t - 4 = 2$ or $20t - 4 = -2$

$20t = 6$ or $20t = 2$

$t = \dfrac{3}{10}s$ or $t = \dfrac{1}{10}s$

Both of these solutions are correct: the ball is 2 feet away from Brian twice during the throw.

(B) Using the same situation, find the time(s) when the ball is 5 feet from Brian.

$|20t - 4| = \boxed{5}$

$20t - 4 = \boxed{5}$ or $20t - 4 = \boxed{-5}$

$20t = \boxed{9}$ or $20t = \boxed{-1}$

$t = \dfrac{\boxed{9}}{20}s$ or $t = \boxed{-\dfrac{1}{20}}s$

One of these solutions represents a time before Alice throws the ball. The function describing the distance to Brian does not apply before Alice throws the ball. Eliminate the invalid solution and write the only correct answer.

$t = \dfrac{\boxed{9}}{20}s$

7. A laser is raised 3 cm up off of a reflective table and pointed so that it hits the table 5 cm from the edge. The laser beam follows a path defined by the absolute value function:

$$v(h) = \frac{3}{5}|h - 5|$$

where v is the vertical height and h is the horizontal position from the edge of the table. Use an absolute value model to find the horizontal position(s) where the laser is 2 cm from the table.

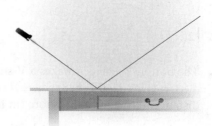

💬 Elaborate

8. Why is important to solve both equations in the disjunction arising from an absolute value equation? Why not just pick one and solve it, knowing the solution for the variable will work when plugged backed into the equation?

9. **Discussion** Discuss how the range of the absolute value function differs from the range of a linear function. Graphically, how does this explain why a linear equation always has exactly one solution while an absolute value equation can have one, two, or no solutions?

10. **Essential Question Check-In** Describe, in your own words, the basic steps to solving absolute value equations and how many solutions to expect.

⭐ Evaluate: Homework and Practice

- Online Homework
- Hints and Help
- Extra Practice

Solve the following absolute value equations by graphing.

1. $|x - 3| + 2 = 5$

2. $2|x + 1| + 5 = 9$

3. $-2|x + 5| + 4 = 1$

4. $\left|\frac{3}{2}(x - 2)\right| + 3 = 2$

Solve each absolute value equation algebraically. Graph the solutions on a number line.

5. $|2x| = 3$

6. $\left|\frac{1}{3}x + 4\right| = 3$

7. $3|2x - 3| + 2 = 3$

8. $-8|-x - 6| + 10 = 2$

Isolate the absolute values in the following equations to determine if they can be solved. If so, find and graph the solution(s). If not, write "no solution".

9. $\frac{1}{4}|x + 2| + 7 = 5$

10. $-3|x - 3| + 3 = 6$

11. $2(|x + 4| + 3) = 6$

12. $5|2x + 4| - 3 = -3$

Solve the absolute value equations.

13. $|3x - 4| + 2 = 1$

14. $7\left|\frac{1}{2}x + 3\frac{1}{2}\right| - 2 = 5$

15. $|2(x + 5) - 3| + 2 = 6$

16. $-5|-3x + 2| - 2 = -2$

17. The bottom of a river makes a V-shape that can be modeled with the absolute value function, $d(h) = \frac{1}{5}|h - 240| - 48$, where d is the depth of the river bottom (in feet) and h is the horizontal distance to the left-hand shore (in feet).

A ship risks running aground if the bottom of its keel (its lowest point under the water) reaches down to the river bottom. Suppose you are the harbormaster and you want to place buoys where the river bottom is 30 feet below the surface. How far from the left-hand shore should you place the buoys?

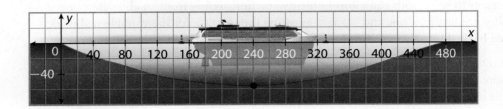

18. Geometry Find the points on the *x*-axis where a circle centered at (3, 0) with a radius of 5 crosses the *x*-axis. Use an absolute value equation and the fact that all points on a circle are the same distance (the radius) from the center.

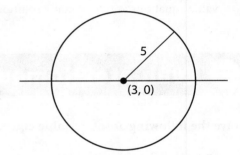

19. A flock of geese is flying past a photographer in a V-formation that can be described using the absolute value function $b(d) = \frac{3}{2}|d - 50|$, where $b(d)$ is the distance (in feet) of a goose behind the leader, and d is the distance from the photographer. If the flock reaches 27 feet behind the leader on both sides, find the distance of the nearest goose to the photographer.

20. Select the value or values of x that satisfy the equation $-\frac{1}{2}|3x - 3| + 2 = 1$.

A. $x = \frac{5}{3}$ B. $x = -\frac{5}{3}$

C. $x = \frac{1}{3}$ D. $x = -\frac{1}{3}$

E. $x = 3$ F. $x = -3$

G. $x = 1$ H. $x = -1$

21. Terry is trying to place a satellite dish on the roof of his house at the recommended height of 30 feet. His house is 32 feet wide, and the height of the roof can be described by the function $h(x) = -\frac{3}{2}|x - 16| + 24$, where x is the distance along the width of the house. Where should Terry

H.O.T.   Focus on Higher Order Thinking

22. Explain the Error While attempting to solve the equation $-3|x - 4| - 4 = 3$ a student came up with the following results. Explain the error and find the correct solution:

$-3|x - 4| - 4 = 3$

$-3|x - 4| = 7$

$|x - 4| = -\frac{7}{3}$

$x - 4 = -\frac{7}{3}$ or $x - 4 = \frac{7}{3}$

$x = \frac{5}{3}$ or $x = -\frac{19}{3}$

23. Communicate Mathematical Ideas Solve this absolute value equation and explain what algebraic properties make it possible to do so.

$3|x - 2| = 5|x - 2| - 7$

24. Justify Your Reasoning This absolute value equation has nested absolute values. Use your knowledge of solving absolute value equations to solve this equation. Justify the number of possible solutions.

$\left| |2x + 5| - 3 \right| = 10$

25. Check for Reasonableness For what type of real-world quantities would the negative answer for an absolute value equation not make sense?

Lesson Performance Task

A snowball comes apart as a child throws it north, resulting in two halves traveling away from the child. The child is standing 12 feet south and 6 feet east of the school door, along an east-west wall. One fragment flies off to the northeast, moving 2 feet east for every 5 feet north of travel, and the other moves 2 feet west for every 5 feet north of travel. Write an absolute value function that describes the northward position, $n(e)$, of both fragments as a function of how far east of the school door they are. How far apart are the fragments when they strike the wall?

2.3 Solving Absolute Value Inequalities

Essential Question: What are two ways to solve an absolute value inequality?

 TEKS **A2.6.F** Solve absolute value linear inequalities.

Explore   Visualizing the Solution Set of an Absolute Value Inequality

You know that when solving an absolute value equation, it's possible to get two solutions. Here, you will explore what happens when you solve absolute value inequalities.

Ⓐ Determine whether each of the integers from −5 to 5 is a solution of the inequality $|x| + 2 < 5$. Write *yes* or *no* for each number in the table. If a number is a solution, plot it on a number line.

Number	Solution?
$x = -5$	no
$x = -4$	no
$x = -3$	no
$x = -2$	yes
$x = -1$	yes
$x = 0$	yes
$x = 1$	yes
$x = 2$	yes
$x = 3$	no
$x = 4$	no
$x = 5$	no

Ⓑ Determine whether each of the integers from −5 to 5 is a solution of the inequality $|x| + 2 > 5$. Write *yes* or *no* for each number in the table. If a number is a solution, plot it on a number line.

Number	Solution?
$x = -5$	yes
$x = -4$	yes
$x = -3$	no
$x = -2$	no
$x = -1$	no
$x = 0$	no
$x = 1$	no
$x = 2$	no
$x = 3$	no
$x = 4$	yes
$x = 5$	yes

Ⓒ State the solutions of the equation $|x| + 2 = 5$ and relate them to the solutions you found for the inequalities in Steps A and B.

Ⓓ If x is any real number and not just an integer, graph the solutions of $|x| + 2 < 5$ on one number line and $|x| + 2 > 5$ on another number line.

Reflect

1. It's possible to describe the solutions of $|x| + 2 < 5$ and $|x| + 2 > 5$ using inequalities that don't involve absolute value. For instance, you can write the solutions of $|x| + 2 < 5$ as $x > -3$ and $x < 3$. Notice that the word *and* is used because x must be both greater than -3 and less than 3. How would you write the solutions of $|x| + 2 > 5$? Explain.

2. Describe the solutions of $|x| + 2 \le 5$ and $|x| + 2 \ge 5$ using inequalities that don't involve absolute value.

🔧 Explain 1 Solving Absolute Value Inequalities Graphically

You can use a graph to solve an absolute value inequality of the form $f(x) > g(x)$ or $f(x) < g(x)$, where $f(x)$ is an absolute value function and $g(x)$ is a constant function. Graph each function separately on the same coordinate plane and determine the intervals on the x-axis where one graph lies above or below the other. For $f(x) > g(x)$, you want to find the x-values for which the graph $f(x)$ is above the graph of $g(x)$. For $f(x) < g(x)$, you want to find the x-values for which the graph of $f(x)$ is below the graph of $g(x)$.

Example 1 **Solve the inequality graphically.**

Ⓐ $|x + 3| + 1 > 4$

The inequality is of the form $f(x) > g(x)$, so determine the intervals on the x-axis where the graph of $f(x) = |x + 3| + 1$ lies above the graph of $g(x) = 4$.

The graph of $f(x) = |x + 3| + 1$ lies above the graph of $g(x) = 4$ to the left of $x = -6$ and to the right of $x = 0$, so the solution of $|x + 3| + 1 > 4$ is $x < -6$ or $x > 0$.

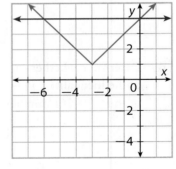

Ⓑ $|x - 2| - 3 < 1$

The inequality is of the form $f(x) < g(x)$, so determine the intervals on the x-axis where the graph of $f(x) = |x - 2| - 3$ lies below the graph of $g(x) = 1$.

The graph of $f(x) = |x - 2| - 3$ lies below the graph of

$g(x) = 1$ between $x = \boxed{-2}$ and $x = \boxed{6}$, so the solution of

$|x - 2| - 3 < 1$ is $x > \boxed{-2}$ and $x < \boxed{6}$.

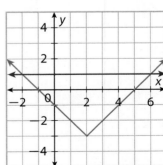

© Houghton Mifflin Harcourt Publishing Company

3. Suppose the inequality in Part A is $|x + 3| + 1 \geq 4$ instead of $|x + 3| + 1 > 4$. How does the solution change?

4. In Part B, what is another way to write the solution $x > -2$ and $x < 6$?

5. **Discussion** Suppose the graph of an absolute value function $f(x)$ lies entirely above the graph of the constant function $g(x)$. What is the solution of the inequality $f(x) > g(x)$? What is the solution of the inequality $f(x) < g(x)$?

Your Turn

6. Solve $|x + 1| - 4 \leq -2$ graphically.

⚙ Explain 2 Solving Absolute Value Inequalities Algebraically

To solve an absolute value inequality algebraically, start by isolating the absolute value expression. When the absolute value expression is by itself on one side of the inequality, apply one of the following rules to finish solving the inequality for the variable.

Solving Absolute Value Inequalities Algebraically
1. If $|x| > a$ where a is a positive number, then $x < -a$ or $x > a$.
2. If $|x| < a$ where a is a positive number, then $-a < x < a$.

Example 2 Solve the inequality algebraically. Graph the solution on a number line.

Ⓐ $|4 - x| + 15 > 21$

$\qquad |4 - x| > 6$

$\qquad 4 - x < -6 \quad$ or $\quad 4 - x > 6$

$\qquad\quad -x < -10 \quad$ or $\quad -x > 2$

$\qquad\qquad x > 10 \quad$ or $\qquad x < -2$

The solution is $x > 10$ or $x < -2$.

Ⓑ $|x + 4| - 10 \leq -2$

$\qquad |x + 4| \leq \boxed{8}$

$\qquad x + 4 \geq \boxed{-8} \quad$ and $\quad x + 4 \leq \boxed{8}$

$\qquad\qquad x \geq \boxed{-12} \quad$ and $\qquad x \leq \boxed{4}$

The solution is $x \geq \boxed{-12}$ and $x \leq \boxed{4}$,

or $\boxed{-12} \leq x \leq \boxed{4}$.

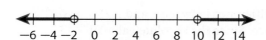

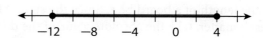

7. In Part A, suppose the inequality were $|4 - x| + 15 > 14$ instead of $|4 - x| + 15 > 21$. How would the solution change? Explain.

8. In Part B, suppose the inequality were $|x + 4| - 10 \leq -11$ instead of $|x + 4| - 10 \leq -2$. How would the solution change? Explain.

Your Turn

Solve the inequality algebraically. Graph the solution on a number line.

9. $3|x - 7| \geq 9$

10. $|2x + 3| < 5$

🔑 Explain 3   Solving a Real-World Problem with Absolute Value Inequalities

Absolute value inequalities are often used to model real-world situations involving a margin of error or *tolerance*. Tolerance is the allowable amount of variation in a quantity.

Example 3

Ⓐ A machine at a lumber mill cuts boards that are 3.25 meters long. It is acceptable for the length to differ from this value by at most 0.02 meters. Write and solve an absolute value inequality to find the range of acceptable lengths.

🧩 Analyze Information

Identify the important information.

- The boards being cut are $\boxed{3.25}$ meters long.
- The length can differ by at most 0.02 meters.

🧩 Formulate a Plan

Let the length of a board be ℓ. Since the sign of the difference between ℓ and 3.25 doesn't matter, take the absolute value of the difference. Since the absolute value of the difference can be at most 0.02, the inequality that models the situation is

$$\left| \ell - \boxed{3.25} \right| \leq \boxed{0.02} .$$

🧩 Solve

$$|\ell - 3.25| \leq 0.02$$

$$\ell - 3.25 \geq -0.02 \text{ and } \ell - 3.25 \leq 0.02$$

$$\ell \geq \boxed{3.23} \text{ and } \qquad \ell \leq \boxed{3.27}$$

So, the range of acceptable lengths is $\boxed{3.23} \leq \ell \leq \boxed{3.27}$

The bounds of the range are positive and close to $\boxed{3.25}$, so this is a reasonable answer.

The answer is correct since $\boxed{3.23} + 0.02 = 3.25$ and $\boxed{3.27} - 0.02 = 3.25$.

Your Turn

11. A box of cereal is supposed to weigh 13.8 oz, but it's acceptable for the weight to vary as much as 0.1 oz. Write and solve an absolute value inequality to find the range of acceptable weights.

 Elaborate

12. Describe the values of x that satisfy the inequalities $|x| < a$ and $|x| > a$ where a is a positive constant.

13. How do you algebraically solve an absolute value inequality?

14. Explain why the solution of $|x| > a$ is all real numbers if a is a negative number.

15. **Essential Question Check-In** How do you solve an absolute value inequality graphically?

⭐ Evaluate: Homework and Practice

• Online Homework
• Hints and Help
• Extra Practice

1. Determine whether each of the integers from −5 to 5 is a solution of the inequality $|x - 1| + 3 \geq 5$. If a number is a solution, plot it on a number line.

2. Determine whether each of the integers from −5 to 5 is a solution of the inequality $|x + 1| - 2 \leq 1$. If a number is a solution, plot it on a number line.

Solve each inequality graphically.

3. $2|x| \leq 6$

4. $|x - 3| - 2 > -1$

5. $\frac{1}{2}|x| + 2 < 3$

6. $|x + 2| - 4 \geq -2$

Match each graph with the corresponding absolute value inequality. Then give the solution of the inequality.

A. $2|x| + 1 > 3$ **B.** $2|x + 1| < 3$ **C.** $2|x| - 1 > 3$ **D.** $2|x - 1| < 3$

7.
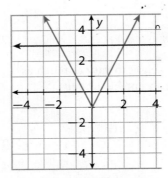

8.
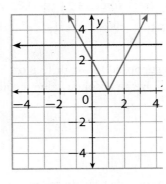

9.
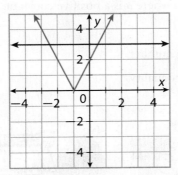

10.
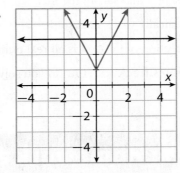

Solve each absolute value inequality algebraically. If the inequality has a solution, graph the solution on a number line.

11. $2\left|x - \dfrac{7}{2}\right| + 3 > 4$

12. $|2x + 1| - 4 < 5$

13. $3|x + 4| + 2 \geq 5$

14. $|x + 11| - 8 \leq -3$

15. $-5|x - 3| - 5 < 15$

16. $8|x + 4| + 10 < 2$

Solve each problem using an absolute value inequality.

17. The thermostat for a house is set to 68 °F, but the actual temperature may vary by as much as 2 °F. What is the range of possible temperatures?

18. The balance of Jason's checking account is $320. The balance varies by as much as $80 each week. What are the possible balances of Jason's account?

19. On average, a squirrel lives to be 6.5 years old. The lifespan of a squirrel may vary by as much as 1.5 years. What is the range of ages that a squirrel lives?

20. You are playing a history quiz game where you must give the years of historical events. In order to score any points at all for a question about the year in which a man first stepped on the moon, your answer must be no more than 3 years away from the correct answer, 1969. What is the range of answers that allow you to score points?

21. The speed limit on a road is 30 miles per hour. Drivers on this road typically vary their speed around the limit by as much as 5 miles per hour. What is the range of typical speeds on this road?

22. **Represent Real-World Problems** A poll of likely voters shows that the incumbent will get 51% of the vote in an upcoming election. Based on the number of voters polled, the results of the poll could be off by as much as 3 percentage points. What does this mean for the incumbent?

23. **Explain the Error** A student solved the inequality $|x - 1| - 3 > 1$ graphically. Identify and correct the student's error.

    I graphed the functions $f(x) = |x - 1| - 3$ and $g(x) = 1$. Because the graph of $g(x)$ lies above the graph of $f(x)$ between $x = -3$ and $x = 5$, the solution of the inequality is $-3 < x < 5$.

    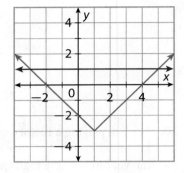

24. **Multi-Step** Recall that a literal equation or inequality is one in which the constants have been replaced by letters.

    a. Solve $|ax + b| > c$ for x. Write the solution in terms of a, b, and c. Assume that $a > 0$ and $c > 0$.

    b. Use the solution of the literal inequality to find the solution of $|10x + 21| > 14$.

    c. Explain why you must assume that $a > 0$ and $c > 0$ before you begin solving the literal inequality.

Lesson Performance Task

The distance between the Sun and each planet in our solar system varies because the planets travel in elliptical orbits around the Sun. Here is a table of the average distance and the variation in the distance for the five innermost planets in our solar system.

	Average Distance	Variation
Mercury	36 million miles	7.5 million miles
Venus	67.2 million miles	0.5 million miles
Earth	92.75 million miles	1.75 million miles
Mars	141 million miles	13 million miles
Jupiter	484 million miles	24 million miles

a. Write and solve an inequality to represent the range of distances that can occur between the Sun and each planet.

b. Calculate the percentage variation (variation divided by average distance) in the orbit of each of the planets. Based on these percentages, which planet has the most elliptical orbit?

Absolute Value Functions, Equations, and Inequalities

Essential Question: How can you use absolute value functions to solve real-world problems?

Key Vocabulary

absolute value *(valor absoluto)*
absolute-value equation
   (ecuación de valor absoluto)
coefficient *(coeficiente)*
disjunction *(disyunción)*
domain *(dominio)*
function *(función)*
inequality *(desigualdad)*
parameter *(parámetro)*
range *(rango)*
symmetry *(simetría)*
vertex *(vértice)*

KEY EXAMPLE   (Lesson 2.1)

Given the function $g(x) = \left| \dfrac{1}{3}(x + 6) \right| - 1$, **predict what the graph will look like compared to the parent function,** $f(x) = |x|$.

The graph of $g(x)$ will be the graph of $f(x)$ translated down 1 unit and left 6 units. There will also be a horizontal stretch of $f(x)$ by a factor of 3.

KEY EXAMPLE   (Lesson 2.2)

Solve $6\left|2x + 3\right| + 1 = 25$ **algebraically.**

$6\lvert 2x + 3 \rvert + 1 = 24$	Subtract 1 from both sides.
$\lvert 4x + 3 \rvert = 4$	Divide both sides by 6.
$4x + 3 = 4 \quad$ or $\quad 4x + 3 = -4$	Rewrite as two equations.
$4x = 1 \qquad$ or $\quad 4x = -7$	*Subtract 3 from all four sides.*
$x = \dfrac{1}{4} \qquad$ or $\quad x = -\dfrac{7}{4}$	Solve for x.
So, $x = \dfrac{1}{4} \qquad$ or $-\dfrac{7}{4}$.	

Subtract 3 from all four sides.

KEY EXAMPLE   (Lesson 2.3)

Solve $\lvert x + 2 \rvert - 6 < 4$ **algebraically, then graph the solution on a number line.**

$$\lvert x + 2 \rvert - 4 < 4$$

$\lvert x + 2 \rvert < 8$	Add 4 to both sides.
$x + 2 < 8 \quad$ or $\quad x + 2 > -8$	Rewrite as two inequalities.
$x < 6 \quad$ or $\quad x > -10$	

The solution is $x < 6$ or $x > -10$.

Subtract 2 from all four sides.

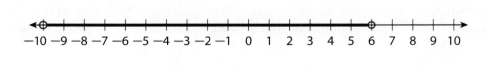

EXERCISES

Solve. *(Lessons 2.2, 2.3)*

1. $-10|x + 2| = -70$

2. $|3x + 7| = 27$

3. $\frac{1}{7}|8 + x| \leq 5$

4. $|x - 2| - 5 > 10$

5. Explain how the graph of $g(x) = \left|\frac{3}{7}(x - 4)\right| + 2$ compares to the graph of $h(x) = \frac{3}{7}(x - 4) + 2$. *(Lesson 2.1)*

6. Leroy wants to place a chimney on his roof. It is recommended that the chimney be set at a height of at least 25 feet. The height of the roof is described by the function $r(x) = -\frac{4}{3}|x - 10| + 35$, where x is the width of the roof. Where should Leroy place the chimney if the house is 40 feet wide? *(Lessons 2.3)*

MODULE PERFORMANCE TASK
What Is the Purity of Gold?

You have three gold rings labeled 10 karat, 14 karat, and 18 karat, and would like to know if the rings are correctly labeled. The table shows the results of an analysis of the rings.

Ring Label	Actual Percentage of Gold
10-karat	40.6%
14-karat	59.5%
18-karat	71.2%

In the United States, jewelry manufacturers are legally allowed a half karat tolerance. Determine which of the rings, if any, have an actual percentage of gold that falls outside this tolerance.

Use your own paper to complete the task. Be sure to write down all your data and assumptions. Then use graphs, numbers, words, or algebra to explain how you reached your conclusion.

2.1–2.3 Absolute Value Functions, Equations, and Inequalities

- Online Homework
- Hints and Help
- Extra Practice

Solve. *(Lesson 2.1)*

1. $|-2x - 3| = 6$

2. $\frac{1}{4}|-4 - 3x| = 2$

3. $|3x + 8| = 2$

4. $4|x + 7| + 3 = 59$

Solve each inequality using the method indicated. *(Lesson 2.2)*

5. $|5x + 2| \leq -13$ (algebraically)

6. $|x - 2| + 1 \leq 5$ (graphically)

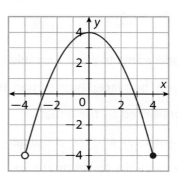

ESSENTIAL QUESTION

7. Write a real world situation that could be modeled by $|x - 14| = 3$. *(Lesson 2.1)*

Assessment Readiness

1. Which function, when graphed, is reflected over the x-axis when compared to $f(x) = |x|$?

   A. $g(x) = 3|x - 4|$

   B. $hx = -\frac{1}{2}|x|$

   C. $j(x) = |x + 3| + 2$

   D. $k(x) = |x| - 10$

2. Solve $\frac{2}{3}|x - 4| + 2 = 5$ for x.

   A. $x = 5$

   B. $x = 11$ or $x = -3$

   C. $x = 8.5$ or $x = -0.5$

   D. $x = 2$ or $x = 6$

3. What happens to $y = 2^{-x}$ as $x \to -\infty$?

   A. $y \to -\infty$

   B. $y \to \infty$

   C. $y \to 0$

   D. $y \to -3$

4. Laurie wants to put a portable cellular phone mini-tower on her roof. The tower cannot be placed higher than 30 feet off the ground. The slant of her roof can be represented by the equation $r(x) = -\frac{1}{4}x + 60$, where x is the distance from the central peak and $r(x)$ is the height off the ground. If her roof is 40 feet across, can she place the tower on the roof? If so, where? Explain.

Assessment Readiness

Personal Math Trainer

• Online Homework
• Hints and Help
• Extra Practice

1. Consider the function $f(x) = 2(x - 1)^2 + 5$. Select the correct statement.

   A. The domain is $-0 < x < \infty$.

   B. The domain is $-1 < x < \infty$.

   C. The range is $y \geq 5$.

   D. The range is $y \geq 7$.

2. Consider the function $g(x) = -3f(x + 1) - 1$. Select the correct statement.

   A. When compared to $f(x) = 2x$, $g(x)$ will have a vertical stretch of $\frac{1}{3}$.

   B. W.hen compared to $f(x) = 2x$, $g(x)$ will be reflected over the x-axis.

   C. When compared to $f(x) = 2x$, $g(x)$ will be translated right 1 unit.

   D. When compared to $f(x) = 2x$, $g(x)$ will be translated up 3 units.

3. What is the inverse function $f^{-1}(x)$ for $f(x) = \frac{1}{2}x - 5$? Select the correct answer.

   A. $f^{-1}(x) = 2x - 10$

   B. $f^{-1}(x) = \frac{1}{2}x + 5$

   C. $f^{-1}(x) = 2x + 10$

   D. $f^{-1}(x) = x + 10$

4. Consider the absolute value equation $3|x - 2| + 6 = 12$. What are the solutions of the equation? Select the correct answer.

   A. $x = 2, x = -2$

   B. Only $x = 4$

   C. $x > 2$

   D. $x = 4, x = 0$

5. Look at each function. For which function will the graph be stretched in the vertical direction when compared to $f(x) = |x|$? Select the correct answer.

   A. $g(x) = 2|x + 1| - 4$

   B. $h(x) = |x - 2| - 1$

   C. $j(x) = |x - 7| + 2$

   D. $k(x) = -\left|x + \frac{1}{2}\right| - 6$

6. A triathlete is training for her next race and starts by swimming 2 miles in 1 hour. She rests for 1 hour and then rides her bike 100 miles in 5 hours. She rests another hour and runs 20 miles in 5 hours. Draw a graph showing the distance she travels over time. Explain your choice. *(Lesson 1.2)*

7. The maximum number of oranges in a cubic foot box can be modeled by the inequality $|x - 17| \leq 5$, depending on the size of the oranges. Solve the inequality to find the highest and lowest amounts of oranges in a box. *(Lesson 2.3)*

Performance Tasks

★ **8.** The revenue from an amusement park ride is given by the admission price of $3 times the number of riders. As part of a promotion, the first 10 riders ride for free.

    A. What kind of transformation describes the change in the revenue based on the promotion?

    B. Write a function rule for this transformation.

© Houghton Mifflin Harcourt Publishing Company

★★ **9.** An automotive mechanic charges $50 to diagnose the problem in a vehicle and $65 per hour for labor to fix it.

   A. If the mechanic increases his diagnostic fee to $60, what kind of transformation is the graph of the total repair bill?

   B. If the mechanic increases his labor rate to $75 per hour, what kind of transformation is this to the graph of the total repair bill?

   C. If it took 3 hours to repair your car, which of the two rate increase would have a greater effect on your total bill?

★★★**10.** **Diving** Scuba divers must know that the deeper the dive, the greater the water pressure in pounds per square inch (psi) for fresh water diving, as shown in the table.

   A. Write the pressure as a function of depth, and identify a reasonable domain and range for this function.

   B. Find the inverse of the function from part **A**. What does the inverse function represent?

   C. The point (25.9, 25.9) is an approximate solution to both the function from part **A** and its inverse. What does this point mean in the context of the problem?

Depth (feet)	Pressure (psi)
34	29.4
68	44.1
102	58.8

Community Theater Owner A community theater currently sells 200 season tickets at $50 each. In order to increase its season-ticket revenue, the theater surveys its season-ticket holders to see if they would be willing to pay more. The survey finds that for every $5 increase in the price of a season ticket, the theater would lose 10 season-ticket holders. What action, if any, should the theater owner take to increase revenue?

a. Let n be the number of $5 price increases in the cost of a season ticket. Write an expression for the cost of a season ticket after n price increases, and an expression for the number of season ticket-holders after n price increases.

b. Use the expressions from part **a** to create a revenue function, $R(n)$, from the survey information.

c. Determine a constraint on the value of n. That is, write and solve an inequality that represents an upper bound on the value of n, then state a reasonable domain for the revenue function.

d. Graph the revenue function. Be sure to label the axes with the quantities they represent and indicate the axis scales by showing numbers for some grid lines.

e. Write a brief paragraph describing what actions the theater owner should take to maximize revenue. Include what happens to the number of season-ticket holders as well as the season-ticket prices.

UNIT 2

Quadratic Functions, Equations, and Relations

MATH IN CAREERS

Toy Manufacturer A toy manufacturer uses math to calculate the cost of manufacturing, including labor and materials, as well as to predict sales, determine profits, and keep track of orders and inventory. Toy manufacturers study market trends and use statistics to understand the economics of supply and demand for their products. They may also apply three-dimensional modeling to determine the amount of materials needed for toy construction.

If you are interested in a career as a toy manufacturer, you should study these mathematical subjects:
- Algebra
- Geometry
- Trigonometry
- Business Math
- Technical Math

Research other careers that require understanding how to predict sales of goods. Check out the career activity at the end of the unit to find out how **Toy Manufacturers** use math.

Reading Start-Up

Vocabulary

Review Words
✔ axis of symmetry *(eje de simetría)*
✔ discriminant *(discriminante)*
✔ elimination *(eliminación)*
✔ parabola *(parábola)*
✔ quadratic formula *(fórmula cuadrática)*
✔ quadratic formula *(fórmula cuadrática)*
✔ quadratic function *(función cuadrática)*
✔ substitution *(sustitución)*
✔ vertex *(vértice)*

Preview Words
complex number *(número complejo)*
directrix *(directriz)*
focus *(foco)*
imaginary number *(número imaginario)*
matrix *(matriz)*

Visualize Vocabulary

Use the ✔ words to complete the graphic. Place one word in each of the four sections of the frame.

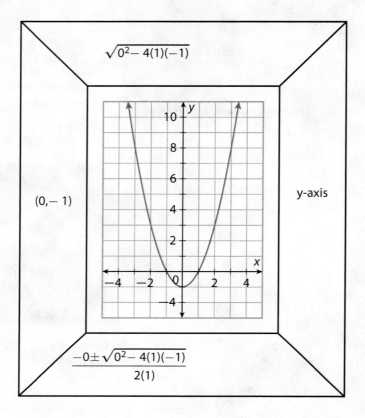

$$\sqrt{0^2 - 4(1)(-1)}$$

(0,− 1)

y-axis

$$\frac{-0 \pm \sqrt{0^2 - 4(1)(-1)}}{2(1)}$$

Understand Vocabulary

To become familiar with some of the vocabulary terms in the module, consider the following. You may refer to the module, the glossary, or a dictionary.

1. Every point on a parabola is equidistant from a fixed line, called the ___?___, and a fixed point, called the ___?___.

2. A ___?___ is any number that can be written as $a + bi$, where a and b are real numbers and $i = \sqrt{-1}$.

3. A ___?___ is a rectangular array of numbers.

Active Reading

Four-Corner Fold Before beginning each lesson, create a four-corner fold to help you organize the characteristics of key concepts. As you study each lesson, define new terms, including an example and a graph or diagram where applicable.

Quadratic Functions

Essential Question: How can graphing quadratic functions be used to solve real-world problems?

REAL WORLD VIDEO
Many modern athletic stadiums have a huge video display board and other state-of-the art features. Quadratic functions can be used in designing stadiums as well as in the modeling of aspects of the games that are played there.

MODULE PERFORMANCE TASK PREVIEW
What Is the Path of the Punt?

In 2013 a player for the Dallas Cowboys kicked a punt from his own 28 yard line that hit the bottom of the video board in the stadium. How can you use a quadratic function to figure out how far the punt would have traveled if it had not hit the board? Let's suit up and find out!

Are YOU Ready?

Complete these exercises to review skills you will need for this module.

Writing Linear Equations

• Online Homework
• Hints and Help
• Extra Practice

Example 1

Write the equation of a line passing through $(-5, 7)$ with slope -3.

$y = -3(x - (-5)) + 7$ Let $m = -3$, $h = -5$, and $k = 7$

$y = -3x - 8$ in the equation $y = m(x - h) + k$.

Write the equation of a line for the given point and slope.

1. $(0, 4); -2$

2. $(-6, 6); 5$

3. $(-7, -2); 10$

Quadratic Functions

Example 2

Find the vertex for the graph of the equation $y = 2x^2 - 4x - 3$.

$y = 2(x^2 - 2x) - 3$ Factor the first two terms.

$y = 2(x^2 - 2x + 1) - 3 - 2 \cdot 1$ *Complete the square and balance the equation.*

$y = 2(x - 1)^2 - 5$ Factor. The equation is now in vertex form of

The vertex is $(1, -5)$. $y = a(x - h)^2 + k$, where (h, k) is the vertex.

Find the vertex for each quadratic equation.

4. $y = 2x^2 - 20x + 10$

5. $y = 3x^2 - 24x + 47$

6. $y = -1(x^2 + 6x + 7)$

Transforming Quadratic Functions

Example 3

Write the equation of $y = -4(x + 1)^2 - 3$ after a transformation 2 units left and 8 units up.

The vertex $(-1, -3)$ is moved to $(-1-2, -3+8)$, or $(-3, 5)$. So the new equation is $y = -4(x + 3)^2 + 5$.

Write the equation of $y = 0.5(x - 9)^2 + 1$ after each transformation.

7. 4 units right, 6 units down   **8.** 10 units left, 2 units up   **9.** 5 units left, 5 units down

3.1 Quadratic Functions in Vertex Form

Essential Question: What does the vertex form of a quadratic function reveal about the function?

 A2.4.D: Transform a quadratic function $f(x) = ax^2 + bx + c$ to the form $f(x) = a(x - h)^2 + k$ to identify the different attributes of $f(x)$.

⊘ Explore Investigating Attributes of a Quadratic Function in Vertex Form

You have seen before that the graph of the function $g(x) = a \cdot f\left(\frac{1}{b}(x - h)\right) + k$ is a transformation of the graph of a parent function $f(x)$, with the parameters a, b, h, and k indicating the specific transformations. For the parent quadratic function $f(x) = x^2$ and $b = 1$, the equation of the transformation is $f(x) = a(x - h)^2 + k$. This is called the *vertex form of a quadratic function* since the vertex of the graph is located at (h, k).

Remember that when $a > 0$, the graph of $f(x) = ax^2$ opens upward, so the graph of $g(x) = -ax^2$, which is the reflection of $f(x)$ in the x-axis, opens downward. In general, the graph of a quadratic function in vertex form opens upward when $a > 0$ and downward when $a < 0$, as illustrated by the graphs.

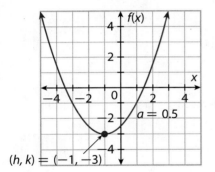

$f(x) = 0.5\big(x - (-1)\big)^2 - 3$

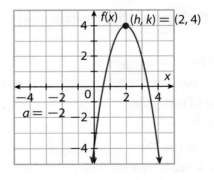

$f(x) = -2(x - 2)^2 + 4$

Ⓐ For the function in vertex form $f(x) = 0.75(x + 3)^2 - 2$, $h = $ ▮ . Copy and complete the table.

x	$f(x) = 0.75(x+3)^2 - 2$	x	$f(x) = 0.75(x+3)^2 - 2$
$h - 4 = $ ▮	$f(h - 4) = $ ▮	$h + 1 = $ ▮	$f(h + 1) = $ ▮
$h - 2 = $ ▮	$f(h - 2) = $ ▮	$h + 2 = $ ▮	$f(h + 2) = $ ▮
$h - 1 = $ ▮	$f(h - 1) = $ ▮	$h + 4 = $ ▮	$f(h + 4) = $ ▮
$h = $ ▮	$f(h) = $ ▮		

What do you observe about the values of $f(x)$ for values of x to either side of $x = h$?

What does your observation say about the axis of symmetry of the graph?

B In Step A, you saw that for a quadratic function in vertex form, $f(h - 1) = f(h + 1)$, $f(h - 2) = f(h + 2)$, and so on.

For $f(x) = 3(x + 2)^2 - 1$: $a =$ ▢, $h =$ ▢, $k =$ ▢

Copy and complete the table.

$f(x) = 3(x + 2)^2 - 1$
$f(h) = 3\left(\boxed{}\right)^2 - 1 = \boxed{}$
$f(h - 1) = f(h + 1) = 3\left(\pm\boxed{}\right)^2 - 1 = \boxed{}$
$f(h - 2) = f(h + 2) = 3\left(\pm\boxed{}\right)^2 - 1 = \boxed{}$
$f(h - 3) = f(h + 3) = 3\left(\pm\boxed{}\right)^2 - 1 = \boxed{}$
$f(h - 4) = f(h + 4) = 3\left(\pm\boxed{}\right)^2 - 1 = \boxed{}$

When $x = h$, $(x + 2)^2 =$ ▢ and $3(x + 2)^2 =$ ▢ . Is the value of $f(x)$ greater than, less than, or equal to the parameter k?

When $x \neq h$,

is $(x + 2)^2$ positive or negative?

$a(x + 2)^2$ is equal to $3(x + 2)^2$ Is this value positive or negative?

is the value of $f(x)$ greater than, less than, or equal to the parameter k?

So when $x \neq h$

is a positive or negative?

does the function have a maximum or minimum value of k?

For $f(x) = -2(x - 6)^2 + 4$: $a =$ ▢ , $h =$ ▢ , $k =$ ▢

Copy and complete the table.

$f(x) = -2(x - 6)^2 + 4$
$f(h) = -2\left(\boxed{}\right)^2 + 4 = \boxed{}$
$f(h - 1) = f(h + 1) = -2\left(\pm\boxed{}\right)^2 + 4 = \boxed{}$
$f(h - 2) = f(h + 2) = -2\left(\pm\boxed{}\right)^2 + 4 = \boxed{}$
$f(h - 3) = f(h + 3) = -2\left(\pm\boxed{}\right)^2 + 4 = \boxed{}$
$f(h - 4) = f(h + 4) = -2\left(\pm\boxed{}\right)^2 + 4 = \boxed{}$

When $x = h$, $(x - 6)^2 = $ ▮ and $-2(x - 6)^2 = $ ▮. Is the value of $f(x)$
greater than, less than, or equal to the parameter k?

When $x \neq h$,

    is $(x - 6)^2$ positive or negative?

    $a(x - 6)^2$ is equal to $-2(x - 6)^2$. Is this value positive or negative?

    is the value of $f(x)$ greater than, less than, or equal to the parameter k?

So when $x \neq h$

    is a positive or negative?

    does the function have a maximum or minimum value of k?

Reflect

1. Find $f(h + d)$ and $f(h - d)$ for a general quadratic function in vertex form, $f(x) = a(x - h)^2 + k$. How does this verify your observation in Step A? Do the values of a and k affect this result?

2. What are the roles of the parameters a, h, and k in determining the maximum or minimum value of a quadratic function $f(x) = a(x - h)^2 + k$?

3. **Discussion** How can you find the range of $f(x) = a(x - h)^2 + k$ without computing any function values?

4. **Discussion** Describe the behavior of the graph of $f(x) = a(x - h)^2 + k$ on either side of $x = h$ when $a > 0$ and when $a < 0$.

⚙ Explain 1   Identifying the Attributes of a Quadratic Function in Vertex Form

Attributes of a quadratic function $f(x) = a(x - h)^2 + k$

The graph has vertex (h, k) and axis of symmetry $x = h$.

When $a > 0$:

- $f(x)$ has a minimum value of k when $x = h$.
- The domain of $f(x)$ is $\{x \mid x \in \Re\}$.
- The range of $f(x)$ is $\{y \mid y \geq k\}$.
- $f(x)$ is decreasing on $(-\infty, h)$ and increasing on $(h, +\infty)$.

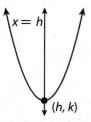

When $a < 0$:

- $f(x)$ has a maximum value of k when $x = h$.
- The domain of $f(x)$ is $\{x \mid x \in \Re\}$.
- The range of $f(x)$ is $\{y \mid y \leq k\}$.
- $f(x)$ is increasing on $(-\infty, h)$ and decreasing on $(h, +\infty)$.

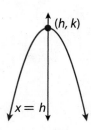

Example 1 Identify the axis of symmetry of the graph of the function. Then give the function's maximum or minimum value, domain, range, and the intervals where the function is increasing or decreasing.

 $f(x) = 4(x - 3)^2 + 5$

Find a, h, and k in the vertex form $f(x) = a(x - h)^2 + k$.

$f(x) = 4(x - 3)^2 + 5$, so $a = 4$, $h = 3$, and $k = 5$.

Axis of symmetry: $x = h$, so $x = 3$

Since $a > 0$, $f(x)$ has a minimum value of k, or 5.

Domain: $\{x|\, x \in \mathfrak{R}\}$; Range: $\{y|\, y \geq k\}$, so $\{y|\, y \geq 5\}$

Decreasing on $(-\infty, h)$, so decreasing on $(-\infty, 3)$; Increasing on $(h, +\infty)$, so increasing on $(3, +\infty)$

Ⓑ $f(x) = -11(x + 5)^2 - 1.6$

Find a, h, and k in the vertex form $f(x) = a(x - h)^2 + k$.

$f(x) = -11(x + 5)^2 - 1.6 = -11\left(x - \left(\boxed{-5}\right)\right)^2 + \left(\boxed{-1.6}\right)$,

so $a = \boxed{-11}$, $h = \boxed{-5}$, and $k = \boxed{-1.6}$.

Axis of symmetry: $x = h$, so $x = \boxed{-5}$

Since $a < 0$, $f(x)$ has a maximum value of k, or $\boxed{-1.6}$.

Domain: $\{x|\, x \in \mathfrak{R}\}$; Range: $\{y|\, y \boxed{\leq} k\}$, so $\{y|\, y \boxed{\leq} -1.6\}$

Increasing on $(-\infty, h)$, so increasing on $\left(-\infty, \boxed{-5}\right)$; Decreasing on $(h, +\infty)$, so decreasing

on $\left(\boxed{-5}, +\infty\right)$.

Your Turn

Identify the axis of symmetry. Then give the function's maximum or minimum value, domain, range, and the intervals where the function is increasing or decreasing.

5. $f(x) = -(x - 0.8)^2$

6. $f(x) = \frac{1}{4}(x + 1)^2 + 1$

⚙ Explain 2   Converting from Standard Form to Vertex Form

Some attributes of a quadratic function are not easy to recognize from the standard form $f(x) = ax^2 + bx + c$. By *completing the square*, you can write an equivalent equation in vertex form to make the attributes more apparent. Remember that a *perfect square trinomial* is the square of a binomial.

Examples of perfect square trinomials:

$$x^2 + 12x + 36 = (x + 6)^2 \qquad x^2 - 3x + \frac{9}{4} = \left(x - \frac{3}{2}\right)^2 \qquad x^2 + 2bx + b^2 = (x + b)^2$$

Note that the first and last terms of the trinomials are the squares of the first and last terms of the binomials. The binomial's last term is also *half the coefficient of the trinomial's middle term.*

Rewriting a Quadratic Function $f(x) = ax^2 + bx + c$ by Completing the Square

1. If $a \neq 1$, factor the first two terms as $a\left(x^2 + \frac{b}{a}x\right)$ so that the coefficient of x^2 is 1.

2. Set up to complete the square. The goal is to add a constant term inside the parentheses to form a perfect-square trinomial. Because you are adding a quantity inside the parentheses, you must subtract an equivalent quantity outside the parentheses to keep the expression equivalent.

3. Complete the square by adding $\left(\frac{b}{2a}\right)^2$ inside the parentheses. Because $\left(\frac{b}{2a}\right)^2$ is multiplied by the coefficient a, subtract $a\left(\frac{b}{2a}\right)^2$ outside the parentheses.

4. Simplify, and write the trinomial as the square of a binomial.

Example 2   **Write the quadratic function in vertex form by completing the square. Then identify the maximum or minimum value of the function and the value of x at which it occurs.**

Ⓐ $f(x) = 2x^2 + 12x + 10$

Factor so that the coefficient of x^2 is 1. $f(x) = 2(x^2 + 6x) + 10$

Set up to complete the square. $f(x) = 2\left(x^2 + 6x + \boxed{}\right) + 10 - \boxed{}$

$\frac{b}{a} = 6$; add the square of one half of 6 to complete $f(x) = 2\left(x^2 + 6x + \left(\frac{6}{2}\right)^2\right) + 10 - 2\left(\frac{6}{2}\right)^2$

the square. Since this quantity is multiplied by 2, subtract twice the quantity to keep the expression equivalent.

Simplify. $f(x) = 2(x^2 + 6x + 9) - 8$

Write the trinomial as the square of a binomial. $f(x) = 2(x + 3)^2 - 8$

$f(x) = 2(x + 3)^2 - 8 = 2\left(x - (-3)\right)^2 + (-8)$, so $a = 2$, $h = -3$, and $k = -8$.

The function $f(x)$ has a minimum value of -8 when $x = -3$.

Ⓑ $f(x) = -3x^2 + 24x - 43$

Factor so that the coefficient of x^2 is 1. $f(x) = -3\left(x^2 \boxed{-8}\, x\right) - 43$

Set up to complete the square. $f(x) = -3\left(x^2 - 8x + \boxed{}\right) - 43 - \boxed{}$

$\dfrac{b}{a} = -8$; add the square of one half of -8 $f(x) = -3\left(x^2 - 8x + \left(\dfrac{\boxed{-8}}{\boxed{2}}\right)^2\right) - 43 - \left(\boxed{-3}\right)\left(\dfrac{-8}{2}\right)^2$

to complete the square. Since this quantity is
multiplied by -3, subtract -3 times the
quantity to keep the expression equivalent.

Simplify. $f(x) = -3\left(x^2 - 8x + \boxed{16}\right) + \boxed{5}$

Write the trinomial as the square of a binomial. $f(x) = -3\left(x \boxed{-4}\right)^2 + 5$

$f(x) = -3(x - 4)^2 + 5$, so $a = \boxed{-3}$, $h = \boxed{4}$, and $k = \boxed{5}$.

The function $f(x)$ has a maximum value of $\boxed{5}$ when $x = \boxed{4}$.

Reflect

7. The introduction to this Explain began the process of completing the square for a general quadratic function in standard form, $f(x) = ax^2 + bx + c$. Copy and complete this process:

$f(x) = ax^2 + bx + c$

$f(x) = a\left(x^2 + \dfrac{b}{a}x\right) + c$

$f(x) = a\left(x^2 + \dfrac{b}{a}x + \left(\dfrac{b}{2a}\right)^2\right) + c - a\left(\dfrac{\boxed{}}{\boxed{}}\right)^2$

$f(x) = a\left(x^2 + \dfrac{b}{a}x + \left(\dfrac{b}{2a}\right)^2\right) + c - \dfrac{\boxed{}}{\boxed{}}$

$f(x) = a\left(x + \dfrac{\boxed{}}{\boxed{}}\right)^2 + c - \dfrac{b^2}{4a}$

Explain how this result indicates how you can use the standard form to find the x-coordinate where the function reaches its maximum or minimum value.

Your Turn

Write the quadratic function in vertex form by completing the square. Then identify the maximum or minimum value of the function and the value of x at which it occurs.

8. $f(x) = -2x^2 - 8x + 3$

🔍 Explain 3   Analyzing a Projectile Motion Model

When you throw, hit, or launch an object into the air you can model its height under the influence of gravity as a function of time. A model for projectile motion on Earth is $h(t) = -16t^2 + v_0 t + h_0$, with height h in feet and time t in seconds. In the model, "-16" is a constant that gives the downward acceleration from Earth's gravity in feet per second squared. The constant v_0 is the object's initial vertical velocity in feet per second. The constant h_0 is the object's initial height (at time $t = 0$) in feet.

Example 3   **Use the projectile motion model to answer the questions.**

Ⓐ   A golf ball is hit with an initial upward velocity of 64 feet per second off a 6-foot-high platform at a driving range.

    a.   How long does it take the ball to reach its maximum height? What is that height?

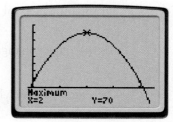

         Use the model $h(t) = -16t^2 + v_0 t + h_0$ with $v_0 = 64$ and $h_0 = 6$:

         $h(t) = -16t^2 + 64t + 6$

         Time at maximum height: $t = -\dfrac{b}{2a} = -\dfrac{64}{2(-16)} = 2$

         Substitute $t = 2$ to find the maximum height:

         $h(2) = -16(2)^2 + 64(2) + 6 = 70$

         The ball reaches its maximum height of 70 feet 2 seconds after it is hit.

         Check your answer by graphing $y = -16x^2 + 64x + 6$ on a graphing calculator and finding the coordinates of the maximum point.

    b.   What is the average rate of change in the ball's height over the time interval from when it is hit to when it reaches its maximum height? Over the time interval from when it is at its maximum height to when it returns to the same height from which it was hit?

         The average rate of change over a time interval is just the change in height over the interval divided by the change in time. For the time interval $[0, 2]$, the ball travels from $(0, 6)$ to $(2, 70)$:

         $\text{average rate of change} = \dfrac{\text{change in height}}{\text{change in time}} = \dfrac{70 - 6}{2 - 0} = 32$

         The average rate of change is 32 feet per second. By symmetry, the time interval on the way back down to the original height is $[2, 4]$, and the average rate of change will be the same, but with the opposite sign, or -32 feet per second.

(B) A pumpkin emerges from an air cannon at a height of 24 feet above the ground with an initial upward velocity of 192 feet per second.

a. How long does it take the pumpkin to reach its maximum height? What is that height?

Use the model $h(t) = -16t^2 + v_0 t + h_0$ with $v_0 = \boxed{192}$ and $h_0 = \boxed{24}$:

$$h(t) = -16t^2 + \boxed{192}\, t + \boxed{24}$$

Time at maximum height: $t = -\dfrac{b}{2a} = -\dfrac{\boxed{192}}{\boxed{2(-16)}} = \boxed{6}$

Substitute $t = 6$ to find the maximum height:

$$h(6) = -16(6)^2 + 192(6) + 24 = \boxed{600}$$

The pumpkin reaches its maximum height of $\boxed{600}$ feet $\boxed{6}$ seconds after it is fired.

b. What is the average rate of change in the pumpkin's height over the time interval from when it is fired to when it reaches its maximum height?

For the time interval $\left[0, \boxed{6}\right]$, the ball travels from $(0, 24)$ to $\left(6, \boxed{600}\right)$:

$$\text{average rate of change} = \frac{\text{change in height}}{\text{change in time}} = \frac{\boxed{600} - 24}{\boxed{6} - 0} = \boxed{96}$$

The average rate of change is $\boxed{96}$ feet per second.

Reflect

9. Copy and complete the table for the model in Example 3 part B. What do you notice about the average rate of change of the height over the intervals?

Time Interval	Height Over Time Interval	Average Rate of Change of Height Over Interval
from 0 s to 2 s	from 24 ft to 344 ft	
from 2 s to 4 s	from 344 ft to 536 ft	
from 4 s to 6 s	from 536 ft to 600 ft	
from 6 s to 8 s	from 600 ft to 536 ft	
from 8 s to 10 s	from 536 ft to 344 ft	
from 10 s to 12 s	from 344 ft to 24 ft	

10. You can rewrite the models in Example 3 parts A and B as $h(t) = -16(t - 2)^2 + 70$ and $h(t) = -16(t - 6)^2 + 600$. Because both models have the coefficient -16, the graphs have the same shape: they are both translations of $-16x^2$. How do the average rates of change you found reflect this fact?

11. The rate of change for a linear function, which is its slope, is constant. Use the table from question 9 to describe the behavior of the average rate of change for a quadratic function.

12. On what real-world parameters does the time it takes a projectile to reach its maximum height depend? Explain your reasoning.

> **Your Turn**

Use the projectile motion model to answer the questions.

13. A pebble is tossed from a cliff. It is released from a height 110 feet above the base of the cliff with an initial upward velocity of 32 feet per second. How long does it take the pebble to reach its maximum height above the base of the cliff? What is that height?

💬 Elaborate

14. How is the vertex form of a quadratic function related to transformations of the graph of the parent quadratic function $f(x) = x^2$?

15. **Essential Question Check-In** What does the value of a in the vertex form of a quadratic function reveal about the function?

⭐ Evaluate: Homework and Practice

- Online Homework
- Hints and Help
- Extra Practice

1. For the function $f(x) = a(x - h)^2 + k$, $f(h + 5) = -19$ and $f(h - 2) = -4$. Find $f(h - 5)$ and $f(h + 2)$. Is a positive or negative? Explain.

Identify the axis of symmetry. Then give the function's maximum or minimum value, domain, range, and the intervals where the function is increasing or decreasing.

2. $f(x) = 5(x - 3)^2 + 6$

3. $f(x) = -7(x - 8)^2 + 1$

4. $f(x) = -6(x + 4)^2 - 8$

5. $f(x) = 2(x + 2)^2 + 9$

6. Match each quadratic function in vertex form with the coordinates of the graph of its vertex.

A. $f(x) = a(x - h)^2 + k$ a. $(-h, k)$

B. $f(x) = a(x - h)^2 - k$ b. (h, k)

C. $f(x) = a(x + h)^2 - k$ c. $(h, -k)$

D. $f(x) = a(x + h)^2 + k$ d. $(-h, -k)$

Write the quadratic function in vertex form by completing the square. Then identify the maximum or minimum value and the value of *x* at which it occurs.

7. $f(x) = x^2 + 6x - 3$

8. $f(x) = x^2 - 10x + 11$

9. $f(x) = 3x^2 + 24x + 53$

10. $f(x) = 9x^2 + 18x - 3$

11. Multi-Step The height *h* above the roadway of the main cable of the Golden Gate Bridge can be modeled by the function $h(x) = \frac{1}{9000}x^2 - \frac{7}{15}x + 500$, where *x* is the distance in feet from the left tower.

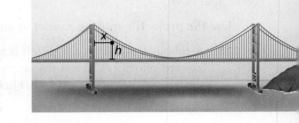

  a. Complete the square to write the function in vertex form.

  b. What is the vertex, and what does it represent?

  c. The left and right towers have the same height. What is the distance in feet between them? Explain.

Use the projectile motion model to answer the questions.

12. A technician is launching an aerial firework from a 200-foot tower. The firework's upward velocity at launch will be 176 feet per second. Professional fireworks are usually timed to explode as they reach their highest point.

  a. How long does it take the firework to reach its maximum height? What is that height? Check your answer by graphing the model using a graphing calculator.

  b. What is the average rate of change in the firework's height over first half second it is rising? over the last half second it is rising?

13. A circus juggler on a high wire tosses a juggling pin upward with an initial vertical velocity of 24 feet per second from a height of 32 feet.

   a. How long does it take the pin to reach its maximum height? What is that height?

   b. The juggler misses the pin on its way down. How long after the pin is tossed does it pass the juggler on the way down? How do you know?

14. When height is measured in meters and time in seconds, the equation for projectile motion becomes $h(t) = -4.9t^2 + v_0 t + h_0$. A fishing boat with two people on it runs out of gas while out in a bay. The people set off an emergency flare from a height of 2 meters above the water. The flare has an initial vertical velocity of 30 meters per second. How long does it take the flare to reach its maximum height? What is that height?

H.O.T. Focus on Higher Order Thinking

15. Explain the Error Two attempts to write $f(x) = 2x^2 - 8x$ in vertex form are shown. Which is incorrect? Explain the error.

   A. $f(x) = 2x^2 - 8x$

   $f(x) = 2(x^2 - 4x)$

   $f(x) = 2(x^2 - 4x + 4) - 4$

   $f(x) = 2(x - 2)^2 - 4$

   B. $f(x) = 2x^2 - 8x$

   $f(x) = 2(x^2 - 4x)$

   $f(x) = 2(x^2 - 4x + 4) - 8$

   $f(x) = 2(x - 2)^2 - 8$

16. Communicate Mathematical Ideas You can rewrite a quadratic function that is in standard form in vertex form by completing the square. How can you also use the fact that the maximum or minimum of a quadratic function in standard form occurs when $x = -\frac{b}{2a}$ to rewrite it in vertex form?

17. Analyze Relationships The functions f and g are defined by $f(x) = x^2 + 2x - 2$ and $g(x) = (x + 1)^2 - 3$. Do f and g represent the same function? Explain.

18. Justify Reasoning Over a given time interval, a golf ball in flight has an average rate of change in height of 0. Does this mean the ball was moving horizontally? Explain.

Lesson Performance Task

A player bumps a volleyball with an initial vertical velocity of 20 ft/s.

a. Use the function $h(t) = -16t^2 + v_0 t + h_0$, where v_0 is the initial velocity and h_0 is the initial height to write a function h in standard form for the ball's height in feet in terms of time t in seconds after the ball is hit.

b. Complete the square to rewrite h in vertex form.

c. What is the maximum height of the ball?

d. Suppose the volleyball were hit under the same conditions, but with an initial velocity of 32 ft/s. How much higher would the ball go?

3.2 Writing Quadratic Functions

Essential Question: What information identifies the parameters for writing a quadratic function in vertex form?

 TEKS A2.4.B: Write the equation of a parabola using given attributes, including vertex, ...axis of symmetry, and direction of opening.

 Resource Locker

Explore Identifying Information for Writing a Quadratic Function in Vertex Form

A given parabola has an axis of symmetry of $x = 1$, a range of $-\infty$ to 4, and opens downward. What does this information tell you that you can use to write the equation of this quadratic function in vertex form?

(A) The parabola opens downward. What do you know about the value of a in the equation of the parabola? Use $<$, $>$, or $=$.

a ▢ 0

(B) The axis of symmetry is $x = 1$. What does this tell you about the vertex of the parabola?

The ▢-value of the vertex of the parabola is ▢.

(C) The range of the parabola is $(-\infty, 4)$. What does this tell you about the vertex of the parabola?

The ▢-value of the vertex of the parabola is ▢.

Reflect

1. What other value do you need to write the equation of this parabola in vertex form? Explain what you would need to find this value and how you would find it.

2. Suppose the range was $(4, \infty)$ and the parabola opened upward. What would be different about the equation of the parabola? What would be the same?

Explain 1 Writing a Quadratic Function Given a Parabola's Vertex, Direction of Opening, and Another Point

Recall that the vertex form of a quadratic function is $f(x) = a(x - h)^2 + k$, where (h, k) is the vertex of the function. Also, recall that if $a < 0$, then the parabolic graph of the function opens downward and the vertex is the maximum point on the parabola, and that if $a > 0$, then the parabolic graph of the function opens upward and the vertex is the minimum point on the parabola. Knowing this information, and one other point on the parabola, will allow you to write the equation of the quadratic function associated with a given parabola.

Example 1 Use the vertex, direction of opening, and another point on each parabola to write its quadratic function in vertex form.

Ⓐ vertex: $(3, 2)$; point: $(5, -6)$; direction of opening: downward

Identify h and k from the vertex. $\qquad h = 3, k = 2$

Substitute h and k into the vertex form of a quadratic function. $\qquad f(x) = a(x - 3)^2 + 2$

Substitute the other point into this equation to solve for a. $\qquad -6 = a(5 - 3)^2 + 2$

$$-6 = a(2)^2 + 2$$

$$-6 = 4a + 2$$

$$-8 = 4a$$

$$-2 = a$$

Substitute a into the vertex form of the function. $\qquad f(x) = -2(x - 3)^2 + 2$

Ⓑ vertex: $(-1, 5)$; point: $(0, 8)$; direction of opening: upward

Identify h and k from the vertex. $\qquad h = \boxed{-1}, k = \boxed{5}$

Substitute h and k from the vertex form of a quadratic function. $\qquad f(x) = a\left(x - \boxed{(-1)}\right)^2 + \boxed{5}$

Substitute the other point into this equation to solve for a. $\qquad \boxed{8} = a\left(\boxed{0 + 1}\right)^2 + \boxed{5}$

$$\boxed{8} = a\left(\boxed{1}\right)^2 + \boxed{5}$$

$$\boxed{8} = \boxed{1}\,a + \boxed{5}$$

$$\boxed{3} = \boxed{1}\,a$$

$$\boxed{3} = a$$

Substitute a into the vertex form of the function. $\qquad f(x) = \boxed{3}\left(\boxed{x + 1}\right)^2 + \boxed{5}$

Your Turn

3. vertex: $(3, -3)$; point: $(2, -7)$; direction of opening: downward

 Explain 2 ## Writing a Quadratic Function Given a Parabola's Axis of Symmetry, Direction of Opening, and Two Non-Vertex Points

When given the axis of symmetry of a parabola, two non-vertex points, and the direction of opening, you can write the quadratic function in vertex form. Recall that the axis of symmetry of a parabola always passes through the vertex. Therefore, if the line of symmetry is $x = h$, then the x-value of the vertex is h. You can use the two non-vertex points to set up a system of two linear equations in a and k and then solve those equations for a and k. The direction the parabola opens determines whether the value of a will be positive or negative.

Example 2 Write the quadratic function for the parabola that will satisfy the given conditions.

Ⓐ The parabola opens upward, has $x = 4$ as the axis of symmetry, and contains the non-vertex points (3, 5) and (7, 12).

The axis of symmetry, $x = 4$ gives the value of h in the vertex form of the function.

$$f(x) = a(x - 4)^2 + k$$

Substitute each of the two points for x and $f(x)$ into the function to obtain a system of two linear equations in two unknowns.

$f(x) = a(x - 4)^2 + k$	$f(x) = a(x - 4)^2 + k$
$5 = a(3 - 4)^2 + k$ Substitute (3, 5).	$12 = a(7 - 4)^2 + k$ Substitute (7, 12).
$5 = a(-1)^2 + k$ Simplify.	$12 = a(3)^2 + k$ Simplify.
$5 = a + k$	$12 = 9a + k$

The system is $\begin{cases} a + k = 5 \\ 9a + k = 12 \end{cases}$. Solve the first equation for k.

$a + k = 5$
$\quad k = 5 - a$

Substitute for k in the second equation and solve for a.

$12 = 9a + k$

$12 = 9a + 5 - a$ Substitute.

$12 = 8a + 5$ Simplify.

$\quad 7 = 8a$ Subtract 5 from each side.

$\quad a = \dfrac{7}{8}$ Divide each side by 8.

Substitute $a = \dfrac{7}{8}$ into the first equation and solve for k.

$a + k = 5$

$\dfrac{7}{8} + k = 5$ Substitute.

$\quad k = 5 - \dfrac{7}{8}$ Solve for k.

$\quad k = \dfrac{33}{8}$ Simplify.

Therefore, the function of the parabola in vertex form is $f(x) = \dfrac{7}{8}(x - 4)^2 + \dfrac{33}{8}$.

Ⓑ The parabola opens upward, has $x = -5$ as the axis of symmetry, and contains the non-vertex points $(-8, 7)$ and $(5, 20)$.

The axis of symmetry, $x = \boxed{-5}$ gives the value of h in the vertex form of the function.

$$f(x) = a\left(x - \boxed{(-5)}\right)^2 + k$$

Substitute each of the two points for x and $f(x)$ into the function to obtain a system of two linear equations in two unknowns.

$f(x) = a(x + 5)^2 + k$	$f(x) = a(x + 5)^2 + k$
$7 = a(-8 + 5)^2 + k$ Substitute $\boxed{(-8, 7)}$.	$\boxed{20} = a\left(\boxed{5} + 5\right)^2 + k$ Substitute (5, 20)
$7 = a(-3)^2 + k$ Simplify.	$20 = a\left(\boxed{10}\right)^2 + k$ Simplify.
$7 = \boxed{9a + k}$	$20 = \boxed{100a + k}$

The system is $\begin{cases} 9a + k = 7 \\ 100a + k = 20 \end{cases}$. Solve the first equation for k.

$9a + k = 7$
$\quad k = 7 - 9a$

Substitute for k in the second equation and solve for a.

$20 = 100a + k$

$20 = 100a + 7 - 9a$ Substitute.

$20 = \boxed{91a} + 7$ Simplify.

$13 = 91a$ Substract 7 from each side.

$a = \dfrac{13}{91}$ Divide each side by 91.

$a = \boxed{\dfrac{1}{7}}$ Simplify.

Substitute $a = \boxed{\dfrac{1}{7}}$ into the first equation and solve for k.

$9a + k = 7$

$9\left(\boxed{\dfrac{1}{7}}\right) + k = 7$ Substitute.

$k = 7 - 9\left(\dfrac{1}{7}\right)$ Solve for k.

$k = 7 - \boxed{\dfrac{9}{7}}$ Simplify.

$k = \boxed{\dfrac{40}{7}}$ Substract.

Therefore, the function of the parabola in vertex form is $f(x) = \dfrac{1}{7}\left(x + 5^2\right) + \dfrac{40}{7}$.

Reflect

4. Given the axis of symmetry and two points, what else can you immediately determine about the parabola?

Your Turn

Write the quadratic function for the parabola that will satisfy the given conditions.

5. The parabola opens downward, has $x = 6$ as an axis of symmetry, and contains the non-vertex points $(15, 3)$ and $(13, 6)$.

⊘ Explain 3   Modeling with Quadratic Functions

You can find the solution to a real-world problem using information given in the problem to write a quadratic function and use the function to estimate an answer.

(A) A bald eagle grabs a fish from a mountain lake and flies to an altitude of 256 feet above the lake. At that point, the fish manages to squirm free and falls back down into a river flowing out of the lake. After falling 3 seconds, the fish is 112 feet above the surface of the lake it was taken from. If the surface of the river where the fish lands is 144 feet below the surface level of the lake, for how many seconds did the fish fall?

🧩 Analyze Information

Identify the important information.
- The function modeling the height of the fish is quadratic with respect to time.
- The vertex of the parabola is at $(0, 256)$.
- A second point on the parabola is $(3, 112)$.

🧩 Formulate a Plan

You want to find the number of seconds the fish fell.

The vertex of the parabola is given, so write the function $h(t)$ in vertex form: $h(t) = a\left(t - h^2\right) + k$.

Use the non-vertex point to find a.

Then find t such that $h(t) = \boxed{-144}$.

Solve

The vertex is $(0, 256)$. Substitute these values into $h(t)$.

$$h(t) = a(t - 0)^2 + 256$$

Substitute the values of the non-vertex point into the function and solve for a.

Substitute a into the function.

$$h(t) = a(t - 0)^2 + 256$$

$$\boxed{112} = a\left(\boxed{3} - 0\right)^2 + 256$$

$$\boxed{112} = a\left(\boxed{3}\right)^2 + 256$$

$$-144 = 9a$$

$$a = \boxed{-16}$$

$$h(t) = \boxed{-16}\, t^2 + 256$$

$$\boxed{-144} = -16t^2 + 256$$

$$-400 = -16t^2$$

$$\boxed{25} = t^2$$

$$t^2 = 25$$

$$t = \boxed{5}$$

The fish hits the surface of the river 5 seconds after being dropped.

Justify and Evaluate

Check your answer by substituting 5 into $h(t)$ and seeing if

$$h(t) = -144: -16(5 - 0)^2 + 256 = -16(5)^2 + 256 = -400 + 256 = -144$$

Your Turn

6. During a competition, an archer fires an arrow at a target on a hill. The arrow reaches a maximum height of 127 feet 2.75 seconds after it was fired. The arrow hits the target 5 seconds after the archer releases it. If the arrow is released from a height of 6 feet, how far above the ground on which the archer is standing is the target? Assume the relationship between time and height is quadratic.

Elaborate

7. **Discussion** If you are given two points in the coordinate plane, can you create a parabola that passes through both points and opens in a specified direction?

8. **Essential Question Check-in** Describe the minimum amount of information required to create a unique parabola. Explain your answer.

☆ Evaluate: Homework and Practice

1. A given parabola has an axis of symmetry of $x = 5$, a range of 7 to ∞, and opens upward. What does this information tell you that you can use to write the equation of this quadratic function in vertex form?

2. A given parabola has an axis of symmetry of $x = -4$, a range of $-\infty$ to 10, and opens downward. What does this information tell you that you can use to write the equation of this quadratic function in vertex form?

Use the vertex, direction of opening, and another point on each parabola to write its quadratic function in vertex form.

3. vertex: $(0, 0)$; point: $(2, 8)$; opens upward

4. vertex: $(2, 1)$; point: $(3, 2)$; opens upward

5. vertex: $(-6, 4)$; point: $(-5, 0)$; opens downward

6. vertex: $(-5, 10)$; point: $(-8, -8)$; opens downward

Write the quadratic function for the parabola that has the given axis of symmetry, points, and direction of opening.

7. axis of symmetry: $x = 3$; points: $(1, 9)$, $(4, 3)$; direction of opening: upward

8. axis of symmetry: $x = -2$; points: $(-3, 2)$, $(0, -13)$; direction of opening: downward

9. axis of symmetry: $x = -3$; points: $(-7, -2)$, $(-5, -8)$; direction of opening: upward

10. axis of symmetry: $x = 4$; points: $(3, -2)$, $(6, -26)$; direction of opening: downward

Find the solution to the real-world problem using the given information to write a quadratic function. If necessary, estimate to answer the question.

11. A soccer player who is 27 feet from a goal attempted to kick the ball into the goal. The ball reached a maximum height of 10 feet when it was 15 feet from the soccer player. What is the height of the ball when it reaches the goal? Will the ball go into the goal or go over it? The goal has a height of 8 feet.

12. A surveyor finds that the cross-section of the bottom of a circular pond has the shape of a parabola. The pond is 24 feet in diameter. The middle of the pond is the deepest part at 8 feet deep. At a point 2 feet from the shore the water is 3 feet deep. How deep is the pond at a point 6 feet from the shore?

13. A horizontal pedestrian bridge is supported from a parabolic arch. The bridge goes above a roadway that is 40 feet wide. At ground level, the main span of the bridge is 90 feet wide. At the edge of the roadway, 25 feet from where the arch touches the ground, the arch is 16 feet high. How tall is the arch at its tallest point?

14. A golfer needs to hit a ball a distance of 500 feet, but there is a 60-foot tall tree that is 100 feet before where the shot needs to land. Given that the maximum height of the shot is 120 feet, and that the intended distance of 500 feet is reached, by how much did the ball clear the tree?

Explain whether each function fits the given data.

The parabola opens upwards and has $x = 8$ as an axis of symmetry.

15. $f(x) = 2(x - 8)^2 + k$

16. $f(x) = -4(x - 8)^2 + k$

17. $f(x) = \frac{1}{2}(x + 8)^2 + k$

18. $f(x) = 71(x - 8)^2 + k$

19. $f(x) = -9(x - 8)^2 + k$

20. $f(x) = (x - 8)^2 + k$

H.O.T. Focus on Higher Order Thinking

21. Explain the Error A student was given the following information and asked to find the function of the parabola in vertex form. Find the student's error and the correct function.

axis of symmetry: $x = 5$; points: $(3, -20)$, $(6, 1)$; direction of opening: downward

From the axis of symmetry, $f(x) = a(x + 5)^2 + k$.

$f(x) = a(x + 5)^2 + k$

$-20 = a(3 + 5)^2 + k$ Substitute $(3, -20)$.

$-20 = a(8)^2 + k$ Simplify.

$-20 = 64a + k$

$f(x) = a(x + 5)^2 + k$

$1 = a(6 + 5)^2 + k$ Substitute $(6, 1)$.

$1 = a(11)^2 + k$ Simplify.

$1 = 121a + k$

The system is $\begin{cases} 64a + k = -20 \\ 121a + k = 1 \end{cases}$.

First solve for a.

$-57a = -21$

$a = \dfrac{7}{19}$

Then substitute $a = \frac{7}{19}$ into the second equation and solve for k.

$$121\left(\frac{7}{19}\right) + k = 1$$

$$k = 1 - 121\left(\frac{7}{19}\right)$$

$$k = -\frac{828}{19}$$

$$f(x) = \frac{7}{19}(x + 5)^2 - \frac{828}{19}$$

22. **Make a Conjecture** Is it possible to find a unique quadratic function given only the axis of symmetry, a non-vertex point, and the average rate of change between the point and vertex? Explain why or why not.

23. **Communicate Mathematical Ideas** Is there a unique quadratic function with points (1, 5) and (5, 5) and axis of symmetry $x = 3$? Why or why not?

Lesson Performance Task

At a test track, the time it takes a driver to stop a car once a signal is given is being measured. The car travels down a straight section of track at a known speed, and a light flashes. The driver applies the brakes, and the distance it takes for the car to stop is measured. The stopping distance can be modeled as a quadratic function of speed. If the quadratic model has an axis of symmetry of $s = -10$, what is the function modeling the stopping time if the driver stops in 75 feet if he is traveling 30 miles per hour?

Now, take the function you found and convert it to standard form, if necessary. The terms all represent different aspects of the situation, with the term representing road conditions, the linear term representing the driver's reaction time, and the quadratic term representing the condition of the car's brakes and tires. Examine the effects of varying the constant term and the coefficients of the variable terms. What could these changes represent?

© Houghton Mifflin Harcourt Publishing Company

3.3 Fitting Quadratic Functions to Data

Essential Question: How can you find the equation of a quadratic function to model data?

 A2.8.B: Use regression methods available through technology to write ... a quadratic function ... from a given set of data. Also A2.4.E, A2.8.C

⊘ Explore Investigating Quadratic Function Models for Data

You have worked in various situations with quadratic functions in standard form, $f(x) = ax^2 + bx + c$; in vertex form, $f(x) = a(x - h)^2 + k$ where (h, k) gives the coordinates of the vertex of the graph; and in intercept form, $f(x) = a(x - x_1)(x - x_2)$ where x_1 and x_2 give the x-intercepts of the graph.

When you have a set of data values that reasonably can be modeled by a quadratic function, you may use any of the above forms to write the function.

Ⓐ A science class collects the following lab data. The students plot the points as shown. The teacher then asks students to find a reasonable quadratic model for the data.

x	3	4	5	6	7	8	9	10	11	12
f(x)	0	18	28	31	33	33	27	21	13	2

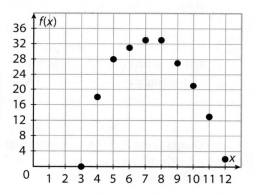

Angelíque estimates the vertex to be (7.5, 34), so that $f(x) = a(x - 7.5)^2 + 34$. She chooses the point (4, 18), substitutes its coordinates for $(x, f(x))$ in the equation, and solves for a to obtain the model $f(x) = -1.31(x - 7.5)^2 + 34$. Her graph is shown.

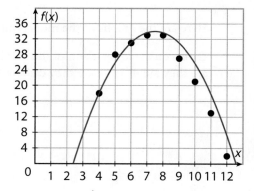

The vertex of the model is at (7.5, 34), so the axis of

symmetry is and the maximum is .

The x-intercepts of the graph of the model are

about _____ .

Is the model a good fit for the data? Explain.

B Beto observes the intercept at $x = 3$, and uses $x = 12$ as an approximation for the other x-intercept, so that $f(x) = a(x - 3)(x - 12)$. He chooses the point $(7, 33)$, substitutes its coordinates for $(x, f(x))$ in the equation, and solves for a to obtain the model $f(x) = -1.65(x - 3)(x - 12)$. His graph is shown.

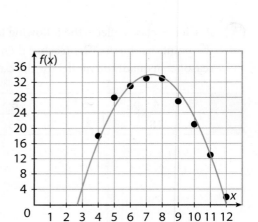

The intercepts of the model are 3 and 12.

The axis of symmetry of a parabola is halfway between the x-intercepts, or at $x = \dfrac{x_1 + x_2}{2}$,

so the model's axis of symmetry is $x = \dfrac{\boxed{} + \boxed{}}{2} = \boxed{}$.

Because the vertex is on the axis of symmetry, the model's maximum is

$f\left(\boxed{}\right) = -1.65\left(\boxed{} - 3\right)\left(7.5 - \boxed{}\right)$. So, to the

nearest tenth, the maximum is $\boxed{}$.

Is the model a good fit for the data? Explain.

C Charla enters the ordered pairs into her graphing calculator and performs *quadratic regression* to find the equation of the best-fitting quadratic model. The result is approximately $f(x) = -1.56x^2 + 23.1x - 51.6$. The graph is shown.

Using the statistics calculation features on her calculator, Charla finds that the x-intercepts are about 2.7 and 12.1, the axis of symmetry is about $x = 7.4$, and the maximum is about 33.9.

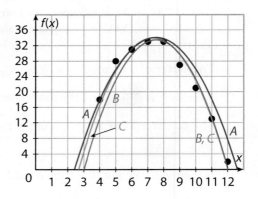

Here are the graphs of the models all together:

Give a quick comparison of the graphs of the models. How are they alike? How are they different?

Reflect

1. Look at the graph of Angelíque's model. Keeping her original estimate for the vertex, what might she have done differently that would have made her model closer to the other two?

2. **Discussion** What are some reasons that you might use each of the methods in this Explore to find a quadratic model for a data set?

© Houghton Mifflin Harcourt Publishing Company

 Explain 1 # Roughly Fitting a Quadratic Function In Vertex Form To Data

When you can make a reasonable estimate of the vertex for a quadratic model on a data plot, you can find an equation for the model. First, visually estimate the axis of symmetry. It may help to sketch parabolic curves among the data points. Use your estimate to approximate the maximum or minimum of the model curve.

Using your estimate of the vertex (which may be a data point) and the coordinates of a second point, solve for the parameter a to find a model in vertex form. The second point does not have to be a data point, but should be a point that you expect to lie on or very near the graph of an appropriate model.

Example 1 **Find an approximate quadratic function model for the graphed data by estimating the coordinates of the vertex and using one other point.**

(A) The yearly average high temperature in Oakdale is **60°F**. The ordered pairs (m, D) give the month of the year m (where January is month 1) and the number of degrees D (Fahrenheit) by which the average high temperature for the months May through October exceeds the yearly average high.

(5, 10), (6, 19), (7, 25), (8, 21), (9, 14), (10, 1)

So for example, in June $(m = 6)$, the average high is 19° above the yearly average, or $60 + 19 = 79°$. The graph of the data is shown.

Estimate the vertex.

Notice that the points for August and September are a little higher than the points for May and June. This indicates that the best estimate for the axis of symmetry is a little to the right of $m = 7$, and so the model's maximum will be a little more than 25. Estimate (7.2, 25.5) for the vertex. Use this with another point, say (10, 1), to find a model.

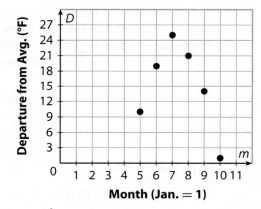

Write the vertex form.
Substitute (7.2, 25.5) for (h, k).
Substitute (10, 1) for $(x, f(x))$.
Solve for a.

$$f(x) = a(x - h)^2 + k$$
$$f(x) = a(x - 7.2)^2 + 25.5$$
$$1 = a(10 - 7.2)^2 + 25.5$$
$$-24.5 = a(2.8)^2$$
$$\frac{-24.5^2}{(2.8)^2} = a$$
$$a = -3.125$$

So, $f(x) = -3.125(x - 7.2)^2 + 25.5$.
An approximate model is $D = -3.1(m - 7.2)^2 + 25.5$.

The graph is shown.

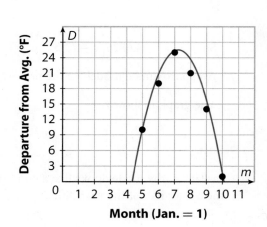

B Engineers conduct a traffic study on a road that has more traffic than it was designed for. At 10-minute intervals from 7:30 to 9:10 AM, they record how many vehicles pass a given point in 1 minute. The ordered pairs (t, V) give the results, where t indicates the time of recording (0 for 7:30, 1 for 7:40, and so on) and V indicates how many vehicles in excess of the designed maximum passed in that minute (a negative sign means the number was below the maximum).

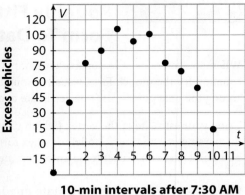

10-min intervals after 7:30 AM

$(0, -28)$ $(1, 40)$, $(2, 78)$, $(3, 90)$, $(4, 111)$, $(5, 99)$, $(6, 106)$, $(7, 78)$, $(8, 70)$, $(9, 54)$, $(10, 14)$

Estimate the vertex.

From looking at the graph, reasonable estimates for the vertex may vary quite a bit. From the overall symmetry and considering the fact that the engineers would not want to underestimate the maximum, (5, 115) is a reasonable estimate. Pick a second point not too near the vertex that seems to fit the overall trend, say (1, 40), to find a model.

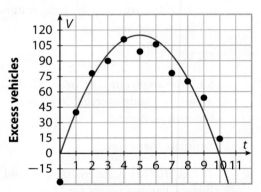

10-min intervals after 7:30 AM

Write the vertex form.

$$f(x) = a(x - h)^2 + k$$

Substitute $\boxed{5}$, $\boxed{115}$ for (h, k).

$$f(x) = a\left(x - \boxed{5}\right)^2 + \boxed{115}$$

Substitute $\boxed{1}$, $\boxed{40}$ for $(x, f(x))$.

$$\boxed{40} = a\left(\boxed{1} - 5\right)^2 + 115$$

Solve for a.

$$\boxed{-75} = a\left(\boxed{-4}\right)^2$$

$$\frac{\boxed{-75}}{\boxed{16}} = a$$

$$a = -4.6875$$

So, $f(x) = -4.6875\left(x - \boxed{5}\right)^2 + \boxed{115}$.

An approximate model (to the nearest tenth) is $V = \boxed{-4.7(t - 5)^2 + 115}$.

The graph is shown.

Reflect

3. In Part A, the model looks like a good fit for the warmer half of the year. How might a quadratic model for the cooler half of the year differ?

4. In Part B, the model looks like a reasonably good fit for the morning rush hour period. Is there another portion of the day that might be modeled by a similar curve? Explain. Why would the engineers be most interested in the models for these portions of the day?

Your Turn

5. The yearly average low temperature in Houston, Texas is 60°F. The ordered pair (m, D) give the month m (counting October as $m = 1$, November as $m = 2$, and so on), and the number of degrees D (Fahrenheit) by which the average low temperature for the months October through April departs from the yearly average low.

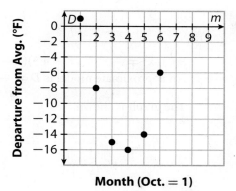

Month (Oct. = 1)

$(1, 1), (2, -8), (3, -15), (4, -16), (5, -14), (6, -6), (7, 0)$

So for example, in January ($m = 4$), the average low is 16° below the yearly average, or $60 - 16 = 44°$. The graph of the data is shown.

Copy the graph on a coordinate grid. Find an approximate quadratic function model for the graphed data by estimating the coordinates of the vertex and using one other point. Then sketch your graph for $D \leq 0$ on your grid.

Explain 2 Roughly Fitting a Quadratic Function in Intercept Form to Data

Finding a model in intercept form is very similar to finding a model in vertex form, except that this time you begin with estimates for the x-intercepts of the model.

Example 2 Find an approximate quadratic function model for the graphed data by estimating the x-intercepts and using one other point.

Ⓐ Use the scenario from Example 1, Part A for your model. The data and graph are repeated here.

$(5, 10), (6, 19), (7, 25), (8, 21), (9, 14), (10, 1)$

Estimate the x-intercepts.

On the right side of the graph, you can see that the x-intercept is a tiny bit to the right of 10. Estimate 10.1. On the left side, it is apparent that the graph is negative when x is 4, so estimate the intercept as a little farther to the right, say 4.3.

Notice that the axis of symmetry of the model is $x = \dfrac{4.3 + 10.1}{2} = 7.2$, which is the same as in the vertex model in Example 1.

Use the intercept estimates, 4.3 and 10.1, along with another point, say (7, 25), to write a model.

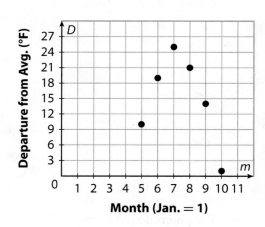

Month (Jan. = 1)

Write the intercept form.

Substitute 4.3 for x_1 and 10.1 for x_2.

Substitute (7, 25) for $(x, f(x))$.

Solve for a.

$$f(x) = a(x - x_1)(x - x_2)$$
$$f(x) = a(x - 4.3)(x - 10.1)$$
$$25 = a(7 - 4.3)(7 - 10.1)$$
$$25 = a(2.7)(-3.1)$$
$$\frac{25}{(2.7)(-3.1)} = a$$
$$a \approx -2.987$$

So, $f(x) = -2.987(x - 4.3)(x - 10.1)$.
An approximate model is $D = -3.0(m - 4.3)(m - 10.1)$.

The graph is shown.

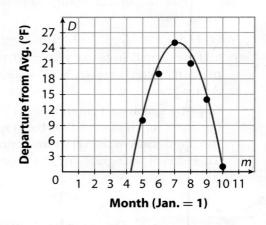

Month (Jan. = 1)

(B) Use the scenario from Example 1, Part B for your model. The data and graph are repeated here.

(0, –28) (1, 40), (2, 78), (3, 90), (4, 111), (5, 99), (6, 106), (7, 78), (8, 70), (9, 54), (10, 14)

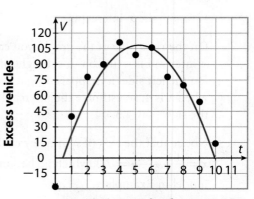

10-min intervals after 7:30 AM

Estimate the x-intercepts.

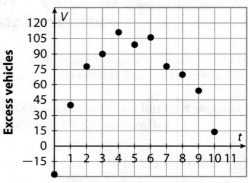

10-min intervals after 7:30 AM

The points do not all clearly lie along a single curve, but 0.5 and 10 look to be reasonable estimates. Pick a second point that is not near the intercepts, say (6, 106), to write a model.

Write the intercept form.

$$f(x) = a(x - x_1)(x - x_2)$$

Substitute $\boxed{0.5}$ for x_1 and $\boxed{10}$ for x_2.

$$f(x) = a\left(x - \boxed{0.5}\right)\left(x - \boxed{10}\right)$$

Substitute $\left(\boxed{6}, \boxed{106}\right)$ for $(x, f(x))$.

$$106 = a\left(\boxed{6} - 0.5\right)\left(\boxed{6} - 10\right)$$

Solve for a.

$$106 = a\left(\boxed{5.5}\right)\left(\boxed{-4}\right)$$

$$\frac{106}{-22} = a$$

$$a \approx -4.818$$

So, $f(x) = -4.818\left(x - \boxed{0.5}\right)\left(x - \boxed{10}\right)$.

An approximate model (to the nearest tenth) is $V = \boxed{-4.8(t - 0.5)(t - 10)}$.

The graph is shown.

Your Turn

6. Use the scenario and your coordinate grid from YourTurn 5. Find an approximate quadratic function model for the graphed data by estimating the x-intercepts and using one other point. Then sketch your graph for $D \leq 0$ on your grid.

⚙ Explain 3   Fitting a Quadratic Function To Data Using Technology

You have used a graphing calculator to find the equation of a line of best fit by entering data and then performing linear regression. You can also use a graphing calculator or software application to find a quadratic curve of best fit for a set of data by performing quadratic regression.

Example 3   Use the quadratic regression feature on a graphing calculator to find an approximate quadratic function model for the graphed data.

Ⓐ   Use the scenario from Example 1, Part A for your model. The data and graph are repeated here.

(5, 10), (6, 19), (7, 25), (8, 21), (9, 14), (10, 1)

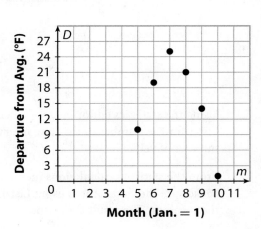

© Houghton Mifflin Harcourt Publishing Company

Using the statistics editor on your calculator, enter the data, using List 1 for the month and List 2 for the number of degrees.

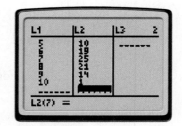

From the statistics calculations menu, select quadratic regression. Make sure the calculator is using List 1 for the x-values and List 2 for the y-values. The result is shown.

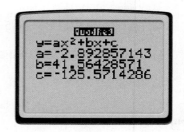

An approximate model is $D = -2.9m^2 + 41.6m - 125.6$.

Using the statistics calculation features on a graphing calculator, you can find that the x-intercepts are about 4.3 and 10.0, the axis of symmetry is about $x = 7.2$, and the maximum is about 23.7.

The graph is shown.

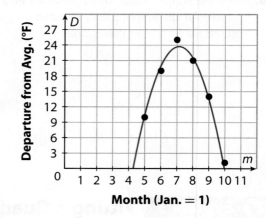

Month (Jan. = 1)

(B) Use the scenario from Example 1, Part B for your model. The data and graph are repeated here.

(0, −28) (1, 40), (2, 78), (3, 90), (4, 111), (5, 99), (6, 106), (7, 78), (8, 70), (9, 54), (10, 14)

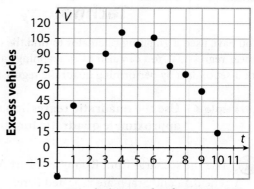

10-min intervals after 7:30 AM

Using the statistics editor on your calculator, enter the data, using List 1 for the number of the time interval and List 2 for the excess number of vehicles.

From the statistics calculations menu, select quadratic regression. Make sure the calculator is using List 1 for the x-values and List 2 for the y-values. The result is shown.

An approximate model (to the nearest tenth) is

$V = \boxed{-4.4t^2 + 45.6t - 10.4}$.

Graph the quadratic regression model and use the statistics calculation features on your calculator to find the following (round to the nearest tenth):

The x-intercepts are about $\boxed{0.2}$ and $\boxed{10.1}$.

The axis of symmetry is about $\boxed{x = 5.2}$.

The maximum is about $\boxed{107.7}$.

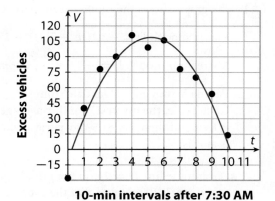

10-min intervals after 7:30 AM

Reflect

7. A graphing calculator will give you the most accurate quadratic model of a set of data. Can you think of any disadvantages of using quadratic regression?

Your Turn

Find an approximate quadratic function model for the graphed data by estimating the x-intercepts and using one other point.

8. Use the scenario from YourTurn 5. Use the quadratic regression feature on a graphing calculator to find an approximate quadratic function model for the graphed data. Then sketch your graph for $D \leq 0$ on a coordinate grid.

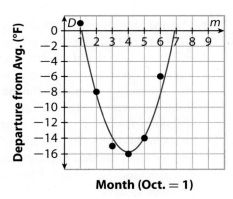

Month (Oct. = 1)

🖉 Explain 4   Solving a Real-World Problem

Once you have a suitable model for a data set, you can use it to make predictions and draw conclusions for appropriate intervals of the domain and range. Remember to be careful, however, about applying the model outside the region of your data, where it may not be appropriate.

One way to make a prediction is simply to substitute a value for a variable in the model and solve for the other variable, but you may also use the graph of the model.

Example 4   Use the indicated quadratic models to answer the questions.

Ⓐ The graph shows the models from part A of Examples 1 and 3:

Vertex model: $D = -3.1(m - 7.2)^2 + 25.5$

Regression model: $D = -2.9m^2 + 41.6m - 125.6$

Padma is moving to Oakdale from Centerville. In Centerville, the greatest monthly average high temperature is 84°, and there is a 105-day period where the average high is at least 70°.

a. Graph the line $D = 24$ on the grid. What does this line represent? (Remember that the average yearly high temperature in Oakdale is 60°.) What different conclusions might Padma reach using the graphs of the two models to compare Oakdale to Centerville? Explain.

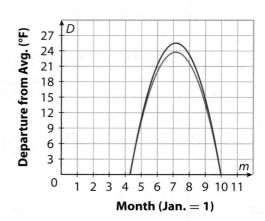

b. Graph the line $D = 10$ on the grid. What does this line represent? Compare the predictions of the models for how long the period is in Oakdale with an average high of at least 70°. How does this compare with Centerville?

Draw the lines $D = 24$ and $D = 10$ on the graph.

c. The line $D = 24$ represents a temperature of $60 + 24 = 84°$. From the regression model, Padma could conclude that the hottest part of summer is nearly identical, since the maximum of the model for Oakdale is almost exactly 84, which is the maximum for Centerville. From the vertex model, she could conclude that there is about a 45-day period where the average high is at or above 84 degrees in Oakdale, which means Oakdale is significantly hotter. This is because the graph of the Oakdale model is above 84° for about a month and a half, or about 45 days.

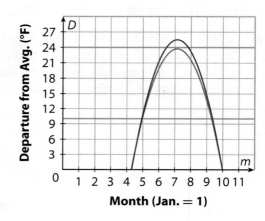

d. The line $D = 10$ represents a temperature of $60 + 10 = 70°$. The models are nearly identical near 70°. They both predict a period of about four and a half months, or about 135 days, in Oakdale with an average high of at least 70°. This is about 30 days longer than the period for Centerville.

Ⓑ The graph shows the models from part B of Examples 1 and 2:

Vertex model: $V = -4.7(t - 5)^2 + 115$

Intercept model: $V = -4.8(t - 0.5)(t - 10)$

The engineers propose a short-term plan to raise the safe capacity of the road by 60 vehicles per minute. Graph the line $V = 60$ on the grid. What does it represent in relation to the graphs? Do the models differ significantly in the conclusions they might lead you to make in evaluating the plan? Explain.

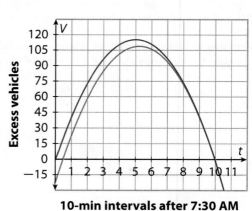

10-min intervals after 7:30 AM

First draw the line $V = 60$ on the graph.

Now consider how the line is related to how many of the passing vehicles are counted as excess vehicles, to answer the questions.

The line represents a new, higher baseline above which passing vehicles are counted as excess vehicles in terms of safety. The models would not likely lead to significantly different conclusions. The vertex model has traffic exceeding the new baseline at about 7:45 instead of 7:50. Both then have traffic above the new baseline until about 8:55. The vertex model shows a maximum of about 55 vehicles above the baseline, while the intercept model has a maximum of about 50 vehicles above the baseline. But these are minor differences as far as evaluating the overall effectiveness of the plan.

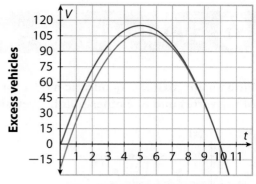

10-min intervals after 7:30 AM

Your Turn

9. The line $D = -15$ along with the vertex form model from Your Turn 6 and the quadratic regression model from Your Turn 8 are shown on the graph. Use the graph to answer the following questions.

   a. What does the line represent?

   b. The line intersects each model twice. What do these intersection points represent?

   c. Use the graphs to estimate roughly how long each model predicts the average low temperatures will be below 45 degrees. Explain how you got your answers.

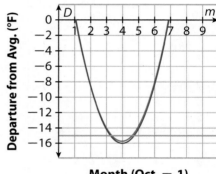

Month (Oct. = 1)

💬 Elaborate

10. How do the data sets modeled in the lesson emphasize the importance of being careful about using the model to make predictions outside the domain represented by the data?

11. **Discussion** Three students have modeled a data set, each using a different one of the methods used in the Examples. Give two ways they can compare their models. What are the advantages of each?

12. **Essential Question Check-In** When you have a scatter plot for which a quadratic model is appropriate, how can you decide how to proceed to find a model?

• Online Homework
• Hints and Help
• Extra Practice

Find an approximate quadratic model for the data by estimating the coordinates of the vertex and one other point. Then sketch a graph of the model.

1.

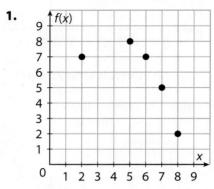

2.

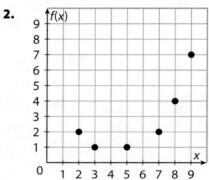

Find an approximate quadratic model for the data by estimating the x-intercepts and one other point. Then sketch a graph of the model.

3.

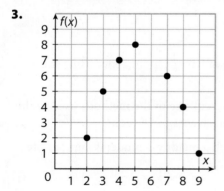

4.

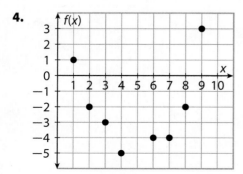

5. Use the quadratic regression feature on a graphing calculator to find an approximate quadratic function model for the data in Evaluate Exercise 2. Then sketch the graph with the graph of your model, and compare the graphs.

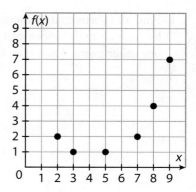

6. Use the quadratic regression feature on a graphing calculator to find an approximate quadratic function model for the data in Evaluate Exercise 4. Then sketch the graph with the graph of your model, and compare the graphs.

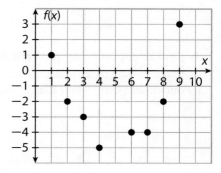

7. A town is holding its annual music festival 6 months from now. Based on last year's ticket sales and survey results of how many tickets could be sold at different prices, a study group presents the table and graph shown. The variable c represents the cost of a ticket (in dollars), and P represents the estimated overall profit (in thousands of dollars) the town would make at that ticket price.

c	25	30	35	40	45	50	55	60
p	2	17	28	30	34	26	21	7

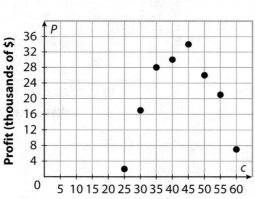

a. Find an approximate quadratic function model for data by estimating the coordinates of the vertex and using one other point. Then sketch your graph.

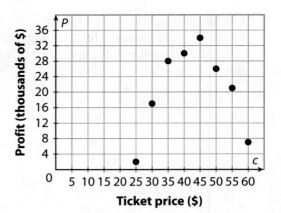

b. Find an approximate quadratic function model for the graphed data by estimating the x-intercepts and using one other point. Then sketch your graph.

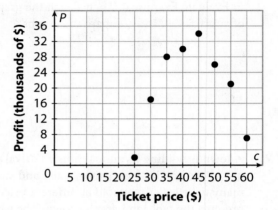

c. Use the quadratic regression feature on a graphing calculator to find an approximate quadratic function model for the graphed data. Then sketch your graph.

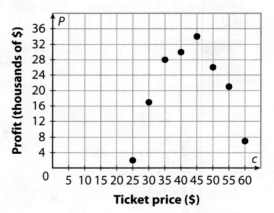

d. What do the x-intercepts of the models represent?

e. What do the models predict for the ticket cost (to the nearest dollar) that the town should choose to maximize profit? What is this profit (to the nearest thousand dollars)?

8. Consider the following data set.

x	10	8	13	9	11	14	6	4	12	7	5
f(x)	9.14	8.14	8.74	8.77	9.29	8.1	6.13	3.1	9.13	7.26	4.74

a. Use a graphing calculator to create a scatter plot.

b. Find a quadratic regression model for the data, and add its graph to the scatter plot.

c. Trace along the model to the right (or use the Table feature). To the nearest tenth, what does the model predict for the rightmost x-intercept?

H.O.T. Focus on Higher Order Thinking

9. Multi-Step Problem A school is making digital backups of 16 mm educational film reels in its library's archives. The table shows approximate run times of the films for a given diameter of film on the reel.

a. Use the quadratic regression feature on a graphing calculator to find a model for the run time T as a function of diameter d.

b. What does the model predict for the run time of a film reel with a diameter of 15 inches?

c. Use the calculator to graph the data points and the regression model. Visually make a rough estimate of the x-intercept. What does it mean in the context? What does it indicate about a reasonable domain for the model?

d. On the same screen, graph the horizontal line $y = 60$. Use the calculator to find the intersection of this line with the model. What prediction by the model does the point of intersection indicate?

Film Run Times (16 mm)	
Diameter (in.)	**Run Time (min)**
3	2.25
5	8
7	15.75
8	31.5
12	63
14	84

10. Communicate Mathematical Ideas A student entered a data set into a graphing calculator and had it perform a quadratic regression. She noticed that the coefficient a in the model was very close to 0. Why might it be a good idea for her to plot the data and examine it to see if a different model might be more appropriate?

Lesson Performance Task

Every year a hole forms in the ozone layer over the Antarctic as temperatures plummet during the winter months in the Southern Hemisphere. As temperatures warm in the spring, the ozone levels return to normal and the hole closes. The table provides data on the average size of the ozone hole for a series of key dates during the Antarctic winter and spring.

Calendar Date	Day Number	Area of the Ozone Hole (million km²)
Aug 15	0	4
Sept 1	17	18
Sept 15	31	23
Oct 1	47	24
Oct 15	61	22
Nov 1	78	17
Nov 15	92	10

a. Find a quadratic function that roughly models the changes in area. You can either plot ordered pairs for the day number/ area and sketch a curve or use a graphing calculator to find a regression.

b. Based on your model, on approximately what calendar date would you predict that the area of the ozone hole will return to zero?

Quadratic Functions

Essential Question: How can graphing quadratic functions be used to solve real-world problems?

Key Vocabulary
completing the square
   (*completar el cuadrado*)
standard form of a quadratic
   function (*forma estándar de
   una ecuación cuadrática*)
vertex form of a quadratic
   function (*forma en vértice de
   una ecuación cuadrática*)

KEY EXAMPLE   (Lesson 3.1)

Identify the axis of symmetry of the graph of $f(x) = 3(x - 2)^2 - 4$, then give the function's maximum or minimum value, domain, range, and the intervals where the function is increasing or decreasing.

$f(x) = a(x - h)^2 + k$, so for $f(x) = 3(x - 2)^2 - 4$, $a = 3$, $h = 2$, and $k = -4$.

The axis of symmetry is $x = h$, so $x = 2$. $f(x)$ has a minimum value of -4.

Domain: $\{x | x \in \Re\}$ Range: $\{y | y \geq -4\}$

Decreasing on $(-\infty, 2]$ and increasing on $[3, +\infty)$.

KEY EXAMPLE   (Lesson 3.2)

Write the equation of a quadratic given that the vertex is (5, 14), a point not on the vertex is (8, −4), and it opens downward.

$h = 5, k - 14$	Identify h and k into the vertex form of a quadratic function.
$f(x) = a(x - 5)^2 + 14$	Substitute h and k into the vertex form of a quadratic function.
$-4 = a(8 - 5)^2 + 14$	Substitute the other point into this equation to solve for a.
$-4 = a(3)^2 + 14$	
$-4 = 9a + 14$	
$-18 = 9a$	
$-2 = a$	
$f(x) = -2(x - 5)^2 + 14$	Substitute a into the vertex form of the function.

KEY EXAMPLE   (Lesson 3.3)

Use a calculator to find the line of best fit for the following data points: $(-1, 5)$, $(0, -1)$, $(2, -3)$, $(2, -1.5)$, $(3, 5)$, and $(4, 10)$.

Put the data points into STAT using List 1 for the x-values and List 2 for the y-values. From the statistics calculations menu, select quadratic regression. The result is shown.

```
QuadReg
 y=ax²+bx+c
 a=1.677083333
 b=-3.802083333
 c=-.75
 R²=.9448902719
```

So, the equation of the line is approximately $f(x) = 1.7x^2 - 3.8x - 0.8$ when rounded to the nearest tenth.

EXERCISES

Find the quadratic equation given the vertex, another point, and the direction it opens. *(Lesson 3.2)*

1. Vertex: (2, 3), Point: (5, 9), Open: Upward

2. Vertex: (0, −5), Point: (6, −10), Open: Downward

Use a calculator to find the best fit line for the given data points. Round to the nearest tenth. *(Lesson 3.3)*

3. (−4, 18), (−2, −1), (0, 0), (3, 20)

4. (−6, −20), (−4, −4), (1, 4), (3, −10)

5. Identify the axis of symmetry of the graph of $f(x) = -2(x + 4)^2 - 4$ then give the function's maximum or minimum value, domain, range, and the intervals where the function is increasing or decreasing. Explain your answer. *(Lesson 3.1)*

MODULE PERFORMANCE TASK

What is the Path of a Punt?

The Dallas Cowboys stadium has a giant video board that is 72 feet high by 160 feet long. The bottom of the board is 90 feet above the playing field. In a game in 2013, a Dallas player kicked a punt from his own 28 yard line that hit the bottom of the video board. If we assume that the punt hit the board directly above the 50 yard line, where do you think the punt would have landed if it had not hit the video board?

Start by listing the information you will need to solve the problem. Then complete the task. Be sure to write down all your data and assumptions. Then use graphs, numbers, words, or algebra to explain how you reached your conclusion.

(Ready) to Go On?

3.1–3.3 Quadratic Functions

• Online Homework
• Hints and Help
• Extra Practice

Copy and complete the table. Identify the axis of symmetry of the given function, then give the function's maximum or minimum value, domain, range, and the intervals where the function is increasing or decreasing. *(Lesson 3.1)*

1.

	$f(x) = 2(x - 3)^2 + 1$	$f(x) = -\frac{1}{2}(x + 1)^2 + 2$
Axis of Symmetry		
Max or Min Value		
Domain		
Range		
Increasing/Decreasing		

Find the equation of the quadratic function using the given information. *(Lesson 3.2)*

2. Vertex: (1, 3); Point: (4, 21); Open: Up

3. Vertex: (4, −2); Point: (0, −6); Open: Down

ESSENTIAL QUESTION

4. Write the best fit line to represent the data points (1, 2), (4, 5), and (7, 2). Then write a real world example to fit the equation. *(Lessons 3.1, 3.2, 3.3)*

Assessment Readiness

1. A parabola goes through the points $(-4, -1)$, $(-2, -3)$, and $(0, -1)$. Which description of the parabola is correct?

   A. The parabola opens downward and has its axis of symmetry at $x = -2$.

   B. The parabola opens upward and has its axis of symmetry at $x = -2$.

   C. The parabola opens downward and has its axis of symmetry at $x = 0$.

   D. The parabola opens upward and has its axis of symmetry at $x = 0$.

2. What is the range of the quadratic equation $f(x) = -(x + 3)^2 + 1$?

   A. $\{y | y \in i\}$

   B. $\{y | y \geq -1\}$

   C. $\{y | y \geq -3\}$

   D. $\{y | y \leq 1\}$

3. Solve $-|x - 4| = -10$ for x.

   A. $x = -6$ or $x = 14$

   B. $x = 6$ or $x = 14$

   C. $x = 4$ or $x = -4$

   D. No solution

4. Elana is making some yarn art by attaching pieces of yarn to a grid in the shapes of different functions, allowing them to cross and make an original design. One strip of yarn is in the shape of a parabola that opens upward, has a vertex at $(5, 4)$ on the grid, and passes through the point $(-3, 0)$. What is the equation of the parabola Elana makes with the yarn? Show your work.

Quadratic Equations and Inequalities

TEKS

Essential Question: How can you use quadratic equations and inequalities to solve real-world problems?

REAL WORLD VIDEO
Safe drivers are aware of stopping distances and carefully judge how fast they can travel based on road conditions. Stopping distance is one of many everyday functions that can be modeled with quadratic equations.

MODULE PERFORMANCE TASK PREVIEW
Can You Stop in Time?

When a driver applies the brakes, the car continues to travel for a certain distance until coming to a stop. The stopping distance for a vehicle depends on many factors, including the initial speed of the car and road conditions. How far will a car travel after the brakes are applied? Let's hit the road and find out!

Are (YOU) Ready?

Complete these exercises to review skills you will need for this module.

Personal Math Trainer

• Online Homework
• Hints and Help
• Extra Practice

One-Step Inequalities

Example 1   Solve $-2x \leq 9$ for x.
$x \geq -4.5$

Divide both sides by -2. Because you are dividing by a negative number, flip the inequality symbol.

Solve each inequality.

1. $n - 12 > 9$

2. $-3p < -27$

3. $\dfrac{k}{4} \geq -1$

Exponents

Example 2   Simplify $\dfrac{3a^5b^2}{9a^2b}$.

$$\dfrac{3a^5b^2}{9a^2b} = \dfrac{3^1a^5b^2}{3^2a^2b^1} = \dfrac{a^{5-2}b^{2-1}}{3^{2-1}} = \dfrac{a^3b}{3}$$

Subtract exponents when dividing.

Simplify each expression.

4. $\dfrac{16p^2}{2p^4}$

5. $5vw^5 \cdot 2v^4$

6. $\dfrac{3x^7y}{6x^4y^2}$

Solving Quadratic Equations by Factoring

Example 3   Factor to solve $x^2 + 2x - 15 = 0$ for x.

Pairs of factors of -15 are:
1 and -15
3 and -5
5 and -3
15 and -1

The pair with the sum of the middle term, 2, is 5 and -3.

$(x + 5)(x - 3) = 0$

Either $x + 5 = 0$ or $x - 3 = 0$, so x-values are -5 and 3.

Factor to solve each equation.

7. $x^2 - 7x + 6 = 0$

8. $x^2 - 18x + 81 = 0$

9. $x^2 - 16 = 0$

4.1 Solving Quadratic Equations by Taking Square Roots

Essential Question: What is an imaginary number, and how is it useful in solving quadratic equations?

 **TEKS A2.4.F:** Solve quadratic ... equations.

 Explore **Investigating Ways of Solving Simple Quadratic Equations**

There are many ways to solve a quadratic equation. Here, you will use three methods to solve the equation $x^2 = 16$: by graphing, by factoring, and by taking square roots.

(A) Solve $x^2 = 16$ by graphing.

First treat each side of the equation as a function, and graph the two functions, which in this case are $f(x) = x^2$ and $g(x) = 16$, on the same coordinate plane. Use a scale of -10 to 10 for the x-axis and -2 to 18 for the y-axis.

Then identify the x-coordinates of the points where two graphs intersect.

$x =$ ▮ or $x =$ ▮

(B) Solve $x^2 = 16$ by factoring.

This method involves rewriting the equation so that 0 is on one side in order to use the *zero-product property*, which says that the product of two numbers is 0 if and only if at least one of the numbers is 0.

Write the equation. $x^2 = 16$

Subtract 16 from both sides. $x^2 - $ ▮ $ = 0$

Factor the difference of two squares. $\left(x + \boxed{}\right)(x - 4) = 0$

Apply the zero-product property. $x + $ ▮ $ = 0$ or $x - 4 = 0$

Solve for x. $x = $ ▮   or $x = 4$

(C) Solve $x^2 = 16$ by taking square roots.

A real number x is a *square root* of a nonnegative real number a provided $x^2 = a$. A square root is written using the radical symbol $\sqrt{}$. Every positive real number a has both a positive square root, written $\sqrt{a}$, and a negative square root, written $-\sqrt{a}$. For instance, the square roots of 9 are $\pm\sqrt{9}$ (read "plus or minus the square root of 9"), or ± 3. The number 0 has only itself as its square root: $\pm\sqrt{0} = 0$.

Write the equation. $x^2 = 16$

Use the definition of square root. $x = \pm\sqrt{16}$

Simplify the square roots. $x = $ ▮

1. Which of the three methods would you use to solve $x^2 = 5$? Explain, and then use the method to find the solutions.

2. Can the equation $x^2 = -9$ be solved by any of the three methods? Explain.

Explain 1 Finding Real Solutions of Simple Quadratic Equations

When solving a quadratic equation of the form $ax^2 + c = 0$ by taking square roots, you may need to use the following properties of square roots to simplify the solutions. (In a later lesson, these properties are stated in a more general form and then proved.)

Property Name	Words	Symbols	Numbers
Product property of square roots	The square root of a product equals the product of the square roots of the factors.	$\sqrt{ab} = \sqrt{a} \cdot \sqrt{b}$ where $a \geq 0$ and $b \geq 0$	$\sqrt{12} = \sqrt{4 \cdot 3}$ $= \sqrt{4} \cdot \sqrt{3}$ $= 2\sqrt{3}$
Quotient property of square roots	The square root of a fraction equals the quotient of the square roots of the numerator and the denominator.	$\sqrt{\dfrac{a}{b}} = \dfrac{\sqrt{a}}{\sqrt{b}}$ where $a \geq 0$ and $b > 0$	$\sqrt{\dfrac{5}{9}} = \dfrac{\sqrt{5}}{\sqrt{9}}$ $= \dfrac{\sqrt{5}}{3}$

Using the quotient property of square roots may require an additional step of *rationalizing the denominator* if the denominator is not a rational number. For instance, the quotient property allows you to write $\sqrt{\dfrac{2}{7}}$ as $\dfrac{\sqrt{2}}{\sqrt{7}}$, but $\sqrt{7}$ is not a rational number. To rationalize the denominator, multiply $\dfrac{\sqrt{2}}{\sqrt{7}}$ by $\dfrac{\sqrt{7}}{\sqrt{7}}$ (a form of 1) and get this result: $\dfrac{\sqrt{2}}{\sqrt{7}} \cdot \dfrac{\sqrt{7}}{\sqrt{7}} = \dfrac{\sqrt{14}}{\sqrt{49}} = \dfrac{\sqrt{14}}{7}$.

Example 1 Solve the quadratic equation by taking square roots.

 $2x^2 - 16 = 0$

Add 16 to both sides.	$2x^2 = 16$
Divide both sides by 2.	$x^2 = 8$
Use the definition of square root.	$x = \pm\sqrt{8}$
Use the product property.	$x = \pm\sqrt{4} \cdot \sqrt{2}$
Simplify.	$x = \pm 2\sqrt{2}$

(B) $-5x^2 + 9 = 0$

Subtract 9 from both sides.	$-5x^2 =$	$\boxed{-9}$
Divide both sides by $\boxed{-5}$.	$x^2 =$	$\boxed{\dfrac{9}{5}}$
Use the definition of square root.	$x =$	$\pm\sqrt{\boxed{\dfrac{9}{5}}}$
Use the quotient property.	$x =$	$\pm\dfrac{\boxed{\sqrt{9}}}{\boxed{\sqrt{5}}}$
Simplify the numerator.	$x =$	$\pm\dfrac{\boxed{3}}{\boxed{\sqrt{5}}}$
Rationalize the denominator.	$x =$	$\pm\boxed{\dfrac{3\sqrt{5}}{5}}$

Your Turn

Solve the quadratic equation by taking square roots.

3. $x^2 - 24 = 0$

4. $-4x^2 + 13 = 0$

🔧 Explain 2 Solving a Real-World Problem Using a Simple Quadratic Equation

Two commonly used quadratic models for falling objects near Earth's surface are the following:

- Distance fallen (in feet) at time t (in seconds): $d(t) = 16t^2$

- Height (in feet) at time t (in seconds): $h(t) = h_0 - 16t^2$ where h_0 is the object's initial height (in feet)

For both models, time is measured from the instant that the object begins to fall. A negative value of t would represent a time before the object began falling, so negative values of t are excluded from the domains of these functions. This means that for any equation of the form $d(t) = c$ or $h(t) = c$ where c is a constant, a negative solution should be rejected.

Example 2 **Write and solve an equation to answer the question. Give the exact answer and, if it's irrational, a decimal approximation (to the nearest tenth of a second).**

(A) If you drop a water balloon, how long does it take to fall 4 feet?

Using the model $d(t) = 16t^2$, solve the equation $d(t) = 4$.

Write the equation.	$16t^2 = 4$
Divide both sides by 16.	$t^2 = \dfrac{1}{4}$
Use the definition of square root.	$t = \pm\sqrt{\dfrac{1}{4}}$
Use the quotient property.	$t = \pm\dfrac{1}{2}$

Reject the negative value of t. The water balloon falls 4 feet in $\frac{1}{2}$ second.

Ⓑ The rooftop of a 5-story building is 50 feet above the ground. How long does it take the water balloon dropped from the rooftop to pass by a third-story window at 24 feet?

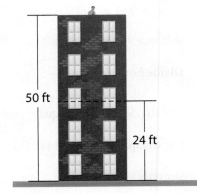

50 ft

24 ft

Using the model $h(t) = h_0 - 16t^2$, solve the equation $h(t) = 24$. (When you reach the step at which you divide both sides by -16, leave 16 in the denominator rather than simplifying the fraction because you'll get a rational denominator when you later use the quotient property.)

Write the equation. $\boxed{50} - 16t^2 = \boxed{24}$

Subtract 50 from both sides. $-16t^2 = \boxed{-26}$

Divide both sides by -16. $t^2 = \boxed{\dfrac{26}{16}}$

Use the definition of square root. $t = \pm\sqrt{\boxed{\dfrac{26}{16}}}$

Use the quotient property to simplify. $t = \pm\boxed{\dfrac{\sqrt{26}}{4}}$

Reject the negative value of t. The water balloon passes by the third-story window

in $\boxed{\dfrac{\sqrt{26}}{4}} \approx \boxed{1.3}$ seconds.

Reflect

5. **Discussion** Explain how the model $h(t) = h_0 - 16t^2$ is built from the model $d(t) = 16t^2$.

Your Turn

Write and solve an equation to answer the question. Give the exact answer and, if it's irrational, a decimal approximation (to the nearest tenth of a second).

6. How long does it take the water balloon described in Part B to hit the ground?

7. On the moon, the distance d (in feet) that an object falls in time t (in seconds) is modeled by the function $d(t) = \frac{8}{3}t^2$. Suppose an astronaut on the moon drops a tool. How long does it take the tool to fall 4 feet?

You know that the quadratic equation $x^2 = 1$ has two real solutions, the equation $x^2 = 0$ has one real solution, and the equation $x^2 = -1$ has no real solutions. By creating a new type of number called *imaginary numbers*, mathematicians allowed for solutions of equations like $x^2 = -1$.

Imaginary numbers are the square roots of negative numbers. These numbers can all be written in the form bi where b is a nonzero real number and i, called the **imaginary unit**, represents $\sqrt{-1}$. Some examples of imaginary numbers are the following:

- $2i$
- $-5i$
- $-\dfrac{i}{3}$ or $-\dfrac{1}{3}i$
- $i\sqrt{2}$ (Write the i in front of the radical symbol for clarity.)
- $\dfrac{i\sqrt{3}}{2}$ or $\dfrac{\sqrt{3}}{2}i$

Given that $i = \sqrt{-1}$, you can conclude that $i^2 = -1$. This means that the square of any imaginary number is a negative real number. When squaring an imaginary number, use the power of a product property of exponents: $(ab)^m = a^m \cdot b^m$.

Example 3 **Find the square of the imaginary number.**

(A) $5i$

$$(5i)^2 = 5^2 \cdot i^2$$
$$= 25(-1)$$
$$= -25$$

(B) $-i\sqrt{2}$

$$(-i\sqrt{2})^2 = \left(\boxed{-\sqrt{2}}\right)^2 \cdot i^2$$
$$= \boxed{2}(-1)$$
$$= \boxed{2}$$

Reflect

8. By definition, i is a square root of -1. Does -1 have another square root? Explain.

Your Turn

Find the square of the imaginary number.

9. $-2i$

10. $\dfrac{\sqrt{3}}{3}i$

Finding Imaginary Solutions of Simple Quadratic Equations

Using imaginary numbers, you can solve simple quadratic equations that do not have real solutions.

Example 4 Solve the quadratic equation by taking square roots. Allow for imaginary solutions.

Ⓐ $x^2 + 12 = 0$

Write the equation.	$x^2 + 12 = 0$
Subtract 12 from both sides.	$x^2 = -12$
Use the definition of square root.	$x = \pm\sqrt{-12}$
Use the product property.	$x = \pm\sqrt{(4)(-1)(3)} = \pm 2i\sqrt{3}$

Ⓑ $4x^2 + 11 = 6$

Write the equation.	$4x^2 + 11 = 6$
Subtract 11 from both sides.	$\boxed{4}\ x^2 = \boxed{-5}$
Divide both sides by $\boxed{4}$.	$x^2 = \boxed{-\dfrac{5}{4}}$
Use the definition of square root.	$x = \pm\sqrt{\boxed{-\dfrac{5}{4}}}$
Use the qoutient property.	$x = \pm\boxed{\dfrac{\sqrt{5}}{2}i}$

Your Turn

Solve the quadratic equation by taking square roots. Allow for imaginary solutions.

11. $\frac{1}{4}x^2 + 9 = 0$

12. $-5x^2 + 3 = 10$

💬 **Elaborate**

13. The quadratic equations $4x^2 + 32 = 0$ and $4x^2 - 32 = 0$ differ only by the sign of the constant term. Without actually solving the equations, what can you say about the relationship between their solutions?

14. What kind of a number is the square of an imaginary number?

15. Why do you reject negative values of t when solving equations based on the models for a falling object near Earth's surface, $d(t) = 16t^2$ for distance fallen and $h(t) = h_0 - 16t^2$ for height during a fall?

16. Essential Question Check-In Describe how to find the square roots of a negative number.

★ Evaluate: Homework and Practice

1. Solve the equation $x^2 - 2 = 7$ using the indicated method.

   a. Solve by graphing.

   b. Solve by factoring.

   c. Solve by taking square roots.

2. Solve the equation $2x^2 + 3 = 5$ using the indicated method.

   a. Solve by graphing.

   b. Solve by factoring.

   c. Solve by taking square roots.

Solve the quadratic equation by taking square roots.

3. $4x^2 = 24$

4. $-\dfrac{x^2}{5} + 15 = 0$

5. $2(5 - 5x^2) = 5$

6. $3x^2 - 8 = 12$

Write and solve an equation to answer the question. Give the exact answer and, if it's irrational, a decimal approximation (to the nearest tenth of a second).

7. A squirrel in a tree drops an acorn. How long does it take the acorn to fall 20 feet?

8. A person washing the windows of an office building drops a squeegee from a height of 60 feet. How long does it take the squeegee to pass by another window washer working at a height of 20 feet?

Geometry Determine the lengths of the sides of the rectangle using the given area. Give answers both exactly and approximately (to the nearest tenth).

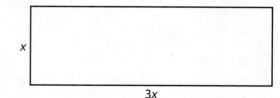

9. The area of the rectangle is 45 cm².

10. The area of the rectangle is 54 cm².

Find the square of the imaginary number.

11. $3i$

12. $i\sqrt{5}$

13. $-i\dfrac{\sqrt{2}}{2}$

14. $-4i\sqrt{3}$

Solve the quadratic equation by taking square roots. Allow for imaginary solutions.

15. $x^2 = -81$

16. $x^2 + 64 = 0$

17. $5x^2 - 4 = -8$

18. $7x^2 + 10 = 0$

Determine whether the quadratic equation has real solutions or imaginary solutions by solving the equation.

19. $15x^2 - 10 = 0$

20. $\frac{1}{2}x^2 + 12 = 4$

21. $5(2x^2 - 3) = 4(x^2 - 10)$

22. $5x^2 - 4 = 10x^2 - 20$

Geometry Determine the length of the sides of each square using the given information. Give answers both exactly and approximately (to the nearest tenth).

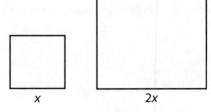

23. The area of the larger square is 42 cm² more than the area of the smaller square.

24. If the area of the larger square is decreased by 28 cm², the result is half of the area of the smaller square.

25. Determine whether each of the following numbers is real or imaginary.

    a. i

    b. a square root of 5

    c. $(2i)^2$

    d. $(-5)^2$

    e. $\sqrt{-3}$

    f. $-\sqrt{10}$

26. **Critical Thinking** When a batter hits a baseball, you can model the ball's height using a quadratic function that accounts for the ball's initial vertical velocity. However, once the ball reaches its maximum height, its vertical velocity is momentarily 0 feet per second, and you can use the model $h(t) = h_0 - 16t^2$ to find the ball's height h (in feet) at time t (in seconds) as it falls to the ground.

   a. Suppose a fly ball reaches a maximum height of 67 feet and an outfielder catches the ball 3 feet above the ground. How long after the ball begins to descend does the outfielder catch the ball?

   b. Can you determine (without writing or solving any equations) the total time the ball was in the air? Explain your reasoning and state any assumptions you make.

27. **Represent Real-World Situations** The aspect ratio of an image on a screen is the ratio of image width to image height. An HDTV screen shows images with an aspect ratio of 16:9. If the area of an HDTV screen is 864 in², what are the dimensions of the screen?

28. **Explain the Error** Russell wants to calculate the amount of time it takes for a load of dirt to fall from a crane's clamshell bucket at a height of 16 feet to the bottom of a hole that is 32 feet deep. He sets up the following equation and tries to solve it.

$$16 - 16t^2 = 32$$
$$-16t^2 = 16$$
$$t^2 = -1$$
$$t = \pm\sqrt{-1}$$
$$t = \pm i$$

Does Russell's answer make sense? If not, find and correct Russell's error.

Lesson Performance Task

A suspension bridge uses two thick cables, one on each side of the road, to hold up the road. The cables are suspended between two towers and have a parabolic shape. Smaller vertical cables connect the parabolic cables to the road. The table gives the lengths of the first few vertical cables starting with the shortest one.

Displacement from the Shortest Vertical Cable (m)	Height of Vertical Cable (m)
0	3
1	3.05
2	3.2
3	3.45

Find a quadratic function that describes the height (in meters) of a parabolic cable above the road as a function of the horizontal displacement (in meters) from the cable's lowest point. Use the function to predict the distance between the towers if the parabolic cable reaches a maximum height of 48 m above the road at each tower.

4.2 Complex Numbers

Essential Question: What is a complex number, and how can you add, subtract, and multiply complex numbers?

 TEKS **A2.7.A:** Add, subtract, and multiply complex numbers.

Resource Locker

Explore Exploring Operations Involving Complex Numbers

In this lesson, you'll learn to perform operations with *complex numbers*, which have a form similar to linear binomials such as $3 + 4x$ and $2 - x$.

(A) Add the binomials $3 + 4x$ and $2 - x$.

Group like terms.
$$(3 + 4x) + (2 - x) = \left(3 + \boxed{}\right) + \left(4x + \boxed{}\right)$$

Combine like terms.
$$= \left(\boxed{} + \boxed{}\right)$$

(B) Subtract $2 - x$ from $3 + 4x$.

Rewrite as addition.
$$(3 + 4x) - (2 - x) = (3 + 4x) + \left(-2 + \boxed{}\right)$$

Group like terms.
$$= \left(3 + \boxed{}\right) + \left(4x + \boxed{}\right)$$

Combine like terms.
$$= \left(\boxed{} + \boxed{}\right)$$

(C) Multiply the binomials $3 + 4x$ and $2 - x$.

Use FOIL.
$$(3 + 4x)(2 - x) = 6 + (-3x) + \boxed{} + \boxed{}$$

Combine like terms.
$$= 6 + \boxed{} + \boxed{}$$

Reflect

1. In Step A, you found that $(3 + 4x) + (2 - x) = 5 + 3x$. Suppose $x = i$ (the imaginary unit). What equation do you get?

2. In Step B, you found that $(3 + 4x) + (2 - x) = 1 + 5x$. Suppose $x = i$ (the imaginary unit). What equation do you get?

3. In Step C, you found that $(3 + 4x)(2 - x) = 6 + 5x - 4x^2$. Suppose $x = i$ (the imaginary unit). What equation do you get? How you can further simplify the right side of this equation?

⚙ Explain 1   Defining Complex Numbers

A **complex number** is any number that can be written in the form $a + bi$, where a and b are real numbers and $i = \sqrt{-1}$. For a complex number $a + bi$ a is called the *real part* of the number, and b is called the *imaginary part*. (Note that "imaginary part" refers to the real multiplier of i; it does not refer to the imaginary number bi.) The Venn diagram shows some examples of complex numbers.

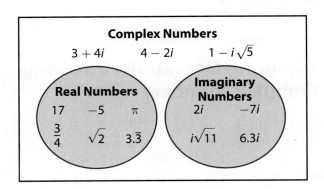

Notice that the set of real numbers is a subset of the set of complex numbers. That's because a real number a can be written in the form $a + 0i$ (whose imaginary part is 0). Likewise, the set of imaginary numbers is also a subset of the set of complex numbers, because an imaginary number bi (where $b \neq 0$) can be written in the form $0 + bi$ (whose real part is 0).

Example 1   **Identify the real and imaginary parts of the given number. Then tell whether the number belongs to each of the following sets: real numbers, imaginary numbers, and complex numbers.**

Ⓐ $9 + 5i$

The real part of $9 + 5i$ is 9, and the imaginary part is 5. Because both the real and imaginary parts of $9 + 5i$ are nonzero, the number belongs only to the set of complex numbers.

Ⓑ $-7i$

The real part of $-7i$ is 0, and the imaginary part is -7. Because the real part is 0, the number belongs to these sets: imaginary numbers and complex numbers.

Your Turn

Identify the real and imaginary parts of the given number. Then tell whether the number belongs to each of the following sets: real numbers, imaginary numbers, and complex numbers.

4.   11

5. $-1 + i$

🎯 Explain 2   Adding and Subtracting Complex Numbers

To add or subtract complex numbers, add or subtract the real parts and the imaginary parts separately.

Example 2   Add or subtract the complex numbers.

Ⓐ $(-7 + 2i) + (5 - 11i)$

     Group like terms. $(-7 + 2i) + (5 - 11i) = (-7 + 5) + (2i + (-11i))$

     Combine like terms. $= -2 + (-9i)$

     Write addition as subtraction. $= -2 - 9i$

Ⓑ $(18 + 27i) - (2 + 3i)$

     Group like terms. $(18 + 27i) - (2 + 3i) = \left(18 - \boxed{2}\right) + \left(\boxed{27i} - 3i\right)$

     Combine like terms. $= \boxed{16} + \boxed{24}\,i$

Reflect

6. Is the sum $(a + bi) + (a - bi)$ where a and b are real numbers, a real number or an imaginary number? Explain.

Your Turn

Add or subtract the complex numbers.

7. $(17 - 16i) - (9 + 10i)$

8. $(16 + 17i) + (-8 - 12i)$

🎯 Explain 3   Multiplying Complex Numbers

To multiply two complex numbers, use the distributive property to multiply each part of one number with each part of the other. Use the fact that $i^2 = -1$ to simplify the result.

Example 3   Multiply the complex numbers.

Ⓐ $(4 + 9i)(6 - 2i)$

     Use the distributive property. $(4 + 9i)(6 - 2i) = 24 - 8i + 54i - 18i^2$

     Substitute -1 for i^2. $= 24 - 8i + 54i - 18(-1)$

     Combine like terms. $= 42 + 46i$

Ⓑ $(-3 + 12i)(7 + 4i)$

Use the distributive property. $(-3 + 12i)(7 + 4i) = \boxed{-21} - 12i + \boxed{84i} + 48i^2$

Substitute -1 for i^2. $= \boxed{-21} - 12i + \boxed{84i} + 48(-1)$

Combine like terms. $= \boxed{-69} + \boxed{72}\ i$

Reflect

9. Is the product of $(a + bi)(a - bi)$, where a and b are real numbers, a real number or an imaginary number? Explain.

Your Turn

Multiply the complex numbers.

10. $(6 - 5i)(3 - 10i)$

11. $(8 + 15i)(11 + i)$

🔧 Explain 4 Solving a Real-World Problem Using Complex Numbers

Electrical engineers use complex numbers when analyzing electric circuits. An electric circuit can contain three types of components: resistors, inductors, and capacitors. As shown in the table, each type of component has a different symbol in a circuit diagram, and each is represented by a different type of complex number based on the phase angle of the current passing through it.

Circuit Component	Symbol in Circuit Diagram	Phase Angle	Representation as a Complex Number
Resistor	⏦ (resistor symbol)	0°	A real number a
Inductor	⏦ (inductor symbol)	90°	An imaginary number bi where $b > 0$
Capacitor	⏦ (capacitor symbol)	−90°	An imaginary number bi where $b < 0$

A diagram of an alternating current (AC) electric circuit is shown along with the *impedance* (measured in ohms, Ω) of each component in the circuit. An AC power source, which is shown on the left in the diagram and labeled 120 V (for volts), causes electrons to flow through the circuit. Impedance is a measure of each component's opposition to the electron flow.

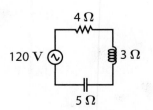

© Houghton Mifflin Harcourt Publishing Company

Example 4   Use the diagram of the electric circuit to answer the following questions.

(A) The total impedance in the circuit is the sum of the impedances for the individual components. What is the total impedance for the given circuit?

Write the impedance for each component as a complex number.

- Impedance for the resistor: 4
- Impedance for the inductor: $3i$
- Impedance for the capacitor: $-5i$

Then find the sum of the impedances.

Total impedance $= 4 + 3i + (-5i) = 4 - 2i$

(B) Ohm's law for AC electric circuits says that the voltage V (measured in volts) is the product of the current I (measured in amps) and the impedance Z (measured in ohms): $V = I \cdot Z$. For the given circuit, the current I is $24 + 12i$ amps. What is the voltage V for each component in the circuit?

Use Ohm's law, $V = I \cdot Z$, to find the voltage for each component. Remember that Z is the impedance from Part A.

Voltage for the resistor $= I \cdot Z = (24 + 12i)\left(\boxed{4} \right) = 96 + \boxed{48}\, i$

Voltage for the inductor $= I \cdot Z = (24 + 12i)\left(\boxed{3i} \right) = -36 + \boxed{72}\, i$

Voltage for the capacitor $= I \cdot Z = (24 + 12i)\left(\boxed{-5i} \right) = \boxed{60} - 120i$

Reflect

12. Find the sum of the voltages for the three components in Part B. What do you notice?

Your Turn

13. Suppose the circuit analyzed in Example 4 has a second resistor with an impedance of $2\,\Omega$ added to it. Find the total impedance. Given that the circuit now has a current of $18 + 6i$ amps, also find the voltage for each component in the circuit.

💬 Elaborate

14. What kind of number is the sum, difference, or product of two complex numbers?

15. When is the sum of two complex numbers a real number? When is the sum of two complex numbers an imaginary number?

16. Discussion What are the similarities and differences between multiplying two complex numbers and multiplying two binomial linear expressions in the same variable?

17. Essential Question Check-In How do you add and subtract complex numbers?

• Online Homework
• Hints and Help
• Extra Practice

1. Find the sum of the binomials $3 + 2x$ and $4 - 5x$. Explain how you can use the result to find the sum of the complex numbers $3 + 2i$ and $4 - 5i$.

2. Find the product of the binomials $1 - 3x$ and $2 + x$. Explain how you can use the result to find the product of the complex numbers $1 - 3i$ and $2 + i$.

Identify the real and imaginary parts of the given number. Then tell whether the number belongs to each of the following sets: real numbers, imaginary numbers, and complex numbers.

3. $5 + i$

4. $7 - 6i$

5. 25

6. $i\sqrt{21}$

Add.

7. $(3 + 4i) + (7 + 11i)$

8. $(2 + 3i) + (6 - 5i)$

9. $(-1 - i) + (-10 + 3i)$

10. $(-9 - 7i) + (6 + 5i)$

Subtract.

11. $(2 + 3i) - (7 + 6i)$

12. $(4 + 5i) - (14 - i)$

13. $(-8 - 3i) - (-9 - 5i)$

14. $(5 + 2i) - (5 - 2i)$

Multiply.

15. $(2 + 3i)(3 + 5i)$

16. $(7 + i)(6 - 9i)$

17. $(-4 + 11i)(-5 - 8i)$

18. $(4 - i)(4 + i)$

Use the diagram of the electric circuit and the given current to find the total impedance for the circuit and the voltage for each component.

19.

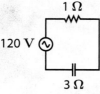

The circuit has a current of $12 + 36i$ amps.

20.

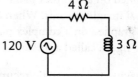

The circuit has a current of $19.2 - 14.4i$.

21.

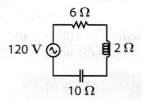

The circuit has a current of $7.2 + 9.6i$ amps.

22.

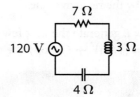

The circuit has a current of $16.8 + 2.4i$ amps.

23. Match each product on the right with the corresponding expression on the left.

A. $(3 - 5i)(3 + 5i)$ a. $-16 + 30i$

B. $(3 + 5i)(3 + 5i)$ b. -34

C. $(-3 - 5i)(3 + 5i)$ c. 34

D. $(3 - 5i)(-3 - 5i)$ d. $16 - 30i$

H.O.T.   **Focus on Higher Order Thinking**

24. Explain the Error While attempting to multiply the expression $(2 - 3i)(3 + 2i)$ a student made a mistake. Explain and correct the error.

$$(2 - 3i)(3 + 2i) = 6 - 9i + 4i - 6i^2$$

$$= 6 - 9(-1) + 4(-1) - 6(1)$$

$$= 6 + 9 - 4 - 6$$

$$= 5$$

25. Critical Thinking Show that $\sqrt{3} + i\sqrt{3}$ and $-\sqrt{3} - i\sqrt{3}$ are the square roots of $6i$.

26. Justify Reasoning What type of number is the product of two complex numbers that differ only in the sign of their imaginary parts? Prove your conjecture.

Lesson Performance Task

Just as real numbers can be graphed on a real number line, complex numbers can be graphed on a complex *plane*, which has a horizontal real axis and a vertical imaginary axis. When a Julia set that involves complex numbers is graphed on a complex plane, the result can be an elaborate self-similar figure called a *fractal*.

Consider Julia sets having the quadratic recursive rule $f(n + 1) = \left(f(n)\right)^2 + c$ for some complex number $f(0)$ and some complex constant c. For a given value of c, a complex number $f(0)$ either belongs or doesn't belong to the "'filled-in" Julia set corresponding to c depending on what happens with the sequence of numbers generated by the recursive rule.

a. Letting $c = i$, generate the first few numbers in the sequence defined by $f(0) = 1$ and $f(n + 1) = \left(f(n)\right)^2 + i$. Copy the table below. Record your results in the table.

n	$f(n)$	$f(n + 1) = \left(f(n)\right)^2 + i$
0	$f(0) = 1$	$f(1) = \left(f(0)\right)^2 + i = (1)^2 + i = 1 + i$
1	$f(1) = 1 + i$	$f(2) = \left(f(1)\right)^2 + i = (1 + i)^2 + i = $ ▮
2	$f(2) = $ ▮	$f(3) = \left(f(2)\right)^2 + i = \left(\text{▮}\right)^2 + i = $ ▮
3	$f(3) = $ ▮	$f(4) = \left(f(3)\right)^2 + i = \left(\text{▮}\right)^2 + i = $ ▮

b. The *magnitude* of a complex number $a + bi$ is the real number $\sqrt{a^2 + b^2}$. In the complex plane, the magnitude of a complex number is the number's distance from the origin. If the magnitudes of the numbers in the sequence generated by a Julia set's recursive rule where $f(0)$ is the starting value remain bounded, then $f(0)$ belongs to the "filled-in" Julia set. If the magnitudes increase without bound, then $f(0)$ doesn't belong to the "filled-in" Julia set. Based on your completed table for $f(0) = 1$, would you say that the number belongs to the "filled-in" Julia set corresponding to $c = i$? Explain.

c. Would you say that $f(0) = i$ belongs to the "filled-in" Julia set corresponding to $c = i$? Explain.

4.3 Finding Complex Solutions of Quadratic Equations

Resource Locker

Essential Question: How can you find the complex solutions of any quadratic equation?

 TEKS **A2.4.F:** Solve quadratic … equations.

⊘ Explore   Investigating Real Solutions of Quadratic Equations

Ⓐ Copy and complete the table.

$ax^2 + bx + c = 0$	$ax^2 + bx = -c$	$f(x) = ax^2 + bx$	$g(x) = -c$
$2x^2 + 4x + 1 = 0$			
$2x^2 + 4x + 2 = 0$			
$2x^2 + 4x + 3 = 0$			

Ⓑ Copy the graph of $f(x) = 2x^2 + 4x$, shown below. Graph each $g(x)$ on your graph. Copy and complete the table.

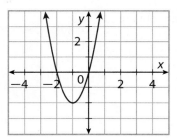

Equation	Number of Real Solutions
$2x^2 + 4x + 1 = 0$	
$2x^2 + 4x + 2 = 0$	
$2x^2 + 4x + 3 = 0$	

Ⓒ Repeat Steps A and B when $f(x) = -2x^2 + 4x$.

$ax^2 + bx + c = 0$	$ax^2 + bx = -c$	$f(x) = ax^2 + bx$	$g(x) = -c$
$-2x^2 + 4x - 1 = 0$			
$-2x^2 + 4x - 2 = 0$			
$-2x^2 + 4x - 3 = 0$			

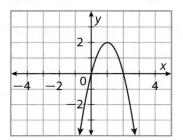

Equation	Number of Real Solutions
$-2x^2 + 4x - 1 = 0$	
$-2x^2 + 4x - 2 = 0$	
$-2x^2 + 4x - 3 = 0$	

1. Look back at Steps A and B. Notice that the minimum value of $f(x)$ in Steps A and B is -2. Identify the number of real solutions the equation $f(x) = g(x)$ has for the given values of $g(x)$. Then copy and complete the table.

Value of g(x)	Number of Real Solutions of f(x) = g(x)
$g(x) = -2$	
$g(x) > -2$	
$g(x) < -2$	

2. Look back at Step C. Notice that the maximum value of $f(x)$ in Step C is 2. Identify the number of real solutions the equation $f(x) = g(x)$ has for the given values of $g(x)$. Then copy and complete the table.

Value of g(x)	Number of Real Solutions of f(x) = g(x)
$g(x) = 2$	
$g(x) > 2$	
$g(x) < 2$	

3. You can generalize Reflect 1: For $f(x) = ax^2 + bx$ where $a > 0$, $f(x) = g(x)$ where $g(x) = -c$ has real solutions when $g(x)$ is greater than or equal to the minimum value of $f(x)$. The minimum value of $f(x)$ is

$$f\left(-\frac{b}{2a}\right) = a\left(-\frac{b}{2a}\right)^2 + b\left(-\frac{b}{2a}\right) = a\left(\frac{b^2}{4a^2}\right) - \frac{b^2}{2a} = \frac{b^2}{4a} - \frac{b^2}{2a} = \frac{b^2}{4a} - \frac{2b^2}{4a} = -\frac{b^2}{4a}.$$

So, $f(x) = g(x)$ has real solutions when $g(x) \geq -\frac{b^2}{4a}$. Since $g(x) = -c$, you obtain:

Write the inequality. $\qquad\qquad\qquad g(x) \geq -\dfrac{b^2}{4a}$

Substitute $-c$ for $g(x)$. $\qquad\qquad -c \geq -\dfrac{b^2}{4a}$

Add $\frac{b^2}{4a}$ to both sides. $\qquad\qquad \dfrac{b^2}{4a} - c \geq 0$

Multiply both sides by $4a$, which is positive. $\qquad b^2 - 4ac \geq 0$

In other words, the equation $ax^2 + bx + c = 0$ where $a > 0$ has real solutions when $b^2 - 4ac \geq 0$.

Generalize the results of Reflect 2 in a similar way. What do you notice?

⊘ Explain 1 Finding Complex Solutions by Completing the Square

Recall that completing the square for the expression $x^2 + bx$ requires adding $\left(\frac{b}{2}\right)^2$ to it, resulting in the perfect square trinomial $x^2 + bx + \left(\frac{b}{2}\right)^2$, which you can factor as $\left(x + \frac{b}{2}\right)^2$. Don't forget that when $x^2 + bx$ appears on one side of an equation, adding $\left(\frac{b}{2}\right)^2$ to it requires adding $\left(\frac{b}{2}\right)^2$ to the other side as well.

Example 1 Solve the equation by completing the square. State whether the solutions are real or non-real.

(A) $3x^2 + 9x - 6 = 0$

1. Write the equation in the form $x^2 + bx = c$.

$$3x^2 + 9x - 6 = 0$$

$$3x^2 + 9x = 6$$

$$x^2 + 3x = 2$$

2. Identify b and $\left(\frac{b}{2}\right)^2$.

$$b = 3$$

$$\left(\frac{b}{2}\right)^2 = \left(\frac{3}{2}\right)^2 = \frac{9}{4}$$

3. Add $\left(\frac{b}{2}\right)^2$ to both sides of the equation.

$$x^2 + 3x + \frac{9}{4} = 2 + \frac{9}{4}$$

4. Solve for x.

$$\left(x + \frac{3}{2}\right)^2 = 2 + \frac{9}{4}$$

$$\left(x + \frac{3}{2}\right)^2 = \frac{17}{4}$$

$$x + \frac{3}{2} = \pm\sqrt{\frac{17}{4}}$$

$$x + \frac{3}{2} = \pm\frac{\sqrt{17}}{2}$$

$$x = -\frac{3}{2} \pm \frac{\sqrt{17}}{2}$$

$$x = \frac{-3 \pm \sqrt{17}}{2}$$

There are two real solutions: $\frac{-3 + \sqrt{17}}{2}$
and $\frac{-3 - \sqrt{17}}{2}$.

(B) $x^2 - 2x + 7 = 0$

1. Write the equation in the form $x^2 + bx = c$.

$$x^2 - 2x = -7$$

2. Identify b and $\left(\frac{b}{2}\right)^2$.

$$b = \boxed{-2}$$

$$\left(\frac{b}{2}\right)^2 = \left(\frac{\boxed{-2}}{2}\right)^2 = \boxed{1}$$

3. Add $\left(\frac{b}{2}\right)^2$ to both sides.

$$x^2 - 2x + \boxed{1} = -7 + \boxed{1}$$

4. Solve for x.

$$x^2 + 2x \; \boxed{1} = -7 + \boxed{1}$$

$$\left(x - \boxed{1}\right)^2 = \boxed{-6}$$

$$x - \boxed{1} = \pm\sqrt{\boxed{-6}}$$

$$x = 1 \pm \sqrt{\boxed{-6}}$$

There are two non-real solutions:
$\boxed{1 + i\sqrt{6}}$ and $\boxed{1 - i\sqrt{6}}$.

Reflect

4. How many complex solutions do the equations in Parts A and B have? Explain.

Your Turn

Solve the equation by completing the square. State whether the solutions are real or non-real.

5. $x^2 + 8x + 17 = 0$

6. $x^2 + 10x - 7 = 0$

⚙ Explain 2 Identifying Whether Solutions Are Real or Non-real

By completing the square for the general quadratic equation $ax^2 + bx + c = 0$, you can obtain the *quadratic formula*, $x = \frac{-b \pm \sqrt{b^2 - 4ac}}{2a}$, which gives the solutions of the general quadratic equation. In the quadratic formula, the expression under the radical sign, $b^2 - 4ac$, is called the *discriminant*, and its value determines whether the solutions of the quadratic equation are real or non-real.

Value of Discriminant	Number and Type of Solutions
$b^2 - 4ac > 0$	Two real solutions
$b^2 - 4ac = 0$	One real solution
$b^2 - 4ac < 0$	Two non-real solutions

Example 2   Answer the question by writing an equation and determining whether the solutions of the equation are real or non-real.

Ⓐ A ball is thrown in the air with an initial vertical velocity of 14 m/s from an initial height of 2 m. The ball's height h (in meters) at time t (in seconds) can be modeled by the quadratic function $h(t) = -4.9t^2 + 14t + 2$. Does the ball reach a height of 12 m?

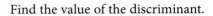

Set $h(t)$ equal to 12. $-4.9t^2 + 14t + 2 = 12$

Subtract 12 from both sides. $-4.9t^2 + 14t + 10 = 0$

Find the value of the discriminant.

$14^2 - 4(-4.9)(-10) = 196 - 196 = 0$

Because the discriminant is zero, the equation as one real solution, so the ball does reach a height of 12 m.

Ⓑ A person wants to create a vegetable garden and keep the rabbits out by enclosing it with 100 feet of fencing. The area of the garden is given by the function $A(w) = w(50 - w)$ where w is the width (in feet) of the garden. Can the garden have an area of 700 ft²?

Set $A(w)$ equal to 700. $w(50 - w) = \boxed{700}$

Multiply on the left side. $50w - w^2 = \boxed{700}$

Subtract 700 from both sides. $-w^2 + 50w - \boxed{700} = 0$

Find the value of the discriminant. $50^2 - 4(-1)(-700) = 2500 - 2800 = -300$

Because the discriminant is negative, the equation has two non-real solutions, so the garden cannot have an area of 700 ft².

Answer the question by writing an equation and determining if the solutions are real or non-real.

7. A hobbyist is making a toy sailboat. For the triangular sail, she wants the height h (in inches) to be twice the length of the base b (in inches). Can the area of the sail be 10 in²?

🔑 Explain 3   Finding Complex Solutions Using the Quadratic Formula

When using the quadratic formula to solve a quadratic equation, be sure the equation is in the form $ax^2 + bx + c = 0$.

Example 3   Solve the equation using the quadratic formula. Check a solution by substitution.

Ⓐ $-5x^2 - 2x - 8 = 0$

Write the quadratic formula. $x = \dfrac{-b \pm \sqrt{b^2 - 4ac}}{2a}$

Substitute values. $= \dfrac{-(-2) \pm \sqrt{-2^2 - 4(-5)(-8)}}{2(-5)}$

Simplify. $= \dfrac{2 \pm \sqrt{-156}}{-10} = \dfrac{1 \pm i\sqrt{39}}{-5}$

So, the two solutions are $-\dfrac{1}{5} - \dfrac{i\sqrt{39}}{5}$ and $-\dfrac{1}{5} + \dfrac{i\sqrt{39}}{5}$.

Check by substituting one of the values.

Substitute. $-5\left(-\dfrac{1}{5} - \dfrac{i\sqrt{39}}{5}\right)^2 - 2\left(-\dfrac{1}{5} - \dfrac{i\sqrt{39}}{5}\right) - 8 \overset{?}{=} 0$

Square. $-5\left(\dfrac{1}{25} + \dfrac{2i\sqrt{39}}{25} - \dfrac{39}{25}\right) - 2\left(-\dfrac{1}{5} - \dfrac{i\sqrt{39}}{5}\right) - 8 \overset{?}{=} 0$

Distribute. $-\dfrac{1}{5} - \dfrac{2i\sqrt{39}}{5} + \dfrac{39}{5} + \dfrac{2}{5} + \dfrac{2i\sqrt{39}}{5} - 8 \overset{?}{=} 0$

Simplify. $\dfrac{40}{5} - 8 \overset{?}{=} 0$

$0 = 0$

(B) $7x^2 + 2x + 3 = -1$

Write the equation with 0 on one side. $\qquad$ $7x^2 + 2x + \boxed{4} = 0$

Write the quadratic formula. $\quad x = \dfrac{-b \pm \sqrt{b^2 - 4ac}}{2a}$

Substitute values. $= \dfrac{-\boxed{2} \pm \sqrt{\left(\boxed{2}\right)^2 - 4\boxed{7}\boxed{4}}}{2\boxed{7}}$

Simplify. $= \dfrac{-\boxed{2} \pm \sqrt{-\boxed{108}}}{14}$

$= \dfrac{-\boxed{2} \pm \boxed{6}\,i\sqrt{\boxed{3}}}{14} = \dfrac{-\boxed{1} \pm \boxed{3}\,i\sqrt{\boxed{3}}}{7}$

So, the two solutions are $-\dfrac{1}{7} + \dfrac{3i\sqrt{3}}{7}$ and $-\dfrac{1}{7} - \dfrac{3i\sqrt{3}}{7}$.

Check by substituting one of the values.

Substitute. $\quad 7\left(-\dfrac{1}{7} + \dfrac{3i\sqrt{3}}{7}\right)^2 + 2\left(-\dfrac{1}{7} + \dfrac{3i\sqrt{3}}{7}\right)^2 + 4 \stackrel{?}{=} 0$

Square. $\quad 7\left(\dfrac{1}{49} - \dfrac{6i\sqrt{3}}{49} - \dfrac{27}{49}\right)^2 + 2\left(-\dfrac{1}{7} + \dfrac{3i\sqrt{3}}{7}\right)^2 + 4 \stackrel{?}{=} 0$

Distribute. $\quad \dfrac{1}{7} - \dfrac{6i\sqrt{3}}{7} - \dfrac{27}{7} - \dfrac{2}{7} + \dfrac{6i\sqrt{3}}{7} + 4 \stackrel{?}{=} 0$

Simplify. $\qquad\qquad\qquad\qquad\qquad -\dfrac{28}{7} + 4 \stackrel{?}{=} 0$

$\qquad\qquad\qquad\qquad\qquad\qquad\qquad 0 = 0$

Your Turn

Solve the equation using the quadratic formula. Check a solution by substitution.

8. $6x^2 - 5x - 4 = 0$ $\qquad\qquad\qquad$ **9.** $x^2 + 8x + 12 = 2x$

💬 Elaborate

10. Discussion Suppose that the quadratic equation $ax^2 + bx + c = 0$ has $p + qi$ where $q \neq 0$ as one of its solutions. What must the other solution be? How do you know?

11. Discussion You know that the graph of the quadratic function $f(x) = ax^2 + bx + c$ has the vertical line $x = -\dfrac{b}{2a}$ as its axis of symmetry. If the graph of $f(x)$ crosses the x-axis, where do the x-intercepts occur relative to the axis of symmetry? Explain.

12. Essential Question Check-In Why is using the quadratic formula to solve a quadratic equation easier than completing the square?

☆ Evaluate: Homework and Practice

1. The graph of $f(x) = x^2 + 6x$ is shown. Use the graph to determine how many real solutions the following equations have: $x^2 + 6x + 6 = 0$, $x^2 + 6x + 9 = 0$, and $x^2 + 6x + 12 = 0$. Explain.

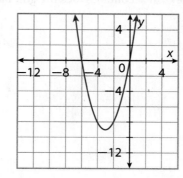

2. The graph of $f(x) = -\frac{1}{2}x^2 + 3x$ is shown. Use the graph to determine how many real solutions the following equations have: $-\frac{1}{2}x^2 + 3x - 3 = 0$, $-\frac{1}{2}x^2 + 3x - \frac{9}{2} = 0$, and $-\frac{1}{2}x^2 + 3x - 6 = 0$. Explain.

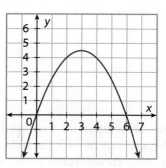

Solve the equation by completing the square. State whether the solutions are real or non-real.

3. $x^2 + 4x + 1 = 0$

4. $x^2 + 2x + 8 = 0$

5. $x^2 - 5x = -20$

6. $5x^2 - 6x = 8$

7. $7x^2 + 13x = 5$

8. $-x^2 - 6x - 11 = 0$

Without solving the equation, state the number of solutions and whether they are real or non-real.

9. $-16x^2 + 4x + 13 = 0$

10. $7x^2 - 11x + 10 = 0$

11. $-x^2 - \frac{2}{5}x = 1$

12. $4x^2 + 9 = 12x$

Answer the question by writing an equation and determining whether the solutions of the equation are real or non-real.

13. A gardener has 140 feet of fencing to put around a rectangular vegetable garden. The function $A(w) = 70w - w^2$ gives the garden's area A (in square feet) for any width w (in feet). Does the gardener have enough fencing for the area of the garden to be 1300 ft²?

14. A golf ball is hit with an initial vertical velocity of 64 ft/s. The function $h(t) = -16t^2 + 64t$ models the height h (in feet) of the golf ball at time t (in seconds). Does the golf ball reach a height of 60 ft?

15. As a decoration for a school dance, the student council creates a parabolic arch with balloons attached to it for students to walk through as they enter the dance. The arch is given by equation $y = x(5 - x)$, where x and y are measured in feet and where the origin is at one end of the arch. Can a student who is 6 feet 6 inches tall walk through the arch without ducking?

16. A small theater company currently has 200 subscribers who each pay $120 for a season ticket. The revenue from season-ticket subscriptions is $24,000. Market research indicates that for each $10 increase in the cost of a season ticket, the theater company will lose 10 subscribers. A model for the projected revenue R (in dollars) from season-ticket subscriptions is $R(p) = (120 + 10p)(200 - 10p)$, where p is the number of $10 price increases. According to this model, is it possible for the theater company to generate $25,600 in revenue by increasing the price of a season ticket?

Solve the equation using the quadratic formula. Check a solution by substitution.

17. $x^2 - 8x + 27 = 0$

18. $x^2 - 30x + 50 = 0$

19. $x + 3 = x^2$

20. $2x^2 + 7 = 4x$

© Houghton Mifflin Harcourt Publishing Company · Image Credits: ©Aflo Foto Agency/Alamy

21. Copy and complete the table. Place an X in the appropriate column to classify each equation by the number and type of its solutions.

Equation	Two Real Solutions	One Real Solution	Two Non-Real Solutions
$x^2 - 3x + 1 = 0$			
$x^2 - 2x + 1 = 0$			
$x^2 - x + 1 = 0$			
$x^2 + 1 = 0$			
$x^2 + x + 1 = 0$			
$x^2 + 2x + 1 = 0$			
$x^2 + 3x + 1 = 0$			

H.O.T. Focus on Higher Order Thinking

22. Explain the Error A student used the method of completing the square to solve the equation $-x^2 + 2x - 3 = 0$. Describe and correct the error.

$$-x^2 + 2x - 3 = 0$$
$$-x^2 + 2x = 3$$
$$-x^2 + 2x + 1 = 3 + 1$$
$$(x + 1)^2 = 4$$
$$x + 1 = \pm\sqrt{4}$$
$$x + 1 = \pm 2$$
$$x = -1 \pm 2$$

So, the two solutions are $-1 + 2 = 1$ and $-1 - 2 = -3$.

23. Make a Conjecture Describe the values of c for which the equation $x^2 + 8x + c = 0$ has two real solutions, one real solution, and two non-real solutions.

24. Analyze Relationships When you rewrite $y = ax^2 + bx + c$ in vertex form by completing the square, you obtain these coordinates for the vertex: $\left(-\frac{b}{2a}, c - \frac{b^2}{4a}\right)$. Suppose the vertex of the graph of $y = ax^2 + bx + c$ is located on the x-axis. Explain how the coordinates of the vertex and the quadratic formula are in agreement in this situation.

Lesson Performance Task

Matt and his friends are enjoying an afternoon at a baseball game. A batter hits a towering home run, and Matt shouts, "Wow, that must have been 110 feet high!" The ball was 4 feet off the ground when the batter hit it, and the ball came off the bat traveling vertically at 80 feet per second.

a. Model the ball's height h (in feet) at time t (in seconds) using the projectile motion model $h(t) = -16t^2 + v_0 t + h$ where v_0 is the projectile's initial vertical velocity (in feet per second) and h_0 is the projectile's initial height (in feet). Use the model to write an equation based on Matt's claim, and then determine whether Matt's claim is correct.

b. Did the ball reach of a height of 100 feet? Explain.

c. Let h_{max} be the ball's maximum height. By setting the projectile motion model equal to h_{max}, show how you can find h_{max} using the discriminant of the quadratic formula.

d. Find the time at which the ball reached its maximum height.

4.4 Solving Quadratic Inequalities

Essential Question: How can you find the solutions of a quadratic inequality algebraically?

 TEKS **A2.4.H** Solve quadratic inequalities.

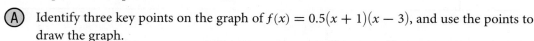 Explore Using the Graph of a Quadratic Function in Intercept Form to Solve Quadratic Inequalities

You are familiar with two forms of a quadratic function: standard form, $f(x) = ax^2 + bx + c$, and vertex form, $f(x) = a(x - h)^2 + k$. A third form of a quadratic function is *intercept form*, $f(x) = a(x - x_1)(x - x_2)$ where a, x_1, and x_2 are constants and $a \neq 0$. In this Explore, you will use the graph of a quadratic function in intercept form to solve quadratic inequalities.

(A) Identify three key points on the graph of $f(x) = 0.5(x + 1)(x - 3)$, and use the points to draw the graph.

- An x-intercept is a value of x for which $f(x) = 0$. Solving $a(x - x_1)(x - x_2) = 0$ using the zero-product property gives two x-intercepts: x_1 and x_2.

  So, what are the x-intercepts of the graph of $f(x) = 0.5(x + 1)(x - 3)$, and what are the coordinates of the corresponding points on the graph of $f(x)$?

- The symmetry of the graph of a quadratic function tells you that if two points on the graph have the same y-coordinate, then the horizontal line segment connecting the two points is bisected by the graph's vertical axis of symmetry. Since $(x_1, 0)$ and $(x_2, 0)$ are two points with the same y-coordinate on the graph of $f(x) = a(x - x_1)(x - x_2)$, the axis of symmetry passes halfway between the points, which means that the axis of symmetry is the vertical line $x = \frac{x_1 + x_2}{2}$.

  So, what is the equation of the axis of symmetry for the graph of $f(x) = 0.5(x + 1)(x - 3)$?

- The axis of symmetry for the graph of a quadratic function passes through the graph's vertex, which means that the vertex of the graph of $f(x) = a(x - x_1)(x - x_2)$ has an x-coordinate of $\frac{x_1 + x_2}{2}$.

  So, what are the coordinates of the vertex of the graph of $f(x) = 0.5(x + 1)(x - 3)$?

- Using the information you've gathered about the graph of $f(x) = 0.5(x + 1)(x - 3)$, draw the graph on a coordinate plane.

Ⓑ Use the graph of $f(x) = 0.5(x + 1)(x - 3)$ from Step A. Copy and complete the table. For each graphical interpretation, state whether the graph of $f(x)$ is above, below, on or above, or on or below the x-axis.

Inequality	Graphical Interpretation of Inequality	Solution Set of Inequality
$0.5(x + 1)(x - 3) < 0$	The inequality asks for the x-values where the graph of $f(x)$ is below the x-axis.	$\{x \mid -1 < x < 3\}$
$0.5(x + 1)(x - 3) \leq 0$	▢	▢
$0.5(x + 1)(x - 3) > 0$	▢	▢
$0.5(x + 1)(x - 3) \geq 0$	▢	▢

Ⓒ Describe how you can obtain the graph of $g(x) = -f(x)$ from the graph of $f(x)$. Then draw the graph on a coordinate plane.

Ⓓ Use the graph of $g(x) = -0.5(x + 1)(x - 3)$ from Step C. Copy and complete the table.

Inequality	Solution of Inequality
$-0.5(x + 1)(x - 3) < 0$	▢
$-0.5(x + 1)(x - 3) \leq 0$	▢
$-0.5(x + 1)(x - 3) > 0$	▢
$-0.5(x + 1)(x - 3) \geq 0$	▢

Reflect

1. In terms of the constants x_1 and x_2 where $x_1 < x_2$, what is the solution set of the inequality $a(x - x_1)(x - x_2) > 0$ where a is a positive constant? Explain.

2. In terms of the constants x_1 and x_2 where $x_1 < x_2$, what is the solution set of the inequality $a(x - x_1)(x - x_2) > 0$ where a is a negative constant? Explain.

3. In terms of the constant x_1, what is the solution set of the inequality $a(x - x_1)^2 > 0$ where a is a positive constant? Explain.

4. In terms of the constant x_1, what is the solution set of the inequality $a(x - x_1)^2 > 0$ where a is a negative constant? Explain.

⚙ Explain 1 Solving Quadratic Inequalities Algebraically

Given a quadratic inequality in a single variable x, you can solve the related quadratic equation to obtain what are called *critical values*. The solutions of the inequality are the values of x that occur either between the critical values or beyond them. The critical values themselves are also solutions of the inequality if the inequality involves $\geq$ or $\leq$.

You know several methods for solving a quadratic equation. Given an equation of the form $ax^2 + bx + c = 0$, you may find that you can factor it so that you can set each factor equal to 0 (using the zero-product property) to obtain the critical values. If factoring doesn't work, then use the quadratic formula to obtain the critical values instead.

Example 1 Solve the inequality algebraically.

Ⓐ $x^2 + 2x + 1 > 9$

Rewrite the inequality with 0 on one side.
$x^2 + 2x + 1 > 9$
$x^2 + 2x - 8 > 0$

Solve the related quadratic equation. In this case, you can factor the quadratic expression.

$x^2 + 2x - 8 = 0$ $x + 4 = 0$ or $x - 2 = 0$

$(x + 4)(x - 2) = 0$ $x = -4$ or $x = 2$

So, the critical values of the inequality are -4 and 2.

Choose an x-value between the critical values, such as 0. Check to see if 0 satisfies the original inequality.

$x^2 + 2x + 1 > 9$ $0^2 + 2(0) + 1 \overset{?}{>} 9$

$1 \not> 9$

Since an x-value that is between the critical values is not a solution of the inequality, the solutions must be beyond the critical values. Note that the critical values themselves are not solutions. So, the solution set is $\{x \mid x < -4 \text{ or } x > 2\}$.

Ⓑ $2x^2 + 1 \leq 4x$

Rewrite the inequality with 0 on one side.

$2x^2 + 1 \leq 4x$

$\boxed{2x^2 - 4x + 1} \leq 0$

Solve the related quadratic equation. In this case, the quadratic expression isn't factorable, so use the quadratic formula.

$2x^2 - 4x + 1 = 0$

$x = \dfrac{-\left(\boxed{-4}\right) \pm \sqrt{(-4)^2 - 4(2)(1)}}{2(2)}$

$= \dfrac{\boxed{4} \pm \sqrt{8}}{4}$

$= \dfrac{\boxed{4} \pm 2\sqrt{2}}{4} = \dfrac{\boxed{2} \pm \sqrt{2}}{2}$

So, the critical values of the inequality are $\boxed{\dfrac{2+\sqrt{2}}{2}} \approx 1.7$ and $\boxed{\dfrac{2-\sqrt{2}}{2}} \approx 0.3.$

Choose an x-value between the critical values, such as 1. Check to see if 1 satisfies the original inequality.

$$2x^2 + 1 \le 4x$$

$$2\left(\boxed{1}\right)^2 + 1 \overset{?}{\le} 4\left(\boxed{1}\right)$$

$$3 \boxed{\le} 4$$

Since an x-value that is between the critical values is a solution of the inequality

and the critical values themselves are also solutions, the solution set is $\left\{ x \middle| \boxed{\dfrac{2-\sqrt{2}}{2}} \le x \le \boxed{\dfrac{2+\sqrt{2}}{2}} \right\}.$

Reflect

5. **Discussion** It's possible to skip having to check an x-value if you think in terms of the graph of a quadratic function as you did in the Explore. Explain how this would work for Part A and for Part B.

Your Turn

Solve the inequality algebraically.

6. $x^2 - 6x + 10 \ge 2$

7. $3x^2 < 3x + 2$

⚙ Explain 2 Solving a Real-World Problem Using Quadratic Inequalities

In real-world situations, variables often must have nonnegative or whole-number values. You must take these constraints into account when solving a problem that leads to a quadratic inequality.

Example 2 Answer the question by writing and solving a quadratic inequality.

(A) A football thrown by a quarterback follows a path given by the equation $y = -0.01x^2 + 0.8x + 7$ where x and y are measured in feet and the origin is on the football field directly below where the quarterback releases the ball. If the ball can be caught or knocked down at any height less than 10 feet, at what distances from the quarterback can the ball be caught or knocked down?

Write the inequality.

$-0.01x^2 + 0.8x + 7 < 10$

Rewrite the inequality with 0 on one side.

$-0.01x^2 + 0.8x - 3 < 0$

Solve the related quadratic equation. $-0.01x^2 + 0.8x - 3 = 0$

© Houghton Mifflin Harcourt Publishing Company

$$x = \frac{-0.8 \pm \sqrt{(0.8)^2 - 4(-0.01)(-3)}}{2(-0.01)}$$

$$= \frac{-0.8 \pm \sqrt{0.52}}{-0.02} \approx \frac{-0.8 \pm 0.72}{-0.02}$$

$$x = 4 \text{ or } x = 76$$

Checking any x-value between 4 and 76 shows that it is not a solution of the inequality. The critical values are not solutions either. So, the approximate solution set of the inequality is $\{x \,|\, x < 4 \text{ or } x > 26\}$.

The ball's path begins at $x = 0$ feet and ends when the ball hits the ground. To find how far the ball is from the quarterback when it hits the ground, solve $-0.01x^2 + 0.8x + 7 = 0$.

$$x = \frac{-0.8 \pm \sqrt{(0.8)^2 - 4(-0.01)(7)}}{2(-0.01)}$$

$$= \frac{-0.8 \pm \sqrt{0.92}}{-0.02} \approx \frac{-0.8 \pm 0.96}{-0.02}$$

$$x = -8 \text{ or } x = 88$$

Reject the negative solution. Since the ball hits the ground about 88 feet away from the quarterback, it can be caught or knocked down between 0 feet and 4 feet from the quarterback and then again between about 76 feet and 88 feet from the quarterback.

Ⓑ A club charges $12 annual dues and has 1000 members. A survey of the members indicates that for every $1 increase in the annual dues, the club will lose 40 members. This means that the revenue R from dues, which is currently $12,000, will become

$$R(d) = (12 + d)(1000 - 40d) = -40d^2 + \boxed{520}\, d + 12,000$$ where d is a whole number of

$1 increases in dues. For what amounts can the dues be increased so that the revenue from dues will be at least $13,000?

Write the inequality. $-40d^2 + \boxed{520}\, d + 12,000 \qquad \geq 13,000$

Rewrite the inequality with 0 on one side. $-40d^2 + \boxed{520}\, d - 1000 \ \geq 0$

Solve the related quadratic equation using the quadratic formula.

To simplify the calculations, begin by dividing both sides of the equation by -40.

$$d^2 - \boxed{13}\, d + 25 = 0$$

$$d = \frac{-\left(\boxed{-13}\right) \pm \sqrt{\left(\boxed{-13}\right)^2 - 4(1)(25)}}{2(1)} = \frac{\boxed{13} \pm \sqrt{\boxed{69}}}{2}$$

$$x \approx 10.65 \text{ or } x \approx 2.35$$

Checking any d-value between 2.35 and 10.65 shows that it is a solution of the inequality, as are the approximate critical values. So, the approximate solution set of the inequality is $\{d \,|\, 2.35 \leq d \leq 10.65\}$. Since d represents a whole number of $1 increases in dues, the

dues can be increased by a minimum of $3 and a maximum of $\boxed{10}$, with the resulting revenue from dues being at least $13,000.

8. A person standing on the ground outside a building throws a set of keys directly upward to a person standing on a second-floor balcony. The person on the ground releases the keys with an initial vertical velocity of 28 ft/s from a height of 4 ft. The function $h(t) = -16t^2 + 28t + 4$ models the height (in feet) of the keys at time t (in seconds) after the keys are thrown. The person standing on the balcony can catch the keys once they reach a height of 14 ft. For what period of time are the keys high enough to be caught?

9. A farmer creates a rectangular pen by using one side of a barn as one side of the pen and using fencing for the other three sides. The farmer has 80 ft of fencing, and the side of the barn is 40 ft long. If x represents the length of the fenced side of the pen that is parallel to the barn, then the length of each of the two fenced sides of the pen that are perpendicular to the barn is $\frac{80-x}{2} = 40 - 0.5x$ ft. For what values of x is the area of the pen at least 600 ft^2?

 Elaborate

10. Describe how to solve a quadratic inequality graphically.

11. What are critical values when solving a quadratic inequality?

12. When solving a real-world problem that leads to a quadratic inequality, what must you take into consideration when identifying the solutions of the inequality?

13. **Essential Question Check-In** When solving a quadratic inequality, you solve a related quadratic equation. What are two methods for solving the equation?

⭐ Evaluate: Homework and Practice

- Online Homework
- Hints and Help
- Extra Practice

Graph the quadratic function. Then copy and complete the table.

1. $f(x) = 3(x - 2)(x - 4)$

Inequality	Solution of Inequality
$3(x - 2)(x - 4) < 0$	⬛
$3(x - 2)(x - 4) \le 0$	⬛
$3(x - 2)(x - 4) > 0$	⬛
$3(x - 2)(x - 4) \le 0$	⬛

2. $f(x) = -\frac{1}{3}(x + 4)(x - 2)$

Inequality	Solution of Inequality
$-\frac{1}{3}(x + 4)(x - 2) < 0$	⬛
$-\frac{1}{3}(x + 4)(x - 2) \le 0$	⬛
$-\frac{1}{3}(x + 4)(x - 2) > 0$	⬛
$-\frac{1}{3}(x + 4)(x - 2) \ge 0$	⬛

Solve the inequality algebraically.

3. $x^2 + x - 4 > 16$

4. $-3x^2 + 3x + 4 \leq -2$

5. $x^2 - 2x < 6$

6. $-x^2 + 4 \geq 2x$

Answer the question by writing and solving a quadratic inequality.

7. **Diving** Relative to the surface of the water, the height h (in feet) of a diver's center of mass during a dive is modeled by the function $h(t) = -16t^2 + 14t + 10$ where t is the time (in seconds) since the dive began. (A person's center of mass is located near the navel.) For what period of time during the dive is the diver's center of mass higher than the diving board, which is 6 feet above the water?

8. **Volleyball** A volleyball player serves the ball. The ball follows a path given by the equation $y = -0.01x^2 + 0.5x + 3$ where x and y are measured in feet and the origin is on the court directly below where the player hits the ball. For what distances from the player is the ball at least as high as the net, which is 8 ft high? If the player is 30 feet away from the net, is the ball likely to go over the net?

9. **Manufacturing** A machine bends a long, flat sheet of metal so that it forms a trough for channeling water. The sides of the trough are the same height and perpendicular to the bottom, and the top of the trough is open. The sheet of metal is 12 inches wide, and the bottom of the trough must have a minimum width of 4 inches. If w represents the width (in inches) of the bottom of the trough, then the height of each side of the trough is $\frac{12 - w}{2} = 6 - 0.5w$ inches. The cross-sectional area A (in square inches) of the trough is $A(w) = w(6 - 0.5w)$. Fwor what values of w is the cross-sectional area at least 15 in²?

10. **Business** A gym has 200 members who pay $30 per month for unlimited use of the gym's equipment. A survey of the members indicates that for each $5 increase in the monthly fee, the gym will lose 20 members. This means that the revenue R from fees, which is currently $6000 per month, will become $R(f) = (30 + 5f)(200 - 20f) = -100f^2 + 400f + 6000$ where f is a whole number of $5 fee increases. For what numbers of $5 fee increases will the revenue from fees actually be less than its current value?

11. Match each solution set on the right with the corresponding inequality on the left.

A. $x^2 + x > 6$

a. $\left\{ x \mid x < 2 \text{ or } x > 3 \right\}$

B. $x^2 - x < 6$

b. $\left\{ x \mid -2 < x < 3 \right\}$

C. $-x^2 + 5x > 6$

c. $\left\{ x \mid 2 < x < 3 \right\}$

D. $-x^2 + 5x < 6$

d. $\left\{ x \mid x < -3 \text{ or } x > 2 \right\}$

12. **Communicate Mathematical Ideas** Explain why solving the inequality $x^2 - 2x - 30 < 5$ is equivalent to solving the inequality $x^2 - 2x - 35 < 0$. Give both an algebraic and a graphical explanation.

13. **Construct Arguments** Given the inequality $a(x - x_1)(x - x_2) < 0$ where a is a positive constant and x_1 and x_2 are constants such that $x_1 < x_2$, give a convincing algebraic argument why the solution set is $\left\{ x | x_1 < x < x_2 \right\}$.

14. **Draw Conclusions** Suppose you use the quadratic formula when finding the critical values for a quadratic inequality you're solving, and the formula gives you values that are non-real. What conclusion can you draw? Give a specific example to support your conclusion.

Lesson Performance Task

A home gardener has 40 feet of fencing for a rectangular herb garden. The garden will be next to a shed, so the fencing will enclose only three sides of the garden. The side of the shed to which the fencing will be attached is 14 feet long.

a. Let x be the length of the two sides of the fence that are attached to the side of the shed. Write a function that gives the area A of the garden in terms of x.

b. The gardener wants the garden to have an area of at least 150 ft². For what values of x is $A(x) \geq 150$? What areas are possible for those x-values?

c. The side of the fence that is parallel to the side of the shed cannot be longer than the side of shed. What constraint does this fact place on the values of x? How does this constraint affect the possible areas of the garden?

Quadratic Equations and Inequalities

Essential Question: How can you use quadratic equations and inequalities to solve real-world problems?

Key Vocabulary
complex number
   (*número complejo*)
imaginary number
   (*número imaginario*)
imaginary unit
   (*unidad imaginaria*)
pure imaginary number
   (*número imaginario puro*)

KEY EXAMPLE   (Lessons 4.1, 4.2)

Take square roots to solve the quadratic equations.

$3x^2 - 27 = 9$		$x^2 + 20 = 0$	
$3x^2 = 36$	Add 27 to both sides.	$x^2 = -20$	Subtract 20 on both sides.
$x^2 = 12$	Divide both sides by 3.	$x = \pm\sqrt{-20}$	Square root
$x = \pm\sqrt{12}$	Square root	$x = \pm\sqrt{(-1)(5)(4)}$	Product Property
$x = \pm\sqrt{4} \cdot \sqrt{3}$	Product property	$x = \pm 2i\sqrt{5}$	Simplify.
$x = \pm 2\sqrt{3}$	Simplify.		

KEY EXAMPLE   (Lesson 4.3)

Solve $2x^2 + 4x - 8 = 0$ by completing the square.

$2x^2 + 4x = 8$	Write the equation in the form $x^2 + bx = c$.
$x^2 + 2x = 4$	
$x^2 + 2x + 1 = 4 + 1$	Add $\left(\frac{b}{2}\right)^2$ to both sides of the equation.
$x + 1^2 = 5$	Solve for x.
$x + 1 = \pm\sqrt{5}$	
$x = -1 \pm\sqrt{5}$	

KEY EXAMPLE   (Lesson 4.4)

Solve $x^2 - 4x - 5 \le 7$ by factoring.

$x^2 - 4x - 12 \le 0$	Rewrite the inequality with 0 on one side.
$x^2 - 4x - 12 = 0$	Solve the related quadratic equation.
$(x - 6)(x + 2) = 0$	
$x - 6 = 0$ or $x + 2 = 0$	
$x = 6$ or $x = -2$	
$0^2 + 3(0) - 5 \le 7$	Test a point between the x values.
$-5 \le 7$	

Since the test point is true, the solution is between the x values.

$-2 \le x \le 6$

EXERCISES

Solve using the method stated. *(Lessons 4.1, 4.3, 4.4)*

1. $x^2 - 16 = 0$ (square root)

2. $2x^2 - 10 = 0$ (square root)

3. $3x^2 - 6x - 12 = 0$ (completing the square)

4. $x^2 + 6x + 10 = 0$ (completing the square)

5. $x^2 - 4x + 4 = 0$ (factoring)

6. $x^2 - x - 30 \geq 0$ (factoring)

7. Explain if a quadratic equation can be solved using factoring. *(Lessons 4.1, 4.3, 4.4)*

8. Can completing the square solve any quadratic equation? Explain. *(Lessons 4.1, 4.3, 4.4)*

MODULE PERFORMANCE TASK

Can You Stop in Time?

A driver sees a tree fall across the road 125 feet in front of the car. The driver is barely able to stop the car before hitting the tree. What was the maximum speed in miles per hour that the car could have been traveling when the driver saw the tree fall?

The equation for braking distance is d is $\dfrac{s^2}{2\mu g}$, where d is braking distance, s is speed of the car, μ is the coefficient of friction between the tires and the road, and g is the acceleration due to gravity, 32.2 ft/s^2.

Start by listing on your own paper the information you will need and the steps you will take to solve the problem. Then complete the task, using numbers, words, or algebra to explain how you reached your conclusion.

(Ready) to Go On?

4.1–4.4 Quadratic Equations and Inequalities

- Online Homework
- Hints and Help
- Extra Practice

Solve the equations or inequalities by taking square roots, completing the square, factoring, or the quadratic formula. *(Lessons 4.1, 4.2, 4.3, 4.4)*

1. $2x^2 - 16 = 0$

2. $2x^2 - 6x - 20 = 0$

3. $2x^2 + 2x - 2 = 0$

4. $x^2 + x = 30$

5. $x^2 - 5x = 24$

6. $-4x^2 + 8 = 24$

7. $x^2 + 30 > 24$

8. $x^2 + 4x + 3 \leq 0$

ESSENTIAL QUESTION

9. Write a real world situation that could be modeled by the equation $7m \cdot 5m = 875$. *(Lesson 4.1)*

Assessment Readiness

1. Which of the following equations, when graphed, has two x-intercepts?
   - **A.** $x^2 + 16 = 0$
   - **B.** $2x^2 - 20 = 10$
   - **C.** $-3x^2 - 6 = 0$
   - **D.** $-0.5x^2 = 13$

2. What are the solutions of $-4x^2 + bx - 16 = 0$?
   - **A.** $x = \pm 4$
   - **B.** $x = \dfrac{1 \pm i\sqrt{15}}{2}$
   - **C.** $x = \pm 4i$
   - **D.** $x = \dfrac{1 \pm \sqrt{15}}{2}$

3. What is the inverse of $f(x) = x^2 + 25$?
   - **A.** $f'(x) = x - 25$
   - **B.** $f'(x) = \pm\sqrt{x - 25}$
   - **C.** $f'(x) = \pm\sqrt{x + 25}$
   - **D.** $f'(x) = \dfrac{x - 25}{2}$

4. Consider the inequality $ax^2 + bx \leq 25$. For what values of a and b would you solve this inequality by taking a square root? For what values of a would the square root result in an imaginary number? Explain your answers.

Quadratic Relations and Systems of Equations and Inequalities

TEKS

Essential Question: How can you use systems of equations and inequalities to solve real-world problems?

REAL WORLD VIDEO
Video game designers need a solid understanding of algebra, including systems of quadratic equations, in order to program realistic interactions within the game environment.

© Houghton Mifflin Harcourt Publishing Company · Image Credits: ©ZUMA Press, Inc./Alamy

MODULE PERFORMANCE TASK PREVIEW

How Can You Hit a Moving Target with a Laser Beam?

Video games can be a lot of fun. They can also help players to develop and hone skills such as following instructions, using logic in problem solving, hand-eye coordination, and fine motor and spatial abilities. Video game designers often use mathematics to program realistic interactions in the video world. How can math be used to aim a particle beam to hit a virtual clay disk flying through the air? Set your sights on the target and let's get started!

Complete these exercises to review skills you will need for this chapter.

Graphing Linear Nonproportional Relationships

- Online Homework
- Hints and Help
- Extra Practice

Example 1

Graph $y = -2x - 3$.

x	0	−2	−3
y	−3	1	3

Make a table of values. Plot the points and draw a line through them.

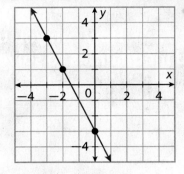

Graph each equation.

1. $y = -x + 5$

2. $y = 3x - 2$

Multi-Step Equations

Example 2

Solve $4(x - 2) = 12$ for x.

$4x - 8 = 12$ Distribute.

$4x = 20$ *Add 8 to both sides.*

$x = 5$ Divide by 4.

Solve each equation.

3. $5 - 3x = 7(x - 1)$

4. $3x + 2(x - 1) = 28$

5. $2(6 - 5x) = 5x + 9$

Solving Systems of Two Linear Equations

Example 3

Solve the system $\begin{cases} y = 2x + 8 \\ 3x + 2y = 2 \end{cases}$.

$3x + 2(2x + 8) = 2$ Substitute.

$x = -2$ *Solve for x.*

$y = 2(-2) + 8 = 4$ Solve for y.

The solution is $(-2, 4)$.

Solve each system.

6. $\begin{cases} y = 10 - 3x \\ 5x - y = 6 \end{cases}$

7. $\begin{cases} 2x - 3y = 4 \\ -x + 2y = 3 \end{cases}$

8. $\begin{cases} 5x - 2y = 4 \\ 3x + 2y = -12 \end{cases}$

5.1 Parabolas

Essential Question: How is the distance formula connected with deriving equations for both vertical and horizontal parabolas?

TEKS A2.4.B Write the equation of a parabola using given attributes, including ... focus, directrix ...

Resource Locker

 Explore   **Deriving the Standard-Form Equation of a Parabola**

A **parabola** is defined as a set of points equidistant from a line (called the **directrix**) and a point (called the **focus**). The focus will always lie on the axis of symmetry, and the directrix will always be perpendicular to the axis of symmetry. This definition can be used to derive the equation for a horizontal parabola opening to the right with its vertex at the origin using the distance formula. (The derivations of parabolas opening in other directions will be covered later.)

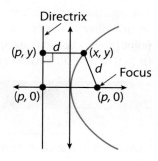

Directrix

(p, y) d (x, y)

d Focus

$(p, 0)$ $(p, 0)$

(A) The coordinates for the focus are given by ▮.

(B) Write down the expression for the distance from a point (x, y) to the coordinates of the focus:

$$d = \sqrt{\left(\boxed{} - \boxed{}\right)^2 + \left(\boxed{} - \boxed{}\right)^2}$$

(C) The distance from a point to a line is measured by drawing a perpendicular line segment from the point to the line. Find the point where a horizontal line from (x, y) intersects the directrix (defined by the line $x = -p$ for a parabola with its vertex on the origin).

▮

(D) Write down the expression for the distance from a point, (x, y) to the point from Step C:

$$d = \sqrt{\left(\boxed{} - \boxed{}\right)^2 + \left(\boxed{} - \boxed{}\right)^2}$$

(E) Setting the two distances the same and simplifying gives.

$$\sqrt{(x - p)^2 + y^2} = \sqrt{(x + p)^2}$$

To continue solving the problem, square both sides of the equation and evaluate the squared binomials.

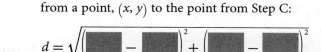

$$\boxed{}\, x^2 + \boxed{}\, xp + \boxed{}\, p^2 + y^2 = \boxed{}\, x^2 + \boxed{}\, xp + \boxed{}\, p^2$$

(F) Collect terms.

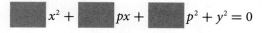

$$\boxed{}\, x^2 + \boxed{}\, px + \boxed{}\, p^2 + y^2 = 0$$

(G) Finally, simplify and arrange the equation into the **standard form for a horizontal parabola** (with vertex at $(0, 0)$):

$$y^2 = \boxed{}$$

1. Why was the directrix placed on the line $x = -p$?

2. **Discussion** How can the result be generalized to arrive at the standard form for a horizontal parabola with a vertex at (h, k): $(y - k)^2 = 4p(x - h)$?

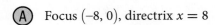 **Explain 1** **Writing the Equation of a Parabola with Vertex at $(0, 0)$**

The equation for a horizontal parabola with vertex at $(0, 0)$ is written in the standard form as $y^2 = 4px$. It has a vertical directrix along the line $x = -p$, a horizontal axis of symmetry along the line $y = 0$, and a focus at the point $(p, 0)$. The parabola opens toward the focus, whether it is on the right or left of the origin $(p > 0$ or $p < 0)$. Vertical parabolas are similar, but with horizontal directrices and vertical axes of symmetry:

Parabolas with Vertices at the Origin		
	Vertical	**Horizontal**
Equation in standard form	$x^2 = 4py$	$y^2 = 4px$
$p > 0$	Opens upward	Opens rightward
$p < 0$	Opens downward	Opens leftward
Focus	$(0, p)$	$(p, 0)$
Directrix	$y = -p$	$x = -p$
Axis of Symmetry	$x = 0$	$y = 0$

Example 1 Find the equation of the parabola from the description of the focus and directrix. Then make a sketch showing the parabola, the focus, and the directrix.

(A) Focus $(-8, 0)$, directrix $x = 8$

A vertical directrix means a horizontal parabola.

Confirm that the vertex is at $(0, 0)$:

   a. The y-coordinate of the vertex is the same as the focus: 0.

   b. The x-coordinate is halfway between the focus (-8) and the directrix $(+8)$: 0.

   c. The vertex is at $(0, 0)$.

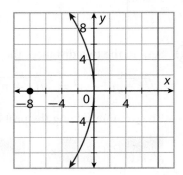

Use the expression for a horizontal parabola, $y^2 = 4px$, and replace p with the x coordinate of the focus: $y^2 = 4(-8)x$

Simplify: $y^2 = -32x$

Plot the focus and directrix and sketch the parabola.

Ⓑ Focus $(0, -2)$, directrix $y = 2$

A horizontal directrix means a vertical parabola.

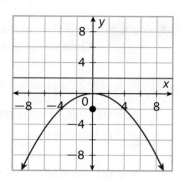

Confirm that the vertex is at $(0, 0)$:

a. The x-coordinate of the vertex is the same as the focus: 0.

b. The y-coordinate is halfway between the focus, $\boxed{-2}$ and the directrix, $\boxed{2}$: 0

c. The vertex is at $(0, 0)$.

Use the expression for a vertical parabola, $\boxed{x^2 = 4py}$, and replace p with the x coordinate of the focus: $x^2 = 4 \cdot \boxed{-2} \cdot y$

Simplify: $x^2 = \boxed{-8y}$

Plot the focus, the directrix, and the parabola.

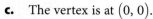

Find the equation of the parabola from the description of the focus and directrix. Then make a sketch showing the parabola, the focus, and the directrix.

3. Focus $(2, 0)$, directrix $x = -2$

4. Focus $\left(0, -\frac{1}{2}\right)$, directrix $y = \frac{1}{2}$

🔧 Explain 2 Writing the Equation of a Parabola with Vertex at (h, k)

The standard equation for a parabola with a vertex (h, k) can be found by translating from $(0, 0)$ to (h, k): substitute $(x - h)$ for x and $(y - k)$ for y. This also translates the focus and directrix each by the same amount.

Parabolas with Vertex (h, k)		
	Vertical	**Horizontal**
Equation in standard form	$(x - h)^2 = 4p(y - k)$	$(y - k)^2 = 4p(x - h)$
$p > 0$	Opens upward	Opens rightward
$p < 0$	Opens downward	Opens leftward
Focus	$(h, k + p)$	$(h + p, k)$
Directrix	$y = k - p$	$x = h - p$
Axis of Symmetry	$x = h$	$y = k$

p is found halfway from the directrix to the focus:

- For vertical parabolas: $p = \dfrac{(y \text{ value of focus}) - (y \text{ value of directrix})}{2}$

- For horizontal parabolas: $p = \dfrac{(x \text{ value of focus}) - (x \text{ value of directrix})}{2}$

The vertex can be found from the focus by relating the coordinates of the focus to h, k, and p.

Example 2 Find the equation of the parabola from the description of the focus and directrix. Then make a sketch showing the parabola, the focus, and the directrix.

(A) Focus $(3, 2)$, directrix $y = 0$

A horizontal directrix means a vertical parabola.

$$p = \frac{(y \text{ value of focus}) - (y \text{ value of directrix})}{2} = \frac{2 - 0}{2} = 1$$

$h =$ the x-coordinate of the focus $= 3$

Solve for k: The y-value of the focus is $k + p$, so $k + p = 2$

$k + 1 = 2$

$k = 1$

Write the equation: $(x - 3)^2 = 4(y - 1)$

Plot the focus, the directrix, and the parabola.

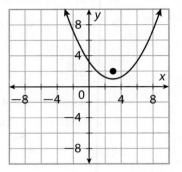

(B) Focus $(-1, -1)$, directrix $x = 5$

A vertical directrix means a horizontal parabola.

$$p = \frac{(x \text{ value of focus}) - (x \text{ value of directrix})}{2} = \frac{\boxed{-1} - \boxed{5}}{2} = \boxed{-3}$$

$k =$ the y-coordinate of the focus $= \boxed{-1}$

Solve for h: The x-value of the focus is $h + p$, so

$h + p = \boxed{-1}$

$h + (-3) = \boxed{-1}$

$h = \boxed{2}$

Write the equation: $(y + 1)^2 = \boxed{-12}\left(x - \boxed{2}\right)$

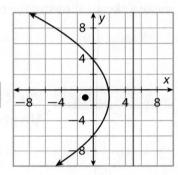

Your Turn

Find the equation of the parabola from the description of the focus and directrix. Then make a sketch showing the parabola, the focus, and the directrix.

5. Focus $(5, -1)$, directrix $x = -3$

6. Focus $(-2, 0)$, directrix $y = 4$

Explain 3 **Rewriting the Equation of a Parabola to Graph the Parabola**

A **second-degree equation in two variables** is an equation constructed by adding terms in two variables with powers no higher than 2. The general form looks like this:

$ax^2 + by^2 + cx + dy + e = 0$

Expanding the standard form of a parabola and grouping like terms results in a second-degree equation with either $a = 0$ or $b = 0$, depending on whether the parabola is vertical or horizontal. To graph an equation in this form requires the opposite conversion, accomplished by completing the square of the squared variable.

Example 3 Convert the equation to the standard form of a parabola and graph the parabola, the focus, and the directrix.

Ⓐ $x^2 - 4x - 4y + 12 = 0$

Isolate the x terms and complete the square on x.

Isolate the x terms. $\qquad\qquad\qquad\qquad x^2 - 4x = 4y - 12$

Add $\left(\dfrac{-4}{2}\right)^2$ to both sides. $\qquad\qquad\quad x^2 - 4x + 4 = 4y - 8$

Factor the perfect square trinomial on the left side. $\qquad (x - 2)^2 = 4y - 8$

Factor out 4 from the right side. $\qquad\qquad\qquad (x - 2)^2 = 4(y - 2)$

This is the standard form for a vertical parabola. Now find p, h, and k from the standard form in order to graph the parabola, focus, and directrix.

$4p = 4$ $\qquad\qquad$ Vertex $= (2, 2)$

$p = 1$ $\qquad\qquad\;\;$ Focus $= (2, k + p) = (2, 3)$

$h = 2$ $\qquad\qquad\;\;$ Directrix:

$k = 2$ $\qquad\qquad\qquad\;\; y = k - p$

$\qquad\qquad\qquad\qquad\quad\;\; y = 1$

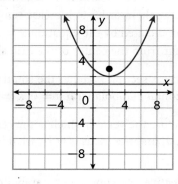

Ⓑ $y^2 + 2x + 8y + 18 = 0$

Isolate the $\boxed{y}$ terms. $\qquad\qquad\qquad y^2 + 8y = -2x - 18$

Add $\left(\dfrac{\boxed{8}}{2}\right)^2$ to both sides. $\qquad\quad y^2 + 8y + \boxed{16} = -2x - \boxed{2}$

Factor the perfect square trinomial. $\qquad \left(y + \boxed{4}\right)^2 = -2x - \boxed{2}$

Factor out $\boxed{-2}$ on the right. $\qquad\quad \left(y + \boxed{4}\right)^2 = \boxed{-2}\left(x + \boxed{1}\right)$

Identify features to graph:

$p = \boxed{-\dfrac{1}{2}}$, $h = \boxed{-1}$, $k = \boxed{-4}$

Vertex $= \left(\boxed{-1}, \boxed{-4} \right)$

Focus $= \left(\boxed{-\dfrac{3}{2}}, \boxed{-4} \right)$

Directrix: $x = \boxed{-\dfrac{1}{2}}$

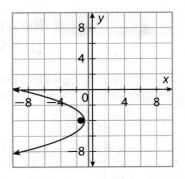

Your Turn

Convert the equation to the standard form of a parabola and graph the parabola, the focus, and the directrix.

7. $y^2 - 12x - 4y + 64 = 0$

8. $x^2 + 8x - 16y - 48 = 0$

🔧 Explain 4 Solving a Real-World Problem

Parabolic shapes occur in a variety of applications in science and engineering that take advantage of the concentrating property of reflections from the parabolic surface at the focus.

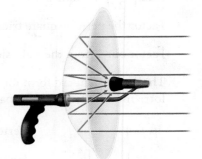

(A) Parabolic microphones are so-named because they use a parabolic dish to bounce sound waves toward a microphone placed at the focus of the parabola in order to increase sensitivity. The dish below has a cross section dictated by the equation $x = 32y^2$ where x and y are in inches. How far from the center of the dish should the microphone be placed?

The cross section matches the standard form of a horizontal parabola with $h = 0$, $k = 0$, $p = 8$.

Therefore the vertex, which is the center of the dish, is at $(0, 0)$ and the focus is at $(8, 0)$, 8 inches away.

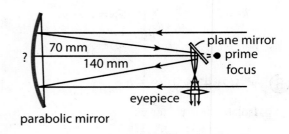

parabolic mirror

(B) A reflective telescope uses a parabolic mirror to focus light rays before creating an image with the eyepiece. If the focal length (the distance from the bottom of the mirror's bowl to the focus) is 140 mm and the mirror has a 70 mm diameter (width), what is the depth of the bowl of the mirror?

The distance from the bottom of the mirror's bowl to the focus is p. The vertex location is not specified (or needed), so use $(0, 0)$ for simplicity. The equation for the mirror is a horizontal parabola (with x the distance along the telescope and y the position out from the center).

$$\left(y - \boxed{0} \right)^2 = 4p \left(x - \boxed{0} \right)$$

$$y^2 = \boxed{560}\, x$$

Since the diameter of the bowl of the mirror is 70 mm, the points at the rim of the mirror have y-values of 35 mm and -35 mm. The x-value of either point will be the same as the x-value of the point directly above the bottom of the bowl, which equals the depth of the bowl. Since the points on the rim lie on the parabola, use the equation of the parabola to solve for the x-value of either edge of the mirror.

$$\boxed{35}^2 = \boxed{560}\,x$$

$$x \approx \boxed{2.19} \text{ mm}$$

The bowl is approximately 2.19 mm deep.

Your Turn

9. A football team needs one more field goal to win the game. The goalpost that the ball must clear is 10 feet ($\sim$3.3 yd) off the ground. The path of the football after it is kicked for a 35-yard field goal is given by the equation $y - 11 = -0.0125\,(x - 20)^2$, in yards. Does the team win?

Elaborate

10. Examine the graphs in this lesson and determine a relationship between the separation of the focus and the vertex, and the shape of the parabola. Demonstrate this by finding the relationship between p for a vertical parabola with vertex of $(0, 0)$ and a, the coefficient of the quadratic parent function $y = ax^2$.

11. **Essential Question Check-In** How is the distance formula used to go from the definition of a parabola based on focus and directrix to an equation that relates x and y?

☆ Evaluate: Homework and Practice

- Online Homework
- Hints and Help
- Extra Practice

Find the equation of the parabola with vertex at $(0, 0)$ from the description of the focus and directrix and plot the parabola, the focus, and the directrix.

1. Focus at $(3, 0)$, directrix: $x = -3$

2. Focus at $(0, -5)$, directrix: $y = 5$

3. Focus at $(-1, 0)$, directrix: $x = 1$

4. Focus at $(0, 2)$, directrix: $y = -2$

Find the equation of the parabola with the given information.

5. Vertex: $(-3, 6)$; Directrix: $x = -2.25$

6. Vertex: $(6, 20)$; Focus: $(6, -11)$

Find the equation of the parabola with vertex at (h, k) from the description of the focus and directrix and plot the parabola, the focus, and the directrix.

7. Focus at $(5, 3)$, directrix: $y = 7$

8. Focus at $(-3, 3)$, directrix: $x = 3$

Convert the equation to the standard form of a parabola and graph the parabola, the focus, and the directrix.

9. $y^2 - 20x - 6y - 51 = 0$

10. $x^2 - 14x - 12y + 73 = 0$

11. Communications The equation for the cross section of a parabolic satellite television dish is $y = \frac{1}{50}x^2$, measured in inches. How far is the focus from the vertex of the cross section?

12. Engineering The equation for the cross section of a spotlight is $y + 5 = \frac{1}{12}x^2$, measured in inches. Where is the bulb located with respect to the vertex of the cross section?

13. When a ball is thrown into the air, the path that the ball travels is modeled by the parabola $y - 7 = -0.0175(x - 20)^2$, measured in feet. What is the maximum height the ball reaches? How far does the ball travel before it hits the ground?

14. The equation of the cables for a suspension bridge is modeled by the equation $y - 55 = 0.0025x^2$, in feet. How far is the lowest point of the cables above the bridge?

15. Match each equation to its graph.

a. $y + 1 = \frac{1}{16}(x - 2)^2$

b. $y - 1 = \frac{1}{16}(x + 2)^2$

c. $x + 1 = -\frac{1}{16}(y - 2)^2$

A.

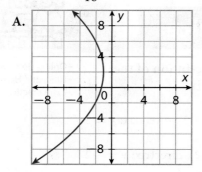

B.

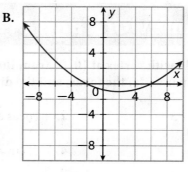

C.

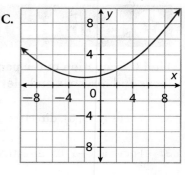

Derive the equation of the parabolas with the given information.

16. An upward pointing parabola with a focus at $(0, p)$ and a directrix at $(y = -p)$

17. A rightward pointing parabola with a focus at $(-p, 0)$ and a directrix at $(y = -p)$

18. **Multi-Step** A tennis player hits a tennis ball while standing just behind the back end of the court. The path of the ball is modeled by the equation $y - 4 = -\frac{4}{1521}(x - 39)^2$. The tennis net is 3 feet high, and the total length of the court is 78 feet.

   a. Explain why the ball will go over the net.

   b. How far is the net located from the player?

   c. Will the ball land inside the court?

19. **Critical Thinking** The latus rectum of a parabola is the line segment perpendicular to the axis of symmetry through the focus, with endpoints on the parabola. Find the length of the latus rectum of the parabola. Justify your answer. Hint: Set the coordinate system such that the vertex is at the origin and it open rightward with the focus at $(p, 0)$.

20. **Explain the Error** Lois uses the parabola $y - 8 = -\frac{1}{18}(x + 2)^2$ and the distance formula to find the distance from the vertex of the parabola to the focus to be 12.7 units. Her work is shown.

$$d = \sqrt{(x - h)^2 + (y - k)^2}$$
$$= \sqrt{(-2 - 0)^2 + (8 + 4.5)^2}$$
$$= \sqrt{(-2)^2 + 12.5^2}$$
$$= \sqrt{4 + 156.25}$$
$$\approx 12.7$$

   a. Explain what Lois did wrong, and then find the correct answer.

   b. Is it necessary to use the distance formula to solve for the distance? Explain.

Lesson Performance Task

Parabolic microphones are used for field audio during sports events. The microphones are manufactured such that the equation of their cross section is $x = \frac{1}{34} y^2$, in inches. The feedhorn part of the microphone is located at the focus.

a. How far is the feedhorn from the edge of the parabolic surface of the microphone?

b. What is the diameter of the microphone? Explain your reasoning.

c. If the diameter is increased by 5 inches, what is the new equation of the cross section of the microphone?

5.2 Solving Linear-Quadratic Systems

Essential Question: How can you solve a system composed of a linear equation in two variables and a quadratic equation in two variables?

 TEKS A2.3.C: Solve, algebraically, systems of two equations in two variables consisting of a linear equation and a quadratic equation. Also A2.3.A, A2.3.D

⊘ Explore Investigating Intersections of Lines and Graphs of Quadratic Equations

There are many real-world situations that can be modeled by linear or quadratic functions. What happens when the two situations overlap? Examine graphs of linear functions and quadratic functions and determine the ways they can intersect.

Ⓐ Examine the two graphs below and determine the ways a line could intersect the parabola.

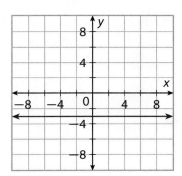 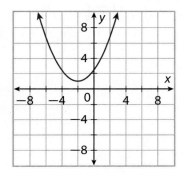

Ⓑ Sketch three graphs of a line and a parabola: one that intersects in one point, one that intersects in two points, and one that does not intersect.

Ⓒ So a linear function and a quadratic function can intersect at ▓▓▓ points.

Reflect

1. If a line intersects a circle at one point, what is the relationship between the line and the radius of the circle at that point?

2. **Discussion** Does a line have to be horizontal to intersect a parabola at exactly one point?

Explain 1 **Solving Linear-Quadratic Systems Graphically**

Graph each equation by hand and find the set of points where the two graphs intersect.

Example 1 Solve the given linear-quadratic system graphically.

Ⓐ $\begin{cases} 2x - y = 3 \\ y + 6 = 2(x + 1)^2 \end{cases}$

Plot the line and the parabola.

Solve each equation for y.

$2x - y = 3$

$$y = 2x - 3$$
$$y + 6 = 2(x + 1)^2$$
$$y = 2(x + 1)^2 - 6$$

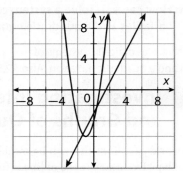

Find the approximate points of intersection: $(-1.4, -5.7)$ and $(0.4, -2.3)$.

Exact solutions are $\left(\frac{-1 - \sqrt{3}}{2}, -\sqrt{3} - 4 \right)$ and $\left(\frac{-1 + \sqrt{3}}{2}, \sqrt{3} - 4 \right)$.

Ⓑ $\begin{cases} 3x + y = 4.5 \\ y = \frac{1}{2}(x - 3)^2 \end{cases}$

Solve each equation for y.

$3x + y = 4.5$

$$y = \boxed{-3x + 4.5}$$
$$y = \boxed{\frac{1}{2}(x - 3)^2}$$

Plot the line and the parabola on a coordinate grid.

Find the approximate point(s) of intersection: $(0, 4.5)$.

Your Turn

Solve the given linear-quadratic system graphically.

3. $\begin{cases} y + 3x = 0 \\ y - 6 = -3x^2 \end{cases}$

4. $\begin{cases} y + 1 = \frac{1}{2}(x - 3)^2 \\ x - y = 6 \end{cases}$

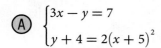 # Solving Linear-Quadratic Systems Algebraically

Use algebra to find the solution. Use substitution or elimination.

Example 2 Solve the given linear-quadratic system algebraically.

(A) $\begin{cases} 3x - y = 7 \\ y + 4 = 2(x + 5)^2 \end{cases}$

Solve this system using elimination.
First line up the terms.

$$7 + y = 3x$$
$$4 + y = 2(x + 5)^2$$

Subtract the second equation from
the first to eliminate the y variable.

$$7 + y = 3x$$
$$-\underline{\left(4 + y = 2(x + 5^2)\right)}$$
$$3 = 3x - 2(x + 5)^2$$

$$3 = 3x - 2(x + 5)^2$$
$$3 = 3x - 2(x^2 + 10x + 25)$$
$$3 = 3x - 2x^2 - 20x - 50$$
$$0 = -2x^2 - 17x - 53$$

Solve the resulting equation for x
using the quadratic formula.

$$2x^2 + 17x + 53 = 0$$
$$x = \frac{-17 \pm \sqrt{17^2 - 4 \cdot 2 \cdot 53}}{2 \cdot 2}$$
$$= \frac{-17 \pm \sqrt{289 - 424}}{4}$$

There is no real number equivalent to $\sqrt{-135}$, so the system
has no solution.

$$= \frac{-17 \pm \sqrt{-135}}{4}$$

(B) $\begin{cases} y = \frac{1}{4}(x - 3)^2 \\ 3x - 2y = 13 \end{cases}$

Solve the system by substitution. The first equation is already solved for y. Substitute the
expression $\frac{1}{4}(x - 3)^2$ for y in the second equation.

$$3x - 2\left(\frac{1}{4}(x - 3)^2\right) = 13$$

$$13 = 3x - 2\left(\frac{1}{4}(x - 3)^2\right)$$
$$13 = 3x - \boxed{\frac{1}{2}}(x - 3)^2$$
$$13 = 3x - \frac{1}{2}\left(\boxed{x^2 - 6x + 9}\right)$$
$$13 = 3x - \frac{1}{2}x^2 + 3x - \frac{9}{2}$$
$$13 = -\frac{1}{2}x^2 + \boxed{6x} - \frac{9}{2}$$
$$0 = -\frac{1}{2}x^2 + 6x - \frac{35}{2}$$

Now, solve for x by factoring.

$$0 = x^2 \boxed{-12x + 35}$$
$$0 = \left(x \boxed{-5}\right)\left(x \boxed{-7}\right)$$
$$x = \boxed{-5} \text{ or } x = \boxed{-7}$$

So the line and the parabola intersect at two points. Use the *x*-coordinates of the intersections to find the points.

Solve $3x - 2y = 13$ for *y*.

$$3x - 2y = 13$$

$$-2y = 13 - 3x$$

$$y = \boxed{-\left(\dfrac{13 - 3x}{2}\right)}$$

Find *y* when $x = 5$ and when $x = 7$.

$$y = -\dfrac{13 - 3 \cdot 5}{2} \qquad\qquad y = -\dfrac{13 - 3 \cdot 7}{2}$$

$$= -\dfrac{13 - 15}{2} \qquad\qquad = -\dfrac{13 - 21}{2}$$

$$= -\dfrac{-2}{2} \qquad\qquad = -\dfrac{-8}{2}$$

$$= 1 \qquad\qquad\qquad = 4$$

So the solutions to the system are $(5, 1)$ and $(7, 4)$.

Reflect

5. How can you check algebraic solutions for reasonableness?

Your Turn

Solve the given linear-quadratic system algebraically.

6.
$$\begin{cases} x - 6 = -\frac{1}{6}y^2 \\ 2x + y = 6 \end{cases}$$

7.
$$\begin{cases} x - y = 7 \\ x^2 - y = 7 \end{cases}$$

Explain 3   Solving Real-World Problems

You can use the techniques from the previous examples to solve real-world problems.

Example 3   Solve each problem.

(A) A tour boat travels around an island in a pattern that can be modeled by the equation $36x^2 + 25y^2 = 900$. A fishing boat approaches the island on a path that can be modeled by the equation $3x - 2y = -8$. Is there a danger of collision? If so, where?

Write the system of equations.

$$\begin{cases} 36x^2 + 25y^2 = 900 \\ 3x - 2y = -8 \end{cases}$$

Solve the second equation for *x*.

$$3x - 2y = -8$$

$$3x = 2y - 8$$

$$x = \dfrac{2y - 8}{3}$$

Substitute for *x* in the first equation.

$$36x^2 + 25y^2 = 900$$

$$36\left(\frac{2y - 8}{3}\right)^2 + 25y^2 = 900$$

$$36\left(\frac{4y^2 - 32y + 64}{9}\right) + 25y^2 = 900$$

$$4\left(4y^2 - 32y + 64\right) + 25y^2 = 900$$

$$16y^2 - 128y + 256 + 25y^2 = 900$$

$$41y^2 - 128y - 644 = 0$$

Solve using the quadratic equation.

$$y = \frac{128 \pm \sqrt{128^2 - 4(41)(-664)}}{2(41)}$$

$$= \frac{128 \pm \sqrt{122{,}000}}{82}$$

$$= -2.70 \text{ or } 5.82$$

Collisions can occur when $y \approx -2.70$ or $y \approx 5.82$.

To find the x-values, substitute the y-values into $x = \frac{2y - 8}{3}$.

$$x = \frac{2(-2.70) - 8}{3} \qquad\qquad x = \frac{2(5.82) - 8}{3}$$

$$= \frac{-5.40 - 8}{3} \qquad\qquad\quad = \frac{11.64 - 8}{3}$$

$$= \frac{-13.40}{3} \qquad\qquad\qquad = \frac{3.64}{3}$$

$$= -4.47 \qquad\qquad\qquad\quad = 1.21$$

So the boats could collide at either $(-4.47, -2.70)$ or $(1.21, 5.82)$.

Ⓑ The range of the signal from a radio station is bounded by a circle described by the equation $x^2 + y^2 = 2025$. A stretch of highway near the station is modeled by the equation $y - 15 = \frac{1}{20}x$. At which points, if any, does a car on the highway enter and exit the broadcast range of the station?

Write the system of equations.

$$\begin{cases} x^2 + y^2 = -2025 \\ y - 15 = \dfrac{1}{20}x \end{cases}$$

Solve the second equation for y.

$$y - 15 = \frac{1}{20}x$$

$$y = \boxed{\frac{1}{20}x + 15}$$

Substitute for x in the first equation.

$$x^2 + y^2 = 2025$$

$$x^2 + \left(\boxed{\frac{1}{20}x + 15}\right)^2 = 2025$$

$$x^2 + \boxed{\frac{1}{400}x^2 + \frac{3}{2}x + 225} = 2025$$

$$\boxed{\frac{401}{400}}\,x^2 + \frac{3}{2}x + 225 = 2025$$

$$\frac{401}{400}x^2 + \frac{3}{2}x - \boxed{1800} = 0$$

$$401x^2 + 600x - 720000 = 0$$

Solve using the quadratic formula.

$$y = \frac{-600 \pm \sqrt{600^2 - 4(401)(-720000)}}{2(401)}$$

$$= \frac{600 \pm \sqrt{1{,}155{,}240{,}000}}{802}$$

$$\approx \boxed{-41.63} \text{ or } \boxed{43.13} \text{ (rounded to the nearest hundredth)}$$

To find the y-values, substitute the x-values into $y = \frac{1}{20}x + 15$.

$$y = \frac{1}{20}(-41.63) + 15 \qquad\qquad y = \frac{1}{20}(-43.13) + 15$$

$$= -\frac{41.63}{20} + 15 \qquad\qquad = -\frac{43.13}{20} + 15$$

$$= -2.08 + 15 \qquad\qquad = 2.16 + 15$$

$$= 12.92 \qquad\qquad = 17.16$$

The car will be within the radio station's broadcast area between $(-41.63, 12.92)$ and $(43.13, 17.16)$.

Your Turn

8. An asteroid is traveling toward Earth on a path that can be modeled by the equation $y = \frac{1}{28}x - 7$. It approaches a satellite in orbit on a path that can be modeled by the equation $\frac{x^2}{49} + \frac{y^2}{51} = 1$. What are the approximate coordinates of the points where the satellite and asteroid might collide?

9. The owners of a circus are planning a new act. They want to have a trapeze artist catch another acrobat in mid-air as the second performer comes into the main tent on a zip-line. If the path of the trapeze can be modeled by the parabola $y = \frac{1}{4}x^2 + 16$ and the path of the zip-line can be modeled by $y = 2x + 12$, at what point can the trapeze artist grab the second acrobat?

Elaborate

10. A parabola opens to the left. Identify an infinite set of parallel lines that will intersect the parabola only once.

11. If a parabola can intersect the set of lines $\left\{ x = a \,\middle|\, a \in R \right\}$ in 0, 1, or 2 points, what do you know about the parabola?

12. **Essential Question Check-In** How can you solve a system composed of a linear equation in two variables and a quadratic equation in two variables?

⭐ Evaluate: Homework and Practice

1. How many points of intersection are on the graph?

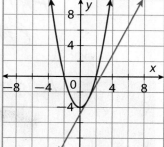

2. How many points of intersection are there on the graph of $\begin{cases} y = x^2 + 3x - 2 \\ y - x = 4 \end{cases}$?

Solve each given linear-quadratic system graphically.

3. $\begin{cases} y = -(x - 2)^2 + 4 \\ y = -5 \end{cases}$

4. $\begin{cases} y - 3 = (x - 1)^2 \\ 2x + y = 5 \end{cases}$

5. $\begin{cases} x = y^2 - 5 \\ -x + 2y = 12 \end{cases}$

6. $\begin{cases} x - 4 = (y + 1)^2 \\ 3x - y = 17 \end{cases}$

7. $\begin{cases} (y - 4)^2 + x^2 = -12x + 20 \\ x = y \end{cases}$

8. $\begin{cases} 5 - y = x^2 + x \\ y + 1 = \frac{3}{4}x \end{cases}$

Solve each linear-quadratic system algebraically.

9. $\begin{cases} 6x + y = -16 \\ y + 7 = x^2 \end{cases}$

10. $\begin{cases} y - 5 = (x - 2)^2 \\ x + 2y = 6 \end{cases}$

11. $\begin{cases} y^2 - 26 = -x^2 \\ x - y = 6 \end{cases}$

12. $\begin{cases} y - 3 = x^2 - 2x \\ 2x + y = 1 \end{cases}$

13. $\begin{cases} y = x^2 + 1 \\ y - 1 = x \end{cases}$

14. $\begin{cases} y = x^2 + 2x + 7 \\ y - 7 = x \end{cases}$

Write and solve a system of equations to find the solutions.

15. Jason is driving his car on a highway at a constant rate of 60 miles per hour when he passes his friend Alan whose car is parked on the side of the road. Alan has been waiting for Jason to pass so that he can follow him to a nearby campground. To catch up to Jason's passing car, Alan accelerates at a constant rate. The distance d, in miles, that Alan's car travels as a function of time t, in hours, since Jason's car has passed is given by $d = 3600t^2$. How long does it takes Alan's car to catch up with Jason's car?

16. The flight of a cannonball toward a hill is described by the parabola $y = 2 + 0.12x - 0.002x^2$.

The hill slopes upward along a path given by $y = 0.15x$.

Where on the hill does the cannonball land?

17. Amy throws a quarter from the top of a building at the same time that a balloon is released from the ground. The equation describing the height y above ground of the quarter in feet is $y = 64 - 2x^2$, where x is the time in seconds. The equation describing the elevation of the balloon in feet is $y = 6x + 8$, where x is the time in seconds. After how many seconds will the balloon and quarter pass each other? Check your solution for reasonableness.

18. The range of an ambulance service is a circular region bounded by the equation $x^2 + y^2 = 400$. A straight road within the service area is represented by $y = 3x + 20$. Find the length of the road that lies within the range of the ambulance service (round your answer to the nearest hundredth).

Recall that the distance formula is

$$d = \sqrt{(x_2 - x_1)^2 + (y_2 - y_1)^2}.$$

19. Match the equations with their solutions.

a. $\begin{cases} y = x - 2 \\ -x^2 + y = 4x - 2 \end{cases}$ **A.** $(4, 3)\ (-4, -3)$

b. $\begin{cases} y = (x - 2)^2 \\ y = -5x - 8 \end{cases}$ **B.** $(0, -2)\ (5, 3)$

c. $\begin{cases} 4y = 3x \\ x^2 + y^2 = 25 \end{cases}$ **C.** $(2, 0)$

d. $\begin{cases} y = (x - 2)^2 \\ y = 0 \end{cases}$ **D.** No solution

20. A student solved the system $\begin{cases} y - 7 = x^2 - 5x \\ y - 2x = 1 \end{cases}$ graphically and determined the only solution to be (1, 3). Was this a reasonable answer? How do you know?

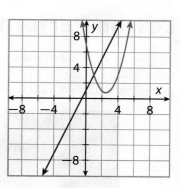

21. Explain the Error A student was asked to come up with a system of equations, one linear and one quadratic, that has two solutions. The student gave $\begin{cases} y^2 = -(x + 1)^2 + 9 \\ y = x^2 - 4x + 3 \end{cases}$ as the answer. What did the student do wrong?

22. Analyze Relationships The graph shows a quadratic function and a linear function $y = d$. If the linear function were changed to $y = d + 3$, how many solutions would the new system have? If the linear function were changed to $y = d - 5$, how many solutions would the new system have? Give reasons for your answers.

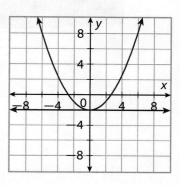

23. Make a Conjecture Given $y = 100x^2$ and $y = 0.0001x^2$, what can you say about any line that goes through the vertex of each but is not horizontal or vertical?

24. Communicate Mathematical Ideas Explain why a system of a linear equation and a quadratic equation cannot have an infinite number of solutions.

Lesson Performance Task

Suppose an aerial freestyle skier goes off a ramp with her path represented by the equation $y = -0.024(x - 25)^2 + 40$. If the surface of the mountain is represented by the linear equation $y = -0.5x + 25$, find the distance in feet the skier lands from the beginning of the ramp.

5.3 Solving Linear Systems in Three Variables

Essential Question: How can you find the solution(s) of a system of three linear equations in three variables?

TEKS A2.3.B Solve systems of three linear equations in three variables by using Gaussian elimination, technology with matrices, and substitution. Also A2.3.A, A2.4.A

Explore   Recognizing Ways that Planes Can Intersect

Recall that a linear equation in two variables defines a line. Consider a *linear equation in three variables*. An example is shown.

$$5 = 3x + 2y + 6z$$

A **linear equation in three variables** has three distinct variables, each of which is either first degree or has a coefficient of zero.

Just as the two numbers that satisfy a linear equation in two variables are called an ordered pair, the three numbers that satisfy a linear equation in three variables are called an **ordered triple** and are written (x, y, z).

The set of all ordered pairs satisfying a linear equation in two variables forms a line. Likewise the set of all ordered triples satisfying a linear equation in three variables forms a plane.

Three linear equations in three variables, considered together, form **a system of three linear equations in three variables**. The solutions of a system like this depend on the ways three planes can intersect.

(A) The diagrams show some ways three planes can intersect. How many points lie on all 3 planes?

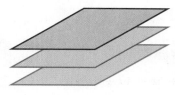
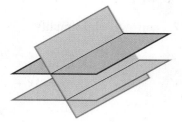
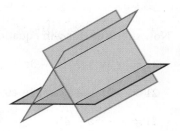

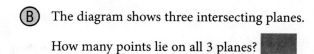

(B) The diagram shows three intersecting planes.

How many points lie on all 3 planes?

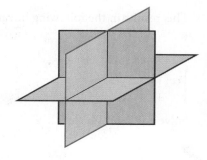

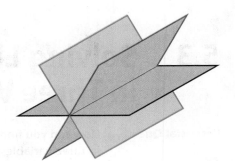

(C) The diagram shows planes intersecting in a different way.

Describe the intersection. ▮▮▮

How many points lie in all 3 planes? ▮▮▮

1. **Discussion** Give an example of three planes that intersect at exactly one point.

🔑 Explain 1 Solving a System of Three Linear Equations Using Substitution

A system of three linear equations is solved in the same manner as a system of two linear equations. It just has more steps.

Example 1 **Solve the system using substitution.**

(A)
$$\begin{cases} -2x + y + 3z = 20 & \boxed{1} \\ -3x + 2y + z = 21 & \boxed{2} \\ 3x - 2y + 3z = -9 & \boxed{3} \end{cases}$$

Choose an equation and variable to start with. The easiest equations to solve are those that have a variable with a coefficient of 1. Solve for y.

$$-2x + y + 3z = 20$$

$$y = 2x - 3z + 20$$

Now substitute for y in equations $\boxed{2}$ and $\boxed{3}$ and simplify.

$21 = -3x + 2(2x - 3z + 20) + z$ $-9 = 3x - 2(2x - 3z + 20) + 3z$

$21 = -3x + 4x - 6z + 40 + z$ $-9 = 3x - 4x + 6z - 40 + 3z$

$21 = x - 5z + 40$ $-9 = -x + 9z - 40$

$-19 = x - 5z \quad \boxed{4}$ $31 = -x + 9z \quad \boxed{5}$

This results in the following linear system in two variables:

$$\begin{cases} -19 = x - 5z & \boxed{4} \\ 31 = -x + 9z & \boxed{5} \end{cases}$$

Solve equation $[4]$ for x.

$$x = 5z - 19$$

© Houghton Mifflin Harcourt Publishing Company

Substitute into equation [5] and solve for z. Then use the value for z to find the values of x.

$31 = -(5z - 19) + 9z$ $31 = -x + 9(3)$

$31 = 4z + 19$ $31 = -x + 27$

$3 = z$ $-4 = x$

Finally, solve the equation for y when $x = -4$ and $z = 3$.

$y = 2x - 3z + 20$

$y = 2(-4) - 3(3) + 20$

$y = 3$

Therefore, the solution to the system of three linear equations is the ordered triple $(-4, 3, 3)$.

(B) There is a unique parabolic function passing through any three noncollinear points in the coordinate plane provided that no two of the points have the same x-coordinate. Find the parabola that passes through the points $(2, 1)$, $(-1, 4)$, and $(-2, 3)$.

The general form of a parabola is the quadratic equation $y = ax^2 + bx + c$. In order to find the equation of the parabola, we must identify the values of a, b, and c. Since each point lies on the parabola, substituting the coordinates of each point into the general equation produces a different equation.

$$\begin{cases} 1 = a(2)^2 + b(2) + c \\ 4 = a(-1)^2 + b(-1) + c \\ \boxed{3} = a\left(\boxed{-2}\right)^2 + b\left(\boxed{-2}\right) + c \end{cases} \Rightarrow \begin{cases} 1 = 4a + 2b + c \quad \boxed{1} \\ 4 = a - b + c \quad \boxed{2} \\ 3 = 4a - 2b + c \quad \boxed{3} \end{cases}$$

Choose an equation in which it is easier to isolate a variable. Solve equation [2] for c.

$c = 4 - a + \boxed{b}$ [2]

Now substitute for $c =$ in equations [1] and [3].

$1 = 4a + 2b + \left(\boxed{4 - a + b}\right)$ $3 = 4a - 2b + \left(\boxed{4 - a + b}\right)$

$1 = \boxed{3a} + 3b + 4$ $3 = 3a - \boxed{b} + 4$

$\boxed{-3} = 3a + 3b$ [4] $\boxed{-1} = 3a - b$ [5]

This results in the following linear system in two variables:

$$\begin{cases} 3a + 3b = -3 & [4] \\ 3a - b = -1 & [5] \end{cases}$$

Solve equation [5] for b.

$b = 3a + \boxed{1}$

Substitute into equation [4] and solve for a. Then use the value for a to find the values of b.

$$3a + 3 + \left(\boxed{3a + 1}\right) = -3 \qquad\qquad 3\left(-\frac{1}{2}\right) + 3b = -3$$

$$3a + 9a + \boxed{3} = -3 \qquad\qquad\qquad \boxed{-\frac{3}{2}} + 3b = -3$$

$$12a = \boxed{-6} \qquad\qquad\qquad\qquad 3b = \boxed{-\frac{3}{2}}$$

$$a = \boxed{-\frac{1}{2}} \qquad\qquad\qquad\qquad b = \boxed{-\frac{1}{2}}$$

Then use the values a and b to solve for c.

$$c = 4 - a + b = 4 - \left(-\frac{1}{2}\right) + \left(-\frac{1}{2}\right) = 4$$

So the equation of the parabola connecting $(2, 1)$, $(-1, 4)$, and $(-2, 3)$ is

$$y = \boxed{-\frac{1}{2}}\, x^2 - \boxed{\frac{1}{2}}\, x + \boxed{4}\,.$$

Your Turn

3. $$\begin{cases} x + 2y + z = 8 \\ 2x + y - z = 4 \\ x + y - 3z = 7 \end{cases}$$

4. $$\begin{cases} 2x - y - 3z = 1 \\ 4x + 3y + 2z = -4 \\ -3x + 2y + 5z = -3 \end{cases}$$

🔑 Explain 2   Solving a System of Three Linear Equations Using Elimination

You can also solve systems of three linear equations using elimination.

Example 2

Ⓐ $$\begin{cases} -2x + y + 3z = 20 \quad \boxed{1} \\ -3x + 2y + z = 21 \quad \boxed{2} \\ 3x - 2y + 3z = -9 \quad \boxed{3} \end{cases}$$

Begin by looking for variables with coefficients that are either the same or additive inverses of each other. When subtracted or added, these pairs will eliminate that variable. Subtract equation $\boxed{3}$ from equation $\boxed{1}$ to eliminate the z variable.

$$\boxed{1} \qquad -2x + y + 3z = 20$$
$$\boxed{3} \qquad \underline{3x - 2y + 3z = -9}$$
$$\qquad -5x + 3y + 0 = 29 \quad \boxed{4}$$

Next multiply $\boxed{2}$ by -3 and add it to $\boxed{1}$ to eliminate the same variable.

$$\boxed{1} \quad -2x + y + 3z = 20 \qquad\qquad -2x + y + 3z = 20$$

$$\boxed{2} \quad \underline{-3(-3x + 2y + z = 21)} \quad \Rightarrow \quad \underline{9x - 6y - 3z = -63}$$

$$7x - 5y + 0 = -43 \quad \boxed{5}$$

This results in the system of two linear equations below.

$$\begin{cases} -5x + 3y = 29 \quad \boxed{4} \\ \ \ 7x - 5y = -43 \quad \boxed{5} \end{cases}$$

To solve this system, multiply $\boxed{4}$ by 5 and add the result to the product of $\boxed{5}$ and 3.

$$\boxed{4} \qquad 5(-5x + 3y = 29) \qquad\qquad -25 + 15y = 145$$

$$\boxed{5} \qquad \underline{3(7x - 5y = -43)} \quad \Rightarrow \quad \underline{21x - 15y = -129}$$

$$-4x + 0 = 16$$

$$-4x = 16$$

$$x = -4$$

Substitute to solve for y and z.

$$-5x + 3y = 29 \quad [4] \qquad\qquad -3x + 2y + z = 21 \quad [2]$$

$$-5(-4) + 3y = 29 \qquad\qquad -3(-4) + 2(3) + z = 21$$

$$y = 3 \qquad\qquad\qquad z = 3$$

The solution to the system is the ordered triple $(-4, 3, 3)$.

Ⓑ
$$\begin{cases} x + 2y + 3z = 9 \quad \boxed{1} \\ x + 3y + 2z = 5 \quad \boxed{2} \\ x - 4y - z = -5 \quad \boxed{3} \end{cases}$$

Begin by subtracting equation $\boxed{2}$ from equation $\boxed{1}$ to eliminate x.

$$\boxed{1} \qquad x + 2y + 3z = 9$$

$$\boxed{2} \qquad \underline{x + 3y + 2z = 5}$$

$$0x - y + z = 4 \quad \boxed{4}$$

Now subtract equation $\boxed{3}$ from equation $\boxed{1}$ to eliminate x.

$$\boxed{1} \qquad x + 2y + 3z = 9$$

$$\boxed{3} \qquad \underline{x + 4y - z = 5}$$

$$0x - 2y + 4z = 14 \quad \boxed{5}$$

This results in a system of two linear equations:

$$\begin{cases} -y + z = 4 \\ -2y + 4z = 14 \end{cases}$$

$\boxed{4}$

$\boxed{5}$

To solve this system, multiply equation $\boxed{5}$ by $-\dfrac{1}{2}$ and add it to equation $\boxed{4}$.

$\boxed{4}$ $\qquad -y + z = 4 \qquad\qquad -y + z = 4$

$\boxed{5}$ $\qquad \underline{-\frac{1}{2}(-2y + 4z = 14)} \quad\Rightarrow\quad \underline{y - 2z = -7}$

$$\qquad\qquad\qquad\qquad\qquad\qquad 0y - z = -3$$

$$\qquad\qquad\qquad\qquad\qquad\qquad\quad z = 3$$

Substitute to solve for y and x.

$-y + z = 4 \qquad [4] \qquad\qquad x + 2y + 3z = 4 \qquad [1]$

$-y + 3 = 4 \qquad\qquad\qquad\quad x + 2(-1) + 3(3) = 9$

$\qquad y = -1 \qquad\qquad\qquad\qquad\qquad\quad x = 2$

The solution to the system is the ordered triple $\left(2, -1, 3\right)$.

Your Turn

5. $\begin{cases} x + 2y + z = 8 \\ 2x + y - z = 4 \\ x + y + 3z = 7 \end{cases}$ $\quad\boxed{1}\ \boxed{2}\ \boxed{3}$

6. $\begin{cases} 2x - y - 3z = 1 \\ 4x + 3y + 2z = -4 \\ -3x + 2y + 5z = -3 \end{cases}$ $\quad\boxed{1}\ \boxed{2}\ \boxed{3}$

⚙ Explain 3 Solving a System of Three Linear Equations Using Matrices

You can represent systems of three linear equations in a *matrix*. A **matrix** is a rectangular array of numbers enclosed in brackets. Matrices are referred to by size: an *m*-by-*n* matrix has *m* rows and *n* columns.

A system of three linear equations can be written in a 3-by-4 matrix as follows. First rearrange the equations so all of the variables are to the left of the equals sign and the constant term is to the right. Then, each row corresponds to an equation and each of the first three columns represents a variable. Each entry represents the coefficient of the variable represented by the column in the equation related to the row. The fourth column is the constants that were to the right of the equals sign.

The system $\begin{cases} 2x + y + 3z = 20 \\ 5x + 2y + z = 21 \\ 3x - 2y + 7z = 9 \end{cases}$ is expressed as $\begin{bmatrix} 2 & 1 & 3 & 20 \\ 5 & 2 & 1 & 21 \\ 3 & -2 & 7 & -9 \end{bmatrix}$ in matrix form.

Gaussian Elimination is a formalized process of using matrices to eliminate two of the variables in each equation in the system. This results in an easy way to view the solution set. The process involves using *elementary row operations* to generate equivalent matrices that lead to a solution.

The **elementary row operations** are

(1) Multiplying a row by a constant – When performing row multiplication, the product of the original value and the constant replaces each value in the row.

(2) Adding two rows – In row addition, each value in the second row mentioned in the addition is replaced by the sum of the values in the equivalent column of the two rows being summed. These operations can also be performed together.

The elimination can be continued past this point to a matrix in which the solutions can be simply read directly out of the matrix. You can use a graphing calculator to perform these operations. The commands are shown in the table.

Command	Meaning	Syntax
*row(	replace each value in the row indicated with the product of the current value and the given number	*row(value,matrix,row)
row+(	replace rowB with the sum of rowA and the current rowB	row+(matrix,rowA,rowB)
*row+(	replace rowB with the product of the given value and rowA added to the current value of rowB	*row+(value,matrix,rowA,rowB)

Example 3 **Solve the system of three linear equations using matrices.**

Ⓐ
$$\begin{cases} -2x + y + 3z = 20 \\ -3x + 2y + z = 21 \\ 3x - 2y + 3z = -9 \end{cases}$$

Input the system as a 3-by-4 matrix. Multiply the first row by –0.5. Enter the command into your calculator. Press enter to view the result.

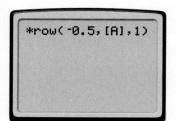

To reuse the resulting matrix, store it into Matrix B. Add 3 times row 1 to row 2. Press enter to view the result. Remember to store the result into a new matrix.

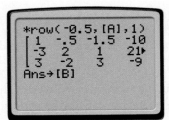

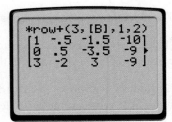

Multiply row 2 by 2. Add −3 times row 1 to row 3. Add 0.5 times row 2 to row 3.

Multiply row 3 by 0.25. Add 7 times row 3 to row 2. Add 1.5 times row 3 to row 1.

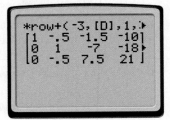

Add 0.5 times row 2 to row 1.

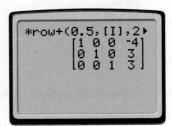

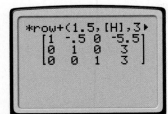

The first row tells us that $x = -4$, the second row tells us that $y = 3$, and the third row tells us that $z = 3$. So the solution is the ordered triple $(-4, 3, 3)$.

Ⓑ $\begin{cases} x + 2y + 3z = 9 \\ x + 3y + 2z = 5 \\ x + 4y - z = -5 \end{cases}$

Write as a matrix.

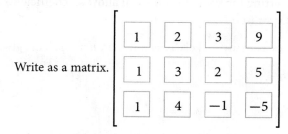

$$\begin{bmatrix} 1 & 2 & 3 & 9 \\ 1 & 3 & 2 & 5 \\ 1 & 4 & -1 & -5 \end{bmatrix}$$

Perform row operations.

$-r1 + r2$

$$\begin{bmatrix} 1 & 2 & 3 & 9 \\ 0 & 1 & -1 & -4 \\ 1 & 4 & -1 & -5 \end{bmatrix}$$

$-r1 + r3$

$$\begin{bmatrix} 1 & 2 & 3 & 9 \\ 0 & 1 & -1 & -4 \\ 0 & 2 & -4 & -14 \end{bmatrix}$$

$-2r2 + r3$

$$\begin{bmatrix} 1 & 2 & 3 & 9 \\ 0 & 1 & -1 & -4 \\ 0 & 0 & -2 & -6 \end{bmatrix}$$

$-0.5r3$

$$\begin{bmatrix} 1 & 2 & 3 & 9 \\ 0 & 1 & -1 & -4 \\ 0 & 0 & 1 & 3 \end{bmatrix}$$

$r3 + r2$

$$\begin{bmatrix} 1 & 2 & 3 & 9 \\ 0 & 1 & 0 & -1 \\ 0 & 0 & 1 & 3 \end{bmatrix}$$

$-3r3 + r1$

$$\begin{bmatrix} 1 & 2 & 0 & 0 \\ 0 & 1 & 0 & -1 \\ 0 & 0 & 1 & 3 \end{bmatrix}$$

$2r2 + r1$

$$\begin{bmatrix} 1 & 0 & 0 & 2 \\ 0 & 1 & 0 & -1 \\ 0 & 0 & 1 & 3 \end{bmatrix}$$

The solution is the ordered triple $(2, -1, 3)$.

Your Turn

7. $\begin{cases} x + 2y + z = 8 \\ 2x + y - z = 4 \\ x + y + 3z = 7 \end{cases}$

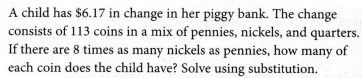

🎸 Explain 4   Solving a Real-World Problem

Example 4

Ⓐ A child has $6.17 in change in her piggy bank. The change consists of 113 coins in a mix of pennies, nickels, and quarters. If there are 8 times as many nickels as pennies, how many of each coin does the child have? Solve using substitution.

Begin by setting up a system of equations, and use p for the number of pennies, n for the number of nickels, and q for the number of quarters. Use the relationships in the problem statement to write the equations.

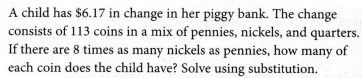

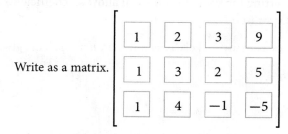

The total number of coins is the sum of the number of each coin. So, the first equation is $p + n + q = 113$.

The total value of the coins is \$6.17 or 617 cents (converting the value to cents will allow all coefficients to be integers). The second equation will be $p + 5n + 25q = 617$.

The third relationship given is that there are eight times as many nickels as pennies or, $n = 8p$. This gives the following system of equations:

$$\begin{cases} p + n + q = 113 & \boxed{1} \\ p + 5n + 25q = 617 & \boxed{2} \\ n = 8p & \boxed{3} \end{cases}$$

Equation $\boxed{3}$ is already solved for n. Substitute for n in equations $\boxed{1}$ and $\boxed{2}$ simplify.

$p + (8p) + q = 113$ $p + 5(8p) + 25q = 617$

$9p + q = 113$ $\boxed{4}$ $p + 40p + 25q = 617$

          $41p + 25q = 617$ $\boxed{5}$

This results in the following linear system in two variables:

$$\begin{cases} 9p + q = 113 & \boxed{4} \\ 41p + 25q = 617 & \boxed{5} \end{cases}$$

Solve equation $\boxed{4}$ for q.

$9p + q = 113$

$q = 113 - 9p$

Substitute for q in equation $\boxed{5}$ and solve for p.

Evaluate at $p = 12$ to find q and n.

$41p + 25(113 - 9p) = 617$ $q = 113 - 9p$ $n = 8p$

$41p + 2825 - 225p = 617$ $q = 113 - 9(12)$ $n = 8(12)$

$12 = p$ $q = 5$ $n = 96$

The child's piggy bank contains 12 pennies, 96 nickels, and 5 quarters.

(B) A student is shopping for clothes. The student needs to buy an equal number of shirts and ties. He also needs to buy four times as many shirts as pants. Shirts cost \$35, ties cost \$25, and pants cost \$40. If the student spends \$560, how many shirts, pants, and ties did he get?

Begin by setting up a system of equations, using s for the number of shirts, t for the number of ties, and p for the number pairs of pants. Use the relationships in the problem statement to write the equations.

The number of shirts is equal to the number of ties. So, the first equation is $s = t$.

The number of shirts is equal to 4 times the number of pairs of pants, so a second equation is $s = \boxed{4p}$.

The total the student spent is the sum of the cost of the shirts, the ties, and the pairs of pants.

$35s + 25t + 40p = \boxed{560}$

The system of equations is below.

$$\begin{cases} s = t & \boxed{1} \\ s = 4p & \boxed{2} \\ 35s + 25t + 40p = 560 & \boxed{3} \end{cases}$$

Equation $\boxed{1}$ is already solved for t. Solve equation $\boxed{2}$ for p.

$4p = s$

$p = \boxed{\dfrac{1}{4}s}$

Substitute for p and t in equation $\boxed{3}$ and solve for s.

$35s + 25(s) + 40\left(\dfrac{1}{4}s\right) = 560$

$35s + 25s + 10s = 560$

$\boxed{70}\,s = 560$

$s = \boxed{8}$

Evaluate the equation solved for p above at $s = 8$ to find p.

$p = \dfrac{1}{4}s$

$p = \dfrac{1}{4}(8) = 2$

Recall that $s = t$, so $t = 8$.

The student bought $\boxed{8}$ shirts, $\boxed{8}$ ties, and $\boxed{2}$ pairs of pants.

Your Turn

8. Louie Dampier is the leading scorer in the history of the American Basketball Association (ABA). His 13,726 points were scored on two-point baskets, three-point baskets, and one-point free throws. In his ABA career, Dampier made 2144 more two-point baskets than free throws and 1558 more free throws than three-point baskets. How many three-point baskets, two-point baskets, and free throws did Dampier make?

💬 Elaborate

9. If you are given a system of linear equations in three variables, but the system only has two equations, what happens when you try to solve it?

10. **Discussion** Why does a system need to have at least as many equations as unknowns to have a unique solution?

11. **Essential Question Check-In** How can you find the solution to a system of three linear equations in three variables?

Solve the system using substitution.

1. $\begin{cases} 4x + y - 2z = -6 & [1] \\ 2x - 3y + 3z = 9 & [2] \\ x - 2y = 0 & [3] \end{cases}$

2. $\begin{cases} x + 5y + 3z = 4 & [1] \\ 4y - z = 3 & [2] \\ 6x - 2y + 4z = 0 & [3] \end{cases}$

Solve the system using elimination.

3. $\begin{cases} 4x + y - 2z = -6 & [1] \\ 2x - 3y + 3z = 9 & [2] \\ x - 2y = 0 & [3] \end{cases}$

4. $\begin{cases} x + 5y + 3z = 4 & [1] \\ 4y - z = 3 & [2] \\ 6x - 2y + 4z = 0 & [3] \end{cases}$

5. $\begin{cases} 2x - y + 3z = -12 & [1] \\ -x + 2y - 3z = 15 & [2] \\ y + 5z = -6 & [3] \end{cases}$

Solve the system of three linear equations using matrices.

6. $\begin{cases} 4x + y - 2z = -6 & [1] \\ 2x - 3y + 3z = 9 & [2] \\ x - 2y = 0 & [3] \end{cases}$

7. $\begin{cases} x + 5y + 3z = 4 & [1] \\ 4y - z = 3 & [2] \\ 6x - 2y + 4z = 0 & [3] \end{cases}$

Solve the system of linear equations using your method of choice.

8. $\begin{cases} 2x - y + 3z = 5 & [1] \\ -6x + 3y - 9z = -15 & [2] \\ 4x - 2y + 6z = 10 & [3] \end{cases}$

9. $\begin{cases} 3x + 4y - z = -7 & [1] \\ x - 5y + 2z = 19 & [2] \\ 5x + y - 2z = 5 & [3] \end{cases}$

10. Find the equation of the parabola passing through the points $(3, 7)$, $(30, -11)$, and $(0, -1)$.

11. Geometry In triangle XYZ, the measure of angle X is eight times the sum of the measures of angles Y and Z. The measure of angle Y is three times the measure of angle Z. What are the measures of the angles?

12. The combined age of three relatives is 120 years. James is three times the age of Dan, and Paul is two times the sum of the ages of James and Dan. How old is each person?

13. Economics At a stock exchange there were a total of 10,000 shares sold in one day. Stock A had four times as many shares sold as Stock B. The number of shares sold for Stock C was equal to the sum of Stock A and Stock B. How many shares of each stock were sold?

14. **Communicate Mathematical Ideas** Explain how you know when a system has infinitely many solutions or when it has no solutions.

15. **Explain the Error** When given this system of equations, a student was asked to solve using matrices. Find and correct the student's error.

$$\begin{cases} 5x + 7y + 9x = 0 \\ x - y + z = -3 \\ 8x + y = 12 \end{cases}$$

$$\begin{bmatrix} 5 & 7 & 9 \\ 1 & -1 & 1 \\ 8 & 1 & 0 \end{bmatrix}$$

16. **Critical Thinking** Explain why the following system of equations cannot be solved.

$$\begin{cases} 7x + y + 6z = 1 \\ -x - 4y + 8z = 9 \end{cases}$$

Lesson Performance Task

A company that manufactures inline skates needs to order three parts—part A, part B, and part C. For one shipping order the company needs to buy a total of 6000 parts. There are four times as many B parts as C parts. The total number of A parts is one-fifth the sum of the B and C parts. On previous orders, the costs had been $0.25 for part A, $0.50 for part B, and $0.75 for part C, resulting in a cost of $3000 for all the parts in one order. When filling out an order for new parts, the company sees that it now costs $0.60 for part A, $0.40 for part B, and $0.60 for part C. Will the company be able to buy the same quantity of parts at the same price as before with the new prices?

© Houghton Mifflin Harcourt Publishing Company • Image Credits: ©Henry Westheim Photography/Alamy

5.4 Solving Systems of Linear Inequalities

Resource Locker

Essential Question: How can you represent the solutions of a system of two or more linear inequalities?

 TEKS **A2.3.F** Solve systems of two or more linear inequalities in two variables. Also A2.3.E, A2.3.G

⊘ Explore Turning a System of Equations into a System of Inequalities

What does the graph of a system of inequalities look like? Start with a system of equations. $y = x + 2$ $y = -2x + 1$

Ⓐ Plot the lines on a coordinate grid.

Ⓑ How many regions do the two lines divide the graph into?

Ⓒ Consider what it means to replace the equals sign with an inequality. Replace the top equation by the inequality $y \geq x + 2$.

How is this different? It means that besides the points on the line $y = x + 2$, the solution will now also include every point with a y-value greater than any point on the line. Indicate this on the graph by lightly shading the two regions above the line represented by $y = x + 2$.

Ⓓ Now replace the second equation with the inequality $y < -2x + 1$.

How is this different? It means that the solution will now include every point with a y-value less than any point on the line $y = -2x + 1$. Indicate this by lightly shading the two regions below the line.

However, because this inequality is non-inclusive, the solution will not contain the points on the line itself. Indicate this by converting the solid line to a dashed line.

Ⓔ How many regions of the graph were shaded in both steps?

Ⓕ Pick a point that is in the darkest region of the graph and check that it agrees with both inequalities.

  $\boxed{} \geq \boxed{} + 2$ Is this statement true or false? $\boxed{}$

  $\boxed{} < -2 \boxed{} + 1$ Is this statement true or false? $\boxed{}$

Reflect

1. **Discussion** Why did a dashed line replace the solid line in only the second inequality?

Explain 1 — Graphing a System of Linear Inequalities in Two Variables

Graphing a system of linear inequalities is just like graphing a single inequality, except the region indicated as the solution should agree with **all** the inequalities in the system. The borders of each inequality in the system are shown with the corresponding solid or dashed line, using a solid line if the inequality is inclusive ($\geq$ or $\leq$) or a dashed line if the inequality is exclusive ($>$ or $<$).

Example 1   Plot each system of inequalities on the graph and give the coordinates of two points in the solution set.

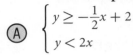

Ⓐ $\begin{cases} y \geq -\frac{1}{2}x + 2 \\ y < 2x \end{cases}$

Plot a line along $y = -\frac{1}{2}x + 2$. Since the inequality is inclusive, the line should be solid.

Shade the half-plane that holds solutions to the inequality $y \geq -\frac{1}{2}x + 2$ (above and to the right of the line).

Plot a line along $y = 2x$. Since the inequality is exclusive, the line should be dashed.

Shade the half-plane that holds solutions to the inequality $y < 2x$ (below and to the right of the line).

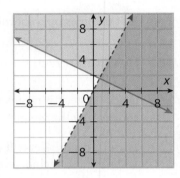

The region that is in both half-planes will be shaded the darkest. This represents the solutions of the system. The regions that were shaded only once are useful to help find solution but they **do not** represent valid solutions of the system; they are regions that represent solutions to only one of the two inequalities.

Points: $(2, 2)$ and $(4, 2)$ are in the solution set.

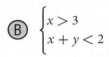

Ⓑ $\begin{cases} x > 3 \\ x + y < 2 \end{cases}$

Plot a dashed line along $\boxed{x} = 3$.

Determine the half-plane that holds solutions to the inequality $x > 3$ (to the right of the line.)

Plot a dashed line along $y = \boxed{-x} + 2$.

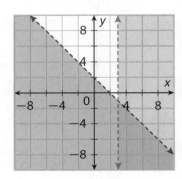

Determine the half-plane that holds solutions to the inequality $x + y < 2$ (below the line.)

Shade each region to indicate the solution. The region that is in both half-planes will be double-shaded.

Sample Points: $(4, -4), (6, -6)$

Your Turn

Plot each system of inequalities on the graph and give the coordinates of two points in the solution set.

2. $\begin{cases} x + y < 4 \\ y \geq 2x - 2 \end{cases}$ **3.** $\begin{cases} 2y + 2x - 3 < 0 \\ y - 3x < 1 \end{cases}$

⚙ Explain 2   Solving a Real-World Problem

Example 2   Use the four-step problem solving method (Analyze, Formulate a Plan, Solve, Justify and Evaluate) to solve the problem.

Ⓐ Sandy makes $2 profit on every cup of juice that she sells and $1 on every fruit bar that she sells. She wants to sell at least 5 fruit bars per day and at least 5 cups of juice per day. She wants to earn at least $25 per day. Show and describe all the possible combinations of juice and fruit bars that Sandy needs to sell to meet her goals, and pick two possible combinations that meet her goals.

🧩 Analyze Information

Identify the important information
- Profit on juice is $2 per cup.
- Profit on fruit bars is $1 each.
- Profit should be $25 or more.
- She wants to sell at least 5 fruit bars.
- She wants to sell at least 5 cups of juice.

🧩 Formulate a Plan

You want to find an equation relating profit to number of fruit bars and number of cups of juice sold. Then convert her sales and profit goals into inequalities and plot them to see where the solutions are.

🧩 Solve

Let c represent the number of juice cups sold, and b represent the number of fruit bars sold. Profit (p) is given by the equation $p = 2c + b$.

The inequalities that represent her daily sales and profit goals are given by

$c \geq 5$	Sell at least 5 cups of juice.
$b \geq 5$	Sell at least 5 fruit bars.
$2c + b \geq 25$	Earn at least $25 profit.

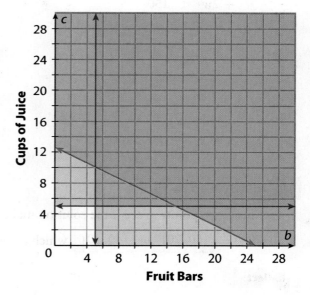

🧩 Justify and Evaluate

This solution seems reasonable because the solution region includes areas of large sales and profits increase with increasing sales. Sandy can meet her sales goal if she sells at the points (8, 9) or (6, 12), corresponding to $8 from sales of fruit bars and $18 from sales of juice, or $6 from sales of fruit bars and $24 from sales of juice. This type of solution is called an unbounded solution. The solution region is not contained in a finite area on the graph.

© Houghton Mifflin Harcourt Publishing Company

B Vance wants to fence in a rectangular area for his dog. He wants the length of the rectangle to be at least 30 feet and the perimeter to be no more than 150 feet. Graph all possible dimensions of the rectangle.

 Analyze

Identify the important information
- Rectangular area.
- The length is at least 30 feet.
- The perimeter is at most 150 feet.

 Formulate a Plan

You are looking for a solution to the dimensions of the rectangle (width and length). To find the limits on width you will need to relate width and length to perimeter with an equation.

perimeter $=$ $\boxed{2}$ $\times$ length $+$ $\boxed{2}$ $\times$ width

 Solve

Using l and w for length and width, write the inequalities that represent Vance's requirements for the fence:

$l \boxed{\geq} 30$

$\boxed{2l} + 2w \boxed{\leq} 150$

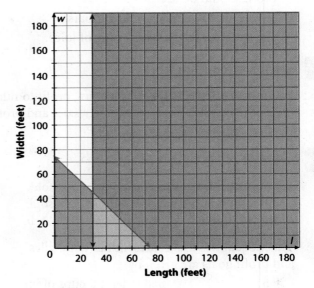

 Justify and Evaluate

Check two points to see if the solution makes sense.

$(l, w) = \boxed{(50, 20)}$ or $\boxed{(40, 30)}$, which are both in the solution region.

Reflect

4. Think about the difference between a real-world quantity like amount of flour and one like the balance of a bank account. There is a boundary on cups of flour that is not stated explicitly but does limit the choice of real numbers that can represent cups of flour. How is this different from an account balance?

5. In the first example, think of a statement that would make the solution bounded, or limit how much profit Sandy could make.

6. Olivia is painting a logo for a billboard and wants to use a combination of blue paint and red paint to completely cover a 5000 square foot billboard. A gallon of paint can cover 500 square feet. Red paint costs $20 per gallon and blue paint costs $30 per gallon. She only has $250 to spend. Make a graph showing all the possible combinations of paint that meet her goals.

7. Dustin decides to try selling whole-wheat muffins and bagels at his farm stand. He has $60 to spend on ingredients and eight hours to prepare the muffins and bagels that he will sell on opening day. One dozen muffins costs $10 to make and takes 1 hour, while one dozen bagels costs $15 to make and takes 2 hours. Make a graph showing all the possible combinations of food that meet his goals.

💬 Elaborate

8. When graphing inequalities, how can you check that you shaded the correct areas?

9. Will the point where the two lines intersect always be a solution? Why or why not?

10. **Essential Question Check-In** What is the difference between the way a "less than" inequality is graphed and the way a "less than or equal to" inequality is graphed?

☆ Evaluate: Homework and Practice

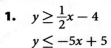

- Online Homework
- Hints and Help
- Extra Practice

Plot the following system of inequalities on a coordinate grid using a scale of -10 to 10 on each axis. Give the coordinates of two points in the solution set.

1. $y \geq \frac{1}{2}x - 4$
    $y \leq -5x + 5$

2. $y < 2x - 2$
    $y < -2x + 4$

3. $x - y > 2$
    $2x + 3y \leq 4$

4. $-3y \leq 6x + 1$
    $-x - 2y - 2 > 0$

5. $y \leq 2x + 5$
    $y \geq 2x - 5$

6. $3x - 2y \leq 12$
    $3x - 2y > -6$

7. $y \geq -2x + 2$
    $2x + y < 10$

8. $9x + 3y \leq 10$
    $3x + y > -5$

9. $y \leq \frac{1}{2}x - 4$
    $y \geq \frac{1}{2}x + 6$

10. $3x - 5y > 6$
    $5y - 3x > 10$

11. $x > 3$
    $y \geq -2$
    $x + y < 6$

12. $y < 2x + 1$
    $2x + 3y < 18$
    $y - x \geq -4$

Write the system of inequalities shown by each graph.

13.

14.

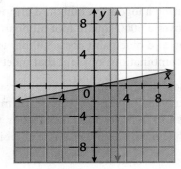

15.

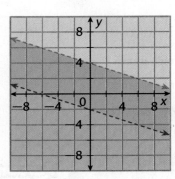

16.

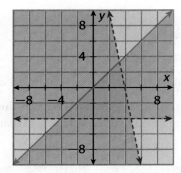

17. A surf shop makes profits of $150 for each surfboard and $100 for each wakeboard. The owner sells at least 3 surfboards and at least 6 wakeboards per month. The shop owner wants to earn at least $2000 per month. Graph all possible combinations of surfboard and wakeboard sales that would satisfy the store owner's earnings goal.

18. Alice is serving pepper jack cheese and cheddar cheese on a platter. She wants to have more than 2 pounds of each. Pepper jack cheese costs $4 per pound and cheddar cheese costs $2 per pound. Alice wants to spend at most $20 on cheese. Graph all possibile combinations of the two cheeses Alice could buy.

19. In one week, Ed can mow at most 9 lawns and rake at most 7 lawns. He charges $20 for mowing and $10 for raking. He needs to earn more than $120 in one week. Graph all the possible combinations of mowing and raking that Ed can do to meet his goal.

20. Linda works at a pharmacy for $15 an hour. She also baby-sits for $10 an hour. Linda needs to earn more than $90 per week, but she does not want to work more than 20 hours per week. Graph the number of hours Linda could work at each job to meet her goals.

21. Tony wants to plant at least 40 acres of corn and at least 50 acres of soybeans. He has 200 acres on which to plant. Graph all the possible combinations of the number of acres of corn and of soybeans Tony could plant.

22. Match each set of inequalities with the correct graph.

a. $\begin{cases} y < x \\ y \le -2x + 1 \end{cases}$

b. $\begin{cases} y \ge x \\ y > -2x + 1 \end{cases}$

c. $\begin{cases} y > x \\ y \ge -2x + 1 \end{cases}$

d. $\begin{cases} y \le x \\ y > -2x + 1 \end{cases}$

A.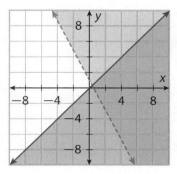

B.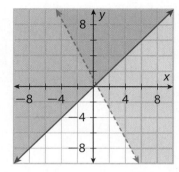

C.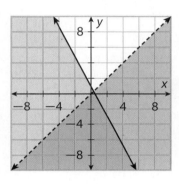

D.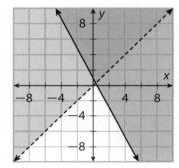

H.O.T. Focus on Higher Order Thinking

23. Explain the Error Two students wrote a system of linear inequalities to describe the graph. Which student is incorrect? Explain the error.

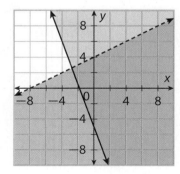

Student A	Student B
$y < \frac{1}{2}x + 4$	$y \ge \frac{1}{2}x + 4$
$y \ge -3x + 6$	$y < -3x + 6$

24. Critical Thinking Can the solutions of a system of linear inequalities be the points on a line? Give an example or explain why not.

25. Make a Conjecture What must be true of the boundary lines in a system of two linear inequalities if there is no solution of the system? Explain.

Lesson Performance Task

Ingrid has 6 nephews and 4 nieces and is going to buy them all presents. She wants to buy the same present for each of the nephews and the same present for each of the nieces. Ingrid plans to spend at least $180 but no more than $240. She wants the prices of the presents to be within $4 of each other. Find and graph the solution set. What do you notice about the solution region on the graph?

Quadratic Relations and Systems of Equations and Inequalities

Essential Question: How can you use systems of equations and inequalities to solve real-world problems?

KEY EXAMPLE (Lesson 5.2)

Solve the system using elimination.

$$\begin{cases} 5x + y = 10 \\ y + 2 = 3(x + 4)^2 \end{cases}$$

First, line up the terms.

$$y + 2 = 3(x + 4)^2$$
$$y - 10 = -5x$$

$$\begin{array}{l} y - 10 = -5x \\ \underline{-y + -2 = -3(x + 4)^2} \\ -12 = 5x - 3(x + 4)^2 \end{array}$$

Subtract the second equation from the first.

$$-12 = 5x - 3(x + 4)^2$$
$$-12 = 5x - 3x^2 - 24x - 48$$
$$0 = -3x^2 - 19x - 36$$

Solve the resulting equation for x.

$$x = \frac{19 \pm \sqrt{(-19)^2 - 4(-3)(-36)}}{2(-3)}$$

$$x = \frac{19 \pm i\sqrt{71}}{-6}$$

There is no real number equivalent, so the system has no solution.

KEY EXAMPLE (Lesson 5.4)

Solve the system by graphing.

$$\begin{cases} y \geq -\frac{3}{4}x - 1 \\ y < 4x \end{cases}$$

$y \geq -\frac{3}{4}x - 1$ will have a solid line, and will be shaded above.

$y < 4x$ will have a broken line, and will be shaded below.

So, the solution to the system of inequalities is the overlapping shading.

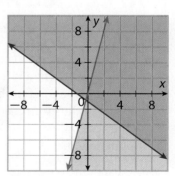

Key Vocabulary

directrix *(directriz)*

focus of a parabola *(foco de una parábola)*

linear equation in three variables *(ecuación lineal en tres variables)*

matrix *(matriz)*

ordered triple *(tripleta ordenada)*

system of linear inequalities *(sistema de desigualdades lineales)*

EXERCISES

Find the solution to the system of equations using graphing or elimination. *(Lessons 5.1, 5.2, 5.3)*

1. $\begin{cases} -4x + 3y = 1 \\ y = x^2 - x - 1 \end{cases}$

2. $\begin{cases} x - 3y = 2 \\ y = x^2 + 2x - 34 \end{cases}$

3. $\begin{cases} 3x + 5y - 2z = -7 \\ -2x + 7y + 6z = -3 \\ 8x + 3y - 10x = -11 \end{cases}$

4. $\begin{cases} 3x + 24y + 9z = 9 \\ x - 8y - 3z = 37 \\ 2x - 16y - 6x = 75 \end{cases}$

Graph the solution to each inequality. *(Lesson 5.4)*

5. $\begin{cases} y \geq \frac{2}{3}x - 4 \\ y \leq -\frac{1}{5}x + 4 \end{cases}$

6. $\begin{cases} y < 2x - 3 \\ y + \frac{2}{3}x \geq 2 \end{cases}$

MODULE PERFORMANCE TASK

How Can You Hit a Moving Target with a Laser Beam?

A video game designer is creating a game similar to skeet shooting, where a player will use a laser beam to hit a virtual clay disk launched into the air. The disk is launched from the ground and, if nothing blows it up, it reaches a maximum height of 30 meters and returns to the ground 60 meters away. The laser is fired from a height of 5 meters above the ground. Where should the designer point the laser to hit the disk at its maximum height?

Use your own paper to complete the task. Be sure to write down all your data and assumptions. Then use graphs, numbers, words, or algebra to explain how you reached your conclusion.

(Ready) to Go On?

5.1–5.4 Quadratic Relations and Systems of Equations and Inequalities

• Online Homework
• Hints and Help
• Extra Practice

Solve the system of equations using any method. *(Lessons 5.1, 5.2, 5.3)*

1. $\begin{cases} y - 8 = 4x \\ y + 12 = x^2 - 8x \end{cases}$

2. $\begin{cases} y = x + 2 \\ 2y - 12 = 2x^2 - 8x \end{cases}$

Solve the system of in equalities by graphing. *(Lesson 5.4)*

3. $\begin{cases} y > -x - 2 \\ y < -5x + 2 \end{cases}$

4. $\begin{cases} y - 2x \geq -3 \\ y \geq -3 \\ x + y \leq 3 \end{cases}$

ESSENTIAL QUESTION

5. Describe a real world situation that might involve three inequalities. *(Lesson 5.4)*

Assessment Readiness

1. If a parabola has a focus at $(-5, 0)$ and a directrix of $x = 5$, in which direction does it open?

   A. upward

   B. downward

   C. leftward

   D. rightward

2. What is the solution of the system of equations $\begin{cases} y = (x + 3)^2 + 1 \\ y = -2x - 6 \end{cases}$?

   A. $(-4, 2)$

   B. $(-3, 1)$

   C. $(0, -6)$

   D. $(5, -16)$

3. What is the domain of the function $f(x) = |x + 5| - 2$?

   A. $\left\{ x \mid x \in \mathbf{R} \right\}$

   B. $\left\{ x \mid x \geq -2 \right\}$

   C. $\left\{ x \mid x \geq -5 \right\}$

   D. $\left\{ x \mid x \leq 5 \right\}$

4. Celeste attempted to graph the system

   $$\begin{cases} y < \frac{1}{2}x - 2 \\ y + \frac{1}{4}x \geq 2 \end{cases}$$

   Her graph is shown. She concluded that there is no solution. Describe one of her mistakes.

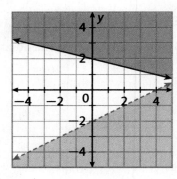

Assessment Readiness

• Online Homework
• Hints and Help
• Extra Practice

1. Consider the function $f(x) = 3(x - 7)^2 + 2$. Select the correct statement.

   A. The range is $\{y \mid y \in \Re\}$.

   B. The vertex of $f(x)$ is $(7, -2)$.

   C. The axis of symmetry for $f(x)$ is $x = 7$.

   D. The domain is $\{x \mid x > 7\}$.

2. Which of the following equations has real roots? Select the correct answer.

   A. $x^2 - 25 = 0$

   B. $-\dfrac{1}{2}x^2 - 3 = 0$

   C. $3x^2 + 4 = 2$

   D. $-x^2 - 16 = 0$

3. Consider the equation $3x^2 - 12x + 15 = 0$. Select the correct statement.

   A. After completing the square, $x = -2 \pm \sqrt{11}$.

   B. Solving this equation involves factoring a monomial.

   C. If solving this equation using factoring, then $(x - 5)(x + 1) = 0$.

   D. To solve this equation using complete the square, $\left(\dfrac{b}{2}\right)^2 = \left(\dfrac{-12}{2}\right)^2 = 36$.

4. Consider the system of equations $\begin{cases} y = 2x^2 - 3x + 5 \\ y - 3 = x \end{cases}$.
   Select the correct statement.

   A. The only way to solve this equation is by elimination.

   B. Another way to write this system is $\begin{cases} y = 2x^2 - 3x + 5 \\ y = x + 3 \end{cases}$

   C. There are three possible solutions to the system.

   D. The system has no solution.

5. Look at each focus and directrix. For which choice is the resulting parabola vertical? Select the correct answer.

   A. Focus $(0, 1)$, Directrix $x = -2$

   A. Focus $(5, -1)$, Directrix $x = \dfrac{1}{2}$

   C. Focus $(6, -3)$, Directrix $x = 2$

   D. Focus $(-4, -2)$, Directrix $y = -3$

6. Marcia shoots an arrow that hits a bull's–eye 80 feet away. Before hitting the bull's–eye, the arrow reaches a maximum height of 16 feet at the midway point, 40 feet. If the bull's–eye is considered to be at (80, 0), what function could represent the path of the arrow if x is the horizontal distance from Marcia and $h(x)$ represents the height of the arrow in relation to the horizontal distance?
(Lesson 3.2)

7. Consider the inequality $-4x^2 + x \geq 3$. What method should be used to most easily solve the inequality if you have a choice between taking the square root, completing the square, or factoring? Explain your reasoning, and then solve the equation. *(Lesson 4.4)*

★ **8.** Keille is building a rectangular pen for a pet rabbit. She can buy wire fencing in a roll of 40 ft or a roll of 80 ft. The graph shows the area of pens she can build with each type of roll.

A. Describe the function for an 80 ft roll of fencing as a transformation of the function for a 40 ft roll of fencing.

B. Is the largest pen Keille can build with an 80 ft roll of fencing twice as large as the largest pen she can build with a 40 ft roll of fencing? Explain.

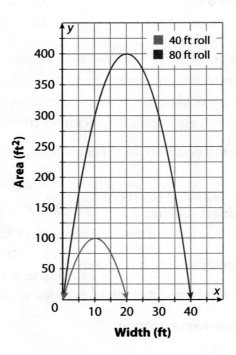

★★ **9.** **Biology** The spittlebug is the world's highest jumping animal relative to its body length of about 6 millimeters. The height h of a spittlebug's jump in millimeters can be model by the function $h(t) = -4000t^2 + 3000t$, where t is the time in seconds.

   A. What is the maximum height that the spittlebug will reach?

   B. What is the ratio of a spittlebug's maximum jumping height to its body length? In the best human jumpers, this ratio is about 1.38. Compare the ratio for spittlebugs with the ratio for the best human jumpers.

★★★**10.** **Safety** The light produced by high-pressure sodium vapor streetlamps for different energy usages is shown in the table.

High-Presure Sodium Vapor Streetlamps					
Energy Use (watts)	35	50	70	100	150
Light Output (lumens)	2250	4000	5800	9500	16,000

   A. Find a quadratic model for the light output with respect to energy use.

   B. Find a liner model for the light output with respect to energy use.

   C. Apply each model to estimate the light output in lumens of a 200-watt bulb.

   D. Which model gives the better estimate? Explain.

Toy Manufacturer A company is marketing a new toy. The function $s(p) = -50p^2 + 3000p$ models how the total sales s of the toy, in dollars, depends on the price p of the toy, in dollars.

a. Complete the square to write the function in vertex form.

b. Graph the function. Be sure to label the axes with the quantities they represent and indicate the axis scales by showing numbers for some grid lines.

c. What is the vertex of the graph? What does the vertex represent in this situation?

d. The model predicts that total sales will be $40,000 when the toy price is $20. At what other price does the model predict that the total sales will be $40,000? Use the symmetry of the graph to support your answer.

e. According to the model, at what nonzero price should the manufacturer expect to sell no toys? How can you determine this price using the graph?

UNIT 3

Polynomial Functions, Expressions, and Equations

MATH IN CAREERS

Statistician Statisticians use math to describe patterns and relationships. Statisticians design surveys and collect data, and rely on mathematical modeling and computational methods to analyze their findings. They use these findings and analyses to help solve problems in various fields, such as business, engineering, the sciences, and government.

If you are interested in a career as a statistician, you should study these mathematical subjects:
- Algebra
- Geometry
- Calculus
- Differential Equations
- Probability
- Statistics

Research other careers that require understanding and analyzing data. Check out the career activity at the end of the unit to find out how **Statisticians** use math.

Reading Start-Up

Vocabulary

Review Words

✔ coefficient *(coeficiente)*

✔ factor *(factor)*

✔ parameter *(parámetro)*

✔ real number *(número real)*

✔ term *(término)*

✔ transformation *(transformación)*

Preview Words

binomial *(binomio)*

cubic function *(función cúbica)*

monomial *(monomio)*

polynomial *(polinomio)*

root *(raíz)*

trinomial *(trinomio)*

Visualize Vocabulary

Use the review words. Copy and complete the chart.

_____?_____	one of the products that exactly divides a polynomial
_____?_____	a rational or irrational number
_____?_____	a number, variable, product, or quotient in an expression
_____?_____	one of the constants in a function or equation that may be changed
_____?_____	a change in the size, position, or shape of a figure or graph
_____?_____	a numerical factor in a term of an algebraic expression

Understand Vocabulary

To become familiar with some of the vocabulary terms in the module, consider the following. You may refer to the module, the glossary, or a dictionary.

1. A polynomial with two terms is a __?__.

2. A polynomial function of degree 3 is a __?__.

3. A __?__ of an equation is any value of the variable that makes the equation true.

Active Reading

Key-Term Fold Before beginning the unit, create a key-term fold to help you organize what you learn. Write a vocabulary term on each tab of the key-term fold. Under each tab, write the definition of the term and an example.

Polynomial Functions

Essential Question: How can polynomial functions help to solve real-world problems?

REAL WORLD VIDEO
Engineers who design roller coasters use mathematics, including polynomial functions, to model the shape of the track.

MODULE PERFORMANCE TASK PREVIEW

What's the Function of a Roller Coaster?

Nothing compares with riding a roller coaster. The thrill of a steep drop, the breathtaking speed, and the wind in your face make the ride unforgettable. How can a polynomial function model the path of a roller coaster? Hang on to your seat and let's find out!

Are (YOU) Ready?

Complete these exercises to review skills you will need for this chapter.

Classifying Polynomials

Example 1 Classify the polynomial $2x^4 + x^3 - 1$ by its degree and number of terms.

Because the greatest exponent is 4, this is a quartic polynomial.

Because the polynomial has three terms, it is a trinomial.

The polynomial $2x^4 + x^3 - 1$ is a quartic trinomial.

- Online Homework
- Hints and Help
- Extra Practice

Classify the polynomial by its degree and number of terms.

1. $3x^3$

2. $9x - 3y + 7$

3. $x^2 - 4$

Transforming Cubic Functions

Example 2 The graph of $f(x) = 0.5(x - 3)^3 + 2$ is transformed 4 units right and 5 units down. Write the new function.

The inflection point is $(3, 2)$. Its location after the transformation is $(3 + 4, 2 - 5)$, or $(7, -3)$.

After the transformation, the function is $f'(x) = 0.5(x - 7)^3 - 3$.

Write the new function after the given transformation.

4. $g(x) = 0.25(x - 6)^3 - 1$
10 units left, 7 units down

5. $h(x) = (x + 9)^3 - 5$
6 units right, 4 units up

6. $f(x) = -0.5(x + 8)^3 + 12$
1 unit left, 3 units up

6.1 Graphing Cubic Functions

Essential Question: How are the graphs of $f(x) = a(x - h)^3 + k$ and $f(x) = \left(\frac{1}{b}(x - h)\right)^3 + k$ related to the graph of $f(x) = x^3$?

 TEKS **A2.2.A** ...analyze key attributes such as domain, range, intercepts, symmetries, asymptotic behavior, and maximum and minimum given an interval. Also A2.6.A.

⊘ Explore 1 Graphing and Analyzing $f(x) = x^3$

You know that a quadratic function has the standard form $f(x) = ax^2 + bx + c$ where a, b, and c are real numbers and $a \neq 0$. Similarly, *a* **cubic function** has the standard form $f(x) = ax^3 + bx^2 + cx + d$ where a, b, c and d are all real numbers and $a \neq 0$. You can use the basic cubic function, $f(x) = x^3$, as the parent function for a family of cubic functions related through transformations of the graph of $f(x) = x^3$.

(A) Copy and complete the table, graph the ordered pairs, and then pass a smooth curve through the plotted points to obtain the graph of $f(x) = x^3$.

x	$y = x^3$
-2	
-1	
0	
1	
2	

(B) Use the graph to analyze the function Then copy and complete the table.

Attributes of $f(x) = x^3$	
Domain	$\mathbb{R}$
Range	
End behavior	As $x \to +\infty$, $f(x) \to$ ⬛.
	As $x \to -\infty$, $f(x) \to$ ⬛.
Zeros of the function	$x = 0$
Where the function has positive values	$x > 0$
Where the function has negative values	
Where the function is increasing	
Where the function is decreasing	The function never decreases.
Is the function even $\left(f(-x) = f(x)\right)$, odd $\left(f(-x) = -f(x)\right)$, or neither?	⬛ , because $(x)^3 =$ ⬛ .

Reflect

1. How would you characterize the rate of change of the function on the intervals $[-1, 0]$ and $[0, 1]$ compared with the rate of change on the intervals $[-2, -1]$ and $[1, 2]$? Explain.

2. A graph is said to be *symmetric about the origin* (and the origin is called the graph's *point of symmetry*) if for every point (x, y) on the graph, the point $(-x, -y)$ is also on the graph. Is the graph of $f(x) = x^3$ symmetric about the origin? Explain.

Explore 2 Predicting Transformations of the Graph of $f(x) = x^3$

You can apply familiar transformations to cubic functions. Check your predictions using a graphing calculator.

Ⓐ Predict the effect of the parameter h on the graph of $g(x) = (x - h)^3$ for each function.

a. The graph of $g(x) = (x - 2)^3$ is a translation of the graph of $f(x)$.

Is the translation right, up, left, or down 2 units?

b. The graph of $g(x) = (x + 2)^3$ is a translation of the graph of $f(x)$.

Is the translation right, up, left, or down 2 units?

Ⓑ Predict the effect of the parameter k on the graph of $g(x) = x^3 + k$ for each function.

a. The graph of $g(x) = x^3 + 2$ is a translation of the graph of $f(x)$.

Is the translation right, up, left, or down 2 units?

b. The graph of $g(x) = x^3 - 2$ is a translation of the graph of $f(x)$.

Is the translation right, up, left, or down 2 units?

Ⓒ Predict the effect of the parameter a on the graph of $g(x) = ax^3$ for each function.

a. The graph of $g(x) = 2x^3$ is a ▮▮▮ of the graph of $f(x)$ by a

factor of ▮▮▮ .

b. The graph of $g(x) = -\frac{1}{2}x^3$ is a ▮▮▮ of the graph of $f(x)$ by a

factor of ▮▮▮ as well as a reflection across the ▮▮▮ .

Ⓓ Predict the effect of the parameter b on the graph of $g(x) = \left(\frac{1}{b}x\right)^3$ for the following values of b.

a. The graph of $g(x) = \left(\frac{1}{2}x\right)^3$ is a [   ] of the graph of $f(x)$ by a factor of [   ].

b. The graph of $g(x) = (2x)^3$ is a [   ] of the graph of $f(x)$ by a factor of [   ].

c. The graph of $g(x) = \left(-\frac{1}{2}x\right)^3$ is a [   ] of the graph of $f(x)$ by a factor of [   ] as well as a [   ] across the [   ].

d. The graph of $g(x) = (-2x)^3$ is a [   ] of the graph of $f(x)$ by a factor of [   ] as well as a [   ] across the [   ].

Reflect

3. The graph of $g(x) = (-x)^3$ is a reflection of the graph of $f(x) = x^3$ across the y-axis, while the graph of $h(x) = -x^3$ is a reflection of the graph of $f(x) = x^3$ across the x-axis. If you graph $g(x)$ and $h(x)$ on a graphing calculator, what do you notice? Explain why this happens.

🖉 Explain 1 Graphing Combined Transformations of $f(x) = x^3$

When graphing transformations of $f(x) = x^3$, it helps to consider the effect of the transformations on the three reference points on the graph of $f(x)$: $(-1, -1)$, $(0, 0)$, and $(1,1)$. The table lists the three points and the corresponding points on the graph of $g(x) = a\left(\frac{1}{b}(x - h)\right)^3 + k$. Notice that the point $(0, 0)$, which is the point of symmetry for the graph of $f(x)$, is affected only by the parameters h and k. The other two reference points are affected by all four parameters.

$f(x) = x^3$		$g(x) = a\left(\dfrac{1}{b}(x - h)\right)^3 + k$	
x	y	x	y
-1	-1	$-b + h$	$-a + k$
0	0	h	k
1	1	$b + h$	$a + k$

Example 1 Identify the transformations of the graph of $f(x) = x^3$ that produce the graph of the given function $g(x)$. Then graph $g(x)$ on the same coordinate plane as the graph of $f(x)$ by applying the transformations to the reference points $(-1, -1)$, $(0, 0)$, and $(1, 1)$.

Ⓐ $g(x) = 2(x - 1)^3 - 1$

The transformations of the graph of $f(x)$ that produce the graph of $g(x)$ are:

- a vertical stretch by a factor of 2
- a translation of 1 unit to the right and 1 unit down

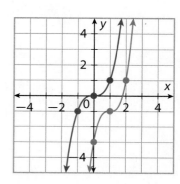

Note that the translation of 1 unit to the right affects only the *x*-coordinates of points on the graph of $f(x)$, while the vertical stretch by a factor of 2 and the translation of 1 unit down affect only the *y*-coordinates.

$f(x) = x^3$		$g(x) = 2(x-1)^3 - 1$	
x	*y*	*x*	*y*
-1	-1	$-1 + 1 = 0$	$2(-1) - 1 = -3$
0	0	$0 + 1 = 1$	$2(0) - 1 = -1$
1	1	$1 + 1 = 2$	$2(1) - 1 = 1$

Ⓑ $g(x) = \left(2(x+3)\right)^3 + 4$

The transformations of the graph of $f(x)$ that produce the graph of $g(x)$ are:

- a horizontal compression by a factor of $\frac{1}{2}$
- a translation of 3 units to the left and 4 units up

Note that the horizontal compression by a factor of $\frac{1}{2}$ and the translation of 3 units to the left affect only the *x*-coordinates of points on the graph of $f(x)$, while the translation of 4 units up affects only the *y*-coordinates.

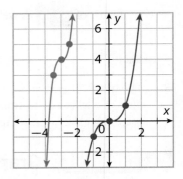

$f(x) = x^3$		$g(x) = \left(2(x+3)\right)^3 + 4$	
x	*y*	*x*	*y*
-1	-1	$\boxed{\frac{1}{2}}(-1) + \boxed{-3} = \boxed{-3\frac{1}{2}}$	$-1 + \boxed{4} = \boxed{3}$
0	0	$\boxed{\frac{1}{2}}(0) + \boxed{-3} = \boxed{-3}$	$0 + \boxed{4} = \boxed{4}$
1	1	$\boxed{\frac{1}{2}}(1) + \boxed{-3} = \boxed{-2\frac{1}{2}}$	$1 + \boxed{4} = \boxed{5}$

Your Turn

Identify the transformations of the graph of $f(x) = x^3$ that produce the graph of the given function $g(x)$. Then graph $g(x)$ on the same coordinate plane as the graph of $f(x)$ by applying the transformations to the reference points $(-1, -1)$, $(0, 0)$, and $(1, 1)$.

4. $g(x) = -\frac{1}{2}(x - 3)^3$

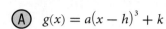

Explain 2 Writing Equations for Combined Transformations of $f(x) = x^3$

Given the graph of the transformed function $g(x) = a\left(\frac{1}{b}(x - h)\right)^3 + k$, you can determine the values of the parameters by using the same reference points that you used to graph $g(x)$ in the previous example.

Example 2 A general equation for a cubic function $g(x)$ is given along with the function's graph. Write a specific equation by identifying the values of the parameters from the reference points shown on the graph.

(A) $g(x) = a(x - h)^3 + k$

Identify the values of h and k from the point of symmetry.

$(h, k) = (2, 1)$, so $h = 2$ and $k = 1$.

Identify the value of a from either of the other two reference points.

The rightmost reference point has general coordinates $(h + 1, a + k)$. Substituting 2 for h and 1 for k and setting the general coordinates equal to the actual coordinates gives this result:

$(h + 1, a + k) = (3, a + 1) = (3, 4)$, so $a = 3$.

Write the function using the values of the parameters: $g(x) = 3(x - 2)^3 + 1$

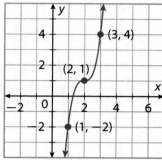

(B) $g(x) = \left(\frac{1}{b}x - h\right)^3 + k$

Identify the values of h and k from the point of symmetry.

$(h, k) = \left(-4, \boxed{1}\right)$, so $h = -4$ and $k = \boxed{1}$.

Identify the value of b from either of the other two reference points.

The rightmost reference point has general coordinates

$(b + h, 1 + k)$. Substituting -4 for h and 1 for k and setting the general coordinates equal to the actual coordinates gives this result:

$\left(b + h, 1 + \boxed{1}\right) = \left(b - 4, \boxed{2}\right) = (-3.5, 2)$, so $b = \boxed{0.5}$.

Write the function using the values of the parameters, and then simplify.

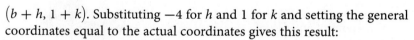

$$g(x) = \left(\frac{1}{\boxed{0.5}}\left(x - \boxed{-4}\right)\right)^3 + \boxed{1}$$

or

$$g(x) = \left(\boxed{2}\left(x + \boxed{4}\right)\right)^3 + \boxed{1}$$

A general equation for a cubic function $g(x)$ is given along with the function's graph. Write a specific equation by identifying the values of the parameters from the reference points shown on the graph.

5. $g(x) = a(x - h)^3 + k$

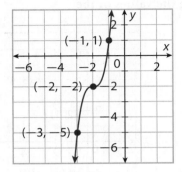

6. $g(x) = \left(\dfrac{1}{b}(x - h)\right)^3 + k$

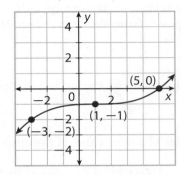

⚙ Explain 3 Modeling with a Transformation of $f(x) = x^3$

You may be able to model a real-world situation that involves volume with a cubic function. Sometimes mass may also be involved in the problem. Mass and volume are related through *density*, which is defined as an object's mass per unit volume. If an object has mass m and volume V, then its density d is $d = \dfrac{m}{V}$. You can rewrite the formula as $m = dV$ to express mass in terms of density and volume.

Example 3 Use a cubic function to model the situation, and graph the function using calculated values of the function. Then use the graph to obtain the indicated estimate.

(A) Estimate the length of an edge of a child's alphabet block (a cube) that has a mass of 23 g and is made from oak with a density of 0.72 g/cm³.

Let ℓ represent the length (in centimeters) of an edge of the block. Since the block is a cube, the volume V (in cubic centimeters) is $V(\ell) = \ell^3$. The mass m (in grams) of the block is $m(\ell) = 0.72 \cdot V(\ell) = 0.72\ell^3$. Make a table of values for this function.

Length (cm)	Mass (g)
0	0
1	0.72
2	5.76
3	19.44
4	46.08

Draw the graph of the mass function, recognizing that the graph is a vertical compression of the graph of the parent cubic function by a factor of 0.72. Then draw the horizontal line $m = 23$ and estimate the value of ℓ where the graphs intersect.

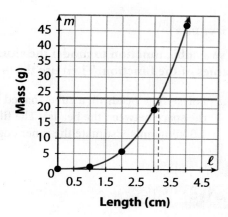

The graphs intersect where $\ell \approx 3.2$, so the edge length of the child's block is about 3.2 cm.

Ⓑ Estimate the radius of a steel ball bearing with a mass of 75 grams and a density of 7.82 g/cm³.

Let r represent the radius (in centimeters) of the ball bearing. The volume V (in cubic centimeters) of the ball bearing is $V(r) = \boxed{\frac{4}{3}\pi}\, r^3$. The mass m (in grams) of the ball bearing is $m(r) = 7.82 \cdot V(r) = \boxed{32.76}\, r^3$.

Radius (cm)	Mass (g)
0	0
0.5	4.10
1	32.76
1.5	110.57
2	262.08

Draw the graph of the mass function, recognizing that the graph is a vertical stretch of the graph of the parent cubic function by a factor of 7.82. Then draw the horizontal line $m = \boxed{75}$ and estimate the value of r where the graphs intersect.

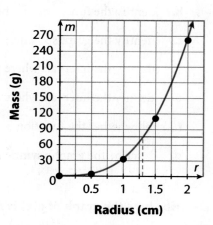

The graphs intersect where $r \approx \boxed{1.3}$, so the radius of the steel ball bearing is about 1.3 cm.

Reflect

7. **Discussion** Why is it important to plot multiple points on the graph of the volume function.

Your Turn

Use a cubic function to model the situation, and graph the function using calculated values of the function. Then use the graph to obtain the indicated estimate.

8. Polystyrene beads fill a cube-shaped box with an effective density of 0.00076 kg/cm³ (which accounts for the space between the beads). The filled box weighs 6 kilograms while the empty box had weighed 1.5 kilograms. Estimate the inner edge length of the box.

💬 Elaborate

9. Identify which transformations (stretches or compressions, reflections, and translations) of $f(x) = x^3$ change the following attributes of the function.

   a. End behavior

   b. Location of the point of symmetry

   c. Symmetry about a point

10. **Essential Question Check-In** Describe the transformations you must perform on the graph of $f(x) = x^3$ to obtain the graph of $f(x) = a(x - h)^3 + k$.

☆ Evaluate: Homework and Practice

- Online Homework
- Hints and Help
- Extra Practice

1. Graph the parent cubic function $f(x) = x^3$ and use the graph to answer each question.

   a. State the function's domain and range.

   b. Identify the function's end behavior.

   c. Identify the graph's x- and y-intercepts.

   d. Identify the intervals where the function has positive values and where it has negative values.

   e. Identify the intervals where the function is increasing and where it is decreasing.

   f. Tell whether the function is even, odd, or neither. Explain.

   g. Describe the graph's symmetry.

Describe how the graph of $g(x)$ is related to the graph of $f(x) = x^3$.

2. $g(x) = (x - 4)^3$

3. $g(x) = -5x^3$

4. $g(x) = x^3 + 2$

5. $g(x) = (3x)^3$

6. $g(x) = (x + 1)^3$

7. $g(x) = \frac{1}{4}x^3$

8. $g(x) = x^3 - 3$

9. $g(x) = \left(-\frac{2}{3}x\right)^3$

© Houghton Mifflin Harcourt Publishing Company

Identify the transformations of the graph of $f(x) = x^3$ that produce the graph of the given function $g(x)$. Then graph $g(x)$ on the same coordinate plane as the graph of $f(x)$ by applying the transformations to the reference points $(-1, -1)$, $(0, 0)$, and $(1, 1)$.

10. $g(x) = \left(\frac{1}{3}x\right)^3$

11. $g(x) = \frac{1}{3}x^3$

12. $g(x) = (x - 4)^3 - 3$

13. $g(x) = (x + 1)^3 + 2$

14. $g(x) = -2x^3 + 3$

15. $g(x) = \left(-2(x - 2)\right)^3$

16. $g(x) = -3(x + 1)^3 - 1$

17. $g(x) = \left(-\frac{1}{4}(x - 1)\right)^3 + 2$

A general equation for a cubic function $g(x)$ is given along with the function's graph. Write a specific equation by identifying the values of the parameters from the reference points shown on the graph.

18. $g(x) = \left(\frac{1}{b}(x - h)\right)^3 + k$

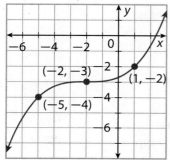

19. $g(x) = a(x - h)^3 + k$

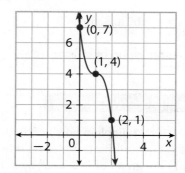

20. $g(x) = \left(\frac{1}{b}(x - h)\right)^3 + k$

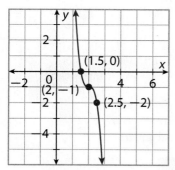

21. $g(x) = a(x - h)^3 + k$

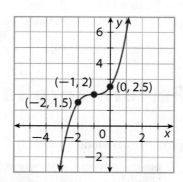

Use a cubic function to model the situation, and graph the function using calculated values of the function. Then use the graph to obtain the indicated estimate.

22. Estimate the edge length of a cube of gold with a mass of 1 kg. The density of gold is 0.019 kg/cm³.

23. A proposed design for a habitable Mars colony is a semispherical biodome used to maintain a breathable atmosphere for the colonists. Estimate the radius of the biodome if it is required to contain 5.5 billion cubic feet of air.

24. **Multiple Response** Identify the transformations of the graph of the parent cubic function that result in the graph of $g(x) = \left(3(x-2)\right)^3 + 1$.

   A. Horizontal stretch by a factor of 3

   B. Horizontal compression by a factor of $\frac{1}{3}$

   C. Vertical stretch by a factor of 3

   D. Vertical compression by a factor of $\frac{1}{3}$

   E. Translation 1 unit up

   F. Translation 1 unit down

   G. Translation 2 units left

   H. Translation 2 units right

H.O.T. Focus on Higher Order Thinking

25. **Justify Reasoning** Explain how horizontally stretching (or compressing) the graph of $f(x) = x^3$ by a factor of b can be equivalent to vertically compressing (or stretching) the graph of $f(x) = x^3$ by a factor of a.

26. **Critique Reasoning** A student reasoned that $g(x) = (x-h)^3$ can be rewritten as $g(x) = x^3 - h^3$, so a horizontal translation of h units is equivalent to a vertical translation of $-h^3$ units. Is the student correct? Explain.

Lesson Performance Task

Julio wants to purchase a spherical aquarium and fill it with salt water, which has an average density of 1.027 g/cm³. He has found a company that sells four sizes of spherical aquariums.

Aquarium Size	Diameter (cm)
Small	15
Medium	30
Large	45
Extra large	60

a. If the stand for Julio's aquarium will support a maximum of 50 kg, what is the largest size tank that he should buy? Explain your reasoning.

b. Julio's friend suggests that he could buy a larger tank if he uses fresh water, which has a density of 1.0 g/cm³. Do you agree with the friend? Why or why not?

6.2 Graphing Polynomial Functions

Resource Locker

Essential Question: How do you sketch the graph of a polynomial function in intercept form?

 TEKS A2.7.I Write the domain and range of a function in interval notation … Also A2.2.A

Explore 1 Investigating the End Behavior of the Graphs of Simple Polynomial Functions

Linear, quadratic, and cubic functions belong to a more general class of functions called *polynomial functions*, which are categorized by their degree. Linear functions are polynomial functions of degree 1, quadratic functions are polynomial functions of degree 2, and cubic functions are polynomial functions of degree 3. In general, a **polynomial function of degree n** has the standard form $p(x) = a_n x^n + a_{n-1} x^{n-1} + \ldots + a_2 x^2 + a_1 x + a_0$, where $a_n, a_{n-1}, \ldots, a_2, a_1$, and a_0 are real numbers called the *coefficients* of the expressions $a_n x^n, a_{n-1} x^{n-1}, \ldots, a_2 x^2, a_1 x$, and a_0, which are the *terms* of the polynomial function. (Note that the constant term, a_0, appears to have no power of x associated with it, but since $x^0 = 1$, you can write a_0 as $a_0 x^0$ and treat a_0 as the coefficient of the term.)

A polynomial function of degree 4 is called a *quartic* function, while a polynomial function of degree 5 is called a *quintic* function. After degree 5, polynomial functions are generally referred to by their degree, as in "a sixth-degree polynomial function."

Ⓐ Use a graphing calculator to graph the polynomial functions $f(x) = x$, $f(x) = x^2$, $f(x) = x^3$, $f(x) = x^4$, $f(x) = x^5$, and $f(x) = x^6$. Then use the graph of each function to determine the function's domain, range, and end behavior. (Use interval notation for the domain and range.)

Function	Domain	Range	End Behavior	
$f(x) = x$			As $x \to +\infty$, $f(x) \to$	.
			As $x \to -\infty$, $f(x) \to$	.
$f(x) = x^2$			As $x \to +\infty$, $f(x) \to$	.
			As $x \to -\infty$, $f(x) \to$	.
$f(x) = x^3$			As $x \to +\infty$, $f(x) \to$	.
			As $x \to -\infty$, $f(x) \to$	.
$f(x) = x^4$			As $x \to +\infty$, $f(x) \to$	.
			As $x \to -\infty$, $f(x) \to$	.
$f(x) = x^5$			As $x \to +\infty$, $f(x) \to$	.
			As $x \to -\infty$, $f(x) \to$	.
$f(x) = x^6$			As $x \to +\infty$, $f(x) \to$	.
			As $x \to -\infty$, $f(x) \to$	.

Ⓑ Use a graphing calculator to graph the polynomial functions $f(x) = -x$, $f(x) = -x^2$, $f(x) = -x^3$, $f(x) = -x^4$, $f(x) = -x^5$, and $f(x) = -x^6$. Then use the graph of each function to determine the function's domain, range, and end behavior. (Use interval notation for the domain and range.)

Function	Domain	Range	End Behavior
$f(x) = -x$			As $x \to +\infty$, $f(x) \to$ ▢ . As $x \to -\infty$, $f(x) \to$ ▢ .
$f(x) = -x^2$			As $x \to +\infty$, $f(x) \to$ ▢ . As $x \to -\infty$, $f(x) \to$ ▢ .
$f(x) = -x^3$			As $x \to +\infty$, $f(x) \to$ ▢ . As $x \to -\infty$, $f(x) \to$ ▢ .
$f(x) = -x^4$			As $x \to +\infty$, $f(x) \to$ ▢ . As $x \to -\infty$, $f(x) \to$ ▢ .
$f(x) = -x^5$			As $x \to +\infty$, $f(x) \to$ ▢ . As $x \to -\infty$, $f(x) \to$ ▢ .
$f(x) = -x^6$			As $x \to +\infty$, $f(x) \to$ ▢ . As $x \to -\infty$, $f(x) \to$ ▢ .

Reflect

1. How can you generalize the results of this Explore for $f(x) = x^n$ and $f(x) = -x^n$ where n is positive whole number?

⊘ Explore 2 Investigating the *x*-intercepts and Turning Points of the Graphs of Polynomial Functions

The cubic function $f(x) = x^3$ has three factors, all of which happen to be x. One or more of the x's can be replaced with other linear factors in x, such as $x - 2$, without changing the fact that the function is cubic. In general, a polynomial function of the form $p(x) = a(x - x_1)(x - x_2)...(x - x_n)$ where a, x_1, x_2,..., and x_n are real numbers (that are not necessarily distinct) has degree n where n is the number of variable factors.

The graph of $p(x) = a(x - x_1)(x - x_2)...(x - x_n)$ has x_1, x_2,..., and x_n as its x-intercepts, which is why the polynomial is said to be in *intercept form*. Since the graph of $p(x)$ intersects the x-axis only at its x-intercepts, the graph must move away from and then move back toward the x-axis between each pair of successive x-intercepts, which means that the graph has a *turning point* between those x-intercepts. Also, instead of crossing the x-axis at an x-intercept, the graph can be *tangent* to the x-axis, and the point of tangency becomes a turning point because the graph must move toward the x-axis and then away from it near the point of tangency.

The y-coordinate of each turning point is a maximum or minimum value of the function. A maximum or minimum value is called *global* or *absolute* if the function never takes on a value that is greater than the maximum or less than the minimum. On the other hand, a maximum or minimum value is called *local* or *relative* if the function does take on values that are greater than the maximum or less than the minimum somewhere outside an interval where the maximum or minimum value occurs.

(A) Use a graphing calculator to graph the cubic functions $f(x) = x^3$, $f(x) = x^2(x - 2)$, and $f(x) = x(x - 2)(x + 2)$. Then use the graph of each function to answer the questions in the table.

Function	$f(x) = x^3$	$f(x) = x^2(x - 2)$	$f(x) = x(x - 2)(x + 2)$
How many distinct factors does $f(x)$ have?			
What are the graph's x-intercepts?			
Is the graph tangent to the x-axis or does it cross the x-axis at each x-intercept?			
How many turning points does the graph have?			
How many global maximum values? How many local?			
How many global minimum values? How many local?			

(B) Use a graphing calculator to graph the quartic functions $f(x) = x^4$, $f(x) = x^3(x - 2)$, $f(x) = x^2(x - 2)(x + 2)$, and $f(x) = x(x - 2)(x + 2)(x + 3)$. Then use the graph of each function to answer the questions in the table.

Function	$f(x) = x^4$	$f(x) = x^3(x - 2)$	$f(x) = x^2(x - 2)$ $(x + 2)$	$f(x) = x(x - 2)$ $(x + 2)(x + 3)$
How many distinct factors?				
What are the x-intercepts?				
Tangent to or cross the x-axis at x-intercepts?				
How many turning points?				
How many global maximum values? How many local?				
How many global minimum values? How many local?				

Reflect

2. What determines how many x-intercepts the graph of a polynomial function in intercept form has?

3. What determines whether the graph of a polynomial function in intercept form crosses the x-axis or is tangent to it at an x-intercept?

4. Suppose you introduced a factor of -1 into each of the quartic functions in Step B. (For instance, $f(x) = x^4$ becomes $f(x) = -x^4$.) How would your answers to the questions about the functions and their graphs change?

Sketching the Graph of Polynomial Functions in Intercept Form

Given a polynomial function in intercept form, you can sketch the function's graph by using the end behavior, the *x*-intercepts, and the sign of the function values on intervals determined by the *x*-intercepts. The sign of the function values tells you whether the graph is above or below the *x*-axis on a particular interval. You can find the sign of the function values by determining the sign of each factor and recognizing what the sign of the product of those factors is.

Example 1 Sketch the graph of the polynomial function.

Ⓐ $f(x) = x(x + 2)(x - 3)$

Identify the end behavior. For the function $p(x) = a(x - x_1)(x - x_2)\ldots(x - x_n)$, the end behavior is determined by whether the degree n is even or odd and whether the constant factor a is positive or negative. For the given function $f(x)$, the degree is 3 and the constant factor a, which is 1, is positive, so $f(x)$ has the following end behavior:

As $x \to +\infty$, $f(x) \to +\infty$.

As $x \to -\infty$, $f(x) \to -\infty$.

Identify the graph's *x*-intercepts, and then use the sign of $f(x)$ on intervals determined by the *x*-intercepts to find where the graph is above the *x*-axis and where it's below the *x*-axis.

The *x*-intercepts are $x = 0$, $x = -2$, and $x = 3$. These three *x*-intercepts divide the *x*-axis into four intervals: $x < -2$, $-2 < x < 0$, $0 < x < 3$, and $x > 3$.

Interval	Sign of the Constant Factor	Sign of *x*	Sign of *x* + 2	Sign of *x* − 3	Sign of $f(x) = x(x + 2)(x - 3)$
$x < -2$	+	−	−	−	−
$-2 < x < 0$	+	−	+	−	+
$0 < x < 3$	+	+	+	−	−
$x > 3$	+	+	+	+	+

So, the graph of $f(x)$ is above the *x*-axis on the intervals $-2 < x < 0$ and $x > 3$, and it's below the *x*-axis on the intervals $x < -2$ and $0 < x < 3$.

Sketch the graph.

While you should be precise about where the graph crosses the *x*-axis, you do not need to be precise about the *y*-coordinates of points on the graph that aren't on the *x*-axis. Your sketch should simply show where the graph lies above the *x*-axis and where it lies below the *x*-axis.

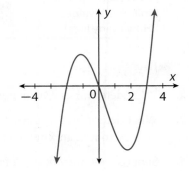

Ⓑ $f(x) = -(x-4)(x-1)(x+1)(x+2)$

Identify the end behavior.

As $x \rightarrow +\infty$, $f(x) \rightarrow \boxed{-\infty}$.

As $x \rightarrow -\infty$, $f(x) \rightarrow \boxed{-\infty}$.

Identify the graph's x-intercepts, and then use the sign of $f(x)$ on intervals determined by the x-intercepts to find where the graph is above the x-axis and where it's below the x-axis.

The x-intercepts are $x = \boxed{-2}$, $x = \boxed{-1}$, $x = \boxed{1}$, $x = \boxed{4}$.

Interval	Sign of the Constant Factor	Sign of $x-4$	Sign of $x-1$	Sign of $x+1$	Sign of $x+2$	Sign of $f(x) = -(x-4)(x-1)(x+1)(x+2)$
$x < \boxed{-2}$	−	−	−	−	−	−
$\boxed{-2} < x < \boxed{-1}$	−	−	−	−	+	+
$\boxed{-1} < x < \boxed{1}$	−	−	+	+	+	−
$\boxed{1} < x < \boxed{4}$	−	−	+	+	+	+
$x > \boxed{4}$	−	+	+	+	+	−

So, the graph of $f(x)$ is above the x-axis on the intervals

$\boxed{-2} < x < \boxed{-1}$ and $\boxed{1} < x < \boxed{4}$, and

it's below the x-axis on the intervals $x < \boxed{-2}$, $\boxed{-1} < x < \boxed{1}$,

and $x > \boxed{4}$.

Sketch the graph.

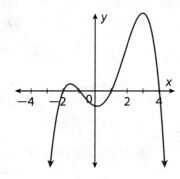

Sketch the graph of the polynomial function.

5. $f(x) = -x^2(x-4)$

⚙ Explain 2 Modeling with a Polynomial Function

You can use cubic functions to model real-world situations. For example, you find the volume of a box (a rectangular prism) by multiplying the length, width, and height. If each dimension of the box is given in terms of x, then the volume is a cubic function of x.

To create an open-top box out of a sheet of cardboard that is 9 inches long and 5 inches wide, you make a square flap of side length x inches in each corner by cutting along one of the flap's sides and folding along the other side. (In the first diagram, a solid line segment in the interior of the rectangle indicates a cut, while a dashed line segment indicates a fold.) After you fold up the four sides of the box (see the second diagram), you glue each flap to the side it overlaps. To the nearest tenth, find the value of x that maximizes the volume of the box.

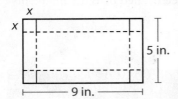

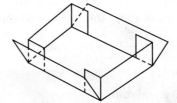

 Analyze Information

Identify the important information.

A square flap of side length x inches is made in each corner of a rectangular sheet of cardboard. The sheet of cardboard measures 9 inches by 5 inches.

 Formulate a Plan

Find the dimensions of the box once the flaps have been made and the sides have been folded up. Create a volume function for the box, graph the function on a graphing calculator, and use the graph to find the value of x that maximizes the volume.

 Solve

1. Write expressions for the dimensions of the box.

    Length of box: $9 - \boxed{2x}$

    Width of box: $5 - \boxed{2x}$

    Height of box: $\boxed{x}$

2. Write the volume function and determine its domain.

    $V(x) = \left(9 - \boxed{2x}\right)\left(5 - \boxed{2x}\right)\boxed{x}$

    Because the length, width, and height of the box must all be positive, the volume function's domain is determined by the following three constraints:

    $9 - 2x > 0$, or $x < \boxed{4.5}$

    $5 - 2x > 0$, or $x < \boxed{2.5}$

    $x > 0$

    Taken together, these constraints give a domain of $0 < x < \boxed{2.5}$.

3. Use a graphing calculator to graph the volume function on its domain.

Adjust the viewing window so you can see the maximum. From the graphing calculator's **CALC** menu, select **4: maximum** to locate the point where the maximum value occurs.

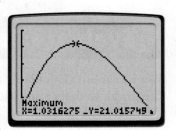

So, $V(x) \approx 21.0$ when $x \approx \boxed{1.0}$, which means that the box has a maximum volume of about 21 cubic inches when square flaps with a side length of 1 inch are made in the corners of the sheet of cardboard.

Justify and Evaluate

Making square flaps with a side length of 1 inch means that the box will be 7 inches long, 3 inches wide, and 1 inch high, so the volume is 21 cubic inches. As a check on this result, consider making square flaps with a side length of 0.9 inch and 1.1 inches:

$V(0.9) = (9 - 1.8)(5 - 1.8)(0.9) = \boxed{20.736}$

$V(1.1) = (9 - 2.2)(5 - 2.2)(1.1) = \boxed{20.944}$

Both volumes are slightly less than 21 cubic inches, which suggests that 21 cubic inches is the maximum volume.

Reflect

6. **Discussion** Although the volume function has three constraints on its domain, the domain involves only two of them. Why?

Your Turn

7. To create an open-top box out of a sheet of cardboard that is 25 inches long and 13 inches wide, you make a square flap of side length x inches in each corner by cutting along one of the flap's sides and folding along the other. (In the diagram, a solid line segment in the interior of the rectangle indicates a cut, while a dashed line segment indicates a fold.) Once you fold up the four sides of the box, you glue each flap to the side it overlaps. To the nearest tenth, find the value of x that maximizes the volume of the box.

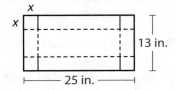

Elaborate

8. Compare and contrast the domain, range, and end behavior of $f(x) = x^n$ when n is even and when n is odd.

9. **Essential Question Check-In** For a polynomial function in intercept form, why is the constant factor important when graphing the function?

Use a graphing calculator to graph the polynomial function. Then use the graph to determine the function's domain, range, and end behavior. (Use interval notation for the domain and range.)

1. $f(x) = x^7$

2. $f(x) = -x^9$

3. $f(x) = x^{10}$

4. $f(x) = -x^8$

Use a graphing calculator to graph the function. Then use the graph to determine the number of turning points and the number and type (global or local) of any maximum or minimum values.

5. $f(x) = x(x + 1)(x + 3)$

6. $f(x) = (x + 1)^2(x - 1)(x - 2)$

7. $f(x) = -x(x - 2)^2$

8. $f(x) = -(x - 1)(x + 2)^3$

Sketch the graph the polynomial function.

9. $f(x) = x^2(x - 2)$

10. $f(x) = -(x + 1)(x - 2)(x - 3)$

11. $f(x) = x(x + 2)^2(x - 1)$

12. To create an open-top box out of a sheet of cardboard that is 6 inches long and 3 inches wide, you make a square flap of side length x inches in each corner by cutting along one of the flap's sides and folding along the other. Once you fold up the four sides of the box, you glue each flap to the side it overlaps. To the nearest tenth, find the value of x that maximizes the volume of the box.

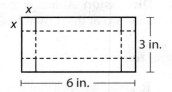

13. The template shows how to create a box from a square sheet of cardboard that has a side length of 36 inches. In the template, solid line segments indicate cuts, dashed line segments indicate folds, and grayed rectangles indicate pieces removed. The vertical strip that is 2 inches wide on the left side of the template is a flap that will be glued to the side of the box that it overlaps when the box is folded up. The horizontal strips that are $\frac{x}{2}$ inches wide at the top and bottom of the template are also flaps that will overlap to form the top and bottom of the box when the box is folded up. Write a volume function for the box in terms of x only. (You will need to determine a relationship between x and y first.) Then, to the nearest tenth, find the dimensions of the box with maximum volume

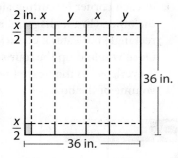

Write a cubic function in intercept form for the given graph, whose x-intercepts are integers. Assume that the constant factor a is either 1 or -1.

14.

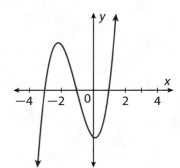

15.

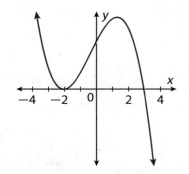

Write a quartic function in intercept form for the given graph, whose x-intercepts are integers. Assume that the constant factor a is either 1 or -1.

16.

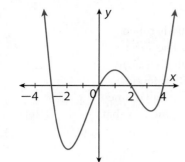

17.

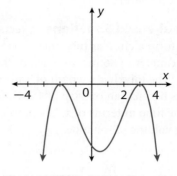

18. Multiple Response Identify all statements that apply to the graph of $f(x) = (x - 1)^2(x + 2)$.

A. The x-intercepts are $x = 1$ and $x = -2$.

B. The x-intercepts are $x = -1$ and $x = 2$.

C. The graph crosses the x-axis at $x = 1$ and is tangent to the x-axis at $x = -2$.

D. The graph crosses the x-axis at $x = -1$ and is tangent to the x-axis at $x = 2$.

E. The graph is tangent to the x-axis at $x = 1$ and crosses the x-axis at $x = -2$.

F. The graph is tangent to the x-axis at $x = -1$ and crosses the x-axis at $x = 2$.

G. A local minimum occurs on the interval $-2 < x < 1$, and a local maximum occurs at $x = 1$.

H. A local maximum occurs on the interval $-2 < x < 1$, and a local minimum occurs at $x = 1$.

I. A local minimum occurs on the interval $-1 < x < 2$, and a local maximum occurs at $x = 2$.

J. A local maximum occurs on the interval $-1 < x < 2$, and a local minimum occurs at $x = 2$.

H.O.T. Focus on Higher Order Thinking

19. Explain the Error A student was asked to sketch the graph of the function $f(x) = x^2(x - 3)$. Describe what the student did wrong. Then sketch the correct graph.

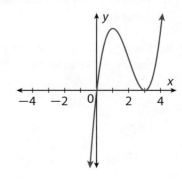

20. Make a Prediction Knowing the characteristics of the graphs of cubic and quartic functions in intercept form, sketch the graph of the quintic function $f(x) = x^2(x + 2)(x - 2)^2$.

21. Represent Real-World Situations A rectangular piece of sheet metal is rolled and riveted to form a circular tube that is open at both ends, as shown. The sheet metal has a perimeter of 36 inches. Each of the two sides of the rectangle that form the two ends of the tube has a length of x inches, and the tube has a circumference of $x - 1$ inches because an overlap of 1 inch is needed for the rivets. Write a volume function for the tube in terms of x. Then, to the nearest tenth, find the value of x that maximizes the volume of the tube.

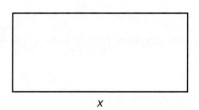

x

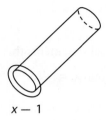

$x - 1$

Lesson Performance Task

The template shows how to create a box with a lid from a sheet of card stock that is 10 inches wide and 24 inches long. In the template, solid line segments indicate cuts, and dashed line segments indicate folds. The square flaps, each with a side length of x inches, are glued to the sides they overlap when the box is folded up. The box has a bottom and four upright sides. The lid, which is attached to one of the upright sides, has three upright sides of its own. Assume that the three sides of the lid can be tucked inside the box when the lid is closed.

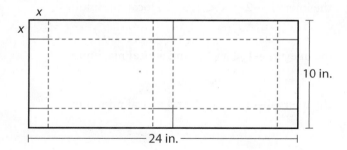

x

x

10 in.

24 in.

a. Write a polynomial function that represents the volume of the box, and state its domain.

b. Use a graphing calculator to find the value of x that will produce the box with maximum volume. What are the dimensions of that box? Lesson Performance Task

© Houghton Mifflin Harcourt Publishing Company

Polynomial Functions

Essential Question: How can polynomial functions help to solve real-world problems?

KEY EXAMPLE (Lesson 6.1)

Identify the transformations of the graph $f(x) = x^3$ that produce the graph of the function $g(x) = \frac{1}{3}(x + 2)^3$. Then create a table with the corresponding input and output values.

- a vertical compression by a factor of $\frac{1}{3}$
- a translation of 2 units to the left

x	$f(x) = x^3$	$g(x) = \frac{1}{3}(x + 2)^3$
-1	-1	$\frac{1}{3}(-1 + 2)^3 = \frac{1}{3}$
0	0	$\frac{1}{3}(0 + 2)^3 = \frac{8}{3}$
1	1	$\frac{1}{3}(1 + 2)^3 = 9$

KEY EXAMPLE (Lesson 6.2)

Use a graphing calculator to graph $g(x) = x(x - 2)^2 (x + 3)$. Then use the graph to determine the number of turning points and minimums or maximums.

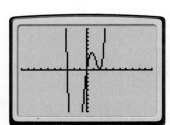

According to the graph, there are three turning points, one local maximum, one local minimum, and one global minimum.

Identify the transformations of the graph $f(x) = x^3$ that produce the graph of the function. *(Lesson 6.1)*

1. $g(x) = \left(-\frac{1}{4}(x+2)\right)^3 + 3$

2. $h(x) = \frac{1}{3}(x-4)^3$

Use the graphing calculator to graph each function, then use the graph to determine the number of turning points, maximums, and minimums. *(Lesson 6.2)*

3. $s(x) = x(x+2)(x+1)^2$

4. $h(x) = x^2(x-3)(x+2)(x-2)$

7. Write a real world situation that could be modeled by the equation $V(w) = w(5w)(3w)$. *(Lesson 6.2)*

MODULE PERFORMANCE TASK

What's the Function of a Roller Coaster?

An engineer is designing part of a roller coaster track that can be modeled by the polynomial function

$$f(x) = 2.0 \times 10^{-6}x^4 - 0.0011x^3 + 0.195x^2 - 12.25x + 250$$

where $f(x)$ is the height in feet of a roller coaster car above ground level, and x is the horizontal distance in feet. For this section of track, the domain is $0 \le x \le 250$.

The factored form of this function is

$$f(x) = 2.0 \times 10^{-6}(x-200)(x-250)(x-50)^2.$$

Describe the experience of a rider who is riding a roller coaster on this track.

Be sure to write down all your data and assumptions. Then use graphs, numbers, words, or algebra to explain how you reached your conclusion.

(Ready) to Go On?

6.1–6.2 Polynomial Functions

• Online Homework
• Hints and Help
• Extra Practice

Identify the transformations of the graph of $f(x) = x^3$ that produce the graph of $g(x) = -\frac{1}{4}(x + 4)^3$. Apply the transformations to the reference points $(-1, -1)$, $(0, 0)$, and $(1, 1)$ *(Lesson 6.1)*

1. Changes to x.

2. Changes to y.

3. Apply the transformations using the changes to x and y.

$f(x) = x^3$		$g(x) = -\frac{1}{4}(x + 4)^3$	
x	y	x	y

Graph the given function on your graphing calculator. Use the graph to state the number of turning points in the graph, and the x-intercepts. *(Lesson 6.2)*

4. $g(x) = x^2(x - 3)$

5. $h(x) = (x - 4)(x - 3)(x + 2)^2$

ESSENTIAL QUESTION

6. Give a real world example of a cubic function. *(Lesson 6.1)*

Assessment Readiness

1. Which function, when graphed, has an inflection point that is above and to the left of the inflection point of $f(x) = (x - 3)^3 + 5$?

   A. $y = (x + 6)^3 + 2$

   B. $y = -3x^3 + 2$

   C. $y = -(x - 1)^3 + 7$

   D. $y = (x - 5)^3$

2. How many turning points are there in the graph of $h(x) = x(x - 1)(x + 3)^3$?

   A. 2

   B. 3

   C. 4

   D. 6

3. What is the solution or solutions of the system of equations $\begin{cases} y = x^2 - 5 \\ y = 3x - 5 \end{cases}$?

   A. $(5, 10)$

   B. $(-3, 4), (2, 1)$

   C. $(0, -5), (3, 4)$

   D. $(2, -1)$

4. What are the x-intercepts of the graph of $y = x^4 - 81$?

   A. -81

   B. $9, -9$

   C. $3, -3$

   D. $9, 3, -3, -9$

5. An ottoman shaped like a rectangular prism has a length of x, a width two inches shorter than the length, and a height two inches taller than the length. Write the function that represents the volume, then find the length, width, and height of the ottoman if the volume is 5760 in^3.

Polynomials

Essential Question: How can you use polynomials to solve real-world problems?

REAL WORLD VIDEO
Meteorologists use mathematics and computer models to analyze climate patterns and forecast weather. For example, polynomial functions can be used to model temperature patterns.

MODULE PERFORMANCE TASK PREVIEW
What's the Temperature?

The weather is always a topic for conversation. Is it hot or cold outside? Is it T-shirt and shorts weather, or should you bundle up? What were the high and low temperatures for a particular day? You might suspect that the outdoor temperature follows a pattern. How can you use a polynomial to model the temperature? Let's find out!

Are (YOU) Ready?

Complete these exercises to review skills you will need for this chapter.

Adding and Subtracting Polynomials

Example 1

Subtract.

$$\left(7a^3 - 4a^2 + 11\right) - \left(3a^2 - 2a + 5\right)$$

$$7a^3 - 4a^2 + 11 - 3a^2 + 2a - 5 \qquad \textit{Multiply by } -1.$$

$$7a^3 - 7a^2 + 2a + 5 \qquad \textit{Combine like terms.}$$

- Online Homework
- Hints and Help
- Extra Practice

Add or subtract the polynomials.

1. $\left(m^5 + 4m^2 + 6\right) - \left(3m^5 - 8m^2\right)$

2. $\left(k^2 + 3k + 1\right) + \left(k^2 - 8\right)$

Algebraic Expressions

Example 2

Simplify the expression $5x^3 - 10x^2 + x^3 + 10$.

$$6x^3 - 10x^2 + 10 \qquad \textit{Combine like terms.}$$

Simplify each expression.

3. $6x - 2x^2 - 2x$

4. $(5x)(2x^2) - x^2$

5. $4(2x - 3y) + 2(x + y)$

Multiplying Polynomials

Example 3

Multiply. $(2a - b)(a + ab + b)$

$$(2a - b)(a + ab + b) = 2a(a + ab + b) - b(a + ab + b)$$

$$= 2a \cdot a + 2a \cdot ab + 2a \cdot b - b \cdot a - b \cdot ab - b \cdot b$$

$$= 2a^2 + 2a^2b + 2ab - ab - ab^2 - b^2$$

$$= 2a^2 + 2a^2b + ab - ab^2 - b^2$$

Multiply the polynomials.

6. $\left(x^2 - 4\right)(x + y)$

7. $(3m + 2)\left(3m^2 - 2m + 1\right)$

7.1 Adding and Subtracting Polynomials

Essential Question: How do you add or subtract two polynomials, and what type of expression is the result?

 TEKS **A2.7.B** Add, subtract…polynomials.

Explore   Identifying and Analyzing Monomials and Polynomials

A polynomial function of degree n has the *standard form* $p(x) = a_n x^n + a_{n-1} x^{n-1} + \ldots + a_2 x^2 + a_1 x + a_0$, where $a_n, a_{n-1}, \ldots, a_2, a_1,$ and a_0 are real numbers. The expression $a_n x^n + a_{n-1} x^{n-1} + \ldots a_2 x^2 + a_1 x + a_0$ is called a **polynomial**, and each term of a polynomial is called a **monomial**. A monomial is the product of a number and one or more variables with whole-number exponents. A polynomial is a monomial or a sum of monomials. The *degree of a monomial* is the sum of the exponents of the variables, and the *degree of a polynomial* is the degree of the monomial term with the greatest degree. The *leading coefficient* of a polynomial is the coefficient of the term with the greatest degree.

(A) Identify the monomials: x^3, $y + 3y^2 - 5y^3 + 10$, $a^2 bc^{12}$, 76

Monomials: [ ]

Not monomials: [ ]

(B) Identify the degree of each monomial.

Monomial	x^3	$a^2 bc^{12}$	76
Degree			

(C) Identify the terms of the polynomial $y + 3y^2 - 5y^3 + 10$. [ ]

(D) Identify the coefficient of each term.

Term	y	$3y^2$	$-5y^3$	10
Coefficient				

(E) Identify the degree of each term.

Term	y	$3y^2$	$-5y^3$	10
Degree				

(F) Write the polynomial in standard form. [ ]

(G) What is the leading coefficient of the polynomial? [ ]

1. **Discussion** How can you find the degree of a polynomial with multiple variables in each term?

🔑 Explain 1 Adding Polynomials

To add polynomials, combine like terms.

Example 1 Add the polynomials.

Ⓐ $\left(4x^2 - x^3 + 2 + 5x^4\right) + \left(-x + 6x^2 + 3x^4\right)$

$5x^4$	$-x^3$	$+4x^2$		$+2$	Write in standard form.

$$\begin{array}{ccccc} 5x^4 & -x^3 & +4x^2 & & +2 \\ +3x^4 & & +6x^2 & -x & \\ \hline 8x^4 & -x^3 & +10x^2 & -x & +2 \end{array}$$

Write in standard form.
Align like terms.
Add.

Ⓑ $\left(10x - 18x^3 + 6x^4 - 2\right) + \left(-7x^4 + 5 + x + 2x^3\right)$

$\left(6x^4 - 18x^3 + 10x - 2\right) + \left(-7x^4 + 2x^3 + x + 5\right)$ Write in standard form.

$= \left(6x^4 - \boxed{7x^4}\right) + \left(\boxed{-18x^3} + 2x^3\right) + \left(\boxed{10x} + x\right) + \left(-2 + \boxed{5}\right)$ Group like terms.

$= \boxed{-x^4} - 16x^3 + \boxed{11x} + 3$ Add.

Reflect

2. Is the sum of two polynomials always a polynomial? Explain.

Your Turn

Add the polynomials.

3. $\left(17x^4 + 8x^2 - 9x^7 + 4 - 2x^3\right) + \left(11x^3 - 8x^2 + 12\right)$

4. $\left(-8x + 3x^{11} + x^6\right) + \left(4x^4 - x + 17\right)$

🔑 Explain 2 Subtracting Polynomials

To subtract polynomials, combine like terms.

Example 2 Subtract the polynomials.

Ⓐ $\left(12x^3 + 5x - 8x^2 + 19\right) - \left(6x^2 - 9x + 3 - 18x^3\right)$

Write in standard form.
Align like terms and add the opposite.
Add.

$$\begin{array}{cccc} 12x^3 & -8x^2 & +5x & +19 \\ +18x^3 & -6x^2 & +9x & -3 \\ \hline 30x^3 & -14x^2 & +14x & +16 \end{array}$$

(B) $\left(-4x^2 + 8x^3 + 19 - 5x^5\right) - \left(9 + 2x^2 + 10x^5\right)$

Write in standard form and add the opposite.

$\left(-5x^5 + 8x^3 - 4x^2 + 19\right) + \left(-10x^5 - 2x^2 - 9\right)$

Group like terms

$= \left(-5x^5 - \boxed{10x^5}\right) + \left(\boxed{8x^3}\right) + \left(\boxed{-4x^2} - 2x^2\right) + \left(\boxed{19} - 9\right)$

Add

$= \boxed{-15x^5} + 8x^3 - \boxed{6x^2} + 10$

Reflect

5. Is the difference of two polynomials always a polynomial? Explain.

Your Turn

Subtract the polynomials.

6. $\left(23x^7 - 9x^4 + 1\right) - \left(-9x^4 + 6x^2 - 31\right)$

7. $\left(7x^3 + 13x - 8x^5 + 20x^2\right) - \left(-2x^5 + 9x^2\right)$

🎸 Explain 3   Modeling with Polynomial Addition and Subtraction

Polynomial functions can be used to model real-world quantities. If two polynomial functions model quantities that are two parts of a whole, the functions can be added to find a function that models the quantity as a whole. If the polynomial function for the whole and a polynomial function for a part are given, subtraction can be used to find the polynomial function that models the other part of the whole.

Example 3   **Find the polynomial that models the problem and use it to estimate the quantity.**

(A) The data from the U.S. Census Bureau for 2005–2009 shows that the number of male students enrolled in high school in the United States can be modeled by the function $M(x) = -10.4x^3 + 74.2x^2 - 3.4x + 8320.2$, where x is the number of years after 2005 and $M(x)$ is the number of male students in thousands. The number of female students enrolled in high school in the United States can be modeled by the function $F(x) = -13.8x^3 + 55.3x^2 + 141x + 7880$, where x is the number of years after 2005 and $F(x)$ is the number of female students in thousands. Estimate the total number of students enrolled in high school in the United States in 2009.

In the equation $T(x) = M(x) + F(x)$, $T(x)$ is the total number of students in thousands.

Add the polynomials.

$\left(-10.4x^3 + 74.2x^2 - 3.4x + 8320.2\right) + \left(-13.8x^3 + 55.3x^3 + 141x + 7880\right)$

$= \left(-10.4x^3 - 13.8x^3\right) + \left(74.2x^2 + 55.3x^2\right) + \left(-3.4x + 141x\right) + \left(8320.2 + 7880\right)$

$= -24.2x^3 + 129.5x^2 + 137.6x + 16{,}200.2$

The year 2009 is 4 years after 2005, so substitute 4 for x.

$-24.2(4)^3 + 129.5(4)^2 + 137.6(4) + 16{,}200.2 \approx 17{,}274$

About 17,274 thousand students were enrolled in high school in the United States in 2009.

(B) The data from the U.S. Census Bureau for 2000–2010 shows that the total number of overseas travelers visiting New York and Florida can be modeled by the function $T(x) = 41.5x^3 - 689.1x^2 + 4323.3x + 2796.6$, where x is the number of years after 2000 and $T(x)$ is the total number of travelers in thousands. The number of overseas travelers visiting New York can be modeled by the function $N(x) = -41.6x^3 + 560.9x^2 - 1632.7x + 6837.4$, where x is the number of years after 2000 and $N(x)$ is the number of travelers in thousands. Estimate the total number of overseas travelers to Florida in 2008.

In the equation $F(x) = T(x)\ \boxed{-}\ N(x)$, $F(x)$ is the number of travelers to Florida in thousands.

Subtract the polynomials.

$$\left(41.5x^3 - 689.1x^2 + 4323.3x + 2796.6\right)\ \boxed{-}\ \left(-41.6x^3 + 560.9x^2 - 1632.7x + 6837.4\right)$$

$$= \left(41.5x^3 - 689.1x^2 + 4323.3x + 2796.6\right) + \left(41.6x^3 - 560.9x^2 + 1632.7x - 6837.4\right)$$

$$= \left(41.5x^3 + \boxed{41.6x^3}\right) + \left(\boxed{-689.1x^2} - 560.9x^2\right) + \left(\boxed{4323.3x} + 1632.7x\right) + \left(2796.6 - \boxed{6837.4}\right)$$

$$= \boxed{83.1}\ x^3 - \boxed{1250}\ x^2 + \boxed{5956}\ x - \boxed{4040.8}$$

The year 2008 is 8 years after 2000, so substitute $\boxed{8}$ for x.

$83.1(8)^3 - 1250(8)^2 + 5956(8) - 4040.8 \approx \boxed{6154}$

About $\boxed{6154}$ thousand overseas travelers visited Florida in 2008.

Your Turn

8. According to the data from the U.S. Census Bureau for 1990–2009, the number of commercially owned automobiles in the United States can be modeled by the function $A(x) = 1.4x^3 - 130.6x^2 + 1831.3x + 128,141$, where x is the number of years after 1990 and $A(x)$ is the number of automobiles in thousands. The number of privately-owned automobiles in the United States can be modeled by the function $P(x) = -x^3 + 24.9x^2 - 177.9x + 1709.5$, where x is the number of years after 1990 and $P(x)$ is the number of automobiles in thousands. Estimate the total number of automobiles owned in 2005.

💬 Elaborate

9. How is the degree of a polynomial related to the degrees of the monomials that comprise the polynomial?

10. How is polynomial subtraction based on polynomial addition?

11. How would you find the model for a whole if you have polynomial functions that are models for the two distinct parts that make up that whole?

12. **Essential Question Check-In** What is the result of adding or subtracting polynomials?

⭐ Evaluate: Homework and Practice

1. Write the polynomial $-23x^7 + x^9 - 6x^3 + 10 + 2x^2$ in standard form, and then identify the degree and leading coefficient.

Add the polynomials.

2. $(82x^8 + 21x^2 - 6) + (18x + 7x^8 - 42x^2 + 3)$

3. $(15x - 121x^{12} + x^9 - x^7 + 3x^2) + (x^7 - 68x^2 - x^9)$

4. $(16 - x^2) + (-18x^2 + 7x^5 - 10x^4 + 5)$

5. $(x + 1 - 3x^2) + (8x - 21x^2 + 1)$

6. $(64 + x^3 - 8x^2) + (7x + 3 - x^2) + (19x^2 - 7x - 2)$

7. $(x^4 - 7x^3 + 2 - x) + (2x^3 - 3) + (1 - 5x^3 - x^4 + x)$

Subtract the polynomials.

8. $(-2x + 23x^5 + 11) - (5 - 9x^3 + x)$

9. $(7x^3 + 68x^4 - 14x + 1) - (-10x^3 + 8x + 23)$

10. $(57x^{18} - x^2) - (6x - 71x^3 + 5x^2 + 2)$

11. $(9x - 12x^3) - (5x^3 + 7x - 2)$

12. $(3x^5 - 9) - (11 + 13x^2 - x^4) - (10x^2 + x^4)$

13. $(10x^2 - x + 4) - (5x + 7) + (6x - 11)$

Find the polynomial that models the problem and use it to estimate the quantity.

14. A rectangle has a length of x and a width of $5x^3 + 4 - x^2$. Find the perimeter of the rectangle when the length is 5 feet.

15. A rectangle has a perimeter of $6x^3 + 9x^2 - 10x + 5$ and a length of x. Find the width of the rectangle when the length is 21 inches.

16. Cho is making a garden, where the length is x feet and the width is $4x - 1$ feet. He wants to add garden stones around the perimeter of the garden once he is done. If the garden is 4 feet long, how many feet will Cho need to cover with garden stones?

17. Employment The data from the U.S. Census Bureau for 1980–2010 shows that the median weekly earnings of full-time male employees who have at least a bachelor's degree can be modeled by the function $M(x) = 0.009x^3 - 0.29x^2 + 30.7x + 439.6$, where x is the number of years after 1980 and $M(x)$ is the median weekly earnings in dollars. The median weekly earnings of all full-time employees who have at least a bachelor's degree can be modeled by the function $T(x) = 0.012x^3 - 0.46x^2 + 56.1x + 732.3$, where x is the number of years after 1980 and $T(x)$ is the median weekly earnings in dollars. Estimate the median weekly earnings of a full-time female employee with at least a bachelor's degree in 2010.

18. Business From data gathered in the period 2008–2012, the yearly amount of U.S. exports can be modeled by the function $E(x) = -228x^3 + 2552.8x^2 - 6098.5x + 11,425.8$, where x is the number of years after 2008 and $E(x)$ is the amount of exports in billions of dollars. The yearly amount of U.S. imports can be modeled by the function $l(x) = -400.4x^3 + 3954.4x^2 - 11,128.8x + 17,749.6$, where x is the number of years after 2008 and $l(x)$ is the amount of imports in billions of dollars. Estimate the total amount the United States imported and exported in 2012.

19. Education From data gathered in the period 1970–2010, the number of full-time students enrolled in a degree-granting institution can be modeled by the function $F(x) = 8.7x^3 - 213.3x^2 + 2015.5x + 3874.9$, where x is the number of years after 1970 and $F(x)$ is the number of students in thousands. The number of part-time students enrolled in a degree-granting institution can be modeled by the function $P(x) = 12x^3 - 285.3x^2 + 2217x + 1230$, where x is the number of years after 1970 and $P(x)$ is the number of students in thousands. Estimate the total number of students enrolled in a degree-granting institution in 2000.

20. Geography The data from the U.S. Census Bureau for 1982–2003 shows that the surface area of the United States that is covered by rural land can be modeled by the function $R(x) = 0.003x^3 - 0.086x^2 - 1.2x + 1417.4$, where x is the number of years after 1982 and $R(x)$ is the surface area in millions of acres. The total surface area of the United States can be modeled by the function $T(x) = 0.0023x^3 + 0.034x^2 - 5.9x + 1839.4$, where x is the number of years after 1982 and is the surface area in millions of acres. Estimate the surface area of the United States that is not covered by rural land in 2001.

21. Determine which polynomials are monomials.

a. $4x^3y$

b. $12 - x^2 + 5x$

c. $152 + x$

d. 783

e. x

f. $19x^{-2}$

g. $4x^4x^2$

22. Explain the Error Colin simplified $\left(16x + 8x^2y - 7xy^2 + 9y - 2xy\right) - \left(-9xy + 8xy^2 + 10x^2y + x - 7y\right)$. His work is shown below. Find and correct Colin's mistake.

$$\left(16x + 8x^2y - 7xy^2 + 9y - 2xy\right) - \left(-9xy + 8xy^2 + 10x^2y + x - 7y\right)$$
$$= \left(16x + 8x^2y - 7xy^2 + 9y - 2xy\right) + \left(9xy - 8xy^2 - 10x^2y - x + 7y\right)$$
$$= \left(16x - x\right) + \left(8x^2y - 7xy^2 - 8xy^2 - 10x^2y\right) + \left(9y + 7y\right) + \left(-2xy + 9xy\right)$$
$$= 15x - 17x^2y^2 + 16y + 7xy$$

23. Critical Reasoning Janice is building a fence around a portion of her rectangular yard. The length of yard she will enclose is x, and the width is $2x^2 - 98x + 5$, where the measurements are in feet. If the length of the enclosed yard is 50 feet and the cost of fencing is $13 per foot, how much will Janice need to spend on fencing?

24. Multi-Step Find a polynomial expression for the perimeter of a trapezoid with legs of length x and bases of lengths $7x^3 + 2x$ and $x^2 + 3x - 10$ where each is measured in inches.

a. Find the perimeter of the trapezoid if the length of one leg is 6 inches.

b. If the length is increased by 5 inches, will the perimeter also increase? By how much?

25. Communicate Mathematical Ideas Present a formal argument for why the set of polynomials is closed under addition and subtraction. Use the polynomials $ax^m + bx^m$ and $ax^m - bx^m$, for real numbers a and b and whole number m, to justify your reasoning.

Lesson Performance Task

The table shows the average monthly maximum and minimum temperatures for Death Valley throughout one year.

Month	Maximum Temperature	Minimum Temperature
January	67	40
February	73	46
March	82	55
April	91	62
May	101	73
June	110	81
July	116	88
August	115	86
September	107	76
October	93	62
November	77	48
December	65	38

Use a graphing calculator to find a good fourth-degree polynomial regression model for both the maximum and minimum temperatures. Then find a function that models the range in monthly temperatures and use the model to estimate the range during September. How does the range predicted by your model compare with the range shown in the table?

7.2 Multiplying Polynomials

Essential Question: How do you multiply polynomials, and what type of expression is the result?

 TEKS **A2.7.B** ...multiply polynomials.

Resource
Locker

⊘ Explore **Analyzing a Visual Model for Polynomial Multiplication**

The volume of a rectangular prism is the product of the length, width, and height of that prism. If the dimensions are all known, then the volume is a simple calculation. What if some of the dimensions are given as **binomials**? A binomial is a polynomial with two terms. How would you find the volume of a rectangular prism that is $x + 3$ units long, $x + 2$ units wide, and x units high? The images below show two methods for finding the solution.

$V = \text{length} \times \text{width} \times \text{height}$
$= (x + 3)(x + 2)x$

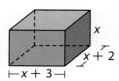

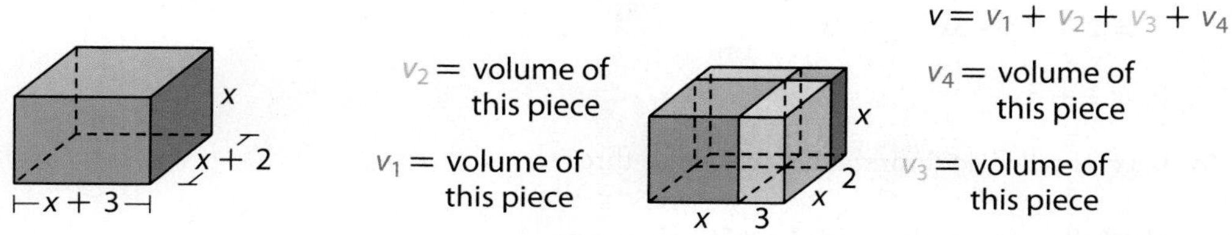

x

$x + 2$

⊢ $x + 3$ ⊣

$v_2 = $ volume of this piece

$v_1 = $ volume of this piece

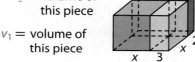

x

x 3

$v = v_1 + v_2 + v_3 + v_4$

$v_4 = $ volume of this piece

$v_3 = $ volume of this piece

Ⓐ The first model shows the rectangular prism, and its volume is calculated directly as the product of two binomials and a monomial.

Ⓑ The second image divides the rectangular prism into ▮ smaller prisms, the dimensions of which are each ▮ .

Ⓒ The volume of a cube (V_1) where all sides have a length of x, is ▮ .

Ⓓ The volume of a rectangular prism (V_2) with dimensions x by x by 2 is ▮ .

Ⓔ The volume of a rectangular prism (V_3) with dimensions x by x by 3 is ▮ .

Ⓕ The volume of a rectangular prism (V_4) with dimensions x by 3 by 2 is ▮ .

Ⓖ So the volume of the rectangular prism is the sum of the volumes of the four smaller regions.

$V_1 + V_2 + V_3 + V_4 = $ ▮ $+$ ▮ $+$ ▮ $+$ ▮

$= $ ▮

1. If all three dimensions were binomials, how many regions would the rectangular prism be divided into?

2. **Discussion** Can this method be applied to finding the volume of other simple solids? Are there solids that this process would be difficult to apply to? Are there any solids that this method cannot be applied to?

🔑 Explain 1 Multiplying Polynomials

Multiplying polynomials involves using the product rule for exponents and the distributive property. The product of two monomials is the product of the coefficients and the sum of the exponents of each variable.

$$5x \cdot 6x^3 = 30x^{1+3} \qquad\qquad -2x^2y^4z \cdot 5y^2z = -10x^2y^{4+2}z^{1+1}$$

$$= 30x^4 \qquad\qquad\qquad\qquad = -10x^2y^6z^2$$

When multiplying two binomials, the distributive property is used. Each term of one polynomial must be multiplied by each term of the other.

$$(2+3x)(1+x) = 2(1+x) + 3x(x+1)$$

$$= 2(1) + 2(x) + 3x(x) + 3x(1)$$

$$= 2 + 2x + 3x^{1+1} + 3x$$

$$= 2 + 5x + 3x^2$$

The polynomial $2 + 5x + 3x^2$ is called a **trinomial** because it has three terms.

Example 1 **Perform the following polynomial multiplications.**

Ⓐ $(x+2)(1-4x+2x^2)$

Find the product by multiplying horizontally.

$(x+2)(2x^2 - 4x + 1)$	Write the polynomials in standard form.
$x(2x^2) + x(-4x) + x(1) + 2(2x^2) + 2(-4x) + 2(1)$	Distribute the x and the 2.
$2x^3 - 4x^2 + x + 4x^2 - 8x + 2$	Simplify.
$2x^3 - 7x + 2$	Combine like terms.

Therefore, $(x+2)(2x^2 - 4x + 1) = 2x^3 - 7x + 2.$

(B) $(3x - 4)(2 + x - 7x^2)$

Find the product by multiplying vertically.

$$-7x^2 + \boxed{x} + 2$$
$$\underline{\qquad 3x - 4}$$

$$\boxed{28x^2} - 4x - 8 \qquad\qquad\text{Multipy } -4 \text{ and } (-7x^2 + x + 2).$$

$$\boxed{-21x^3} + 3x^2 + 6x \qquad\qquad\text{Multipy } \boxed{3x} \text{ and } (-7x^2 + x + 2).$$

$$-21x^3 + \boxed{31x^2} + 2x - 8 \qquad\qquad\text{Combine like terms.}$$

Write each polynomial in standard form.

Therefore, $(3x - 4)(2 + x - 7x^2) = -21x^3 + 31x^2 + 2x - 8$.

Your Turn

Multiply.

3. $(3 + 2x)(4 - 7x + 5x^2)$

4. $(x - 6)(3 - 8x - 4x^2)$

⊘ Explain 2   Modeling with Polynomial Multiplication

Many real-world situations can be modeled with polynomial functions. Sometimes, a situation will arise in which a model is needed that combines two quantities modeled by polynomial functions. In this case, the desired model would be the product of the two known models.

Example 2   **Find the polynomial function modeling the desired relationship.**

(A) Mr. Silva manages a manufacturing plant. From 1990 through 2005, the number of units produced (in thousands) can be modeled by $N(x) = 0.02x^2 + 0.2x + 3$. The average cost per unit (in dollars) can be modeled by $C(x) = -0.002x^2 - 0.1x + 2$, where x is the number of years since 1990. Write a polynomial $T(x)$ that can be used to model Mr. Silva's total manufacturing cost for those years.

The total manufacturing cost is the product of the number of units made and the cost per unit.

$T(x) = N(x) \cdot C(x)$

Multiply the two polynomials.

$$
\begin{array}{r}
0.02x^2 + 0.2x + 3 \\
\times \ -0.002x^2 - 0.1x + 2 \\
\hline
0.04x^2 + 0.4x + 6 \\
-0.002x^3 \quad - 0.02x^2 - 0.3x \\
-0.00004x^4 - 0.0004x^3 \ - 0.006x^2 \\
\hline
-0.00004x^4 - 0.0024x^3 \ + 0.014x^2 + 0.1x + 6
\end{array}
$$

Therefore, the total manufacturing cost can be modeled by the following polynomial, where x is the number of years since 1990.

$T(x) = -0.00004x^4 - 0.0024x^3 + 0.014x^2 + 0.1x + 6$

B Ms. Liao runs a small dress company. From 1995 through 2005, the number of dresses she made can be modeled by $N(x) = 0.3x^2 - 1.6x + 14$, and the average cost to make each dress can be modeled by $C(x) = -0.001x^2 - 0.06x + 8.3$, where x is the number of years since 1995. Write a polynomial that can be used to model Ms. Liao's total dressmaking costs, $T(x)$, for those years.

The total dressmaking cost is the product of the number of dresses made and the cost per dress.

$T(x) = N(x) \cdot C(x)$

Multiply the two polynomials.

$$
\begin{array}{r}
0.3x^2 \quad - 1.6x \quad + 14 \\
\times - 0.001x^2 \quad \boxed{-0.06x} \quad + 8.3 \\
\hline
2.49x^2 \quad - 13.28x \quad \boxed{+116.2} \\
-0.018x^3 \quad \boxed{+0.096x^2} \quad - 0.84x \\
-0.0003x^{\boxed{4}} + 0.0016x^3 - 0.014x^2 \\
\hline
-0.0003x^{\boxed{4}} - 0.0164x^3 + 2.572x^2 \quad \boxed{-14.12x} \quad + 116.2
\end{array}
$$

Therefore, the total dressmaking cost can be modeled by the following polynomial, where x is the number of years since 1995.

$T(x) = -0.0003x^4 - 0.0164x^3 + 2.572x^2 - 14.12x + 116.2$

Your Turn

5. Brent runs a small toy store specializing in wooden toys. From 2000 through 2012, the number of toys Brent made can be modeled by $N(x) = 0.7x^2 - 2x + 23$, and the average cost to make each toy can be modeled by $C(x) = -0.004x^2 - 0.08x + 25$, where x is the number of years since 2000. Write a polynomial that can be used to model Brent's total cost for making the toys, $T(x)$, for those years.

🎸 Explain 3   Verifying Polynomial Identities

You have already seen certain special polynomial relationships. For example, a difference of two squares can be easily factored: $x^2 - a^2 = (x + a)(x - a)$. This equation is an example of a **polynomial identity**, a mathematical relationship equating one polynomial quantity to another. Another example of a polynomial identity is

$$(x + a)^2 - (x - a)^2 = 4ax.$$

The identity can be verified by simplifying one side of the equation to match the other.

Example 3   **Verify the given polynomial identity.**

(A) $(x + a)^2 - (x - a)^2 = 4ax$

The right side of the identity is already fully simplified. Simplify the left-hand side.

$$(x + a)^2 - (x - a)^2 = 4ax$$

$x^2 + 2ax + a^2 - (x^2 - 2ax + a^2) = 4ax$ Use the sum of the two squares and the difference of two squares identities.

$x^2 + 2ax + a^2 - x^2 + 2ax - a^2 = 4ax$ Rearrange terms.

$\cancel{x^2} - \cancel{x^2} + 2ax + 2ax + \cancel{a^2} - \cancel{a^2} = 4ax$ Simplify.

$$4ax = 4ax$$

Therefore, $(x + a)^2 - (x - a)^2 = 4ax$ is a true statement.

(B) $(a + b)(a^2 - ab + b^2) = a^3 + b^3$

The right side of the identity is already fully simplified. Simplify the left-hand side.

$$(a + b)(a^2 - ab + b^2) = a^3 + b^3$$

$a(a^2) + a\boxed{\boxed{-ab}} + a(b^2) + b(a^2) + \boxed{b}(-ab) + b(b^2) = a^3 + b^3$ Distribute a and b.

$a^3 - a^2b + ab^2 + \boxed{a^2b} - ab^2 + \boxed{b^3} = a^3 + b^3$ Simplify.

$a^3 - \boxed{a^2b} + a^2b^2 - \boxed{ab^2} + b^3 = a^3 + b^3$ Rearrange terms.

$a^3 \boxed{+} b^3 = a^3 + b^3$ Combine like terms.

Therefore, $(a + b)(a^2 - ab + b^2) = a^3 + b^3$ is a true statement.

6. Show that $a^5 - b^5 = (a - b)(a^4 + a^3b + a^2b^2 + ab^3 + b^4)$.

7. Show that $(a - b)(a^2 + ab + b^2) = a^3 - b^3$.

🖉 Explain 4 Using Polynomial Identities

The most obvious use for polynomial identities is simplifying algebraic expressions, but polynomial identities often turn out to have nonintuitive uses as well.

Example 4 For each situation, find the solution using the given polynomial identity.

Ⓐ The polynomial identity $(x^2 + y^2)^2 = (x^2 - y^2)^2 + (2xy)^2$ can be used to identify Pythagorean triples. Generate a Pythagorean triple using $x = 4$ and $y = 3$.

Substitute the given values into the identity.

$$(4^2 + 3^2)^2 = (4^2 - 3^2)^2 + (2 \cdot 4 \cdot 3)^2$$
$$(16 + 9)^2 = (16 - 9)^2 + (24)^2$$
$$(25)^2 = (7)^2 + (24)^2$$
$$625 = 49 + 576$$
$$625 = 625$$

Therefore, 7, 24, 25 is a Pythagorean triple.

Ⓑ The identity $(x + y)^2 = x^2 + 2xy + y^2$ can be used for mental-math calculations to quickly square numbers.

Find the square of 27.

Find two numbers whose sum is equal to 27.

Let $x = \boxed{20}$ and $y = 7$.

Evaluate.

$$\left(20 + \boxed{7}\right)^2 = 20^2 + \boxed{2 \cdot 20 \cdot 7} + 7^2$$
$$27^2 = 400 + \boxed{280} + 49$$
$$27^2 = \boxed{729}$$

Verify by using a calculator to find 27^2.

$$27^2 = \boxed{729}$$

8. The identity $(x + y)(x - y) = x^2 - y^2$ can be used for mental-math calculations to quickly multiply two numbers in specific situations.

   Find the product of 37 and 43. (Hint: What values should you choose for x and y so the equation calculates the product of 37 and 43?)

9. The identity $(x - y)^2 = x^2 - 2xy + y^2$ can also be used for mental-math calculations to quickly square numbers.

   Find the square of 18. (Hint: What values should you choose for x and y so the equation calculates the square of 18?)

Elaborate

10. What property is employed in the process of polynomial multiplication?

11. How can you use unit analysis to justify multiplying two polynomial models of real-world quantities?

12. Give an example of a polynomial identity and how it's useful.

13. **Essential Question Check-In** When multiplying polynomials, what type of expression is the product?

⭐ Evaluate: Homework and Practice

• Online Homework
• Hints and Help
• Extra Practice

1. The dimensions for a rectangular prism are $x + 5$ for the length, $x + 1$ for the width, and x for the height. What is the volume of the prism?

Perform the following polynomial multiplications.

2. $(3x - 2)(2x^2 + 3x - 1)$

3. $(x^3 + 3x^2 + 1)(3x^2 + 6x - 2)$

4. $(x^2 + 9x + 7)(3x^2 + 9x + 5)$

5. $(2x + 5y)(3x^2 - 4xy + 2y^2)$

6. $(x^3 + x^2 + 1)(x^2 - x - 5)$

7. $(4x^2 + 3x + 2)(3x^2 + 2x - 1)$

Write a polynomial function to represent the new value.

8. The volume of a stock or number of shares traded on a given day is $S(x) = x^5 - 3x^4 + 10x^2 - 6x + 30$. The average cost of a share of a stock on a given day is $C(x) = 0.004x^4 - 0.02x^2 + 0.3x + 4$.

9. A businessman models the number of items (in thousands) that his company sold from 1998 through 2004 as $N(x) = -0.1x^3 + x^2 - 3x + 4$ and the average price per item (in dollars) as $P(x) = 0.2x + 5$, where x represents the number of years since 1998. Write a polynomial $R(x)$ that can be used to model the total revenue for this company.

10. **Biology** A biologist has found that the number of branches on a certain rare tree in its first few years of life can be modeled by the polynomial $b(y) = 4y^2 + y$. The number of leaves on each branch can be modeled by the polynomial $l(y) = 2y^3 + 3y^2 + y$, where y is the number of years after the tree reaches a height of 6 feet. Write a polynomial describing the total number of leaves on the tree.

11. **Physics** An object thrown in the air has a velocity after t seconds that can be described by $v(t) = -9.8t + 24$ (in meters/second) and a height $h(t) = -4.9t^2 + 24t + 60$ (in meters). The object has mass $m = 2$ kilograms. The kinetic energy of the object is given by $K = \frac{1}{2}mv^2$, and the potential energy is given by $U = 9.8mh$. Find an expression for the total kinetic and potential energy $K + U$ as a function of time. What does this expression tell you about the energy of the falling object?

Verify the given polynomial identity.

12. $(x + y + z)^2 = x^2 + y^2 + z^2 + 2xy + 2xz + 2yz$

13. $a^5 + b^5 = (a + b)(a^4 - a^3b + a^2b^2 - ab^3 + b^4)$

14. $x^4 - y^4 = (x - y)(x + y)(x^2 + y^2)$

15. $(a^2 + b^2)(x^2 + y^2) = (ax - by)^2 + (bx + ay)^2$

Evaluate the following polynomials using one or more of these identities.

$(x + y)^2 = x^2 + 2xy + y^2$, $(x + y)(x - y) = x^2 - y^2$, or $(x - y)^2 = x^2 - 2xy + y^2$.

16. 43^2

17. 32^2

18. 89^2

19. 47^2

20. $54 \cdot 38$

21. $58 \cdot 68$

22. Explain the Error Two students used binomial expansion to expand $(a + b)^2$. Which answer is incorrect? Identify the error.

A	B

$$(a + b)^2$$

$$1a^2b^0 + 2a^2b^1 + 1a^0b^2$$

$$a^2 + 2ab + b^2$$

$$(a + b)^2$$

$$1a^2b^2 + 2a^1b^1 + 1a^0b^0$$

$$a^2b^2 + 2ab + 1$$

23. Determine how many terms there will be after performing the polynomial multiplication.

a. $(5x)(3x)$

b. $(3x)(2x + 1)$

c. $(x + 1)(x - 1)$

d. $(x + 2)(3x^2 - 2x + 1)$

H.O.T. Focus on Higher Order Thinking

24. Multi-Step Given the polynomial identity: $x^6 + y^6 = (x^2 + y^2)(x^4 - x^2y^2 + y^4)$

a. Verify directly by expanding the right hand side.

b. Use another polynomial identity to verify this identity. $\left(\text{Note that } a^6 = (a^2)^3 = (a^3)^2\right)$

25. Communicate Mathematical Ideas Explain why the set of polynomials is closed under multiplication.

26. Critical Thinking Explain why every other term of the expansion of $(x - y)^5$ is negative when $(x - y)$ is raised to the fifth power.

Lesson Performance Task

The table presents data about oil wells in the state of Oklahoma from 1992 through 2008.

Year	Number of Wells	Average Daily Oil Production per Well (Barrels)
2008	83,443	2.178
2007	82,832	2.053
2006	82,284	2.108
2005	82,551	2.006
2004	83,222	2.10
2003	83,415	2.12
2002	83,730	2.16
2001	84,160	2.24
2000	84,432	2.24
1999	85,043	2.29
1998	85,691	2.49
1997	86,765	2.62
1996	88,144	2.66
1995	90,557	2.65
1994	91,289	2.73
1993	92,377	2.87
1992	93,192	2.99

a. Given the data in this table, use polynomial regression to find models for the number of producing wells and average daily well output in terms of t years since 1992.

b. Find a function modeling the total daily oil output for the state of Oklahoma.

© Houghton Mifflin Harcourt Publishing Company

7.3 Factoring Polynomials

Essential Question: What are some ways to factor a polynomial, and how is factoring useful?

Resource Locker

TEKS **A2.7.E** Determine linear and quadratic factors of a polynomial expression of degree three and of degree four, including factoring the sum and difference of two cubes and factoring by grouping.

Explore Analyzing a Visual Model for Polynomial Factorization

Factoring a polynomial of degree n involves finding factors of lesser a degree that can be multiplied together to produce the polynomial. When a polynomial has degree 3, for example, you can think of it as a rectangular prism whose dimensions you need to determine.

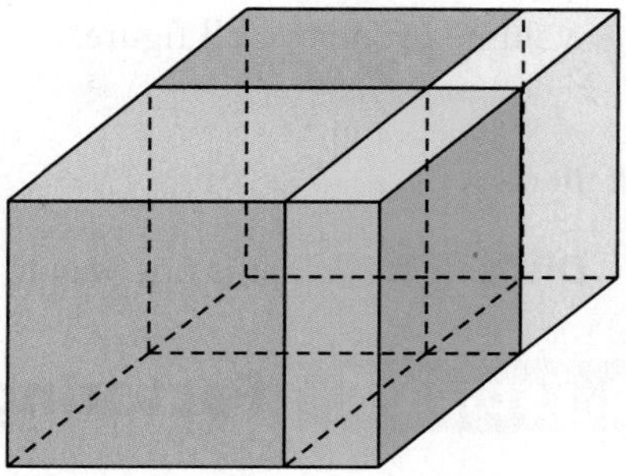

(A) The volumes of the parts of the rectangular prism are as follows:

Red: $V = x^3$

Green: $V = 2x^2$

Yellow: $V = 8x$

Blue: $V = 4x^2$

Total volume: $V = x^3 + 6x^2 + 8x$

(B) The volume of the red piece is found by cubing the length of one side. What is the height of this piece?

(C) The volume of a rectangular prism is $V = lwh$, where l is the length, w is the width, and h is the height of the prism. Notice that the green prism shares two sides with the cube. What are the lengths of these two sides?

(D) What is the length of the third side of the green prism?

(E) You showed that the width of the cube is and the width of the green prism is . What is the width of the entire prism?

You determined that the length of the green piece is *x*. Use the volume of the yellow piece and the information you have derived to find the length of the prism.

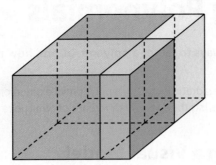

Ⓖ Since the dimensions of the overall prism are x, $x + 2$, and $x + 4$, the volume of the overall prism can be rewritten in factored form as $V = (x)(x + 2)(x + 4)$. Multiply these polynomials together to verify that this is equal to the original given expression for the volume of the overall figure.

Reflect

1. **Discussion** What is one way to double the volume of the prism?

🎯 Explain 1 Factoring Out the Greatest Common Monomial First

Most polynomials cannot be *factored over the integers*, which means to find factors that use only integer coefficients. But when a polynomial can be factored, each factor has a degree less than the polynomial's degree. While the goal is to write the polynomial as a product of linear factors, this is not always possible. When a factor of degree 2 or greater cannot be factored further, it is called an **irreducible factor**.

Example 1 Factor each polynomial over the integers.

Ⓐ $6x^3 + 15x^2 + 6x$

$6x^3 + 15x^2 + 6x$	Write out the polynomial.
$x(6x^2 + 15x + 6)$	Factor out a common monomial, an *x*.
$3x(2x^2 + 5x + 2)$	Factor out a common monomial, a 3.
$3x(2x + 1)(x + 2)$	Factor into simplest terms.

Note: The second and third steps can be combined into one step by factoring out the greatest common monomial.

Ⓑ $2x^3 - 20x$

$2x^3 - 20x$ Write out the polynomial.

$2x(x^2 - 10)$ Factor out the greatest common monomial.

Reflect

2. Why wasn't the factor $x^2 - 10$ further factored?

3. Consider what happens when you factor $x^2 - 10$ over the real numbers and not merely the integers. Find a such that $x^2 - 10 = (x - a)(x + a)$.

Your Turn

4. $3x^3 + 7x^2 + 4x$

⏻ Explain 2 Recognizing Special Factoring Patterns

Remember the factoring patterns you already know:

Difference of two squares: $a^2 - b^2 = (a + b)(a - b)$

Perfect square trinomials: $a^2 + 2ab + b^2 = (a + b)^2$ and $a^2 - 2ab + b^2 = (a - b)^2$

There are two other factoring patterns that will prove useful:

Sum of two cubes: $a^3 + b^3 = (a + b)(a^2 - ab + b^2)$

Difference of two cubes: $a^3 - b^3 = (a - b)(a^2 + ab + b^2)$

Notice that in each of the new factoring patterns, the quadratic factor is irreducible over the integers.

Example 2 Factor the polynomial using a factoring pattern.

Ⓐ $27x^3 + 64$

$27x^3 + 64$ Write out the polynomial.

$27x^3 = (3x)^3$ Check if $27x^3$ is a perfect cube.

$64 = (4)^3$ Check if 64 is a perfect cube.

$a^3 + b^3 = (a + b)(a^2 - ab + b^2)$ Use the sum of two cubes formula to factor.

$(3x)^3 + 4^3 = (3x + 4)((3x)^2 - (3x)(4) + 4^2)$

$27x^3 + 64 = (3x + 4)(9x^2 - 12x + 16)$

Ⓑ $8x^3 - 27$

$8x^3 - 27$	Write out the polynomial.
$8x^3 = (2x)^3$	Check if $8x^3$ is a perfect cube.
$27 = (3)^3$	Check if 27 is a perfect cube.
$a^3 - b^3 = (a - b)(a^2 + ab + b^2)$	Use the difference of two cubes formula to factor.
$8x^3 - 27 = (2x - 3)(4x^2 + 6x + 9)$	

Reflect

5. The equation $8x^3 - 27 = 0$ has three roots. How many of them are real, what are they, and how many are nonreal?

Your Turn

Factor by using a factoring pattern.

6. $40x^4 + 5x$

Explain 3   Factoring by Grouping

Another technique for factoring a polynomial is grouping. If the polynomial has pairs of terms with common factors, factor by grouping terms with common factors and then factoring out the common factor from each group. Then look for a common factor of the groups in order to complete the factorization of the polynomial.

Example 3   **Factor the polynomial by grouping.**

Ⓐ $x^3 + x^2 + x + 1$

Write out the polynomial.	$x^3 - x^2 + x - 1$
Group by common factor.	$(x^3 - x^2) + (x - 1)$
Factor.	$x^2(x - 1) + 1(x - 1)$
Regroup.	$(x^2 + 1)(x - 1)$

Ⓑ $x^4 + x^3 + x + 1$

Write out the polynomial.	$x^4 + x^3 + x + 1$
Group by common factor.	$(x^4 + x^3) + (x + 1)$
Factor.	$x^3(x + 1) + 1(x + 1)$
Regroup.	$(x^3 + 1)(x + 1)$
Apply sum of two cubes to the first term.	$(x^2 - x + 1)(x + 1)(x + 1)$
Substitute this into the expression and simplify.	$(x + 1)^2(x^2 - x + 1)$

Your Turn

Factor by grouping.

7. $x^3 + 3x^2 + 3x + 2$

Explain 4 Solving a Real-World Problem by Factoring a Polynomial

Remember that the zero-product property is used in solving factorable quadratic equations. It can also be used in solving factorable polynomial equations.

Example 4   **Write and solve a polynomial equation for the situation described.**

Ⓐ   A water park is designing a new pool in the shape of a rectangular prism. The sides and bottom of the pool are made of material 5 feet thick. The length must be twice the height (depth), and the interior width must be three times the interior height. The volume of the box must be 6000 cubic feet. What are the exterior dimensions of the pool?

The dimensions of the interior of the pool, as described by the problem, are the following:

$h = x - 5$

$w = 3x - 15$

$l = 2x - 10$

The formula for volume of a rectangular prism is $V = lwh$. Plug the values into the volume equation.

$V = (x - 5)(3x - 15)(2x - 10)$

$V = (x - 5)(6x^2 - 60x + 150)$

$V = 6x^3 - 90x^2 + 450x - 750$

Now solve for $V = 6000$.

$6000 = 6x^3 - 90x^2 + 450x - 750$

$0 = 6x^3 - 90x^2 + 450x - 6750$

Factor the resulting new polynomial.

$6x^3 - 90x^2 + 450x - 6750$

$= 6x^2(x - 15) + 450(x - 15)$

$= (6x^2 + 450)(x - 15)$

The only real root is $x = 15$.

The interior height of the pool will be 10 feet, the interior width 30 feet, and the interior length 20 feet. Therefore, the exterior height is 15 feet, the exterior length is 30 feet, and the exterior width is 40 feet.

Ⓑ Engineering To build a hefty wooden feeding trough for a zoo, its sides and bottom should be 2 feet thick, and its outer length should be twice its outer width and height.

What should the outer dimensions of the trough be if it is to hold 288 cubic feet of water?

Volume = Interior Length(feet) · Interior Width(feet) · Interior Height(feet)

$$288 = (2x - 4)(x - 4)(x - 2)$$
$$288 = 2x^3 - 16x^2 + 40x - 32$$
$$0 = 2x^3 - 16x^2 + 40x - 320$$
$$0 = 2x^2(x - 8) + 40(x - 8)$$
$$0 = 2(x^2 + 20)(x - 8)$$

The only real solution is $x = 8$. The trough is 16 feet long, 8 feet wide, and 8 feet high.

Your Turn

8. **Engineering** A new shed is being designed in the shape of a rectangular prism. The shed's side and bottom should be 3 feet thick. Its outer length should be twice its outer width and height.

   What should the outer dimensions of the shed be if it is to have 972 cubic feet of space?

Elaborate

9. Describe how the method of grouping incorporates the method of factoring out the greatest common monomial.

10. How do you decide if an equation fits in the sum of two cubes pattern?

11. How can factoring be used to solve a polynomial equation of the form $p(x) = a$, where a is a nonzero constant?

12. **Essential Question Check-In** What are two ways to factor a polynomial?

☆ Evaluate: Homework and Practice

Factor the polynomial, or identify it as irreducible.

1. $x^3 + x^2 - 12x$

2. $x^3 + 5$

3. $x^3 - 125$

4. $x^3 + 5x^2 + 6x$

5. $8x^3 + 125$

6. $2x^3 + 6x$

7. $216x^3 + 64$

8. $8x^3 - 64$

9. $10x^3 - 80$

10. $2x^4 + 7x^3 + 5x^2$

11. $x^3 + 10x^2 + 16x$

12. $x^3 + 9769$

Factor the polynomial by grouping.

13. $x^3 + 8x^2 + 6x + 48$

14. $x^3 + 4x^2 - x - 4$

15. $8x^4 + 8x^3 + 27x + 27$

16. $27x^4 + 54x^3 - 64x - 128$

17. $x^3 + 2x^2 + 3x + 6$

18. $4x^4 - 4x^3 - x + 1$

Write and solve a polynomial equation for the situation described.

19. **Engineering** A new rectangular outbuilding for a farm is being designed. The outbuilding's side and bottom should be 4 feet thick. Its outer length should be twice its outer width and height. What should the outer dimensions of the outbuilding be if it is to hold 2304 cubic feet?

20. **Arts** A piece of rectangular crafting supply is being cut for a new sculpture. You want its length to be 4 times its height and its width to be 2 times its height. If you want the wood to be 64 cubic centimeters, what will its length, width, and height be?

21. **Engineering** A new rectangular holding tank is being built. The tank's side and bottom should be 1 foot thick. Its outer length should be twice its outer width and height.

What should the outer dimensions of the tank be if it is to hold 36 cubic feet?

22. **Construction** A piece of granite is being cut for a building foundation. You want its length to be 8 times its height and its width to be 3 times its height. If you want the granite to be 648 cubic yards, what will its length, width, and height be?

23. State which, if any, special factoring pattern each of the following polynomial functions follows:

    a. $x^2 - 4$ **b.** $3x^3 + 5$ **c.** $4x^2 + 25$

    d. $16x^3 + 375$ **e.** $64x^3 - x^2 + 1$

24. **Communicate Mathematical Ideas** What is the relationship between the degree of a polynomial and the degree of its factors?

25. **Critical Thinking** Why is there no sum-of-two-squares factoring pattern?

26. **Explain the Error** Jim was trying to factor a polynomial function and produced the following result:

    $3x^3 + x^2 + 3x + 1$ Write out the polynomial.

    $3x^2(x + 1) + 3(x + 1)$ Group by common factor.

    $3(x^2 + 1)(x + 1)$ Regroup.

    Explain Jim's error.

27. Factoring can also be done over the complex numbers. This allows you to find all the roots of an equation, not just the real ones.

    Copy and complete the steps to show how to use a special factor identity to factor $x^2 + 4$ over the complex numbers.

    $x^2 + 4$ Write out the polynomial.

    $x^2 - (-4)$ _____?_____

    $(x + \boxed{})(x - \boxed{})$ Factor.

    $(x + 2i)(\boxed{})$ Simplify.

28. Find all the complex roots of the equation $x^4 - 16 = 0$.

29. Factor $x^3 + x^2 + x + 1$ over the complex numbers.

Lesson Performance Task

Sabrina is building a rectangular raised flower bed. The boards on the two shorter sides are 6 inches thick, and the boards on the two longer sides are 4 inches thick. Sabrina wants the outer length of her bed to be 4 times its height and the outer width to be 2 times its height. She also wants the boards to rise 4 inches above the level of the soil in the bed. What should the outer dimensions of the bed be if she wants it to hold 3136 cubic inches of soil?

7.4 Dividing Polynomials

Essential Question: What are some ways to divide polynomials, and how do you know when the divisor is a factor of the dividend?

 TEKS **A2.7.C** Determine the quotient of a polynomial of degree three and of degree four when divided by a polynomial of degree one and of degree two. Also A2.7.D

Resource Locker

Explore   Evaluating a Polynomial Function Using Synthetic Substitution

Polynomials can be written in something called nested form. A polynomial in nested form is written in such a way that evaluating it involves an alternating sequence of additions and multiplications. For instance, the nested form of $p(x) = 4x^3 + 3x^2 + 2x + 1$ is $p(x) = x\big(x(4x + 3) + 2\big) + 1$, which you evaluate by starting with 4, multiplying by the value of x, adding 3, multiplying by x, adding 2, multiplying by x, and adding 1.

(A) Given $p(x) = 4x^3 + 3x^2 + 2x + 1$, find $p(-2)$.

You can set up an array of numbers that captures the sequence of multiplications and additions needed to find $p(a)$. Using this array to find $p(a)$ is called **synthetic substitution**.

Given $p(x) = 4x^3 + 3x^2 + 2x + 1$, find $p(-2)$ by using synthetic substitution. The dashed arrow indicates bringing down, the diagonal arrows represent multiplication by -2, and the solid down arrows indicate adding.

The first two steps are to bring down the leading number, 4, then multiply by the value you are evaluating at, -2.

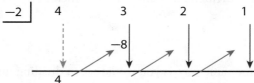

(B) Copy the diagram. Then add 3 and -8.

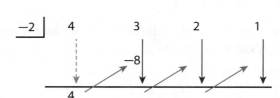

(C) Multiply the previous answer by -2.

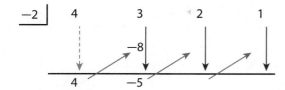

(D) Continue this sequence of steps until you reach the last addition.

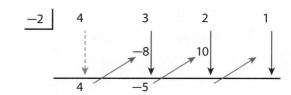

(E) $p(-2) =$

1. **Discussion** After the final addition, what does this sum correspond to?

⊘ Explain 1   Dividing Polynomials Using Long Division

Recall that arithmetic long division proceeds as follows.

$$
\begin{array}{r}
\text{Divisor} \quad\;\; 23 \leftarrow \text{Quotient} \\
12\overline{)\,277\,} \leftarrow \text{Dividend} \\
\underline{24} \\
37 \\
\underline{36} \\
1 \leftarrow \text{Remainder}
\end{array}
$$

Notice that the long division leads to the result $\frac{dividend}{divisor} = quotient + \frac{remainder}{divisor}$. Using the numbers from above, the arithmetic long division leads to $\frac{277}{12} = 23 + \frac{1}{12}$. Multiplying through by the divisor yields the result $dividend = (divisor)(quotient) + remainder$. (This can be used as a means of checking your work.)

Example 1   **Given a polynomial divisor and dividend, use long division to find the quotient and remainder. Write the result in the form** $dividend = (divisor)(quotient) + remainder$ **and then carry out the multiplication and addition as a check.**

Ⓐ $\left(4x^3 + 2x^2 + 3x + 5\right) \div \left(x^2 + 3x + 1\right)$

Begin by writing the dividend in standard form, including terms with a coefficient of 0 (if any).

$4x^3 + 2x^2 + 3x + 5$

Write division in the same way as you would when dividing numbers.

$$x^2 + 3x + 1\overline{)\,4x^3 + 2x^2 + 3x + 5\,}$$

Find the value you need to multiply the divisor by so that the first term matches with the first term of the dividend. In this case, in order to get $4x^3$, we must multiply x^2 by $4x$. This will be the first term of the quotient.

$$
\begin{array}{r}
4x \\
x^2 + 3x + 1\overline{)\,4x^3 + 2x^2 + 3x + 5\,}
\end{array}
$$

Next, multiply the divisor through by the term of the quotient you just found and subtract that value from the dividend. $\left(x^2 + 3x + 1\right)(4x) = 4x^3 + 12x^2 + 4x$, so subtract $4x^3 + 12x^2 + 4x$ from $4x^3 + 2x^2 + 3x + 5$.

$$
\begin{array}{r}
4x \\
x^2 + 3x + 1\overline{)\,4x^3 + 2x^2 + 3x + 5\,} \\
\underline{-\left(4x^3 + 12x^2 + 4x\right)} \\
-10x^2 - x + 5
\end{array}
$$

Taking this difference as the new dividend, continue in this fashion until the largest term of the remaining dividend is of lower degree than the divisor.

$$
\begin{array}{r}
4x - 10 \\
x^2 + 3x + 1 \overline{)\; 4x^3 + 2x^2 + 3x + 5} \\
\underline{-\left(4x^3 + 12x^2 + 4x\right)} \\
-10x^2 - x + 5 \\
\underline{-\left(-10x^2 - 30x - 10\right)} \\
29x + 15
\end{array}
$$

Since $29x + 5$ is of lower degree than $x^2 + 3x + 1$, stop. $29x + 15$ is the remainder.

Write the final answer.

$4x^3 + 2x^2 + 3x + 5 = \left(x^2 + 3x + 1\right)(4x - 10) + 29x + 15$

Check.

$$4x^3 + 2x^2 + 3x + 5 = \left(x^2 + 3x + 1\right)(4x - 10) + 29x + 15$$
$$= 4x^3 + 12x^2 + 4x - 10x^2 - 30x - 10 + 29x + 15$$
$$= 4x^3 + 2x^2 + 3x + 5$$

(B) $\left(6x^4 + 5x^3 + 2x + 8\right) \div \left(x^2 + 2x - 5\right)$

Write the dividend in standard form, including terms with a coefficient of 0.

$6x^4 + 5x^3 + 0x^2 + 2x + 8$

Write the division in the same way as you would when dividing numbers.

$x^2 + 2x - 5 \overline{)\; 6x^4 + 5x^3 + 0x^2 + 2x + 8}$

Divide.

$$
\begin{array}{r}
6x^2 - \boxed{7x} + \boxed{44} \\
x^2 + 2x - 5 \overline{)\; 6x^4 + 5x^3 + 0x^2 + 2x + 8} \\
\underline{-\left(6x^4 + 12x^3 - 30x^2\right)} \\
-7x^3 + 30x^2 + 2x \\
\underline{-\left(-7x^3\; \boxed{-14x^2 + 35x}\right)} \\
\boxed{44x^2 - 33x} + 8 \\
\underline{-\left(\;\boxed{44x^2 + 88x - 220}\;\right)} \\
\boxed{-121x + 228}
\end{array}
$$

Write the final answer.

$6x^4 + 5x^3 + 2x + 8 = \boxed{(x^2 + 2x - 5)(6x^2 - 7x + 44) - 121x + 228}$

Check.

$$6x^4 + 5x^3 + 2x + 8 = (x^2 + 2x - 5)(6x^2 - 7x + 44) - 121x + 228$$
$$= 6x^4 - 7x^3 + 44x^2 + 12x^3 - 14x^2 + 88x - 30x^2 + 35x - 220 - 121x + 228$$
$$= 6x^4 + 5x^3 + 2x + 8$$

Reflect

2. How do you include the terms with 0 coefficients?

Your Turn

Use long division to find the quotient and remainder. Write the result in the form $dividend = (divisor)(qoutient) + remainder$ **and then carry out a check.**

3. $(15x^3 + 8x - 12) \div (3x^2 + 6x + 1)$

4. $(9x^4 + x^3 + 11x^2 - 4) \div (x^2 + 16)$

🔧 Explain 2 Dividing $p(x)$ by $x - a$ Using Synthetic Division

Compare long division with synthetic substitution. There are two important things to notice. The first is that $p(a)$ is equal to the remainder when $p(x)$ is divided by $x - a$. The second is that the numbers to the left of $p(a)$ in the bottom row of the synthetic substitution array give the coefficients of the quotient. For this reason, synthetic substitution is also called **synthetic division**.

Long Division	Synthetic Substitution
$$\begin{array}{r} 3x^2 + 10x + 20 \\ x-2 \overline{)\ 3x^3 + 4x^2 + 0x + 10} \\ \underline{-(3x^3 - 6x^2)} \\ 10x^2 + 0x \\ \underline{-(10x^2 - 20x)} \\ 20x + 10 \\ \underline{-20x - 40} \\ 50 \end{array}$$	$$\begin{array}{r} 2 \rfloor \ \ 3 \ \ \ 4 \ \ \ 0 \ \ \ 10 \\ \ \ \ \ \ \ \ \ \ \ 6 \ \ 20 \ \ 40 \\ \hline 3 \ \ 10 \ \ 20 \ \lfloor 50 \end{array}$$

Example 2 Given a polynomial $p(x)$, use synthetic division to divide by $x - a$ and obtain the quotient and the (nonzero) remainder. Write the result in the form $p(x) = (x - a)$ $(quotient) + p(a)$ then carry out the multiplication and addition as a check.

Ⓐ $(7x^3 - 6x + 9) \div (x + 5)$

By inspection, $a = -5$. Write the coefficients and a in the synthetic division format.

$$-5\rfloor \quad 7 \ \ 0 \ \ -6 \ \ 9$$
$$\overline{} \lfloor$$

Bring down the first coefficient. Then multiply and add for each column.

$$\begin{array}{r} -5\rfloor \quad 7 \ \ \ \ \ \ 0 \ \ \ \ \ \ -6 \ \ \ \ \ \ 9 \\ \ \ \ \ \ \ \ \ \ \ \ -35 \ \ \ 175 \ \ -845 \\ \hline 7 \ \ \ -35 \ \ \ 169 \ \lfloor -839 \end{array}$$

Write the result, using the non-remainder entries of the bottom row as the coefficients.

$$(7x^2 - 6x + 9) = (x + 5)(7x^2 - 35x + 169) - 836$$

Check.

$$(7x^3 - 6x + 9) = (x + 5)(7x^2 - 35x + 169) - 836$$

$$= 7x^3 - 35x^2 - 35x^2 - 175x + 169x + 845 - 836$$

$$= 7x^3 - 6x + 9$$

Ⓑ $(4x^4 - 3x^2 + 7x + 2) \div \left(x - \dfrac{1}{2}\right)$

Find a. Then write the coefficients and a in the synthetic division format.

Find $a = \boxed{\dfrac{1}{2}}$

$$\dfrac{1}{2} \big\rfloor \; 4 \quad 0 \quad -3 \quad 7 \quad 2$$

Bring down the first coefficient. Then multiply and add for each column.

$$\dfrac{1}{2} \big\rfloor \begin{array}{ccccc} 4 & 0 & -3 & 7 & 2 \\ & 2 & 1 & -1 & 3 \\ \hline 4 & 2 & -2 & 6 & \underline{5} \end{array}$$

Write the result.

$$(4x^4 - 3x^2 + 7x + 2) = \boxed{\left(x - \dfrac{1}{2}\right)(4x^3 + 2x^2 - 2x + 6) + 5}$$

Check.

$$(4x^4 - 3x^2 + 7x + 2) = \left(x - \dfrac{1}{2}\right)(4x^3 + 2x^2 - 2x + 6) + 5$$

$$= 4x^4 + 2x^3 - 2x^2 + 6x - 2x^3 - x^2 + x - 3 + 5$$

$$= 4x^4 + 3x^2 + 7x + 2$$

Reflect

5. Can you use synthetic division to divide a polynomial by $x^2 + 3$? Explain.

Your Turn

Given a polynomial $p(x)$, use synthetic division to divide by $x - a$ and obtain the quotient and the (nonzero) remainder. Write the result in the form $p(x) = (x - a)(quotient) + p(a)$. You may wish to perform a check.

6. $(2x^3 + 5x^2 - x + 7) \div (x - 2)$

7. $(6x^4 + 25x^3 - 3x + 5) \div \left(x + \dfrac{1}{3}\right)$

⚙ Explain 3 Using the Remainder Theorem and Factor Theorem

When $p(x)$ is divided by $x - a$, the result can be written in the form $p(x) = (x - a)q(x) + r$ where $q(x)$ is the quotient and r is a number. Substituting a for x in this equation gives $p(a) = (a - a)q(a) + r$. Since $a - a = 0$, this simplifies to $p(a) = r$. This is known as the **Remainder Theorem**.

If the remainder $p(a)$ in $p(x) = (x - a)q(x) + p(a)$ is 0, then $p(x) = (x - a)q(x)$, which tells you that $x - a$ is a factor of $p(x)$. Conversely, if $x - a$ is a factor of $p(x)$, then you can write $p(x)$ as $p(x) = (x - a)q(x)$, and when you divide $p(x)$ by $x - a$, you get the quotient $q(x)$ with a remainder of 0. These facts are known as the **Factor Theorem**.

Example 3 Determine whether the given binomial is a factor of the polynomial $p(x)$. If so, find the remaining factors of $p(x)$.

(A) $p(x) = x^3 + 3x^2 - 4x - 12; (x + 3)$

Use synthetic division.

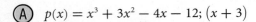

$$\begin{array}{r|rrrr} -3 & 1 & 3 & -4 & -12 \\ & & -3 & 0 & 12 \\ \hline & 1 & 0 & -4 & \boxed{0} \end{array}$$

Since the remainder is 0, $x + 3$ is a factor.

Write $q(x)$ and then factor it.

$q(x) = x^2 - 4 = (x + 2)(x - 2)$

So, $p(x) = x^3 + 3x^2 - 4x - 12 = (x + 2)(x - 2)(x + 3)$.

(B) $p(x) = x^4 - 4x^3 - 6x^2 + 4x + 5; (x + 1)$

Use synthetic division.

$$\begin{array}{r|rrrrr} -1 & 1 & -4 & -6 & 4 & 5 \\ & & -1 & 5 & 1 & -5 \\ \hline & 1 & -5 & -1 & 5 & \boxed{0} \end{array}$$

Since the remainder is 0, $(x + 1)$ is a factor. Write $q(x)$.

$q(x) = \boxed{x^3 - 5x^2 - x + 5}$

Now factor $q(x)$ by grouping.

$q(x) = \boxed{x^3 - 5x^2 - x + 5}$

$\quad = \boxed{x^2(x - 5) - (x - 5)}$

$\quad = \boxed{(x^2 - 1)(x - 5)}$

$\quad = \boxed{(x + 1)(x - 1)(x - 5)}$

So, $p(x) = x^4 - 4x^3 - 6x^2 + 4x + 5 = \boxed{(x + 1)(x + 1)(x - 1)(x - 5)}$.

Determine whether the given binomial is a factor of the polynomial $p(x)$. If it is, find the remaining factors of $p(x)$.

8. $p(x) = 2x^4 + 8x^3 + 2x + 8; (x + 4)$

9. $p(x) = 3x^3 - 2x + 5; (x - 1)$

⚙ Explain 4   Solving a Real-World Problem Using Polynomial Division

Example 3   Solve the problem using polynomial division.

Ⓐ   The profit P (in millions of dollars) for a clock factory can be modeled by $P = -13x^3 + 21x$ where x is the number of clocks produced (in millions). The company now produces 1 million clocks and makes a profit of $8,000,000, but would like to cut back on production. What lesser number of clocks could the company produce and still make the same profit?

$8 = -13x^3 + 21x$

$0 = 13x^3 - 21x + 8$

You know that $x = 1$ is a solution to the equation. This implies that $x - 1$ is a factor of $13x^3 - 21x + 8$. Use synthetic division to find the other factors.

```
1|  13   0   -21    8
          13   13   -8
    _____
    13   13   -8   |0
```

So, $(x - 1)(13x^2 + 13x - 8) = 0$.

Recall that the quadratic formula is $x = \dfrac{-b \pm \sqrt{b^2 - 4ac}}{2a}$.

Use the quadratic formula to find that $x \approx 0.4$ is the other positive solution.

The company could still make the same profit producing about 400,000 clocks.

Ⓑ   The profit P (in thousands) for a jewelry store can be modeled by $P = -16x^3 + 32x$ where x is the number of pieces of jewelry produced (in thousands). The company now produces 1000 pieces and makes a profit of $16,000, but would like to cut back on production. What lesser number of pieces of jewelry could the store produce and still make the same profit?

$16 = -16x^3 + 32x$

$0 = \boxed{16x^3 - 32x + 16}$

You know that $x = 1$ is a solution to the equation. This implies that $x - 1$ is a factor of

$\boxed{16x^3 - 32x + 16}$. Use synthetic division to find the other factors.

$$\begin{array}{r} 1\rvert\ \ 16\quad 0\quad -32\quad 16 \\ \underline{16\quad 16\ -16\quad\ \ } \\ 16\quad 16\ -16\quad\ \lvert\underline{0} \end{array}$$

So, $(x - 1)\left(\boxed{16x^2 + 16x - 16}\right) = 0$.

Factor out the GCF.

$$0 = (x - 1)\left(\boxed{16x^2 + 16x - 16}\right)$$

$$= \boxed{16(x - 1)(x^2 + x - 1)}$$

Recall that the quadratic formula is $x = \dfrac{-b \pm \sqrt{b^2 - 4ac}}{2a}$.

Use the quadratic formula to find that $x \approx \boxed{0.6}$ is the other positive solution.

The company could still make the same profit producing about 600 pieces of jewelry.

Your Turn

10. The total number of dollars donated each year to a small charitable organization has followed the trend $d(t) = 2t^3 + 10t^2 + 2000t + 10{,}000$, where d is dollars and t is the number of years since 1990. The average number of dollars per donor can be expressed by $t + 5$. Write an expression describing the total number of donors each year.

💬 Elaborate

11. Compare long division and synthetic division of polynomials.

12. How does knowing one linear factor of a polynomial help find the other factors?

13. What conditions must be met in order to use synthetic division?

14. **Essential Question Check-In** How do you know when the divisor is a factor of the dividend?

☆ Evaluate: Homework and Practice

- Online Homework
- Hints and Help
- Extra Practice

Given $p(x)$, find $p(-3)$ by using synthetic substitution.

1. $p(x) = 8x^3 + 7x^2 + 2x + 4$

2. $p(x) = x^3 + 6x^2 + 7x - 25$

3. $p(x) = 2x^3 + 5x^2 - 3x$

4. $p(x) = -x^4 + 5x^3 - 8x + 45$

Given a polynomial divisor and dividend, use long division to find the quotient and remainder. Write the result in the form *dividend* $= ($*divisor*$)($*quotient*$) +$ *remainder*. **You may wish to carry out a check.**

5. $\left(18x^3 - 3x^2 + x - 1\right) \div \left(x^2 - 4\right)$

6. $\left(6x^4 + x^3 - 9x + 13\right) \div \left(x^2 + 8\right)$

7. $\left(x^4 + 6x - 2.5\right) \div \left(x^2 + 3x + 0.5\right)$

8. $\left(x^3 + 250x^2 + 100x\right) \div \left(\dfrac{1}{2}x^2 + 25x + 9\right)$

Given a polynomial $p(x)$, use synthetic division to divide by $x - a$ and obtain the quotient and the (nonzero) remainder. Write the result in the form $p(x) = (x - a)(\text{quotient}) + p(a)$. You may wish to carry out a check.

9. $(7x^3 - 4x^2 - 400x - 100) \div (x - 8)$

10. $(8x^4 - 28.5x^2 - 9x + 10) \div (x + 0.25)$

11. $(2.5x^3 + 6x^2 - 5.5x - 10) \div (x + 1)$

12. $(-25x^4 - 247x^3 + 50x^2 + 200x + 10) \div (x + 10)$

Determine whether the given binomial is a factor of the polynomial $p(x)$. If so, find the remaining factors of $p(x)$.

13. $p(x) = x^3 + 2x^2 - x - 2;\ (x + 2)$

14. $p(x) = 2x^4 + 6x^3 - 5x - 10;\ (x + 2)$

15. $p(x) = x^3 - 22x^2 + 157x - 360;\ (x - 8)$

16. $p(x) = 3x^4 - 6x^3 - 6x^2 - 3x - 30;\ (x - 2)$

17. $p(x) = 4x^3 - 12x^2 + 2x - 5;\ (x - 3)$

18. The volume of a rectangular prism is modeled by the function $V(x) = x^3 - 8x^2 + 19x - 12$. Given $V(1) = 0$ and $V(3) = 0$, identify the other value of x for which $V(x) = 0$, which will give the missing dimension of the prism.

19. Given that the height of a rectangular prism is $x + 2$ and the volume is $x^3 - x^2 - 6x$, write an expression that represents the area of the top face of the prism.

20. **Physics** A Van de Graaff generator is a machine that produces very high voltages by using small, safe levels of electric current. One machine has a current that can be modeled by $I(t) = t + 2$, where $t > 0$ represents time in seconds. The power of the system can be modeled by $P(t) = 0.5t^3 + 6t^2 + 10t$. Write an expression that represents the voltage of the system. Recall that $V = \frac{P}{I}$.

21. **Geometry** The volume of a hexagonal pyramid is modeled by the function $V(x) = \frac{1}{3}x^3 + \frac{4}{3}x^2 + \frac{2}{3}x - \frac{1}{3}$. Given the height $x + 1$, use polynomial division to find an expression for the area of the base. (Hint: For a pyramid, $V = \frac{1}{3}Bh$.)

22. **Explain the Error** Two students used synthetic division to divide $3x^3 - 2x - 8$ by $x - 2$. Determine which solution is correct. Find the error in the other solution.

A.				B.			
2⌋	3	0	−2	−8	2⌋	3	0	−2	−8
		6	12	20			−6	12	−20
	3	6	10	12		3	−6	10	−28

23. **Multi-Step** Use synthetic division to divide $p(x) = 3x^3 - 11x^2 - 56x - 50$ by $(3x + 4)$. Then check the solution.

24. **Critical Thinking** The polynomial $ax^3 + bx^2 + cx + d$ is factored as $3(x - 2)(x + 3)(x - 4)$. What are the values of a and d? Explain.

25. **Analyze Relationships** Investigate whether the set of whole numbers, the set of integers, and the set of rational numbers are closed under each of the four basic operations. Then consider whether the set of polynomials in one variable is closed under the four basic operations, and determine whether polynomials are like whole numbers, integers, or rational numbers with respect to closure. Use the table to organize.

	Whole Numbers	Integers	Rational Numbers	Polynomials
Addition				
Subtraction				
Multiplication				
Division (by nonzero)				

Lesson Performance Task

The table gives the attendance data for all divisions of NCAA Women's Basketball.

			NCAA Women's Basketball Attendance

Season	Years since 2006–2007	Number of teams in all 3 divisions	Attendance (in thousands) for all 3 divisions
2006–2007	0	1003	10,878.3
2007–2008	1	1013	11,120.8
2008–2009	2	1032	11,160.3
2009–2010	3	1037	11,134.7
2010–2011	4	1048	11,160.0
2011–2012	5	1055	11,201.8

Enter the data from the second, third, and fourth columns of the table and perform polynomial regression on the data pairs (t, T) and (t, A) where $t =$ years since the 2006–2007 season, $T =$ number of teams, and $A =$ attendance (in thousands). For each set of data pairs, choose the regression model having the least degree that best fits the data.

Then create a model for the average attendance per team: $A_{avg}(t) = \frac{A(t)}{T(t)}$. Carry out the division to write $A_{avg}(t)$ in the form *quadratic quotient* $+ \frac{remainder}{T(t)}$.

Use an online computer algebra system to carry out the division of $A(t)$ by $T(t)$.

Essential Question: How can you use polynomials to solve real-world problems?

Key Vocabulary

binomial *(binomio)*

monomial *(monomio)*

polynomial *(polinomio)*

synthetic división *(división sintética)*

trinomial *(trinomio)*

KEY EXAMPLE (Lesson 7.1)

Subtract: $(5x^4 - x^3 + 2x + 1) - (2x^3 + 3x^2 - 4x - 7)$

$$
\begin{array}{r}
5x^4 \;\;- x^3 \;\; 0x^2 \;\;\; 2x \;\;\; 1 \\
+ \;\;\;\;\; -2x^3 \;\; -3x^2 \;\;\; 4x \;\;\; 7 \\
\hline
5x^4 - 3x^3 \;\; -3x^2 + 6x + 8
\end{array}
$$

Write in standard form.

Align like terms and add the opposite.

Add.

Therefore, $(5x^4 - x^3 + 2x + 1) - (2x^3 + 3x^2 - 4x - 7) = 5x^4 - 3x^3 - 3x^2 + 6x + 8$.

KEY EXAMPLE (Lesson 7.2)

Multiply: $(3x - 2)(2x^2 - 5x + 1)$

$(3x - 2)(2x^2 - 5x + 1)$

$3x(2x^2) + 3x(-5x) + 3x(1) + (-2)(2x^2) + (-2)(-5x) + (-2)(1)$

$6x^3 - 15x^2 + 3x - 4x^2 + 10x - 2$

$6x^3 - 19x^2 + 13x - 2$

Therefore, $(3x - 2)(2x^2 - 5x + 1) = 6x^3 - 19x^2 + 13x - 2$.

Write in standard form.

Distribute the 3x and the −2.

Simplify.

Combine like terms.

KEY EXAMPLE (Lesson 7.4)

Divide: $(x^3 + 10x^2 + 13x + 36) \div (x + 9)$

$$
\begin{array}{r}
x^2 + x + 4 \\
x + 9 \overline{)\; x^3 + 10x^2 + 13x + 36} \\
+.-\left(x^3 + \;\; 9x^2\right) \\
\hline
x^2 + 13x \\
-\left(x^2 + \;\; 9x\right) \\
\hline
4x + 36 \\
-\left(4x + 36\right) \\
\hline
0
\end{array}
$$

In order to get x^3, multiply by x^2.

Multiply the divisor through by x^2, then subtract.

In order to get x^2, multiply by x.

Multiply the divisor through by x, then subtract.

In order to get 4x, multiply by 4.

Multiply the divisor through by 4, then subtract.

Therefore, $(x^3 + 10x^2 + 13x + 36) \div (x + 9) = x^2 + x + 4$.

EXERCISES

Solve. *(Lessons 7.1, 7.2, 7.4)*

1. $(9x^2 + 2x + 12) + (7x^2 + 10x - 13)$

2. $(6x^6 - 4x^5) - (10x^5 - 15x^4 + 8)$

3. $(x - 3)(4x^2 - 2x + 3)$

4. $(3x^3 - 2x^2 + 4x + 7) \div (x^2 + 2x)$

5. Mr. Alonzo runs a car repair garage. The average income from repairing a car can be modeled by $C(x) = 45x + 150$. If, for one year, the number of cars repaired can be modeled by $N(x) = 9x^2 + 7x + 6$, write a polynomial that can be used to model Mr. Alonzo's business income for that year. Explain. *(Lesson 7.2)*

MODULE PERFORMANCE TASK
What's the Temperature?

A meteorologist studying the temperature patterns for Redding, California found the average of the daily minimum and maximum temperatures for each month, but the August temperatures are missing.

Month	Jan	Feb	Mar	Apr	May	June	July	Aug	Sep	Oct	Nov	Dec
Average Max Temperature (°F)	55.3	61.3	62.5	69.6	80.5	90.4	98.3	?	89.3	77.6	62.1	54.7
Average Min Temperature (°F)	35.7	40	41.7	46	52.3	61.8	64.7	?	58.8	49.2	41.4	35.2

How can she find the averages for August? She began by fitting the polynomial function shown below to the data for the average maximum temperature, where x is the month, with $x = 1$ corresponding to January, and the temperature is in degrees Fahrenheit.

$$T_{\max}(x) = 0.0095x^5 - 0.2719x^4 + 2.5477x^3 - 9.1882x^2 + 17.272x + 45.468$$

She also thinks that a vertical compression of this function will create a function that fits the average minimum temperature data for Redding.

Use this information to find the average high and low temperature for August. Use graphs, numbers, words, or algebra to explain how you reached your conclusion.

(Ready) to Go On?

7.1–7.4 Polynomials

- Online Homework
- Hints and Help
- Extra Practice

Factor the polynomial. *(Lesson 7.3)*

1. $3x^2 + 4x - 4$

2. $2x^3 + 4x^2 - 30x$

3. $9x^2 - 25$

4. $4x^2 - 16x + 16$

Complete the polynomial operation. *(Lesson 7.1, 7.2, 7.4)*

5. $\left(8x^3 - 2x^2 - 4x + 8\right) + \left(5x^2 + 6x - 4\right)$

6. $\left(-4x^2 - 2x + 8\right) - \left(x^2 + 8x - 5\right)$

7. $5x(x + 2)(3x - 7)$

8. $\left(3x^3 + 12x^2 + 11x - 2\right) \div (x + 2)$

ESSENTIAL QUESTION

9. Write a real world situation that would require adding polynomials. *(Lesson 7.1)*

Assessment Readiness

1. Which of the following polynomials can be divided without a remainder?
   A. $(3x^3 - 5x^2 - 10x - 2) \div (x + 1)$
   B. $(2x^2 - 5x - 1) \div (x - 3)$
   C. $(x^3 - 4x^2 + 2x - 3) \div (x + 2)$
   D. $(2x^3 - 2x + 3) \div (x - 5)$

2. Factor $x^3 - x^2 - 6x$ completely.
   A. $x^2(x - 6)$
   B. $x(x + 2)(x - 3)$
   C. $(x - 3)(x - 6)(x + 1)$
   D. $(x + 2)(x - 3)$

3. How many turning points are there in the graph of $h(x) = (x + 5)(x + 4)(x - 2)^2$?
   A. 1
   B. 3
   C. 5
   D. 6

4. If a parabola has a focus at $(3, 2)$ and a directrix of $y = 6$, in which direction does it open?
   A. upward
   B. downward
   C. leftward
   D. rightward

5. A rectangular plot of land has a length of $(2x^2 + 5x - 20)$ and a width of $(3x + 4)$. What is the polynomial representing the area of the plot of land? Explain how you got your answer.

Polynomial Equations

Essential Question: How can you use polynomial equations to solve real-world problems?

LESSON 8.1
Finding Rational Solutions of Polynomial Equations
TEKS **A2.7.D**

LESSON 8.2
Finding Complex Solutions of Polynomial Equations
TEKS **A2.7.D, A2.7.E**

REAL WORLD VIDEO
The population of the Texas horned lizard has decreased rapidly, and the species is now considered threatened. Biologists use polynomials and other mathematical models to study threatened and endangered species.

MODULE PERFORMANCE TASK PREVIEW

What Do Polynomials Have to Do with Endangered Species?

A species is considered to be endangered when the population is so low that the species is at risk of becoming extinct. Biologists use mathematics to model the population of species, and use their models to help them predict the future population and to determine whether or not a species is at risk of extinction. How can a polynomial be used to model a species population? Let's find out!

Are Ready?

Complete these exercises to review skills you will need for this chapter.

Real Numbers

Example 1

Compare $2\sqrt{64}$ and $\sqrt{225}$.

$2\sqrt{64} = 2.8$ and $\sqrt{225} = 15$ *Evaluate the radicals.*

$16 > 15$ *Multiply and compare.*

Since $16 > 15$, $2\sqrt{64} > \sqrt{225}$.

• Online Homework
• Hints and Help
• Extra Practice

Compare. Use $>$ or $<$.

1. $4\sqrt{25}$? $25\sqrt{4}$

2. $0.75\sqrt{144}$? $8\sqrt{16}$

3. $2.2\sqrt{100}$? $3\sqrt{36}$

Add and Subtract Rational Numbers

Example 2

Add $\dfrac{3}{4} + \dfrac{5}{6}$.

$\left(\dfrac{3}{3}\right) \cdot \dfrac{3}{4} + \left(\dfrac{2}{2}\right) \cdot \dfrac{5}{6}$ *The LCM is 12.*

$\dfrac{9}{12} + \dfrac{10}{12}$ *Multiply by 1.*

$\dfrac{19}{12}$ *Add.*

Add or subtract.

4. $\dfrac{1}{3} + \dfrac{5}{8}$

5. $\dfrac{7}{12} - \dfrac{4}{9}$

6. $\dfrac{9}{8} - \dfrac{5}{6}$

Equations Involving Exponents

Example 3

Solve $x^2 + 3x - 10 = 0$ for x.

$(x - 2)(x + 5) = 0$ *Factor.*

Either $(x - 2) = 0$ or $(x + 5) = 0$

$x = 2$ or $x = -5$ *Solve.*

The solutions for x are 2 and −5.

Solve for x.

7. $x^2 - 5x + 4 = 0$

8. $x^2 + 11x + 30 = 0$

9. $x^2 + 6x = 16$

8.1 Finding Rational Solutions of Polynomial Equations

Resource Locker

Essential Question: How do you find the rational roots of a polynomial equation?

 TEKS **A2.7.D** Determine the linear factors of a polynomial function of degree three and of degree four using algebraic methods. Also A2.7.B

 Explore **Relating Zeros and Coefficients of Polynomial Functions**

The zeros of a polynomial function and the coefficients of the function are related. Consider the polynomial function $f(x) = (x + 2)(x - 1)(x + 3)$.

(A) Identify the zeros of the polynomial function.

(B) Multiply the factors to write the function in standard form.

(C) How are the zeros of $f(x)$ related to the standard form of the function?

(D) Now consider the polynomial function $g(x) = (2x + 3)(4x - 5)(6x - 1)$. Identify the zeros of this function.

(E) Multiply the factors to write the function in standard form.

(F) How are the zeros of $g(x)$ related to the standard form of the function?

Reflect

1. In general, how are the zeros of a polynomial function related to the function written in standard form?

2. **Discussion** Does the relationship from the first Reflect question hold if the zeros are all integers? Explain.

3. If you use the zeros, you can write the factored form of $g(x)$ as $g(x) = \left(x + \frac{3}{2}\right)\left(x - \frac{5}{4}\right)\left(x - \frac{1}{6}\right)$, rather than as $g(x) = (2x + 3)(4x - 5)(6x - 1)$. What is the relationship of the factors between the two forms? Give this relationship in a general form.

🔧 Explain 1 Finding Zeros Using the Rational Zero Theorem

If a polynomial function $p(x)$ is equal to $(a_1x + b_1)(a_2x + b_2)(a_3x + b_3)$, where $a_1, a_2, a_3, b_1, b_2,$ and b_3 are integers, the leading coefficient of $p(x)$ will be the product $a_1a_2a_3$ and the constant term will be the product $b_1b_2b_3$. The zeros of $p(x)$ will be the rational numbers $-\frac{b_1}{a_1}, -\frac{b_2}{a_2}, -\frac{b_3}{a_3}$.

Comparing the zeros of $p(x)$ to its coefficient and constant term shows that the numerators of the polynomial's zeros are factors of the constant term and the denominators of the zeros are factors of the leading coefficient. This result can be generalized as the Rational Zero Theorem.

Rational Zero Theorem

If $p(x)$ is a polynomial function with integer coefficients, and if $\frac{m}{n}$ is a zero of $p(x)$ $\left(p\left(\frac{m}{n}\right) = 0\right)$, then m is a factor of the constant term of $p(x)$ and n is a factor of the leading coefficient of $p(x)$.

Example 1 Find the rational zeros of the polynomial function; then write the function as a product of factors. Make sure to test the possible zeros to find the actual zeros of the function.

Ⓐ $f(x) = x^3 + 2x^2 - 19x - 20$

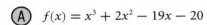

   a. Use the Rational Zero Theorem to find all possible rational zeros.
      Factors of -20: $\pm 1, \pm 2, \pm 4, \pm 5, \pm 10, \pm 20$

   b. Test the possible zeros. Use a synthetic division table to organize the work. In this table, the first row represents the coefficients of the polynomial, the first column represents the divisors, and the last column represents the remainders.

$\frac{m}{n}$	1	2	−19	−20
1	1	3	−16	−36
2	1	4	−11	−42
4	1	6	5	0
5	1	7	16	60

   c. Factor the polynomial. The synthetic division by 4 results in a remainder of 0, so 4 is a zero and the polynomial in factored form is given as follows:

$$(x - 4)(x^2 + 6x + 5) = 0$$

$$(x - 4)(x + 5)(x + 1) = 0$$

$$x = 4, x = -5, \text{ or } x = -1$$

The zeros are $x = 4$, $x = -5$, or $x = -1$.

(B) $f(x) = x^4 - 4x^3 - 7x^2 + 22x + 24$

    a. Use the Rational Zero Theorem to find all possible rational zeros.

        Factors of -24: $\pm 1, \pm 2, \pm 3, \pm 4, \pm 6, \pm 8, \pm 12, \pm 24$

    b. Test the possible zeros. Use a synthetic division table.

$\dfrac{m}{n}$	1	-4	-7	22	24
1	1	-3	-10	12	36
2	1	-2	-11	0	24
3	1	-1	-10	-8	0

    c. Factor the polynomial. The synthetic division by 3 results in a remainder of 0, so 3 is a zero and the polynomial in factored form is given as follows:

        $(x - 3)(x^3 - x^2 - 10x - 8) = 0$

    d. Use the Rational Zero Theorem again to find all possible rational zeros of $g(x) = x^3 - x^2 - 10x - 8$.

        Factors of -8: $\pm 1, \pm 2, \pm 4, \pm 8$

    e. Test the possible zeros. Use a synthetic division table.

$\dfrac{m}{n}$	1	-1	-10	-8
1	1	0	-10	-18
2	1	1	-8	-24
3	1	2	-4	-20
4	1	3	2	0

    f. Factor the polynomial. The synthetic division by 4 results in a remainder of 0, so 4 is a zero and the polynomial in factored form is:

        $(x - 3)(x - 4)(1x^2 + 3x + 2) = 0$

        $(x - 3)(x - 4)(x + 2)(x + 1) = 0$

        $x = 3, x = 4, x = -2,$ or $x = -1$

        The zeros are $x = 3, x = 4, x = -2,$ or $x = -1$.

4. How is using synthetic division on a 4th degree polynomial to find its zeros different than using synthetic division on a 3rd degree polynomial to find its zeros?

5. Suppose you are trying to find the zeros the function $f(x) = x^2 + 1$. Would it be possible to use synthetic division on this polynomial? Why or why not?

6. Using synthetic division, you find that $\frac{1}{2}$ is a zero of $f(x) = 2x^3 + x^2 - 13x + 6$. The quotient from the synthetic division array for $f\left(\frac{1}{2}\right)$ is $2x^2 + 2x - 12$. Show how to write the factored form of $f(x) = 2x^3 + x^2 - 13x + 6$ using integer coefficients.

Your Turn

7. Find the zeros of $f(x) = x^3 - 2x^2 - 8x$.

Explain 2   Solving a Real-World Problem Using the Rational Root Theorem

Since a zero of a function $f(x)$ is a value of x for which $f(x) = 0$, finding the zeros of a polynomial function $p(x)$ is the same thing as find the solutions of the polynomial equation $p(x) = 0$. Because a solution of a polynomial equation is known as a **root**, the Rational Zero Theorem can be also expressed as the Rational Root Theorem.

Rational Root Theorem

If the polynomial $p(x)$ has integer coefficients, then every rational root of the polynomial equation $p(x) = 0$ can be written in the form $\frac{m}{n}$, where m is a factor of the constant term of $p(x)$ and n is a factor of the leading coefficient of $p(x)$.

Ⓐ **Engineering** A pen company is designing a gift container for their new premium pen. The marketing department has designed a pyramidal box with a rectangular base. The base width is 1 inch shorter than its base length and the height is 3 inches taller than 3 times the base length. The volume of the box must be 6 cubic inches. What are the dimensions of the box? Graph the volume function and the line $y = 6$ on a graphing calculator to check your solution.

A. Analyze Information

The important information is that the base width must be 1 inch shorter than

the base length, the height must be 3 inches taller than 3 times the base length,

and the box must have a volume of 6 cubic inches.

B. Formulate a Plan

Write an equation to model the volume of the box.

Let x represent the base length in inches. The base width is $x - 1$ and the height is $3x + 3$, or $3(x + 1)$.

$$\frac{1}{3}\,\ell wh = V$$
$$\frac{1}{3}(x)(x - 1)(3)(x + 1) = 6$$
$$1x^3 - 1x - 6 = 0$$

 C. Solve

Use the Rational Root Theorem to find all possible rational roots.

Factors of -6: $\pm 1, \pm 2, \pm 3, \pm 6$

Test the possible roots. Use a synthetic division table.

$\frac{m}{n}$	1	0	−1	−6
1	1	1	0	−6
2	1	2	3	0
3	1	3	8	18

Factor the polynomial. The synthetic division by 2 results in a remainder of 0, so 2 is a root and the polynomial in factored form is as follows:

$$\left(1x - 2\right)\left(1x^2 + 3x + 8\right) = 0, \text{ or } \left(x - 2\right)\left(x^2 + 3x + 8\right) = 0$$

The quadratic polynomial produces only complex roots, so the only possible answer for the base length is 2 inches. The base width is 1 inch and the height is 9 inches.

 D. Justify and Evaluate

The x-coordinates of the points where the graphs of two functions, f and g, intersect is the solution of the equation $f(x) = g(x)$. Using a graphing calculator to graph the volume function and $y = 6$ results in the graphs intersecting at the point $(2, 6)$. Since the x-coordinate is 2, the answer is correct.

Your Turn

8. **Engineering** A box company is designing a new rectangular gift container. The marketing department has designed a box with a width 2 inches shorter than its length and a height 3 inches taller than its length. The volume of the box must be 56 cubic inches. What are the dimensions of the box?

9. For a polynomial function with integer coefficients, how are the function's coefficients and rational zeros related?

10. Describe the process for finding the rational zeros of a polynomial function with integer coefficients.

11. How is the Rational Root Theorem useful when solving a real-world problem about the volume of an object when the volume function is a polynomial and a specific value of the function is given?

12. **Essential Question Check-In** What does the Rational Root Theorem find?

☆ Evaluate: Homework and Practice

Find the rational zeros of each polynomial function then write each function in factored form.

• Online Homework
• Hints and Help
• Extra Practice

1. $f(x) = x^3 - x^2 - 10x - 8$

2. $f(x) = x^3 + 2x^2 - 23x - 60$

3. $j(x) = 2x^3 - x^2 - 13x - 6$

4. $g(x) = x^3 - 9x^2 + 23x - 15$

5. $h(x) = x^3 - 5x^2 + 2x + 8$

6. $h(x) = 6x^3 - 7x^2 - 9x - 2$

7. $s(x) = x^3 - x^2 - x + 1$

8. $t(x) = x^3 + x^2 - 8x - 12$

9. $A(x) = x^3 - 9x^2 + 27x - 27$

10. $q(x) = x^3 - 4x^2 - 16x + 64$

11. $b(x) = x^3 - 6x^2 - 37x + 210$

12. $R(x) = x^3 - 6x^2 - x + 30$

13. $k(x) = x^4 + 5x^3 - x^2 - 17x + 12$

14. $g(x) = x^4 - 6x^3 + 11x^2 - 6x$

15. $h(x) = x^4 - 2x^3 - 3x^2 + 4x + 4$

16. $f(x) = x^4 - 5x^2 + 4$

17. $j(x) = x^4 + 3x^3 - 12x^2 - 20x + 48$

18. $h(x) = x^4 - 11x^3 + 41x^2 - 61x + 30$

19. **Manufacturing** A company is designing a new rectangular shipping box that must have a volume of 24 cubic inches. The company has created a box with a width that is 2 inches less than its length. The height is 5 inches greater than the length. What are the dimensions?

20. **Manufacturing** A laboratory supply company is designing a new rectangular box in which to ship glass pipes. The company has created a box with a width 2 inches shorter than its length and a height 9 inches taller than twice its length. The volume of each box must be 45 cubic inches. What are the dimensions?

21. Engineering A natural history museum is building a pyramidal glass structure for its tree snake exhibit. Its research team has designed a pyramid with a square base and with a height that is 2 yards more than a side of its base. The volume of the pyramid must be 147 cubic yards. What are the dimensions?

22. Engineering A paper company is designing a new, pyramid-shaped paperweight. Its development team has decided that to make the length of the paperweight 4 inches less than the height and the width of the paperweight 3 inches less than the height. The paperweight must have a volume of 12 cubic inches. What are the dimensions of the paperweight?

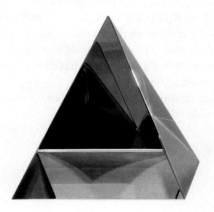

23. Match each polynomial function with its set of roots.

a. $f(x) = (x + 2)(x - 4)\left(x - \dfrac{3}{2}\right)$

A. $x = 2, x = 3, x = 4$

b. $f(x) = \left(x - \dfrac{1}{2}\right)\left(x - \dfrac{5}{4}\right)\left(x + \dfrac{7}{3}\right)$

B. $x = -2, x = -4, x = \dfrac{3}{2}$

c. $f(x) = (x - 2)(x - 2)(x - 2)$

C. $x = \dfrac{1}{2}, x = \dfrac{5}{4}, x = \dfrac{-7}{3}$

d. $f(x) = \left(x + \dfrac{4}{5}\right)\left(x - \dfrac{6}{7}\right)(x - 4)$

D. $x = \dfrac{-4}{5}, x = \dfrac{6}{7}, x = 4$

24. Identify the zeroes of $f(x) = (x + 3)(x - 4)(x - 3)$, write the function in standard form, and state how the zeros are related to the standard form.

H.O.T. Focus on Higher Order Thinking

25. Critical Thinking Consider the polynomial function $g(x) = 2x^3 - 6x^2 + \pi x + 5$. Is it possible to use the Rational Zero Theorem and synthetic division to factor this polynomial? Explain.

26. Explain the Error Sabrina was told to find the zeros of the polynomial function $h(x) = x(x - 4)(x + 2)$. She stated that the zeros of this polynomial are $x = 0$, $x = -4$, and $x = 2$. Explain her error.

27. Justify Reasoning If $\dfrac{c}{b}$ is a rational zero of a polynomial function $p(x)$, explain why $bx - c$ must be a factor of the polynomial.

28. Justify Reasoning A polynomial function $p(x)$ has degree 3, and its zeros are -3, 4, and 6. What do you think is the equation of $p(x)$? Do you think there could be more than one possibility? Explain.

Lesson Performance Task

For the years from 2001–2010, the number of Americans traveling to other countries by plane can be represented by the polynomial function $A(t) = 20t^4 - 428t^3 + 2760t^2 - 4320t + 33{,}600$, where A is the number of thousands of Americans traveling abroad by airplane and t is the number of years since 2001. In which year were there 40,000,000 Americans traveling abroad? Use the Rational Root Theorem to find your answer.

[Hint: consider the function's domain and range before finding all possible rational roots.]

8.2 Finding Complex Solutions of Polynomial Equations

Resource Locker

Essential Question: What do the Fundamental Theorem of Algebra and its corollary tell you about the roots of the polynomial equation p(x) = 0 where p(x) has degree n?

 A2.7.D Determine the linear factors of a polynomial function of degree three and of degree four using algebraic methods. Also A2.7.B, A2.7.E

⊘ Explore   Investigating the Number of Complex Zeros of a Polynomial Function

You have used various algebraic and graphical methods to find the roots of a polynomial equation $p(x) = 0$ or the zeros of a polynomial function $p(x)$. Because a polynomial can have a factor that repeats, a zero or a root can occur multiple times.

The polynomial $p(x) = x^3 + 8x^2 + 21x + 18 = (x + 2)(x + 3)^2$ has -2 as a zero once and -3 as a zero twice, or *with multiplicity 2.* The **multiplicity** of a zero of $p(x)$ or a root of $p(x) = 0$ is the number of times that the related factor occurs in the factorization.

In this Explore, you will use algebraic methods to investigate the relationship between the degree of a polynomial function and the number of zeros that it has.

(A) Find all zeros of $p(x) = x^3 + 7x^2$. Include any multiplicities greater than 1.

$$p(x) = x^3 + 7x^2$$

Factor out the GCF. $p(x) = \boxed{}(x + 7)$

What are all the zeros of $p(x)$? $\boxed{}$

(B) Find all zeros of $p(x) = x^3 - 64$. Include any multiplicities greater than 1.

$$p(x) = x^3 - 64$$

Factor the difference of two cubes. $p(x) = \left(x \boxed{} 4\right)\left(x^2 + \boxed{} + \boxed{}\right)$

What are the real zeros of $p(x)$?

Solve $x^2 + 4x + 16 = 0$ using the quadratic formula.

$$x = \frac{-b \pm \sqrt{b^2 - 4ac}}{2a}$$

$$x = \frac{\boxed{} \pm \sqrt{4^2 - 4 \cdot 1 \cdot \boxed{}}}{2 \cdot \boxed{}} \quad x = \frac{-4 \pm \sqrt{\boxed{}}}{2} \quad x = \frac{-4 \pm \boxed{} \sqrt{3}}{2}$$

$$x = -2 \pm 2i\sqrt{3}$$

What are the non-real zeros of $p(x)$?

Ⓒ Find all zeros of $p(x) = x^4 + 3x^3 - 4x^2 - 12x$. Include any multiplicities greater than 1.

$$p(x) = x^4 + 3x^3 - 4x^2 - 12x$$

Factor out the GCF.

$$p(x) = x\left(\boxed{}\right)$$

Group terms to begin
factoring by grouping.

$$p(x) = x\left((x^3 + 3x^2) - \left(\boxed{}\right)\right)$$

Factor out common monomials.

$$p(x) = x\left(\boxed{}(x + 3) - \boxed{}(x + 3)\right)$$

Factor out the common binomial.

$$p(x) = x(x + 3)(x^2 - 4)$$

Factor the difference of squares.

$$p(x) = x(x + 3)\left(\boxed{}\right)\left(\boxed{}\right)$$

What are all the zeros of $p(x)$?

Ⓓ Find all zeros of $p(x) = x^4 - 16$. Include any multiplicities greater than 1.

$$p(x) = x^4 - 16$$

Factor the difference of squares.

$$p(x) = \left(\boxed{}\right)(x^2 + 4)$$

Factor the difference of squares.

$$p(x) = \left(\boxed{}\right)\left(\boxed{}\right)(x^2 + 4)$$

What are the real zeros of $p(x)$? $\boxed{}$

Solve $x^2 + 4 = 0$ by taking square roots.

$$x^2 + 4 = 0$$
$$x^2 = -4$$
$$x = \pm\sqrt{-4}$$
$$x = \pm\boxed{}$$

What are the non-real zeros of $p(x)$?

(E) Find all zeros of $p(x) = x^4 + 5x^3 + 6x^2 - 4x - 8$. Include multiplicities greater than 1.

By the Rational Zero Theorem, possible rational zeros are ± 1, ± 2, ± 4, and ± 8.
Use a synthetic division table to test possible zeros.

$\dfrac{m}{n}$	1	5	6	−4	−8
1	1	6	12	8	0

The remainder is 0. Does this indicate that 1 is a zero?

$p(x)$ factors as $(x - 1)\left(\right)$.

Test for zeros in the cubic polynomial.

$\dfrac{m}{n}$	1	6	12	8
1	1	7	19	27
−1	1	5	7	1
2	1	8	28	64
−2	1	4	4	0

▮ a zero.

$p(x)$ factors as $(x - 1)(x + 2)\left(\right)$. The quadratic is a perfect square trinomial.

So, $p(x)$ factors completely as $p(x) = (x - 1) $.

What are all the zeros of $p(x)$? ▮

(F) Copy and complete the table to summarize your results from Steps A–E.

Polynomial Function in Standard Form	Polynomial Function Factored over the Integers	Real Zeros and Their Multiplicities	Non-real Zeros and Their Multiplicities
$p(x) = x^3 + 7x^2$	▮	▮	▮
$p(x) = x^3 - 64$	▮	▮	▮
$p(x) = x^4 + 3x^3 - 4x^2 - 12x$	▮	▮	▮
$p(x) = x^4 - 16$	▮	▮	▮
$p(x) = x^4 + 5x^3 + 6x^2 - 4x - 8$	▮	▮	▮

1. Examine the table. For each function, count the number of unique zeros, both real and non-real. How does the number of unique zeros compare with the degree?

2. Examine the table again. This time, count the total number of zeros for each function, where a zero of multiplicity m is counted as m zeros. How does the total number of zeros compare with the degree?

3. **Discussion** Describe the apparent relationship between the degree of a polynomial function and the number of zeros it has.

Explain 1   Applying the Fundamental Theorem of Algebra to Solving Polynomial Equations

The Fundamental Theorem of Algebra and its corollary summarize what you have observed earlier while finding rational zeros of polynomial functions and in completing the Explore.

The Fundamental Theorem of Algebra

Every polynomial function of degree $n \geq 1$ has at least one zero, where a zero may be a complex number.

Corollary: Every polynomial function of degree $n \geq 1$ has exactly n zeros, including multiplicities.

Because the zeros of a polynomial function $p(x)$ give the roots of the equation $p(x) = 0$, the theorem and its corollary also extend to finding all roots of a polynomial equation.

Example 1   Solve the polynomial equation by finding all roots.

(A) $2x^3 - 12x^2 - 34x + 204 = 0$

The polynomial has degree 3, so the equation has exactly 3 roots.

$$2x^3 - 12x^2 - 34x + 204 = 0$$

Divide both sides by 2. $x^3 - 6x^2 - 17x + 102 = 0$

Group terms. $(x^3 - 6x^2) - (17x - 102) = 0$

Factor out common monomials. $x^2(x - 6) - 17(x - 6) = 0$

Factor out the common binomial. $(x^2 - 17)(x - 6) = 0$

One root is $x = 6$. Solving $x^2 - 17 = 0$ gives $x^2 = 17$, or $x = \pm\sqrt{17}$.

The roots are $-\sqrt{17}$, $\sqrt{17}$, and 6.

(B) $x^4 - 6x^2 - 27 = 0$

The polynomial has degree 4, so the equation has exactly 4 roots.

Notice that $x^4 - 6x^2 - 27$ has the form $u^2 - 6u - 27$, where $u = x^2$. So, you can factor it like a quadratic trinomial.

$$x^4 - 6x^2 - 27 = 0$$

Factor the trinomial. $\left(x^2 - \boxed{9}\right)\left(x^2 + \boxed{3}\right) = 0$

Factor the difference of squares. $\left(x + \boxed{3}\right)\left(x - \boxed{3}\right)(x^2 + 3) = 0$

The real roots are -3 and 3. Solving $x^2 + 3 = 0$ gives $x^2 = -3$, or

$$x = \pm\sqrt{-3} = \pm\boxed{i}\sqrt{\boxed{3}}.$$

The roots are -3, 3, $-i\sqrt{3}$, $i\sqrt{3}$.

Reflect

4. Restate the Fundamental Theorem of Algebra and its corollary in terms of the roots of equations.

Your Turn

Solve the polynomial equation by finding all roots.

5. $8x^3 - 27 = 0$

6. $p(x) = x^4 - 13x^3 + 55x^2 - 91x$

🖋 Explain 2   Writing a Polynomial Function From Its Zeros

You may have noticed in finding roots of quadratic and polynomial equations that any irrational or complex roots come in pairs. These pairs reflect the "$\pm$" in the quadratic formula. For example, for any of the following number pairs, you will never have a polynomial equation for which only one number in the pair is a root.

$$\sqrt{5} \text{ and } -\sqrt{5};\ 1 + \sqrt{7} \text{ and } 1 - \sqrt{7};\ i \text{ and } -i;\ 2 + 14i \text{ and } 2 - 14i;\ \frac{11}{6} + \frac{1}{6}i\sqrt{3} \text{ and } \frac{11}{6} - \frac{1}{6}i\sqrt{3}$$

The irrational root pairs $a + b\sqrt{c}$ and $a - b\sqrt{c}$ are called *irrational conjugates*. The complex root pairs $a + bi$ and $a - bi$ are called *complex conjugates*.

Irrational Root Theorem

If a polynomial $p(x)$ has rational coefficients and $a + b\sqrt{c}$ is a root of the equation $p(x) = 0$, where a and b are rational and $\sqrt{c}$ is irrational, then $a - b\sqrt{c}$ is also a root of $p(x) = 0$.

Complex Conjugate Root Theorem

If $a + bi$ is an imaginary root of a polynomial equation with real-number coefficients, then $a - bi$ is also a root.

Because the roots of the equation $p(x) = 0$ give the zeros of a polynomial function, corresponding theorems apply to the zeros of a polynomial function. You can use this fact to write a polynomial function from its zeros. Because irrational and complex conjugate pairs are a sum and difference of terms, the product of irrational conjugates is always a rational number and the product of complex conjugates is always a real number.

$$\left(2 - \sqrt{10}\right)\left(2 + \sqrt{10}\right) = 2^2 - \left(\sqrt{10}\right)^2 = 4 - 10 = -6 \left(1 - i\sqrt{2}\right)\left(1 + i\sqrt{2}\right) = 1^2 - \left(i\sqrt{2}\right)^2 = 1 - (-1)(2) = 3$$

Example 2 **Write the polynomial function with least degree and a leading coefficient of 1 that has the given zeros.**

 A 5 and $3 + 2\sqrt{7}$

Because irrational zeros come in conjugate pairs, $3 - 2\sqrt{7}$ must also be a zero of the function.

Use the 3 zeros to write a function in factored form, then multiply to write it in standard form.

$$p(x) = \left[x - \left(3 + 2\sqrt{7}\right)\right]\left[x - \left(3 - 2\sqrt{7}\right)\right](x - 5)$$

Multiply the first two factors using FOIL.
$$= \left[x^2 - \left(3 - 2\sqrt{7}\right)x - \left(3 + 2\sqrt{7}\right)x + \left(3 + 2\sqrt{7}\right)\left(3 - 2\sqrt{7}\right)\right](x - 5)$$

Multipy the conjugates.
$$= \left[x^2 - \left(3 - 2\sqrt{7}\right)x - \left(3 + 2\sqrt{7}\right)x + \left(9 - 4 \cdot 7\right)\right](x - 5)$$

Combine like terms.
$$= \left[x^2 + \left(-3 + 2\sqrt{7} - 3 - 2\sqrt{7}\right)x + (-19)\right](x - 5)$$

Simplify.
$$= \left[x^2 - 6x - 19\right](x - 5)$$

Distributive property
$$= x\left(x^2 - 6x - 19\right) - 5\left(x^2 - 6x - 19\right)$$

Multiply.
$$= x^3 - 6x^2 - 19x - 5x^2 + 30x + 95$$

Combine like terms.
$$= x^3 - 11x^2 + 11x + 95$$

The polynomial function is $p(x) = x^3 - 11x^2 + 11x + 95$.

Ⓑ 2, 3 and $1 - i$

Because complex zeros come in conjugate pairs, $1 + i$ must also be a zero of the function.

Use the 4 zeros to write a function in factored form, then multiply to write it in standard form.

$$p(x) = \left[x - (1 + i)\right]\left[x - \boxed{\left(1 - i\right)}\right](x - 2)(x - 3)$$

Multiply the first
two factors using FOIL.
$$= \left[x^2 - (1 - i)x - \boxed{\left(1 + i\right)}x + (1 + i)(1 - i)\right](x - 2)(x - 3)$$

Multipy the conjugates.
$$= \left[x^2 - (1 - i)x - (1 + i)x + \left(1 - \boxed{\left(-1\right)}\right)\right](x - 2)(x - 3)$$

Combine like terms.
$$= \left[x^2 + (-1 + i - 1 + i)x + 2\right](x - 2)(x - 3)$$

Simplify.
$$= \boxed{\left(x^2 - 2x + 2\right)}(x - 2)(x - 3)$$

Multipy the binomials.
$$= (x^2 - 2x + 2)\ \boxed{\left(x^2 - 5x + 6\right)}$$

Distributive property
$$= x^2(x^2 - 5x + 6)\boxed{-\ 2x}\ (x^2 - 5x + 6) + 2(x^2 - 5x + 6)$$

Multipy.
$$= (x^4 - 5x^3 - 6x^2) + \left(-2x^3 + 10x^2 - 12x\right) + \left(2x^2 - 10x + 12\right)$$

Combine like terms.
$$= \boxed{x^4 - 7x^3 + 18x^2 - 22x + 12}$$

The polynomial function is $p(x) = x^4 - 7x^3 + 18x^2 - 22x + 12$.

Reflect

7. Restate the Irrational Root Theorem in terms of the zeros of polynomial functions.

8. Restate the Complex Conjugates Zero Theorem in terms of the roots of equations.

Your Turn

Write the polynomial function with the least degree and a leading coefficient of 1 that has the given zeros.

9. $2 + 3i$ and $4 - 7\sqrt{2}$

Explain 3 Solving a Real-World Problem by Graphing Polynomial Functions

You can use graphing to help you locate or approximate any real zeros of a polynomial function. Though a graph will not help you find non-real zeros, it can indicate that the function has non-real zeros. For example, look at the graph of $p(x) = x^4 - 2x^2 - 3$.

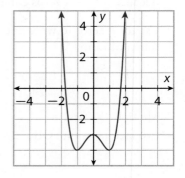

The graph intersects the x-axis twice, which shows that the function has two real zeros. By the corollary to the Fundamental Theorem of Algebra, however, a fourth degree polynomial has four zeros. So, the other two zeros of $p(x)$ must be non-real. The zeros are $-\sqrt{3}$, $\sqrt{3}$, i, and $-i$. (A polynomial whose graph has a turning point on the x-axis has a real zero of even multiplicity at that point. If the graph "bends" at the x-axis, there is a real zero of odd multiplicity greater than 1 at that point.)

(A) The following polynomial models approximate the total oil consumption C (in millions of barrels per day) for North America (NA) and the Asia Pacific region (AP) over the period from 2001 to 2011, where t is in years and $t = 0$ represents 2001.

$$C_{NA}(t) = 0.00494t^4 - 0.0915t^3 + 0.442t^2 - 0.239t + 23.6$$

$$C_{AP}(t) = 0.00877t^3 - 0.139t^2 + 1.23t - 21.1$$

Use a graphing calculator to plot the functions and approximate the x-coordinate of the intersection in the region of interest. What does this represent in the context of this situation? Determine when oil consumption in the Asia Pacific region overtook oil consumption in North America using the requested method.

Graph $Y1 = 0.00494x^4 - 0.0915x^3 + 0.442x^2 - 0.239x + 23.6$ and $Y2 = 0.00877x^3 - 0.139x^2 + 1.23x + 21.1$. Use the "Calc" menu to find the point of intersection. Here are the results for Xmin = 0, Xmax = 10, Ymin = 20, Ymax = 30. (The graph for the Asia Pacific is the one that rises upward on all segments.)

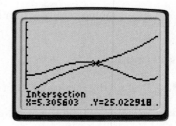

The functions intersect at about $x = 5$, which represents the year 2006. This means that the models show oil consumption in the Asia Pacific equaling and then overtaking oil consumption in North America about 2006.

(B) Find a single polynomial model for the situation in Example 3A whose zero represents the time that oil consumption for the Asia Pacific region overtakes consumption for North America. Plot the function on a graphing calculator and use it to find the x-intercept.

Let the function $C_D(t)$ represent the difference in oil consumption in the Asia Pacific and North America.

A difference of 0 indicates the time that consumption is equal.

$$\boxed{C_D(t)} = \boxed{C_{AP}(t)} - C_{NA}(t)$$

$$= -0.00877t^3 - 0.139t^2 + 1.23t + 21.1 - \left(0.00494t^4 - 0.0915t^3 + 0.442t^2 - 0.239t + 23.6\right)$$

Remove parentheses and rearrange terms.

$$= -0.00494t^4 + 0.00877t^3 + 0.0915t^3 - 0.139t^2 - 0.442t^2 + 1.23t + 0.239t + 21.1 - 23.6$$

Combine like terms. Round to three significant digits.

$$= -0.00494t^4 + 0.100t^3 - 0.581t^2 + 1.47t - 2.50$$

Graph $C_D(t)$ and find the x-intercept. (The graph with Ymin $= -4$, Ymax $= 6$ is shown.)

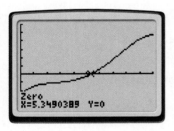

Zero
X=5.3490389 Y=0

Within the rounding error, the results for the x-coordinate of the intersection of $C_{NA}(t)$ and $C_{AP}(t)$ and the x-intercept of $C_D(t)$ are the same.

Your Turn

10. An engineering class is designing model rockets for a competition. The body of the rocket must be cylindrical with a cone-shaped top. The cylinder part must be 60 cm tall, and the height of the cone must be twice the radius, as shown. The volume of the payload region must be 558π cm^3 in order to hold the cargo. Use a graphing calculator to graph the rocket's payload volume as a function of the radius x. On the same screen, graph the constant function for the desired payload. Find the intersection to find x.

Elaborate

11. What does the degree of a polynomial function $p(x)$ tell you about the zeros of the function or the roots of the equation $p(x) = 0$?

12. A polynomial equation of degree 5 has the roots 0.3, 2, 8, and 10.6 (each of multiplicity 1). What can you conclude about the remaining root? Explain your reasoning.

13. Discussion Describe two ways you can use graphing to determine when two polynomial functions that model a real-world situation have the same value.

14. Essential Question Check-In What are possible ways to find all the roots of a polynomial equation?

⭐ Evaluate: Homework and Practice

• Online Homework
• Hints and Help
• Extra Practice

Find all zeros of $p(x)$. Include any multiplicities greater than 1.

1. $p(x) = 3x^3 - 10x^2 + 10x - 4$

2. $p(x) = x^3 - 3x^2 + 4x - 12$

Solve the polynomial equation by finding all roots.

3. $2x^3 - 3x^2 + 8x - 12 = 0$

4. $x^4 - 5x^3 + 3x^2 + x = 0$

Write the polynomial function with least degree and a leading coefficient of 1 that has the given zeros.

5. $0, \sqrt{5}$, and 2

6. $4i$, 2, and -2

7. $1, -1$ (multiplicity 3), and $3i$

8. 3(multiplicity of 2) and $3i$

9. Forestry Height and trunk volume measurements from 10 giant sequoias between the heights of 220 and 275 feet in California give the following model, where h is the height in feet and V is the volume in cubic feet.

$$V(h) = 0.131h^3 - 90.9h^2 + 21,200h - 1,627,400$$

The "President" tree in the Giant Forest Grove in Sequoia National Park has a volume of about 45,100 cubic feet. Use a graphing calculator to plot the function $V(h)$ and the constant function representing the height of the President tree together. (Use a window of 220 to 275 for X and 30,000 to 55,000 for Y.) Find the x-coordinate of the intersection of the graphs. What does this represent in the context of this situation?

10. **Business** Two competing stores, store A and store B, opened the same year in the same neighborhood. The annual revenue R (in millions of dollars) for each store t years after opening can be approximated by the polynomial models shown.

$$R_A(t) = 0.0001\left(-t^4 + 12t^3 - 77t^2 + 600t + 13{,}650\right)$$

$$R_B(t) = 0.0001\left(-t^4 + 36t^3 - 509t^2 + 3684t + 3390\right)$$

Using a graphing calculator, graph the models from $t = 0$ to $t = 10$, with a range of 0 to 2 for R. Find the x-coordinate of the intersection of the graphs, and interpret the graphs.

11. **Personal Finance** A retirement account contains cash and stock in a company. The cash amount is added to each week by the same amount until week 32, then that same amount is withdrawn each week. The functions shown model the balance B (in thousands of dollars) over the course of the past year, with the time t in weeks.

$$B_C(t) = -0.12|t - 32| + 13$$

$$B_S(t) = 0.00005t^4 - 0.00485t^3 + 0.1395t^2 - 1.135t + 15.75$$

Use a graphing calculator to graph both models (Use 0 to 20 for range.). Find the x-coordinate of any points of intersection. Then interpret your results in the context of this situation.

12. Match each equation with all of its roots.

a. $x^4 + x^3 + 2x^2 + 4x - 8 = 0$ **A.** 1

b. $x^4 - 5x^2 + 4 = 0$ **B.** -2

                                         C. 2

                                         D. -1

                                         E. $2i$

                                         F. $-2i$

13. **Draw Conclusions** Find all of the roots of $x^6 - 5x^4 - 125x^2 + 15{,}625 = 0$. (Hint: Rearrange the terms with a sum of cubes followed by the two other terms.)

14. **Explain the Error** A student is asked to write the polynomial function with least degree and a leading coefficient of 1 that has the zeros $1 + i$, $1 - i$, $\sqrt{2}$, and -3. The student writes the product of factors shown, and multiplies them together to obtain $p(x) = x^4 + \left(1 - \sqrt{2}\right)x^3 - \left(4 + \sqrt{2}\right)x^2 + \left(6 + 4\sqrt{2}\right)x - 6\sqrt{2}$. What error did the student make? What is the correct function?

15. **Critical Thinking** What is the least degree of a polynomial equation that has $3i$ as a root with a multiplicity of 3, and $2 - \sqrt{3}$ as a root with multiplicity 2? Explain.

Lesson Performance Task

In 1984 the MPAA introduced the PG-13 rating to their movie rating system. Recently, scientists measured the incidences of a specific type of violence depicted in movies. The researchers used specially trained coders to identify the specific type of violence in one half of the top grossing movies for each year since 1985. The trend in the average rate per hour of 5-minute segments of this type of violence in movies rated G/PG, PG-13, and R can be modeled as a function of time by the following equations:

$$V_{G/PG}(t) = -0.015t + 1.45$$

$$V_{PG-13}(t) = 0.000577t^3 - 0.0225t^2 + 0.26t + 0.8$$

$$V_R(t) = 2.15$$

V is the average rate per hour of 5-minute segments containing the specific type of violence in movies, and t is the number of years since 1985.

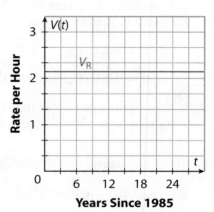

a. Interestingly, in 1985 or $t = 0$, $V_{G/PG}(0) > V_{PG-13}(0)$. Can you think of any reasons why this would be true?

b. What do the equations indicate about the relationship between $V_{G/PG}(t)$ and $V_{PG-13}(t)$ as t increases?

Copy the graph shown. On the same coordinate grid graph the models for $V_{G/PG}(t)$ and $V_{PG-13}(t)$ and find the year in which $V_{PG-13}(t)$ will be greater than $V_{G/PG}(t)$.

Polynomial Equations

Essential Question: How can you use polynomial equations to solve real-world problems?

Key Vocabulary

root *(raíz)*
multiplicity *(multiplicidad)*

KEY EXAMPLE   *(Lesson 8.1)*

Find the rational zeros of $f(x) = x^3 + 6x^2 + 11x + 6$; then write the function as a product of factors.

Factors of 6: $\pm 1, \pm 2, \pm 3, \pm 6$

Use the Rational Zero Theorem.

$\frac{m}{n}$	1	6	11	6
1	1	7	18	24
2	1	8	27	60
3	1	9	38	120
6	1	12	83	504
−1	1	5	6	0

Test the roots in a synthetic division table.

$(x + 1)(x^2 + 5x + 6)$

$(x + 1)(x + 2)(x + 3)$

Factor the trinomial.

$x = -1, x = -2, x = -3$

KEY EXAMPLE   *(Lesson 8.2)*

Find all the zeros of $m(x) = 2x^4 - 4x^3 + 8x^2 - 16x$.

$2x^4 - 4x^3 - 8x^2 - 16x$

$2x(x^3 - 2x^2 - 4x + 8)$ *Factor out the GCF.*

$2x((x^3 - 2x^2) - (4x - 8))$ *Group the terms.*

$2x(x^2(x - 2) - 4(x - 2))$ *Factor out common monomials.*

$2x(x^2 - 4)(x - 2)$ *Factor out the common binomial.*

$2x(x + 2)(x - 2)(x - 2)$ *Difference of two squares*

So, the zeros of $m(x)$ are $0, -2, 2$ (mult. 2).

EXERCISES

Rewrite the function as a product of factors, and state all of the zeros. *(Lessons 8.1, 8.2)*

1. $r(x) = x^3 + 13x^2 + 48x + 36$

2. $m(x) = 3x^4 - 3x^2$

3. $n(x) = x^3 + 5x^2 - 8x - 12$

4. $p(x) = x^3 - 8$

5. $b(x) = x^4 - 81$

6. $t(x) = 15x^3 + 27x^2 - 6x$

7. Give an example of a fourth degree polynomial equation with all real zero answers. Explain how you got your equation. *(Lessons 8.1)*

© Houghton Mifflin Harcourt Publishing Company

MODULE PERFORMANCE TASK

What Do Polynomials Have to Do With Endangered Species?

A biologist has been studying a particular species of frog in an area for many years and has compiled population data. She used the data to create a model of the population, given here, where x is the year since 2000.

$$P(x) = -x^4 + 27x^3 - 198x^2 + 372x + 1768$$

Describe the trends for the population, and explain what the model predicts for the future population of this species of frog.

Be sure to write down all your data and assumptions. Then use graphs, numbers, words, or algebra to explain how you reached your conclusions.

(Ready) to Go On?

8.1–8.2 Polynomial Functions

- Online Homework
- Hints and Help
- Extra Practice

Write the function as a product of factors. *(Lesson 8.1)*

1. $f(x) = 7x^3 - 14x^2 - x + 2$

2. $g(x) = 3x^2 + 2x - 8$

3. $h(x) = 4x^2 - 25$

4. $t(x) = 8x^3 - 512$

List the roots. *(Lessons 8.1, 8.2)*

5. $m(x) = x^4 + 3x^2 - 18$

6. $r(x) = x^3 + 3x^2 - x - 3$

7. $q(x) = x^3 - 1$

8. $p(x) = 9x^2 - 100$

ESSENTIAL QUESTION

9. Give an example of how factoring polynomials might be used in Geometry. *(Lesson 8.1)*

Assessment Readiness

1. Which of the following polynomials has all real roots?

   A. $f(x) = x^4 - 4x^2 - 5$

   B. $g(x) = x^2 - 9$

   C. $h(x) = x^4 - 256$

   D. $k(x) = x^3 - 27$

2. A parabola goes through the points $(6, 4)$, $(-4, 14)$, and $(0, -2)$. Which description of the parabola is correct?

   A. The parabola opens upward and its vertex is at $(2, -4)$.

   B. The parabola opens downward and its vertex is at $(2, -4)$.

   C. The parabola opens upward and its vertex is at $(0, -2)$.

   D. The parabola opens downward and its vertex is at $(0, -2)$.

3. By analyzing a quickly growing oil town, an analyst states that the predicted population P of the town t years from now can be modeled by the function $P(t) = 5x^3 - 2x^2 + 15{,}000$. If we assume the function is true, in approximately how many years will the town have a population of 225,000?

   A. 53 years

   B. 35 years

   C. 22 years

   D. 10 years

4. Explain why some polynomial functions have imaginary roots. Describe the way a polynomial with imaginary roots looks on a graph.

Assessment Readiness

1. Identify the transformations of the graph of $f(x) = x^3$ that produce the graph of the function $g(x) = -2(x - 5)^3$. Select the correct statement.

   A. When compared to $f(x)$, the graph of $g(x)$ is not reflected across the x-axis.

   B. When compared to $f(x)$, the graph of $g(x)$ is vertically compressed by a factor of $\frac{1}{2}$.

   C. When compared to $f(x)$ the graph of $g(x)$ is translated 5 units to the right.

   D. When compared to $f(x)$, the graph of $g(x)$ is translated 5 units vertically.

2. Consider the polynomial $3x^3 + 9x^2 - 12x$. Select the correct statement.

   A. The polynomial cannot be factored as it is written.

   B. The completely factored polynomial is $3x(x - 3)(x + 4)$.

   C. At an intermediate step, the factored polynomial is $3x(3x^2 + 9x - 2)$.

   D. $3x$ can be factored out of every term.

3. Consider the polynomial operation $3x(x - 2)(5x + 2)$. Which of the following expressions is equivalent to this operation? Select the correct answer.

   A. $(3x^2 - 6x)(5x + 2)$ **C.** $15x^3 - 24x^2 + 12x$

   B. $3x(x^2 - 8x - 4)$ **D.** $3x(5x^2 - 5x - 2)$

4. Consider the polynomial function $g(x) = 3x^3 + 6x^2 - 9x$. Select the correct statement.

   A. The polynomial has no common monomial.

   B. The polynomial has only real roots.

   C. The polynomial has only complex roots.

   D. The roots of the polynomial are 0, −3, 1, 3.

5. Identify the zeros of $m(x) = x^4 - 16$. Select the correct answer.

   A. $\pm\frac{1}{2}$ **C.** $2 \pm 2i$

   B. 0 **D.** $\pm 2i, \pm 2i$

6. Use a graphing calculator to graph the function $f(x) = -x(x + 1)(x - 4)^2$, and then use the graph to determine the number of turning points and minimums or maximums. *(Lesson 6.2)*

7. Ms. Flores grows tomatoes on her farm. The price per pound of tomatoes can be modeled by $P(x) = 20x + 4$. If the total income that she wants to earn from tomatoes for one year can be modeled by $\ell(x) = 60x^3 - 8x^2 + 136x + 28$, write a polynomial that can be used to model the pounds of tomatoes Ms. Flores needs to grow in one year. *(Lesson 7.4)*

Performance Tasks

★ **8. Measurement** A bottom for a box can be made by cutting congruent squares from each of the four corners of a piece of cardboard. The volume of a box made from an 8.5-by-11-inch piece of cardboard would be represented by $v(x) = x(11 - 2x)(8.5 - 2x)$, where x is the side length of one square.

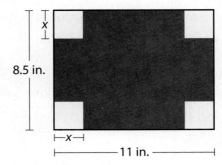

A. Express the volume as a sum of monomials.

B. Find the volume when $x = 1$ inch.

★★ **9. Astronomy** The volume of several planets in cubic kilometers can be modeled by $v(d) = \frac{1}{6}\pi d^3$, where d is the diameter of the planet in kilometers. The mass of each planet in kilograms in terms of diameter d can be modeled by
$M(d) = (3.96 \times 10^{12})d^3 - (6.50 \times 10^{17})d^2 + (2.56 \times 10^{22})d - 5.56 \times 10^{25}$.

A. The density of a planet in kilograms per cubic kilometer can be found by dividing the planet's mass by its volume. Use polynomial division to find a model for the density of a planet in terms of its diameter.

B. Use the model to estimate the density of Jupiter, with diameter $d = 142{,}984$ km.

★★★ **10. Business** The profit of a small business (in thousands of dollars) since it was founded can be modeled by the polynomial
$f(t) = -t^4 + 44t^3 - 612t^2 + 2592t$, where t represents the number of years since 1980.

A. Factor $f(t)$ completely.

B. What was the company's profit in 1985?

C. Find and interpret $f(15)$.

D. What can you say about the company's long-term prospects?

Statistician According to data from the U.S. Census Bureau, the total number of people in the United States labor force can be approximated by the function $T(x) = -0.011x^2 + 2x + 107$, where x is the number of years since 1980 and $T(x)$ is the number of workers in millions. The number of women in the United States labor force can be approximated by the function $W(x) = -0.012x^2 + 1.26x + 45.5$.

a. Use the function $T(x)$ to estimate the number of workers in millions in 2010.

b. Write a polynomial function $M(x)$ that models the number of men in the labor force, and explain how you found your function.

c. Use the function found in part b to estimate the number of male workers in millions in 2010.

d. Explain how you could have found the answer to part c without using the function $M(x)$.

UNIT 4

Rational Functions, Expressions, and Equations

MATH IN CAREERS

Chemist Chemists study the properties and composition of substances. They use the mathematics of ratios and proportions to determine the atomic composition of materials and the quantities of atoms needed to synthesize materials. They use geometry to understand the physical structures of chemical compounds. Chemists also use mathematical models to understand and predict behavior of chemical interactions, including reaction rates and activation energies.

If you are interested in a career as a chemist, you should study these mathematical subjects:

- Geometry
- Algebra
- Calculus
- Differential Equations
- Statistics

Research other careers that require using mathematical models to predict behavior. Check out the career activity at the end of the unit to find out how **Chemists** use math.

© Houghton Mifflin Harcourt Publishing Company • Image Credits: © Erik Isakson/Blend Images/Corbis

Visualize Vocabulary

Use the ✓ words. Copy and complete the chart.

_____?_____	the set of output values of a function or relation
_____?_____	a linear relationship between two variables, x and y, that can be written in the form $y = kx$, where k is a nonzero constant
_____?_____	the multiplicative inverse of a number; the product of a number and its reciprocal is 1
_____?_____	the simplest function with the defining characteristics of the function family
_____?_____	the set of all possible input values of a relation or function
_____?_____	an algebraic expression whose numerator and denominator are polynomials and whose denominator has a degree ≥ 1.

Review Words

✔ direct variation
  (variación directa)

✔ domain
  (dominio)

✔ parent function
  (función madre)

✔ range
  (rango)

✔ rational expression
  (expresión racional)

✔ reciprocal
  (recíproco)

Preview Words

asymptote
  (asíntota)

closure
  (cerradura)

inverse variation
  (variación inversa)

rational function
  (función racional)

Understand Vocabulary

To become familiar with some of the vocabulary terms in the module, consider the following. You may refer to the module, the glossary, or a dictionary.

1. ___?___ is a relationship between two variables, x and y, that can be written in the form $y = \frac{k}{x}$, where k is a nonzero constant and $x \neq 0$.

2. A line that a graph approaches as the value of the variable becomes extremely large or small is an ___?___.

3. A function whose rule can be written as a rational expression is a ___?___.

Active Reading

Double-Door Fold Before beginning each lesson, create a double-door fold to compare the characteristics of two expressions, functions, or variations. This can help you identify the similarities and differences between the topics.

© Houghton Mifflin Harcourt Publishing Company

Rational Functions

Essential Question: How can you use rational functions to solve real-world problems?

REAL WORLD VIDEO
As a consumer, you may shop around for the best deal on a new bike helmet. Check out the video to see how sporting goods manufacturers can use rational functions to help set pricing and sales goals.

MODULE PERFORMANCE TASK PREVIEW

What Is the Profit?

Like any business, a manufacturer of bike helmets must pay attention to ways to minimize costs and maximize profit. Businesses use mathematical functions to calculate and predict various quantities, including profits, costs, and revenue. What are some of the ways a business can use a profit function? Let's find out!

Are (YOU) Ready?

Complete these exercises to review skills you will need for this chapter.

Graphing Linear Nonproportional Relationships

Example 1

Graph $y = -\frac{1}{2}x - 3$

Plot the y-intercept $(0, -3)$

The slope is $-\frac{1}{2}$, so from $(0, -3)$, plot the next point up 1 and left 2.

Draw a line through the two points.

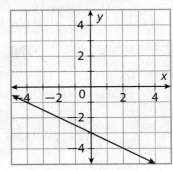

Graph each relationship.

1. $y = 3x - 4$

2. $y = -\frac{3}{4}x + 1$

Direct and Inverse Variation

Example 2

The graph of a direct variation function passes through $(1, 10)$. Write the equation for the function.

$k = \frac{y}{x} = \frac{10}{1} = 10$, so the equation is $y = 10x$.

Example 3

The graph of an inverse variation function passes through $(4, 3)$. Write the equation for the function.

$k = xy = 4 \cdot 3 = 12$, so the equation is $y = \frac{12}{x}$.

Write a direct variation equation for the graph that passes through the point.

3. $(2, 5)$

4. $(3, 6)$

5. $(4, 1)$

Write an inverse variation equation for the graph that passes through the point.

6. $(8, 1)$

7. $(5, 10)$

8. $(2, 6)$

9.1 Inverse Variation

Essential Question: What does it mean for one variable to vary inversely as another variable?

 TEKS **A2.6.L** Formulate and solve equations involving inverse variation.

⊘ Explore   Investigating Inverse Variation

You know that the area A of a rectangle with length ℓ and width w is given by the formula $A = \ell w$. If you hold the width constant and allow the length to vary, the area will vary also. For instance, if $w = 2$, then the equation relating A and ℓ is $A = 2\ell$, A is said to *vary directly* as ℓ and 2 is called the *constant of variation*. In general, any equation of the form $y = ax$, where a is a nonzero constant, is a *direct variation*, and its graph is a line that passes through the origin. For instance, the graph of $A = 2\ell$ is shown. The graph is a ray rather than a line because length and area are nonnegative quantities.

In this Explore, you will consider what happens to the length and width of a rectangle if you hold the area constant.

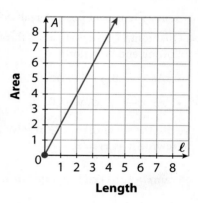

(A) Let the area of a rectangle be 12 square units. Copy and complete the table, which lists possible positive-integer lengths and widths for the rectangle. Note that it doesn't matter whether the width is less than, equal to, or greater than the length.

Length	Width
1	12
2	
3	
4	
6	
12	

(B) On a copy of the coordinate grid shown, draw each of the rectangles having the lengths and widths in the table from Step A. Each rectangle should have its lower-left corner at the origin. The first rectangle, having a length of 1 and a width of 12, is already drawn for you.

(C) Using your coordinate grid from Step B, draw a smooth curve through the upper-right corners of the rectangles.

(D) Write an equation that gives w in terms of ℓ.

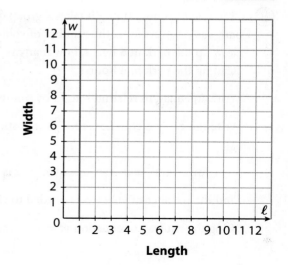

© Houghton Mifflin Harcourt Publishing Company

1. In the direct variation equation $A = 2\ell$, the value of A increases as the value of ℓ increases. For the equation that you wrote in Step D, what can you say about the value of w as the value of ℓ increases?

🔑 Explain 1 Formulating and Solving Inverse Variation Equations

An **inverse variation** is a relationship between two variables x and y that can be written in the form $y = \frac{a}{x}$ where $a \neq 0$. In this relationship, y is said to vary inversely as x, and a is called the **constant of variation**.

If x and y represent positive real-world quantities, then the graph of $y = \frac{a}{x}$ is a Quadrant I curve that passes through points of the form $\left(x, \frac{a}{x}\right)$ and has the following end behavior:

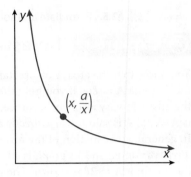

- As $x \rightarrow 0$, $y \rightarrow +\infty$.

- As $x \rightarrow +\infty$, $y \rightarrow 0$.

To use the equation $y = \frac{a}{x}$ to solve problems, you may find it helpful to rewrite it as $xy = a$.

Example 1 Write an equation relating the variables and use it to answer the question.

(A) The time t (in days) that it takes a theater crew to set up a stage for a musical varies inversely as the number of workers w. If 30 workers can set up the stage in 4 days, how many days would it take if only 24 workers are available?

Write an equation relating w and t by finding the constant of variation, a.

Write the general equation. $\quad t = \frac{a}{w}$ $\qquad$ Substitute known values. $4 = \frac{a}{30}$

Solve for a. $\qquad 120 = a$ $\qquad$ So, an equation is $t = \frac{120}{w}$.

Find the amount of time needed to set up the stage with 24 workers.

Using the equation $t = \frac{120}{w}$, substitute 24 for w and get $t = \frac{120}{24} = 5$.

So, 24 workers can set up the stage in 5 days.

(B) The time t (in hours) that it takes a group of volunteers to clean up a city park varies inversely as the number of volunteers v. If 10 volunteers can clean up the park in 6 hours, how many volunteers would be needed to clean up the park in 4 hours?

Write an equation relating v and t by finding the constant of variation, a.

Write the general equation. $t = \frac{a}{v}$ $\quad$ Substitute known values. $10 = \dfrac{a}{\boxed{6}}$

Solve for k. $\boxed{60} = a$ $\quad$ So, an equation t is $t = \dfrac{\boxed{60}}{v}$.

Find the number of volunteers needed to clean up the park in 4 hours.

Using the equivalent equation $vt = \boxed{60}$, substitute 4 for t and solve for v to

get $v = \boxed{15}$.

So, 15 volunteers are needed to clean up the park in 4 hours.

Reflect

2. **Discussion** Using the equivalent equation $xy = a$ for an inverse variation, explain why the point (q, p) must be on the graph of the equation if the point (p, q) is.

3. **Discussion** What does the fact that for every point (p, q) on the graph of $y = \frac{a}{x}$ the point (q, p) is also on the graph tell you about the symmetry of the graph?

Your Turn

Write an equation relating the variables and use it to answer the question.

4. Kim lives in a suburb and drives to work in a city. The time t (in hours) it takes her to get to work varies inversely with her average driving speed s (in miles per hour). When she averages 20 miles per hour in heavy traffic, it takes her 1.5 hours to get to work. How long would the trip take if her average driving speed is 50 miles per hour in light traffic?

5. Boyle's law says that the volume V of a gas held in a container at a constant temperature varies inversely with the pressure P on the gas. The volume of a particular gas is 8 liters at a pressure of 3 atmospheres. What is the pressure when the volume is 6 liters?

Explain 2 Distinguishing between Inverse Variation and Direct Variation

As you know, you can rewrite the inverse variation equation $y = \frac{a}{x}$ as $xy = a$. The alternative form of the equation gives you a way to check for inverse variation in a table of data: If the products of the paired values of the variables are constant (or nearly constant), then inverse variation exists.

A direct variation equation has the form $y = ax$, which you can rewrite as $\frac{y}{x} = a$. So, to check for direct variation in a table of data, see if the ratios of the paired values of the variables are constant.

Example 2 Determine whether the two variables vary inversely or directly. Then write an equation and use it to answer the question.

(A) The table gives the total cost (in dollars) of various numbers of tickets to a school play. What is the cost of 12 tickets?

Tickets, t	3	7	9
Total cost, C	12	28	36

Check both the products tC and the ratios $\frac{C}{t}$ to see which are constant.

Because the ratios $\frac{C}{t}$ are constant, C varies directly as t.

Write the equation. $C = 4t$

Find the cost for 12 tickets. $C = 4(12) = 48$

So, 12 tickets cost $48.

t	C	tC	$\frac{C}{t}$
3	12	36	4
7	28	196	4
9	36	324	4

(B) The table gives the time (in hours) needed to drive to a destination at various average speeds (in miles per hour). What is the time needed to get to the destination when driving at an average speed of 45 miles per hour?

Average Speed, s	12	15	20
Time, t	50	40	30

Check both the products st and the ratios $\frac{t}{s}$ to see which are constant.

s	t	st	$\frac{t}{s}$
12	50	600	$4.1\overline{6}$
15	40	600	$2.\overline{6}$
20	30	600	1.5

Because the products st are constant, s varies inversely as t.

Write the equation. $t = \frac{600}{s}$

Find the time needed to get to the destination when driving at an average speed of 48 miles per hour.

$$t = \frac{\boxed{600}}{48} = \boxed{12.5}$$

So, it takes 12.5 hours to get to the destination when driving at an average speed of 48 miles per hour.

Reflect

6. State the real-world significance of the constant of variation in Part A and Part B.

Your Turn

Determine whether the two variables vary inversely or directly. Then write an equation and use it to answer the question.

7. The table gives the number of pages read from a book for various amounts of time (in hours) spent reading. How many pages can be read in 6 hours?

Time, t	2	3	5
Pages Read, p	40	60	100

8. The table gives the amount (in dollars) that each person owes when a group of people buys a birthday present for a friend. How much does each person owe when 8 people chip in for the present?

Number of People, p	2	4	5
Amount each Owes, A	40	20	16

Elaborate

9. How do direct variation and inverse variation differ?

10. What is another way to write the inverse variation equation $y = \frac{a}{x}$? How is this equation helpful?

11. **Essential Question Check-In** If x and y represent positive real-world quantities that vary inversely, what happens to y as x approaches 0? What happens to y as x increases without bound?

☆ Evaluate: Homework and Practice

• Online Homework
• Hints and Help
• Extra Practice

1. Let the area of a rectangle be 16 square units. On a copy of the coordinate grid shown, draw all rectangles having positive-integer lengths and widths. (Note that it doesn't matter whether the width is less than, equal to, or greater than the length.) Each rectangle should have its lower-left corner at the origin. The first rectangle, having a length of 1 and a width of 16, is already drawn for you. After drawing the rectangles, draw a smooth curve through their upper-right corners.

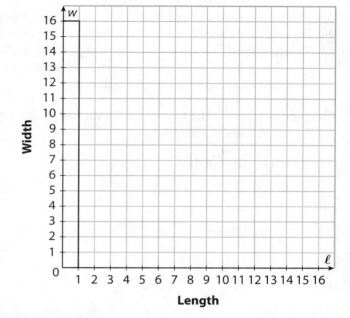

2. Write an equation of the curve that you drew in Evaluate 1. The equation should give the width w of a rectangle in terms of the length ℓ.

Write an equation relating the variables and use it to answer the question.

3. Given that y varies inversely as x, and $y = 8$ when $x = 3$, what is the value of y when $x = 12$?

4. Given that y varies inversely as x, and $y = 10$ when $x = 4$, what is the value of x when $y = 8$?

5. The time t (in hours) that it takes a pump to empty a tank of water varies inversely with the pumping rate r (in gallons per hour). If it takes 3 hours to empty a tank of water when the pumping rate is 80 gallons per hour, how long does it take to empty the tank when the pumping rate is 60 gallons per hour?

6. The number of flowers f that a gardener can plant along a border of a garden varies inversely with the distance d (in inches) between the flowers. If the gardener can fill the border with 30 flowers planted 12 inches apart, how far apart should the gardener plant 36 flowers instead?

7. The number of presents p that Tim can afford to buy varies inversely with their average cost C (in dollars). If Tim can afford 5 presents when their average cost is $12, what average cost would 3 presents have?

8. A club rents a bus for a trip. The cost C (in dollars) that each person pays to cover the cost of the bus varies inversely with the number of people p who go on the trip. It will cost $30 per person if 50 people go on the trip. How much will it cost per person if 40 people go on the trip?

9. For a fundraiser, members of the booster club wash cars by hand. The time t (in minutes) it takes to wash a car varies inversely as the number of people p who are washing the car. If 2 people can wash a car in 20 minutes, how many people would be needed to wash a car in 8 minutes?

10. A gear with 32 teeth meshes with a gear with 40 teeth so that when one gear revolves, the other one does as well. The number of revolutions r that each gear makes varies inversely with the gear's number of teeth t. When the gear with 32 teeth makes 5 revolutions, how many revolutions does the gear with 40 teeth make?

11. Music The frequency f (in hertz) of a vibrating guitar string varies inversely as its length ℓ (in centimeters). If a guitar string 65 centimeters long vibrates with a frequency of 110 hertz, at what frequency would the guitar string vibrate when the guitarist reduces the string's length to 22 centimeters?

12. Physics When a lever is placed on a fulcrum and a force is applied at each end, the lever will be in balance as long as the magnitude m (in pounds) of each force and the distance d (in feet) of each force from the fulcrum satisfy an inverse variation relationship. If a force of 50 pounds is applied to one end of a lever at a distance of 2 feet from the fulcrum, what force must be applied to other end, which is 5 feet from the fulcrum, to bring the lever into balance?

Determine whether the two variables vary inversely or directly. Then write an equation and use it to answer the question.

13. Given the table of data, what is y when $x = 15$?

x	1	3	4
y	30	10	7.5

14. Given the table of data, what is y when $x = 10$?

x	2	5	6
y	30	75	90

15. The table gives the cost (in dollars) per person when friends share in renting a mountain cabin for a weekend. What is the cost per person when 6 friends rent the cabin?

Number of People, p	2	3	5
Cost per Person, C	90	60	36

16. The table gives the amount of gas (in gallons) used when driving a car various distances (in miles) on highways. What amount of gas is used when driving 336 miles on highways?

Distance Driven, d	112	140	224
Amount of Gas, g	4	5	8

17. The table gives the cost (in dollars) of renting a rowboat at a lake for various amounts of time (in hours). What is the cost of renting a rowboat for 3.5 hours?

Time, t	2	2.5	3
Rental Cost, C	28	35	42

18. The table gives the total working time (in hours) that it takes a crew of painters to paint a house. How much time does it take 6 painters to paint the house?

Number of Painters, p	2	3	5
Total Working Time, t	48	32	19.2

19. The table gives the speed of a bicycle (in miles per hour) when a cyclist pedals at various rates (in revolutions per minute of the pedals) with the bicycle in a particular gear. What is the bicycle's speed when the cyclist pedals at a rate of 72 revolutions per minute?

Pedaling Rate, r	30	60	90
Bicycle's Speed, s	5	10	15

20. The table gives the number of laptops sold in a month when a store sells a particular model of laptop at various prices (in dollars). How many laptops would be sold in a month when the store sells the laptop for $500?

Price of Laptop, p	600	720	800
Number of Laptops Sold, ℓ	60	50	45

21. The table gives the number of small figurines that can be placed on a display shelf for various distances (in centimeters) between them. How many figurines can be placed on the shelf when they are 24 centimeters apart?

Distance between Figurines, s	10	15	20
Number of Figurines, f	12	8	6

22. The table gives the amount of water (in gallons) coming out of a garden hose for various amounts of time (in minutes). How much water comes out of the garden hose in 20 minutes?

Time, t	4	9	16
Amount of Water, w	72	162	288

23. Determine whether each of the following situations represents direct variation or inverse variation.

a. When traveling a fixed distance, the travel time is a function of average speed.

b. For items that are priced the same, the total cost is a function of the number of items purchased.

c. When traveling at a fixed speed, the distance traveled is a function of the travel time.

d. For a fixed amount of money, the number of identical items that can be purchased is a function of the cost per item.

24. Justify Reasoning If y varies directly as x, what happens to the value of y when the value of x is doubled? If y varies inversely as x, what happens to the value of y when the value of x is doubled? Use the general equations for direct and inverse variation to justify your reasoning.

25. Explain the Error Boyle's law says that the volume V of a gas held in a container at a constant temperature varies inversely with the pressure P on the gas. The volume of a particular gas is 6 liters at a pressure of 2 atmospheres. Jerry says that if the pressure is changed to 3 atmospheres, the volume will be 9 liters. Explain and correct his error.

26. Represent Real-World Situations The volume V of a gas varies inversely as the pressure P and directly as the temperature T. A particular gas has a volume of 10 liters, a temperature of 300 kelvins, and a pressure of 1.5 atmospheres. If the gas is compressed to a volume of 7.5 liters and is heated to a temperature of 360 kelvins, what will the pressure be? Write an equation and use it to answer the question.

Lesson Performance Task

You have a collection of CDs whose songs you want to transfer to your new MP3 player. The MP3 player has 32,000 megabytes (MB) of storage. An average song lasts 4 minutes and requires 40 MB of storage on a CD.

a. Write a function that gives the average number S of songs that your MP3 player can store if the average file size of a song is s MB.

b. If you were to transfer the songs from your CDs in their current size, how many songs could you expect to store on your MP3 player?

c. The MP3 file format compresses songs without much loss in the quality of the sound. Typically, the MP3 format compresses a CD file to a tenth of its size. How many songs from your CDs can you expect to store as MP3 files on your MP3 player?

d. In general, if you could use a file format that compresses the songs on your CDs by a factor of $\frac{1}{f}$ where $f > 1$, how many songs in that format can you expect to store on your MP3 player?

9.2 Graphing Simple Rational Functions

Essential Question: How are the graphs of $f(x) = a\left(\dfrac{1}{x-h}\right) + k$ and $f(x) = \dfrac{1}{\frac{1}{b}(x-h)} + k$ related to the graph of $f(x) = \dfrac{1}{x}$?

 TEKS **A2.6.G** Analyze the effect on the graphs of $f(x) = \dfrac{1}{x}$ when $f(x)$ is replaced by $af(x)$, $f(bx)$, $f(x-c)$, and $f(x)+d$ for specific positive and negative real values of a, b, c, and d. Also A2.2.A, A2.6.K, A2.7.I

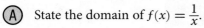 Explore 1 Graphing and Analyzing $f(x) = \dfrac{1}{x}$

A **rational function** is a function of the form $f(x) = \dfrac{p(x)}{q(x)}$ where $p(x)$ and $q(x)$ are polynomials. The most basic rational function with a variable expression in the denominator is $f(x) = \dfrac{1}{x}$.

(A) State the domain of $f(x) = \dfrac{1}{x}$.

The function accepts all real numbers except [   ], because division by [   ] is undefined. So, the function's domain is as follows:

- As an inequality: $x <$ [   ] or $x >$ [   ]

- In set notation: $\left\{ x \mid x \neq \boxed{} \right\}$

- In interval notation (where the symbol $\cup$ means *union*):

  $\left(-\infty, \boxed{} \right) \cup \left(\boxed{}, +\infty \right)$

(B) Determine the end behavior of $f(x) = \dfrac{1}{x}$.

First, copy and complete the tables.

x Increases without Bound		x Decreases without Bound	
x	$f(x) = \dfrac{1}{x}$	**x**	$f(x) = \dfrac{1}{x}$
100		−100	
1000		−1000	
10,000		−10,000	

Next, summarize the results.

- As $x \rightarrow +\infty$, $f(x) \rightarrow$ [   ].

- As $x \rightarrow -\infty$, $f(x) \rightarrow$ [   ].

(C) Be more precise about the end behavior of $f(x) = \frac{1}{x}$, and determine what this means for the graph of the function.

You can be more precise about the end behavior by using the notation $f(x) \to 0^+$, which means that the value of $f(x)$ approaches 0 from the positive direction (that is, the value of $f(x)$ is positive as it approaches 0), and the notation $f(x) \to 0^-$, which means that the value of $f(x)$ approaches 0 from the negative direction. So, the end behavior of the function is more precisely summarized as follows:

- As $x \to +\infty$, $f(x) \to$ [ ] .

- As $x \to -\infty$, $f(x) \to$ [ ] .

The end behavior indicates that the graph of $f(x)$ approaches, but does not cross, the

[ ] -axis, so that axis is an asymptote for the graph.

(D) Examine the behavior of $f(x) = \frac{1}{x}$ near $x = 0$, and determine what this means for the graph of the function.

First, copy and complete the tables.

x Approaches 0 from the Positive Direction	
x	$f(x) = \frac{1}{x}$
0.01	[ ]
0.001	[ ]
0.0001	[ ]

x Approaches 0 from the Negative Direction	
x	$f(x) = \frac{1}{x}$
−0.01	[ ]
−0.001	[ ]
−0.0001	[ ]

Next, summarize the results.

- As $x \to 0^+$, $f(x) \to$ [ ] .

- As $x \to 0^-$, $f(x) \to$ [ ] .

The behavior of $f(x) = \frac{1}{x}$ near $x = 0$ indicates that the graph of $f(x)$ approaches, but does

not cross, the [ ] , so that axis is also an asymptote for the graph.

(E) Graph $f(x) = \frac{1}{x}$.

First, determine the sign of $f(x)$ on the two parts of its domain.

- When x is a negative number, $f(x)$ is a [ ] number.

- When x is a negative number, $f(x)$ is a [ ] number.

Next, copy and complete the tables.

Negative Values of x	
x	$f(x) = \dfrac{1}{x}$
−2	
−1	
−0.5	

Positive Values of x	
x	$f(x) = \dfrac{1}{x}$
0.5	
1	
2	

Finally, use the information from this step and all previous steps to draw the graph. Draw asymptotes as dashed lines.

(F) State the range of $f(x) = \dfrac{1}{x}$.

The function takes on all real numbers except ▓, so the function's range is as follows:

- As an inequality: $y < $ ▓ or $y > $ ▓
- In set notation: $\left\{ y \mid y \neq \boxed{} \right\}$
- In interval notation (where the symbol ∪ **means** *union*): $\left(-\infty, \boxed{} \right) \cup \left(\boxed{}, +\infty \right)$

(G) Identify the intervals where the function is increasing and where it is decreasing.

(H) Determine whether $f(x) = \dfrac{1}{x}$ is an even function, an odd function, or neither.

Reflect

1. How does the graph of $f(x) = \dfrac{1}{x}$ show that the function has no zeros?

2. **Discussion** A graph is said to be *symmetric about the origin* (and the origin is called the graph's *point of symmetry*) if for every point (x, y) on the graph, the point $(-x, -y)$ is also on the graph. Is the graph of $f(x) = \dfrac{1}{x}$ symmetric about the origin? Explain.

3. What line is a line of symmetry for the graph of $f(x) = \dfrac{1}{x}$?

⊘ Explore 2 Predicting Transformations of the Graph of $f(x) = \dfrac{1}{x}$

In an earlier lesson, you learned how to transform the graph of a function using reflections across the x- and y-axes, vertical and horizontal stretches and compressions, and translations. Here, you will apply those transformations to the graph of the cubic function $f(x) = \dfrac{1}{x}$.

(A) Predict the effect of the parameter h on the graph of $g(x) = \dfrac{1}{x - h}$ for each function.

a. The graph of $g(x) = \dfrac{1}{x - 3}$ is a ▓ of the graph of $f(x)$ ▓ 3 units.

b. The graph of $g(x) = \dfrac{1}{x + 3}$ is a ▓ of the graph of $f(x)$ ▓ 3 units.

Check your predictions using a graphing calculator.

Ⓑ Predict the effect of the parameter k on the graph of $g(x) = \frac{1}{x} + k$ for each function.

a. The graph of $g(x) = \frac{1}{x} + 3$ is a [   ] of the graph of $f(x)$ [   ] 3 units.

b. The graph of $g(x) = \frac{1}{x} - 3$ is a [   ] of the graph of $f(x)$ [   ] 3 units.

Check your predictions using a graphing calculator.

Ⓒ Predict the effect of the parameter a on the graph of $g(x) = a\left(\frac{1}{x}\right)$ for each function.

a. The graph of $g(x) = 2\left(\frac{1}{x}\right)$ is a [   ] of the graph of $f(x)$ by a factor of [   ].

b. The graph of $g(x) = 0.5\left(\frac{1}{x}\right)$ is a [   ] of the graph of $f(x)$ by a factor of [   ].

c. The graph of $g(x) = -0.5\left(\frac{1}{x}\right)$ is a [   ] of the graph of $f(x)$ by a factor of [   ] as well as a reflection across the x-axis.

d. The graph of $g(x) = -2\left(\frac{1}{x}\right)$ is a [   ] of the graph of $f(x)$ by a factor

of [   ] as well as a [   ] across the [   ].

Check your predictions using a graphing calculator.

Ⓓ Predict the effect of the parameter b on the graph of $g(x) = \frac{1}{\frac{1}{b}x}$ for each function.

a. The graph of $g(x) = \frac{1}{0.5x}$ is a [   ] of the graph of $f(x)$ by a factor of [   ].

b. The graph of $g(x) = \frac{1}{2x}$ is a [   ] of the graph of $f(x)$ by a factor of [   ].

c. The graph of $g(x) = \frac{1}{-0.5x}$ is a [   ] of the graph of $f(x)$ by a factor of [   ] as well as a [   ] across the [   ].

d. The graph of $g(x) = \frac{1}{-2x}$ is a [   ] of the graph of $f(x)$ by a factor of [   ] as well as

a [   ] across the [   ].

Reflect

4. For each function from Step D, there is a function from Step C that has an identical graph even though the graphs of the two functions involve different transformations of the graph of $f(x)$. Using the letters and numbers in the lists below, match each function from Step D with a function from Step C and show why the functions are equivalent.

Functions from Step D

1. $g(x) = \dfrac{1}{0.5x}$

2. $g(x) = \dfrac{1}{2x}$

3. $g(x) = \dfrac{1}{-0.5x}$

4. $g(x) = \dfrac{1}{-2x}$

Functions from Step C

a. $g(x) = 2\left(\frac{1}{x}\right)$

b. $g(x) = 0.5\left(\frac{1}{x}\right)$

c. $g(x) = -0.5\left(\frac{1}{x}\right)$

d. $g(x) = -2\left(\frac{1}{x}\right)$

⚙ Explain 1 Graphing Simple Rational Functions

When graphing transformations of $f(x) = \frac{1}{x}$, it helps to consider the effect of the transformations on the following features of the graph of $f(x)$: the vertical asymptote, $x = 0$; the horizontal asymptote, $y = 0$; and two reference points, $(-1, -1)$ and $(1, 1)$. The table lists these features of the graph of $f(x)$ and the corresponding features of the graph of $g(x) = a\left(\dfrac{1}{\frac{1}{b}(x - h)}\right) + k$. Note that the asymptotes are affected only by the parameters h and k, while the reference points are affected by all four parameters.

Feature	$f(x) = \frac{1}{x}$	$g(x) = a\left(\dfrac{1}{\frac{1}{b}(x-h)}\right) + k$
Vertical asymptote	$x = 0$	$x = h$
Horizontal asymptote	$y = 0$	$y = h$
Reference point	$(-1, -1)$	$(-b + h, -a + k)$
Reference point	$(1, 1)$	$(b + h, a + k)$

Example 1   Identify the transformations of the graph of $f(x) = \frac{1}{x}$ that produce the graph of the given function $g(x)$. Then graph $g(x)$ on the same coordinate plane as the graph of $f(x)$ by applying the transformations to the asymptotes $x = 0$ and $y = 0$ to the reference points $(-1, -1)$ and $(1, 1)$. Also state the domain and range of $g(x)$ using inequalities, set notation, and interval notation.

Ⓐ $g(x) = 3\left(\dfrac{1}{x - 1}\right) + 2$

The transformations of the graph of $f(x)$ that produce the graph of $g(x)$ are:

- a vertical stretch by a factor of 3
- a translation of 1 unit to the right and 2 units up

Note that the translation of 1 unit to the right affects only the x-coordinates, while the vertical stretch by a factor of 3 and the translation of 2 units up affect only the y-coordinates.

Feature	$f(x) = \frac{1}{x}$	$g(x) = 3\left(\dfrac{1}{x - h}\right) + 2$
Vertical asymptote	$x = 0$	$x = 1$
Horizontal asymptote	$y = 0$	$y = 2$
Reference point	$(-1, -1)$	$\left(-1 + 1, 3(-1) + 2\right) = (0, -1)$
Reference point	$(1, 1)$	$\left(1 + 1, 3(1) + 2\right) = (2, 5)$

Domain of $g(x)$:

　　Inequality: $x < 1$ or $x > 1$

　　Set notation: $\left\{x \,\middle|\, x \neq 1\right\}$

　　Interval notation: $(-\infty, 1) \cup (1, +\infty)$

Range of $g(x)$:

　　Inequality: $y < 2$ or $y > 2$

　　Set notation: $\left\{y \,\middle|\, y \neq 2\right\}$

　　Interval notation: $(-\infty, 2) \cup (2, +\infty)$

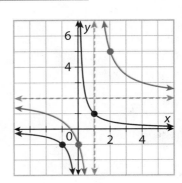

Ⓑ $g(x) = \dfrac{1}{2(x+3)} - 1$

The transformations of the graph of $f(x)$ that produce the graph of $g(x)$ are:

- a horizontal compression by a factor of $\dfrac{1}{2}$
- a translation of 3 units to the left and 1 unit down

Note that the horizontal compression by a factor of $\dfrac{1}{2}$ and the translation of 3 units to the left affect only the x-coordinates of points on the graph of $f(x)$, while the translation of 1 unit down affects only the y-coordinates.

Feature	$f(x) = \dfrac{1}{x}$	$g(x) = \dfrac{1}{2(x+3)} - 1$
Vertical asymptote	$x = 0$	$x = \boxed{-3}$
Horizontal asymptote	$y = 0$	$y = \boxed{-1}$
Reference point	$(-1, -1)$	$\left(\dfrac{1}{2}\left(\boxed{-1}\right) - 3, \boxed{-1} - 1 \right) = \left(\boxed{-3\frac{1}{2}}, \boxed{-2} \right)$
Reference point	$(1, 1)$	$\left(\dfrac{1}{2}\left(\boxed{1}\right) - 3, \boxed{1} - 1 \right) = \left(\boxed{-2\frac{1}{2}}, \boxed{0} \right)$

Domain of $g(x)$:

Inequality: $x < \boxed{-3}$ or $x > \boxed{-3}$

Set notation: $\left\{ x \mid x \neq \boxed{-3} \right\}$

Interval notation: $\left(-\infty, \boxed{-3} \right) \cup \left(\boxed{-3}, +\infty \right)$

Range of $g(x)$:

Inequality: $y < \boxed{-1}$ or $y > \boxed{-1}$

Set notation: $\left\{ y \mid y \neq \boxed{-1} \right\}$

Interval notation: $\left(-\infty, \boxed{-1} \right) \cup \left(\boxed{-1}, +\infty \right)$

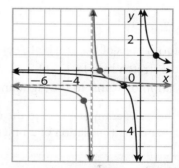

Identify the transformations of the graph of $f(x) = \frac{1}{x}$ that produce the graph of the given function $g(x)$. Then graph $g(x)$ on the same coordinate plane as the graph of $f(x)$ by applying the transformations to the asymptotes $x = 0$ and $y = 0$ to the reference points $(-1, -1)$ and $(1, 1)$. Also state the domain and range of $g(x)$ using inequalities, set notation, and interval notation.

5. $g(x) = -0.5\left(\frac{1}{x+1}\right) - 3$

6. $g(x) = \dfrac{1}{-0.5(x-2)} + 1$

⚙ Explain 2 Rewriting Simple Rational Functions in Order to Graph Them

When given a rational function of the form $g(x) = \frac{mx+n}{px+q}$, where $m \neq 0$ and $p \neq 0$, you can carry out the division of the numerator by the denominator to write the function in the form $g(x) = a\left(\frac{1}{x-h}\right) + k$ or $g(x) = \frac{1}{\frac{1}{b}(x-h)} + k$ in order to graph it.

Example 2 Rewrite the function in the form $g(x) = a\left(\frac{1}{x-h}\right) + k$ or $g(x) = \frac{1}{\frac{1}{b}(x-h)} + k$ and graph it. Also state the domain and range using inequalities, set notation, and interval notation.

Ⓐ $g(x) = \dfrac{3x-4}{x-1}$

Use long division.

$$
\begin{array}{r}
3 \\
x-1{\overline{\smash{\big)}\,3x-4}} \\
\underline{3x-3} \\
-1
\end{array}
$$

So, the quotient is 3, and the remainder is -1. Using the fact that $divided = quotient + \frac{remainder}{divisor}$, you have $g(x) = 3 + \frac{-1}{x-1}$, or $g(x) = -\frac{1}{x-1} + 3$.

The graph of $g(x)$ has vertical asymptote $x = 1$, horizontal asymptote $y = 3$, and reference points $\left(-1+1, -(-1)+3\right) = (0, 4)$ and $\left(1+1, -(1)+3\right) = (2, 2)$.

Domain of $g(x)$:

Inequality: $x < 1$ or $x > 1$

Set notation: $\left\{x \mid x \neq 1\right\}$

Interval notation: $\left(-\infty, 1\right) \cup \left(1, +\infty\right)$

Domain of $g(x)$:

Inequality: $y < 3$ or $y > 3$

Set notation: $\left\{y \mid y \neq 3\right\}$

Interval notation: $\left(-\infty, 3\right) \cup \left(3, +\infty\right)$

Ⓑ $g(x) = \dfrac{4x - 7}{-2x + 4}$

Use long division.

$$-2x + 4 \overline{)\, 4x - 7\,} \quad -2$$

$$\underline{4x - 8}$$

$$\boxed{1}$$

So, the quotient is −2, and the remainder is 1. Using the fact that $divided = quotient + \dfrac{remainder}{divisor}$,

you have $g(x) = \dfrac{-2 + \boxed{1}}{-2x + 4}$, or $g(x) = \dfrac{\boxed{1}}{-2\left(x - \boxed{2}\right)} - 2.$

The graph of $g(x)$ has vertical asymptote $x = \boxed{1}$, horizontal asymptote $y = -2$, and reference points

$\left(-\dfrac{1}{2}(-1) + \boxed{2}, -1 - 2\right) = \left(2\dfrac{1}{2}, -3\right)$ and $\left(-\dfrac{1}{2}(1) + \boxed{2}, 1 - 2\right) = \left(1\dfrac{1}{2}, -1\right).$

Domain of $g(x)$:

Inequality: $x < \boxed{2}$ or $x > \boxed{2}$

Set notation: $\left\{x \mid x \neq \boxed{2}\right\}$

Interval notation: $\left(-\infty, \boxed{2}\right) \cup \left(\boxed{2}, +\infty\right)$

Range of $g(x)$:

Inequality: $y < \boxed{-2}$ or $y > \boxed{-2}$

Set notation: $\left\{y \mid y \neq \boxed{-2}\right\}$

Interval notation: $\left(-\infty, \boxed{-2}\right) \cup \left(\boxed{-2}, +\infty\right)$

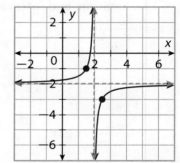

Reflect

7. In Part A, the graph of $g(x)$ is the result of what transformations of the graph of $f(x) = \dfrac{1}{x}$?

8. In Part B, the graph of $g(x)$ is the result of what transformations of the graph of $f(x) = \dfrac{1}{x}$?

Rewrite the function in the form $g(x) = a\left(\dfrac{1}{x-h}\right) + k$ or $g(x) = \dfrac{1}{\frac{1}{b}(x-h)} + k$ and graph it. Also state the domain and range using inequalities, set notation, and interval notation.

9. $g(x) = \dfrac{3x + 8}{x + 2}$

⚙ Explain 3 Writing Simple Rational Functions

When given the graph of a simple rational function, you can write its equation using one of the general forms $g(x) = a\left(\dfrac{1}{x-h}\right) + k$ and $g(x) = \dfrac{1}{\frac{1}{b}(x-h)} + k$ after identifying the values of the parameters using information obtained from the graph.

Example 3

(A) Write the function whose graph is shown. Use the form $g(x) = a\left(\dfrac{1}{x-h}\right) + k$.

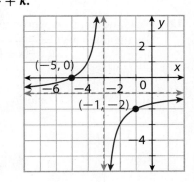

Since the graph's vertical asymptote is $x = 3$, the value of the parameter h is 3. Since the graph's horizontal asymptote is $y = 4$, the value of the parameter k is 4.

Substitute these values into the general form of the function.

$g(x) = a\left(\dfrac{1}{x-3}\right) + 4$

Now use one of the points, such as $(4, 6)$, to find the value of the parameter a.

$g(x) = a\left(\dfrac{1}{x-3}\right) + 4$

$6 = a\left(\dfrac{1}{4-3}\right) + 4$

$6 = a + 4$

$2 = a$

So, $g(x) = 2\left(\dfrac{1}{x-3}\right) + 4$.

(B) Write the function whose graph is shown. Use the form $g(x) = \dfrac{1}{\frac{1}{b}(x-h)} + k$.

Since the graph's vertical asymptote is $x = -3$, the value of the parameter h is -3. Since the graph's horizontal asymptote is $y = \boxed{-1}$, the value of the parameter k is -1.

Substitute these values into the general form of the function.

$g(x) = \dfrac{1}{\frac{1}{b}(x+3)} + \boxed{-1}$

© Houghton Mifflin Harcourt Publishing Company

Now use one of the points, such as $(-5, 0)$, to find the value of the parameter a.

$$g(x) = \dfrac{1}{\frac{1}{b}(x+3)} + \boxed{-1}$$

$$0 = \dfrac{1}{\frac{1}{b}(-5+3)} + \boxed{-1}$$

$$\boxed{1} = \dfrac{1}{\frac{1}{b}(-2)}$$

$$\dfrac{1}{b}(-2) \cdot \boxed{1} = 1$$

$$\dfrac{1}{b} = \boxed{\dfrac{-1}{2}}$$

$$b = \boxed{-2}$$

So, $g(x) = \dfrac{1}{\boxed{\frac{1}{-2}}(x+3)} + \boxed{-1}$, or $g(x) = \dfrac{1}{-0.5(x+3)} - 1$.

Reflect

10. **Discussion** In Parts A and B, the coordinates of a second point on the graph of $g(x)$ are given. In what way can those coordinates be useful?

Your Turn

11. Write the function whose graph is shown.
    Use the form $g(x) = a\left(\dfrac{1}{x-h}\right) + k$.

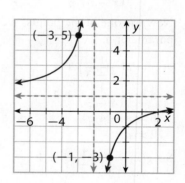

12. Write the function whose graph is shown.
    Use the form $g(x) = \dfrac{1}{\frac{1}{b}(x-h)} + k$.

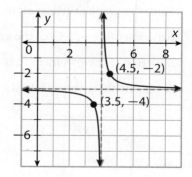

Explain 4 **Modeling with Simple Rational Functions**

In a real-world situation where there is a shared cost and a per-person or per-item cost, you can model the situation using a rational function that has the general form $f(x) = \frac{a}{x - h} + k$ where $f(x)$ is the total cost for each person or item.

Example 4

 A **Mary and some of her friends are thinking about renting a car while staying at a beach resort for a vacation. The cost per person for staying at the beach resort is $300, and the cost of the car rental is $220. If the friends agree to share the cost of the car rental, what is the minimum number of people who must go on the trip so that the total cost for each person is no more than $350?**

 Analyze Information

Identify the important information.

- The cost per person for the resort is $300.

- The cost of the car rental is $220.

- The most that each person will spend is $350.

 Formulate a Plan

Create a rational function that gives the total cost for each person. Graph the function, and use the graph to answer the question.

Solve

Let p be the people who agree to go on the trip. Let $C(p)$ be the cost (in dollars) for each person.

$$C(p) = \frac{\boxed{220}}{p} + \boxed{300}$$

Graph the function, recognizing that the graph involves two transformations of the graph of the parent rational function:

- a vertical stretch by a factor of 220

- a vertical translation of 300 units up

Also draw the line $C(p) = 350$.

The graphs intersect between $p = \boxed{4}$ and $p = \boxed{5}$, so the minimum number of people who must go on the trip in order for the total cost for each person to be no more than $350 is 5.

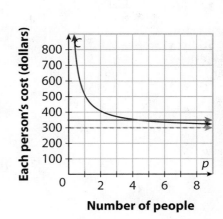

Check the solution by evaluating the function $C(p)$. Since $C(4) = \boxed{355} > 350$ and $C(5) = \boxed{344} < 350$, the minimum number of people who must go on the trip is 5.

Your Turn

13. Justin has purchased a basic silk screening kit for applying designs to fabric. The kit costs $200. He plans to buy T-shirts for $10 each, apply a design that he creates to them, and then sell them. Model this situation with a rational function that gives the average cost of a silk-screened T-shirt when the cost of the kit is included in the calculation. Make a graph of the function to determine the minimum number of T-shirts that brings the average cost below $17.50.

Elaborate

14. Compare and contrast the attributes of $f(x) = \frac{1}{x}$ and the attributes of $g(x) = -\frac{1}{x}$.

15. State the domain and range of $f(x) = a\left(\frac{1}{x-h}\right) + k$ using inequalities, set notation, and interval notation.

16. Given that the model $C(p) = \frac{100}{p} + 50$ represents the total cost C (in dollars) for each person in a group of p people when there is a shared expense and an individual expense, describe what the expressions $\frac{100}{p}$ and 50 represent.

17. **Essential Question Check-In** Describe the transformations you must perform on the graph of $f(x) = \frac{1}{x}$ to obtain the graph of $f(x) = a\left(\frac{1}{x-h}\right) + k$.

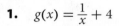 Evaluate: Homework and Practice

- Online Homework
- Hints and Help
- Extra Practice

Describe how the graph of $g(x)$ is related to the graph of $f(x) = \frac{1}{x}$.

1. $g(x) = \frac{1}{x} + 4$

2. $g(x) = 5\left(\frac{1}{x}\right)$

3. $g(x) = \frac{1}{x+3}$

4. $g(x) = \frac{1}{0.1x}$

5. $g(x) = \frac{1}{x} - 7$

6. $g(x) = \frac{1}{x-8}$

7. $g(x) = -0.1\left(\frac{1}{x}\right)$

8. $g(x) = \frac{1}{-3x}$

Identify the transformations of the graph of $f(x) = \frac{1}{x}$ that produce the graph of the given function $g(x)$. Then graph $g(x)$ on the same coordinate plane as the graph of $f(x)$ by applying the transformations to the asymptotes $x = 0$ and $y = 0$ and to the reference points $(-1, -1)$ and $(1, 1)$. Also state the domain and range of $g(x)$ using inequalities, set notation, and interval notation.

9. $g(x) = 3\left(\dfrac{1}{x+1}\right) - 2$

10. $g(x) = \dfrac{1}{-0.5(x-3)} + 1$

11. $g(x) = -0.5\left(\dfrac{1}{x-1}\right) - 2$

12. $g(x) = \dfrac{1}{2(x+2)} + 3$

Rewrite the function in the form $g(x) = a\,\dfrac{1}{(x-h)} + k$ or $g(x) = \dfrac{1}{\frac{1}{b}(x-h)} + k$ and graph it. Also state the domain and range using inequalities, set notation, and interval notation.

13. $g(x) = \dfrac{3x-5}{x-1}$

14. $g(x) = \dfrac{x+5}{0.5x+2}$

15. $g(x) = \dfrac{-4x+11}{x-2}$

16. $g(x) = \dfrac{4x+13}{-2x-6}$

17. Write the function whose graph is shown. Use the form $g(x) = a\left(\dfrac{1}{x-h}\right) + k$.

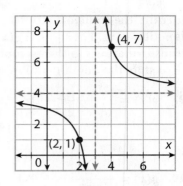

18. Write the function whose graph is shown. Use the form $g(x) = \dfrac{1}{\frac{1}{b}(x-h)} + k$

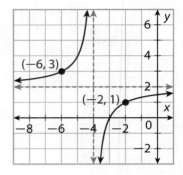

19. Write the function whose graph is shown. Use the form $g(x) = \dfrac{1}{\frac{1}{b}(x-h)} + k$.

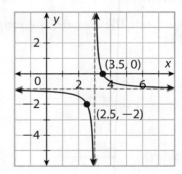

20. Write the function whose graph is shown.
Use the form $g(x) = a\left(\dfrac{1}{x-h}\right) + k$

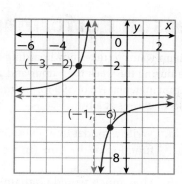

21. Maria has purchased a basic stained glass kit for $100. She plans to make stained glass suncatchers and sell them. She estimates that the materials for making each suncatcher will cost $15. Model this situation with a rational function that gives the average cost of a stained glass suncatcher when the cost of the kit is included in the calculation. Make a graph of the function to determine the minimum number of suncatchers that brings the average cost below $22.50.

22. Amy has purchased a basic letterpress kit for $140. She plans to make wedding invitations. She estimates that the cost of the paper and envelope for each invitation is $2. Model this situation with a rational function that gives the average cost of a wedding invitation when the cost of the kit is included in the calculation. Make a graph of the function to determine the minimum number of invitations that brings the average cost below $5.

23. Multiple Response Identify the transformations of the graph of the parent rational function that result in the graph of $g(x) = \dfrac{1}{2(x-3)} + 1$

A. Horizontal stretch by a factor of 2

B. Horizontal compression by a factor of $\frac{1}{2}$

C. Vertical stretch by a factor of 2

D. Vertical compression by a factor of $\frac{1}{2}$

E. Translation 1 unit up

F. Translation 1 unit down

G. Translation 3 units right

H. Translation 3 units left

H.O.T. Focus on Higher Order Thinking

24. Justify Reasoning Explain why, for positive numbers a and b, a vertical stretch or compression of the graph of $f(x) = \frac{1}{x}$ by a factor of a and, separately, a horizontal stretch or compression of the graph of $f(x)$ by a factor of b result in the same graph when a and b are equal.

25. Communicate Mathematical Ideas Determine the domain and range of the rational function $g(x) = \dfrac{mx + n}{px + q}$ where $p \neq 0$. Give your answer in set notation, and explain your reasoning.

Lesson Performance Task

Graham wants to take snowboarding lessons at a nearby ski resort that charges $40 per week for a class that meets once during the week for 1 hour and gives him a lift ticket valid for 4 hours. The resort also charges a one-time equipment-rental fee of $99 for uninterrupted enrollment in classes. The resort requires that learners pay for three weeks of classes at a time.

a. Write a model that gives Graham's average weekly enrollment cost (in dollars) as a function of the time (in weeks) that Graham takes classes.

b. How much would Graham's average weekly enrollment cost be if he took classes only for the minimum of three weeks?

c. For how many weeks would Graham need to take classes for his average weekly enrollment cost to be at most $60? Describe how you can use a graphing calculator to graph the function from part a in order to answer this question, and then state the answer.

9.3 Graphing More Complicated Rational Functions

Essential Question: What features of the graph of a rational function should you identify in order to sketch the graph? How do you identify those features?

 TEKS **A2.6.K** Determine the asymptotic restrictions on the domain of a rational function and represent domain and range using interval notation, inequalities, and set notation. Also A2.7.I

Explore 1 **Investigating Domains and Vertical Asympotes of More Complicated Rational Functions**

You know that the rational function $f(x) = \frac{1}{x-2} + 3$ has the domain $\{x | x \neq 2\}$ because the function is undefined at $x = 2$. Its graph has the vertical asymptote $x = 2$ because as $x \to 2^+$ (x approaches 2 from the right), $f(x) \to +\infty$, and as $x \to 2^-$ (x approaches 2 from the left), $f(x) \to -\infty$. In this Explore, you will investigate the domains and vertical asymptotes of other rational functions.e

(A) Copy and complete the table. Identify each function's domain based on the x-values for which the function is undefined. Write the domain using an inequality, set notation, and interval notation. Then state the equations of what you think the vertical asymptotes of the function's graph are.

Function	Domain	Possible Vertical Asymptotes
$f(x) = \dfrac{x+3}{x-1}$		
$f(x) = \dfrac{(x+5)(x-1)}{x+1}$		
$f(x) = \dfrac{x-4}{(x+1)(x-1)}$		
$f(x) = \dfrac{2x^2 - 3x + 9}{x^2 - x - 6}$		

(B) Using a graphing calculator, graph each of the functions from Step A, and check to see if vertical asymptotes occur where you expect. Are there any unexpected results?

Ⓒ Examine the behavior of $f(x) = \dfrac{x+3}{x-1}$ near $x = 1$.

First, copy and complete the tables.

x approaches 1 from the right	
x	$f(x) = \dfrac{x+3}{x-1}$
1.1	
1.01	
1.001	

x approaches 1 from the left	
x	$f(x) = \dfrac{x+3}{x-1}$
0.9	
0.99	
0.999	

Next, summarize the results.

- As $x \to 1^+$, $f(x) \to$ ▮.
- As $x \to 1^-$, $f(x) \to$ ▮.

The behaviour of $f(x) = \dfrac{x+3}{x-1}$ near $x = 1$ shows that the graph of $f(x)$ ▮ a vertical asymptote at $x = 1$.

Ⓓ Examine the behavior of $f(x) = \dfrac{(x+5)(x-1)}{(x+1)}$ near $x = -1$.

First, copy and complete the tables.

x approaches −1 from the right	
x	$f(x) = \dfrac{(x+5)(x-1)}{x+1}$
−0.9	
−0.99	
−0.999	

x approaches −1 from the left	
x	$f(x) = \dfrac{(x+5)(x-1)}{x+1}$
−1.1	
−1.01	
−1.001	

Next, summarize the results.

- As $x \to -1^+$, $f(x) \to$ ▮.
- As $x \to -1^-$, $f(x) \to$ ▮.

The behavior of $f(x) = \dfrac{(x+5)(x-1)}{(x+1)}$ near $x = -1$ shows that the graph of $f(x)$ ▮ a vertical asymptote at $x = -1$.

E. Examine the behavior of $f(x) = \dfrac{x-4}{(x+1)(x-1)}$ near $x = -1$ and $x = 1$.

First, copy and complete the tables. Round results to the nearest tenth.

x approaches −1 from the right	
x	$f(x) = \dfrac{x-4}{(x+1)(x-1)}$
−0.9	25.8
−0.99	250.8
−0.999	2500.8

x approaches −1 from the left	
x	$f(x) = \dfrac{x-4}{(x+1)(x-1)}$
−1.1	−24.3
−1.01	−249.3
−1.001	−2499.3

x approaches 1 from the right	
x	$f(x) = \dfrac{x-4}{(x+1)(x-1)}$
1.1	−13.8
1.01	−148.8
1.001	−1498.8

x approaches 1 from the left	
x	$f(x) = \dfrac{x-4}{(x+1)(x-1)}$
0.9	16.3
0.99	151.3
0.999	1501.3

Next, summarize the results.

- As $x \to -1^+$, $f(x) \to +\infty$.
- As $x \to -1^-$, $f(x) \to -\infty$.

- As $x \to 1^+$, $f(x) \to -\infty$.
- As $x \to 1^-$, $f(x) \to +\infty$.

The behavior of $f(x) = \dfrac{x-4}{(x+1)(x-1)}$ near $x = -1$ shows that the graph of $f(x)$ has a vertical asymptote at $x = -1$. The behavior of $f(x) = \dfrac{x-4}{(x+1)(x-1)}$ near $x = 1$ shows that the graph of $f(x)$ has a vertical asymptote at $x = 1$.

Examine the behavior of $f(x) = \dfrac{2x^2 - 3x - 9}{x^2 - x - 6}$ near $x = -2$ and $x = 3$.

First, copy and complete the tables. Round results to the nearest ten thousandth if necessary.

x approaches −2 from the right	
x	$f(x) = \dfrac{2x^2 - 3x - 9}{x^2 - x - 6}$
−1.9	
−1.99	
−1.999	

x approaches −2 from the left	
x	$f(x) = \dfrac{2x^2 - 3x - 9}{x^2 - x - 6}$
−2.1	
−2.01	
−2.001	

x approaches 3 from the right	
x	$f(x) = \dfrac{2x^2 - 3x - 9}{x^2 - x - 6}$
3.1	
3.01	
3.001	

x approaches 3 from the left	
x	$f(x) = \dfrac{2x^2 - 3x - 9}{x^2 - x - 6}$
2.9	
2.99	
2.999	

Next, summarize the results:

- As $x \to -2^+$, $f(x) \to$ ▮ .
- As $x \to -2^-$, $f(x) \to$ ▮ .
- As $x \to 3^+$, $f(x) \to$ ▮ .
- As $x \to 3^-$, $f(x) \to$ ▮ .

The behavior of $f(x) = \dfrac{2x^2 - 3x - 9}{x^2 - x - 6}$ near $x = -2$ shows that the graph of $f(x)$ ▮ a vertical asymptote at $x = -2$. The behavior of $f(x) = \dfrac{2x^2 - 3x - 9}{x^2 - x - 6}$ near $x = 3$ shows that the graph of $f(x)$ ▮ a vertical asymptote at $x = 3$.

Reflect

1. Rewrite $f(x) = \dfrac{2x^2 - 3x - 9}{x^2 - x - 6}$ so that its numerator and denominator are factored. How does this form of the function explain the behavior of the function near $x = 3$?

2. **Discussion** When you graph $f(x) = \dfrac{2x^2 - 3x - 9}{x^2 - x - 6}$ on a graphing calculator, you can't tell that the function is undefined for $x = 3$. How does using the calculator's table feature help? What do you think the graph should look like to make it clear that the function is undefined at $x = 3$?

You can determine the end behavior of a rational function by using polynomial division. When you divide a rational function's numerator (dividend) by its denominator (divisor), you obtain a quotient and a remainder. You can then rewrite the function in the form $f(x) = \text{quotient} + \frac{\text{remainder}}{\text{divisor}}$. Because the degree of the remainder must be less than the degree of the divisor, the expression $\frac{\text{remainder}}{\text{divisor}}$ approaches 0 as x increases or decreases without bound. This means that the function has the same end behavior as the quotient.

Ⓐ The table lists the same rational functions as in the previous Explore. Copy and complete the table. When writing a function in the form $f(x) = \text{quotient} + \frac{\text{remainder}}{\text{divisor}}$, you will need to write numerator and denominator as polynomials in standard form before carrying out the division.

Function	Function in the form $f(x) = \text{quotient} + \dfrac{\text{remainder}}{\text{divisor}}$	End behavior
$f(x) = \dfrac{x+3}{x-1}$		
$f(x) = \dfrac{(x+5)(x-1)}{x+1}$		
$f(x) = \dfrac{x-4}{(x+1)(x-1)}$		
$f(x) = \dfrac{2x^2 - 3x - 9}{x^2 - x - 6}$		

Ⓑ Identify the functions in Step A whose graphs have horizontal asymptotes.

Ⓒ Using a graphing calculator, graph each of the functions in Step A to check its end behavior. Then examine the graph to determine the function's range. Copy and complete the table using an inequality, set notation, and interval notation. (For the third function, you should examine a table of values using an x-value increment of 0.1. Once you have a sense of where the function's minimum and maximum values occur, select **3:minimum** from the **CALC** menu to determine the minimum value and **4:maximum** from the **CALC** menu to determine the maximum value. Round these values to the nearest hundredth, recognizing that the range you give is an approximation of the actual range.)

Function	Range
$f(x) = \dfrac{x+3}{x-1}$	
$f(x) = \dfrac{(x+5)(x-1)}{x+1}$	
$f(x) = \dfrac{x-4}{(x+1)(x-1)}$	
$f(x) = \dfrac{2x^2 - 3x - 9}{x^2 - x - 6}$	

3. What line does the graph of $f(x) = \dfrac{(x+5)(x-1)}{x+1}$ approach as x increases or decreases without bound? Explain.

4. If you rewrite the function $f(x) = \dfrac{x-4}{(x+1)(x-1)}$ as $f(x) = \dfrac{x-4}{x^2-1}$ and then multiply the numerator and denominator by $\dfrac{1}{x^2}$, you get $f(x) = \dfrac{\frac{1}{x} - \frac{4}{x^2}}{1 - \frac{1}{x^2}}$. Using this form of the function, describe what happens to each term in the numerator and denominator as x increases without bound and as x decreases without bound. Then explain how these results give you the function's end behavior.

5. **Discussion** Which of the four functions in this Explore has a graph that crosses its horizontal asymptote? How do you reconcile the fact that a graph is supposed to approach a line but not cross it in order for the line to be an asymptote with the fact that the graph of the function you identified crosses its horizontal asymptote?

⚙ Explain 1 Sketching the Graphs of More Complicated Rational Functions

As you have seen, there can be breaks in the graph of a rational function. These breaks are called *discontinuities*, and there are two kinds:

1. When a rational function has a factor in the denominator that is not also in the numerator, an *infinite discontinuity* occurs at the value of x for which the factor equals 0. On the graph of the function, an infinite discontinuity appears as a vertical asymptote.

2. When a rational function has a factor in the denominator that is also in the numerator, a *point discontinuity* occurs at the value of x for which the factor equals 0. On the graph of the function, a point discontinuity appears as a "hole."

The graph of a rational function can also have a horizontal asymptote. It is determined by the degrees and leading coefficients of the function's numerator and denominator. If the numerator is a polynomial $p(x)$ in standard form with leading coefficient a and the denominator is a polynomial $q(x)$ in standard form with leading coefficient b, then an examination of the function's end behavior gives the following results.

Relationship between Degree of $p(x)$ and Degree of $q(x)$	Equation of Horizontal Asymptote (if one exists)
Degree of $p(x)$ < degree of $q(x)$	$y = 0$
Degree of $p(x)$ = degree of $q(x)$	$y = \dfrac{a}{b}$
Degree of $p(x)$ > degree of $q(x)$	There is no horizontal asymptote. The function instead increases or decreases without bound as x increases or decreases without bound. In particular, when the degree of the numerator is 1 more than the degree of the denominator, the function's graph approaches a slanted line, called a *slant asymptote*, as x increases or decreases without bound.

You can sketch the graph of a rational function by identifying where vertical asymptotes, "holes," and horizontal asymptotes occur. Using the factors of the numerator and denominator, you can also establish intervals on the x-axis where either an x-intercept or a discontinuity occurs and then check the signs of the factors on those intervals to determine whether the graph lies above or below the x-axis.

Example 1 Sketch the graph of the given rational function. (If the degree of the numerator is 1 more than the degree of the denominator, find the graph's slant asymptote by dividing the numerator by the denominator.) Also state the function's domain and range using inequalities, set notation, and interval notation. (If your sketch indicates that the function has maximum or minimum values, use a graphing calculator to find those values to the nearest hundredth when determining the range.)

(A) $f(x) = \dfrac{x+1}{x-2}$

Identify vertical asymptotes and "holes."

The function is undefined when $x - 2 = 0$, or $x = 2$. Since $x - 2$ does not appear in the numerator, there is a vertical asymptote rather than a "hole" at $x = 2$.

Identify horizontal asymptotes and slant asymptotes.

The numerator and denominator have the same degree and the leading coefficient of each is 1, so there is a horizontal asymptote at $y = \frac{1}{1} = 1$.

Identify x-intercepts.

An x-intercept occurs when $x + 1 = 0$, or $x = -1$.

Check the sign of the function on the intervals $x < -1$, $-1 < x < 2$, and $x > 2$.

Interval	Sign of $x+1$	Sign of $x-2$	Sign of $f(x) = \dfrac{x+1}{x-2}$
$x < -1$	$-$	$-$	$+$
$-1 < x < 2$	$+$	$-$	$-$
$x > 2$	$+$	$+$	$+$

Sketch the graph using all this information. Then state the domain and range.

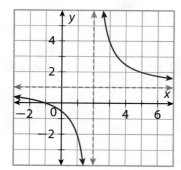

Domain:

Inequality: $x < 2$ or $x > 2$

Set notation: $\left\{ x \mid x \neq 2 \right\}$

Interval notation: $(-\infty, 2) \cup (2, +\infty)$

Range:

Inequality: $y < 1$ or $y > 1$

Set notation: $\left\{ y \mid y \neq 1 \right\}$

Interval notation: $(-\infty, 1) \cup (1, +\infty)$

(B) $f(x) = \dfrac{x^2 + x - 2}{x + 3}$

Factor the function's numerator.

$$f(x) = \frac{x^2 + x - 2}{x + 3} = \frac{(x-1)(x+2)}{x+3}$$

Identify vertical asymptotes and "holes."

The function is undefined when $x + 3 = 0$, or $x = \boxed{-3}$. Since $x + 3$ does not appear in the numerator, there is a vertical asymptote rather than a "hole" at $x = \boxed{-3}$.

Identify horizontal asymptotes and slant asymptotes.

Because the degree of the numerator is 1 more than the degree of the denominator, there is no horizontal asymptote, but there is a slant asymptote. Divide the numerator by the denominator to identify the slant asymptote.

$$
\begin{array}{r}
x - \boxed{2} \\
x + 3 \overline{)\ x^2 + x - 2\ } \\
\underline{x^2 + 3x} \\
-2x - 2 \\
\underline{-2x - 6} \\
4
\end{array}
$$

So, the line $y = x - \boxed{2}$ is the slant asymptote.

Identify x-intercepts.

There are two x-intercepts: when $x - 1 = 0$, or $x = \boxed{1}$, and when $x + 2 = 0$, or $x = \boxed{-2}$.

Check the sign of the function on the intervals $x < -3$, $-3 < x < -2$, $-2 < x < 1$, and $x > 1$.

Interval	Sign of $x + 3$	Sign of $x + 2$	Sign of $x - 1$	Sign of $f(x) = \dfrac{(x-1)(x+2)}{x+3}$
$x < -3$	−	−	−	−
$-3 < x < -2$	+	−	−	+
$-2 < x < 1$	+	+	−	−
$x > 1$	+	+	+	+

Sketch the graph using all this information. Then state the domain and range.

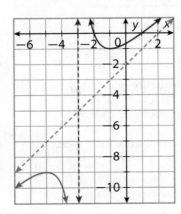

Domain:

Inequality: $x < \boxed{-3}$ or $x > \boxed{-3}$

Set notation: $\left\{ x \mid x \neq \boxed{-3} \right\}$

Interval notation: $\left(-\infty, \boxed{-3} \right) \cup \left(\boxed{-3}, +\infty \right)$

The sketch indicates that the function has a maximum value and a minimum value. Using **3:minimum** from the **CALC** menu on a graphing calculator gives -1 as the minimum value. Using **4:maximum** from the **CALC** menu on a graphing calculator gives -5 as the maximum value.

Range:

Inequality: $y < \boxed{-5}$ or $y > \boxed{-1}$

Set notation: $\left\{ y \mid y < \boxed{-5} \text{ or } y > \boxed{-1} \right\}$ Interval notation: $\left(-\infty, \boxed{-5} \right) \cup \left(\boxed{-1}, +\infty \right)$

Sketch the graph of the given rational function. (If the degree of the numerator is 1 more than the degree of the denominator, find the graph's slant asymptote by dividing the numerator by the denominator.) Also state the function's domain and range using inequalities, set notation, and interval notation. (If your sketch indicates that the function has maximum or minimum values, use a graphing calculator to find those values to the nearest hundredth when determining the range.)

6. $f(x) = \dfrac{x + 1}{x^2 + 3x - 4}$

⊘ Explain 2   Modeling with More Complicated Rational Functions

When two real-world variable quantities are compared using a ratio or rate, the comparison is a rational function. You can solve problems about the ratio or rate by graphing the rational function.

Example 2   **Write a rational function to model the situation, or use the given rational function. State a reasonable domain and range for the function using set notation. Then use a graphing calculator to graph the function and answer the question.**

Ⓐ   A baseball team has won 32 games out of 56 games played, for a winning percentage of $\frac{32}{56} \approx 0.571$. How many consecutive games must the team win to raise its winning percentage to 0.600?

Let w be the number of consecutive games to be won. Then the total number of games won is the function $T_{won}(W) = 32 + w$, and the total number of games played is the function $T_{played}(W) = 56 + w$.

The rational function that gives the team's winning percentage p (as a decimal) is

$p(w) = \dfrac{T_{won}(W)}{T_{played}(W)} = \dfrac{32 + w}{56 + w}$.

The domain of the rational function is $\left\{ w \mid w \geq 0 \text{ and } w \text{ is a whole number} \right\}$. Note that you do not need to exclude -56 from the domain, because only nonnegative whole-number values of w make sense in this situation.

Since the function models what happens to the team's winning percentage from consecutive wins (no losses), the values of $p(w)$ start at 0.571 and approach 1 as w increases without bound. So, the range is

$\left\{ p \mid 0.571 \leq p < 1 \right\}$.

Graph $y = \dfrac{32 + x}{56 + x}$ on a graphing calculator using a viewing window that shows 0 to 10 on the x-axis and 0.5 to 0.7 on the y-axis. Also graph the line $y = 0.6$. To find where the graphs intersect, select **5: intersect** from the **CALC** menu.

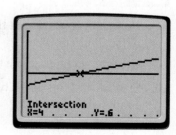

So, the team's winning percentage (as a decimal) will be 0.600 if the team wins 4 consecutive games.

B Two friends decide spend an afternoon canoeing on a river. They travel 4 miles upstream and 6 miles downstream. In still water, they know that their average paddling speed is 5 miles per hour. If their canoe trip takes 4 hours, what is the average speed of the river's current? To answer the question, use the rational function $t(c) = \frac{4}{5-c} + \frac{6}{5+c} = \frac{50 - 2c}{(5-c)(5+c)}$ where c is the average speed of the current (in miles per hour) and t is the time (in hours) spent canoeing 4 miles against the current at a rate of $5 - c$ miles per hour and 6 miles with the current at a rate of $5 + c$ miles per hour.

In order for the friends to travel upstream, the speed of the current must be less than their average paddling speed, so the domain of the function is $\left\{ c \mid 0 \leq c < \boxed{5} \right\}$. If the friends canoed in still water $(c = 0)$, the trip would take a total of $\frac{4}{5} + \frac{6}{5} = \boxed{2}$ hours. As c approaches 5 from the left, the value of $\frac{6}{5+c}$ approaches $\frac{6}{10} = 0.6$ hour, but the value of $\frac{4}{5-c}$ increases without bound. So, the range of the function is $\left\{ t \mid t \geq \boxed{2} \right\}$.

Graph $y = \frac{50 - 2x}{(5-x)(5+x)}$ on a graphing calculator using a viewing window that shows 0 to 5 on the x-axis and 2 to 5 on the y-axis. Also graph the line $y = \boxed{4}$. To find where the graphs intersect, select **5:intersect** from the **CALC** menu. The calculator shows that the average speed of the current is about 3.8 miles per hour.

Your Turn

Write a rational function to model the situation, or use the given rational function. State a reasonable domain and range for the function using set notation. Then use a graphing calculator to graph the function and answer the question.

7. A saline solution is a mixture of salt and water. A $p\%$ saline solution contains $p\%$ salt and $(100 - p)\%$ water by mass. A chemist has 300 grams of a 4% saline solution that needs to be strengthened to a 6% solution by adding salt. How much salt should the chemist add?

💬 Elaborate

8. How can you show that the vertical line $x = c$, where c is a constant, is an asymptote for the graph of a rational function?

9. How can you determine the end behavior of a rational function?

10. **Essential Question Check-In** How do you identify any vertical asymptotes and "holes" that the graph of a rational function has?

State the domain using an inequality, set notation, and interval notation. For any *x*-value excluded from the domain, state whether the graph has a vertical asymptote or a "hole" at that *x*-value. Use a graphing calculator to check your answer.

1. $f(x) = \dfrac{x + 5}{x + 1}$

2. $f(x) = \dfrac{x^2 + 2x - 3}{x^2 - 4x + 3}$

Divide the numerator by the denominator to write the function in the form $f(x) = \text{quotient} + \dfrac{\text{remainder}}{\text{divisor}}$ and determine the function's end behavior. Then, using a graphing calculator to examine the function's graph, state the range using an inequality, set notation, and interval notation.

3. $f(x) = \dfrac{3x + 1}{x - 2}$

4. $f(x) = \dfrac{x}{(x - 2)(x + 3)}$

5. $f(x) = \dfrac{x^2 - 5x + 6}{x - 1}$

6. $f(x) = \dfrac{4x^2 - 1}{x^2 + x - 2}$

Sketch the graph of the given rational function. (If the degree of the numerator is 1 more than the degree of the denominator, find the graph's slant asymptote by dividing the numerator by the denominator.) Also state the function's domain and range using inequalities, set notation, and interval notation. (If your sketch indicates that the function has maximum or minimum values, use a graphing calculator to find those values to the nearest hundredth when determining the range.)

7. $f(x) = \dfrac{x - 1}{x + 1}$

8. $f(x) = \dfrac{x - 1}{(x - 2)(x + 3)}$

9. $f(x) = \dfrac{(x + 1)(x - 1)}{x + 2}$

10. $f(x) = \dfrac{-3x(x - 2)}{(x - 2)(x + 2)}$

11. $f(x) = \dfrac{x^2 + 2x - 4}{x - 1}$

12. $f(x) = \dfrac{2x^2 - 4x}{x^2 + 4x + 4}$

Write a rational function to model the situation, or use the given rational function. State a reasonable domain and range for the function using set notation. Then use a graphing calculator to graph the function and answer the question.

13. A basketball team has won 16 games out of 23 games played, for a winning percentage (expressed as a decimal) of $\frac{16}{23} \approx 0.696$. How many consecutive games must the team win to raise its winning percentage to 0.750?

14. So far this season, a baseball player has had 84 hits in 294 times at bat, for a batting average of $\frac{84}{294} \approx 0.286$. How many consecutive hits must the player get to ravise his batting average to 0.300?

15. A kayaker traveled 5 miles upstream and then 8 miles downstream on a river. The average speed of the current was 3 miles per hour. If the kayaker was paddling for 5 hours, what was the kayaker's average paddling speed? To answer the question, use the rational function $t(s) = \frac{5}{s-3} + \frac{8}{s+3} = \frac{13s-9}{(s-3)(s+3)}$ where s is the kayaker's average paddling speed (in miles per hour) and t is the time (in hours) spent kayaking 5 miles against the current at a rate of $s-3$ miles per hour and 8 miles with the current at a rate of $s+3$ miles per hour.

16. In aviation, *air speed* refers to a plane's speed in still air. A small plane maintains a certain air speed when flying to and from a city that is 400 miles away. On the trip out, the plane flies against a wind, which has an average speed of 40 miles per hour. On the return trip, the plane flies with the wind. If the total flight time for the round trip is 3.5 hours, what is the plane's average air speed? To answer this question, use the rational function $t(s) = \frac{400}{s-40} + \frac{400}{s+40} = \frac{800}{(s-40)(s+40)}$ air speed (in miles per hour) and t is the total flight time (in hours) for the round trip.

17. **Multiple Response** Identify the statements that apply to the rational function

$f(x) = \dfrac{x - 2}{x^2 - x + 6}.$

A. The function's domain is $\left\{x \mid x \neq -2 \text{ and } x \neq 3\right\}$.

B. The function's domain is $\left\{x \mid x \neq -2 \text{ and } x \neq -3\right\}$.

C. The function's range is $\left\{y \mid y \neq 0\right\}$.

D. The function's range is $\left\{y \mid -\infty \; y < +\infty\right\}$.

E. The function's graph has vertical asymptotes at $x = -2$ and $x = 3$.

F. The function's graph has a vertical asymptote at $x = -3$ and a "hole" at $x = 2$.

G. The function's graph has a horizontal asymptote at $y = 0$.

H. The function's graph has a horizontal asymptote at $y = 1$.

H.O.T. Focus on Higher Order Thinking

18. **Draw Conclusions** For what value(s) of a does the graph of $f(x) = \dfrac{x + a}{x^2 + 4x + 3}$ have a "hole"? Explain. Then, for each value of a, state the domain and the range of $f(x)$ using interval notation.

19. **Critique Reasoning** A student claims that the functions $f(x) = \dfrac{4x^2 - 1}{4x + 2}$ and $g(x) = \dfrac{4x + 2}{4x^2 - 1}$ have different domains but identical ranges. Which part of the student's claim is correct, and which is false? Explain.

Lesson Performance Task

In professional baseball, the smallest allowable volume of a baseball is 92.06% of the largest allowable volume, and the range of allowable radii is 0.04 inch.

a. Let r be the largest allowable radius (in inches) of a baseball. Write expressions, both in terms of r, for the largest allowable volume of the baseball and the smallest allowable volume of the baseball. (Use the formula for the volume of a sphere, $V = \frac{4}{3} \pi r^3$.)

b. Write and simplify a function that gives the ratio R of the smallest allowable volume of a baseball to the largest allowable volume.

c. Use a graphing calculator to graph the function from part b, and use the graph to find the smallest allowable radius and the largest allowable radius of a baseball. Round your answers to the nearest hundredth.

Essential Question: How can you use rational functions to solve real-world problems?

Key Vocabulary

asymptote *(asíntota)*

constant of variation
   (constante de variación)

inverse variation
   (variación inversa)

parent function
   (función madre)

rational function
   (función racional)

KEY EXAMPLE   *(Lesson 9.1)*

The variables x and y vary inversely, and $y = 12$ when $x = 3$.
What is the value of y when $x = -4$?

$y = \dfrac{k}{x}$ Find the value of the constant of variation.

$12 = \dfrac{k}{3}$

$36 = k$

The inverse variation equation is $y = \dfrac{36}{x}$. When $x = -4$, $y = \dfrac{36}{-4}, = -9$.

KEY EXAMPLE   *(Lesson 9.3)*

Graph $y = \dfrac{2x^2}{x + 2}$. State the domain, range, x-intercept, and identify any asymptotes.

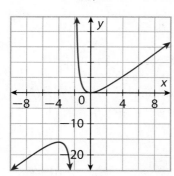

Domain: $x < -2$ or $x > -2$

Range: $y \le -\dfrac{16}{3}$ or $y \ge 0$

The numerator has 0 as its only zero, so the x-intercept is $(0, 0)$.

The denominator has -2 as its only zero, so the graph has a vertical asymptote at $x = -2$.

EXERCISES

Write an equation relating the variables and use it to answer the question. *(Lesson 9.1)*

1. The variables x and y vary inversely. When $x = 6$, $y = 2$. What is y when $x = 15$?

2. For a fixed voltage, the current I flowing in a wire varies inversely as the resistance R of the wire. If the current is 8 amperes when the resistance is 15 ohms, what will the resistance be when the current is 5 amperes?

Describe how the graph of $g(x)$ is related to the graph of $f(x) = \frac{1}{x}$. *(Lesson 9.2)*

3. $g(x) = \dfrac{1}{x + 4}$

4. $g(x) = \dfrac{1}{x - 2} + 3$

Graph the function using a graphing calculator. State the domain, x-intercept(s), and identify asymptotes. *(Lesson 9.3)*

5. $f(x) = \dfrac{x^2 - 3x}{x + 4}$

6. $f(x) = \dfrac{x - 3}{x^2 + 6x + 5}$

MODULE PERFORMANCE TASK

What Is the Profit?

A sporting goods store sells two styles of bike helmets: Style A for \$30 each and Style B for \$40 each. The store is trying to calculate its average profit on each style of helmet, using the rational function $A(x) = \frac{P(x)}{x}$, where $P(x)$ is the profit on the sale of x helmets. The helmet supplier offers a of volume discount for orders up to 500 helmets, using the cost formulas shown in the table. For each style, how does per-helmet profit change as the number of helmets increases? What is the maximum per-helmet profit?

Number of Helmets (x)	100	200	300	400	500
Style A					
Revenue					
Cost: $100 + (20 - 0.01x)x$					
Profit					
Style B					
Revenue					
Cost: $250 + (30 - 0.03x)x$					
Profit					

Copy and complete the table to organize your data. Then use graphs, numbers, words, or algebra to explain how you reached your conclusion.

(Ready) to Go On?

9.1–9.3 Rational Expressions and Equations

- Online Homework
- Hints and Help
- Extra Practice

Write an equation relating the variables and use it to answer the question. *(Lesson 9.1)*

1. The variables x and y vary inversely. When $x = -12$, $y = \frac{2}{3}$. What is y when $x = -3$?

2. The number of hours h needed to pick a field of berries varies inversely as the number of people working p, and $h = 20$ hours when $p = 10$ people. Find h when $p = 25$ people.

Describe how the graph of $g(x)$ is related to the graph of $f(x) = \frac{1}{x}$. *(Lesson 9.2)*

3. $g(x) = \frac{5}{x} - 3$

4. $g(x) = \frac{1}{-0.5(x - 2)} + 4$

Graph the function using a graphing calculator. State the domain, x-intercept(s), and identify asymptotes. *(Lessons 9.2, 9.3)*

5. $f(x) = \frac{2x - 4}{x + 3}$

6. $f(x) = \frac{x^2 - 9}{x - 2}$

ESSENTIAL QUESTION

7. How do you identify the asymptotes of a rational function?

Assessment Readiness

1. Which statement about the graph of $y = \dfrac{2x + 5}{x - 1}$ is false?

   A. The line $x = 1$ is an asymptote.

   B. The line $y = 2$ is an asymptote.

   C. The function is undefined for $x = -1$.

   D. The point $(0, -5)$ lies on the graph.

2. What is the solution set of $x^2 - 64 < 0$?

   A. $x < -8$ or $x > -8$

   B. $-8 < x < 8$

   C. $-64 < x < 64$

   D. $x < -64$ or $x > -64$

3. Which is a factor of $x^3 + 2x^2 - 5x - 6$?

   A. $(x + 2)$

   B. $(x - 2)$

   C. $(x - 5)$

   D. $(x + 6)$

4. The time t in days that it takes a movie crew to build a set varies inversely as the number of workers w. If 25 workers can build the set in 3 days, how long would it take 15 workers to build the set?

   A. 5 days

   B. 15 days

   C. 2 days

   D. 25 days

5. You have subscribed to a cable television service. The cable company charges a one-time installation fee of $30 and a monthly fee of $50. Write a model that gives the average cost per month as a function of months subscribed to the service. After how many months will the average cost be $56? Explain your thinking and identify any asymptotes on the graph of the function.

Rational Expressions and Equations

Essential Question: How can you use rational expressions and equations to solve real-world problems?

REAL WORLD VIDEO
Robotic arms and other prosthetic devices are among the wonders of robotics. Check out some of the other cutting-edge applications of modern robotics.

MODULE PERFORMANCE TASK PREVIEW

Robots and Resistors

Robotics engineers design robots and develop applications for them, such as executing high-precision tasks in factories, cleaning toxic waste, and locating and defusing bombs. People who work in robotics are skilled in areas such as electronics and computer programming. How can a rational expression be used to help design the circuitry for a robot? Let's find out!

Are (YOU) Ready?

Complete these exercises to review skills you will need for this chapter.

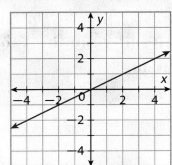

• Online Homework
• Hints and Help
• Extra Practice

Graphing Linear Proportional Relationships

Example 1

Graph $y = \frac{1}{2}x$.

When $x = 0$, $y = 0$, so plot $(0, 0)$ on the graph.

The slope is $\frac{1}{2}$, so from $(0, 0)$, plot the next point up 1 and over 2.

Draw a line through the two points.

Graph each proportional relationship.

1. $y = 2x$

2. $y = \frac{2}{3}x$

Direct and Inverse Variation

Example 2

In a direct variation the constant is 4 and its graph passes through $(x, 10)$. Find x.

$y = kx \longrightarrow 10 = 4x \rightarrow x = 2.5$

Example 3

In an inverse variation the constant is 2.4 and its graph passes through $(6, y)$. Find y.

$k = xy \longrightarrow 2.4 = 6y \longrightarrow y = 0.4$

Find the missing variable for each direct variation.

3. $k = -1; (x, -5)$

4. $k = 3; (9, y)$

5. $k = \frac{1}{3}; (x, -2)$

Find the missing variable for each inverse variation.

6. $k = 8; (x, -10)$

7. $k = -2; (5, y)$

8. $k = 6; (x, 1.5)$

10.1 Adding and Subtracting Rational Expressions

Essential Question: How can you add and subtract rational expressions?

 TEKS **A2.7.F** Determine the sum, difference…of rational expressions with integral exponents of degree one and of degree two.

 Explore   **Identifying Excluded Values**

Given a rational expression, identify the excluded values by finding the zeroes of the denominator. If possible, simplify the expression.

(A) $\dfrac{(1 - x^2)}{x - 1}$

The denominator of the expression is ▮.

(B) Since division by 0 is not defined, the excluded values for this expression are all the values that would make the denominator equal to 0.

$x - 1 = 0$

$x = $ ▮

(C) Begin simplifying the expression by factoring the numerator.

$\dfrac{(1 - x^2)}{x - 1} = \dfrac{(\ \blacksquare\ )(\ \blacksquare\ )}{x - 1}$

(D) Divide out terms common to both the numerator and the denominator.

$\dfrac{(1 - x^2)}{x - 1} = \dfrac{(\ \blacksquare\ )(\ \blacksquare\ )}{-(1 - x)} = -(\ \blacksquare\ ) = \blacksquare$

(E) The simplified expression is

$\dfrac{(1 - x^2)}{x - 1} = \blacksquare$, whenever $x \neq \blacksquare$

(F) What is the domain for this function? What is its range?

Reflect

1. What factors can be divided out of the numerator and denominator?

⚙ Explain 1   Writing Equivalent Rational Expressions

Given a rational expression, there are different ways to write an equivalent rational expression. When common terms are divided out, the result is an equivalent but simplified expression.

Example 1   **Simplify the expressions.**

(A)   Write $\dfrac{3x}{(x+3)}$ as an equivalent rational expression that has a denominator of $(x+3)(x+5)$.

The expression $\dfrac{3x}{(x+3)}$ has a denominator of $(x+3)$.

The factor missing from the denominator is $(x+5)$.

Introduce a common factor, $(x+5)$.

$$\dfrac{3x}{(x+3)} = \dfrac{3x(x+5)}{(x+3)(x+5)}$$

$\dfrac{3x}{(x+3)}$ is equivalent to $\dfrac{3x(x+5)}{(x+3)(x+5)}$.

(B)   Simplify the expression $\dfrac{(x^2+5x+6)}{(x^2+3x+2)(x+3)}$.

Write the expression.	$\dfrac{(x^2+5x+6)}{(x^2+3x+2)(x+3)}$
Factor the numerator and denominator.	$\dfrac{(x+2)(x+3)}{(x+1)(x+2)(x+3)}$
Divide out like terms.	$\dfrac{1}{x+1}$

Your Turn

2.   Write $\dfrac{5}{5x-25}$ as an equivalent expression with a denominator of $(x-5)(x+1)$.

3.   Simplify the expression $\dfrac{(x+x^3)(1-x^2)}{(x^2-x^6)}$.

⚙ Explain 2   Adding and Subtracting Rational Expressions

Adding and subtracting rational expressions is similar to adding and subtracting fractions.

Example 2   **Add or subtract. Identify any excluded values and simplify your answer.**

Ⓐ $\dfrac{x^2 + 4x + 2}{x^2} + \dfrac{x^2}{x^2 + x}$

Factor the denominators. $\dfrac{x^2 + 4x + 2}{x^2} + \dfrac{x^2}{x(x + 1)}$

Identify where the expression is not defined. The first expression is undefined when $x = 0$. The second expression is undefined when $x = 0$ and when $x = -1$.

Find a common denominator. The LCM for x^2 and $x(x + 1)$ is $x^2(x + 1)$.

Write the expressions with a common denominator by multiplying both by the appropriate form of 1.
$$\dfrac{(x + 1)}{(x + 1)} \cdot \dfrac{x^2 + 4x + 2}{x^2} + \dfrac{x^2}{(x + 1)} \cdot \dfrac{x}{x}$$

Simplify each numerator.
$$= \dfrac{x^3 + 5x^2 + 6x + 2}{x^2\,(x + 1)} + \dfrac{x^3}{x^2(x + 1)}$$

Add.
$$= \dfrac{x^3 + 5x^2 + 6x + 2}{x^2\,(x + 1)}$$

Since none of the factors of the denominator are factors of the numerator, the expression cannot be further simplified.

Ⓑ $\dfrac{2x^2}{x^2 - 5x} - \dfrac{x^2 + 3x - 4}{x^2}$

Factor the denominators.
$$\dfrac{2x^2}{\boxed{x(x - 5)}} - \dfrac{x^2 + 3x - 4}{x^2}$$

Identify where the expression is not defined. The first expression is undefined when $x = 0$ and when $x = 5$. The second expression is undefined when $x = 0$.

Find a common denominator. The LCM for $x(x - 5)$ and x^2 is $x^2(x - 5)$.

Write the expressions with a common denominator by multiplying both by the appropriate form of 1.
$$\boxed{\dfrac{x}{x}} \cdot \dfrac{2x^2}{x(x - 5)} - \dfrac{x^2 + 3x - 4}{x^2} \cdot \dfrac{x - 5}{x - 5}$$

Simplify each numerator.
$$= \dfrac{2x^3}{x^2(x - 5)} - \dfrac{x^3 - 2x^2 - 19x + 20}{x^2(x - 5)}$$

Subtract.
$$= \dfrac{\boxed{x^3} + 2x^2 + 19x - 20}{x^2(x - 5)}$$

Since none of the factors of the denominator are factors of the numerator, the expression cannot be further simplified.

Your Turn

Add each pair of expressions, simplifying the result and noting the combined excluded values. Then subtract the second expression from the first, again simplifying the result and noting the combined excluded values.

4. $-x^2$ and $\dfrac{1}{(1 - x^2)}$

5. $\dfrac{x^2}{(4 - x^2)}$ and $\dfrac{1}{(2 - x)}$

⚙ Explain 3   Adding and Subtracting with Rational Models

Rational expressions can model real-world phenomena, and can be used to calculate measurements of those phenomena.

Example 3   Find the sum or difference of the models to solve the problem.

Ⓐ Two groups have agreed that each will contribute $2000 for an upcoming trip. Group A has 6 more people than group B. Let x represent the number of people in group A. Write and simplify an expression in terms of x that represents the difference between the number of dollars each person in group A must contribute and the number each person in group B must contribute.

$$\frac{2000}{x} - \frac{2000}{x - 6} = \frac{2000(x - 6)}{x(x - 6)} - \frac{2000x}{(x - 6)x}$$

$$= \frac{2000x + 12{,}000 - 2000x}{x(x - 6)}$$

$$= \frac{12{,}000}{x(x - 6)}$$

Ⓑ A freight train averages 30 miles per hour traveling to its destination with full cars and 40 miles per hour on the return trip with empty cars. Find the total time in terms of d. Use the formula $t = \frac{d}{r}$.

Let d represent the one-way distance.

Total time: $\dfrac{d}{30} + \dfrac{d}{40}$ $= \dfrac{d \cdot \boxed{40}}{30 \cdot \boxed{40}} + \dfrac{d \cdot \boxed{30}}{40 \cdot \boxed{30}}$

$$= \frac{d \cdot \boxed{40} + d \cdot \boxed{30}}{\boxed{1200}}$$

$$= \frac{\boxed{7}}{\boxed{120}} d$$

6. A hiker averages 1.4 miles per hour when walking downhill on a mountain trail and 0.8 miles per hour on the return trip when walking uphill. Find the total time in terms of d. Use the formula $t = \frac{d}{r}$.

7. Yvette ran at an average speed of 6.20 feet per second during the first two laps of a race and an average speed of 7.75 feet per second during the second two laps of a race. Find her total time in terms of d, the distance around the racecourse.

Elaborate

8. Why do rational expressions have excluded values?

9. How can you tell if your answer is written in simplest form?

10. **Essential Question Check-In** Why do sums or differences of rational expressions combine their excluded terms?

⭐ Evaluate: Homework and Practice

- Online Homework
- Hints and Help
- Extra Practice

Given a rational expression, identify the excluded values by finding the zeroes of the denominator.

1. $\dfrac{x-1}{x^2+3x-4}$

2. $\dfrac{4}{x(x+17)}$

Write the given expression as an equivalent rational expression that has the given denominator.

3. Expression: $\dfrac{x-7}{x+8}$

   Denominator: x^3+8x^2

4. Expression: $\dfrac{3x^3}{3x-6}$

   Denominator: $(2-x)(x^2+9)$

Simplify the given expression.

5. $\dfrac{(-4-4x)}{(x^2-x-2)}$

6. $\dfrac{-x-8}{x^2+9x+8}$

7. $\dfrac{6x^2+5x+1}{3x^2+4x+1}$

8. $\dfrac{x^4-1}{x^2+1}$

Add or subtract the given expressions, simplifying each result and noting the combined excluded values.

9. $\dfrac{1}{1+x} + \dfrac{1-x}{x}$

10. $\dfrac{x+4}{x^2-4} + \dfrac{-2x-2}{x^2-4}$

11. $\dfrac{1}{2+x} - \dfrac{2-x}{x}$

12. $\dfrac{4x^4+4}{x^2+1} - \dfrac{8}{x^2+1}$

13. $\dfrac{x^4-2}{x^2-2} + \dfrac{2}{-x^2+2}$

14. $\dfrac{1}{x^2+3x-4} - \dfrac{1}{x^2-3x+2}$

15. $\dfrac{3}{x^2-4} - \dfrac{x+5}{x+2}$

16. $\dfrac{-3}{9x^2-4} + \dfrac{1}{3x^2+2x}$

17. $\dfrac{x-2}{x+2} + \dfrac{1}{x^2-4} - \dfrac{x+2}{2-x}$

18. $\dfrac{x-3}{x+3} - \dfrac{1}{x-3} + \dfrac{x+2}{3-x}$

19. The owner of store A and store B wants to know the average cost of both stores. Store A has an average cost of $\dfrac{100+2q}{q}$, and store B has an average cost of $\dfrac{200+q}{2q}$, where both stores have the same output, q. Find an expression to represent the cost of both stores.

20. An auto race consists of 8 laps. A driver completes the first 3 laps at an average speed of 185 miles per hour and the remaining laps at an average speed of 200 miles per hour. Let d represent the length of one lap. Find the time in terms of d that it takes the driver to complete the race.

21. The junior and senior classes of a high school are cleaning up a beach. Each class has pledged to clean 1600 meters of shoreline. The junior class has 12 more students than the senior class. Let s represent the number of students in the senior class. Write and simplify an expression in terms of s that represents the difference between the number of meters of shoreline each senior must clean and the meters each junior must clean.

22. Architecture The Renaissance architect Andrea Palladio believed that the height of a room with vaulted ceilings should be the harmonic mean of the length and width. The harmonic mean of two positive numbers a and b is equal to $\dfrac{2}{\frac{1}{a} + \frac{1}{b}}$. Simplify this expression. What are the excluded values? What do they mean in this problem?

23. Match each expression with the correct excluded value(s).

a. $\dfrac{3x + 5}{x + 2}$ **A.** no excluded values

b. $\dfrac{1 + x}{x^2 - 1}$ **B.** $x \neq 0, -2$

c. $\dfrac{3x^4 - 12}{x^2 + 4}$ **C.** $x \neq 1, -1$

d. $\dfrac{3x + 6}{x^2(x + 2)}$ **D.** $x \neq -2$

H.O.T. Focus on Higher Order Thinking

24. Explain the Error George was asked to write the expression $2x - 3$ with excluded values placed one at a time at $x = 1$, $x = 2$, and $x = -3$. He wrote the following expressions:

a. $\dfrac{2x - 3}{x - 1}$

b. $\dfrac{2x - 3}{x - 2}$

c. $\dfrac{2x - 3}{x + 3}$

What error did George make? Write the correct expressions, then write an expression that has all three excluded values.

25. Communicate Mathematical Ideas Write a rational expression with excluded values at $x = 0$ and $x = 17$.

26. Critical Thinking Sketch the graph of the rational equation $y = \dfrac{x^2 + 3x + 2}{x + 1}$. Think about how to graphically show that a graph exists over a domain except at one point.

Lesson Performance Task

A kayaker spends an afternoon paddling on a river. She travels 3 miles upstream and 3 miles downstream in a total of 4 hours. In still water, the kayaker can travel at an average speed of 2 miles per hour. Based on this information, can you estimate the average speed of the river's current? Is your answer reasonable?

Next, assume the average speed of the kayaker is an unknown, k, and not necessarily 2 miles per hour. What is the range of possible average kayaker speeds under the rest of the constraints?

10.2 Multiplying and Dividing Rational Expressions

Essential Question: How can you multiply and divide rational expressions?

 TEKS **A2.7.F** Determine the … product, and quotient of rational expressions with integral exponents of degree one and of degree two.

Explore   Relating Multiplication Concepts

Use the facts you know about multiplying rational numbers to determine how to multiply rational expressions.

Ⓐ How do you multiply $\frac{4}{5} \cdot \frac{5}{6}$?

Multiply 4 by ▮ to find the ▮ of the product, and multiply 5 by ▮ to find the ▮.

Ⓑ $\frac{4}{5} \cdot \frac{5}{6} = \dfrac{▮}{▮}$

Ⓒ To simplify, factor the numerator and denominator.

$20 = ▮$

$30 = ▮$

Ⓓ Cancel common factors in the numerator and denominator to simplify the product.

$$\frac{4}{5} \cdot \frac{5}{6} = \frac{20}{30} = \frac{2\cdot2\cdot5}{2\cdot3\cdot5} = \dfrac{▮}{▮}$$

Ⓔ Based on the steps used for multiplying rational numbers, how can you multiply the rational expression $\frac{x+1}{x-1} \cdot \frac{3}{2(x+1)}$?

Reflect

1. **Discussion** Multiplying rational expressions is similar to multiplying rational numbers. Likewise, dividing rational expressions is similar to dividing rational numbers. How could you use the steps for dividing rational numbers to divide rational expressions?

Explain 1   Multiplying Rational Expressions

To multiply rational expressions, multiply the numerators to find the numerator of the product, and multiply the denominators to find the denominator. Then, simplify the product by cancelling common factors.

Note the excluded values of the product, which are any values of the variable for which the expression is undefined.

Example 1 Find the products and any excluded values.

Ⓐ $\dfrac{3x^2}{x^2-2x-8} \cdot \dfrac{2x^2-6x-20}{x^2-3x-10}$

$\dfrac{3x^2}{x^2-2x-8} \cdot \dfrac{2x^2-6x-20}{x^2-3x-10} = \dfrac{3x^2}{(x+2)(x-4)} \cdot \dfrac{2(x+2)(x-5)}{(x+2)(x-5)}$ 　Factor the numerators and denominators.

$= \dfrac{6x^2(x+2)(x-5)}{(x+2)(x-4)(x+2)(x-5)}$ 　Multiply the numerators and multiply the denominators.

$= \dfrac{6x^2\cancel{(x+2)}\cancel{(x-5)}}{\cancel{(x+2)}(x-4)(x+2)\cancel{(x-5)}}$ 　Cancel the common factors in the numerator and denominator.

$= \dfrac{6x^2}{(x+2)(x-4)}$

Determine what values of x make each expression undefined.

$\dfrac{3x^2}{x^2-2x-8}$: 　The denominator is 0 when $x = -2$ and $x = 4$.

$\dfrac{2x^2-6x-20}{x^2-3x-10}$: 　The denominator is 0 when $x = -2$ and $x = 5$.

Excluded values: $x = -2$, $x = 4$, and $x = 5$

Ⓑ $\dfrac{x^2-8x}{14(x^2+8x+15)} \cdot \dfrac{7x+35}{x+8}$

$\dfrac{x^2-8x}{14(x^2+8x+15)} \cdot \dfrac{7x+35}{x+8} = \dfrac{\boxed{x}\,(x-8)}{14\boxed{(x+3)}(x+5)} \cdot \dfrac{7\boxed{(x+5)}}{x+8}$ 　Factor the numerators and denominators.

$= \dfrac{7x(x-8)\boxed{(x+5)}}{14\boxed{(x+3)}(x+5)(x+8)}$ 　Multiply the numerators and multiply the denominators.

$= \dfrac{\boxed{x(x-8)}}{\boxed{2(x+3)(x+8)}}$ 　Cancel the common factors in the numerator and denominator.

Determine what values of x make each expression undefined.

$\dfrac{x^2-8x}{14(x^2+8x+15)}$: 　The denominator is 0 when $\boxed{x=-3 \text{ and } x=-5}$.

$\dfrac{7x+35}{x+8}$: 　The denominator is 0 when $\boxed{x=-8}$.

Excluded values: $\boxed{x=-3,\ x=-5,\text{ and } x=-8}$

Your Turn

Find the products and any excluded values.

2. $\dfrac{x^2-9}{x^2-5x-24} \cdot \dfrac{x-8}{2x^2-18x}$

3. $\dfrac{x}{x-9} \cdot \dfrac{3x-27}{x+1}$

🔑 Explain 2 Dividing Rational Expressions

To divide rational expressions, change the division problem to a multiplication problem by multiplying by the reciprocal. Then, follow the steps for multiplying rational expressions.

Example 2 Find the quotients and any excluded values.

Ⓐ $\dfrac{(x+7)^2}{x^2} \div \dfrac{x^2+9x+14}{x^2+x-2}$

$\dfrac{(x+7)^2}{x^2} \div \dfrac{x^2+9x+14}{x^2+x-2} = \dfrac{(x+7)^2}{x^2} \cdot \dfrac{x^2+x-2}{x^2+9x+14}$ Multiply by the reciprocal.

$= \dfrac{(x+7)(x+7)}{x^2} \cdot \dfrac{(x+2)(x-1)}{(x+7)(x+2)}$ Factor the numerators and denominators.

$= \dfrac{(x+7)(x+7)(x+2)(x-1)}{x^2(x+7)(x+2)}$ Multiply the numerators and multiply the denominators.

$= \dfrac{\cancel{(x+7)}(x+7)\cancel{(x+2)}(x-1)}{x^2\cancel{(x+7)}\cancel{(x+2)}}$ Cancel the common factors in the numerator and denominator.

$= \dfrac{x+7(x-1)}{x^2}$

Determine what values of x make each expression undefined.

$\dfrac{(x+7)^2}{x}$:   The denominator is 0 when $x=0$.

$\dfrac{x^2+9x+14}{x^2+x-2}$:   The denominator is 0 when $x=-2$ and $x=1$.

$\dfrac{x^2+x-2}{x^2+9x+14}$:   The denominator is 0 when $x=-7$ and $x=-2$.

Excluded values: $x=0$, $x=-7$, $x=1$, and $x=-2$

Ⓑ $\dfrac{6x}{3x-30} \div \dfrac{9x^2-27x-36}{x^2-10x}$

$\dfrac{6x}{3x-30} \div \dfrac{9x^2-27x-36}{x^2-10x} = \dfrac{6x}{3x-30} \cdot \dfrac{\boxed{x^2-10x}}{\boxed{9x^2-27x-36}}$ Multiply by the reciprocal.

$= \dfrac{6x}{3\boxed{x-10}} \cdot \dfrac{x\boxed{x-10}}{9(x+1)\boxed{x-4}}$ Factor the numerators and denominators.

$= \dfrac{6x^2\boxed{x-10}}{27\boxed{x-10}(x+1)\boxed{x-4}}$ Multiply the numerators and multiply the denominators.

$= \dfrac{\boxed{2x^2}}{\boxed{9(x+1)(x-4)}}$ Cancel the common factors in the numerator and denominator.

Determine what values of x make each expression undefined.

$\dfrac{6x}{3x - 30}$:   The denominator is 0 when $\boxed{x = 10}$.

$\dfrac{9x^2 - 27x - 36}{x^2 - 10x}$:   The denominator is 0 when $\boxed{x = 10 \text{ and } x = 0}$.

$\dfrac{x^2 - 10x}{9x^2 - 27x - 36}$:   The denominator is 0 when $\boxed{x = -1 \text{ and } x = 4}$.

Excluded values: $\boxed{x = 0,\ x = 10,\ x = -1, \text{ and } x = 4}$

Your Turn

Find the quotients and any excluded values.

4. $\dfrac{x + 11}{4x} \div \dfrac{2x + 6}{x^2 + 2x - 3}$

5. $\dfrac{20}{x^2 - 7x} \div \dfrac{5x^2 - 40x}{x^2 - 15x + 56}$

🔧 Explain 3   Activity: Investigating Closure

A set of numbers is said to be closed, or to have **closure**, under a given operation if the result of the operation on any two numbers in the set is also in the set.

(A)   Recall whether the set of whole numbers, the set of integers, and the set of rational numbers are closed under each of the four basic operations.

	Addition	**Subtraction**	**Multiplication**	**Division**
Whole Numbers	Closed	Not Closed	Closed	Not Closed
Integers	Closed	Closed	Closed	Not Closed
Rational Numbers	Closed	Closed	Closed	Closed

(B)   Look at the set of rational expressions. Use the rational expressions $\dfrac{p(x)}{q(x)}$ and $\dfrac{r(x)}{s(x)}$ where $p(x)$, $q(x)$, $r(x)$ and $s(x)$ are nonzero. Add the rational expressions.

$$\frac{p(x)}{q(x)} + \frac{r(x)}{s(x)} = \boxed{\frac{p(x)s(x) + q(x)r(x)}{q(x)s(x)}}$$

(C)   Is the set of rational expressions closed under addition? Explain.

Yes; since $q(x)$ and $s(x)$ are nonzero, $q(x)s(x)$ is nonzero. So, $\dfrac{p(x)s(x) + q(x)r(x)}{q(x)s(x)}$ is again a rational expression.

(D)   Subtract the rational expressions.

$$\frac{p(x)}{q(x)} - \frac{r(x)}{s(x)} = \boxed{\frac{p(x)s(x) - q(x)r(x)}{q(x)s(x)}}$$

(E)   Is the set of rational expressions closed under subtraction? Explain.

Yes; since $q(x)$ and $s(x)$ are nonzero, $q(x)s(x)$ is nonzero. So, $\dfrac{p(x)s(x) - q(x)r(x)}{q(x)s(x)}$ is again a rational expression.

Ⓕ Multiply the rational expressions.

$$\frac{p(x)}{q(x)} \cdot \frac{r(x)}{s(x)} = \boxed{\frac{p(x)r(x)}{q(x)s(x)}}$$

Ⓖ Is the set of rational expressions closed under multiplication? Explain.

Yes; since $q(x)$ and $s(x)$ are nonzero, $q(x)s(x)$ is nonzero. So, $\frac{p(x)r(x)}{q(x)s(x)}$ is again a rational expression.

Ⓗ Divide the rational expressions.

$$\frac{p(x)}{q(x)} \div \frac{r(x)}{s(x)} = \boxed{\frac{p(x)s(x)}{q(x)r(x)}}$$

Ⓘ Is the set of rational expressions closed under division? Explain.

Yes; since $q(x)$ and $r(x)$ are nonzero, $q(x)r(x)$ is nonzero. So, $\frac{p(x)s(x)}{q(x)r(x)}$ is again a rational expression.

Reflect

6. Are rational expressions most like whole numbers, integers, or rational numbers? Explain.

🔑 Explain 4 Multiplying and Dividing with Rational Models

Models involving rational expressions can be solved using the same steps to multiply or divide rational expressions.

Example 3 Solve the problems using rational expressions.

Ⓐ Leonard drives 40 miles to work every day. One-fifth of his drive is on city roads, where he averages 30 miles per hour. The other part of his drive is on a highway, where he averages 55 miles per hour. The expression $\frac{d_c r_h + d_h r_c}{r_c r_h}$ represents the total time spent driving, in hours. In the expression, d_c represents the distance traveled on city roads, d_h represents the distance traveled on the highway, r_c is the average speed on city roads, and r_h is the average speed on the highway. Use the expression to find the average speed of Leonard's drive.

The total distance traveled is 40 miles. Find an expression for the average speed, r, of Leonard's drive.

$r =$ Total distance traveled $\div$ Total time

$= 40 \div \dfrac{d_c r_h + d_h r_c}{r_c r_h}$

$= 40 \cdot \dfrac{r_c r_h}{d_c r_h + d_h r_c}$

$= \dfrac{40 r_c r_h}{d_c r_h + d_h r_c}$

Find the values of d_c and d_h.

$d_c = \frac{1}{5}(40) = 8$ miles

$d_h = 40 - 8 = 32$ miles

Solve for r by substituting in the given values from the problem.

$$r = \frac{d_c r_h}{d_c r_h + d_h r_c}$$

$$= \frac{40 \cdot 55 \cdot 30}{8 \cdot 55 + 32 \cdot 30}$$

$$\approx 47 \text{ miles per hour}$$

The average speed of Leonard's drive is about 47 miles per hour.

(B) The fuel efficiency of Tanika's car at highway speeds is 35 miles per gallon. The expression $\frac{48E - 216}{E(E - 6)}$ represents the total gas consumed, in gallons, when Tanika drives 36 miles on a highway and 12 miles in a town to get to her relative's house. In the expression, E represents the fuel efficiency, in miles per gallon, of Tanika's car at highway speeds. Use the expression to find the average rate of gas consumed on her trip.

The total distance traveled is $\boxed{48}$ miles. Find an expression for the average rate of gas consumed, g, on Tanika's trip.

$g = $ Total gas consumed $\div$ Total distance traveled

$$= \frac{48E - 216}{E(E - 6)} \div \boxed{48}$$

$$= \frac{48E - 216}{\boxed{48}\, E(E - 6)}$$

The value of E is $\boxed{35}$.

Solve for g by substituting in the value of E.

$$g = \frac{48\left(\boxed{35}\right) - 216}{48\left(\boxed{35}\right)\left(\boxed{35} - 6\right)}$$

$$= \frac{\boxed{1464}}{\boxed{48{,}720}}$$

$$\approx \boxed{0.03}$$

The average rate of gas consumed on Tanika's trip is about $\boxed{0.03}$ gallon per mile.

Your Turn

7. The distance traveled by a car undergoing constant acceleration, a, for a time, t, is given by $d = v_0 t + \frac{1}{2}at^2$ where v_0 is the initial velocity of the car. Two cars are side by side with the same initial velocity. One car accelerates and the other car does not. Write an expression for the ratio of the distance traveled by the accelerating car to the distance traveled by the nonaccelerating car as a function of time.

💬 Elaborate

8. Explain how finding excluded values when dividing one rational expression by another is different from multiplying two rational expressions.

9. **Essential Question Check-In** How is dividing rational expressions related to multiplying rational expressions?

★ Evaluate: Homework and Practice

1. Explain how to multiply the rational expressions.

$$\frac{x-3}{2} \cdot \frac{x^2 - 3x + 4}{x^2 - 2x}$$

Find the products and any excluded values.

2. $\dfrac{x}{3x-6} \cdot \dfrac{x-2}{x+9}$

3. $\dfrac{5x^2 + 25x}{2} \cdot \dfrac{4x}{x+5}$

4. $\dfrac{x^2 - 2x - 15}{10x + 30} \cdot \dfrac{3}{x^2 - 3x - 10}$

5. $\dfrac{x^2 - 1}{x^2 + 5x + 4} \cdot \dfrac{x^2}{x^2 - x}$

6. $\dfrac{x^2 + 14x + 33}{4x} \cdot \dfrac{x^2 - 3x}{x+3} \cdot \dfrac{8x - 56}{x^2 + 4x - 77}$

7. $\dfrac{9x^2}{x-6} \cdot \dfrac{x^2 - 36}{3x - 6} \cdot \dfrac{3}{4x^2 + 24x}$

Find the quotients and any excluded values.

8. $\dfrac{5x^2 + 10x}{x^2 + 2x + 1} \div \dfrac{20x + 40}{x^2 - 1}$

9. $\dfrac{x^2 - 9x + 18}{x^2 + 9x + 18} \div \dfrac{x^2 - 36}{x^2 - 9}$

10. $\dfrac{-x^2 + x + 20}{5x^2 - 25x} \div \dfrac{x+4}{2x - 14}$

11. $\dfrac{x+3}{x^2 + 8x + 15} \div \dfrac{x^2 - 25}{x-5}$

12. $\dfrac{x^2 - 10x + 9}{3x} \div \dfrac{x^2 - 7x - 18}{x^2 + 2x}$

13. $\dfrac{8x + 32}{x^2 + 8x + 16} \div \dfrac{x^2 - 6x}{x^2 - 2x - 24}$

Let $p(x) = \dfrac{1}{x+1}$ and $q(x) = \dfrac{1}{x-1}$. Find the result and determine whether the result of performing each operation is another rational expression.

14. $p(x) + q(x)$

15. $p(x) - q(x)$

16. $p(x) \cdot q(x)$

17. $p(x) \div q(x)$

18. The distance a race car travels is given by the equation $d = v_0 t + \frac{1}{2}at^2$ where v_0 is the initial speed of the race car, a is the acceleration, and t is the time travelled. Near the beginning of a race, the driver accelerates for 9 seconds at a rate of 4 m/s². The driver's initial speed was 75 m/s. Find the driver's average speed during the acceleration.

19. Julianna is designing a circular track that will consist of three concentric rings, each one set 6 meters apart. Find an expression for the ratio of the length of the outer ring to the length of the middle ring and another for the ratio of the length of the outer ring to length of the inner ring. If the radius of the inner ring is set at 90 meters, how many times longer is the outer ring than the middle ring and the inner ring?

20. Geometry Find a rational expression for the ratio of the surface area of a cylinder to the volume of a cylinder. Then find the ratio when the radius is 3 inches and the height is 10 inches.

H.O.T. Focus on Higher Order Thinking

21. Explain the Error Maria finds an equivalent expression to $\dfrac{x^2 - 4x - 45}{3x - 15} \div \dfrac{6x^2 - 150}{x^2 - 5x}$. Her work is shown. Find and correct Maria's mistake.

$$\dfrac{x^2 - 4x - 45}{3x - 15} \div \dfrac{6x^2 - 150}{x^2 - 5x} = \dfrac{(x - 9)(x + 5)}{3(x - 5)} \div \dfrac{6(x + 5)(x - 5)}{x(x - 5)}$$

$$= \dfrac{6(x - 9)(x + 5)(x + 5)(x - 5)}{3x(x - 5)(x - 5)}$$

$$= \dfrac{2(x - 9)(x - 5)^2}{x(x - 5)}$$

22. Critical Thinking Multiply the rational expression. What do you notice about the expression?

$$\left(\dfrac{3}{x - 4} + \dfrac{x^3 - 4x}{8x^2 - 32} \right) \left(\dfrac{3x + 18}{x^2 + 2x - 24} - \dfrac{x}{8} \right)$$

23. Multi-Step Jordan is making a garden with an area of $x^2 + 13x + 30$ square feet and a length of $x + 3$ feet.

a. Find an expression for the width of Jordan's garden.

b. If Karl makes a garden with an area of $3x^2 + 48x + 180$ square feet and a length of $x + 6$, how many times larger is the width of Jon's garden than Jordan's?

c. If x is equal to 4, what are the dimensions of both Jordan's and Karl's gardens?

Lesson Performance Task

Who has the advantage, taller or shorter runners? Almost all of the energy generated by a long-distance runner is released in the form of heat. For a runner with height H and speed V, the rate hg of heat generated and the rate h_r of heat released can be modeled by $h_g = k_1 H^3 V^2$ and $h_r = k_2 H^2$, k_1 and k_2 being constants. So, how does a runner's height affect the amount of heat she releases as she increases her speed?

10.3 Solving Rational Equations

Essential Question: What methods are there for solving rational equations?

 TEKS A2.6.I Solve rational equations that have real solutions. Also A2.6.H, A2.6.J

Explore   Solving Rational Equations Graphically

A rational equation is an equation that contains one or more rational expressions. The time t in hours it takes to travel d miles can be determined by using the equation $t = \frac{d}{r}$, where r is the average rate of speed. This equation is an example of a rational equation. One method to solving rational equations is by graphing.

Solve the rational equation $\frac{x}{x-3} = 2$ by graphing.

(A) First, identify any excluded values. A number is an excluded value of a rational expression if substituting the number into the expression results in a division by 0, which is undefined. Solve $x - 3 = 0$ for x.

$$x - 3 = 0$$

$$x = \boxed{}$$

(B) So, 3 is an excluded value of the rational equation. Rewrite the equation with 0 on one side.

$$\frac{x}{x-3} = 2$$

$$\boxed{} = 0$$

Subtract $\boxed{}$ from both sides.

(C) Graph the left side of the equation as a function. Substitute y for 0, then copy and complete the table below.

(D) Use the table to graph the function.

x	y	(x, y)
0		
1		
2		
4		
5		
9		

(E) Identify any x-intercepts of the graph.

There is an x-intercept at $\boxed{}$.

(F) Is the value of x an excluded value? What is the solution of $\frac{x}{x-3} = 2$?

1. **Discussion** Why does rewriting a rational equation with 0 on one side help with solving the equation?

⚙ Explain 1 Identifying the LCD of Two Rational Expressions

Given two or more rational expressions, the least common denominator (LCD) is found by factoring each denominator and finding the least common multiple (LCM) of the factors. This technique is useful for the addition and subtraction of expressions with unlike denominators.

Least Common Denominator (LCD) of Rational Expressions

To find the LCD of rational expressions:

1. Factor each denominator completely. Write any repeated factors as powers.

2. List the different factors. If the denominators have common factors, use the highest power of each common factor.

Example 2 **Find the LCD for each set of rational expressions.**

Ⓐ $\dfrac{-2}{3x - 15}$ and $\dfrac{6x}{4x + 28}$

Factor each denominator completely.

$3x - 15 = 3(x - 5)$

$4x + 28 = 4(x + 7)$

List the different factors.

$3, 4, x - 5, x + 7$

The LCD is $3 \cdot 4(x - 5)(x + 7)$,

or $12(x - 5)(x + 7)$.

Ⓑ $\dfrac{-14}{x^2 - 11x + 14}$ and $\dfrac{9}{x^2 - 6x + 9}$

Factor each denominator completely.

$x^2 - 11x + 24 = \boxed{(x - 3)(x - 8)}$

$x^2 - 6x + 9 = \boxed{(x - 3)(x - 3)}$

List the different factors.

$x - 3$ and $x - 8$

Taking the highest power of $(x - 3)$,

the LCD is $(x - 3)^2(x - 8)$.

2. **Discussion** When is the LCD of two rational expressions not equal to the product of their denominators?

Your Turn

Find the LCD for each set of rational expressions.

3. $\dfrac{x+6}{8x-24}$ and $\dfrac{14x}{10x-30}$

4. $\dfrac{12x}{15x+60} = \dfrac{5}{x^2+9x+20}$

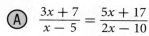 **Explain 2** Solving Rational Equations Algebraically

Rational equations can be solved algebraically by multiplying through by the LCD and solving the resulting polynomial equation. However, this eliminates the information about the excluded values of the original equation. Sometimes an excluded value of the original equation is a solution of the polynomial equation, and in this case the excluded value will be an **extraneous solution** of the polynomial equation. Extraneous solutions are not solutions of an equation.

Example 2   Solve each rational equation algebraically.

(A) $\dfrac{3x+7}{x-5} = \dfrac{5x+17}{2x-10}$

Identify any excluded values.	$x-5=0 \qquad 2x-10=0$
The excluded value is 5.	$x=5 \qquad\qquad x=5$
Identify the LCD.	$2x-10=2(x-5)$
The different factors are 2 and $x-5$.	$x-5=x-5$
The LCD is $2(x-5)$.	
Multiply each term by the LCD.	$\dfrac{3x+7}{x-5}\cdot 2(x-5) = \dfrac{5x+17}{2(x-5)}\cdot 2(x-5)$
Divide out common factors.	$\dfrac{3x+7}{\cancel{x-5}}\cdot 2\,\cancel{(x-5)} = \dfrac{5x+17}{\cancel{2}\,\cancel{(x-5)}}\cdot \cancel{2}\,\cancel{(x-5)}$
Simplify.	$(3x+7)2 = 5x+17$
Use the Distributive Property.	$6x+14 = 5x+17$
Solve for x.	$x+14 = 17$
	$x=3$

The solution $x=3$ is not an excluded value. So, $x=3$ is the solution of the equation.

© Houghton Mifflin Harcourt Publishing Company

Ⓑ $\dfrac{2x-9}{x-7} + \dfrac{x}{2} = \dfrac{5}{x-7}$

Identify any excluded values.

$x - 7 = 0$

$x = \boxed{7}$

The excluded value is 7.

Identify the LCD.

The different factors are 2 and $x - 7$.

The LCD is $2(x - 7)$.

Multiply each term by the LCD. $\dfrac{2x-9}{x-7} \cdot \boxed{2(x-7)} + \dfrac{x}{2} \cdot \boxed{2(x-7)} = \dfrac{5}{x-7} \cdot \boxed{2(x-7)}$

Divide out common factors. $\dfrac{2x-9}{\cancel{x-7}} \cdot \boxed{2\cancel{(x-7)}} + \dfrac{x}{\cancel{2}} \cdot \boxed{\cancel{2}(x-7)} = \dfrac{5}{\cancel{x-7}} \cdot \boxed{2\cancel{(x-7)}}$

Simplify. $\boxed{2}\,(2x-9) + x\left(\boxed{x-7}\right) = 5\left(\boxed{2}\right)$

Use the Distributive Property. $\boxed{4x - 18} + x^2 - 7x = \boxed{10}$

Write in standard form. $\boxed{x^2 - 3x - 28} = 0$

Factor. $\left(\boxed{x-7}\right)\left(\boxed{x+4}\right) = 0$

Use the Zero Product Property. $x - 7 = 0$ or $\boxed{x+4} = 0$

Solve for x. $x = 7$ or $x = \boxed{-4}$

The solution $x = \boxed{7}$ is extraneous because it is an excluded value. The only solution is $x = \boxed{-4}$.

Your Turn

Solve each rational equation algebraically.

5. $\dfrac{8}{x+3} = \dfrac{x+1}{x+6}$

Solving a Real-world Problem with a Rational Equation

Rational equations are used to model real-world situations. These equations can be solved algebraically.

Ⓐ Kelsey is kayaking on a river. She travels 5 miles upstream and 5 miles downstream in a total of 6 hours. In still water, Kelsey can travel at an average speed of 3 miles per hour. What is the average speed of the river's current?

🧩 Analyze Information

Identify the important information:

• The answer will be the average speed of the current.

• Kelsey spent 6 hours kayaking.

• She traveled 5 miles upstream and 5 miles downstream.

• Her average speed in still water is 3 miles per hour.

🧩 Formulate a Plan

Let c represent the speed of the current in miles per hour. When Kelsey is going upstream, her speed is equal to her speed in still water minus c. When Kelsey is going downstream, her speed is equal to her speed in still water plus c.

The variable c is restricted to positive real numbers.

Complete the table.

	Distance (mi)	Average speed (mi/h)	Time (h)
Upstream	5	$3 - c$	$\dfrac{5}{3 - c}$
Downsteam	5	$3 + c$	$\dfrac{5}{3 + c}$

Use the results from the table to write an equation.
total time = time upstream + time downstream

$$6 = \boxed{\dfrac{5}{3 - c}} + \boxed{\dfrac{5}{3 + c}}$$

© Houghton Mifflin Harcourt Publishing Company • Image Credit: ©Robert Michael/Corbis

Solve

$$3 - c = 0 \qquad 3 + c = 0$$

$$\boxed{3} = c \qquad c = \boxed{-3}$$

Excluded values: 3 and -3

LCD: $(3 - c)(3 + c)$

Multiply by the LCD.

$$6 \cdot \boxed{(3-c)(3+c)} = \frac{5}{3-c} \cdot \boxed{(3-c)(3+c)} + \frac{5}{3+c} \cdot \boxed{(3-c)(3+c)}$$

Divide out common factors.

$$6 \cdot \boxed{(3-c)(3+c)} = \frac{5}{3-c} \cdot \boxed{(3-c)(3+c)} + \frac{5}{3+c} \cdot \boxed{(3-c)(3+c)}$$

Simplify.

$$6 \cdot \boxed{(3-c)(3+c)} = 5 \cdot \boxed{3+c} + 5 \cdot \boxed{3-c}$$

Use the Distributive Property.

$$\boxed{54 - 6c^2} = 15 + 5c + \boxed{15 - 5c}$$

Write in standard form.

$$0 = \boxed{6\,c^2 - 24}$$

Factor.

$$0 = 6(c+2)\left(\boxed{c-2}\right)$$

Use the Zero Product Property.

$$c + 2 = 0 \text{ or } \boxed{c-2} = 0$$

Solve for c.

$$c = \boxed{-2} \text{ or } c = \boxed{2}$$

There are no extraneous solutions. The solutions are $c = -2$ or $c = 2$.

Justify and Evaluate

The solution $c = \boxed{-2}$ is unreasonable because the speed of the current cannot be negative, but the solution $c = \boxed{2}$ is reasonable because the speed of the current can be positive. If the speed of the current is 2 miles per hour, it would take Kelsey 5 hour(s) to go upstream and 1 hour(s) to go downstream, which is a total of 6 hours.

Reflect

6. Why does the domain of the variable have to be restricted in real-world problems that can be modeled with a rational equation?

7. Kevin can clean a large aquarium tank in about 7 hours. When Kevin and Lara work together, they can clean the tank in 4 hours. Write and solve a rational equation to determine how long, to the nearest tenth of an hour, it would take Lara to clean the tank if she works by herself. Explain whether the answer is reasonable.

💬 Elaborate

8. Why is it important to check solutions to rational equations?

9. Why can extraneous solutions to rational equations exist?

10. Essential Question Check In How can you solve a rational equation without graphing?

⭐ Evaluate: Homework and Practice

- Online Homework
- Hints and Help
- Extra Practice

Copy and complete the table. Then solve the rational equation by graphing.

1. $\dfrac{x}{x+4} = -3$

x	y	(x, y)
−8		
−6		
−5		
−3.5		
−2		
0		

2. $\dfrac{x}{2x-10} = 3$

x	y	(x, y)
0		
3		
4		
5.5		
7		
10		

Find the LCD for each set of rational expressions.

3. $\dfrac{x}{2x + 16}$ and $\dfrac{-4x}{3x - 27}$

4. $\dfrac{x^2 - 4}{5x - 30}$ and $\dfrac{5x + 13}{7x - 42}$

5. $\dfrac{4x + 12}{x^2 + 5x + 6}$ and $\dfrac{5x + 15}{10x + 20}$

6. $\dfrac{-11}{x^2 - 3x - 28}$ and $\dfrac{2}{x^2 - 2x - 24}$

7. $\dfrac{12}{3x^2 - 21x - 54}$ and $\dfrac{-1}{21x^2 - 84}$

8. $\dfrac{3x}{5x^2 - 40x - 60}$ and $\dfrac{17}{-7x^2 + 56x + 84}$

Solve each rational equation algebraically.

9. $\dfrac{9}{4x} - \dfrac{5}{6} = -\dfrac{13}{12x}$

10. $\dfrac{3}{x + 1} + \dfrac{2}{7} = 2$

11. $\dfrac{56}{x^2 - 2x - 15} - \dfrac{6}{x + 3} = \dfrac{7}{x - 5}$

12. $\dfrac{x^2 - 29}{x^2 - 10x + 21} = \dfrac{6}{x - 7} + \dfrac{5}{x - 3}$

13. $\dfrac{5}{2x + 6} - \dfrac{1}{6} = \dfrac{2}{x + 4}$

14. $\dfrac{5}{x^2 - 3x + 2} - \dfrac{1}{x - 2} = \dfrac{x + 6}{3x - 3}$

For 15 and 16, write a rational equation for each real-world application. Do not solve.

15. A save percentage in lacrosse is found by dividing the number of saves by the number of shots faced. A lacrosse goalie saved 9 of 12 shots. How many additional consecutive saves *s* must the goalie make to raise his save percentage to 0.850?

16. Jake can mulch a garden in 30 minutes. Together, Jake and Ross can mulch the same garden in 16 minutes. How much time *t*, in minutes, will it take Ross to mulch the garden when working alone?

17. Geometry A new ice skating rink will be approximately rectangular in shape and will have an area of 18,000 square feet. Using an equation for the perimeter *P*, of the skating rink in terms of its width *W*, what are the dimensions of the skating rink if the perimeter is 580 feet?

18. Water flowing through both a small pipe and a large pipe can fill a water tank in 9 hours. Water flowing through the large pipe alone can fill the tank in 17 hours. Write an equation that can be used to find the amount of time *t*, in hours, it would take to fill the tank using only the small pipe.

19. A riverboat travels at an average of 14 km per hour in still water. The riverboat travels 110 km east up the Ohio River and 110 km west down the same river in a total of 17.5 hours. To the nearest tenth of a kilometer per hour, what was the speed of the current of the river?

20. A baseball player's batting average is equal to the number of hits divided by the number of at bats. A professional player had 139 hits in 515 at bats in 2012 and 167 hits in 584 at bats in 2013. Write and solve an equation to find how many additional consecutive hits h the batter would have needed to raise his batting average in 2012 to be at least equal to his average in 2013.

21. The time required to deliver and install a computer network at a customer's location is $t = 5 + \frac{2d}{r}$, where t is time in hours, d is in the distance (in miles), from the warehouse to the customer's location, and r is the average speed of the delivery truck. If it takes 8.2 hours for an employee to deliver and install a network for a customer located 80 miles from the warehouse, what is the average speed of the delivery truck?

22. Art A glassblower can produce several sets of simple glasses in about 3 hours. When the glassblower works with an apprentice, the job takes about 2 hours. How long would it take the apprentice to make the same number of sets of glasses when working alone?

23. Which of the following equations have at least two excluded values? Identify all that apply.

A. $\dfrac{3}{x} + \dfrac{1}{5x} = 1$

B. $\dfrac{x-4}{x-2} + \dfrac{3}{x} = \dfrac{5}{6}$

C. $\dfrac{x}{x-6} + 1 = \dfrac{5}{2x-12}$

D. $\dfrac{2x-3}{x^2 - 10x + 25} + \dfrac{3}{7} = \dfrac{1}{x-5}$

E. $\dfrac{7}{x+2} + \dfrac{3x-4}{x^2 + 5x + 6} = 9$

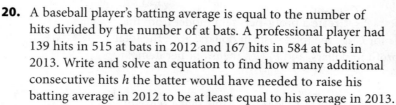

H.O.T. Focus on Higher Order Thinking

24. Critical Thinking An equation has the form $\frac{a}{x} + \frac{x}{b} = c$, where a, b, and c are constants and $b \neq 0$. How many solutions could this equation have? Explain.

25. Multiple Representations Write an equation whose graph is a straight line, but with an open circle at $x = 4$.

26. Justify Reasoning Explain why the excluded values do not change when multiplying by the LCD to add or subtract rational expressions.

27. Critical Thinking Describe how you would find the inverse of the rational function
$f(x) = \dfrac{x-1}{x-2}, x \neq 2$. Then find the inverse.

Lesson Performance Task

Kasey creates comedy sketch videos and posts them on a popular video website and is selling an exclusive series of sketches on DVD. The total cost to make the series of sketches is $989. The materials cost $1.40 per DVD and the shipping costs $2.00 per DVD. Kasey plans to sell the DVDs for $12 each.

a. Let d be the number of DVDs Kasey sells. Create a profit-per-item model from the given information by writing a rule for $C(d)$, the total costs in dollars, $S(d)$, the total sales income in dollars, $P(d)$, the profit in dollars, and $P_{PI}(d)$, the profit per item sold in dollars.

b. What is the profit per DVD if Kasey sells 80 DVDs? Does this value make sense in the context of the problem?

c. Then use the function $P_{PI}(d)$ from part a to find how many DVDs Kasey would have to sell to break even. Identify all excluded values.

Rational Expressions and Equations

Essential Question: How can you use rational expressions and equations to solve real-world problems?

Key Vocabulary

closure *(cerradura)*

extraneous solution
  (solución extraña)

rational expression
  (expresión racional)

reciprocal *(recíproco)*

KEY EXAMPLE   *(Lesson 10.1)*

Add the expression $\frac{1}{3+x} + \frac{3-x}{x}$, simplify the result, and note the excluded values.

$$\frac{1}{3+x} + \frac{3-x}{x} = \frac{1x}{(3+x)x} + \frac{(3-x)(3+x)}{x(3+x)}$$ Write with like denominators.

$$= \frac{x+(9-x^2)}{x(x+3)}$$ Add.

$$= \frac{-x^2+x+9}{x(x+3)}, x \neq -3, 0$$ Simplify.

KEY EXAMPLE   *(Lesson 10.2)*

Find the quotient of $\frac{x+3}{x+2} \div \frac{x^2-9}{2x-4}$ and note any excluded values.

$$\frac{x+3}{x+2} \div \frac{x^2-9}{2x-4} = \frac{x+3}{x+2} \cdot \frac{2x-4}{x^2-9}$$ Multiply by the reciprocal.

$$= \frac{x+3}{x+2} \cdot \frac{2(x-2)}{(x+3)(x-3)}$$ Factor the numerators and denominators.

$$= \frac{2\cancel{(x+3)}(x-2)}{(x+2)\cancel{(x+3)}(x-3)}$$ Multiply and cancel the common factors.

$$= \frac{2(x-2)}{(x+2)(x-3)} ; x \neq \pm2, \pm3$$

KEY EXAMPLE   *(Lesson 10.3)*

Solve the rational equation algebraically.

$$\frac{x}{x-3} + \frac{x}{2} = \frac{6x}{2x-6}$$

$$2\cancel{(x-3)}\frac{x}{\cancel{x-3}} + 2(x-3)\frac{x}{\cancel{2}} = 2\cancel{(x-3)}\frac{6x}{\cancel{2x-6}}$$ Multiply each term by the LCD and divide out common factors.

$$2x + x(x-3) = 6x$$ Simplify.

$$x^2 - 7x = 0$$ Write in standard form.

$$x(x-7) = 0$$ Factor.

$$x = 0 \text{ or } x = 7$$ Solve for x.

Add or subtract the given expressions, simplify the result, and note the excluded values. *(Lesson 10.1)*

1. $\dfrac{6x + 6}{x^2 - 9} + \dfrac{-3x - 3}{x^2 - 9}$

2. $\dfrac{4}{x^2 - 1} - \dfrac{x + 2}{x - 1}$

Multiply or divide the given expressions, simplify the result, and note the excluded values. *(Lesson 10.2)*

3. $\dfrac{x^2 - 4x - 5}{3x - 15} \cdot \dfrac{4}{x^2 - 2x - 3}$

4. $\dfrac{x + 2}{x - 4} \div \dfrac{x}{3x - 12}$

Solve each rational equation algebraically. *(Lesson 10.3)*

5. $x - \dfrac{10}{x} = 3$

6. $\dfrac{5}{x + 1} = \dfrac{2}{x + 4}$

MODULE PERFORMANCE TASK

Robots and Resistors

An engineer is designing part of a circuit that will control a robot. The circuit must have a certain total resistance to function properly. The engineer plans to use several resistors in *parallel*, which means each resistor is on its own branch of the circuit. The resistors available for this project are 20, 50, 80, and 200-ohm.

How can the engineer design a parallel circuit with a total resistance of 10 ohms using a maximum of 5 resistors, at least two of which must be different values? Find at least two possible circuit configurations that meet these criteria.

For another part of the circuit, the engineer wants to use resistors in parallel to create a total resistance of 6 ohms. Can she do it using the available resistor values? If so, how? If not, explain why not.

Begin by listing all of the information you will need to solve the problem. Be sure to write down all your data and assumptions. Then use graphs, numbers, words, or algebra to explain how you reached your conclusion.

(Ready) to Go On?

10.1–10.3 Rational Expressions and Equations

- Online Homework
- Hints and Help
- Extra Practice

Perform the indicated operations, simplify the result and note any excluded values.
(Lessons 10.1, 10.2)

1. $\dfrac{4}{x+5} + \dfrac{2x}{x^2-25}$

2. $\dfrac{3x+2}{x-2} - \dfrac{x+5}{x-2}$

3. $\dfrac{x+3}{x+2} \cdot \dfrac{2x-4}{x^2-9}$

4. $\dfrac{x-3}{x-4} \div \dfrac{x-2}{x^2-16}$

Solve each rational equation. *(Lesson 10.3)*

5. $\dfrac{3}{x+2} + \dfrac{3}{2x+4} = \dfrac{x}{2x+4}$

6. $\dfrac{x}{x-8} = \dfrac{24-2x}{x-8}$

7. $\dfrac{8x}{x^2-4} - \dfrac{4}{x+2} = \dfrac{8}{x^2-4}$

8. $\dfrac{3x}{x+1} + \dfrac{6}{2x} = \dfrac{7}{x}$

ESSENTIAL QUESTION

9. How do you add or subtract rational expressions and identify any excluded values?

Assessment Readiness

1. A hiker averages 0.6 mile per hour walking up a mountain trail and 1.3 miles per hour walking down the trail. Find the total time in terms of d. Use the formula $t = \dfrac{d}{r}$.

   A. $\dfrac{13}{60}d$

   B. $\dfrac{7}{10}d$

   C. $\dfrac{19}{20}d$

   D. $\dfrac{95}{39}d$

2. If each of the following expressions is defined, which is equivalent to $x - 3$?

   A. $\dfrac{(x-3)(x+5)}{x+3} \cdot \dfrac{x+3}{x+5}$

   B. $\dfrac{(x+3)(x+5)}{x-5} \div \dfrac{x+5}{x-5}$

   C. $\dfrac{x+3}{x+5} + \dfrac{x-3}{x+5}$

   D. $\dfrac{5x-5}{x-5} - \dfrac{x-3}{x-5}$

3. Which equation does **not** have real roots?

   A. $x^2 - 12 = 0$

   B. $x^2 + 25 = 0$

   C. $x^2 - 4x = -3$

   D. $-8x^2 + 20 = 0$

4. What are the x-intercepts of the graph of $y = x^4 - 256$?

   A. -256

   B. $16, -16$

   C. $4, -4$

   D. $16, 4, -4, -16$

5. A restaurant has two pastry ovens. When both ovens are used, it takes about 3 hours to bake the bread needed for one day. When only the large oven is used, it takes about 4 hours to bake the bread for one day. About how long would it take to bake the bread for one day if only the small oven were used? Explain how you got your answer.

Assessment Readiness

Personal Math Trainer
• Online Homework
• Hints and Help
• Extra Practice

1. What are the asymptotes of $y = \frac{3x^3}{x-5}$? Select the correct answer.

   A. $x = 0, x = 5$

   B. $x = 5$

   C. $x = -5$

   D. $y = 3$

2. How is the graph of $g(x) = 1 + \frac{1}{x+5}$ related to the graph of $f(x) = \frac{1}{x}$? Select the correct statement.

   A. g is f translated 1 unit up and 5 units left

   B. g is f translated 1 unit up and 5 units right

   C. g is f translated 1 unit down and 5 units left

   D. g is f translated 1 unit down and 5 units right

3. Which equation has the solutions $x = -6, 4$? Select the correct answer.

   A. $x + 2 = \frac{24}{x+6}$

   B. $\frac{x+2}{x} = 24$

   C. $x - 4 = \frac{24}{x}$

   D. $x + 2 = \frac{24}{x}$

4. Which of the following expressions has the excluded values $x \neq 0, 2$? Select the correct answer.

   A. $\frac{1}{x+2} + \frac{4+x}{x}$

   B. $\frac{1}{x-2} + \frac{4+x}{x}$

   C. $\frac{1}{x^2-2} + \frac{4+x}{x^2+2}$

   D. $\frac{x}{x+4} + \frac{x-2}{2}$

5. Which of the following operations simplifies to $\frac{(x+1)(x+3)}{(x+4)}$? Select the correct answer.

   A. $\frac{x+1}{x-3} \div \frac{4}{x^2+9}$

   B. $\frac{x+1}{x+4} \div \frac{x+4}{x+1}$

   C. $\frac{x+1}{x-3} \div \frac{x+4}{x^2-9}$

   D. $\frac{x+4}{x^2-9} \div \frac{x+1}{x-3}$

6. The time t it takes Sam to drive to his grandmother's house is inversely proportional to the speed v at which he drives. Write an equation for the one-way travel time. If it takes Sam 5 hours driving 50 miles per hour, how long would it take him if he drove at 65 miles per hour? *(Lesson 9.3)*

7. A town has two trucks to collect garbage. When both trucks are in use, they take 6 hours to collect all the garbage. When only the small truck is in use, it takes 24 hours to collect the garbage. How long would it take to collect the garbage if only the large truck is in service? *(Lesson 10.3)*

Performance Tasks

★ 8. For a car moving with initial speed v_0 and acceleration a, the distance d that the car travels in time t is given by $d = v_0 t + \frac{1}{2}at^2$.

   A. Write a rational expression in terms of t for the average speed of the car during a period of acceleration. Simplify the expression.

   B. During a race, a driver accelerates for 3 s at a rate of 10 ft/s² in order to pass another car. The driver's initial speed was 264 ft/s. What was the driver's average speed during the acceleration?.

★★ 9. The average speed for the winner of the 2002 Indy 500 was 25 mi/h greater than the average speed for the 2001 winner. In addition, the 2002 winner completed the 500 mi race 32 min faster than the 2001 winner.

   A. Let s represent the average speed of the 2001 winner in miles per hour. Write expressions in terms of s for the time in hours that it took the 2001 and 2002 winners to complete the race.

   B. Write a rational equation that can be used to determine s. Solve your equation to find the average speed of the 2001 winner to the nearest mile per hour.

★★★**10. Architecture** The Renaissance architect Andrea Palladio preferred that the length and width of rectangular rooms be limited to certain ratios. These ratios are listed in the table. Palladio also believed that the height of a room with vaulted ceilings should be the harmonic mean of the length.

Rooms with a Width of 30ft		
Length-to-Width Ratio	Length (ft)	Height (ft)
2:1		
3:2		
4:3		
5:3		
$\sqrt{2}$:1		

A. The harmonic mean of two positive numbers a and b is equal to $\dfrac{2}{\frac{1}{a} + \frac{1}{b}}$. Simplify this expression.

B. Copy and complete the table for a rectangular room with a width of 30 feet that meets Palladio's requirements for its length and height. If necessary, round to the nearest tenth.

C. A Palladian room has a length-to-width ratio of 4:3. If the length of this room is doubled, what effect should this change have on the room's width and height, according to Palladio's principles?

Chemist A chemist mixes 5 mL of an acid with 15 mL of water. The concentration of acid in the acid-and-water mix is $\frac{5}{5+15} = \frac{5}{20} = 25\%$. If the chemist adds more acid to the mix, then the concentration C becomes a function of the additional amount a of acid added to the mix.

a. Write a rule for the function $C(a)$.

b. What is a reasonable domain for this function? Explain.

c. What concentration of acid does pure water have? What concentration of acid does pure acid have? So, what are the possible values of $C(a)$?

d. Graph the function. Be sure to label the axes with the quantities they represent and indicate the axis scales by showing numbers for some grid lines.

e. Analyze the function's rule to determine the vertical asymptote of the function's graph. Why is the asymptote irrelevant in this situation?

f. Analyze the function's rule to determine the horizontal asymptote of the function's graph. What is the relevance of the asymptote in this situation?

Radical Functions, Expressions, and Equations

MATH IN CAREERS

Nutritionist Nutritionists provide services to individuals and institutions, such as schools and hospitals. Nutritionists must be able to calculate the amounts of different substances in a person's diet, including calories, fat, vitamins, and minerals. They must also calculate measures of fitness, such as body mass index. Nutritionists must use statistics when reviewing nutritional studies in scientific journals.

If you are interested in a career as a nutritionist, you should study these mathematical subjects:

- Algebra
- Statistics
- Business Math

Research other careers that require proficiency in understanding statistics in scientific articles. Check out the career activity at the end of the unit to find out how **Nutritionists** use math.

Reading Start-Up

© Houghton Mifflin Harcourt Publishing Company

Vocabulary

Review Words

✔ composition of functions
   (composición de funciones)
   extraneous solution
   (solución extraña)
✔ inverse function
   (función inversa)
✔ many-to-one function
   (función muchos a uno)
✔ one-to-one function
   (función uno a uno)
   radical expression
   (expresión radical)

Preview Words

   cube root function
   (función de raíz cúbica)
   index (índice)
   square root function
   (función de raíz cuadrada)

Visualize Vocabulary

Use the ✓ words. Copy and complete the graphic. Put just one word in each section of the square.

The function that results from exchanging the input and output values of a function.	A function where each element of the range may correspond to more than one element of the domain.
A function where each element of the range corresponds to only one element of the domain.	A series of two functions in which the output of one function is used as the input for the other.

Function Types

Understand Vocabulary

To become familiar with some of the vocabulary terms in the module, consider the following. You may refer to the module, the glossary, or a dictionary.

1. A function whose rule contains a variable under a square-root sign

   is a __?__.

2. A function whose rule contains a variable under a cube-root sign

   is a __?__.

3. In the radical expression $\sqrt[n]{x}$, n is the __?__.

Active Reading

Pyramid Fold Before beginning a module, create a pyramid fold to help you take notes from each lesson in the module. The three sides of the pyramid can summarize information about function families, their graphs, and their characteristics.

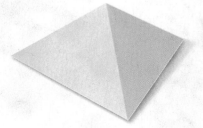

Radical Functions

Essential Question: How can you use radical functions to solve real-world problems?

REAL WORLD VIDEO
A rocket must generate enough thrust to achieve escape velocity from Earth's gravitational field. Check out some of the calculations and preparations that go into a successful launch.

MODULE PERFORMANCE TASK PREVIEW
We Have Liftoff!

If you throw a ball straight up, it will eventually come back down. But if you could throw it with enough initial velocity, it would escape Earth's surface and go into orbit. If you could throw it even faster, it might even escape the solar system. What is the escape velocity for Earth, the minimum velocity for an object to leave Earth's surface and not return? What about the velocity necessary to escape other planets? Let's take off and find out!

Are (YOU) Ready?

Complete these exercises to review skills you will need for this chapter.

Exponents

Example 1   Simplify .

$$x^2 \cdot x^3 - 2x^4 \cdot x = x^{2+3} - 2x^{4+1}$$
$$= x^5 - 2x^5$$
$$= -x^5$$

Simplify each expression.

1. $5x^3 \cdot 2x$

2. $-x^4 \cdot x^3$

3. $4x^2\left(2xy - x^2\right)$

Inverse Linear Functions

Example 2   Write the inverse function of $y = x + 9$. $x^2 \cdot x^3 - 2x^4 \cdot x$

$$y - 9 = x + 9 - 9$$ Subtract.

$$y - 9 = x$$ Simplify.

The inverse function of $y = x + 9$ is $x = y - 9$.

Example 3   Write the inverse function of $y = \frac{x}{-22}$.   Multiply.

$$(-22)y = -\frac{x}{22}(-22)$$ Simplify.

$$-22y = x$$

The inverse function of $y = \frac{x}{-22}$ is $x = -22y$.

Write the inverse of each function.

4. $y = x - 6$

5. $y = 7x$

6. $y = \frac{1}{2}x$

7. $y = x + 11$

8. $y = -18x$

9. $y = 21 + x$

11.1 Inverses of Simple Quadratic and Cubic Functions

Resource Locker

Essential Question: What functions are the inverses of quadratic functions and cubic functions, and how can you find them?

 TEKS **A2.2.B** Graph and write the inverse of a function using notation such as $f^{-1}(x)$.
Also A2.2.A, A2.2.C, A2.7.I

⊘ Explore   Finding the Inverse of a Many-to-One Function

The function $f(x)$ is defined by the following ordered pairs: $(-2, 4)$, $(-1, 2)$, $(0, 0)$, $(1, 2)$, and $(2, 4)$.

Ⓐ Find the inverse function of $f(x)$, $f^{-1}(x)$, by reversing the coordinates in the ordered pairs.

Ⓑ Is the inverse also a function? Explain.

Ⓒ If necessary, restrict the domain of $f(x)$ such that the inverse, $f^{-1}(x)$, is a function.

The domain of $f(x)$ should be restricted to $\left\{ x \mid x \geq \boxed{} \right\}$.

Ⓓ With the restricted domain of $f(x)$, what ordered pairs define the inverse function $f^{-1}(x)$?

Reflect

1. **Discussion** Look again at the ordered pairs that define $f(x)$. Without switching the order of the coordinates, how could you have known that the inverse of $f(x)$ would not be a function?

2. How will restricting the domain of $f(x)$ affect the range of its inverse?

⊘ Explain 1   Finding and Graphing the Inverse of a Simple Quadratic Function

The function $f(x) = x^2$ is a many-to-one function, so its domain must be restricted in order to find its inverse function. If the domain is restricted to $x \geq 0$, then the inverse function is $f^{-1}(x) = \sqrt{x}$; if the domain is restricted to $x \leq 0$, then the inverse function is $f^{-1}(x) = -\sqrt{x}$.

The inverse of a quadratic function is a **square root function**, which is a function whose rule involves $\sqrt{x}$. **The parent square root function** is $g(x) = \sqrt{x}$. A square root function is defined only for values of x that make the expression under the radical sign nonnegative.

Example 1 **Restrict the domain of each quadratic function and find its inverse. Confirm the inverse relationship using composition. Graph the function and its inverse.**

(A) $f(x) = 0.5x^2$

Restrict the domain. $\left\{x | x \geq 0\right\}$

Find the inverse.

Replace $f(x)$ with y.	$y = 0.5x^2$
Multiply both sides by 2.	$2y = x^2$
Use the definition of positive square root.	$\sqrt{2y} = x$
Switch x and y to write the inverse.	$\sqrt{2x} = y$
Replace y with $f^{-1}(x)$.	$f^{-1}(x) = \sqrt{2x}$

Confirm the inverse relationship using composition.

$$f^{-1}(f(x)) = f^{-1}(0.5x^2)$$
$$= \sqrt{2(0.5x^2)}$$
$$= \sqrt{x^2}$$
$$= x \text{ for } x \geq 0$$

Since $f^{-1}(f(x)) = x$ for $x \geq 0$, it has been confirmed that $f^{-1}(x) = \sqrt{2x}$ for $x \geq 0$ is the inverse function of $f(x) = 0.5x^2$ for $x \geq 0$.

Graph $f^{-1}(x)$ by graphing $f(x)$ and reflecting $f(x)$ over the line $y = x$.

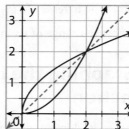

(B) $f(x) = x^2 - 7$

Find the inverse.

Replace $f(x)$ with y.	$\boxed{y} = x^2 - 7$
Add 7 to both sides.	$\boxed{y + 7} = x^2$
Use the definition of positive square root.	$\boxed{\sqrt{y + 7}} = x$
Switch x and y to write the inverse.	$\sqrt{y + 7} = y$
Replace y with $f^{-1}(x)$.	$\sqrt{y + 7} = f^{-1}(x)$
Restrict the domain.	$\left\{x | x \geq -7\right\}$

Confirm the inverse relationship using composition.

$$f^{-1}\big(f(x)\big) = f^{-1}\boxed{\left(x^2 - 7\right)}$$
$$= \boxed{\sqrt{(x^2 - 7) + 7}}$$
$$= \boxed{\sqrt{x^2}}$$
$$= \boxed{x \text{ for } x \geq 0}$$

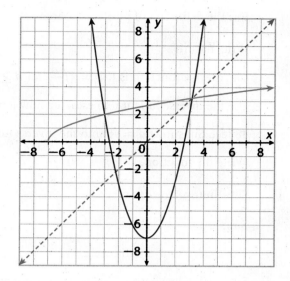

Since $f^{-1}\big(f(x)\big) = x$ for $x \geq 0$ it has been

confirmed that $f^{-1}(x) = \sqrt{x + 7}$ for $x \geq -7$

is the inverse function of $f(x) = x^2 - 7$ for $x \geq 0$.

Graph $f^{-1}(x)$ by graphing $f(x)$ and reflecting

$f(x)$ over the line $y = x$.

Your Turn

Restrict the domain of each quadratic function and find its inverse. Confirm the inverse relationship using composition. Graph the function and its inverse.

3. $f(x) = 3x^2$ 　　　　　　　　　　4. $f(x) = 5x^2$

🔧 Explain 2　Finding the Inverse of a Quadratic Model

In many instances, quadratic functions are used to model real-world applications. It is often useful to find and interpret the inverse of a quadratic model. Note that when working with real-world applications, it is more useful to use the notation $x(y)$ for the inverse of $y(x)$ instead of the notation $y^{-1}(x)$.

Example 2　**Find the inverse of each of the quadratic functions. Use the inverse to solve the application.**

(A)　The function $d(t) = 16t^2$ gives the distance d in feet that a dropped object falls in t seconds. Write the inverse function $t(d)$ to find the time t in seconds it takes for an object to fall a distance of d feet. Then estimate how long it will take a penny dropped into a well to fall 48 feet.

The original function $d(t) = 16t^2$ is a quadratic function with a domain restricted to $t \geq 0$.

Find the inverse function.

Write $d(t)$ as d. 　　　　　　　　　　$d = 16t^2$

Divide both sides by 16. 　　　　　　　　$\dfrac{d}{16} = t^2$

Use the definition of positive square root.

$$\sqrt{\frac{d}{16}} = t$$

Write t as $t(d)$.

$$\sqrt{\frac{d}{16}} = t(d)$$

The inverse function is $t(d) = \sqrt{\frac{d}{16}}$ for $d \geq 0$.

Use the inverse function to estimate how long it will take a penny dropped into a well to fall

48 feet. Substitute $d = 48$ into the inverse function.

Write the function.

$$t(d) = \sqrt{\frac{d}{16}}$$

Substitute 48 for d.

$$t(48) = \sqrt{\frac{48}{16}}$$

Simplify.

$$t(48) = \sqrt{3}$$

Use a calculator to estimate.

$$t(48) \approx 1.7$$

So, it will take about 1.7 seconds for a penny to fall 48 feet into the well.

(B) The function $E(v) = 4v^2$ gives the kinetic energy E in Joules of an 8-kg object that is travelling at a velocity of v meters per second. Write and graph the inverse function $v(E)$ to find the velocity v in meters per second required for an 8-kg object to have a kinetic energy of E Joules. Then estimate the velocity required for an 8-kg object to have a kinetic energy of 60 Joules.

The original function $E(v) = 4v^2$ is a quadratic function with a domain restricted

to $v \geq 0$. Find the inverse function.

Write $E(v)$ as E.

$$\boxed{E} = 4v^2$$

Divide both sides by 4.

$$\frac{E}{4} = v^2$$

Use the definition of positive square root.

$$\boxed{\sqrt{\frac{E}{4}}} = v$$

Write v as $v(E)$.

$$v(E) = \sqrt{\frac{E}{4}}$$

The inverse function is $v(E) = \sqrt{\frac{E}{4}}$ for $E \geq 0$.

Use the inverse function to estimate the velocity required for an 8-kg object to have a kinetic energy of 60 Joules.

Substitute $E = 60$ into the inverse function.

Write the function.

$$v(E) = \boxed{\sqrt{\frac{E}{4}}}$$

Substitute 60 for E.

$$v\left(\boxed{60}\right) = \boxed{\sqrt{\frac{60}{4}}}$$

Simplify.

$$v(60) = \sqrt{15}$$

$$v(60) \approx 3.9$$

So, an 8-kg object with kinetic energy of 60 Joules is traveling at a velocity of 3.9 meters per second.

Find the inverse of the quadratic function. Use the inverse to solve the application.

5. The function $A(r) = \pi r^2$ gives the area of a circular object with respect to its radius r. Write the inverse function $r(A)$ to find the radius r required for area of A. Then estimate the radius of an circular object that has an area of 40 cm².

⚙ Explain 3 Finding and Graphing the Inverse of a Simple Cubic Function

Note that the function $f(x) = x^3$ is a one-to-one function, so its domain does not need to be restricted in order to find its inverse function. The inverse of $f(x) = x^3$ is $f^{-1}(x) = \sqrt[3]{x}$.

The inverse of a cubic function is a **cube root function**, which is a function whose rule involves $\sqrt[3]{x}$. The **parent cube root function** is $g(x) = \sqrt[3]{x}$.

Example 3 Find the inverse of each cubic function. Confirm the inverse relationship using composition. Graph the function and its inverse.

Ⓐ $f(x) = 0.5x^3$

Find each inverse. Graph the function and its inverse.

Replace $f(x)$ with y. $y = 0.5x^3$

Multiply both sides by 2. $2y = x^3$

Use the definition of cube root. $\sqrt[3]{2y} = x$

Switch x and y to write the inverse. $\sqrt[3]{2x} = y$

Replace y with $f^{-1}(x)$. $\sqrt[3]{2x} = f^{-1}(x)$

Confirm the inverse relationship using composition.

$$f^{-1}\big(f(x)\big) = f^{-1}\big(0.5x^3\big)$$
$$= \sqrt[3]{2\big(0.5x^3\big)}$$
$$= \sqrt[3]{x^3}$$
$$= x$$

Since $f^{-1}\big(f(x)\big) = x$, it has been confirmed that $f^{-1}(x) = \sqrt[3]{2x}$ is the inverse function of $f(x) = 0.5x^3$.

Graph $f^{-1}(x)$ by graphing $f(x)$ and reflecting $f(x)$ over the line $y = x$.

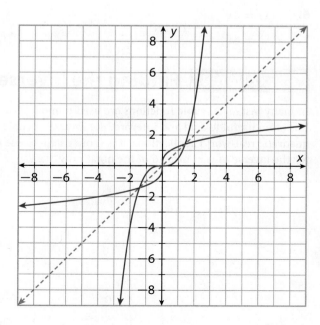

Ⓑ $f(x) = x^3 - 9$

Find the inverse.

Replace $f(x)$ with y. $\boxed{y} = x^3 - 9$

Add 9 to both sides. $\boxed{y + 9} = x^3$

Use the definition of cube root. $\boxed{\sqrt[3]{y + 9}} = x$

Switch x and y to write the inverse. $\sqrt[3]{x + 9} = y$

Replace y with $f^{-1}(x)$. $\sqrt[3]{x + 9} = f^{-1}(x)$

Confirm the inverse relationship using composition.

$f^{-1}\big(f(x)\big) = f^{-1}\Big(\boxed{x^3 - 9}\Big)$

$\phantom{f^{-1}\big(f(x)\big)} = \boxed{\sqrt[3]{(x^3 - 9) + 9}}$

$\phantom{f^{-1}\big(f(x)\big)} = \boxed{\sqrt[3]{x^3}}$

$\phantom{f^{-1}\big(f(x)\big)} = \boxed{x}$

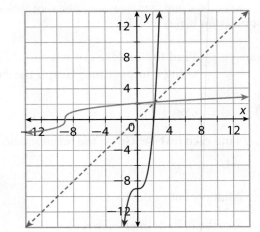

Since $f^{-1}\big(f(x)\big) = \boxed{x}$, it has been confirmed that

$f^{-1}(x) = \boxed{\sqrt[3]{x + 9}}$ is the inverse function of

$f(x) = x^3 - 9$.

Graph $f^{-1}(x)$ by graphing $f(x)$ and reflecting $f(x)$

over the line $y = x$.

Your Turn

Find each inverse. Graph the function and its inverse.

6. $f(x) = 2x^3$

7. $f(x) = 6x^3$

🖉 Explain 4 Finding the Inverse of a Cubic Model

In many instances, cubic functions are used to model real-world applications.
It is often useful to find and interpret the inverse of cubic models. As with
quadratic real-world applications, it is more useful to use the notation $x(y)$
for the inverse of $y(x)$ instead of the notation $y^{-1}(x)$.

Example 4 Find the inverse of each of the following cubic functions.

(A) The function $m(L) = 0.00001L^3$ gives the mass m in kilograms of a red snapper of length L centimeters. Find the inverse function $L(m)$ to find the length L in centimeters of a red snapper that has a mass of m kilograms.

The original function $m(L) = 0.00001L^3$ is a cubic function.

Find the inverse function.

Write $m(L)$ as m. $\qquad m = 0.00001L^3$

Multiply both sides by 100,000. $\qquad 100{,}000m = L^3$

Use the definition of cube root. $\quad \sqrt[3]{100{,}000m} = L$

Write L as $L(m)$. $\qquad \sqrt[3]{100{,}000m} = L(m)$

The inverse function is $L(m) = \sqrt[3]{100{,}000m}$.

(B) The function $A(r) = \dfrac{4}{3}\pi r^3$ gives the surface area A of a sphere with radius r. Find the inverse function $r(A)$ to find the radius r of a sphere with surface area A.

The original function $A(r) = \dfrac{4}{3}\pi r^3$ is a cubic function.

Find the inverse function.

Write $A(r)$ as A. $\qquad\qquad\qquad \boxed{A} = \dfrac{4}{3}\pi r^3$

Divide both sides by $\dfrac{4}{3}\pi$. $\qquad \boxed{\dfrac{3}{4\pi}A} = r^3$

Use the definition of cube root. $\qquad \boxed{\sqrt[3]{\dfrac{3}{4\pi}A}} = r$

Write r as $r(A)$. $\qquad\qquad\qquad \sqrt[3]{\dfrac{3}{4\pi}A} = r(A)$

The inverse function is $r(A) = \sqrt[3]{\dfrac{3}{4\pi}A}$.

Your Turn

8. The function $m(r) = \dfrac{44}{3}\pi r^3$ gives the mass in grams of a spherical lead ball with a radius of r centimeters. Find the inverse function $r(m)$ to find the radius r of a lead sphere with mass m.

⊙ Elaborate

9. What is the general form of the inverse function for the function $f(x) = ax^2$? State any restrictions on the domains.

10. What is the general form of the inverse function for the function $f(x) = ax^3$? State any restrictions on the domains.

11. **Essential Question Check-In** Why must the domain be restricted when finding the inverse of a quadratic function, but not when finding the inverse of a cubic function?

★ Evaluate: Homework and Practice

• Online Homework
• Hints and Help
• Extra Practice

Restrict the domain of the quadratic function and find its inverse. Confirm the inverse relationship using composition. Graph the function and its inverse.

1. $f(x) = 0.2x^2$

2. $f(x) = 8x^2$

3. $f(x) = x^2 + 10$

Restrict the domain of the quadratic function and find its inverse. Confirm the inverse relationship using composition.

4. $f(x) = 15x^2$

5. $f(x) = x^2 - \dfrac{3}{4}$

6. $f(x) = 0.7x^2$

7. The function $d(s) = \dfrac{1}{14.9}s^2$ models the average depth d in feet of the water over which a tsunami travels, where s is the speed in miles per hour. Write the inverse function $s(d)$ to find the speed required for a depth of d feet. Then estimate the speed of a tsunami over water with an average depth of 1500 feet.

8. The function $x(T) = 9.8\left(\dfrac{T}{2\pi}\right)^2$ gives the length x in meters for a pendulum to swing for a period of T seconds. Write the inverse function to find the period of a pendulum in seconds. The period of a pendulum is the time it takes the pendulum to complete one back-and-forth swing. Find the period of a pendulum with length of 5 meters.

Find the inverse of each cubic function. Confirm the inverse relationship using composition. Graph the function and its inverse.

9. $f(x) = 0.25x^3$

10. $f(x) = -12x^3$

Find the inverse of the cubic function. Confirm the inverse relationship using composition.

11. $f(x) = x^3 - \dfrac{5}{6}$

12. $f(x) = x^3 + 9$

13. The function $m(r) = 31r^3$ models the mass in grams of a spherical zinc ball as a function of the ball's radius in centimeters. Write the inverse model to represent the radius r in cm of a spherical zinc ball as a function of the ball's mass m in g.

14. The function $m(r) = 21r^3$ models the mass in grams of a spherical titanium ball as a function of the ball's radius in centimeters. Write the inverse model to represent the radius r in centimeters of a spherical titanium ball as a function of the ball's mass m in grams.

15. The weight w in pounds that a shelf can support can be modeled by $w(d) = 82.9d^3$ where d is the distance, in inches, between the supports for the shelf. Write the inverse model to represent the distance d in inches between the supports of a shelf as a function of the weight w in pounds that the shelf can support.

H.O.T. Focus on Higher Order Thinking

16. Explain the Error A student was asked to find the inverse of the function $f(x) = \left(\dfrac{x}{2}\right)^3 + 9$. What did the student do wrong? Find the correct inverse.

$$f(x) = \left(\dfrac{x}{2}\right)^3 + 9$$
$$y = \left(\dfrac{x}{2}\right)^3 + 9$$
$$y - 9 = \left(\dfrac{x}{2}\right)^3$$
$$2y - 18 = x^3$$
$$\sqrt[3]{2y - 18} = x$$
$$y = \sqrt[3]{2y - 18}$$
$$f^{-1}(x) = \sqrt[3]{2y - 18}$$

17. Make a Conjecture The function $f(x) = x^2$ must have its domain restricted to have its inverse be a function. The function $f(x) = x^3$ does not need to have its domain restricted to have its inverse be a function. Make a conjecture about which power functions need to have their domains restricted to have their inverses be functions and which do not.

18. Multi-Step A framing store uses the function $\left(\dfrac{c - 0.2}{0.5}\right)^2 = a$ to determine the total area of a piece of glass with respect to the cost before installation of the glass. Write the inverse function for the cost c in dollars of glass for a picture with an area of a in square inches. Then write a new function to represent the total cost C the store charges if it costs $6.00 for installation. Use the total cost function to estimate the cost if the area of the glass is 192 cm².

Lesson Performance Task

One method used to irrigate crops is the center-pivot irrigation system. In this method, sprinklers rotate in a circle to water crops. The challenge for the farmer is to determine where to place the pivot in order to water the desired number of acres. The farmer knows the area but needs to find the radius of the circle necessary to define that area. How can the farmer determine this from the formula for the area of a circle $A = \pi r^2$? Find the formula the farmer could use to determine the radius necessary to irrigate a given number of acres, A. (Hint: One acre is 43,560 square feet.) What would be the radius necessary for the sprinklers to irrigate an area of 133 acres?

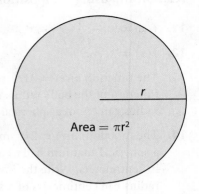

Area = πr^2

11.2 Graphing Square Root Functions

Essential Question: How can you use transformations of a parent square root function to graph functions of the form $g(x) = a\sqrt{(x-h)} + k$ or $g(x) = \sqrt{\frac{1}{b}(x-h)} + k$?

 TEKS **A2.4.C** Determine the effect on the graphs of $f(x) = \sqrt{x}$ when $f(x)$ is replaced by $af(x)$, $f(x) + d$, $f(bx)$, and $f(x - c)$ for specific positive and negative values of a, b, c, and d. Also A2.2.A, A2.7.I

⊘ Explore   Graphing and Analyzing the Parent Square Root Function

Although you have seen how to use imaginary numbers to evaluate square roots of negative numbers, graphing complex numbers and complex valued functions is beyond the scope of this course. For purposes of graphing functions based on the square roots (and in most cases where a square root function is used in a real-world example), the domain and range should both be limited to real numbers.

The square root function is the inverse of a quadratic function with a domain limited to positive real numbers. The quadratic function must be a one-to-one function in order to have an inverse, so the domain is limited to one side of the vertex. The square root function is also a one-to-one function as all inverse functions are.

(A)   The domain of the square root function (limited to real numbers) is given by $\left\{ x \mid x \geq \boxed{} \right\}$.

(B)   Copy and complete the table.

x	$f(x) = \sqrt{x}$
0	
1	
4	
9	

(C)   Plot the points on a coordinate grid, and connect them with a smooth curve.

(D)   Recall that the range of this function is the inverse of the parent quadratic $\left(f(x) = x^2 \right)$ with a domain limited to the nonnegative real numbers. Write the range of this square root function.

$\left\{ y \mid y \geq \boxed{} \right\}$

(E)   The graph appears to be getting flatter as x increases, indicating that the rate of change $\boxed{}$ as x increases.

(F)   Describe the end behavior of the square root function, $f(x) = \sqrt{x}$.

$f(x) \rightarrow \boxed{}$ as $x \rightarrow \boxed{}$

Reflect

1. **Discussion** Why does the end behavior of the square root function only need to be described at one end?

2. The solution to the equation $x^2 = 4$ is sometimes written as $x = \pm 2$. Explain why the inverse of $f(x) = x^2$ cannot similarly be written as $g(x) = \pm\sqrt{x}$ in order to use all reals as the domain of $f(x)$.

Explore 2 Predicting the Effects of Parameters on the Graphs of Square Root Functions

You have learned how to transform the graph of a function using reflections across the x- and y-axes, vertical and horizontal stretches and compressions, and translations. Here, you will apply those transformations to the graph of the square root function $f(x) = \sqrt{x}$.

When transforming the parent function $f(x) = \sqrt{x}$, you can get functions of the form

$g(x) = a\sqrt{(x - h)} + k$ or $g(x) = \sqrt{\frac{1}{b}(x - h)} + k$.

For each parameter, predict the effect on the graph of the parent function, and then confirm your prediction with a graphing calculator.

(A) Predict the effect of the parameter, h, on the graph of $g(x) = \sqrt{x - h}$ for each function.

  a. $g(x) = \sqrt{x - 2}$: The graph is a ⬛ of the graph of $f(x)$ ⬛ 2 units.

  b. $g(x) = \sqrt{x + 2}$: The graph is a ⬛ of the graph of $f(x)$ ⬛ 2 units.

  Check your answers using a graphing calculator.

(B) Predict the effect of the parameter k on the graph of $g(x) = \sqrt{x} + k$ for each function.

  a. $g(x) = \sqrt{x} + 2$: The graph is a ⬛ of the graph of $f(x)$ ⬛ 2 units.

  b. $g(x) = \sqrt{x} - 2$: The graph is a ⬛ of the graph of $f(x)$ ⬛ 2 units.

  Check your answers using a graphing calculator.

(C) Predict the effect of the parameter a on the graph of $g(x) = a\sqrt{x}$ for each function.

  a. $g(x) = 2\sqrt{x}$: The graph is a ⬛ stretch of the graph of $f(x)$ by a factor of ⬛ .

  b. $g(x) = \frac{1}{2}\sqrt{x}$: The graph is a ⬛ compression of the graph of $f(x)$ by a factor of ⬛ .

  c. $g(x) = -\frac{1}{2}\sqrt{x}$: The graph is a ⬛ compression of the graph of $f(x)$ by a factor of ⬛ as well as a ⬛ across the ⬛ .

  d. $g(x) = -2\sqrt{x}$: The graph is a ⬛ stretch of the graph of $f(x)$ by a factor of ⬛ as well as a ⬛ across the ⬛ .

  Check your answers using a graphing calculator.

D. Predict the effect of the parameter, b, on the graph of $g(x) = \sqrt{\frac{1}{b}x}$ for each function.

a. $g(x) = \sqrt{\frac{1}{2}x}$: The graph is a ▮▮▮▮ stretch of the graph of $f(x)$ by a factor of ▮▮▮▮ .

b. $g(x) = \sqrt{2x}$: The graph is a ▮▮▮▮ compression of the graph of $f(x)$ by a factor of ▮▮▮▮ .

c. $g(x) = \sqrt{-\frac{1}{2}x}$: The graph is a ▮▮▮▮ stretch of the graph of $f(x)$ by a factor of ▮▮▮▮ as well as a ▮▮▮▮ across the ▮▮▮▮ .

d. $g(x) = \sqrt{-2x}$: The graph is a ▮▮▮▮ compression of the graph of $f(x)$ by a factor of ▮▮▮▮ as well as a ▮▮▮▮ across the ▮▮▮▮ .

Check your answers using a graphing calculator.

Reflect

3. **Discussion** Describe what the effect of each of the transformation parameters is on the domain and range of the transformed function.

Explain 1 Graphing Square Root Functions

When graphing transformations of the square root function, it is useful to consider the effect of the transformation on two reference points, $(0, 0)$ and $(1, 1)$, that lie on the parent function, and where they map to on the transformed function, $g(x)$.

$f(x) = \sqrt{x}$		$g(x) = a\sqrt{x-h} + k$		$g(x) = \sqrt{\frac{1}{b}(x-h)} + k$	
x	y	x	y	x	y
0	0	h	k	h	k
1	1	$h+1$	$k+a$	$h+b$	$k+1$

The reference points can be found by recognizing that the initial point of the graph is translated from $(0, 0)$ to (h, k). From the initial point, find the next reference point by going up or down by $|a|$ or left or right by $|b|$, depending on the parameter used and its sign.

Transformations of the square root function also affect the domain and range. In order to work with real valued inputs and outputs, the domain of the square root function cannot include values of x that result in a negative-valued expression. Negative values of x can be in the domain, as long as they result in nonnegative values of the expression that is inside the square root. Similarly, the value of the square root function is positive by definition, but multiplying the square root function by a negative number, or adding a constant to it changes the range and can result in negative values of the transformed function.

Example 1 For each of the transformed square root functions, find the transformed reference points and use them to plot the transformed function on the same graph with the parent function. Describe the domain and range using set notation.

(A) $g(x) = 2\sqrt{x - 3} - 2$

To find the domain:

Square root input must be nonnegative.	$x - 3 \geq 0$
Solve the inequality for x.	$x \geq 3$

The domain is $\left\{ x \mid x \geq 3 \right\}$.

To find the range:

The square root function is nonnegative.	$\sqrt{x - 3} \geq 0$
Multiply by 2	$2\sqrt{x - 3} \geq 0$
Subtract 2.	$2\sqrt{x - 3} - 2 \geq -2$
Subraction in $g(x)$.	$g(x) \geq -2$

Since $g(x)$ is greater than or equal to -2 for all x in the domain,

the range is $\left\{ y \mid y \geq -2 \right\}$.

$(0, 0) \rightarrow (3, -2)$

$(1, 1) \rightarrow (4, 0)$

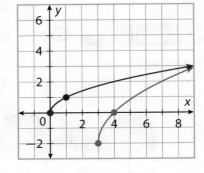

(B) $g(x) = \sqrt{-\frac{1}{2}(x - 2)} + 1$

To find the domain:

Square root input must be nonnegative.	$-\frac{1}{2}(x - 2) \geq \boxed{0}$
Multiply both sides by -2.	$x - 2 \boxed{\leq} 0$
Add 2 to both sides.	$\boxed{x} \leq 2$

Expressed in set notation, the domain is $\left\{ x \mid \boxed{x \leq 2} \right\}$.

To find the range:

The square root function is nonnegative.	$\sqrt{-\frac{1}{2}(x - 2)} \boxed{\geq} 0$
Add 1 both sides	$\sqrt{-\frac{1}{2}(x - 2)} + 1 \geq \boxed{1}$
Substistute in $\boxed{g(x)}$.	$g(x) \geq 1$

Since $g(x)$ is greater than 1 for all x in the domain,

the range (in set notation) is $\left\{ y \mid \boxed{y \geq 1} \right\}$.

$(0, 0) \rightarrow \boxed{(2, 1)}$

$(1, 1) \rightarrow \boxed{(0, 2)}$

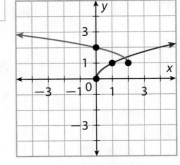

For each of the transformed square root functions, find the transformed reference points and use them to plot the transformed function on the same graph with the parent function. Describe the domain and range using set notation.

4. $g(x) = -3\sqrt{x-2} + 3$

5. $g(x) = \sqrt{\frac{1}{3}(x+2)} + 1$

⊘ Explain 2   Writing Square Root Functions

Given the graph of a square root function and the form of the transformed function, either $g(x) = a\sqrt{x-h} + k$ or $g(x) = \sqrt{\frac{1}{b}(x-h)} = k$, the transformation parameters can be determined from the transformed reference points. In either case, the initial point will be at (h, k) and readily apparent. The parameter a can be determined by how far up or down the second point (found at $x = h+1$) is from the initial point, or the parameter b can be determined by how far to the left or right the second point (found at $y = k+1$) is from the initial point.

Example 2   Write the function that matches the graph using the indicated transformation format.

Ⓐ $g(x) = \sqrt{\frac{1}{b}(x-h)} + k$

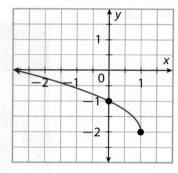

Initial point: $(h, k) = (1, -2)$

Second point:

$$(h + b, k + 1) = (0, -1)$$

$$1 + b = 0$$

$$b = -1$$

The function is $g(x) = \sqrt{-1(x-1)} - 2$.

Ⓑ $g(x) = a\sqrt{x-h} + k$

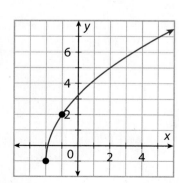

Initial point: $(h, k) = \left(\boxed{-2}, \boxed{-1} \right)$

Second point:

$$\left(h + 1, k + \boxed{a} \right) = \left(-1, \boxed{2} \right)$$

$$\boxed{-1} + a = 2$$

$$a = \boxed{3}$$

The function is $g(x) = \boxed{3} \sqrt{x \boxed{+} 2} - \boxed{1}$.

Write the function that matches the graph using the indicated transformation format.

6. $g(x) = \sqrt{\frac{1}{b}(x - h)} + k$

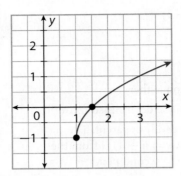

7. $g(x) = a\sqrt{(x - h)} + k$

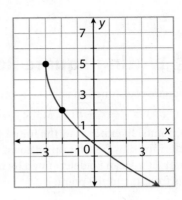

⚙ Explain 3   Modeling with Square Root Functions

Square root functions that model real-world situations can be used to investigate average rates of change.

Recall that the average rate of change of the function $f(x)$ over an interval from x_1 to x_2 is given by

$$\frac{f(x_2) - f(x_1)}{x_2 - x_1}.$$

Example 3   Use a calculator to evaluate the model at the indicated points, and connect the points with a curve to complete the graph of the model. Calculate the average rates of change over the first and last intervals and explain what the rate of change represents.

Ⓐ The approximate period T of a pendulum (the time it takes a pendulum to complete one swing) is given in seconds by the formula $T = 0.32\sqrt{\ell}$, where ℓ is the length of the pendulum in inches. Use lengths of 2, 4, 6, 8, and 10 inches.

First find the points for the given x-values.

Length (inches)	Period (seconds)
2	0.45
4	0.64
6	0.78
8	0.91
10	1.01

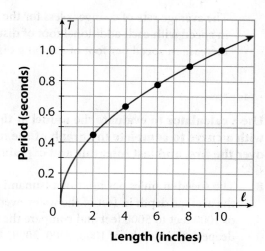

Plot the points and draw a smooth curve through them.

Find the average increase in period per inch increase in the pendulum length for the first interval and the last interval.

First interval:

$$\text{rate of change} = \frac{0.64 - 0.45}{4 - 2}$$
$$= 0.095$$

Last Interval:

$$\text{rate of change} = \frac{1.01 - 0.91}{10 - 8}$$
$$= 0.05$$

The average rate of change is less for the last interval. The average rate of change represents the increase in pendulum period with each additional inch of length. As the length of the pendulum increases, the increase in period time per inch of length becomes less.

(B) A car with good tires is on a dry road. The speed, in miles per hour, from which the car can stop in a given distance d, in feet, is given by $s(d) = \sqrt{96d}$. Use distances of 20, 40, 60, 80, and 100 feet.

First, find the points for the given x-values.

Distance	20	40	60	80	100
Speed	43.8	62.0	75.9	87.6	98.0

Plot the points and draw a smooth curve through them.

First interval:

$$\text{rate of change} = \frac{\boxed{62.0} - \boxed{43.8}}{40 - 20}$$
$$= \boxed{0.91}$$

Last Interval:

$$\text{rate of change} = \frac{\boxed{98.0} - \boxed{87.6}}{100 - 80}$$
$$= \boxed{0.52}$$

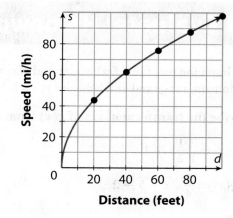

The average rate of change is less for the last interval. The average rate of change represents the increase in speed with each additional foot of distance. As the available stopping distance increases, the additional increase in speed per foot of stopping distance decreases.

Your Turn

Use a calculator to evaluate the model at the indicated points, and connect the points with a curve to complete the graph of the model. Calculate the average rates of change over the first and last intervals and explain what the rate of change represents.

8. The speed in miles per hour of a tsunami can be modeled by the function $s(d) = 3.86 \sqrt{d}$, where d is the average depth in feet of the water over which the tsunami travels. Graph this function from depths of 1000 feet to 5000 feet and compare the change in speed with depth from the shallowest interval to the deepest. Use depths of 1000, 2000, 3000, 4000, and 5000 feet for the x-values.

💬 Elaborate

9. What is the difference between the parameters inside the radical (b and h) and the parameters outside the radical (a and k)?

10. Which transformations change the square root function's end behavior?

11. Which transformations change the square root function's initial point location?

12. Which transformations change the square root function's domain?

13. Which transformations change the square root function's range?

14. **Essential Question Check-In** Describe in your own words the steps you would take to graph a function of the form $g(x) = a\sqrt{x - h} + k$ or $g(x) = \sqrt{\frac{1}{b}(x - h)} + k$ if you were given the values of h and k and using either a or b.

⭐ Evaluate: Homework and Practice

- Online Homework
- Hints and Help
- Extra Practice

1. Graph the functions $f(x) = \sqrt{x}$ and $g(x) = -\sqrt{x}$ on the same grid. Describe the domain, range and end behavior of each function. How are the functions related?

Describe the transformations of $g(x)$ from the parent function $f(x) = \sqrt{x}$.

2. $g(x) = \sqrt{\frac{1}{2}x} + 1$

3. $g(x) = -5\sqrt{x + 1} - 3$

4. $g(x) = \frac{1}{4}\sqrt{x - 5} - 2$

5. $g(x) = \sqrt{-7(x - 7)}$

Describe the domain and range of each function using set notation.

6. $g(x) = \sqrt{\frac{1}{3}(x-1)}$

7. $g(x) = 3\sqrt{x+4} + 3$

8. $g(x) = \sqrt{-5(x+1)} + 2$

9. $g(x) = -7\sqrt{x-3} - 5$

Plot the transformed function $g(x)$ on a coordinate grid with the parent function, $f(x) = \sqrt{x}$.

10. $g(x) = -\sqrt{x} + 3$

11. $g(x) = \sqrt{\frac{1}{3}(x+4)} - 1$

12. $g(x) = \sqrt{-\frac{2}{3}\left(x - \frac{1}{2}\right)} - 2$

13. $g(x) = 4\sqrt{x+3} - 4$

Write the function that matches the graph using the indicated transformation format.

14. $g(x) = \sqrt{\frac{1}{b}(x-h)} + k$

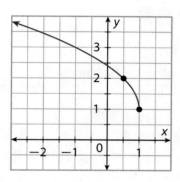

15. $g(x) = \sqrt{\frac{1}{b}(x-h)} + k$

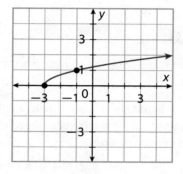

16. $g(x) = a\sqrt{x-h} + k$

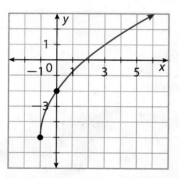

17. $g(x) = a\sqrt{x-h} + k$

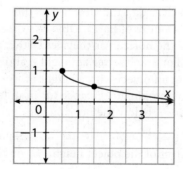

Use a calculator to evaluate the model at the indicated points, and connect the points with a curve to complete the graph of the model. Calculate the average rates of change over the first and last intervals and explain what the rate of change represents.

18. A farmer is trying to determine how much fencing to buy to make a square holding pen with a 6-foot gap for a gate. The length of fencing, f, in feet, required as a function of area, A, in square feet, is given by $f(A) = 4\sqrt{A} - 6$. Evaluate the function from 20 ft² to 100 ft² by calculating points every 20 ft².

19. The speed, s, in feet per second, of an object dropped from a height, h, in feet, is given by the formula $s(h) = \sqrt{64h}$. Evaluate the function for heights of 0 feet to 25 feet by calculating points every 5 feet.

20. Water is draining from a tank at an average speed, s, in feet per second, characterized by the function $s(d) = 8\sqrt{d-2}$, where d is the depth of the water in the tank in feet. Evaluate the function for depths of 2, 3, 4, and 5 feet.

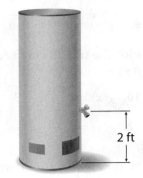

2 ft

21. A research team studies the effects from an oil spill to develop new methods in oil clean-up. In the spill they are studying, the damaged oil tanker spilled oil into the ocean, forming a roughly circular spill pattern. The spill expanded out from the tanker, increasing the area at a rate of 100 square meters per hour.

    The radius of the circle is given by the function $r = \sqrt{\dfrac{100}{\pi}t}$, where t is the time (in hours) after the spill begins. Evaluate the function at hours 0, 1, 2, 3, and 4.

22. Name the transformations of the parent function $f(x) = \sqrt{x}$ that result in the function $g(x) = \sqrt{-2(x-3)} + 2$.

H.O.T. Focus on Higher Order Thinking

23. **Draw Conclusions** Describe the transformations to $f(x) = \sqrt{x}$ that result in the function $g(x) = \sqrt{-8x + 16} + 3$.

24. **Analyze Relationships** Show how a horizontally stretched square root function can sometimes be replaced by a vertical compression by equating the two forms of the transformed square root function.

$$g(x) = a\sqrt{x} = \sqrt{\dfrac{1}{b}x}$$

    What must you assume about a and b for this replacement to result in the same function?

25. **Multi-Step** On a clear day, the view across the ocean is limited by the curvature of Earth. Objects appear to disappear below the horizon as they get farther from an observer. For an observer at height h above the water looking at an object with a height of H (both in feet), the approximate distance (d) in miles at which the object drops below the horizon is given by $d(h) = 1.21\sqrt{h + H}$.

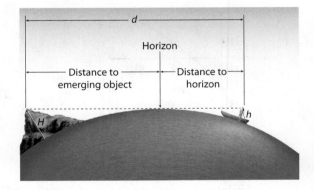

    a. What is the effect of the object height, H, on the graph of $d(h)$?

    b. What is the domain of the function $d(h)$? Explain your answer.

    c. Plot two functions of distance required to see an object over the horizon versus observer height: one for seeing a 2-foot-tall buoy and one for seeing a 20-foot-tall sailboat. Calculate points every 10 feet from 0 to 40 feet.

    d. Where is the greatest increase in viewing distance with observer height?

Lesson Performance Task

With all the coffee beans that come in for processing, a coffee manufacturer cannot sample all of them. Suppose one manufacturer uses the function $s(x) = \sqrt{x} + 1$ to determine how many beans that it must take from x containers in order to obtain a good representative sample. How does this function relate to the function $f(x) = \sqrt{x}$? Graph both functions. How many samples should be taken from a shipment of 45 containers of beans? Explain why this can only be a whole number answer.

11.3 Fitting Square Root Functions to Data

Essential Question: How can you find the equation of a square root function to model data?

 TEKS **A2.4.E** Formulate…square root equations using technology given a table of data.

⊘ Explore Investigating the Inverse Relationship between General Quadratic Functions and Radical Functions

Investigate the relationship between the quadratic function $f(x) = 4x^2 - 16x + 21$ and its inverse.

Ⓐ First, complete the square so that the function is in vertex form. Factor the first two terms so that the coefficient of x^2 is 1.

$$f(x) = 4x^2 - 16x + 21$$

$$f(x) = \boxed{}$$

Ⓑ Using the vertex form of $f(x) = 4x^2 - 16x + 21$, give the vertex of the function.

Ⓒ The graph of $f(x)$ is the graph of $y = x^2$ $\boxed{}$ stretched by a factor of 4, translated

to the right $\boxed{}$ unit(s), and translated $\boxed{}$ 5 units.

Ⓓ The inverse of $f(x)$ will be a square root function. Does $f(x)$ pass the horizontal line test?

Ⓔ Based on your answer to Step D, will the domain of $f(x)$ have to be restricted so that a positive square root function will be its inverse? If so, give the restricted domain.

Ⓕ Use the vertex of $f(x)$ to predict the initial point of its inverse $f^{-1}(x)$.

The initial point of $f^{-1}(x)$ is $\boxed{}$.

Ⓖ Find $f^{-1}(x)$ by only using the positive square root.

$$f(x) = 4(x - 2)^2 + 5$$

$$f^{-1}(x) = \boxed{}.$$

Ⓗ The inverse of $f(x) = 4(x - 2)^2 + 5$ is $f^{-1}(x) = \sqrt{\dfrac{x-5}{4}} + 2$. What is the initial point of $f^{-1}(x)$?

Ⓘ The graph of $f^{-1}(x)$ is the graph of $y = \sqrt{x}$ $\boxed{}$ stretched by a factor of 4,

translated to the $\boxed{}$ 5 units, and translated up $\boxed{}$ unit(s).

1. Find the range of $f(x)$ and the domain and range of $f^{-1}(x)$. How do the restricted domain and range of $f(x)$ compare to the domain and range of $f^{-1}(x)$?

⏺ Explain 1 Roughly Fitting a Square Root Function to Data

A square root function in the form $y = a\sqrt{x - h} + k$ can be fit to model a set of data that appear to follow a square root model by visually estimating the model's initial point, selecting one other point in the data, and solving for a.

Example 1 Look at the data in the plot, estimate the initial point, and draw a curve similar to a square root function that appears to go through the data points. Solve for the estimated square root function.

Ⓐ The data represents the number of bacteria in refrigerated food, where x is the number of bacteria and y is the temperature in degrees Celsius.

x	y
100	1
105	1.4
120	2
125	2.2
140	2.4
145	2.5
180	3

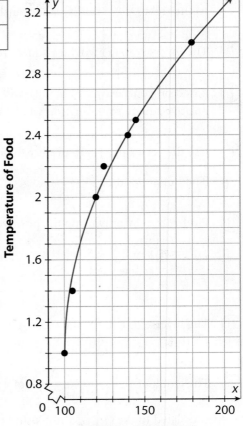

Determine the values of h and k by estimating the location of the vertex (initial point) of the square root function on the graph.

$\text{vertex} = (100, 1)$ 　　　　 $h = 100$ 　　　　 $k = 1$

Substitute $h = 100$ and $k = 1$ into $y = a\sqrt{x - h} + k$.

$$y = a\sqrt{x - 100} + 1$$

To find the value of a, substitute the coordinates of any other point into $y = a\sqrt{x - 100} + 1$ and solve for a. In this case, use $x = 120$ and $y = 2$.

$$2 = a\sqrt{120 - 100} + 1$$

$$1 = a\sqrt{20}, \text{ so } 0.224 \approx a$$

The vertex form of the function is $y = 0.224\sqrt{x - 100} + 1$.

(B) The data represents the radar-detected speed, s, in inches per second, of a dropped object at the end of a fall as a function of its starting height, v, in inches.

Starting Height (v) (inches)	Speed at Sensor (s) (inches/second)
30	56
35	101
45	129
70	193
90	226
125	273
150	313
200	354

Determine the values h and k by estimating the location of the vertex (initial point) of the square root function on the graph.

vertex $= (30, 56)$

$h = \boxed{30}$

$k = \boxed{56}$

$s(v) = a\sqrt{v - \boxed{30}} + \boxed{56}$

Find the value of a by using another point on the curve, substituting it in, and solving for a.

Reference Point $= \left(125, \boxed{273}\right)$

$\boxed{273} = a\sqrt{\boxed{125} - h} + k$

$273 - \boxed{56} = a\sqrt{125 - \boxed{30}}$

$a = \dfrac{\boxed{217}}{\sqrt{\boxed{95}}}$

$\approx \boxed{22.26}$

The vertex form of the function is

$s(v) = 22.6\sqrt{v - 30} + 56.$

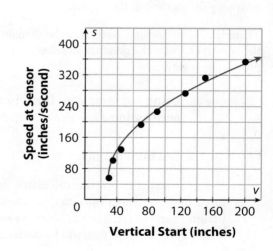

Reflect

2. **Discussion** How did you arrive at your estimate for the vertex? Can you think of another way to estimate the vertex? Discuss the merits or demerits of each approach.

Your Turn

Make a copy of the given graph, estimate the initial point, and draw a curve shaped similar to a square root function that appears to go through the data points. Solve for the estimated square root function.

3. Thomas opens a new boat dealership at the beginning of 2008 and sees his sales grow every year. The data represent the years and the number of boats sold each year.

Year	Sales
2008	37
2009	45
2010	50
2011	54
2012	54
2013	57
2014	57
2015	64

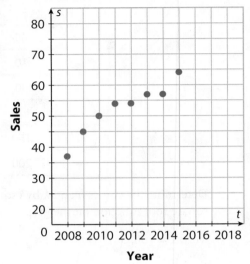

Explain 2 Fitting a Square Root Function to Data Using Technology

Graphing calculators can be used to fit a selection of function types to a data set, as you have seen in previous lessons involving linear and quadratic models. Regression to a square root model is not usually available on a graphing calculator but a quadratic regression is. The results of a quadratic regression can be solved to find an inverse function following the method in the Explore.

There are two options for restricting the domain of a quadratic function so that it is a one-to-one function, and the correct choice is the one that includes the given data set. The data determine if the square root function will be positive or negative.

Example 2 Using the same data from Example 1, find a square root model by performing a quadratic regression.

(A) Use the data from Example 1A.

Using the statistics on your calculator, enter the data, using List 1 for the temperature and List 2 for the number of bacteria. Entering the data this way will switch the variables x and y from Example 1A. The variables are switched as this will act as the inverse function of the square root function that will be derived from the quadratic regression.

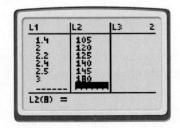

From the statistics calculations menu, select quadratic regression.

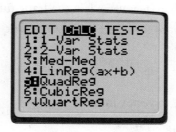

Push ENTER twice and you should see a result like this:

An approximate model is $y = 21x^2 - 44x + 124$.

Complete the square so that the function is in vertex form.

$$y = 21x^2 - 44x + 124$$

$$= 21(x^2 - 2.1x) + 124$$

$$= 21(x^2 - 2.1x + 1.10) - 23.2 + 124$$

$$= 21(x - 1.05)^2 + 101$$

The restricted domain of y that includes the data points is given by $x \geq 1.05$.

You can find the inverse by using the positive square root function written in vertex form.

$$y = \sqrt{\frac{1}{21}(x - 101)} + 1.05$$

$$= 0.218\sqrt{x - 101} + 1.05$$

Comparing this function to the function from Example 1A shows that they are very similar. Plotting this function and comparing its graph to the graph of the function in Example 1A, you can see that they are nearly indistinguishable.

(B) Use the data from Example 1B.

If the square root function is $s(v)$, then its inverse is a quadratic function, $\boxed{v(s)}$. To find the quadratic function in standard form, perform a quadratic regression on the data from Example 1B.

$$v(s) = \boxed{0.001657}\ s^2 - \boxed{0.1194}\ s + \boxed{31.48}$$

Complete the square to convert $v(s)$ to vertex form.

$$v(s) = 0.001657s^2 - 0.1194s + 31.48$$

$$= 0.001657\left(s^2 - \boxed{72.06}\ s\right) + 31.48$$

$$= 0.001657\left(s^2 - 72.06s + \boxed{1298.16}\right) - \boxed{2.15} + 31.48$$

$$= 0.001657\left(s^2 - 72.06s + \boxed{1298.16}\right) + \boxed{29.33}$$

$$= 0.001657\left(s - \boxed{36.03}\right)^2 + \boxed{29.33}$$

The restricted domain of $v(s)$ that includes the data is $s \boxed{\geq} 36.03$.

The inverse of $v(s)$ can be written in vertex form using a positive square root as:

$$s(v) = \sqrt{\dfrac{v - \boxed{29.33}}{\boxed{0.001657}}} + \boxed{36.03}$$

$$= \boxed{24.57}\ \sqrt{v - 29.33} + 36.03$$

Plot this function and your previous function from Example 1B on the same grid and compare them.

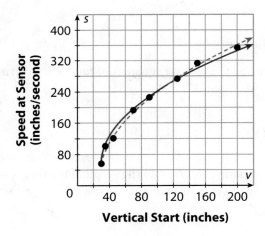

4. Use the data from Your Turn 3 and perform a quadratic regression to find a square root function using your graphing calculator. Plot this function and your previous function from Your Turn 3 on the same grid and compare them.

⚙ Explain 3   Solving a Real-World Problem

Models can be used to make predictions in the real world even at points along a curve that do not correspond to any existing data points.

Example 3   Read the problem description and solve using the four-step problem solving process.

Ⓐ Use the models from Example 1B and 2B to determine the answer to the problem.

You are conducting a physics experiment using a radar gun to check the speed of a steel ball dropped from varying heights as it passes by the sensor. The data collected is from the table in Example 1B.

You are tasked with testing the durability of a hard plastic shell on a new phone design and you need to test the material by checking for damage after repeated impacts at 360 inches per second to simulate the kind of accidental damage a typical user inflicts over the life of a phone. You decide that the easiest way to set this experiment up is to determine the height required to achieve a speed of 360 inches per second on impact. You tried a series of heights with a radar gun to measure the speed and collected the data shown in Example 1B.

Analyze

Looking over the data you collected, there are no data points with a speed of 360 inches per second, and continued attempts do not seem likely to randomly produce the correct speed. On the other hand, the pattern of the data appears to match a square root function.

Formulate a Plan

Since you cannot easily pick a height and hope it produces the desired speed, you need to use a model or fit function to determine an appropriate height.

You have two methods of fitting the data based on examples in this lesson, one based on estimation of parameters and one based on regression.

Solve

Find the height by solving the equation: $s = a\sqrt{v - h} + k$ using $s = 360$ in./s and the model parameters you found in Examples 1B and 2B.

Estimate model: $\boxed{360} = \boxed{22.26}\;\sqrt{v - \boxed{30}} + \boxed{56}$

Regression model: $\boxed{360} = \boxed{24.57}\;\sqrt{v - \boxed{29.33}} + \boxed{36.03}$

In order to solve this equation, use a graphical approach. Using the curves you made in the previous examples, find the intersection of the two model curves with the constant function $s = \boxed{360}$.

Estimate model: $v = \boxed{217}$

Regression model: $v = \boxed{203}$

 Justify and Evaluate

First check that the graphically solved numbers produce the desired speed.

Estimate model: $s\left(\boxed{217}\right) = \boxed{360}$

Regression model: $s\left(\boxed{203}\right) = \boxed{360}$

The regression model suggests a slightly lower height to reach the same desired speed.

Your Turn

5. Using the graphs of the two models from Your Turns 3 and 4, predict the expected year when boat sales will reach 65. Compare the results of the two models.

Elaborate

6. When selecting a second point in order to determine the value of a, is it better to pick a point near the initial point or farther from it? Explain.

7. Why is a quadratic model used to find the regression equation of a square root model?

8. **Discussion** What are the advantages and disadvantages of estimating a square root function compared to using quadratic regression?

9. **Essential Question Check-In** How can you use a calculator to find the equation of a square root function to model data?

☆ Evaluate: Homework and Practice

Find the inverse positive square root function for each quadratic function by first writing each quadratic function in vertex form. Compare the vertex of the quadratic function with the endpoint of its inverse function. Then compare the domains and ranges, and the transformations from their respective parent functions.

1. $f(x) = x^2 + 4x + 1$

2. $f(x) = -x^2 - 10x - 21$

Estimate and then plot the best fitting square root function to the given data. Then give the domain and range of the function.

3. Body mass index (BMI) is a measure used to determine healthy body mass based on a person's height. BMI is calculated by dividing a person's mass in kilograms by the square of his or her height in meters. The median BMI measures for a group of boys are given in the chart.

Median BMI (B)	Age of Boys (A)
15.4	6
15.5	7
15.8	8
16.2	9
16.6	10

4. An object traveling at a certain speed has a kinetic energy of 20 kJ. Model the speed of the object based on its kinetic energy given in the table below.

Kinetic Energy (kJ)	Speed above Initial Speed (m/s)
20	0.00
80	5.06
185	10.05
330	14.94
525	20.02
1040	29.99
1365	35.01
1730	39.98
2140	44.96
2600	50.01
3095	54.97
3645	60.03

5.

x	y
2	3.1
2.1	2.2
2.4	4.2
3	8.9
4	10.8
5	11
6	13.2
7	13.5

a. Use quadratic regression on a graphing calculator to find the quadratic function. Convert the function to vertex form and indicate the domain and range that contains the data.

b. Find each square root function by inverting the given quadratic regression function. Then graph this square root function and your previous square root function for the given data on the same grid.

c. Use the graph of both models to find the value of x when $y = 12$. Compare the results.

6.

x	y
2	3.1
2.1	2.2
2.4	4.2
3	8.9
4	10.8
5	11
6	13.2
7	13.5

a. Use quadratic regression on a graphing calculator to find the quadratic function. Convert the function to vertex form and indicate the domain and range that contains the data.

b. Find each square root function by inverting the given quadratic regression function. Then graph this square root function and your previous square root function for the given data on the same grid.

c. Use the graph of both models to find the value of x when $y = -2$. Compare the results.

7. Draw Conclusions Copy and complete the table below. Find the residuals for $f(x)$, the model found by roughly fitting a square root function and $r(x)$, the model that is the inverse of the quadratic regression function for the data described in Evaluate 6. Using a scale similar to the one shown, plot the residuals and determine which model is a better fit for the data.

x	y_d	$y_f = f(x)$	$y_d - y_f$	$y_r = r(x)$	$y_d - y_r$
20	0.00				
80	5.06				
185	10.05				
330	14.94				
525	20.02				
1040	29.99				
1365	35.01				
1730	39.98				
2140	44.96				
2600	50.01				
3095	54.97				
3645	60.03				

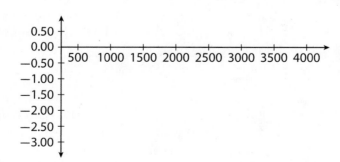

8. Critique Reasoning A student makes the following claim: When roughly fitting a square root function to data, the initial point is always either the leftmost data point or will be to the left of all of the data.

Is the student correct? Justify your answer or find a counterexample.

Lesson Performance Task

The speed of sound is typically given as 767 mi/h, but that value is only accurate if the temperature is 68°F. We can calculate the speed of sound, s, in air in miles per hour using the function $s = \sqrt{k(T + C)}$, where T is the temperature in degrees Fahrenheit, and k and C are constants. The table contains some values returned by this function.

Temperature (°F)	Speed of Sound in Air (mi/h)
−460	0
−100	634
0	717
68	768
212	866

a. Determine the values of the constants k and C of the function.

b. Suppose one day in Antarctica it is −110 °F and in Texas it is 110 °F. What is the difference in the speed of sound in these two locations?

c. How much longer would it take to hear a very loud sound from 5 miles away in Antarctica than in Texas?

11.4 Graphing Cube Root Functions

Essential Question: How can you use transformations of parent cube root functions to graph functions of the form $f(x) = a\sqrt[3]{(x - h)} + k$ or $g(x) = \sqrt[3]{\frac{1}{b}(x - h)} + k$?

 TEKS **A2.6.A** Analyze the effect on the graphs of ... $f(x) = \sqrt[3]{x}$ when $f(x)$ is replaced by $af(x)$, $f(bx)$, $f(x - c)$, and $f(x) + d$ for specific positive and negative real values of a, b, c, and d. Also A2.2.A, A2.7.I

Resource Locker

Explore 1 Graphing and Analyzing the Parent Cube Root Function

The cube root parent function is $f(x) = \sqrt[3]{x}$. To graph $f(x)$, choose values of x and find corresponding values of y. Choose both negative and positive values of x.

Graph the function $f(x) = \sqrt[3]{x}$. Identify the domain and range of the function.

(A) Make a table of values.

x	y	(x, y)
−8		
−1		
0		
1		
8		

(B) Use the table to graph the function.

(C) Identify the domain and range of the function.

The domain is the ▮.

The range is ▮.

(D) Does the graph of $f(x) = \sqrt[3]{x}$ have any symmetry?

The graph has ▮.

Reflect

1. Can the radicand in a cube root function be negative?

Predicting the Effects of Parameters on the Graphs of Cube Root Functions

Given the parent function $f(x) = \sqrt[3]{x}$, predict the effect of parameters on the graphs of cube root functions.

(A) Predict the effect of the parameter, h, on the graph of $g(x) = \sqrt[3]{x - h}$ for each function.

a. $g(x) = \sqrt[3]{x - 3}$: The graph is a [   ] of the graph of $f(x)$ [   ] 3 units.

b. $g(x) = \sqrt[3]{x + 3}$: The graph is a [   ] of the graph of $f(x)$ [   ] 3 units.

Check your answers using a graphing calculator.

(B) Predict the effect of the parameter k on the graph of $g(x) = \sqrt[3]{x} + k$ for each function.

a. $g(x) = \sqrt[3]{x} + 3$: The graph is a [   ] of the graph of $f(x)$ [   ] 3 units.

b. $g(x) = \sqrt[3]{x} - 3$: The graph is a [   ] of the graph of $f(x)$ [   ] 3 units.

Check your answers using a graphing calculator.

(C) Predict the effect of the parameter a on the graph of $g(x) = a\sqrt[3]{x}$ for each function.

a. $g(x) = 3\sqrt[3]{x}$: The graph is a [   ] stretch of the graph of $f(x)$ by a factor of [   ].

b. $g(x) = \frac{1}{3}\sqrt[3]{x}$: The graph is a [   ] compression of the graph of $f(x)$ by a factor of [   ].

c. $g(x) = -\frac{1}{3}\sqrt[3]{x}$: The graph is a [   ] compression of the graph of $f(x)$ by a factor of [   ] as well as a [   ] across the [   ].

d. $g(x) = -3\sqrt[3]{x}$: The graph is a [   ] stretch of the graph of $f(x)$ by a factor of [   ] as well as a [   ] across the [   ].

Check your answers using a graphing calculator.

(D) Predict the effect of the parameter, b, on the graph of $g(x) = \sqrt[3]{\frac{1}{b}x}$ for each function.

a. $g(x) = \sqrt[3]{\frac{1}{3}x}$: The graph is a [   ] stretch of the graph of $f(x)$ by a factor of [   ].

b. $g(x) = \sqrt[3]{3x}$: The graph is a [   ] compression of the graph of $f(x)$ by a factor of [   ].

c. $g(x) = \sqrt[3]{-\frac{1}{3}x}$: The graph is a [   ] stretch of the graph of $f(x)$ by a factor of [   ] as well as a [   ] across the [   ].

d. $g(x) = \sqrt[3]{-3x}$: The graph is a [   ] compression of the graph of $f(x)$ by a factor of [   ] as well as a [   ] across the [   ].

Check your answers using a graphing calculator.

Reflect

2. In $g(x) = \sqrt[3]{x - h} + k$ how do h and k effect the graphs of cube root functions?

🖉 Explain 1 Graphing Cube Root Functions

Transformations of the Cube Root Parent Function $f(x) = \sqrt[3]{x}$

Transformation	$f(x)$ Notation	Examples
Vertical translation	$f(x) + k$	$y = \sqrt[3]{x} + 3$ 3 units up $y = \sqrt[3]{x} - 4$ 4 units down
Horizontal translation	$f(x - h)$	$y = \sqrt[3]{x - 2}$ 2 units right $y = \sqrt[3]{x + 1}$ 1 units left
Vertical stretch/compression	$af(x)$	$y = 6\sqrt[3]{x}$ vertical stretch by 6 $y = \frac{1}{2}\sqrt[3]{x}$ vertical compression by $\frac{1}{2}$
Horizontal stretch/compression	$f\left(\frac{1}{b}x\right)$	$y = \sqrt[3]{\frac{1}{5}x}$ horizontal stretch by 5 $y = \sqrt[3]{3x}$ horizontal compression by $\frac{1}{3}$
Reflection	$-f(x)$ $f(-x)$	$y = -\sqrt[3]{x}$ across x-axis $y = \sqrt[3]{-x}$ across y-axis

For the function $f(x) = a\sqrt[3]{x - h} + k$, (h, k) is the graph's point of symmetry. Use the values of a, h, and k to draw each graph. For example, the point $(1, 1)$ on the graph of the parent function becomes the point $(1 + h, a + k)$ on the graph of the given function.

Example 1 Graph the cube root functions.

(A) Graph $g(x) = 2\sqrt[3]{x - 3} + 5$.

The transformations of the graph of $f(x) = \sqrt[3]{x}$ that produce the graph of $g(x)$ are:

- a vertical stretch by a factor of 2

- a translation of 3 units to the right and 5 units up

Choose points on $f(x) = \sqrt[3]{x}$ and find the transformed corresponding points on $g(x) = 2\sqrt[3]{x - 3} + 5$.

Graph $g(x) = 2\sqrt[3]{x - 3} + 5$ using the transformed points.

$f(x) = \sqrt[3]{x}$	$g(x) = 2\sqrt[3]{x - 3} + 5$
$(-8, -2)$	$(-5, 1)$
$(-1, -1)$	$(2, 3)$
$(0, 0)$	$(3, 5)$
$(1, 1)$	$(4, 7)$
$(8, 2)$	$(11, 9)$

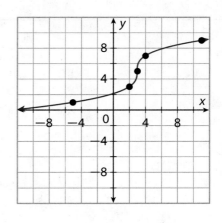

© Houghton Mifflin Harcourt Publishing Company

Ⓑ Graph $g(x) = \sqrt[3]{\frac{1}{2}(x - 10)} + 4$.

The transformations of the graph of $f(x) = \sqrt[3]{x}$ that produce the graph of $g(x)$ are:

- a horizontal stretch by a factor of 2

- a translation of 10 units to the right and 4 units up

Choose points on $f(x) = \sqrt[3]{x}$ and find the transformed corresponding points on $g(x) = \sqrt[3]{\frac{1}{2}(x - 10)} + 4$.

Graph $g(x) = \sqrt[3]{\frac{1}{2}(x - 10)} + 4$ using the transformed points.

$f(x) = \sqrt[3]{x}$	$g(x) = \sqrt[3]{\frac{1}{2}(x - 10)} + 4$
$(-8, -2)$	$(-6, 2)$
$(-1, -1)$	$(8, 3)$
$(0, 0)$	$(10, 4)$
$(1, 1)$	$(12, 5)$
$(8, 2)$	$(26, 6)$

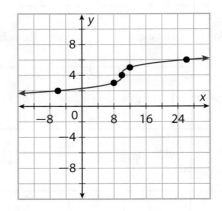

Your Turn

Copy and complete the tables, then graph the cube root functions.

3. Graph $g(x) = \sqrt[3]{x - 3} + 6$.

$f(x) = \sqrt[3]{x}$	$g(x) = \sqrt[3]{x - 3} + 6$
$(-8, -2)$	
$(-1, -1)$	
$(0, 0)$	
$(1, 1)$	
$(8, 2)$	

4. Graph $g(x) = \sqrt[3]{x + 3} - 7$.

$f(x) = \sqrt[3]{x}$	$g(x) = \sqrt[3]{x + 3} - 7$
$(-8, -2)$	
$(-1, -1)$	
$(0, 0)$	
$(1, 1)$	
$(8, 2)$	

Explain 2   Writing Cube Root Functions

Given the graph of the transformed function $g(x) = a\sqrt[3]{\frac{1}{b}(x - h)} + k$, you can determine the values of the parameters by using the reference points $(-1, 1)$, $(0, 0)$, and $(1, 1)$ that you used to graph $g(x)$ in the previous example.

Example 2   **For the given graphs, write a cube root function.**

(A)   Write the function in the form $g(x) = a\sqrt[3]{x - h} + k$.

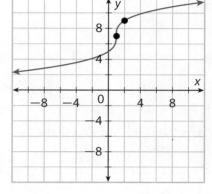

Identify the values of a, h, and k.

Identify the values of h and k from the point of symmetry.

$(h, k) = (1, 7)$, so $h = 1$ and $k = 7$.

Identify the value of a from either of the other two reference points $(-1, 1)$ or $(1, 1)$.

The reference point $(1, 1)$ has general coordinates $(h + 1, a + k)$. Substituting 1 for h and 7 for k and setting the general coordinates equal to the actual coordinates gives this result:

$(h + 1, a + k) = (2, a + 7) = (2, 9)$, so $a = 2$.

$a = 2$ $h = 1$ $k = 7$

The function is $g(x) = 2\sqrt[3]{x - 1} + 7$.

(B)   Write the function in the form $g(x) = \sqrt[3]{\frac{1}{b}(x - h)} + k$.

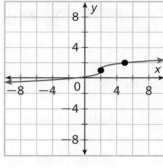

Identify the values of b, h, and k.

Identify the values of h and k from the point of symmetry.

$(h, k) = \left(2, \boxed{1}\right)$ so $h = 2$ and $k = \boxed{1}$.

Identify the value of b from either of the other two reference points.

The rightmost reference point has general coordinates $(b + h, 1 + k)$.
Substituting 2 for h and 1 for k and setting the general coordinates equal to the actual coordinates gives this result:

$\left(b + h, 1 + \boxed{1}\right) = \left(b + 2, \boxed{2}\right) = (5, 2)$, so $b = \boxed{3}$.

$b = \boxed{3}$ $h = \boxed{2}$ $k = \boxed{1}$

The function is $g(x) = \sqrt[3]{\frac{1}{3}(x - 2)} + 1$.

For the given graphs, write a cube root function.

5. Write the function in the form $g(x) = a\sqrt[3]{x-h} + k$.

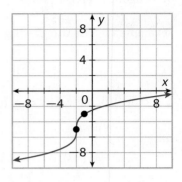

6. Write the function in the form $g(x) = \sqrt[3]{\frac{1}{b}(x-h)} + k$.

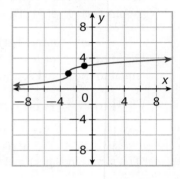

🚀 Explain 3   Modeling with Cube Root Functions

You can use cube root functions to model real-world situations.

Example 3

Ⓐ The shoulder height h (in centimeters) of a particular elephant is modeled by the function $h(t) = 62.1\sqrt[3]{t} + 76$, where t is the age (in years) of the elephant. Graph the function and examine its average rate of change over the equal t-intervals $(0, 20)$, $(20, 40)$, and $(40, 60)$. What is happening to the average rate of change as the t-values of the intervals increase? Use the graph to find the height when $t = 35$.

Graph $h(t) = 62.1\sqrt[3]{t} + 76$.

The graph is the graph of $f(x) = \sqrt[3]{x}$ translated up 76 and stretched vertically by a factor of 62.1. Graph the transformed points $(0, 76)$, $(8, 200.2)$, $(27, 262.3)$, and $(64, 324.4)$. Connect the points with a smooth curve.

First interval:

Average Rate of change $\approx \dfrac{244.6 - 76}{20 - 0}$

$= 8.43$

Second interval:

Average Rate of change $\approx \dfrac{288.4 - 244.6}{40 - 20}$

$= 2.19$

Third interval:

Average Rate of change $\approx \dfrac{319.1 - 288.4}{60 - 40}$

$= 1.54$

The average rate of change is becoming less.

Drawing a vertical line up from 35 gives a value of about 280 cm.

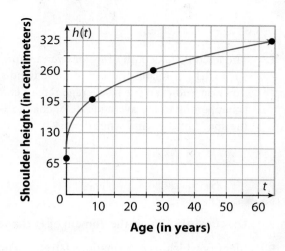

(B) The velocity of a 1400-kilogram car at the end of a 400-meter run is modeled by the function $v = 15.2\sqrt[3]{p}$, where v is the velocity in kilometers per hour and p is the power of its engine in horsepower. Graph the function and examine its average rate of change over the equal p-intervals $(0,60)$, $(60,120)$, and $(120,180)$. What is happening to the average rate of change as the p-values of the intervals increase? Use the function to find the velocity when p is 100 horsepower.

Graph $V = 15.2\sqrt[3]{p}$.

The graph is the graph of $f(x) = \sqrt[3]{x}$ stretched vertically by a factor of 15.2. Graph the transformed points $(0, 0)$, $(8, 30.4)$, $(27, 45.6)$, $(64, 60.8)$, $(125, 76)$, and $(216, 91.2)$. Connect the points with a smooth curve.

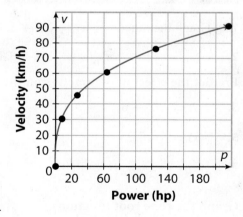

The rate of change over the interval $(0, 60)$ is

$\dfrac{\boxed{59.5} - \boxed{0}}{60 - 0}$ which is about 0.99.

The rate of change over the interval $(60, 120)$ is $\dfrac{\boxed{75.0} - \boxed{59.5}}{120 - 60}$ which is about 0.26.

The rate of change over the interval $(120, 180)$ is $\dfrac{\boxed{85.8} - \boxed{75.0}}{180 - 120}$ which is about 0.18.

The average rate of change is becoming less. Substitute $p = 100$ in the function.

$v = 15.2\sqrt[3]{p}$

$v = 15.2\sqrt[3]{\boxed{100}}$

$v \approx 15.2\left(\boxed{4.64}\right) = \boxed{70.5}$

The velocity is about 70.5 km/h.

7. The fetch is the length of water over a wind that is blowing in the same direction. The function $s(f) = 7.1\sqrt[3]{f}$, relates the speed of the wind s in kilometers per hour to the fetch f in kilometers. Graph the function and examine its average rate of change over the intervals $(20, 80)$, $(80, 140)$, and $(140, 200)$. What is happening to the average rate of change as the f-values of the intervals increase? Use the function to find the speed of the wind when $f = 64$.

 **Elaborate**

8. **Discussion** Why is the domain of $f(x) = \sqrt[3]{x}$ all real numbers?

9. Identify which transformations (stretches or compressions, reflections, and translations) of $f(x) = x^3$ change the following attributes of the function.

   a. Location of the point of symmetry

   b. Symmetry about a point

10. **Essential Question Check-In** How do parameters a, b, h, and k effect the graphs of $f(x) = a\sqrt[3]{(x - h)} + k$ and $g(x) = \sqrt[3]{\frac{1}{b}(x - h)} + k$?

⭐ Evaluate: Homework and Practice

• Online Homework
• Hints and Help
• Extra Practice

1. Graph the function $g(x) = \sqrt[3]{x} + 3$. Identify the domain and range of the function.

2. Graph the function $g(x) = \sqrt[3]{x} - 5$. Identify the domain and range of the function.

Predict the effect of parameters on the graphs of cube root functions.

3. $g(x) = \sqrt[3]{x} + 6$

4. $g(x) = \sqrt[3]{x - 5}$

5. $g(x) = \frac{1}{3}\sqrt[3]{-x}$

6. $g(x) = \sqrt[3]{5x}$

7. $g(x) = -2\sqrt[3]{x} + 3$

8. $g(x) = \sqrt[3]{x + 4} - 3$

Graph the cube root functions.

9. $g(x) = 3\sqrt[3]{x + 4}$

10. $g(x) = 2\sqrt[3]{x} + 3$

11. $g(x) = \sqrt[3]{x - 3} + 2$

For the given graphs, write a cube root function.

12. Write the function in the form $g(x) = a\sqrt[3]{x - h} + k$.

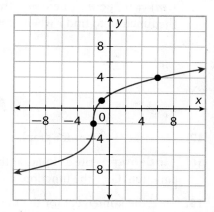

13. Write the function in the form $g(x) = a\sqrt[3]{x - h} + k$.

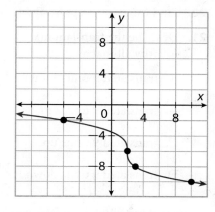

14. Write the function in the form $g(x) = \sqrt[3]{\dfrac{1}{b}(x - h)} + k$.

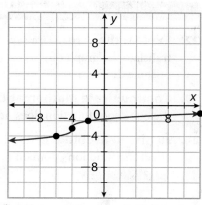

15. The length of the side of a cube is modeled by $s = \sqrt[3]{V}$. Graph the function. Use the graph to find s when $V = 48$.

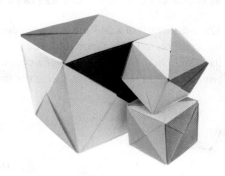

16. The radius of a stainless steel ball can be modeled by $r(m) = 0.31\sqrt[3]{m}$, where m is the mass of the ball. Use the function to find r when $m = 125$.

17. Describe the steps for graphing $g(x) = \sqrt[3]{x + 8} - 11$.

18. **Modeling** Write a situation that can be modeled by a cube root function. Give the function.

19. Find the y-intercept for the function $y = a\sqrt[3]{x - h} + k$.

20. Find the x-intercept for the function $y = a\sqrt[3]{x - h} + k$.

21. Describe the translation(s) used to get $g(x) = \sqrt[3]{x - 9} + 12$ from $f(x) = \sqrt[3]{x}$. Identify all that apply.

   A. translated 9 units right   E. translated 12 units right

   B. translated 9 units left   F. translated 12 units left

   C. translated 9 units up   G. translated 12 units up

   D. translated 9 units down   H. translated 12 units down

H.O.T. Focus on Higher Order Thinking

22. **Explain the Error** Tim says that to graph $g(x) = \sqrt[3]{x - 6} + 3$, you need to translate the graph of $f(x) = \sqrt[3]{x}$ 6 units to the left and then 3 units up. What mistake did he make?

23. **Communicate Mathematical Ideas** Why does the square root function have a restricted domain but the cube root function does not?

24. **Justify Reasoning** Does a horizontal translation and a vertical translation of the function $f(x) = \sqrt[3]{x}$ affect the function's domain or range? Explain.

Lesson Performance Task

The side length of a 243-gram copper cube is 3 centimeters. Use this information to write a model for the radius of a copper sphere as a function of its mass. Then, find the radius of a copper sphere with a mass of 50 grams. How would changing the material affect the function?

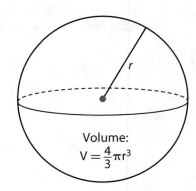

Volume:
$V = \frac{4}{3}\pi r^3$

Essential Question: How can you use radical functions to solve real-world problems?

Key Vocabulary

cube-root function
   (función de raíz cúbica)

index *(índice)*

inverse function
   (función inversa)

square-root function
   (función de raíz cuadrada)

KEY EXAMPLE   *(Lesson 11.2)*

Graph $y = -\sqrt{x-3} + 2$. Describe the domain and range.

Sketch the graph of $y = -\sqrt{x}$.

It begins at the origin and passes through $(1, -1)$.

For $y = -\sqrt{x-3} + 2$, $h = 3$ and $k = 2$.
Shift the graph of $y = -\sqrt{x}$ right 3 units and up 2 units. The graph begins at $(3, 2)$ and passes through $(4, 1)$.

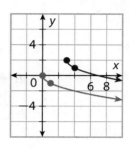

Domain: $\{x : x \geq 3\}$ Range: $\{y : y \leq 2\}$

KEY EXAMPLE   *(Lesson 11.4)*

Graph $y = \sqrt[3]{x+2} - 4$.

Sketch the graph of $y = \sqrt[3]{x}$.

It passes through $(-1, -1)$, $(0, 0)$, and $(1, 1)$.

For $y = \sqrt[3]{x+2} - 4$, $h = -2$ and $k = -4$.
Shift the graph of $y = \sqrt[3]{x}$ left 2 units and down 4 units. The graph passes through $(-3, -5)$, $(-2, -4)$, and $(-1, -3)$.

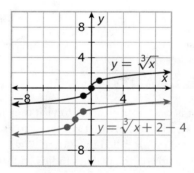

EXERCISES

Find the inverse of each function. Restrict the domain where necessary. *(Lesson 11.1)*

1. $f(x) = 16x^2$

2. $f(x) = x^3 - 20$

Identify the transformations of the graph $f(x) = \sqrt{x}$ that produce the graph of the function. *(Lesson 11.2)*

3. $g(x) = -\sqrt{4x}$

4. $h(x) = \frac{1}{2}\sqrt{x} + 1$

Use the vertex and a second point to fit a square root function to the data. *(Lesson 11.3)*

5. Points: $(3, 5.2), (4, 10), (5, 12.9), (6, 13.1), (7, 15.3), (8, 15.6)$

Identify the transformations of the graph $f(x) = \sqrt[3]{x}$ that produce the graph of the function. *(Lesson 11.4)*

6. $g(x) = 4\sqrt[3]{x}$

7. $h(x) = \sqrt[3]{x - 5} + 3$

MODULE PERFORMANCE TASK

We Have Liftoff!

A rocket scientist is designing a rocket to visit the planets in the solar system. The velocity that is needed to escape a planet's gravitational pull is called the escape velocity. The escape velocity depends on the planet's radius and its mass, according to the equation $V_{escape} = \sqrt{2gR}$, where R is the radius and g is the gravitational constant for the particular planet. The rocket's maximum velocity is exactly double Earth's escape velocity. For which planets will the rocket have enough velocity to escape the planet's gravity?

Planet	Radius (m)	Mass (kg)	g (m/s^2)
Mercury	2.43×10^6	3.20×10^{23}	3.61
Venus	6.07×10^6	4.88×10^{24}	8.83
Mars	3.38×10^6	6.42×10^{23}	3.75
Jupiter	6.98×10^7	1.90×10^{27}	26.0
Saturn	5.82×10^7	5.68×10^{26}	11.2
Uranus	2.35×10^7	8.68×10^{25}	10.5
Neptune	2.27×10^7	1.03×10^{26}	13.3

Begin by listing any additional information you will need to solve the problem. Be sure to write down all your data and assumptions. Then use graphs, numbers, words, or algebra to explain how you reached your conclusions.

11.1–11.4 Radical Functions

- Online Homework
- Hints and Help
- Extra Practice

Find the inverse of each function. State any restrictions on the domain.
(Lesson 11.1)

1. $f(x) = x^2 + 9$

2. $f(x) = -7x^3$

Identify the transformations of the graph $f(x) = \sqrt{x}$ **or** $h(x) = \sqrt[3]{x}$ **that produce the graph of the function.** *(Lessons 11.2, 11.4)*

3. $g(x) = \dfrac{1}{3}\sqrt{x-5} - 4$

4. $g(x) = \sqrt[3]{4x} + 3$

Solve *(Lesson 11.3)*

5. Use the vertex and a second point to fit a square root function to the data.

x	y
16.7	8
16.8	9
17.1	10
17.5	11
17.9	12

ESSENTIAL QUESTION

6. How do you use a parent square root or cube root function to graph a transformation of the function? *(Lessons 11.2, 11.4)*

Assessment Readiness

1. Which function is graphed below?

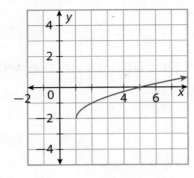

   A. $y = \sqrt{x - 1} - 2$
   B. $y = \sqrt{x - 1} + 2$

   C. $y = \sqrt{x + 1} - 2$
   D. $y = \sqrt{x + 1} + 2$

2. What is the inverse of $f(x) = x^3 - 16$?
   A. $f^{-1}(x) = \sqrt[3]{x - 16}$
   B. $f^{-1}(x) = \sqrt[3]{x + 16}$

   C. $f^{-1}(x) = \sqrt[3]{x} + 16$
   D. $f^{-1}(x) = \sqrt[3]{x} - 16$

3. A plane's average speed when flying from one city to another is 550 mi/h and is 430 mi/h on the return flight. To the nearest mile per hour, what is the plane's average speed for the entire trip?
   A. 360 mi/h
   B. 453 mi/h

   C. 483 mi/h
   D. 490 mi/h

4. The kinetic energy E (in joules) of a 1250 kilogram compact car is given by the equation $E = 625s^2$ where s is the speed of the car (in meters per second). Write an inverse model that gives the speed of the car as a function of its kinetic energy. If the kinetic energy doubles, will the speed double? Explain why or why not.

Radical Expressions and Equations

Essential Question: How can you use radical expressions and equations to solve real-world problems?

REAL WORLD VIDEO
A field biologist studying howler monkeys can use radical functions to calculate sound intensity, which decreases faster than linearly with distance.

MODULE PERFORMANCE TASK PREVIEW
Don't Disturb the Neighbors!

The loudness of a sound is subjective and depends on the listener's sensitivity to the frequencies of the sound waves. An objective measure, sound intensity, can be used to measure sounds. Sound intensity decreases the farther you get from the source of a sound. How far away do your neighbors have to be so that a loud band does not bother them? Let's find out!

Complete these exercises to review skills you will need for this chapter.

Exponents

Example 1

Simplify $\left(x^3\right)^2 + x \cdot x^3 + 3x^4$.

$$\left(x^3\right)^2 + x \cdot x^3 + 3x^4 = \left(x^3\right)\left(x^3\right) + x \cdot x^3 + 3x^4 \qquad \text{Start with the raised power.}$$

$$= x^{3+3} + x^{1+3} + 3x^4 \qquad \text{Add exponents.}$$

$$= x^6 + x^4 + 3x^4 \qquad \text{Simplify.}$$

$$= x^6 + 4x^4 \qquad \text{Add like terms.}$$

- Online Homework
- Hints and Help
- Extra Practice

Simplify each expression.

1. $\left(-x^5\right)^2$

2. $\left(3x^2\right)^3 - x^4 \cdot x^2$

3. $3x(2x)^2$

Inverse Linear Functions

Example 2

Write the inverse function of $y = 10x - 4$.

$$y - 4 = 10x \qquad \text{Isolate the } x\text{-term.}$$

$$\frac{y-4}{10} = \frac{10x}{10} \qquad \text{Divide.}$$

The inverse function of $y = 10x - 4$ is $x = \dfrac{y-4}{10}$.

Write the inverse function.

4. $y = 3x + 1$

5. $y = 2(x - 9)$

6. $y = \dfrac{1}{4}(3x + 4)$

Rational and Radical Exponents

Example 3

Write $\sqrt[9]{a^3}$ using a rational exponent.

$$\sqrt[9]{a^3} = a^{\frac{3}{9}} = a^{\frac{1}{3}}$$

Write each radical expression using a rational exponent.

7. $\sqrt[2]{x^5}$

8. $\sqrt[4]{a^2 b}$

9. $\sqrt[4]{p^8 q^2}$

12.1 Radical Expressions and Rational Exponents

Essential Question: How are rational exponents related to radicals and roots?

 **A2.7.G** Rewrite radical expressions that contain variables to equivalent forms.

Explore Defining Rational Exponents in Terms of Roots

Remember that a number a is an nth root of a number b if $a^n = b$. As you know, a square root is indicated by $\sqrt{}$ and a cube root by $\sqrt[3]{}$. In general, the nth root of a real number a is indicated by $\sqrt[n]{a}$, where n is the **index** of the radical and a is the radicand. (Note that when a number has more than one real root, the radical sign indicates only the principal, or positive, root.)

A *rational exponent* is an exponent that can be expressed as $\frac{m}{n}$, where m is an integer and n is a natural number. You can use the definition of a root and properties of equality and exponents to explore how to express roots using rational exponents.

(A) How can you express a square root using an exponent? That is, if $\sqrt{a} = a^m$, what is m?

Given $\qquad\qquad\qquad\qquad \sqrt{a} = a^m$

Square both sides. $\qquad\qquad \left(\sqrt{a}\right)^2 = \left(a^m\right)^2$

Definition of square root $\qquad \boxed{} = \left(a^m\right)^2$

Power of a power property $\qquad a = a^{\boxed{}}$

Definition of first power $\qquad a^{\boxed{}} = a^{2m}$

The bases are the same, so equate exponents. $\qquad \boxed{} = \boxed{}$

Solve. $\qquad\qquad\qquad\qquad m = \boxed{}$

So, $\qquad\qquad\qquad\qquad \sqrt{a} = a^{\boxed{}}$.

Ⓑ How can you express a cube root using an exponent? That is, if $\sqrt[3]{a} = a^m$, what is m?

Given

$$\sqrt[3]{a} = a^m$$

Cube both sides.

$$\left(\sqrt[3]{a}\right)^3 = \left(a^m\right)^3$$

Definition of cube root

□ = □

Power of a power property

□ = □

Definition of first power

□ = □

The bases are the same, so equate exponents.

□ = □

Solve.

$m =$ □

So,

$$\sqrt[3]{a} = a^{\square}.$$

Reflect

1. **Discussion** Examine the reasoning in Steps A and B. Can you apply the same reasoning for any nth root, $\sqrt[n]{a}$, where n is a natural number? Explain. What can you conclude?

2. For a positive number a, under what condition on n will there be only one real nth root? two real nth roots? Explain.

3. For a negative number a, under what condition on n will there be no real nth roots? one real nth root? Explain.

🎸 Explain 1 Translating Between Radical Expressions and Rational Exponents

In the Explore, you found that a rational exponent $\frac{m}{n}$ with $m = 1$ represents an nth root, or that $a^{\frac{1}{n}} = \sqrt[n]{a}$ for positive values of a. This is also true for negative values of a when the index is odd. When $m \neq 1$, you can think of the numerator m as the power and the denominator n as the root. The following ways of expressing the exponent $\frac{m}{n}$ are equivalent.

© Houghton Mifflin Harcourt Publishing Company

Rational Exponents		
For any natural number n, integer m, and real number a when the nth root of a is real:		
Words	**Numbers**	**Algebra**
The exponent $\frac{m}{n}$ indicates the mth power of the nth root of a quantity.	$27^{\frac{2}{3}} = \left(\sqrt[3]{27}\right)^2 = 3^2 = 9$	$a^{\frac{m}{n}} = \left(\sqrt[n]{a}\right)^m$
The exponent $\frac{m}{n}$ indicates the nth root of the mth power of a quantity.	$4^{\frac{3}{2}} = \sqrt{4^3} = \sqrt{64} = 8$	$a^{\frac{m}{n}} = \sqrt[n]{a^m}$

Notice that you can evaluate each example in the "Numbers" column using the equivalent definition.

$$27^{\frac{2}{3}} = \sqrt[3]{27^2} = \sqrt[3]{729} = 9 \qquad 4^{\frac{3}{2}} = \left(\sqrt{4}\right)^3 = 2^3 = 8$$

Example 1 Translate radical expressions into expressions with rational exponents, and vice versa. Simplify numerical expressions when possible. Assume all variables are positive.

Ⓐ **a.** $(-125)^{\frac{4}{3}}$ **b.** $x^{\frac{11}{8}}$ **c.** $\sqrt[5]{6^4}$ **d.** $\sqrt[4]{x^3}$

a. $(-125)^{\frac{4}{3}} = \left(\sqrt[3]{-125}\right)^4 = (-5)^4 = 625$

b. $x^{11/8} = \sqrt[8]{x^{11}}$ or $\left(\sqrt[8]{x}\right)^{11}$

c. $\sqrt[5]{6^4} = 6^{\frac{4}{5}}$

d. $\sqrt[4]{x^3} = x^{\frac{3}{4}}$

Ⓑ **a.** $\left(\frac{81}{16}\right)^{\frac{3}{4}}$ **b.** $(xy)^{\frac{5}{3}}$ **c.** $\sqrt[3]{11^6}$ **d.** $\sqrt[3]{\left(\frac{2x}{y}\right)^5}$

a. $\left(\frac{81}{16}\right)^{\frac{3}{4}} = \left(\boxed{4}\sqrt{\frac{81}{16}}\right)^{\boxed{3}} = \left(\boxed{\frac{3}{2}}\right)^3 = \boxed{\frac{27}{8}}$

b. $(xy)^{\frac{5}{3}} = \boxed{3}\sqrt{(xy)^{\boxed{5}}}$ or $\left(\boxed{3}\sqrt{xy}\right)^{\boxed{5}}$

c. $\sqrt[3]{11^6} = 11^{\boxed{\frac{6}{3}}} = 11^{\boxed{2}} = \boxed{121}$

d. $\sqrt[3]{\left(\frac{2x}{y}\right)^5} = \left(\frac{2x}{y}\right)^{\boxed{\frac{5}{3}}}$

Reflect

4. How can you use a calculator to show that evaluating $0.001728^{\frac{4}{3}}$ as a power of a root and as a root of a power are equivalent methods?

Your Turn

5. Translate radical expressions into expressions with rational exponents, and vice versa. Simplify numerical expressions when possible. Assume all variables are positive.

a. $\left(-\frac{32}{243}\right)^{\frac{2}{5}}$ **b.** $(3y)^{\frac{b}{c}}$

c. $\sqrt[3]{0.5^9}$ **d.** $\left(\sqrt[u]{st}\right)^v$

⚙ Explain 2 Modeling with Power Functions

The following functions all involve a given power of a variable.

$A = \pi r^2$ (area of a circle)

$V = \frac{4}{3}\pi r^3$ (volume of a sphere)

$T = 1.11 \cdot L^{\frac{1}{2}}$ (the time T in seconds for a pendulum of length L feet to complete one back-and-forth swing)

These are all examples of *power functions*. A power function has the form $y = ax^b$ where a is a real number and b is a rational number.

Example 2   **Solve each problem by modeling with power functions.**

Ⓐ **Biology** The function $R = 73.3\sqrt[4]{M^3}$, known as Kleiber's law, relates the basal metabolic rate R in Calories per day burned and the body mass M of a mammal in kilograms. The table shows typical body masses for some members of the cat family.

Typical Body Mass	
Animal	**Mass (kg)**
House cat	4.5
Cheetah	55
Lion	170

a. Rewrite the formula with a rational exponent.

b. What is the value of R for a cheetah to the nearest 50 Calories?

c. From the table, the mass of the lion is about 38 times that of the house cat. Is the lion's metabolic rate more or less than 38 times the cat's rate? Explain.

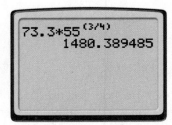

a. Because $\sqrt[n]{a^m} = a^{\frac{m}{n}}$, $\sqrt[4]{M^3} = M^{\frac{3}{4}}$, so the formula is $R = 73.3M^{\frac{3}{4}}$.

b. Substitute 55 for M in the formula and use a calculator.

The cheetah's metabolic rate is about 1500 Calories.

c. Less; find the ratio of R for the lion to R for the house cat.

$$\frac{73.3(170)^{\frac{3}{4}}}{73.3(4.5)^{\frac{3}{4}}} = \frac{170^{\frac{3}{4}}}{4.5^{\frac{3}{4}}} \approx \frac{47.1}{3.1} \approx 15$$

The metabolic rate for the lion is only about 15 times that of the house cat.

© Houghton Mifflin Harcourt Publishing Company • Image Credits: ©Radius Images/Corbis

(B) The function $h(m) = 241m^{-\frac{1}{4}}$ models an animal's approximate resting heart rate h in beats per minute given its mass m in kilograms.

    a. A common shrew has a mass of only about 0.01 kg. To the nearest 10, what is the model's estimate for this shrew's resting heart rate?

    b. What is the model's estimate for the resting heart rate of an American elk with a mass of 300 kg?

    c. Two animal species differ in mass by a multiple of 10. According to the model, about what percent of the smaller animal's resting heart rate would you expect the larger animal's resting heart rate to be?

    a. Substitute 0.01 for m in the formula and use a calculator.

$$h(m) = 241 \left(\boxed{0.01} \right)^{-\frac{1}{4}} \approx \boxed{760}$$

    The model estimates the shrew's resting heart rate to be is about 760 beats per minute.

    b. Substitute 300 for m in the formula and use a calculator.

$$h(m) = 241 \left(\boxed{300} \right)^{-\frac{1}{4}} \approx \boxed{60}$$

    The model estimates the elk's resting heart rate to be about 60 beats per minute.

    c. Find the ratio of $h(m)$ for the larger animal to the smaller animal. Let 1 represent the mass of the smaller animal.

$$\frac{241 \cdot \boxed{10}^{-\frac{1}{4}}}{241 \cdot 1^{-\frac{1}{4}}} = \boxed{10}^{-\frac{1}{4}} = \frac{1}{10^{\boxed{\frac{1}{4}}}} \approx \boxed{0.56}$$

    You would expect the larger animal's resting heart rate to be about 56% of the smaller animal's resting heart rate.

Reflect

6. What is the difference between a power function and an exponential function?

7. In Part B, the exponent is negative. Are the results consistent with the meaning of a negative exponent that you learned for integers? Explain.

Your Turn

8. Use Kleiber's law from Part A.

    a. Find the basal metabolic rate for a 170 kilogram lion to the nearest 50 Calories. Then find the formula's prediction for a 70 kilogram human.

    b. Use your metabolic rate result for the lion to find what the basal metabolic rate for a 70 kilogram human *would* be *if* metabolic rate and mass were directly proportional. Compare the result to the result from Part a.

Elaborate

9. Explain how can you use a radical to write and evaluate the power $4^{2.5}$.

10. When $y = kx$ for some constant k, y varies directly as x. When $y = kx^2$, y varies directly as the square of x; and when $y = k\sqrt{x}$, y varies directly as the square root of x. How could you express the relationship $y = kx^{\frac{3}{5}}$ for a constant k?

11. Essential Question Check-In Which of the following are true? Explain.

- To evaluate an expression of the form $a^{\frac{m}{n}}$, first find the nth root of a. Then raise the result to the mth power.
- To evaluate an expression of the form $a^{\frac{m}{n}}$, first find the mth power of a. Then find the nth root of the result.

⭐ Evaluate: Homework and Practice

- Online Homework
- Hints and Help
- Extra Practice

Translate expressions with rational exponents into radical expressions. Simplify numerical expressions when possible. Assume all variables are positive.

1. $64^{\frac{5}{3}}$

2. $x^{\frac{p}{q}}$

3. $(-512)^{\frac{2}{3}}$

4. $3^{\frac{2}{7}}$

5. $-\left(\dfrac{729}{64}\right)^{\frac{5}{6}}$

6. $0.125^{\frac{4}{3}}$

7. $vw^{\frac{2}{3}}$

8. $(-32)^{0.6}$

Translate radical expressions into expressions with rational exponents. Simplify numerical expressions when possible. Assume all variables are positive.

9. $\sqrt[7]{y^5}$

10. $\sqrt[7]{-6^6}$

11. $\sqrt[3]{3^{15}}$

12. $\sqrt[4]{(\pi z)^3}$

13. $\sqrt[6]{(bcd)^4}$

14. $\sqrt{6^6}$

15. $\sqrt[5]{32^2}$

16. $\sqrt[3]{\left(\dfrac{4}{x}\right)^9}$

17. Music Frets are small metal bars positioned across the neck of a guitar so that the guitar can produce the notes of a specific scale. To find the distance a fret should be placed from the bridge, multiply the length of the string by $2^{-\frac{n}{12}}$, where n is the number of notes higher than the string's root note. Where should a fret be placed to produce a F note on a B string (6 notes higher) given that the length of the string is 64 cm?

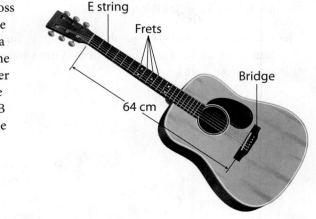

E string

Frets

Bridge

64 cm

18. **Meteorology** The function $W = 35.74 + 0.6215T - 35.75V^{\frac{4}{25}} + 0.4275TV^{\frac{4}{25}}$ relates the windchill temperature W to the air temperature T in degrees Fahrenheit and the wind speed V in miles per hour. Use a calculator to find the wind chill temperature to the nearest degree when the air temperature is 28 °F and the wind speed is 35 miles per hour.

19. **Astronomy** New stars can form inside a cloud of interstellar gas when a cloud fragment, or *clump*, has a mass M greater than the *Jean's mass* M_J. The Jean's mass is $M_J = 100n^{-\frac{1}{2}}(T + 273)^{\frac{3}{2}}$ where n is the number of gas molecules per cubic centimeter and T is the gas temperature in degrees Celsius. A gas clump has $M = 137$, $n = 1000$, and $T = -263$. Will the clump form a star? Justify your answer.

20. **Urban geography** The total wages W in a metropolitan area compared to its total population p can be approximated by a power function of the form $W = a \cdot p^{\frac{9}{8}}$ where a is a constant. About how many times greater does the model predict the total earnings for a metropolitan area with 3,000,000 people will be compared to a metropolitan area with 750,000?

21. Which statement is true?

   A. In the expression $8x^{\frac{3}{4}}$, $8x$ is the radicand.

   B. In the expression $(-16)x^{\frac{4}{5}}$, 4 is the index.

   C. The expression $1024^{\frac{n}{m}}$ represents the nth root of the mth power of 1024.

   D. $50^{-\frac{2}{5}} = -50^{\frac{2}{5}}$

   E. $\sqrt{(xy)^3} = xy^{\frac{3}{2}}$

22. **Critical Thinking** For a negative real number a, under what condition(s) on m and n $(n \neq 0)$ is $a^{\frac{m}{n}}$ a real number? Explain. (Assume $\frac{m}{n}$ is written in simplest form.)

23. **Explain the Error** A teacher asked students to evaluate $10^{-\frac{3}{5}}$ using their graphing calculators. The calculator entries of several students are shown below. Which entry will give the incorrect result? Explain.

24. Critical Thinking The graphs of three functions of the form $y = ax^{\frac{m}{n}}$ are shown for a specific value of a, where m and n are natural numbers. What can you conclude about the relationship of m and n for each graph? Explain.

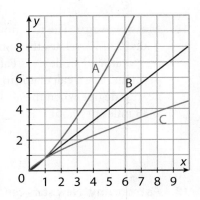

Lesson Performance Task

The formula $W = 35.74 + 0.6215T - 35.75V^{\frac{4}{25}} + 0.4275TV^{\frac{4}{25}}$ relates the wind chill temperature W to the air temperature T in degrees Fahrenheit and the wind speed V in miles per hour. Find the wind chill to the nearest degree when the air temperature is 40 °F and the wind speed is 35 miles per hour. If the wind chill is about 23 °F to the nearest degree when the air temperature is 40 °F, what is the wind speed to the nearest mile per hour?

12.2 Simplifying Radical Expressions

Essential Question: How can you simplify expressions containing rational exponents or radicals involving *n*th roots?

 TEKS A2.7.G Rewrite radical expressions that contain variables to equivalent forms.

 Explore   **Establishing the Properties of Rational Exponents**

In previous courses, you have used properties of integer exponents to simplify and evaluate expressions, as shown here for a few simple examples:

$$4^2 \cdot 4^3 = 4^{2+3} = 4^5 = 1024 \qquad\qquad (4 \cdot x)^2 = 4^2 \cdot x^2 = 16x^2$$

$$\left(4^2\right)^3 = 4^{2\cdot3} = 4^6 = 4096 \qquad\qquad \frac{4^2}{4^3} = 4^{2-3} = 4^{-1} = \frac{1}{4}$$

$$\left(\frac{4}{x}\right)^3 = \frac{4^3}{x^3} = \frac{64}{x^3}$$

Now that you have been introduced to expressions involving rational exponents, you can explore the properties that apply to simplifying them.

Ⓐ   Let $a = 64$, $b = 4$, $m = \frac{1}{3}$, and $n = \frac{3}{2}$. Evaluate each expression by substituting and applying exponents individually, as shown. Copy and complete the table.

Expression	Substitute	Simplify	Result
$a^m \cdot a^n$	$64^{\frac{1}{3}} \cdot 64^{\frac{3}{2}}$	$4 \cdot 512$	2048
$(a \cdot b)^n$	$(64 \cdot 4)^{\frac{3}{2}}$	$256^{\frac{3}{2}}$	
$(a^m)^n$			
$\dfrac{a^n}{a^m}$			
$\left(\dfrac{a}{b}\right)^n$			

(B) Copy and complete the table again. This time, however, apply the rule of exponents that you would use for integer exponents.

Expression	Apply Rule and Substitute	Simplify	Result
$a^m \cdot a^n$	$64^{\frac{1}{3}+\frac{3}{2}}$	$64^{\frac{11}{6}}$	▨
$(a \cdot b)^n$	▨	▨	▨
$(a^m)^n$	▨	▨	▨
$\dfrac{a^n}{a^m}$	▨	▨	▨
$\left(\dfrac{a}{b}\right)^n$	▨	▨	▨

Reflect

1. Compare your results in Steps A and B. What can you conclude?

2. In Steps A and B, you evaluated $\dfrac{a^n}{a^m}$ two ways. Now evaluate $\dfrac{a^m}{a^n}$ two ways, using the definition of negative exponents. Are your results consistent with your previous conclusions about integer and rational exponents?

⚙ Explain 1 Simplifying Rational-Exponent Expressions

Rational exponents have the same properties as integer exponents.

Properties of Rational Exponents		
For all nonzero real numbers a and b and rational numbers m and n		
Words	**Numbers**	**Algebra**
Product of Powers Property To multiply powers with the same base, add the exponents.	$12^{\frac{1}{2}} \cdot 12^{\frac{3}{2}} = 12^{\frac{1}{2}+\frac{3}{2}} = 12^2 = 144$	$a^m \cdot a^n = a^{m+n}$
Quotient of Powers Property To divide powers with the same base, subtract the exponents.	$\dfrac{125^{\frac{2}{3}}}{125^{\frac{1}{3}}} = 125^{\frac{2}{3}-\frac{1}{3}} = 125^{\frac{1}{3}} = 5$	$\dfrac{a^m}{a^n} = a^{m-n}$
Power of a Power Property To raise one power to another, multiply the exponents.	$\left(8^{\frac{2}{3}}\right)^3 = 8^{\frac{2}{3}\cdot 3} = 8^2 = 64$	$(a^m)^n = a^{m \cdot n}$
Power of a Product Property To find a power of a product, distribute the exponent.	$(16 \cdot 25)^{\frac{1}{2}} = 16^{\frac{1}{2}} \cdot 25^{\frac{1}{2}} = 4 \cdot 5 = 20$	$(ab)^m = a^m b^m$
Power of a Quotient Property To find the power of a qoutient, distribute the exponent.	$\left(\dfrac{16}{81}\right)^{\frac{1}{4}} = \dfrac{16^{\frac{1}{4}}}{81^{\frac{1}{4}}} = \dfrac{2}{3}$	$\left(\dfrac{a}{b}\right)^m = \dfrac{a^m}{b^m}$

Example 1 Simplify the expression. Assume that all variables are positive. Exponents in simplified form should all be positive.

 a. $25^{\frac{3}{5}} \cdot 25^{\frac{7}{5}}$

Product of Powers Prop. $= 25^{\frac{3}{5}+\frac{7}{5}}$

Simplify. $\qquad = 25^2$

$\qquad\qquad = 625$

b. $\dfrac{8^{\frac{1}{3}}}{8^{\frac{2}{3}}}$

Quotient of Powes Prop. $= 8^{\frac{1}{3}-\frac{2}{3}}$

Simplify. $\qquad = 8^{-\frac{1}{3}}$

Definition of neg. power $= \dfrac{1}{8^{\frac{1}{3}}}$

Simplify. $\qquad = \dfrac{1}{2}$

Ⓑ **a.** $\left(\dfrac{y^{\frac{4}{3}}}{16y^{\frac{2}{3}}}\right)^{\frac{3}{2}}$ **b.** $\left(27x^{\frac{3}{4}}\right)^{\frac{2}{3}}$

$\boxed{\text{Quotient of Powers}}$ Prop. $= \left(\dfrac{y^{\frac{4}{3}-\frac{2}{3}}}{16}\right)^{\frac{3}{2}}$	Power of a Product Prop. $= \boxed{27}^{\frac{2}{3}}\left(\boxed{x^{\frac{3}{4}}}\right)^{\frac{2}{3}}$
Simplify. $= \left(\dfrac{\boxed{y^{\frac{2}{3}}}}{16}\right)^{\frac{3}{2}}$	Power of a Power Prop. $= 27^{\frac{2}{3}}\left(x^{\boxed{\frac{3}{4}\cdot\frac{2}{3}}}\right)$
$\boxed{\text{Power of a Quotient}}$ Prop. $= \dfrac{\left(y^{\frac{2}{3}}\right)^{\frac{3}{2}}}{16^{\frac{3}{2}}}$	Simplify. $= \boxed{9x^{\frac{1}{2}}}$
$\boxed{\text{Power of a power}}$ Prop. $= \dfrac{y^{\frac{2}{3}\cdot\frac{3}{2}}}{16^{\frac{3}{2}}}$	
Simplify. $= \boxed{\dfrac{y}{64}}$	

Your Turn

Simplify the expression. Assume that all variables are positive. Exponents in simplified form should all be positive.

3. $\left(12^{\frac{2}{3}}\cdot 12^{\frac{4}{3}}\right)^{\frac{3}{2}}$ **4.** $\dfrac{\left(6x^{\frac{1}{3}}\right)^2}{x^{\frac{5}{3}}y}$

🔧 **Explain 2** ## Simplifying Radical Expressions Using the Properties of Exponents

When you are working with radical expressions involving nth roots, you can rewrite the expressions using rational exponents and then simplify them using the properties of exponents.

Example 2 Simplify the expression by writing it using rational exponents and then using the properties of rational exponents. Assume that all variables are positive. Exponents in simplified form should all be positive.

Ⓐ $x\left(\sqrt[3]{2y}\right)\left(\sqrt[3]{4x^2y^2}\right)$

Write using rational exponents.	$= x(2y)^{\frac{1}{3}}\left(4x^2y^2\right)^{\frac{1}{3}}$
Power of a Product Property	$= x\left(2y\cdot 4x^2y^2\right)^{\frac{1}{3}}$
Power of a Powers Property	$= x\left(8x^2y^3\right)^{\frac{1}{3}}$
Power of a Product Property	$= x\left(2x^{\frac{2}{3}}y\right)$
Power of Powers Property	$= 2x^{\frac{5}{3}}y$

© Houghton Mifflin Harcourt Publishing Company

Ⓑ $\dfrac{\sqrt{64y}}{\sqrt[3]{64y}}$

White using rational exponents. $= \dfrac{(64y)^{\frac{1}{2}}}{(64y)^{\frac{1}{3}}}$

Quotient of Powers Property $= (64y)^{\frac{1}{2} - \frac{1}{3}}$

Simplify. $= (64y)^{\boxed{\frac{1}{6}}}$

Power of a Product Property $= \boxed{64^{\frac{1}{6}} y^{\frac{1}{6}}}$

Simplify. $= \boxed{2y^{\frac{1}{6}}}$

Your Turn

5. $\dfrac{\sqrt{x^3}}{\sqrt[3]{x^2}}$

6. $\sqrt[5]{16^3} \cdot \sqrt[4]{4^5} \cdot \sqrt[3]{4^2}$

🎸 **Explain 3** **Simplifying Radical Expressions Using the Properties of nth Roots**

From working with square roots, you know, for example, that $\sqrt{8} \cdot \sqrt{2} = \sqrt{8 \cdot 2} = \sqrt{16} = 4$ and $\dfrac{\sqrt{8}}{\sqrt{2}} \cdot = \sqrt{\dfrac{8}{2}} = \sqrt{4} = 2$. The corresponding properties also apply to *n*th roots.

Properties of *n*th Roots		
For $a > 0$ and $b > 0$		
Words	**Numbers**	**Algebra**
Product of Property of Roots The *n*th root of a product is equal to the product of the *n*th roots.	$\sqrt[3]{16} = \sqrt[3]{8} \cdot \sqrt[3]{2} = 2\sqrt[3]{2}$	$\sqrt[n]{ab} = \sqrt[n]{a} \cdot \sqrt[n]{b}$
Quotient of Property of Roots The *n*th root of a Quotient is equal to the Quotient of the *n*th roots.	$\sqrt{\dfrac{25}{16}} = \dfrac{\sqrt{25}}{\sqrt{16}} = \dfrac{5}{4}$	$\sqrt[n]{\dfrac{a}{b}} = \dfrac{\sqrt[n]{a}}{\sqrt[n]{b}}$

Example 3 Simplify the expression using the properties of *n*th roots. Assume that all variables are positive. Rationalize any irrational denominators.

 $\sqrt[3]{256x^3y^7}$

$$\sqrt[3]{256x^3y^7}$$

Write 256 as a power. $= \sqrt[3]{2^8 \cdot x^3 y^7}$

Product Property of Roots $= \sqrt[3]{2^6 \cdot x^3 y^6} \cdot \sqrt[3]{2^2 \cdot y}$

Factor out perfect cubes. $= \sqrt[3]{2^6} \cdot \sqrt[3]{x^3} \cdot \sqrt[3]{y^6} \cdot \sqrt[3]{4y}$

Simplify. $= 4xy^2 \sqrt[3]{4y}$

(B) $\sqrt[4]{\dfrac{81}{x}}$

$$\sqrt[4]{\dfrac{81}{x}}$$

| Quotient Property of Roots | $= \sqrt[4]{\dfrac{81}{\sqrt[4]{x}}}$ |

Simplify. $= \dfrac{\boxed{3}}{\sqrt[4]{x}}$

Rationalize the denominator. $= \dfrac{3}{\sqrt[4]{x}} \cdot \dfrac{\boxed{\sqrt[4]{x^3}}}{\sqrt[4]{x^3}}$

| Product Property of Roots | $= \dfrac{3\sqrt[4]{x^3}}{\sqrt[4]{x^4}}$ |

Simplify. $= \boxed{\dfrac{3\sqrt[4]{x^3}}{x}}$

Reflect

7. In Part B, why was $\sqrt[4]{x^3}$ used when rationalizing the denominator? What factor would you use to rationalize a denominator of $\sqrt[5]{4y^3}$?

Your Turn

Simplify the expression using the properties of nth roots. Assume that all variables are positive.

8. $\sqrt[3]{216x^{12}y^{15}}$

9. $\sqrt[4]{\dfrac{16}{x^{14}}}$

⚙ Explain 4 Rewriting a Radical-Function Model

When you find or apply a function model involving rational powers or radicals, you can use the properties in this lesson to help you first find a simpler expression for the model.

(A) **Manufacturing** A can that is twice as tall as its radius has the minimum surface area for the volume it contains. The formula $S = 6\pi \left(\dfrac{V}{2\pi}\right)^{\frac{2}{3}}$ expresses the surface area of a can with this shape in terms of its volume.

  a. Use the properties of rational exponents to simplify the expression for the surface area. Then write the approximate model with the coefficient rounded to the nearest hundredth.

  b. Graph the model using a graphing calculator. What is the surface area in square centimeters for a can with a volume of 440 cm³?

a.

$$S = 6\pi \left(\frac{V}{2\pi}\right)^{\frac{2}{3}}$$

Power of a Quotient Property

$$= 6\pi \cdot \frac{V^{\frac{2}{3}}}{(2\pi)^{\frac{2}{3}}}$$

Group Powers of 2π.

$$= \frac{3(2\pi)}{(2\pi)^{\frac{2}{3}}} \cdot V^{\frac{2}{3}}$$

Quotient of Powers Property

$$= 3(2\pi)^{1-\frac{2}{3}} \cdot V^{\frac{2}{3}}$$

Simplify.

$$= 3(2\pi)^{\frac{1}{3}} \cdot V^{\frac{2}{3}}$$

Use a calculator.

$$\approx 5.54 V^{\frac{2}{3}}$$

A simplified model is $S = 3(2\pi)^{\frac{1}{3}} \cdot V^{\frac{2}{3}}$, which gives $S \approx 5.54 V^{\frac{2}{3}}$.

b.

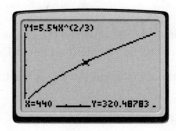

The surface area is about 320 cm².

B **Commercial fishing** The buoyancy of a fishing float in water depends on the volume of air it contains. The radius of a spherical float as a function of its volume is given by $r = \sqrt[3]{\frac{3V}{4\pi}}$.

a. Use the properties of roots to rewrite the expression for the radius as the product of a coefficient term and a variable term. Then write the approximate formula with the coefficient rounded to the nearest hundredth.

b. What should the radius be for a float that needs to contain 4.4 ft³ of air to have the proper buoyancy?

a.

$$r = \sqrt[3]{\frac{3V}{4\pi}}$$

Rewrite radicand.

$$= \sqrt[3]{\frac{3}{4\pi} \cdot \boxed{V}}$$

Product Property of Roots

$$= \sqrt[3]{\frac{3}{4\pi}} \cdot \boxed{\sqrt[3]{V}}$$

Use a calculator

$$\approx \boxed{0.62 \sqrt[3]{V}}$$

The rewritten formula is $r = \boxed{\sqrt[3]{\frac{3}{4\pi}} \cdot \sqrt[3]{V}}$, which gives $r \approx \boxed{0.62 \sqrt[3]{V}}$.

b.

Substitute 4.4 for V.

$$r = 0.62\sqrt[3]{4.4} \approx \boxed{1.02}$$

The radius is about 1.0 feet.

10. Discussion What are some reasons you might want to rewrite an expression involving radicals into an expression involving rational exponents?

11. The surface area as a function of volume for a box with a square base and a height that is twice the side length of the base is $S = 10\left(\dfrac{V}{2}\right)^{\frac{2}{3}}$. Use the properties of rational exponents to simplify the expression for the surface area so that no fractions are involved. Then write the approximate model with the coefficient rounded to the nearest hundredth.

💬 Elaborate

12. In problems with a radical in the denominator, you rationalized the denominator to remove the radical. What can you do to remove a rational exponent from the denominator? Explain by giving an example.

13. Show why $\sqrt[n]{a^n}$ is equal to a for all natural numbers a and n using the definition of nth roots and using rational exponents.

14. Show that the Product Property of Roots is true using rational exponents.

15. Essential Question Check-In Describe the difference between applying the Power of a Power Property and applying the Power of a Product Property for rational exponents using an example that involves both properties.

☆ Evaluate: Homework and Practice

Simplify the expression. Assume that all variables are positive. Exponents in simplified form should all be positive.

- Online Homework
- Hints and Help
- Extra Practice

1. $\left(\left(\dfrac{1}{16}\right)^{-\frac{2}{3}}\right)^{\frac{3}{4}}$

2. $\dfrac{x^{\frac{1}{3}} \cdot x^{\frac{5}{6}}}{x^{\frac{1}{6}}}$

3. $\dfrac{9^{\frac{3}{2}} \cdot 9^{\frac{1}{2}}}{9^{-2}}$

4. $\left(\dfrac{16^{\frac{5}{3}}}{16^{\frac{5}{6}}}\right)^{\frac{9}{5}}$

5. $\dfrac{2xy}{\left(x^{\frac{1}{3}}y^{\frac{2}{3}}\right)^{\frac{3}{2}}}$

6. $\dfrac{3y^{\frac{3}{4}}}{2xy^{\frac{3}{2}}}$

Simplify the expression by writing it using rational exponents and then using the properties of rational exponents. Assume that all variables are positive. Exponents in simplified form should all be positive.

7. $\sqrt[4]{25} \cdot \sqrt[3]{5}$

8. $\dfrac{\sqrt[4]{2^{-2}}}{\sqrt[9]{2^{-9}}}$

9. $\dfrac{\sqrt[4]{3^3} \cdot \sqrt[3]{x^2}}{\sqrt{3x}}$

10. $\dfrac{\sqrt[4]{x^4 y^6} \cdot \sqrt{x^6}}{y}$

11. $\dfrac{\sqrt[6]{s^4 t^9}}{\sqrt[3]{st}}$

12. $\sqrt[4]{27} \cdot \sqrt{3} \cdot \sqrt[6]{81^3}$

Simplify the expression using the properties of *n*th roots. Assume that all variables are positive. Rationalize any irrational denominators.

13. $\dfrac{\sqrt[4]{36} \cdot \sqrt[4]{216}}{\sqrt[4]{6}}$

14. $\sqrt[4]{4096 x^6 y^8}$

15. $\dfrac{\sqrt[3]{x^8 y^4}}{\sqrt[3]{x^2 y}}$

16. $\sqrt[5]{\dfrac{125}{w^6}} \cdot \sqrt[5]{25v}$

17. Weather The volume of a sphere as a function of its surface area is given by $V = \dfrac{4\pi}{3}\left(\dfrac{S}{4\pi}\right)^{\frac{3}{2}}$.

a. Use the properties of roots to rewrite the expression for the radius as the product of a simplified coefficient term (with positive exponents) and a variable term. Then write the approximate formula with the coefficient rounded to the nearest thousandth.

b. A spherical weather balloon has a surface area of 500 ft². What is the approximate volume of the balloon?

18. Amusement parks An amusement park has a ride with a free fall of 128 feet. The formula $t = \sqrt{\dfrac{2d}{g}}$ gives the time t in seconds it takes the ride to fall a distance of d feet. The formula $v = \sqrt{2gd}$ gives the velocity v in feet per second after the ride has fallen d feet. The letter g represents the gravitational constant.

a. Rewrite each formula so that the variable d is isolated. Then simplify each formula using the fact that $g \approx 32$ ft/s².

b. Find the time it takes the ride to fall halfway and its velocity at that time. Then find the time and velocity for the full drop.

c. What is the ratio of the time it takes for the whole drop to the time it takes for the first half? What is the ratio of the velocity after the second half of the drop to the velocity after the first half? What do you notice?

19. Which choice(s) is/are equivalent to $\sqrt{2}$?

A. $\left(\sqrt[8]{2}\right)^4$

B. $\dfrac{2^3}{2^{-\frac{5}{2}}}$

C. $\left(4^{\frac{2}{3}} \cdot 2^{\frac{2}{3}}\right)^{\frac{1}{4}}$

D. $\dfrac{\sqrt[3]{2^2}}{\sqrt[6]{2}}$

E. $\dfrac{\sqrt{2^{-\frac{3}{4}}}}{\sqrt{2^{-\frac{7}{4}}}}$

20. Home Heating A propane storage tank for a home is shaped like a cylinder with hemispherical ends, and a cylindrical portion length that is 4 times the radius.

The formula $S = 12\pi \left(\dfrac{3V}{16\pi}\right)^{\frac{2}{3}}$ expresses the surface area of a tank with this shape in terms of its volume.

a. Use the properties of rational exponents to rewrite the expression for the surface area so that the variable V is isolated. Then write the approximate model with the coefficient rounded to the nearest hundredth.

b. Graph the model using a graphing calculator. What is the surface area in square feet for a tank with a volume of 150 ft^3 ?

H.O.T. Focus on Higher Order Thinking

21. Critique Reasoning Aaron's work in simplifying an expression is shown. What mistake(s) did Aaron make? Show the correct simplification.

$$625^{-\frac{1}{3}} \div 625^{-\frac{4}{3}}$$
$$= 625^{-\frac{1}{3} - \left(-\frac{4}{3}\right)}$$
$$= 625^{-\frac{1}{3}\left(-\frac{3}{4}\right)}$$
$$= 625^{\frac{1}{4}}$$
$$= 5$$

22. Critical Thinking Use the definition of nth root to show that the Product Property of Roots is true, that is, that $\sqrt[n]{ab} = \sqrt[n]{a} \cdot \sqrt[n]{b}$. (Hint: Begin by letting x be the nth root of a and letting y be the nth root of b.)

23. Critical Thinking For what real values of a is $\sqrt[4]{a}$ greater than a? For what real values of a is $\sqrt[5]{a}$ greater than a?

Lesson Performance Task

You've been asked to help decorate for a school dance, and the theme chosen is "The Solar System." The plan is to have a bunch of papier-mâché spheres serve as models of the planets, and your job is to paint them. All you're told are the volumes of the individual spheres, but you need to know their surface areas so you can get be sure to get enough paint. How can you write a simplified equation using rational exponents for the surface area of a sphere in terms of its volume?

(The formula for the volume of a sphere is $V = \frac{4}{3}\pi r^3$ and the formula for the surface area of a sphere is $A = 4\pi r^2$.)

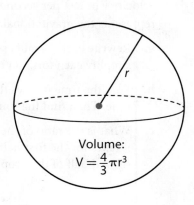

Volume:
$V = \frac{4}{3}\pi r^3$

12.3 Solving Radical Equations

Essential Question: How can you solve equations involving square roots and cube roots?

 TEKS **A2.4.F** Solve…square root equations. Also A2.4.G, A2.6.B, A2.7.H

 Explore   **Investigating Solutions of Square Root Equations**

When solving quadratic equations, you have learned that the number of real solutions depends upon the values in the equation, with different equations having 0, 1, or 2 real solutions. How many real solutions does a square root equation have? In the Explore, you will investigate graphically the numbers of real solutions for different square root equations.

(A)   Remember that you can graph the two sides of an equation as separate functions to find solutions of the equation: a solution is any x-value where the two graphs intersect.

The graph of $y = \sqrt{x - 3}$ is shown on a calculator window of $-4 \leq x \leq 16$ and $-2 \leq y \leq 8$. Reproduce the graph on your calculator. Then add the graph of $y = 2$.

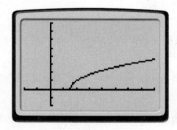

How many solutions does the equation $\sqrt{x - 3} = 2$ have? [ ] How do you know?

On your calculator, replace the graph of $y = 2$ with the graph of $y = -1$.

How many solutions does the equation $\sqrt{x - 3} = -1$ have? [ ] How do you know?

(B)   Graph $y = \sqrt{x - 3} + 2$ on your calculator (you can use the same viewing window as in Step A).

Add the graph of $y = 3$ to the graph of $y = \sqrt{x - 3} + 2$.

How many solutions does $\sqrt{x - 3} + 2 = 3$ have? [ ]

Replace the graph of $y = 3$ with the graph of $y = 1$.

How many solutions does $\sqrt{x - 3} + 2 = 1$ have? [ ]

(C) Graph both sides of $\sqrt{4x-4} = x + 1$ as separate functions on your calculator.

How many solutions does $\sqrt{4x-4} = x + 1$ have?

Replace the graph of $y = x + 1$ with the graph of $y = \frac{1}{2}x$.

How many solutions does $\sqrt{4x-4} = \frac{1}{2}x$ have?

Replace the graph of $y = \frac{1}{2}x$ with the graph of $y = 2x - 5$.

How many solutions does $\sqrt{4x-4} = 2x - 5$ have?

(D) Graph both sides of $\sqrt{2x-3} = \sqrt{x}$ as separate functions on your calculator.

How many solutions does $\sqrt{2x-3} = \sqrt{x}$ have?

Replace the graph of $y = \sqrt{x}$ with the graph of $y = \sqrt{2x+3}$.

How many solutions does $\sqrt{2x-3} = \sqrt{2x+3}$ have?

Reflect

1. For a square root equation of the form $\sqrt{bx-h} = c$, what can you conclude about the number of solutions based on the sign of c?

2. For a square root equation of the form $\sqrt{bx-h} + k = c$, what can you conclude about the number of solutions based on the values of k and c?

3. For a cube root equation of the form $\sqrt[3]{bx-h} = c$, will the number of solutions depend on the sign of c? Explain.

4. The graphs in the second part of Step D appear to be get closer and closer as x increases. How can you be sure that they never meet, that is, that $\sqrt{2x-3} = \sqrt{2x+3}$ really has no solutions?

⊘ Explain 1 Solving Square Root and $\frac{1}{2}$-Power Equations

A *radical equation* contains a variable within a radical or a variable raised to a (non-integer) rational power. To solve a square root equation, or, equivalently, an equation involving the power $\frac{1}{2}$, you can square both sides of the equation and solve the resulting equation.

Because opposite numbers have the same square, squaring both sides of an equation may introduce an apparent solution that is not an actual solution (an extraneous solution). For example, while the only solution of $x = 2$ is 2, the equation that is the square of each side, $x^2 = 4$, has two solutions, -2 and 2. But -2 is not a solution of the original equation.

© Houghton Mifflin Harcourt Publishing Company

Example 1 Solve the equation. Check for extraneous solutions.

(A) $2 + \sqrt{x + 10} = x$

$$2 + \sqrt{x + 10} = x$$

Isolate the radical. $\sqrt{x + 10} = x - 2$

Square both sides. $\left(\sqrt{x + 10}\right)^2 = (x - 2)^2$

Simplify. $x + 10 = x^2 - 4x + 4$

Simplify. $0 = x^2 - 5x - 6$

Factor. $0 = (x - 6)(x + 1)$

Zero Product Property $x = 6 \text{ or } x = -1$

Check:

$2 + \sqrt{x + 10} = x$ $2 + \sqrt{x + 10} = x$

$2 + \sqrt{6 + 10} \stackrel{?}{=} x$ $2 + \sqrt{-1 + 10} \stackrel{?}{=} -1$

$2 + \sqrt{16} \stackrel{?}{=} 6$ $2 + \sqrt{9} \stackrel{?}{=} -1$

$6 = 6 \checkmark$ $5 \neq -1 \checkmark$

$x = 6$ is a solution. $x = -1$ is not a solution.

The solution is $x = 6$.

(B) $(x + 6)^{\frac{1}{2}} - (2x - 4)^{\frac{1}{2}} = 0$

Rewrite with radicals. $\sqrt{x + 6} - \sqrt{2x - 4} = 0$

Isolate radicals on each side. $\sqrt{x + 6} = \boxed{\sqrt{2x - 4}}$

Square both sides. $\left(\sqrt{x + 6}\right)^2 = \left(\boxed{\sqrt{2x - 4}}\right)$

Simplify. $\boxed{x + 6} = \boxed{2x - 4}$

Solve. $\boxed{10} = x$

Check:

$$\sqrt{x + 6} - \sqrt{2x - 4} = 0$$

$$\sqrt{10 + 6} - \sqrt{2\boxed{10} - 4} \stackrel{?}{=} 0$$

$$\boxed{\sqrt{16}} - \boxed{\sqrt{16}} \stackrel{?}{=} 0$$

$$\boxed{0} = 0$$

The solution is $x = 10$.

5. Graph the solution from Part A on a graphing calculator. How can you tell from the graph that there is an extraneous solution?

6. Solve $(x + 5)^{\frac{1}{2}} - 2 = 1$.

⚿ Explain 2 Solving Cube Root and $\frac{1}{3}$-Power Equations

You can solve radical equations that involve roots other than square roots by raising both sides to the index of the radical. So, to solve a cube root equation, or, equivalently, an equation involving the power $\frac{1}{3}$, you can cube both sides of the equation and solve the resulting equation.

Example 2 Solve the equation.

(A) $\sqrt[3]{x + 2} + 7 = 5$

$$\sqrt[3]{x + 2} + 7 = 5$$

Isolate the radical. $\sqrt[3]{x + 2} = -2$

Cube both sides. $\left(\sqrt[3]{x + 2}\right)^3 = (-2)^3$

Simplify. $x + 2 = -8$

Solve for x $x = -10$

The solution is $x = -10$.

(B) $\sqrt[3]{x - 5} = x + 1$

$$\sqrt[3]{x - 5} = x + 1$$

Cube both sides. $\left(\sqrt[3]{x - 5}\right)^3 = (x + 1)^3$

Simplify $\boxed{x - 5} = \boxed{x^3 + 3x^2 + 3x + 1}$

Simplify. $0 = \boxed{x^3 + 3x^2 + 2x + 6}$

Begin to factor by grouping. $0 = x^2 \left(\boxed{x + 3}\right) + 2 \left(\boxed{x + 3}\right)$

Complete factoring $0 = (x^2 + 2)\left(\boxed{x + 3}\right)$

By the Zero Product Property, $\boxed{x^2 + 2} = 0$ or $\boxed{x + 3} = 0$.

Because there are no values of x for which $x^2 = \boxed{-2}$, the only solution is $\boxed{x = -3}$.

7. **Discussion** Part A shows checking for extraneous solutions, while Part B does not. While it is always wise to check your answers, can a cubic equation have an extraneous solution? Explain your answer.

8. Solve $2(x - 50)^{\frac{1}{3}} = -10$.

Explain 3   Solving a Real-World Problem

Ⓐ **Driving** The speed s in miles per hour that a car is traveling when it goes into a skid can be estimated by using the formula $s = \sqrt{30fd}$, where f is the coefficient of friction and d is the length of the skid marks in feet.

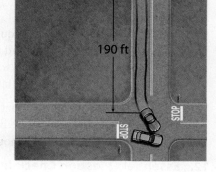

After an accident, a driver claims to have been traveling the speed limit of 55 mi/h. The coefficient of friction under the conditions at the time of the accident was 0.6, and the length of the skid marks is 190 feet. Is the driver telling the truth about the car's speed? Explain.

Use the formula to find the length of a skid at a speed of 55 mi/h. Compare this distance to the actual skid length of 190 feet.

$$s = \sqrt{30fd}$$

Substitute 55 for s and 0.6 for f $55 = \sqrt{30(0.6)d}$

Simplify. $55 = \sqrt{18d}$

Square both sides. $55^2 = \left(\sqrt{18d}\right)^2$

Simplify. $3025 = 18d$

Solve for d. $168 \approx d$

If the driver had been traveling at 55 mi/h, the skid marks would measure about 168 feet. Because the skid marks actually measure 190 feet, the driver must have been driving faster than 55 mi/h.

Ⓑ **Construction** The diameter d in inches of a rope needed to lift a weight of w tons is given by the formula $d = \frac{\sqrt{15w}}{\pi}$. How much weight can be lifted with a rope with a diameter of 1.0 inch?

Use the formula for the diameter as a function of weight, and solve for the weight given the diameter.

$$d = \frac{\sqrt{15w}}{\pi}$$

Substitute. $\boxed{1.0} = \frac{\sqrt{15w}}{\pi}$

Square both sides. $\boxed{\pi} = \boxed{\sqrt{15w}}$

Isolate the radical. $\left(\boxed{\pi}\right)^2 = \left(\sqrt{15w}\right)^2$

Simplify. $\boxed{\pi^2} = 15w$

Solve for w. $\boxed{0.66} \approx w$

A rope with a diameter of 1.0 can hold about 0.66 ton, or about 1300 pounds.

9. **Biology** The trunk length (in inches) of a male elephant can be modeled by $l = 23\sqrt[3]{t} + 17$, where t is the age of the elephant in years. If a male elephant has a trunk length of 100 inches, about what is his age?

💬 Elaborate

10. A student asked to solve the equation $\sqrt{4x + 8} + 9 = 1$ isolated the radical, squared both sides, and solved for x to obtain $x = 14$, only to find out that the apparent solution was extraneous. Why could the student have stopped trying to solve the equation after isolating the radical?

11. When you see a cube root equation with the radical expression isolated on one side and a constant on the other, what should you expect for the number of solutions? Explain. What are some reasons you should check your answer anyway?

12. **Essential Question Check-In** Solving a quadratic equation of the form $x^2 = a$ involves taking the square root of both sides. Solving a square root equation of the form $\sqrt{x} = b$ involves squaring both sides of the equation. Which of these operations can create an equation that is not equivalent to the original equation? Explain how this affects the solution process.

⭐ Evaluate: Homework and Practice

- Online Homework
- Hints and Help
- Extra Practice

Solve the equation.

1. $\sqrt{x - 9} = 5$

2. $\sqrt{3x} = 6$

3. $\sqrt{x + 3} = x + 1$

4. $\sqrt{(15x + 10)} = 2x + 3$

5. $(x + 4)^{\frac{1}{2}} = 6$

6. $(45 - 9x)^{\frac{1}{2}} = x - 5$

7. $(x - 6)^{\frac{1}{2}} = x - 2$

8. $4(x - 2)^{\frac{1}{2}} = (x + 13)^{\frac{1}{2}}$

9. $5 - \sqrt[3]{x-4} = 2$

10. $2\sqrt[3]{3x + 2} = \sqrt[3]{4x - 9}$

11. $\sqrt[3]{69x + 35} = x + 5$

12. $\sqrt[3]{x + 5} = x - 1$

13. $(x + 7)^{\frac{1}{3}} = (4x)^{\frac{1}{3}}$

14. $(5x + 1)^{\frac{1}{4}} = 4$

15. $(-9x - 54)^{\frac{1}{3}} = -2x + 3$

16. $2(x - 1)^{\frac{1}{5}} = (2x - 17)^{\frac{1}{5}}$

17. **Driving** The formula for the speed versus skid length in Example 3A assumes that all 4 wheel brakes are working at top efficiency. If this is not true, another parameter is included in the equation so that the equation becomes $s = \sqrt{30fdn}$ where n is the percent braking efficiency as a decimal. Accident investigators know that the rear brakes failed on a car, reducing its braking efficiency to 60%. On a dry road with a coefficient of friction of 0.7, the car skidded 250 feet. Was the car going above the speed limit of 60 mi/h when the skid began?

18. **Anatomy** The surface area S of a human body in square meters can be approximated by $S = \sqrt{\frac{hm}{36}}$ where h is height in meters and m is mass in kilograms. A basketball player with a height of 2.1 meters has a surface area of about 2.7 m^2. What is the player's mass?

19. **Biology** The approximate antler length L (in inches) of a deer buck can be modeled by $L = 9\sqrt[3]{t} + 15$ where t is the age in years of the buck. If a buck has an antler length of 36 inches, what is its age?

20. **Amusement Parks** For a spinning amusement park ride, the velocity v in meters per second of a car moving around a curve with radius r meters is given by $v = \sqrt{ar}$ where a is the car's acceleration in m/s². If the ride has a maximum acceleration of 30 m/s² and the cars on the ride have a maximum velocity of 12 m/s, what is the smallest radius that any curve on the ride may have?

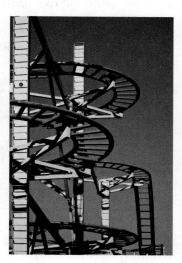

21. For each radical equation, state the number of solutions that exist.

A. $\sqrt{x-4} = -5$

B. $\sqrt{x-4} + 6 = 11$

C. $4 = -2\sqrt[3]{x+2}$

D. $\sqrt{x+40} = 0$

E. $\sqrt[3]{2x+5} = -18$

22. **Critical Thinking** For an equation of the form $\sqrt{x + a} = b$ where b is a constant, does the sign of a affect whether or not there is a solution for a given value of b? If so, how? If not, why not?

23. **Explain the Error** Below is a student's work in solving the equation $2\sqrt{3x + 3} = 12$. What mistake did the student make? What is the correct solution?

$$2\sqrt{3x + 3} = 12$$

$$2\left(\sqrt{3x + 3}\right)^2 = 12^2$$

$$2(3x + 3) = 144$$

$$6x + 6 = 144$$

$$x = 23$$

24. **Communicate Mathematical Ideas** Describe the key difference between solving radical equations for which you solve by raising both sides to an even power and those you solve by raising both sides to an odd power.

25. **Critical Thinking** How could you solve an equation for which one side is a rational power radical expression and the other side is a constant? Give an example. Under what condition would you have to be especially careful to check your solutions?

Lesson Performance Task

For many years scientists have used a scale known as the Fujita Scale to categorize different types of tornados in relation to the velocity of the winds produced. The formula used to generate the scale is given by $V = k(F + 2)^{\frac{3}{2}}$. The scale employs a constant, k, and the tornado's category number to determine wind speed. If you wanted to determine the different category numbers, how could you solve the radical equation for the variable F? (The value for k is about 14.1.)

Copy and complete the table. Solve the equation for F then verify the different categories using the minimum wind velocity. Do the values seem reasonable given the value for k?

Fujita Tornado Scale			
Damage Level	**Category**	**Minimum Wind Velocity (mi/h)**	**Calculations**
Moderate	F1	73	
Significant	F2	113	
Severe	F3	158	
Devastating	F4	207	
Incredible	F5	261	

Radical Expressions and Equations

Essential Question: How can you use radical expressions and equations to solve real-world problems?

Key Vocabulary

extraneous solution
(*solución extraña*)
radical expression
(*expresión radical*)
rational exponent
(*exponente racional*)

KEY EXAMPLE   (Lesson 12.1)

Evaluate the expression.

$$\left(\sqrt[4]{16}\right)^5 = 2^5 = 32$$
$$27^{\frac{4}{3}} = \left(\sqrt[3]{27}\right)^4 = 3^4 = 81$$

KEY EXAMPLE   (Lesson 12.2)

Write the expression in simplest form. Assume all variables are positive.

$$\sqrt[3]{48} = \sqrt[3]{8 \cdot 6} = \sqrt[3]{8} \cdot \sqrt[3]{6} = 2\sqrt[3]{6}$$
$$\left(\frac{x^4}{y^8}\right)^{\frac{1}{2}} = \frac{\left(x^4\right)^{\frac{1}{2}}}{\left(y^8\right)^{\frac{1}{2}}} = \frac{x^{4 \cdot \frac{1}{2}}}{y^{8 \cdot \frac{1}{2}}} = \frac{x^2}{y^4}$$

KEY EXAMPLE   (Lesson 12.3)

Solve the equation. $\sqrt{x + 15} = x - 5$

$\left(\sqrt{x + 15}\right)^2 = (x - 5)^2$	Square both sides.
$x + 15 = x^2 - 10x + 25$	
$x^2 - 11x + 10 = 0$	Write in standard form.
$(x - 10)(x - 1) = 0$	Factor.
$x = 10 \text{ or } x = 1$	Solve for x.
$\sqrt{10 + 15} \stackrel{?}{=} 10 - 5 \quad \sqrt{1 + 15} \stackrel{?}{=} 1 - 5$	Check.
$5 = 5 \qquad\qquad 4 \neq -4$	

The solution $x = 1$ is extraneous. The only solution is $x = 10$.

EXERCISES

Evaluate the expression. *(Lesson 12.1)*

1. $\sqrt[3]{-64}$

2. $81^{\frac{1}{4}}$

3. $256^{\frac{3}{4}}$

Write the expression in simplest form. Assume that all variables are positive. *(Lesson 12.2)*

4. $\sqrt[3]{80}$

5. $\left(3^4 \cdot 5^4\right)^{-\frac{1}{4}}$

6. $\left(25a^{10}b^{16}\right)^{\frac{1}{2}}$

7. $\sqrt[5]{\dfrac{c}{d^8}}$

Solve each equation. *(Lesson 12.3)*

8. $\sqrt[3]{5x-4} = 2$

9. $\sqrt{x+6} - 7 = -2$

MODULE PERFORMANCE TASK

Don't Disturb the Neighbors!

The faintest sound an average person can detect has an intensity of 1×10^{-12} watts per square meter, where watts are a unit of power. The intensity of a sound is given by $l = \dfrac{P}{4\pi d^2}$, where P is the power of the sound and d is the distance from the source. Yolanda wants to throw a party at her house and plans to invite a band to perform. The power of the sound from the band's speakers is typically 3.0 watts. Yolanda's neighborhood has a rule that between 7 p.m. and 11 p.m., a sound intensity up to $l = 5.0 \times 10^{-5}$ W/m² is acceptable; after 11 p.m., the acceptable intensity is $l = 5.0 \times 10^{-7}$ W/m². How far away would Yolanda's closest neighbors need to be for the band to play till 11 p.m.? How far would they need to be for the band to play all night?

Start by listing the information you will need to solve the problem. Then complete the task. Be sure to write down all your data and assumptions. Then use graphs, numbers, words, or algebra to explain how you reached your conclusion.

(Ready) to Go On?

12.1–12.3 Radical Expressions and Equations

- Online Homework
- Hints and Help
- Extra Practice

Simplify each expression. Assume that all variables are positive. *(Lessons 12.1, 12.2)*

1. $32^{\frac{1}{5}}$

2. $\left(\sqrt[3]{64}\right)^4$

3. $\sqrt[3]{27x^6}$

4. $\sqrt[4]{2x^6y^8}$

Solve each equation. *(Lesson 12.3)*

5. $\sqrt{10x} = 3\sqrt{x+1}$

6. $\sqrt[3]{2x-2} = 6$

7. $(4x+7)^{\frac{1}{2}} = 3$

8. $(x+3)^{\frac{1}{3}} = -6$

ESSENTIAL QUESTION

9. How do you solve a radical equation and identify any extraneous roots?

Assessment Readiness

1. Which expression can be simplified to a rational number?

   A. $\sqrt{2} + \sqrt{2}$

   B. $\sqrt{4} \cdot \sqrt{20}$

   C. $(\sqrt{12})^2$

   D. $\sqrt{\dfrac{16}{2}}$

2. What is the solution of the equation $(3x + 1)^{\frac{1}{3}} = -2$?

   A. -9

   B. -3

   C. 3

   D. 9

3. Which is equivalent to $(4 - 3i)(2 - i)$?

   A. $5 - 10i$

   B. $5 + 10i$

   C. $8 - 10i$

   D. $8 + 10i$

4. At what point does the graph of $f(x) = \dfrac{2x^2 - 5x - 3}{x - 3}$ have a hole?

   A. $(-0.5, 0)$

   B. $(-0.5, -3.5)$

   C. $(3, 0)$

   D. $(3, 7)$

5. The formula $S = \sqrt{\dfrac{A}{4.828}}$ can be used to approximate the side length s of a regular octagon with area A. A stop sign is shaped like a regular octagon with a side length of 12.4 in. To the nearest square inch, what is the area of the stop sign? Explain how you got your answer.

Assessment Readiness

Personal **Math Trainer**
• Online Homework
• Hints and Help
• Extra Practice

1. How is the graph of $g(x) = \frac{1}{3}\sqrt{x-1}$ related to the graph of $f(x) = \sqrt{x}$? Select the correct statement.

   A. A vertical stretching by a factor of 3 and a translation 1 unit right

   B. A vertical compression by a factor of $\frac{1}{3}$ and a translation 1 unit up

   C. A vertical compression by a factor of $\frac{1}{3}$ and a translation 1 unit right

   D. A vertical compression by a factor of $\frac{1}{3}$ and a translation 1 unit left

2. Which function represents the transformation of the graph of $f(x) = \sqrt[3]{x}$ by a vertical stretch by a factor of 5 and a translation 1 unit left and 2 units down. Select the correct answer.

   A. $g(x) = 2\sqrt[3]{x+1} - 5$

   B. $g(x) = \frac{1}{5}\sqrt[3]{x+1} - 2$

   C. $g(x) = 5\sqrt[3]{x-1} + 2$

   D. $g(x) = 5\sqrt[3]{x+1} - 2$

3. What is the inverse of $f(x) = \frac{1}{2}x^3 + 5$ Select the correct answer.

   A. $f^{-1}(x) = \sqrt[3]{2(x-5)}$

   B. $f^{-1}(x) = \sqrt[3]{\frac{1}{2}(x-5)}$

   C. $f^{-1}(x) = \sqrt[3]{2(x+5)}$

   D. $f^{-1}(x) = \sqrt[3]{2x} - 10$

4. Which expression can be simplified to 25? Select the correct answer.

   A. $\left(\sqrt[2]{125}\right)^3$

   B. $\left(\sqrt[3]{125}\right)^2$

   C. $\left(\sqrt{125}\right)^{\frac{1}{3}}$

   D. $\sqrt[3]{125}$

5. Which expression can be simplified to $\frac{2x^2}{\sqrt[3]{y}}$? Assume that all variables are positive. Select the correct answer.

   A. $\sqrt[3]{\frac{8x^6}{y}}$

   B. $\sqrt[2]{\frac{8x^6}{y^3}}$

   C. $\sqrt[3]{\frac{6x^6}{y}}$

   D. $\sqrt[3]{\frac{8x^9}{3y}}$

6. A company produces canned tomatoes. They want the height h of each can to be twice the diameter d. Write an equation for the surface area A of the can in terms of the radius r. If the company wants to use no more than 90 square inches of metal for each can, what is the maximum radius of the can they will produce? *(Lesson 11.1)*

7. The period T of a pendulum in seconds is given by $T = 2\pi\sqrt{\frac{L}{9.81}}$, where L is the length of the pendulum in meters. If you want to use a pendulum as a clock, with a period of 2 seconds, how long should the pendulum be? *(Lesson 12.3)*

Performance Tasks

★ **8.** The formula $P = 73.3\sqrt[4]{m^3}$, known as Kleiber's law, relates the metabolism rate P of an organism in Calories per day and the body mass m of the organism in kilograms. The table shows the typical body mass of several members of the cat family.

Typical Body Mass	
Animal	**Mass(kg)**
House cat	4.5
Cheetah	55.0
Lion	170.0

  A. What is the metabolism rate of a cheetah to the nearest Calorie per day?

  B. Approximately how many more Calories of food does a lion need to consume each day than a house cat does?

★★ **9.** On a clear day, the approximate distance d in miles that a person can see is given by $d = 1.2116\sqrt{h}$, where h is the person's height in feet above the ocean.

  A. To the nearest tenth of a mile, how far can the captain on a clipper ship 15 feet above the ocean see?

  B. How much farther, to the nearest tenth of a mile, will a sailor at the top of a mast 120 feet above the ocean be able to see than will the captain?

  C. A pirate ship is approaching the clipper ship at a relative speed of 10 miles per hour. Approximately how many minutes sooner will the sailor be able to see the pirate ship than will the captain?

★★★**10.** The time it takes a pendulum to make one complete swing back and forth depends on its string length, as shown in the table.

String Length (m)	2	4	6	8	10
Time (s)	2.8	4.0	4.9	5.7	6.3

A. Graph the relationship between string length and time, and identify the parent function which best describes the data.

B. The function $T(x) = 2\pi\sqrt{\frac{x}{9.8}}$ gives the period in seconds of a pendulum of length x. The period of a pendulum is the time it takes the pendulum to complete one back-and-forth swing. Describe the graph of T as a transformation of $f(x) = \sqrt{x}$.

C. By what factor must the length of a pendulum be increased to double its period?

Nutritionist Body mass index (BMI) is a measure used to determine healthy body mass based on a person's height. BMI is calculated by dividing a person's mass in kilograms by the square of his or her height in meters. The median BMI measures for a group of boys, ages 2 to 10 years are given in the chart below.

Age of Boys	2	3	4	5	6	7	8	9	10
Median BMI	16.6	16.0	15.6	15.4	15.4	15.5	15.8	16.2	16.6

a. Create a scatter plot for the data in the table, treating age as the independent variable x and median BMI as the dependent variable y.

b. Use a calculator to find a quadratic regression model for the data. What is your model?

c. Give the domain of $f(x)$ based on the data set. Because $f(x)$ is quadratic, it is not one-to-one and its inverse is not a function. Restrict the domain of $f(x)$ to values of x for which $f(x)$ is increasing so that its inverse will be a function. What is the restricted domain of $f(x)$?

d. Find and graph the inverse of $f(x)$. What does $f^{-1}(x)$ model?

UNIT 6

Exponential and Logarithmic Functions and Equations

MODULE 13

Exponential Functions

TEKS A2.2.A, A2.5.A, A2.5.B

MODULE 14

Modeling with Exponential and Other Functions

TEKS A2.8.A, A2.8.B, A2.8.C

MODULE 15

Logarithmic Functions

TEKS A2.2.A, A2.2.B, A2.2.C, A2.5.A, A2.5.B, A2.5.C, A2.7.I

MODULE 16

Logarithmic Properties and Exponential and Logarithmic Equations

TEKS A2.5.B, A2.5.C, A2.5.D

MATH IN CAREERS

Nuclear Medicine Technologist
Nuclear medicine technologists use technology to create images, or *scans*, of parts of a patient's body. They must understand the mathematics of exponential decay of radioactive materials. Nuclear medicine technologists analyze data from the scan, which are presented to a specialist for diagnosis.

If you are interested in a career as a nuclear medicine technologist, you should study these mathematical subjects:
- Algebra
- Statistics
- Calculus

Check out the career activity at the end of the unit to find out how **Nuclear Medicine Technologists** use math.

Reading Start-Up

Vocabulary

Review Words

asymptote
(asíntota)

inverse function
(función inversa)

✔ translation
(traslación)

✔ vertical compression
(compresión vertical)

✔ vertical stretch
(estiramiento vertical)

Preview Words

explicit formula
(fórmula explícita)

geometric sequence
(sucesión geométrica)

logarithmic function
(función logarítmica)

recursive formula
(fórmula recurrente)

Visualize Vocabulary

Use the ✓ words. Copy and complete the graphic.

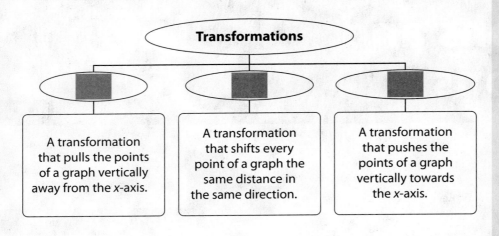

Transformations

A transformation that pulls the points of a graph vertically away from the *x*-axis.

A transformation that shifts every point of a graph the same distance in the same direction.

A transformation that pushes the points of a graph vertically towards the *x*-axis.

Understand Vocabulary

To become familiar with some of the vocabulary terms in the module, consider the following. You may refer to the module, the glossary, or a dictionary.

1. A sequence in which the ratio of successive terms is a constant r, where $r \neq 0$ or 1 , is a ___?___.

2. A ___?___ is a rule for a sequence in which one or more previous terms are used to generate the next term.

3. A ___?___ is the inverse of an exponential function.

Active Reading

Booklet Before beginning the unit, create a booklet to help you organize what you learn. Each page of the booklet should correspond to a lesson in the unit and summarize the most important information form the lesson. Include definitions, examples, and graphs to help you recall the main elements of the lesson. Highlight the main idea and use colored pencils to help you illustrate any important concepts or differences.

Exponential Functions

© Houghton Mifflin Harcourt Publishing Company • Image Credits: ©Adam Hart-Davis/Science Photo Library

Essential Question: How can you use exponential functions to solve real-world problems?

REAL WORLD VIDEO
Check out how exponential functions can be used to model the path of a bouncing ball and other real-world patterns.

MODULE PERFORMANCE TASK PREVIEW
That's the Way the Ball Bounces

The height that a ball reaches after bouncing off a hard surface depends on several factors, including the height from which the ball was dropped and the material the ball is made of. The height of each successive bounce will be less than the previous bounce. How can mathematical modeling be used to represent a bouncing ball? Let's find out!

Are (YOU) Ready?

Complete these exercises to review skills you will need for this chapter.

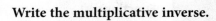

- Online Homework
- Hints and Help
- Extra Practice

Real Numbers

Example 1 Write the multiplicative inverse of 0.3125.

$$0.3125 = \frac{3125}{10,000}$$ Write the decimal as a fraction.

$$= \frac{5}{16} \rightarrow \frac{16}{5}$$ Simplify, then take the reciprocal.

The multiplicative inverse of 0.3125 is $\frac{16}{5}$.

Write the multiplicative inverse.

1. 1.125

2. -0.6875

3. 0.444

Exponential Functions

Example 2 Evaluate $12(1.5)^{x-5}$ for $x = 8$.

$12(1.5)^{8-5}$ Substitute.

$12(1.5)^3$ Simplify.

$12(3.375) = 40.5$ Evaluate the exponent. Multiply.

Evaluate each expression.

4. $30(1.1)^{5x}$; $x = 0.4$

5. $8(2.5)^{\frac{x}{3}}$; $x = 12$

6. $2(x)^{2x+9}$; $x = -3$

Geometric Sequences

Example 3 List the first four terms of the sequence if $t_1 = 2$ and $t_n = -3t_{n-1}$.

$t_2 = -3t_{2-1} = -3t_1 = -3 \cdot 2 = -6$ Find the second term.

$t_3 = -3t_{3-1} = -3t_2 = -3 \cdot (-6) = 18$ Find the third term.

$t_4 = -3t_{4-1} = -3t_3 = -3 \cdot 18 = -54$ Find the fourth term.

The first four terms are 2, –6, 18, and –54.

List the first four terms of the sequence.

7. $t_1 = 0.02$

$t_n = 5t_{n-1}$

8. $t_1 = 3$

$t_n = 0.5t_{n-1}$

13.1 Geometric Sequences

Essential Question: How can you define a geometric sequence algebraically?

 TEKS **A2.5.B** Formulate exponential ... equations that model real-world situations, including exponential relationships written in recursive notation. Also A2.5.A, A2.7.I

Resource Locker

⊘ Explore   Investigating Geometric Sequences

As a tree grows, limbs branch off of the trunk, then smaller limbs branch off these limbs and each branch splits off into smaller and smaller copies of itself the same way throughout the entire tree. A mathematical object called a *fractal tree* resembles this growth.

Start by drawing a vertical line at the bottom of a piece of paper. This is Stage 0 of the fractal tree and is considered to be one 'branch'. The length of this branch defines 1 unit.

For Stage 1, draw 2 branches off of the top of the first branch. For this fractal tree, each smaller branch is $\frac{1}{2}$ the length of the previous branch and is at a 45-degree angle from the direction of the parent branch. The first four iterations, Stages 0-3, are shown.

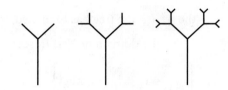

Ⓐ In Stage 2, there are 2 branches drawn on the end of each of the 2 branches drawn in Stage 1. There are ⬛ new branches in Stage 2. Each one of these branches will be $\frac{1}{2}$ the length of its predecessors or ⬛ unit in length.

Ⓑ For Stage 3, there are 8 new branches in total. To draw Stage 4, a total of ⬛ branches must be drawn and to draw Stage 5, a total of ⬛ branches must be drawn. Thus, each stage adds ⬛ times as many branches as the previous stage did.

Ⓒ Copy and complete the table.

Stage	New Branches	Pattern	New Branches as a Power
Stage 0	1	1	2^0
Stage 1	2	$2 \cdot 1$	2^1
Stage 2	4	$2 \cdot 2$	2^2
Stage 3	8	$2 \cdot$ ⬛	⬛
Stage 4	16	$2 \cdot$ ⬛	⬛
Stage 5	32	$2 \cdot$ ⬛	⬛
Stage 6	64	$2 \cdot$ ⬛	⬛

Ⓓ The procedure for each stage after Stage 0 is to draw 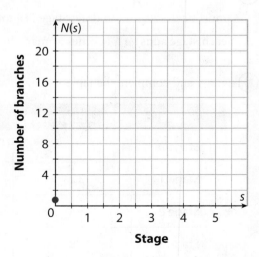 branches on 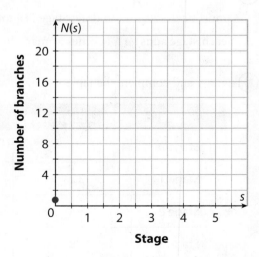 branch added in the previous step.

Ⓔ Using the description above, write an equation for the number of new branches in a stage given the previous stage. Represent stage s as N_s; Stage 3 will be N_3.

$N_4 = $ ⬛ · ⬛ $N_6 = $ ⬛ · ⬛

$N_5 = $ ⬛ · ⬛ $N_s = $ ⬛ · ⬛

Ⓕ Rewrite the rule for Stage s as a function $N(s)$ that has a stage number as an input and the number of new branches in the stage as an output.

$N(s) = $ ⬛

Ⓖ Recall that the domain of a function is the set of all numbers for which the function is defined. $N(s)$ is a function of s and s is the stage number. Since the stage number refers to the ⬛ the tree has branched, it has to be ⬛.
Write the domain of $N(s)$ in set notation.

$$\left\{ s \mid s \text{ is a } \boxed{} \text{ number} \right\}$$

Ⓗ Similarly, the range of a function is the set of all possible values that the function can output over the domain. Let $N(s) = b$, the ⬛.

The range of $N(s)$ is $\left\{ 1, 2, 4 \boxed{}, \boxed{}, \boxed{}, \ldots \right\}$.

The range of $N(s)$ is $\left\{ N \mid N = 2^n, \text{ where } n \text{ is } \boxed{} \right\}$.

Ⓘ Copy and complete the graph shown. Graph the first five values of $N(s)$.

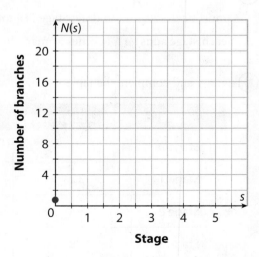

Ⓙ As s increases, $N(s)$ ⬛.

$N(s)$ is ⬛ function.

(K) Copy and complete the table for branch length.

(L) Write $L(s)$ expressing the branch length as a function of the Stage.

$$L(s) = \left(\dfrac{1}{}\right)^{\boxed{}}$$

(M) Write the domain and range of $L(s)$ in set notation.

The domain of $L(s)$ is $\left\{s \mid s \text{ is a } \boxed{} \text{ number}\right\}$.

The range of $L(s)$ is $\left\{1, \dfrac{1}{2}, \dfrac{1}{4}, \boxed{}, \boxed{}, \boxed{}, \dots\right\}$.

The range of $L(s)$ is $\left\{L \mid L = \left(\dfrac{1}{2}\right)^{n}, \text{ where } n \text{ is } \boxed{}\right\}$.

(N) Copy and complete the graph shown. Graph the first five values of $N(s)$.

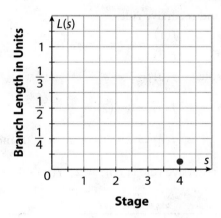

Stage Number	Number of Branches	Branch Length
0	1	1
1	2	$\dfrac{1}{2}$
2	4	$\dfrac{1}{4}$
3	8	$\dfrac{1}{\boxed{}}$
4	16	$\dfrac{1}{\boxed{}}$
5	32	$\dfrac{1}{\boxed{}}$
⋮	⋮	⋮
n	2^{n}	$\dfrac{1}{\boxed{}}$

(O) As s increases, $L(s)$. $L(s)$ is function.

© Houghton Mifflin Harcourt Publishing Company

Reflect

1. What is the total length added at each stage?

2. Is the total length of all the branches a sequence? If so, identify the sequence.

A sequence is a set of numbers related by a common rule. All sequences start with an initial term. In a **geometric sequence**, the ratio of any term to the previous term is constant. This constant ratio is called the **common ratio** and is denoted by r $(r \neq 1)$. In the **explicit form** of the sequence, each term is found by evaluating the function $f(n) = ar^n$ or $f(n) = ar^{n-1}$ where a is the initial value and r is the common ratio, for some whole number n. Note that there are two forms of the explicit rule because it is permissible to call the initial value the first term or to call ar the first term.

A geometric sequence can also be defined recursively $f(n) = r \cdot f(n-1)$ where either $f(0) = a$ or $f(1)$, again depending on the way the terms of the sequence are numbered. $f(n) = r \cdot f(n-1)$ is called the **recursive rule** for the sequence.

Example 1 Write the explicit and recursive rules for a geometric sequence given a table of values.

(A)

n	0	1	2	3	4	$\cdots$	$j-1$	j	$\cdots$
$f(n)$	3	6	12	24	48	$\cdots$	$ar^{(j-1)}$	ar^j	$\cdots$

Determine a and r, then write the explicit and recursive rules.

Find the common ratio: $\dfrac{f(n)}{f(n-1)} = r$. $\dfrac{f(1)}{f(0)} = \dfrac{6}{3} = 2 = r$

Find the initial value, $a = f(0)$, from the table. $f(0) = 3 = a$

Find the explicit rule: $f(n) = ar^n$. $f(n) = 3 \cdot (2)^n$

Write the recursive rule. $f(n) = 2 \cdot f(n-1), n \geq 1$ and $f(0) = 3$

The explicit rule is $f(n) = 3 \cdot (2)^n$ and the recursive rule is $f(n) = 2 \cdot f(n-1), n \geq 1$ and $f(0) = 3$.

(B)

n	1	2	3	4	5	$\cdots$	$j-1$	j	$\cdots$
$f(n)$	$\frac{1}{25}$	$\frac{1}{5}$	1	5	25	$\cdots$	$ar^{(j-1)}$	ar^j	$\cdots$

Determine a and r, then write the explicit and recursive rules.

Find the common ratio: $\dfrac{f(n)}{f(n-1)} = r$. $\dfrac{f\left(\boxed{4}\right)}{f\left(\boxed{3}\right)} = \dfrac{\boxed{5}}{\boxed{1}} = \boxed{5} = r$

Find the initial value, $a = f(1)$, from the table. $f(1) = \boxed{\frac{1}{25}} = a$

Find the explicit rule: $f(n) = ar^{n-1}$. $f(n) = \boxed{\frac{1}{25}} \cdot \left(\boxed{5}\right)^{n-1}$

Write the recursive rule. $f(n) = \boxed{5} \cdot f(n-1), n \geq \boxed{2}$ and $f(1) = \boxed{5}$

The explicit rule is $f(n) = \boxed{\frac{1}{25} \cdot (5)^{n-1}}$ and the recursive rule is $f(n) = \boxed{5} \cdot f(n-1), n \geq \boxed{2}$ where $f(1) = \boxed{5}$.

3. **Discussion** If you were told that a geometric sequence had an initial value of $f(5) = 5$, could you write an explicit and a recursive rule for the function? What would the explicit rule be?

Your Turn

Write the explicit and recursive rules for a geometric sequence given a table of values.

4.

n	0	1	2	3	4	5	6	...
f(n)	$\frac{1}{27}$	$\frac{1}{9}$	$\frac{1}{3}$	1	3	9	27	...

5.

n	1	2	3	4	5	6	7	...
f(n)	0.001	0.01	0.1	1	10	100	1000	...

Explain 2 Graphing Geometric Sequences

To graph a geometric sequence given an explicit or a recursive rule you can use the rule to generate a table of values and then graph those points on a coordinate plane. Since the domain of a geometric sequence consists only of whole numbers, its graph consists of individual points, not a smooth curve.

Example 2 Given either an explicit or recursive rule for a geometric sequence, use a table to generate values and draw the graph of the sequence.

(A) Explicit rule: $f(n) = 2 \cdot 2^n$, $n \geq 0$

Use a table to generate points.

n	0	1	2	3	4	5	...
f(n)	2	4	8	16	32	64	...

Plot the first three points on the graph.

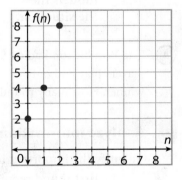

(B) Recursive rule: $f(n) = 0.5 \cdot f(n-1)$, $n \geq 1$ and $f(0) = 16$

Use a table to generate points.

n	0	1	2	3	4	5	6	...
f(n)	16	8	4	2	1	0.5	0.25	...

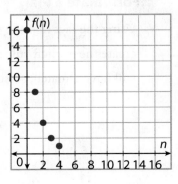

© Houghton Mifflin Harcourt Publishing Company

Given either an explicit or recursive rule for a geometric sequence, use a table to generate values and draw the graph of the sequence.

6. $f(n) = 3 \cdot 2^{n-1}, n \geq 1$

n	1	2	3	4	5	$\cdots$
$f(n)$						$\cdots$

7. $f(n) = 3 \cdot f(n-1), n \geq 2$ and $f(1) = 2$

n	1	2	3	4	5	$\cdots$
$f(n)$						$\cdots$

🔧 Explain 3   Modeling With a Geometric Sequence

Given a real-world situation that can be modeled by geometric sequence, you can use an explicit or a recursive rule to answer a question about the situation.

Example 3   Write both an explicit and recursive rule for the geometric sequence that models the situation. Use the sequence to answer the question asked about the situation.

(A) The Wimbledon Ladies' Singles Championship begins with 128 players. Each match, two players play and only one moves to the next round. The players compete until there is one winner. How many rounds must the winner play?

🧩 Analyze Information

Identify the important information:

- The first round requires 64 matches, so $a =$ 64 .

- The next round requires half as many matches, so $r = \dfrac{1}{2}$.

🧩 Formulate a Plan

Using the fact that the domain starts at 1 and the first round has 128 players,

create the explicit rule and the recursive rule for the tournament. The final round

will have 1 match, so substitute this value into the explicit rule and solve for n.

Solve

The explicit rule is $f(n)$ $\boxed{64 \cdot \left(\frac{1}{2}\right)^{n-1}}$, $n = \geq 1$.

The recursive rule is $f(n) = \boxed{\frac{1}{2}} \cdot f(n-1)$, $n \geq 2$ and $f(1) = \boxed{64}$.

The final round will have 1 match, so substitute 1 for $f(n)$ into the explicit rule and solve for n.

$$f(n) = 64 \cdot \left(\frac{1}{2}\right)^{n-1}$$

$$\boxed{1} = 64 \cdot \left(\frac{1}{2}\right)^{n-1}$$

$$\boxed{\frac{1}{64}} = \left(\frac{1}{2}\right)^{n-1}$$

$$\left(\frac{1}{2}\right)^{\boxed{6}} = \left(\frac{1}{2}\right)^{n-1}$$

Two powers with the same positive base other than 1 are equal if and only if the exponents are equal.

$$\left(\frac{1}{2}\right)^{\boxed{6}} = \left(\frac{1}{2}\right)^{n-1}$$

$$\boxed{6} = n - 1$$

$$\boxed{7} = n$$

The winner must play in 7 rounds.

 Justify and Evaluate

The answer of 7 rounds makes sense because using the explicit rule gives

$f(7) = \boxed{1}$ and the final round will have 1 match(es). This result can be checked

using the recursive rule, which again results in $f(7) = \boxed{1}$.

Your Turn

Write both an explicit and recursive rule for the geometric sequence that models the situation. Use the sequence to answer the question asked about the situation.

8. A particular type of bacteria divides into two new bacteria every 20 minutes. A scientist growing the bacteria in a laboratory begins with 200 bacteria. How many bacteria are present 4 hours later?

 Elaborate

9. Describe the difference between an explicit rule for a geometric sequence and a recursive rule.

10. How would you decide to use $n = 0$ or $n = 1$ as the starting value of n for a geometric sequence modeling a real-world situation?

11. **Essential Question Check-In** How can you define a geometric sequence in an algebraic way? What information do you need to write these rules?

You are creating self-similar fractal trees. You start with a trunk of length 1 unit (at Stage 0). Then the trunk splits into two branches each one-third the length of the trunk. Then each one of these branches splits into two new branches, with each branch one-third the length of the previous one.

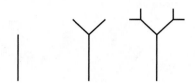

1. Can the length of the new branches at each stage be described with a geometric series? Explain. If so, find the explicit form of the length of each branch.

2. Can the number of new branches at each stage be described with geometric series? Explain. If so, find the recursive rule of the length of number of new branches.

3. Can the total length of the new branches at each stage be modeled with a geometric sequence? Explain. (The total length of the new branches is the sum of the lengths of all the new branches.)

Write the explicit and recursive rules for a geometric sequence given a table of values.

4.

n	0	1	2	3	4	$\cdots$
f(n)	0.1	0.3	0.9	2.7	8.1	$\cdots$

5.

n	0	1	2	3	4	$\cdots$
f(n)	100	10	1	0.1	0.01	$\cdots$

6.

n	1	2	3	4	5	$\cdots$
f(n)	1000	100	10	1	0.1	$\cdots$

7.

n	1	2	3	4	5	$\cdots$
f(n)	10^{50}	10^{47}	10^{44}	10^{41}	10^{38}	$\cdots$

Given either an explicit or recursive rule for a geometric sequence, use a table to generate values and draw the graph of the sequence.

8. $f(n) = \left(\dfrac{1}{2}\right) \cdot 4^n, n \geq 0$

n	0	1	2	3	4	$\cdots$
f(n)						$\cdots$

9. $f(n) = 2f(n-1), n \geq 1$ and $f(0) = 0.5$

n	0	1	2	3	4	⋯
$f(n)$						⋯

10. $f(n) = 0.5 \cdot f(n-1), n \geq 2$ and $f(1) = 8$

n	1	2	3	4	5	⋯
$f(n)$						⋯

11. $f(n) = \frac{2}{3} \cdot f(n-1), n \geq 2$ and $f(1) = 1$

n	1	2	3	4	5	⋯
$f(n)$						⋯

Write both an explicit and recursive rule for the geometric sequence that models the situation. Use the sequence to answer the question asked about the situation.

12. The Alphaville Youth Basketball committee is planning a single-elimination tournament. The committee wants the winner to play 4 games. How many teams should the committee invite?

13. An online video game tournament begins with 1024 players. Four players play in each game. In each game there is only one winner, and only the winner advances to the next round. How many games will the winner play?

14. **Genealogy** You have 2 biological parents, 4 biological grandparents, and 8 biological great-grandparents.

a. How many direct ancestors do you have if you trace your ancestry back 6 generations? How many direct ancestors do you have if you go back 12 generations?

b. **What if...?** How does the explicit rule change if you are considered the first generation?

15. Fractals Waclaw Sierpinski designed various fractals. He would take a geometric figure, shade it in, and then start removing the shading to create a fractal pattern.

a. The Sierpinski triangle is a fractal based on a triangle. In each iteration, the center of each shaded triangle is removed.

Given that the area of the original triangle is 1 square unit, write a sequence for the area of the nth iteration of the Sierpinski triangle. (The first iteration is the original triangle.)

b. The Sierpinski carpet is a fractal based on a square. In each iteration, the center of each shaded square is removed.

Given that the area of the original square is 1 square unit, write a sequence for the area of the nth iteration of the Sierpinski carpet. (The first iteration is the original square.)

c. Find the shaded area of the fourth iteration of the Sierpinski carpet.

16. A piece of paper is 0.1 millimeter thick. When folded, the paper is twice as thick.

a. Find both the explicit and recursive rule for this geometric sequence.

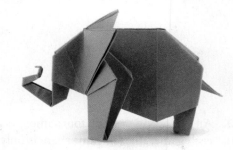

b. Studies have shown that you can fold a piece of paper a maximum of 7 times. How thick will the paper be if it is folded on top of itself 7 times?

c. Assume that you could fold the paper as many times as you want. How many folds would be required for the paper to be taller than Mount Everest at 8850 meters? (Hint: Use a calculator to generate two large powers of 2 and check if the required number of millimeters is between those two powers. Continue to refine your guesses.)

© Houghton Mifflin Harcourt Publishing Company • Image Credits: ©imagefactory/Shutterstock

17. Justify Reasoning Suppose you have the following table of points of a geometric sequence. The table is incomplete so you do not know the initial value. Explain why each of the following can or cannot be the rules for the function in the table.

n	. . .	4	5	6	7	. . .
f(n)	. . .	6	12	24	48	. . .

a. $f(n) = 2^n$

b. $f(n) = \frac{3}{8} \cdot (2)^n$

c. $f(n) = 2 \cdot f(n-1)$, $n \geq 1$ and $f(0) = 6$

d. $f(n) = \frac{3}{4} \cdot (2)^{n-1}$

e. $f(n) = 2 \cdot f(n-1)$, $n \geq 1$ and $f(0) = \frac{3}{8}$

f. $f(n) = 2 \cdot f(n-1)$, $n \geq 1$ and $f(1) = \frac{3}{4}$

g. $f(n) = (1.5) \cdot (2)^{n-2}$

h. $f(n) = 3 \cdot (2)^{n-3}$

18. Communicate Mathematical Ideas Show that the rules $f(n) = ar^n$ for $n \geq 0$ and $f(n) = ar^{n-1}$ for $n \geq 1$ for a geometric sequence are equivalent.

Lesson Performance Task

Have you ever heard of musical octaves? Octaves are defined as the interval between the same musical note in a higher or lower pitch. Octaves are geometric sequences. For example, the table shows the frequencies produced by playing the note D in ascending octaves, D_0 being the lowest D note audible to the human ear.

Scale of D's	
Note	**Frequency (Hz)**
D_0	18.35
D_1	35.71
D_2	73.42
D_3	146.83

a. Explain how to write an explicit rule and a recursive rule for the frequency of D notes in hertz, where $n = 1$ represents D_1.

b. The note commonly called "middle D" is D_4. Use the explicit rule or the recursive rule from part **a** to predict the frequency for middle D.

c. Humans generally cannot hear sounds with frequencies greater than 20,000 Hz. What is the first D note that humans cannot hear? Explain.

13.2 Exponential Growth Functions

Essential Question: How is the graph of $g(x) = ab^{x-h} + k$ where $b > 1$ related to the graph of $f(x) = b^x$?

 TEKS **A2.5.A** Determine the effects on the key attributes on the graphs of $f(x) = b^x$ ... where b is 2, 10, ... when $f(x)$ is replaced by $af(x)$, $f(x) + d$, and $f(x - c)$ for specific positive and negative real values of a, c, and d. Also A2.2.A, A2.5.B, A2.5.D, A2.7.I

Resource Locker

⊘ Explore 1 Graphing and Analyzing $f(x) = 2^x$ and $f(x) = 10^x$

An **exponential function** is a function of the form $f(x) = b^x$, where the base b is a positive constant other than 1 and the exponent x is a variable. Notice that there is no single parent exponential function because each choice of the base b determines a different function.

Ⓐ Copy and complete the input-output table for each of the parent exponential functions below.

x	$f(x) = 2^x$
−3	
−2	
−1	
0	
1	
2	
3	

x	$p(x) = 10^x$
−3	
−2	
−1	
0	
1	
2	
3	

Ⓑ Graph the parent functions $f(x) = 2^x$ and $p(x) = 10^x$ by plotting points.

Ⓒ What is the domain of each function?

Domain of $f(x) = 2^x$: $\left\{ x \middle| \right\}$

Domain of $p(x) = 10^x$: $\left\{ x \middle| \right\}$

Ⓓ What is the range of each function?

Range of $f(x) = 2^x$: $\left\{ y \middle| \right\}$

Range of $p(x) = 10^x$: $\left\{ y \middle| \right\}$

Ⓔ What is the y-intercept of each function?

y-intercept of $f(x) = 2^x$: $\left(0, \right)$

y-intercept of $p(x) = 10^x$: $\left(0, \right)$

Ⓕ What is the trend of each function?

In both $f(x) = 2^x$ and $p(x) = 10^x$, as the value of x increases, the value of y ____.

1. Will the domain be the same for every exponential function? Why or why not?

2. Will the range be the same for every exponential function in the form $f(x) = b^x$, where b is a positive constant? Why or why not?

3. Will the value of the y-intercept be the same for every exponential function? Why or why not?

⊘ Explore 2 Predicting Transformations of the Graphs of $f(x) = 2^x$ and $f(x) = 10^x$

Based on your experience with transforming the parent function $f(x)$ in previous lessons, make predictions about the effect of varying the parameters in $g(x) = af(x - c) + d$. Confirm your predictions using a graphing calculator.

The graph of $f(x) = 2^x$ is shown, as is a separate graph of $p(x) = 10^x$.

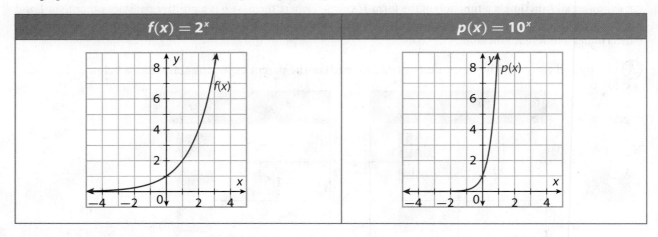

For Parts A–D, predict what the graph of each function will look like, and then sketch the graph based on the graph shown on your calculator. Show $f(x)$ and its two transformations of on one graph and show $p(x)$ and its two transformations on another graph.

(A) The graph of $g_1(x) = \frac{1}{4}(2^x)$ will be the graph of $f(x) = 2^x$ vertically by a

factor of ▨.

The graph of $g_2(x) = 3(2^x)$ will be the graph of $f(x) = 2^x$ vertically ▨ by a

factor of ▨.

The graph of $q_1(x) = 2(10^x)$ will be the graph of $p(x) = 10^x$ vertically by a

factor of ▨.

The graph of $q_2(x) = \frac{1}{5}(10^x)$ will be the graph of $p(x) = 10^x$ vertically ▨ by a

factor of ▨.

Ⓑ The graph of $g_1(x) = -\frac{3}{4}(2^x)$ will be the graph of $f(x) = 2^x$ reflected across the [ ]

and vertically [ ] by a factor of [ ].

The graph of $g_2(x) = -5(2^x)$ will be the graph of $f(x) = 2^x$ reflected across the [ ]

and vertically [ ] by a factor of [ ].

The graph of $q_1(x) = -\frac{5}{4}(10^x)$ will be the graph of $p(x) = 10^x$ reflected across the [ ]

and vertically [ ] by a factor of [ ].

The graph of $q_2(x) = -\frac{1}{4}(10^x)$ will be the graph of $p(x) = 10^x$ reflected across the [ ]

and vertically [ ] by a factor of [ ].

Ⓒ The graph of $g_1(x) = 2^{x+1}$ will be the graph of $f(x) = 2^x$ translated [ ] unit to the [ ].

The graph of $g_2(x) = 2^{x-4}$ will be the graph of $f(x) = 2^x$ translated [ ] units to the [ ].

The graph of $q_1(x) = 10^{x+2}$ will be the graph of $p(x) = 10^x$ translated [ ] unit to the [ ].

The graph of $q_2(x) = 10^{x-3}$ will be the graph of $p(x) = 10^x$ translated [ ] units to the [ ].

Ⓓ The graph of $g_1(x) = 2^x + 3$ will be the graph of $f(x) = 2^x$ translated [ ] units [ ].

The graph of $g_2(x) = 2^x - \frac{5}{2}$ will be the graph of $f(x) = 2^x$ translated [ ] units [ ].

The graph of $q_1(x) = 10^x + 5$ will be the graph of $p(x) = 10^x$ translated [ ] units [ ].

The graph of $q_2(x) = 10^x - 2$ will be the graph of $p(x) = 10^x$ translated [ ] units [ ].

Reflect

4. **Discussion** Identify the values of a that make the domain and range of $g(x) = af(x)$ different than that of $f(x) = b^x$.

5. Identify the values of h that make the domain and range of $g(x) = f(x - h)$ different than that of $f(x) = b^x$.

6. Identify the values of k that make the domain and range of $g(x) = f(x) + k$ different than that of $f(x) = b^x$.

⌖ Explain 1 Graphing Combined Transformations of $f(x) = b^x$ Where $b > 1$

A given exponential function $g(x) = a(b^{x-h}) + k$ with base b can be graphed by recognizing the difference between the given function and its parent function, $f(x) = b^x$. These differences define the parameters of the transformation, where k represents the vertical translation, h is the horizontal translation, and a represents either the vertical stretch or compression of the exponential function and whether it is reflected across the x-axis. You can use these parameters to see what happens to two reference points during the transformation. Two points that are easily visualized on the parent exponential function are $(0, 1)$ and $(1, b)$. The parent exponential function also has an asymptote at $y = 0$.

The given function is the parent function translated horizontally h units to the right, stretched or compressed by a factor of a, and translated up h units. Also, if $a < 0$, then the parent function is reflected across the x-axis before it is translated vertically. The point $(0, 1)$ becomes $(h, a + k)$ and $(1, b)$ becomes $(1 + h, ab + k)$. The asymptote becomes $y = k$.

The graphs of $f(x) = 2^x$ and $p(x) = 10^x$ are shown below with the reference points and asymptotes labeled.

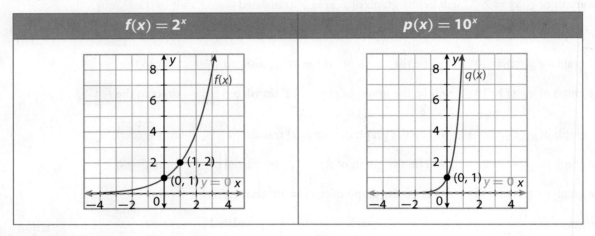

$f(x) = 2^x$	$p(x) = 10^x$

Example 1 State the domain and range of the given function. Then identify the new values of the reference points and the asymptote. Use these values to graph the function.

Ⓐ $g(x) = -3(2^{x-2}) + 1$

The domain of $g(x) = 3(2^{x-2}) + 1$ is $\left\{ x | -\infty < x < \infty \right\}$.

The range of $g(x) = -3(2^{x-2}) + 1$ is $\left\{ y | y < 1 \right\}$.

Examine $g(x)$ and identify the parameters.

$a = -3$, which means that the function is reflected across the x-axis and vertically stretched by a factor of 3.

$h = 2$, so the function is translated 2 units to the right.

$k = 1$, so the function is translated 1 unit up.

The point $(0, 1)$ becomes $(h, a + k)$.

$(h, a + k) = (2, -3 + 1)$

$\qquad\qquad = (2, -2)$

$(1, b)$ becomes $(1 + h, ab + k)$.

$$(1 + h, ab + k) = (1 + 2, -3(2) + 1)$$
$$= (3, -6 + 1)$$
$$= (3, -5)$$

The asymptote becomes $y = k$.

$$y = k \quad \rightarrow \quad y = 1$$

Plot the transformed points and asymptote and draw the curve.

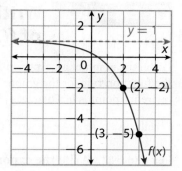

(B) $q(x) = 1.5(10^{x-3}) - 5$

The domain of $q(x) = 1.5(10^{x-3}) - 5$ is $\left\{ x \middle| \left[-\infty < x < \infty \right] \right\}$.

The range of $q(x) = 1.5(10^{x-3}) - 5$ is $\left\{ y \middle| \left[y > -5 \right] \right\}$.

Examine $q(x)$ and identify the parameters.

$a = \boxed{1.5}$ so the function is stretched vertically by a factor of 1.5.

$h = \boxed{3}$ so the function is translated 3 units to the right.

$k = \boxed{-5}$ so the function is translated 5 units down.

The point $(0,1)$ becomes $(h, a + k)$.

$$(h, a + k) = (3, 1.5 - 5) = (3, -3.5)$$

$(1, b)$ becomes $(1 + h, ab + k)$.

$$(1 + h, ab + k) = (1 + 3, 1.5(10) - 5) = (4, 10)$$

The asymptote becomes $y = k$.

$$y = k \quad \rightarrow \quad y = \boxed{-5}$$

Plot the transformed points and asymptote and draw the curve.

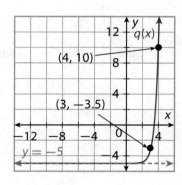

Your Turn

7. $g(x) = 4(2^{x+2}) - 6$

8. $q(x) = -\dfrac{3}{5}(10^{x+2}) + 3$

Explain 2 **Writing Equations for Combined Transformations of $f(x) = b^x$ Where $b > 1$**

Given the graph of an exponential function, you can use your knowledge of the transformation parameters to write the function rule for the graph. Recall that the asymptote will give the value of k and the x-coordinate of the first reference point is h. Then let y_1 be the y-coordinate of the first point and solve the equation $y_1 = a + k$ for a.

Finally, use a, h, and k to write the function in the form $g(x) = a\left(b^{x-h}\right) + k$.

Example 2 Write the exponential function that will produce the given graph, using the specified value of b. Verify that the second reference point is on the graph of the function. Then state the domain and range of the function in set notation.

Ⓐ Let $b = 2$.

The asymptote is $y = 1$, showing that $k = 1$.

The first reference point is $\left(-\dfrac{1}{3}, -\dfrac{1}{3}\right)$. This shows that $h = -\dfrac{1}{3}$ and

that $a + k = -\dfrac{1}{3}$.

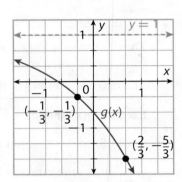

Substitute $k = 1$ and solve for a.

$$a + k = -\dfrac{1}{3}$$

$$a + 1 = -\dfrac{1}{3}$$

$$a = -\dfrac{4}{3}$$

$$h = -\dfrac{1}{3}$$

$$k = 1$$

Substitute these values into $g(x) = a\left(b^{x-h}\right) + k$ to find $g(x)$.

$$g(x) = a\left(b^{x-h}\right) + k$$

$$= -\dfrac{4}{3}\left(2^{x+\frac{1}{3}}\right) + 1$$

Verify that $g\left(\dfrac{2}{3}\right) = -\dfrac{5}{3}$.

$$g\left(\dfrac{2}{3}\right) = -\dfrac{4}{3}\left(2^{\frac{2}{3}+\frac{1}{3}}\right) + 1$$

$$= -\dfrac{4}{3}\left(2^1\right) + 1$$

$$= -\dfrac{4}{3}\left(2\right) + 1$$

$$= \dfrac{3}{3} - \dfrac{8}{3}$$

$$= -\dfrac{5}{3}$$

The domain of $g(x)$ is $\left\{x \mid -\infty < x < +\infty\right\}$.

The range of $g(x)$ is $\left\{y \mid y < 1\right\}$.

Ⓑ Let $b = 10$.

The asymptote is $y = \boxed{6}$, showing that $k = \boxed{6}$.

The first reference point is $(-4, 4.4)$. This shows that $h = \boxed{-4}$ and

that $a + k = \boxed{4.4}$. Substitute for k and solve for a.

$$a + k = \boxed{4.4}$$

$$a + \boxed{6} = \boxed{4.4}$$

$$a = \boxed{-1.6}$$

$$h = \boxed{-4}$$

$$k = \boxed{6}$$

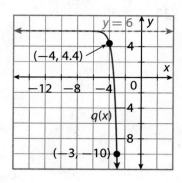

Substitute these values into $q(x) = a\left(b^{x-h}\right) + k$ to find $q(x)$.

$$q(x) = a\left(b^{x-h}\right) + k = \boxed{-1.6}\left(10^{x-(-4)}\right) + \boxed{6}$$

Verify that $q(-3) = -10$.

$$q(-3) = \boxed{-1.6}\left(10^{-3-(-4)}\right) + \boxed{6}$$

$$= \boxed{-1.6}\left(10^{\boxed{1}}\right) + \boxed{6}$$

$$= \boxed{-16} + \boxed{6}$$

$$= \boxed{-10}$$

The domain of $q(x)$ is $\left\{x \mid -\infty < x < +\infty\right\}$.

The range of $q(x)$ is $\left\{y \mid y < 6\right\}$.

Your Turn

Write the exponential function that will produce the given graph, using the specified value of b. Verify that the second reference point is on the graph of the function. Then state the domain and range of the function in set notation.

9. $b = 2$

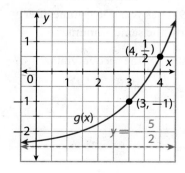

10. $b = 10$

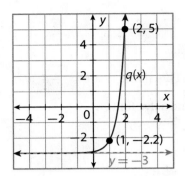

Explain 3   Modeling with Exponential Growth Functions

An **exponential growth function** has the form $f(t) = a(1 + r)^t$ where $a > 0$ and r is a constant percent increase (expressed as a decimal) for each unit increase in time t. That is, since $f(t + 1) = (1 + r) \cdot f(t) = f(t) + r \cdot f(t)$, the value of the function increases by $r \cdot f(t)$ on the interval $[t, t + 1]$. The base $1 + r$ of an exponential growth function is called the **growth factor**, and the constant percent increase r, in decimal form, is called the **growth rate**.

Example 3   **Find the function that corresponds with the given situation. Then use the graph of the function to make a prediction.**

Ⓐ   Tony purchased a rare guitar in 2000 for \$12,000. Experts estimate that its value will increase by 14% per year. Use a graph to find the number of years it will take for the value of the guitar to be \$60,000.

Write a function to model the growth in value for the guitar.

$$f(t) = a(1 + r)^t$$
$$= 12,000(1 + 0.14)^t$$
$$= 12,000(1.14)^t$$

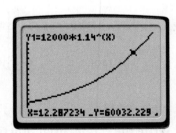

Use a graphing calculator to graph the function.

Use the graph to predict when the guitar will be worth \$60,000.

Use the TRACE feature to find the t-value where $f(t) \approx 60,000$.

So, the guitar will be worth \$60,000 approximately 12.29 years after it was purchased.

Ⓑ   At the same time that Tony bought the \$12,000 guitar, he also considered buying another rare guitar for \$15,000. Experts estimated that this guitar would increase in value by 9% per year. Determine after how many years the two guitars will be worth the same amount.

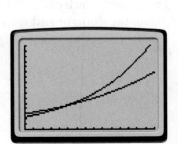

Write a function to model the growth in value for the second guitar.

$$g(t) = a(1 + r)^t$$
$$= \boxed{15,000}\left(1 + \boxed{0.09}\right)^t$$
$$= \boxed{15,000}\left(\boxed{1.09}\right)^t$$

Use a graphing calculator to graph the two functions.

Use the graph to predict when the two guitars will be worth the same amount.

Use the intersection feature to find the *t*-value where $g(t) = \boxed{f(t)}$.

So, the two guitars will be worth the same amount 4.98 years after 2000.

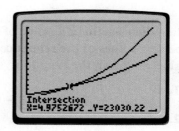

Reflect

11. In part A, find the average rates of change over the intervals $(0, 4)$, $(4, 8)$, and $(8, 12)$. Do the rates increase, decrease, or stay the same?

Your Turn

Find the function that corresponds with the given situation. Then graph the function on a calculator and use the graph to make a prediction.

12. John researches a baseball card and finds that it is currently worth \$3.25. However, it is supposed to increase in value 11% per year. In how many years will the card be worth \$26?

💬 Elaborate

13. How are reference points helpful when graphing transformations of $f(x) = b^x$ or when writing equations for transformed graphs?

14. Give the general form of an exponential growth function and describe its parameters.

15. **Essential Question Check-In** Which transformations of $f(x) = b^x$ change the function's end behavior? Which transformations change the function's *y*-intercept?

☆ Evaluate: Homework and Practice

- Online Homework
- Hints and Help
- Extra Practice

Describe the effect of each transformation on the parent function. Graph the parent function and its transformation. Then determine the domain, range, and *y*-intercept of each function.

1. $f(x) = 2^x$ and $g(x) = 2(2^x)$

2. $f(x) = 2^x$ and $g(x) = -5(2^x)$

3. $f(x) = 2^x$ and $g(x) = 2^{x+2}$

4. $f(x) = 2^x$ and $g(x) = 2^x + 5$

5. $f(x) = 10^x$ and $g(x) = 2(10^x)$

6. $f(x) = 10^x$ and $g(x) = -4(10^x)$

7. $f(x) = 10^x$ and $g(x) = 10^{x-2}$

8. $f(x) = 10^x$ and $g(x) = 10^x - 6$

9. Describe the graph of $g(x) = 2^{(x-3)} - 4$ in terms of $f(x) = 2^x$.

10. Describe the graph of $g(x) = 10^{(x+7)} + 6$ in terms of $f(x) = 10^x$.

State the domain and range of the given function. Then identify
the new values of the reference points and the asymptote. Use these
values to graph the function.

11. $h(x) = 2\left(3^{x+2}\right) - 1$

12. $k(x) = -0.5\left(4^{x-1}\right) + 2$

13. $f(x) = 3\left(6^{x-7}\right) - 8$

14. $f(x) = -3\left(2^{x+1}\right) + 3$

15. $h(x) = -\dfrac{1}{4}\left(5^{x+1}\right) - \dfrac{3}{4}$

16. $p(x) = 2\left(4^{x-3}\right) - 5$

Write the exponential function that will produce the given graph,
using the specified value of *b*. Verify that the second reference point
is on the graph of the function. Then state the domain and range of
the function in set notation.

17. $b = 2$

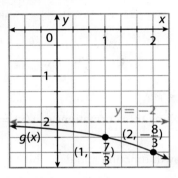

18. $b = 2$

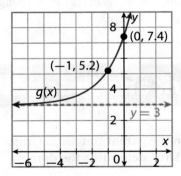

19. $b = 10$

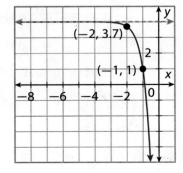

20. $b = 10$

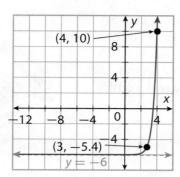

Find the function that corresponds with the given situation. Then graph the function on a calculator and use the graph to make a prediction.

21. A certain stock opens with a price of $0.59. Over the first three days, the value of the stock increases on average by 50% per day. If this trend continues, how many days will it take for the stock to be worth $6?

22. Sue has a lamp from her great-grandmother. She has it appraised and finds it is worth $1000. She wants to sell it, but the appraiser tells her that the value is appreciating by 8% per year. In how many years will the value of the lamp be $2000?

23. The population of a small town is 15,000. If the population is growing by 5% per year, how long will it take for the population to reach 25,000?

24. Bill invests $3000 in a bond fund with an interest rate of 9% per year. If Bill does not withdraw any of the money, in how many years will his bond fund be worth $5000?

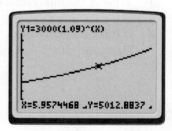

H.O.T. Focus on Higher Order Thinking

25. Analyze Relationships Compare the end behavior of $g(x) = 2^x$ and $f(x) = x^2$. How are the graphs of the functions similar? How are they different?

26. **Explain the Error** A student has a baseball card that is worth $6.35. He looks up the appreciation rate and finds it to be 2.5% per year. He wants to find how much it will be worth after 3 years. He writes the function $f(t) = 6.35(2.5)^t$ and uses the graph of that function to find the value of the card in 3 years.

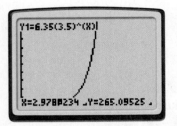

According to his graph, his card will be worth about $265.10 in 3 years. What did the student do wrong? What is the correct answer?

Lesson Performance Task

Like all collectables, the price of an item is determined by what the buyer is willing to pay and the seller is willing to accept. The estimated value of a 1948 Tucker 48 in excellent condition has risen at an approximately exponential rate from about $500,000 in December 2006 to about $1,400,000 in December 2013.

a. Find an equation in the form $V(t) = V_0 (1 + r)^t$, where V_0 is the value of the car in dollars in December 2006, r is the average annual growth rate, t is the time in years since December 2006, and $V(t)$ is the value of the car in dollars at time t. (Hint: Substitute the known values and solve for r.)

b. What is the interpretation for the value of r?

c. If this trend continues, what would be the value of the car in December 2017?

13.3 Exponential Decay Functions

Essential Question: How is the graph of $g(x) = ab^{x-h} + k$ where $0 < b < 1$ related to the graph of $f(x) = b^x$?

 A2.5.B Formulate exponential ... equations that model real-world situations...Also A2.2.A, A2.5.A, A2.5.D, A2.7.I

Explore 1 Graphing and Analyzing $f(x) = \left(\frac{1}{2}\right)^x$ and $f(x) = \left(\frac{1}{10}\right)^x$

Exponential decay functions are exponential functions with bases between 0 and 1 assuming a positive leading coefficient. These functions can be transformed in a manner similar to exponential growth functions. Begin by plotting the parent functions of two of the more commonly used bases: $\frac{1}{2}$ and $\frac{1}{10}$.

(A) To begin, copy and complete the table in order to find points along the function $f(x) = \left(\frac{1}{2}\right)^x$. You may need to review the rules of the properties of exponents, including negative exponents.

(B) What does the end behavior of this function appear to be as x increases?

(C) Plot the points on a graph and draw a smooth curve through them.

x	$f(x) = \left(\frac{1}{2}\right)^x$
−3	8
−2	
−1	
0	
1	
2	
3	

(D) Copy and complete the table for $f(x) = \left(\frac{1}{10}\right)x$.

(E) Plot the points on a graph and draw a smooth curve through them.

x	$f(x) = \left(\frac{1}{10}\right)^x$
−3	1000
−2	
−1	
0	
1	
2	
3	

(F) Copy and fill in the following table of properties:

	$f(x) = \left(\frac{1}{2}\right)^x$	$f(x) = \left(\frac{1}{10}\right)^x$
Domain	$\{x \mid -\infty < x < \infty\}$	$\{x \mid \}$
Range	$\{y \mid \}$	$\{y \mid \}$
End behavior as $x \to \infty$	$f(x) \to $	$f(x) \to $
End behavior as $x \to -\infty$	$f(x) \to $	$f(x) \to $
y-intercept	$\left(, \right)$	$\left(, \right)$

(G) Both of these functions ▮ throughout the domain.

(H) Of the two functions, $f(x) = \left(\dfrac{1}{\boxed{}}\right)^x$ decreases faster.

Reflect

1. **Make a Conjecture** Look at the table of properties for the functions. What do you notice? Make a conjecture about these properties for exponential decay functions of the form $f(x) = \left(\frac{1}{n}\right)^x$, where n is a constant.

⊘ **Explore 2** **Predicting Transformations of the Graphs of**
$$f(x) = \left(\frac{1}{2}\right)^x \text{ and } f(x) = \left(\frac{1}{10}\right)^x$$

Based on your experience with transforming the parent function $f(x)$ in previous lessons, make predictions about the effect of varying the parameters in $g(x) = af(x-c) + d$. Confirm your predictions using a graphing calculator.

(A) The graph of $g_1(x) = 3\left(\frac{1}{2}\right)^x$ will be the graph of $f(x) = \left(\frac{1}{2}\right)^x$ vertically ▮ by a factor of ▮ .

The graph of $g_2(x) = \frac{1}{4}\left(\frac{1}{2}\right)^x$ will be the graph of $f(x) = \left(\frac{1}{2}\right)^x$ vertically ▮ by a factor of ▮ .

(B) The graph of $g_1(x) = -\frac{3}{4}\left(\frac{1}{2}\right)^x$ will be the graph of $f(x) = \left(\frac{1}{2}\right)^x$ reflected across the [ ] and vertically [ ] by a factor of [ ].

The graph of $g_2(x) = -5\left(\frac{1}{2}\right)^x$ will be the graph of $f(x) = \left(\frac{1}{2}\right)^x$ reflected across the [ ] and vertically [ ] by a factor of [ ].

The graph of $q_1(x) = -\frac{5}{4}\left(\frac{1}{10}\right)^x$ will be the graph of $f(x) = \left(\frac{1}{10}\right)^x$ reflected across the [ ] and vertically [ ] by a factor of [ ].

The graph of $q_2(x) = -\frac{1}{4}\left(\frac{1}{10}\right)^x$ will be the graph of $f(x) = \left(\frac{1}{10}\right)^x$ reflected across the [ ] and vertically [ ] by a factor of [ ].

(C) The graph of $g_1(x) = \left(\frac{1}{2}\right)^{x+1}$ will be the graph of $f(x) = \left(\frac{1}{2}\right)^x$ translated [ ] unit to the [ ].

The graph of $g_2(x) = \left(\frac{1}{2}\right)^{x-4}$ will be the graph of $f(x) = \left(\frac{1}{2}\right)^x$ translated [ ] units to the [ ].

The graph of $q_1(x) = \left(\frac{1}{10}\right)^{x+2}$ will be the graph of $f(x) = \left(\frac{1}{10}\right)^x$ translated [ ] units to the [ ].

The graph of $q_2(x) = \left(\frac{1}{10}\right)^{x-3}$ will be the graph of $f(x) = \left(\frac{1}{10}\right)^x$ translated [ ] units to the [ ].

(D) The graph of $g_1(x) = \left(\frac{1}{2}\right)^x + 3$ will be the graph of $f(x) = \left(\frac{1}{2}\right)^x$ translated [ ] units [ ].

The graph of $g_2(x) = \left(\frac{1}{2}\right)^x - \frac{5}{2}$ will be the graph of $f(x) = \left(\frac{1}{2}\right)^x$ translated [ ] units [ ].

The graph of $q_1(x) = \left(\frac{1}{10}\right)^x + 5$ will be the graph of $f(x) = \left(\frac{1}{10}\right)^x$ translated [ ] units [ ].

The graph of $q_2(x) = \left(\frac{1}{10}\right)^x - 2$ will be the graph of $f(x) = \left(\frac{1}{10}\right)^x$ translated [ ] units [ ].

Reflect

2. Which parameters make the domain and range of $g(x)$ differ from those of the parent function? Write the transformed domain and range for $g(x)$ in set notation.

🔑 **Explain 1** **Graphing Combined Transformations of $f(x) = b^x$ Where $0 < b < 1$**

When graphing transformations of $f(x) = b^x$ where $0 < b < 1$, it is helpful to consider the effect of the transformation on two reference points, $(0, 1)$ and $\left(-1, \frac{1}{b}\right)$, vas well as the effect on the asymptote, $y = 0$. The table shows these reference points and the asymptote $y = 0$ for $f(x) = b^x$ and the corresponding points and asymptote for the transformed function, $g(x) = ab^{x-h} + k$.

	$f(x) = b^x$	$g(x) = ab^{x-h} + k$
First reference point	$(0, 1)$	$(h, a + k)$
Second reference point	$\left(-1, \dfrac{1}{b}\right)$	$\left(h - 1, \dfrac{a}{b} + k\right)$
Asymptote	$y = 0$	$y = k$

Example 1 For each of the transformed functions, use the reference points and the asymptote to draw the transformed function on the grid with the parent function. Then describe the domain and range of the transformed function using set notation.

Ⓐ $g(x) = 3\left(\dfrac{1}{2}\right)^{x-2} - 2$

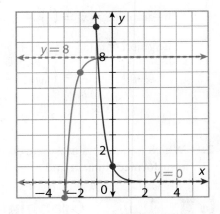

Identify parameters: $a = 3$ $b = \dfrac{1}{2}$ $h = 2$ $k = -2$

Find reference points: $(h, a + k) = (2, 3 - 2) = (2, 1)$

$\left(h - 1, \dfrac{a}{b} + k\right) = \left(2 - 1, \dfrac{3}{\frac{1}{2}} - 2\right) = (1, 4)$

Find the asymptote: $y = -2$

Plot the points and draw the asymptote. Then connect the points with a smooth curve that approaches the asymptote without crossing it.

Domain: $\left\{x \mid -\infty < x < \infty\right\}$ Range: $\left\{y \mid y > -2\right\}$

Ⓑ $g(x) = -\left(\dfrac{1}{10}\right)^{x+2} + 8$

Identify parameters: $a = \boxed{-1}$ $b = \dfrac{1}{10}$ $h = \boxed{-2}$ $k = \boxed{8}$

Find reference points:

$\left(h, \boxed{a + k}\right) = (-2, -1 + 8)\,(-2, 7)$

$\left(h - 1, \dfrac{a}{b} + k\right) = \left(-2 - 1, \dfrac{-1}{\frac{1}{10}} + 8\right) = \left(\boxed{-3}, \boxed{-2}\right)$

Find the asymptote: $y = \boxed{8}$

Plot the points and draw the asymptote. Then connect the points with a smooth curve that approaches the asymptote without crossing it.

Domain: $\left\{x \mid \boxed{-\infty < x < \infty}\right\}$ Range: $\left\{y \mid \boxed{y < 8}\right\}$

Your Turn

Copy the graph shown. For the transformed function, use the reference points and the asymptote to draw the transformed function on the grid with the parent function. Then describe the domain and range of the transformed function using set notation.

3. $g(x) = 3\left(\dfrac{1}{3}\right)^{x+2} - 4$

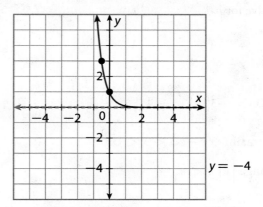

$y = -4$

  Explain 2 ## Writing Equations for Combined Transformations of $f(x) = b^x$ where $0 < b < 1$

Given a graph of an exponential decay function, $g(x) = ab^{x-h} + k$, the reference points and the asymptote can be used to identify the transformation parameters in order to write the function rule.

Example 2 Write the function represented by this graph and state the domain and range using set notation.

(A)

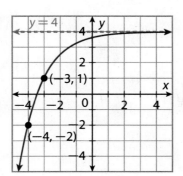

Find k from the asymptote: $k = 4$.

The first reference point is at $(-3, 1)$.

Equate point value with parameters-based expression. $\qquad (-3, 1) = (h, a + k)$

Use the x-coordinate to solve for h. $\qquad h = -3$

Use the y-coordinate to solve for a. $\qquad a = 1 - k$

$\qquad = -3$

The second reference point is at $(-4, -2)$.

Equate point value with parameters-based expression.

$$(-4, -2) = \left(h - 1, \frac{a}{b} + k\right)$$

Equate y-coordinate with parameters.

$$\frac{-3}{b} + 4 = -2$$

Solve for b.

$$\frac{-3}{b} = -6$$

$$b = \frac{-3}{-6}$$

$$= \frac{1}{2}$$

$$g(x) = -3\left(\frac{1}{2}\right)^{x+3} + 4$$

Domain: $\left\{x \mid -\infty < x < \infty\right\}$

Range: $\left\{y \mid y < 4\right\}$

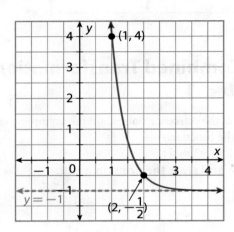

$(1, 4)$

$(2, -\frac{1}{2})$

$y = -1$

Find k from the asymptote: $k = \boxed{-1}$.

The first reference point is at $\left(\boxed{2}, \boxed{-\frac{1}{2}}\right)$, so $\left(\boxed{2}, -\frac{1}{2}\right) = \left(h, \boxed{a + k}\right)$

$$h = \boxed{2} \qquad a = \boxed{-\frac{1}{2}} - k$$

$$= \boxed{\frac{1}{2}}$$

The second reference point is at $\left(\boxed{1}, \boxed{4}\right)$, so $\left(\boxed{1}, 4\right) = \left(h - 1, \boxed{\frac{a}{b} + k}\right)$

$$\frac{\frac{1}{2}}{b} - 1 = \boxed{4}$$

$$\frac{\frac{1}{2}}{b} = \boxed{5}$$

$$b = \frac{\frac{1}{2}}{5}$$

$$= \boxed{\frac{1}{10}}$$

$$g(x) = \boxed{\frac{1}{2}} \left(\frac{1}{10}\right)^{x - \boxed{2}} - \boxed{-1}$$

Domain: $\left\{x \mid -\infty < x < \infty\right\}$

Range: $\left\{y \mid y \boxed{>} -1\right\}$

Reflect

4. Compare the *y*-intercept and the asymptote of the function shown in this table to the function plotted in Example 2A.

x	−5	−4	−3	−2	−1	0	1	2
g(x)	−10	−4	−4	$\frac{1}{2}$	$1\frac{1}{4}$	$1\frac{5}{8}$	$1\frac{13}{16}$	$1\frac{29}{32}$

5. Compare the *y*-intercept and the asymptote of the function shown in this table to the function plotted in Example 2B.

x	−3	−2	−1	0	1	2
g(x)	49	4	−0.5	−0.95	−0.995	−0.9995

Your Turn

Write the function represented by this graph and state the domain and range using set notation.

6.

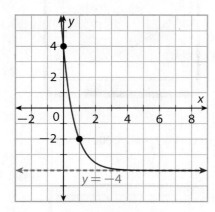

 Explain 3   Modeling with Exponential Decay Functions

Exponential decay functions can be applied to situations in which a quantity decreases by a constant percentage for each unit increase in time.

$$f(t) = a(1 - r)^t$$

In this form of the decay function, r (which must be expressed as a decimal or a fraction rather than a percentage) is called the **decay rate**. The term $(1 - r)$ is known as the **decay factor**. The vertical stretch parameter, a, is also the value of the decay function at the start (when $t = 0$).

Example 3   **Given the description of the decay terms, write the exponential decay function in the form $f(t) = a(1 - r)^t$ and graph it with a graphing calculator.**

(A)   The value of a truck purchased new for $28,000 decreases by 9.5% each year. Write an exponential function for this situation and graph it using a calculator. Use the graph to predict after how many years the value of the truck will be $5000.

"Purchased new for $28,000..." $a = 28,000$

"...decreases by 9.5% each year." $r = 0.095$

Substitute parameter values. $V_T(t) = 28,000(1 - 0.095)^t$

Simplify. $V_T(t) = 28,000(0.905)^t$

Graph the function with a graphing calculator. Use WINDOW to adjust the graph settings so that you can see the function and the function values that are important.

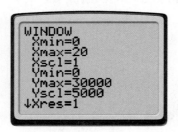
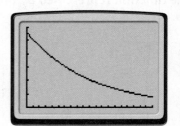

Find when the value reaches $5000 by finding the intersection between $V_T(t) = 28,000(0.905)^t$ and $V_T(t) = 5000$ on the calculator.

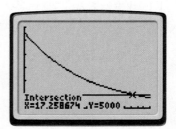

The intersection is at the point $(17.26, 5000)$, which means after 17.26 years, the truck will have a value of $5000.

Ⓑ The value of a sports car purchased new for $45,000 decreases by 15% each year. Write an exponential function for the depreciation of the sports car, and plot it along with the previous example. After how many years will the two vehicles have the same value if they are purchased at the same time?

"Purchased new for $45,000..." $\boxed{a} = 45,000$

"...decreases by 15% each year." $r = \boxed{0.15}$

Substitute parameter values. $V_c(t) = \boxed{45,000}\left(1 - \boxed{0.15}\right)^t$

Simplify. $V_c(t) = 45,000\left(\boxed{0.85}\right)^t$

Add this plot to the graph for the truck value from Example A and find the intersection of the two functions to determine when the values are the same.

The intersection point is $\left(\boxed{7.567}, \boxed{13,155}\right)$.

After $\boxed{7.567}$ years, the values of both vehicles will be

$\$\boxed{13,155}$.

Reflect

7. What reference points could you use if you plotted the value function for the sports car on graph paper? Confirm that the graph passes through them using the calculate feature on a graphing calculator.

8. Using the sports car from example B, calculate the average rate of value change over the course of the first year and the second year of ownership. What happens to the absolute value of the rate of change from the first interval to the second? What does this mean in this situation?

Your Turn

9. On federal income tax returns, self-employed people can depreciate the value of business equipment. Suppose a computer valued at $2765 depreciates at a rate of 30% per year. Use a graphing calculator to determine the number of years it will take for the computer's value to be $350.

💬 Elaborate

10. Which transformations of $f(x) = \left(\frac{1}{2}\right)^x$ or $f(x) = \left(\frac{1}{10}\right)^x$ change the function's end behavior?

11. Which transformations change the location of the graph's y-intercept?

12. **Discussion** How are reference points and asymptotes helpful when graphing transformations of $f(x) = \left(\frac{1}{2}\right)^x$ or $f(x) = \left(\frac{1}{10}\right)^x$ or when writing equations for transformed graphs?

13. Give the general form of an exponential decay function based on a known decay rate and describe its parameters.

14. **Essential Question Check-In** How is the graph of $f(x) = b^x$ used to help graph the function $g(x) = ab^{x-h} + k$?

☆ Evaluate: Homework and Practice

1. Graph the function $f(x) = \left(\frac{1}{3}\right)^x$ by plotting points with integer x-values from -2 to 2.

Describe the transformation(s) from each parent function and give the domain and range of each function.

2. $g(x) = \left(\frac{1}{2}\right)^x + 3$

3. $g(x) = \left(\frac{1}{10}\right)^{x+4}$

4. $g(x) = -\left(\frac{1}{10}\right)^{x-1} + 2$

5. $g(x) = 3\left(\frac{1}{2}\right)^{x+3} - 6$

Copy each graph. For each of the transformed functions, use the reference points and the asymptote to draw the transformed function on the grid with the parent function. Then describe the domain and range of the transformed function using set notation.

6. $g(x) = -2\left(\frac{1}{2}\right)^{x-1} + 2$

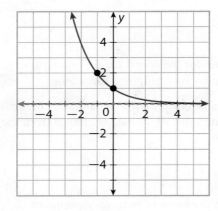

7. $g(x) = \left(\frac{1}{4}\right)^{x+2} + 3$

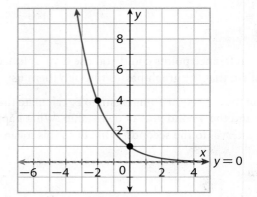

8. $g(x) = \frac{1}{2}\left(\frac{1}{3}\right)^{x-\frac{1}{2}} + 2$

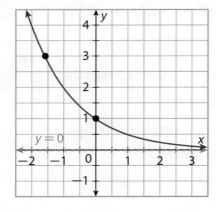

9. $g(x) = 2\left(\frac{1}{4}\right)^{x-2} - 3$

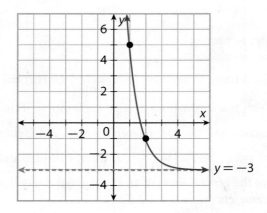

10. $g(x) = -3\left(\dfrac{1}{2}\right)^{x+2} + 7$

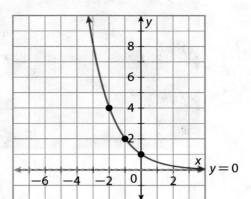

11. $g(x) = -\left(\dfrac{2}{3}\right)^{x+1} + \dfrac{1}{2}$

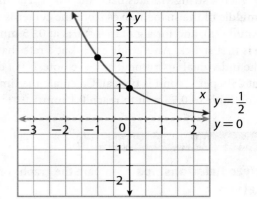

Write the function represented by each graph and state the domain and range using set notation.

12.

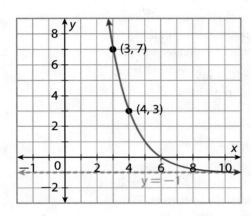

13.

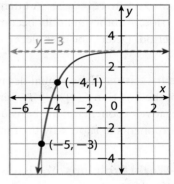

Write the exponential decay function described in the situation and use a graphing calculator to answer each question asked.

14. Medicine A quantity of insulin used to regulate sugar in the bloodstream breaks down by about 5% each minute after the injection. A bodyweight-adjusted dose is generally 10 units. How long does it take for the remaining insulin to be half of the original injection?

15. Paleontology Carbon-14 is a radioactive isotope of carbon that is used to date fossils. There are about 1.5 atoms of carbon-14 for every trillion atoms of carbon in the atmosphere, which known as 1.5 ppt (parts per trillion). Carbon in a living organism has the same concentration as carbon-14. When an organism dies, the carbon-14 content decays at a rate of 11.4% per millennium (1000 years). Write the equation for carbon-14 concentration (in ppt) as a function of time (in millennia) and determine how old a fossil must be that has a measured concentration of 0.2 ppt.

16. **Music** Stringed instruments like guitars and pianos create a note when a string vibrates back and forth. The distance that the middle of the string moves from the center is called the amplitude (a), and for a guitar, it starts at 0.75 mm when a note is first struck. Amplitude decays at a rate that depends on the individual instrument and the note, but a decay rate of about 25% per second is typical. Calculate the time it takes for an amplitude of 0.75 mm to reach 0.1 mm.

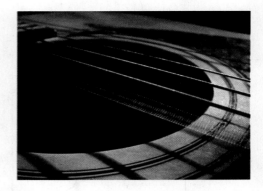

H.O.T. Focus on Higher Order Thinking

17. **Analyze Relationships** Compare the graphs of $f(x) = \left(\frac{1}{2}\right)^x$ and $g(x) = x^{\frac{1}{2}}$.
    Which of the following properties are the same? Explain.

    a. Domain

    c. End behavior as x increases

    b. Range

    d. End behavior as x decreases

18. **Communicate Mathematical Ideas** A quantity becomes half as much during each given time period. Another quantity becomes one-quarter as much during the same given time period. Determine each decay rate, state which is greater, and explain your results.

19. **Multiple Representations** Exponential decay functions are written as transformations of the function $f(x) = b^x$, where $0 < b < 1$. However, it also possible to use negative exponents as the basis of an exponential decay function. Use the properties of exponents to show why the function $f(x) = 2^{-x}$ is an exponential decay function.

20. **Represent Real-World Problems** You buy a video game console for $500 and sell it 5 years later for $100. The resale value decays exponentially over time. Write a function that represents the resale value, R, in dollars over the time, t, in years. Explain how you determined your function.

Lesson Performance Task

Sodium-24 is a radioactive isotope of sodium used as a diagnostic aid in medicine. It undergoes radioactive decay to form the stable isotope magnesium-24 and has a half-life of about 15 hours. This means that, in this time, half the amount of a sample mass of sodium-24 decays to magnesium-24. Suppose we start with an initial mass of of 100 grams sodium-24.

a. Use the half-life of sodium-24 to write an exponential decay function of the form $m_{Na}(t) = m_0(1 - r)^t$, where m_0 is the initial mass of sodium-24, r is the decay rate, t is the time in hours, and $m_{Na}(t)$ is the mass of sodium-24 at time t. What is the meaning of r?

b. The combined amounts of sodium-24 and magnesium-24 must equal m_0, or 100, for all possible values of t. Show how to write a function for $m_{Mg}(t)$, the mass of magnesium-24 as a function of t.

c. Use a graphing calculator to graph $m_{Na}(t)$ and $m_{Mg}(t)$. Describe the graph of $m_{Mg}(t)$ as a series of transformations of $m_{Na}(t)$. What does the intersection of the graphs represent?

13.4 The Base e

Essential Question: How is the graph of $g(x) = ae^{x-h} + k$ related to the graph of $f(x) = e^x$?

 TEKS **A2.5.A** Determine the effects on the key attributes on the graphs of $f(x) = bx$...where b is...e when $f(x)$ is replaced by $af(x)$, $f(x) + d$, and $f(x - c)$ for specific positive and negative real values of a, c, and d. Also A2.2.A, A2.5.B, A2.5.D, A2.7.I

 Resource Locker

⏱ Explore 1 Graphing and Analyzing $f(x) = e^x$

The following table represents the function $f(x) = \left(1 + \frac{1}{x}\right)^x$ for several values of x.

x	1	10	100	1000	...
f(x)	2	2.5937...	2.7048...	2.7169...	...

As the value of x increases without bound, the value of $f(x)$ approaches a number whose decimal value is 2.718... This number is irrational and is called e. You can write this in symbols as $f(x) \to e$ as $x \to +\infty$.

If you graph $f(x)$ and the horizontal line $y = e$, you can see that $y = e$ is the horizontal asymptote of $f(x)$.

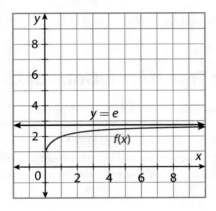

Even though e is an irrational number, it can be used as the base of an exponential function. The number e is sometimes called the natural base of an exponential function and is used extensively in scientific and other applications involving exponential growth and decay.

Ⓐ Copy and complete the table of values below for the function $f(x) = e^x$. Use decimal approximations.

x	−10	−1	−0.5	0	0.5	1	1.5	2
$f(x) = e^x$	4.54×10^{-5}	$\frac{1}{e} = 0.367...$	0.606...		$\sqrt{e} =$			

Ⓑ Plot the points on a graph.

Ⓒ The domain of $f(x) = e^x$ is $\left\{ x \mid \boxed{} \right\}$.

The range of $f(x) = e^x$ is $\left\{ y \mid \boxed{} \right\}$.

Ⓓ Is the function increasing or decreasing? For what values of x is it increasing/decreasing?

Ⓔ The function's y-intercept is $\left(0, \boxed{} \right)$ because $f(0) = e^0 = \boxed{}$ and $x = 0$ is in the domain of the function.

Ⓕ Another point on the graph that can be used as a reference point is $\left(1, \boxed{} \right)$.

Ⓖ Identify the end behavior.

$f(x) \to \boxed{}$ as $x \to \infty$

$f(x) \to \boxed{}$ as $x \to -\infty$

There is a horizontal asymptote at $y = \boxed{}$.

Reflect

1. What is the relationship between the graphs of $f(x) = e^x$, $g(x) = 2^x$, and $h(x) = 3^x$? (Hint: Sketch the graphs on your own paper.)

⊘ Explore 2 Predicting Transformations of the Graph of $f(x) = e^x$

The parent function, $f(x) = e^x$, can be transformed into a different exponential function with base e depending on the value and sign of the constant parameters h, k, and a. As in previous transformation of graphs, the effect of h on the graph of $g(x) = f(x - h)$, the effect of k on the graph of $g(x) = f(x) + k$, and the effect of a on the graph of $g(x) = af(x)$ can all be predicted from the value and sign of the parameters. Predict the effect of each transformation on the following graphs and then use a graphing calculator to confirm your prediction.

Ⓐ Transform $f(x) = e^x$ into $g(x) = e^{x-1}$.

The function $g(x) = e^{x-1}$ is of the form $g(x) = \boxed{}$, so $g(x) = e^{x-1}$ represents a $\boxed{}$ translation by $\boxed{}$ units(s) to the $\boxed{}$.

Ⓑ Transform $f(x) = e^x$ into $g(x) = e^{x+1}$.

The function $g(x) = e^{x+1}$ is of the form $g(x) = \boxed{}$, so $g(x) = e^{x+1}$ represents a $\boxed{}$ translation by $\boxed{}$ units(s) to the $\boxed{}$.

Ⓒ Transform $f(x) = e^x$ into $g(x) = e^x + 2$.

The function $g(x) = e^x + 2$ is of the form $g(x) = \boxed{}$, so $g(x) = e^x + 2$ represents a $\boxed{}$ translation by $\boxed{}$ units(s) $\boxed{}$.

Ⓓ $f(x) = e^x$ into $g(x) = e^x - 2$.

The function $g(x) = e^x - 2$ is of the form $g(x) =$ [ ], so $g(x) = e^x - 2$ represents a translation by [ ] units(s) [ ].

Ⓔ Transform $f(x) = e^x$ into $g(x) = 2e^x$.

The function $g(x) = 2e^x$ is of the form $g(x) =$ [ ], so $g(x) = 2e^x$ represents a vertical [ ] by a factor of [ ].

Ⓕ Transform $f(x) = e^x$ into $g(x) = \frac{1}{2}e^x$.

The function $g(x) = \frac{1}{2}e^x$ is of the form $g(x) =$ [ ], so $g(x) = \frac{1}{2}e^x$ represents a vertical [ ] by a factor of [ ].

Ⓖ Transform $f(x) = e^x$ into $g(x) = -2e^x$.

The function $g(x) = -2e^x$ is of the form $g(x) =$ [ ], so $g(x) = -2e^x$ represents a vertical [ ] by a factor of [ ] and a reflection across the [ ]-axis.

Ⓗ Transform $f(x) = e^x$ into $g(x) = -\frac{1}{2}e^x$.

The function $g(x) = -\frac{1}{2}e^x$ is of the form $g(x) =$ [ ], so $g(x) = -\frac{1}{2}e^x$ represents a vertical [ ] by a factor of [ ] and a reflection across the [ ]-axis.

Reflect

2. **Discussion** Describe the effects of the parameters h, k, and a on the domain, range, and asymptote of $g(x)$ in regards to the domain, range, and asymptote of the parent function $f(x)$.

🔧 Explain 1 Graphing Combined Transformations of $f(x) = e^x$

When graphing combined transformations of $f(x) = e^x$ that result in the function $g(x) = a \cdot e^{x-h} + k$, it helps to focus on two reference points on the graph of $f(x)$, $(0, 1)$ and $(1, e)$, as well as on the asymptote $y = 0$. The table shows these reference points and the asymptote $y = 0$ for $f(x) = e^x$ and the corresponding points and asymptote for the transformed function, $g(x) = a \cdot e^{x-h} + k$.

	$f(x) = e^x$	$g(x) = a \cdot e^{x-h} + k$
First reference point	$(0, 1)$	$(h, a + k)$
Second reference point	$(1, e)$	$(h + 1, ae + k)$
Asymptote	$y = 0$	$y = k$

Example 1 Given a function of the form $g(x) = a \cdot e^{x-h} + k$, identify the reference points and use them to draw the graph. State the transformations that compose the combined transformation, the asymptote, the domain, and range. Write the domain and range using set notation.

(A) $g(x) = 3 \cdot e^{x+1} + 4$

Compare $g(x) = 3 \cdot e^{x+1} + 4$ to the general form $g(x) = a \cdot e^{x-h} + k$ to find that $h = -1$, $k = 4$, and $a = 3$.

Find the reference points of $f(x) = 3 \cdot e^{x+1} + 4$.

$(0, 1) \rightarrow (h, a + k) = (-1, 3 + 4) = (-1, 7)$

$(1, e) \rightarrow (h + 1, ae + k) = (-1 + 1, 3e + 4) = (0, 3e + 4)$

State the transformations that compose the combined transformation.

$h = -1$, so the graph is translated 1 unit to the left.

$k = 4$, so the graph is translated 4 units up.

$a = 3$, so the graph is vertically stretched by a factor of 3.

a is positive, so the graph is not reflected across the x-axis.

The asymptote is vertically shifted to $y = k$, so $y = 4$.

The domain is $\left\{x | -\infty < x < \infty\right\}$.

The range is $\left\{y | y > 4\right\}$.

Use the information to graph the function $g(x) = 3 \cdot e^{x+1} + 4$.

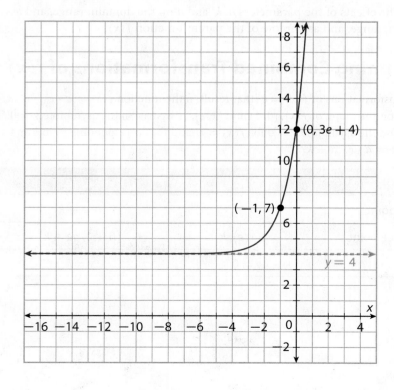

Ⓑ $g(x) = -0.5 \cdot e^{x-2} - 1$

Compare $g(x) = -0.5 \cdot e^{x-2} - 1$ to the general form $g(x) = a \cdot e^{x-h} + k$ to find that $h = \boxed{2}$,

$k = \boxed{-1}$, and $a = \boxed{-0.5}$.

Find the reference points of $g(x) = -0.5 \cdot e^{x-2} - 1$.

$(0, 1) \rightarrow (h, a + k) = \left(\boxed{2}, \boxed{-0.5} + \boxed{-1}\right) = \left(\boxed{2}, \boxed{-1.5}\right)$

$(1, e) \rightarrow (h + 1, ae + k) = \left(\boxed{2} + 1, \boxed{-0.5}e + \boxed{-1}\right) = \left(\boxed{3}, \boxed{-0.5e - 1}\right)$

State the transformations that compose the combined transformation.

$h = \boxed{2}$, so the graph is translated $\boxed{2}$ units to the right.

$k = \boxed{-1}$, so the graph is translated $\boxed{1}$ unit down.

$a = \boxed{-0.5}$, so the graph is vertically stretched by a factor of $\boxed{0.5}$.

a is negative, so the graph is reflected across the $\boxed{x}$-axis.

The asymptote is vertically shifted to $y = k$, so $y = \boxed{-1}$.

The domain is $\left\{x \mid \boxed{-\infty < x < \infty}\right\}$.

The range is $\left\{y \mid \boxed{y < -1}\right\}$.

Use the information to graph the function $g(x) = -0.5 \cdot e^{x-2} - 1$.

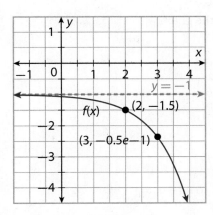

Your Turn

Given a function of the form $g(x) = a \cdot e^{x-h} + k$, identify the reference points and use them to draw the graph. State the asymptote, domain, and range. Write the domain and range using set notation.

3. $g(x) = (-1) \cdot e^{x+2} - 3$

4. $g(x) = 2 \cdot e^{x-1} + 1$

Writing Equations for Combined Transformations of $f(x) = e^x$

If you are given the transformed graph $g(x) = a \cdot e^{x-h} + k$, it is possible to write the equation of the transformed graph by using the reference points $(h, a + k)$ and $(1 + h, ae + k)$.

Example 2   Write the function whose graph is shown. State the domain and range in set notation.

(A)   First, look at the labeled points on the graph.

$(h, a + k) = (4, 6)$

$(1 + h, ae + k) = (5, 2e + 4)$

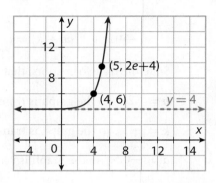

Find a, h, and k.

$(h, a + k) = (4, 6)$, so $h = 4$.

$(1 + h, ae + k) = (5, 2e + 4)$, so $ae + k = 2e + 4$.
Therefore, $a = 2$ and $k = 4$.

Write the equation by substituting the values of a, h, and k into the function $g(x) = a \cdot e^{x-h} + k$.

$g(x) = 2e^{x-4} + 4$

State the domain and range.

Domain: $\left\{ x \mid -\infty < x < \infty \right\}$

Range: $\left\{ y \mid y > 4 \right\}$

(B)   First, look at the labeled points on the graph.

$(h, a + k) = \left(\boxed{-4}, \boxed{-8} \right)$

$(1 + h, ae + k) = \left(\boxed{-3}, \boxed{-2e - 6} \right)$

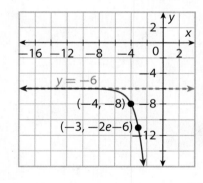

Find a, h, and k.

$(h, a + k) = (-4, -8)$, so $h = \boxed{-4}$.

$(1 + h, ae + k) = (-3, -2e - 6)$, so $ae + k = \boxed{-2e - 6}$.

Therefore, $a = \boxed{-2}$ and $k = \boxed{-6}$.

Write the equation by substituting the values of a, h, and k into the function $g(x) = a \cdot e^{x-h} + k$.

$g(x) = \boxed{-2e^{x+4} - 6}$

State the domain and range.

Domain: $\left\{ x \mid \boxed{-\infty < x < \infty} \right\}$

Range: $\left\{ y \mid \boxed{y < -6} \right\}$

Write the function whose graph is shown. State the domain and range in set notation.

5.

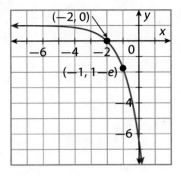

6.

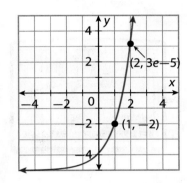

Explain 3 Modeling with Exponential Functions Having Base *e*

Although the function $f(x) = e^x$ has base $e \approx 2.718$, the function $g(x) = e^{cx}$ can have any positive base (other than 1) by choosing an appropriate positive or negative value of the constant c. This is because you can write $g(x)$ as $(e^c)^x$ by using the Power of a Power Property of Exponents.

Example 3 **Solve each problem using a graphing calculator. Then determine the growth rate or decay rate of the function.**

(A) The Dow Jones index is a stock market index for the New York Stock Exchange. The Dow Jones index after for the period 1980-2000 can be modeled by $V_{DJ}(t) = 878e^{0.121t}$, where t is the number of years after 1980. Determine how many years after 1980 the Dow Jones index will reach 3000.

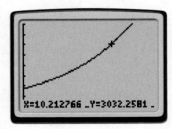

Use a graphing calculator to graph the function.

The value of the function is about 3000 when $x \approx 10.2$. So, the Dow Jones index will reach 3000 after 10.2 years, or after the year 1990.

In an exponential growth model of the form $f(x) = ae^{cx}$, the growth factor $1 + r$ is equal to e^c.

To find r, first rewrite the function in the form $f(x) = a(e^c)^x$.

$$V_{DJ}(t) = 878e^{0.121t}$$

$$= 878(e^{0.121})^t$$

Find r by using $1 + r = e^c$.

$$1 + r = e^c$$

$$1 + r = e^{0.121}$$

$$r = e^{0.121} - 1 \approx 0.13$$

So, the growth rate is about 13%.

Ⓑ The Nikkei 225 index is a stock market index for the Tokyo Stock Exchange. The Nikkei 225 index for the period 1990-2010 can be modeled by $V_{N225}(t) = 23{,}500e^{-0.0381t}$, where t is the number of years after 1990. Determine how many years after 1990 the Nikkei 225 index will reach 15,000.

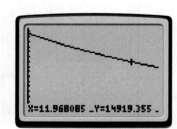

X=11.968085 _Y=14919.355 _

Use a graphing calculator to graph the function.

The value of the function is about 15,000 when $x \approx \boxed{12}$. So, the

Nikkei 225 index will reach 15,000 after $\boxed{12}$ years, or after the year $\boxed{2002}$.

In an exponential decay model of the form $f(x) = ae^{cx}$, the decay factor $\boxed{1 - r}$ is equal to e^c.

To find r, first rewrite the function in the form $f(x) = a(e^c)^x$.

$$V_{N225}(t) = 23{,}500e^{-0.0381t}$$

$$= 23{,}500\left(\boxed{e^{-0.0381}}\right)^t$$

Find r by using $1 - r = e^c$.

$$1 - r = e^c$$

$$1 - r = \boxed{e^{-0.0381}}$$

$$r = \boxed{1 - e^{-0.0381}} \approx \boxed{0.037}$$

So, the growth rate is $\boxed{3.7}$ %.

7. A paleontologist uncovers a fossil of a saber-toothed cat in California. The paleontologist analyzes the fossil and concludes that the specimen contains 15% of its original carbon-14. The percent of original carbon-14 in a specimen after t years can be modeled by $N(t) = 100e^{-0.00012t}$, where t is the number of years after the specimen died. Use a graphing calculator to determine the age of the fossil. Then determine the decay rate of the function.

💬 Elaborate

8. Which transformations of $f(x) = e^x$ change the function's end behavior?

9. Which transformations change the location of the graph's y-intercept?

10. Why can the function $f(x) = ae^{cx}$ be used as an exponential growth model and as an exponential decay model? How can you tell if the function represents growth or decay?

11. **Essential Question Check-In** How are reference points helpful when graphing transformations of $f(x) = e\,x$ or when writing equations for transformed graphs?

⭐ Evaluate: Homework and Practice

- Online Homework
- Hints and Help
- Extra Practice

1. What is the greatest value of $f(x) = \left(1 + \frac{1}{x}\right)^x$ for any positive value of x?

2. Identify the key attributes of $f(x) = e^x$, including the domain and range in set notation, the end behavior, and all intercepts.

Predict the effect of the parameters h, k, or a on the graph of the parent function $f(x) = e^x$. Identify any changes of domain, range, or end behavior.

3. $g(x) = f\left(x - \frac{1}{2}\right)$

4. $g(x) = f(x) - \frac{5}{2}$

5. $g(x) = -\frac{1}{4}f(x)$

6. $g(x) = \frac{27}{2}f(x)$

7. The graph of $f(x) = ce^x$ crosses the y-axis at $(0, c)$, where c is some constant. Where does the graph of $g(x) = f(x) - d$ cross the y-axis?

Given the function of the form $g(x) = a \cdot e^{x-h} + k$, identify the reference points and use them to draw the graph. State the domain and range in set notation.

8. $g(x) = e^{x-1} + 2$

9. $g(x) = -e^{x+1} - 1$

10. $g(x) = \frac{1}{2} e^{x+3} + 2$

11. $g(x) = -\frac{3}{4} e^{x+2} - 4$

12. $g(x) = \frac{3}{2} e^{x-1} - 3$

13. $g(x) = -\frac{5}{3} e^{x-4} + 2$

Write the function whose graph is shown. State the domain and range in set notation.

14.

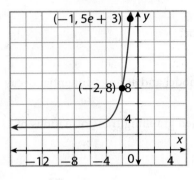

15.

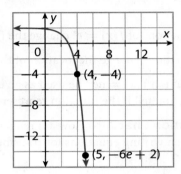

Solve each problem using a graphing calculator. Then determine the growth rate or decay rate of the function.

16. Medicine Technetium-99m, a radioisotope used to image the skeleton and the heart muscle, has a half-life of about 6 hours. Use the decay function $N(t) = N_0 e^{-0.1155t}$, where N_0 is the initial amount and t is the time on hours, to determine how many hours it takes for a 250 milligram dose to decay to 16 milligrams.

17. Ecology The George River herd of caribou in Canada was estimated to be about 4700 in 1954 and grew at an exponential rate to about 472,000 in 1984. Use the exponential growth function $P(t) = P_0 e^{0.154t}$, where P_0 is the initial population, t is the time in years after 1954, and $P(t)$ is the population at time t, to determine after how many years the herd will be 25 million.

18. Chemistry Radioactive plutonium (Pu-239) has a half-life about 24,110 years. Use the function $N(t) = N_0 e^{-0.000029t}$ to find how many years it will take for 20 grams of Pu-239 to decay to 1 gram. N_0 represents the initial amount of Pu-239 and t is the time in years.

19. Population The population of a town was estimated to be about 7200 in 1990 and grew at an exponential rate to about 40,000 in 2010. Use the exponential growth function $P(t) = P_0 e^{0.086t}$, where P_0 is the initial population, t is the time in years after 1990, and $P(t)$ is the population at time t, to determine after how many years the population will be 50,000.

20. Explain the Error A classmate claims that the function $g(x) = -4e^{x-5} + 6$ is the parent function $f(x) = e^x$ reflected across the y-axis, vertically compressed by a factor of 4, translated to the left 5 units, and translated up 6 units. Explain what the classmate described incorrectly and describe $g(x)$ as a series of transformations of $f(x)$.

21. Multi-Step Newton's law of cooling states that the temperature of an object decreases exponentially as a function of time, according to $T = T_s + (T_0 - T_s)e^{-kt}$, where T_0 is the initial temperature of the liquid, T_s is the surrounding temperature, and k is a constant. For a time in minutes, the constant for coffee is approximately 0.283. The corner coffee shop has an air temperature of 70°F and serves coffee at 206°F. Coffee experts say coffee tastes best at 140°F.

a. How long does it take for the coffee to reach its best temperature?

b. The air temperature on the patio outside the coffee shop is 86 °F. How long does it take for coffee to reach its best temperature there?

c. Find the time it takes for the coffee to cool to 71°F in both the coffee shop and the patio. Explain how you found your answer.

22. Analyze Relationships The graphing calculator screen shows the graphs of the functions $f(x) = 2^x$, $f(x) = 10^x$, and $f(x) = e^x$ on the same coordinate grid. Identify the common attributes and common point(s) of the three graphs. Explain why the point(s) is(are) common to all three graphs.

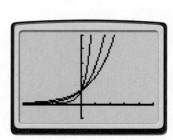

Lesson Performance Task

The ever-increasing amount of carbon dioxide in Earth's atmosphere is an area of concern for many scientists. In order to more accurately predict what the future consequences of this could be, scientists make mathematic models to extrapolate past increases into the future. A model developed to predict the annual mean carbon dioxide level L in Earth's atmosphere in parts per million t years after 1960 is $L(t) = 36.9 \cdot e^{0.0223t} + 280$.

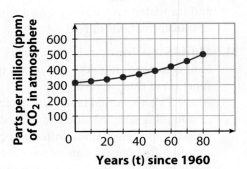

a. Use the function $L(t)$ to describe the graph of $L(t)$ as a series of transformations of $f(t) = e^t$.

b. Find and interpret $L(80)$, the carbon dioxide level predicted for the year 2040. How does it compare to the carbon dioxide level in 2015?

c. Can $L(t)$ be used as a model for all positive values of t? Explain.

Exponential Functions

Essential Question: How can you use exponential functions to solve real-world problems?

© Houghton Mifflin Harcourt Publishing Company

Key Vocabulary

exponential decay
   (decremento exponencial)
exponential function
   (función exponencial)
exponential growth
   (crecimiento exponencial)
geometric sequence
   (sucesión geométrica)

KEY EXAMPLE   *(Lesson 13.1)*

Find the 12ᵗʰ term of the geometric sequence 5, 15, 45, . . .

$r = \dfrac{15}{5} = 3$	Find the common ratio of the sequence.
$a_n = a_1 r^{n-1}$	Write the formula for a geometric sequence
$a_{12} = 5(3)^{12-1}$	Substitute in a_1, r, and n.
$a_{12} = 5(177,147)$	Use a calculator to solve for a_{12}.
$a_{12} = 885,735$	Simplify.

KEY EXAMPLE   *(Lesson 13.3)*

$g(x) = 3^{x+1}$ **is a transformation of the function** $f(x) = 3^x$. **Sketch a graph of** $g(x) = 3^{x+1}$.

$$g(x) = 3^{x+1} = f(x+1)$$

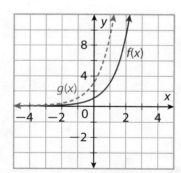

Because $g(x) = 3^{x+1} = f(x+1)$, the graph of g can be obtained by shifting the graph of f one unit to the left, as shown.

The solid line represents $f(x) = 3^x$,.
The dashed line represents $g(x) = 3^{x+1}$.

EXERCISES

1. If the first three terms of a geometric sequence are 3, 12, and 48, what is the seventh term? *(Lesson 13.1)*

Sketch the graphs of the following transformations. *(Lessons 13.2, 13.3, 13.4)*

2. $g(x) = -2(0.5)^x$

3. $f(x) = \left(\dfrac{1}{2}\right)^{-x}$

4. $f(x) = 2e^{x-2} + 1$

5. $g(x) = \left(\dfrac{3}{5}\right)^x$

MODULE PERFORMANCE TASK
That's The Way the Ball Bounces

Kingston is a chemical engineer who is testing the "bounciness" of two novel materials. He formed each material into two equal-sized spheres. Kingston then dropped each sphere on a hard surface and measured the heights the spheres reached after each bounce. The results are shown in the table.

	Heights (cm)					
	h_0	h_1	h_2	h_3	h_4	h_5
Material A	90	63.0	44.1	30.9	21.6	15.1
Material B	90	49.5	27.2	15.0	8.2	4.5

Use the data to create mathematical models for the heights of the spheres. Compare the two materials. One of the two materials will be used for the tip of a pogo stick. Which material should Kingston recommend and why?

Be sure to write down all your data and assumptions. Then use graphs, numbers, words, or algebra to explain how you reached your conclusion.

13.1–13.4 Exponential Functions

- Online Homework
- Hints and Help
- Extra Practice

Write a recursive rule and an explicit rule for each geometric sequence.
(Lesson 13.1)

1. $9, 27, 81, 243, \ldots$

2. $5, -5, 5, -5, \ldots$

State the domain and range for the graphs of the following functions. *(Lessons 13.2, 13.3)*

3. $y = \dfrac{1}{4}^x$

4. $y = \dfrac{1}{3}^{(x-2)} + 2$

5. $y = -3 \cdot 2^{x+2}$

6. $y = 3^{x-2} - 1$

ESSENTIAL QUESTION

7. How can you tell whether an exponential function models exponential growth or exponential decay?

Assessment Readiness

1. Which of the following is a geometric sequence?
   A. 10, 15, 20, 25,...
   B. 5, 15, 45, 135,...
   C. 1, 3, 5, 7,...
   D. $\frac{1}{2}, \frac{3}{4}, 1, 1\frac{1}{4},$...

2. When the base in an exponential function is between 0 and 1, the function shows
   A. exponential decay
   B. exponential growth
   C. the natural base e
   D. a geometric sequence

3. What is the asymptote of the graph of $y = \left(\frac{1}{2}\right)^{x-2} + 3$?
   A. $y = -3$
   B. $y = -2$
   C. $y = 2$
   D. $y = 3$

4. Solve $\frac{3}{4}|x + 3| - 8 = 4$ for x.
   A. $x = 13$ or $x = -19$
   B. $x = 8$ or $x = -3$
   C. $x = -3$
   D. $x = 5$ or $x = -11$

5. The graphs of $f(x) = 2^x$, $f(x) = 10^x$ and $f(x) = e^x$ all pass through a common point. Explain why the point $(0, 1)$ is common to all three functions.

Modeling with Exponential and Other Functions

Essential Question: How can modeling with exponential and other functions help you to solve real-world problems?

REAL WORLD VIDEO
Most people have to save up money for a major purchase like a car or new home. Check out some of the factors to consider when investing for long-term goals.

MODULE PERFORMANCE TASK PREVIEW
Double Your Money!

If you had some money to invest, how would you pick the investment option that would let your money grow fastest? The return on an investment depends on factors such as the length of time of the investment and the return rate. How can you use an exponential model to find out when an investment will double in value? Let's find out!

Are (YOU) Ready?

Complete these exercises to review skills you will need for this chapter.

Writing Linear Equations

Example 1

Write an equation for the line that passes through the points $(2, 3)$ and $(4, -1)$.

$$\frac{-1 - 3}{4 - 2} = \frac{-4}{2} = -2 \qquad \text{Find the slope.}$$

$$\text{So } y = -2x + b \qquad \text{Substitute slope for } m \text{ in } y = mx + b.$$

$$(3) = -2(2) + b \qquad \text{Substitute } (2, 3) \text{ for } x\text{- and } y\text{-values.}$$

$$b = 7 \qquad \text{Solve for } b.$$

The equation is $y = -2x + 7$.

Write an equation for the line that passes through the given points.

1. $(2, -5), (6, -3)$ **2.** $(4, -3), (-2, 15)$ **3.** $(4, 7), (-2, -2)$

Transforming Linear Functions

Example 2

Write the equation of $y = 9x - 2$ after a reflection across the x-axis followed by a reflection across the y-axis.

$$y = -1(9x - 2) \rightarrow y = -9x + 2 \qquad \text{Reflection across the } x\text{-axis}$$

$$y = -9(-x) + 2 \rightarrow y = 9x + 2 \qquad \text{Reflection across the } y\text{-axis}$$

$$\text{So } y = 9x - 2 \qquad \begin{array}{l} \text{reflected across both axes is} \\ y = 9x + 2. \end{array}$$

Write the equation of each function after a reflection across both axes.

4. $y = 2x + 1$ **5.** $y = -3x - 4$ **6.** $y = -0.2x + 6$

Equations Involving Exponents

Example 3

Solve $x^{\frac{2}{3}} = 16$ for x.

$$\left(x^{\frac{2}{3}}\right)^{\frac{3}{2}} = \pm (16)^{\frac{3}{2}} \qquad \text{Raise both sides to the same power.}$$

$$x = \pm \left(16^{\frac{1}{2}}\right)^{3} = \pm (4)^{3} = \pm 64 \qquad \text{Evaluate the right side.}$$

So, $x = \pm 64$.

Solve for x.

7. $x^6 = 4096$ **8.** $x^{\frac{3}{2}} = 27$ **9.** $\frac{1}{3}x^{\frac{2}{5}} = 3$

14.1 Fitting Exponential Functions to Data

Essential Question: What are ways to model data using an exponential function of the form
$f(x) = ab^x$?

 TEKS **A2.8.B** Use regression methods available through technology to write ... an exponential function from a given set of data. Also A2.8.A, A2.8.C

⌗ Explore   Identifying Exponential Functions from Tables of Values

Notice for an exponential function $f(x) = ab^x$ that $f(x + 1) = ab^{x+1}$. By the product of powers property, $ab^{x+1} = a(b^x \cdot b^1) = ab^x \cdot b = f(x) \cdot b$. So, $f(x + 1) = f(x) \cdot b$. This means that increasing the value of x by 1 multiplies the value of $f(x)$ by b. In other words, for successive integer values of x, each value of $f(x)$ is b times the value before it, or, equivalently, the ratio between successive values of $f(x)$ is b. This gives you a test to apply to a given set of data to see whether it represents exponential growth or decay.

Each table gives function values for successive integer values of x. Find the ratio of successive values of $f(x)$ to determine whether each set of data can be modeled by an exponential function.

Ⓐ

x	0	1	2	3	4
f(x)	1	4	16	64	256

$\dfrac{f(1)}{f(0)} = $ ▨ ; $\dfrac{f(2)}{f(1)} = $ ▨ ; $\dfrac{f(3)}{f(2)} = $ ▨ ; $\dfrac{f(4)}{f(3)} = $ ▨

Are the data exponential?

Ⓑ

x	0	1	2	3	4
f(x)	1	7	13	19	25

$\dfrac{f(1)}{f(0)} = $ ▨ ; $\dfrac{f(2)}{f(1)} = $ ▨ ; $\dfrac{f(3)}{f(2)} = $ ▨ ; $\dfrac{f(4)}{f(3)} = $ ▨

Are the data exponential?

Ⓒ

x	0	1	2	3	4
f(x)	1	4	13	28	49

$\dfrac{f(1)}{f(0)} = $ ▨ ; $\dfrac{f(2)}{f(1)} = $ ▨ ; $\dfrac{f(3)}{f(2)} = $ ▨ ; $\dfrac{f(4)}{f(3)} = $ ▨

Are the data exponential?

x	0	1	2	3	4
f(x)	1	0.25	0.0625	0.015625	0.00390625

$\dfrac{f(1)}{f(0)} = $ ▨ ; $\dfrac{f(2)}{f(1)} = $ ▨ ; $\dfrac{f(3)}{f(2)} = $ ▨ ; $\dfrac{f(4)}{f(3)} = $ ▨

Are the data exponential?

Reflect

1. In which step(s) does the table show exponential growth? Which shows exponential decay? What is the base of the growth or decay?

2. In which step are the data modeled by the exponential function $f(x) = 4^{-x}$?

3. What type of function model would be appropriate in each step not modeled by an exponential function? Explain your reasoning.

4. **Discussion** In the introduction to this Explore, you saw that the ratio between successive terms of $f(x) = ab^x$ is b. Find and simplify an expression for $f(x + c)$ where c is a constant. Then explain how this gives you a more general test to determine whether a set of data can be modeled by an exponential function.

Explain 1 Roughly Fitting an Exponential Function to Data

As the answer to the last Reflect question above indicates, if the ratios of successive values of the dependent variable in a data set for equally-spaced values of the independent variable are equal, an exponential function model fits. In the real world, sets of data rarely fit a model perfectly, but if the ratios are approximately equal, an exponential function can still be a good model.

Example 1

Ⓐ **Population Statistics** The table gives the official population of the United States for the years 1790 to 1890.

Year	Total Population
1790	3,929,214
1800	5,308,483
1810	7,239,881
1820	9,638,453
1830	12,860,702
1840	17,063,353
1850	23,191,876
1860	31,443,321
1870	38,558,371
1880	50,189,209
1890	62,979,766

© Houghton Mifflin Harcourt Publishing Company

Create an approximate exponential model for the data set. Then graph your function with a scatter plot of the data and assess its fit.

It appears that the ratio of the population in each decade to the population of the decade before it is pretty close to one and one third, so an exponential model should be reasonable.

For a model of the form $f(x) = ab^x$, $f(0) = a$. So, if x is the number of decades after 1790, the value when $x = 0$ is a, the initial population in 1790, or 3,929,214.

One way to estimate the growth factor, b, is to find the population ratios from decade to decade and average them:

$$\frac{1.35 + 1.36 + 1.33 + 1.33 + 1.33 + 1.36 + 1.36 + 1.23 + 1.30 + 1.26}{10} \approx 1.32$$

An approximate model is $f(x) = 3.93(1.32)^x$, where $f(x)$ is in millions.

The graph is shown.

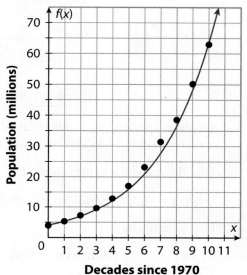

The graph looks like a good fit for the data. All of the points lie on, or close to, the curve.

Another way to estimate b is to choose a point other than $(0, a)$ from the scatter plot that appears would lie on, or very close to, the best-fitting exponential curve. Substitute the coordinates in the general formula and solve for b. For the plot shown, the point $(8, 38.56)$ looks like a good choice.

$$38.56 = 3.93 \cdot b^8$$

$$(9.81)^{\frac{1}{8}} \approx (b^8)^{\frac{1}{8}}$$

$$1.33 \approx b$$

An approximate model is $f(x) = 3.93(1.33)^x$. The graph is shown.

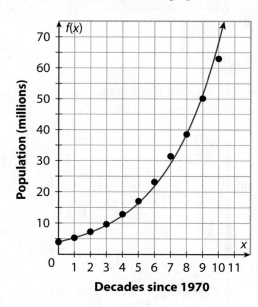

Notice that this function model appears to be even better than the first one for the period from 1790 to 1870, but the first model better represents the data at the end of the 100-year period.

B **Movies** The table shows the decline in weekly box office revenue from its peak for one of 2013's top-grossing summer movies.

Week	Revenue (in Millions of Dollars)
0	95.3
1	55.9
2	23.7
3	16.4
4	8.8
5	4.8
6	3.3
7	1.9
8	1.1
9	0.6

Create an approximate exponential model for the data set. Then graph your function with a scatter plot of the data and assess its fit.

Find the value of a in $f(x) = ab^x$.

When $x = 0$, $f(x) = 95.3$. So, $a = 95.3$.

Find an estimate for b.

Approximate the revenue ratios from week to week and average them:

$$\frac{0.59 + 0.42 + 0.69 + 0.54 + \boxed{0.55 + 0.69 + 0.58 + 0.58 + 0.55}}{\boxed{9}} \approx \boxed{0.58}$$

An approximate model is $f(x) = \boxed{95.3(0.58)^x}$.

The graph looks like a very good fit for the data. All of the points except one (2 weeks after peak revenue) lie on, or very close to, the curve.

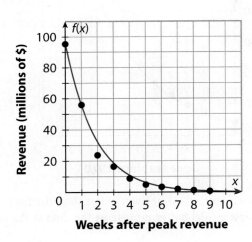

5. **Fisheries** The total catch in tons for Iceland's fisheries from 2002 to 2010 is shown in the table.

Year	Total Catch (Millions of Tons)
2002	2.145
2003	2.002
2004	1.750
2005	1.661
2006	1.345
2007	1.421
2008	1.307
2009	1.164
2010	1.063

Create an approximate exponential model for the data set. Then graph your function with a scatter plot of the data and assess its fit.

🎯 Explain 2 Fitting an Exponential Function to Data Using Technology

Previously you have used a graphing calculator to find a linear regression model of the form $y = ax + b$ to model data, and have also found quadratic regression models of the form $y = ax^2 + bx + c$. Similarly, you can use a graphing calculator to perform exponential regression to produce a model of the form $f(x) = ab^x$.

Example 2

Ⓐ **Population Statistics** Use the data from Example 1 Part A and a graphing calculator to find the exponential regression model for the data, and show the graph of the model with the scatter plot.

Using the STAT menu, enter the number of decades since 1790 in List1 and the population to the nearest tenth of a million in List2.

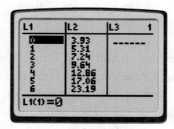

© Houghton Mifflin Harcourt Publishing Company • Image Credits: ©Bob Krist/Corbis

Using the STAT CALC menu, choose "ExpReg" and press ENTER until you see this screen:

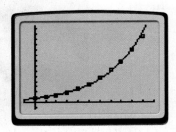

An approximate model is $f(x) = 4.116(1.323)^x$.

Making sure that STATPLOT is turned "On," enter the model into the Y = menu either directly or using the VARS menu and choosing "Statistics," "EQ," and "RegEQ.") The graphs are shown using the ZoomStat window:

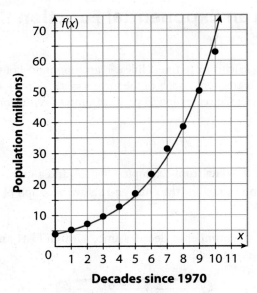

Plotted with the second graph from Example 1 (shown dotted), you can see that the graphs are nearly identical.

Decades since 1970

(B) **Movies** Use the data from Example 1 Part B and a graphing calculator to find the exponential regression model for the data. Graph the regression model on the calculator, then graph the model from Example 1 on the same screen using a dashed curve. How do the graphs of the models compare? What can you say about the actual decline in revenue from one week after the peak to two weeks after the peak compared to what the regression model indicates?

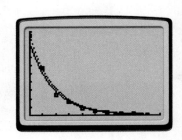

Enter the data and perform exponential regression.

The model (using 3 digits of precision is $f(x) = \boxed{86.2(0.576)^x}$.

The graphs of the models are very close, but the regression equation starts with a lower initial value, and comes closer to the data point that the first model misses by the most. The last several weeks the models appear to be very close together. From the data, the decline from one week after the peak to two weeks after the peak was significantly larger than accounted for by the regression model.

Reflect

6. **Discussion** The U.S. population in 2014 was close to 320 million people. What does the regression model in Part A predict for the population in 2014? What does this tell you about extrapolating far into the future using an exponential model? How does the graph of the scatter plot with the regression model support this conclusion? (Note: The decade-to-decade U.S. growth dropped below 30% to stay after 1880, and below 20% to stay after 1910. From 2000 to 2010, the rate was below 10%.)

Your Turn

7. **Fisheries** Use the data from YourTurn5 and a graphing calculator to find the exponential regression model for the data. Graph the regression model on the calculator, then graph the model from your answer to YourTurn5 on the same screen. How do the graphs of the models compare?

🔑 Explain 3 Solving a Real-World Problem Using a Fitted Exponential Function

In the real world, the purpose of finding a mathematical model is to help identify trends or patterns, and to use them to make generalizations, predictions, or decisions based on the data.

Example 3

Ⓐ The Texas population increased from 20.85 million to 25.15 million from 2000 to 2010.

  a. Assuming exponential growth during the period, write a model where $x = 0$ represents the year 2000 and $x = 1$ represents the year 2010. What was the growth rate over the decade?

  b. Use the power of a power property of exponents to rewrite the model so that b is the yearly growth factor instead of the growth factor for the decade. What is the yearly growth rate for this model? Verify that the model gives the correct population for 2010.

  c. The Texas population was about 26.45 million in 2013. How does this compare with the prediction made by the model?

  d. Find the model's prediction for the Texas population in 2035. Do you think it is reasonable to use this model to guide decisions about future needs for water, energy generation, and transportation needs. Explain your reasoning.

a. For a model of the form $f(x) = ab^x$, a $= f(0)$, so $a = 20.85$. To find an estimate for b, substitute $(x, f(x)) = (1, 25.5)$ and solve for b.

$$f(x) = a \cdot b^x$$

$$25.15 = 20.85 \cdot b^1$$

$$\frac{25.15}{20.85} = b, \text{ so } b \approx 1.206$$

An approximate model is $f(x) = 20.85(1.206)^x$. The growth rate was about 20.6%.

b. Because there are 10 years in a decade, the 10th power of the new b must give 1.206, the growth factor for the decade. So, $b^{10} = 1.206$, or $b = 1.206^{\frac{1}{10}}$. Use the power of a power property:

$$f(x) = 20.85(1.206)^x = 20.85\left(1.206^{\frac{1}{10}}\right)^{10x} \approx 20.85(1.019)^{10x}$$

Because x is decades after 2000, this is equivalent to $f(x) = 20.85(1.019)^x$ where x is years after 2000.

The model gives a 2010 population of $f(x) = 20.85(1.019)^{10} \approx 25.17$. This agrees with the actual population within a rounding error.

c. Substitute $x = 13$ into the model $f(x) = 20.85(1.019)^x$:

$$f(13) = 20.85(1.019)^{13} \approx 26.63$$

The prediction is just a little bit higher than the actual population.

d. For 2035, $x = 35$: $f(35) = 20.85(1.019)^{35} \approx 40.3$. The model predicts a Texas population of about 40 million in 2035. Possible answer: Because it is very difficult to maintain a high growth rate with an already very large population, and with overall population growth slowing, it seems unreasonable that the population would increase from 25 to 40 million so quickly. But because using the model to project even to 2020 gives a population of over 30 million, it seems reasonable to make plans for the population to grow by several million people over a relatively short period.

B The average revenue per theater for the movie in Part B of the previous Examples are shown in the graph. (Note that for this graph, Week 0 corresponds to Week 2 of the graphs from the previous Examples.) The regression model is $y = 5.65(0.896)^x$.

a. From Week 3 to Week 4, there is a jump of over 60% in the average weekly revenue per theater, but the total revenue for the movie for the corresponding week fell by over 30%. What must have occurred for this to be true?

There must have been a sharp reduction in the number of theaters showing the movie.

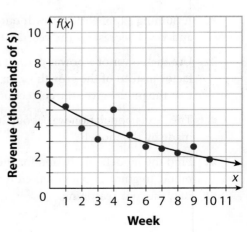

b. A new theater complex manager showing a similar summer movie in a single theater worries about quickly dropping revenue the first few weeks, and wants to stop showing the movie. Suppose you are advising the manager. Knowing that the model shown reflects the long-term trend well for such movies, what advice would you give the manager?

Possible answer: Be careful about removing the movie too quickly. Unless the amount of weekly revenue needed is very high, the model indicates that the longer-term trend may decline more slowly than the short-term trend.

Reflect

8. Discussion Consider the situation in Example 3B about deciding when to stop showing the movie. How does an understanding of what other theater managers might do affect your decision?

Your Turn

9. Graph the regression model for the catch in Icelandic fisheries, $f(x) = 2.119(0.9174^x)$, to find when the model predicts the total catches to drop below 0.5 million tons (remember that $x = 0$ corresponds to 2002). Should the model be used to project actual catch into the future? Why or why not? What are some considerations that the model raises about the fishery?

💬 Elaborate

10. How can you tell whether a given set of data can reasonably be modeled using an exponential function?

11. What are some ways that an exponential growth or decay model can be used to guide decisions, preparations, or judgments about the future?

12. Essential Question Check-In What are some ways to find an approximate exponential model for a set of data without using a graphing calculator?

⭐ Evaluate: Homework and Practice

- Online Homework
- Hints and Help
- Extra Practice

Determine whether each set of data can be modeled by an exponential function. If it can, tell whether it represents exponential growth or exponential decay. If it can't, tell whether a linear or quadratic model is instead appropriate.

1.

x	0	1	2	3	4
f(x)	2	6	18	54	162

2.

x	1	2	3	4	5	6
f(x)	1	2	3	5	8	13

3.

x	0	1	2	3	4
f(x)	2	8	18	32	50

4.

x	5	10	15	20	25
f(x)	76.2	66.2	59.1	50.9	44.6

Three students, Anja, Ben, and Celia, are asked to find an approximate exponential model for the data shown. Use the data and scatter plot for Exercises 5–7.

x	0	1	2	3	4	5	6	7	8	9	10
f(x)	10	6.0	5.4	3.9	3.7	2.3	1.4	1.0	0.9	0.8	0.5

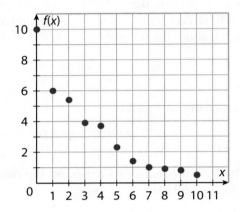

5. To find an approximate exponential model, Anja uses the first data point to find a, and then estimates b by finding the ratio of the first two function values. What is her model?

6. To find his model, Ben uses the first and last data points. What is his model?

7. Celia thinks that because the drop between the first two points is so large, the best model might actually have a y-intercept a little below 10. She uses $(0, 9.5)$ to estimate a in her model. To estimate b, she finds the average of the ratios of successive data values. What is her model? (Use two digits of precision for all quantities.)

8. Classic Cars The data give the estimated value in dollars of a model of classic car over several consecutive years.

15,4300	16,2100	17,300	18,400	19,600	20,700	22,000

a. Find an approximate exponential model for the car's value by averaging the successive ratios of the value. Then make a scatter plot of the data, graph your model with the scatter plot, and assess its fit to the data.

b. In the last year of the data, a car enthusiast spends $15,100 on a car of the given model that is in need of some work. The owner then spends $8300 restoring it. Use your model to create a table of values with a graphing calculator. How long does the function model predict the owner should keep the car before it can be sold for a profit of at least $5000?

9. **Movies** The table shows the average price of a movie ticket in the United States from 2001 to 2010.

Year	2001	2002	2003	2004	2005	2006	2007	2008	2009	2010
Price ($)	5.66	5.81	6.03	6.21	6.41	6.55	6.88	7.18	7.50	7.89

a. Make a scatter plot of the data. Then use the first point and another point on the plot to find an approximate exponential model for the average ticket price. Then graph the model with your scatter plot and assess its fit to the data.

b. Use a graphing calculator to find a regression model for the data, and graph the model with the scatter plot. How does this model compare to your previous model?

c. What does the regression model predict for the average cost in 2014? How does this compare with the actual 2014 cost of about $8.35? A theater owner uses the model in 2010 to project income for 2014 assuming average sales of 490 tickets per day at the predicted price. If the actual price is instead $8.35, did the owner make a good business decision? Explain.

10. **Pharmaceuticals** A new medication is being studied to see how quickly it is metabolized in the body. The table shows how much of an initial dose of 15 milligrams remains in the bloodstream after different intervals of time.

Hours Since Administration	Amount Remaining (mg)
0	15
1	14.3
2	13.1
3	12.4
4	11.4
5	10.7
6	10.2
7	9.8

a. Use a graphing calculator to find a regression model. Use the calculator to graph the model with the scatter plot. How much of the drug is eliminated each hour?

b. The half-life of a drug is how long it takes for half of the drug to be broken down or eliminated from the bloodstream. Using the Table function, what is the half-life of the drug to the nearest hour?

c. Doctors want to maintain at least 7 mg of the medication in the bloodstream for maximum therapeutic effect, but do not want the amount much higher for a long period. This level is reached after 12 hours. A student suggests that this means that a 15 mg dose should be given every 12 hours. Explain whether you agree with the student. (*Hint*: Given the medicine's decay factor, how much will be in the bloodstream after the first few doses?)

11. Housing The average selling price of a unit in a high-rise condominium complex over 5 consecutive years was approximately $184,300; $195,600; $204,500; $215,300; $228,200.

a. Find an exponential regression model where x represents years after the initial year and $f(x)$ is in thousands of dollars.

b. A couple wants to buy a unit in the complex. First, they want to save 20% of the selling price for a down payment. What is the model that represents 20% of the average selling price for a condominium?

c. At the time that the average selling price is $228,200 $\left(\text{or when } x = 4\right)$, the couple has $20,000 saved toward a down payment. They are living with family, and saving $1000 per month. Graph the model from Part *b* and a function that represents the couple's total savings on the same calculator screen. How much longer does the model predict it will take them to save enough money?

12. Business growth The growth in membership in thousands of a rapidly-growing Internet site over its first few years is modeled by $f(x) = 60(3.61)^x$ where x is in years and $x = 0$ represents the first anniversary of the site. Rewrite the model so that the growth factor represents weeks instead of years. What is the weekly growth factor? What does this model predict for the membership 20 weeks after the anniversary?

13. Which data set can be modeled by an exponential function $f(x) = ab^x$?

a. $(0, 0.1), (1, 0.5), (2, 2.5), (3, 12.5)$

b. $(0, 0.1), (1, 0.2), (2, 0.3), (3, 0.4)$

c. $(0, 1), (1, 2), (2, 4), (4, 8)$

d. $(0, 0.8), (1, 0.4), (2, 0.10), (3, 0.0125)$

H.O.T. Focus on Higher Order Thinking

14. Error analysis From the data $(2, 72.2), (3, 18.0), (4, 4.4), (5, 1.1), (6, 0.27)$, a student sees that each change of 1 in x corresponds to a change in $f(x)$ of very close to 0.25, so that an exponential model is appropriate. From the first term, the student obtains $a = 72.2$, and writes the model $f(x) = 72.2(0.25)^x$. The student graphs the model with the data and observes that it does not fit the data well. What did the student do wrong? Correct the student's model.

15. Critical thinking For the data $(0, 5)$, $(1, 4)$, $(2, 3.5)$, $(3, 3.25)$, $(4, 3.125)$, $(5, 3.0625)$, the ratio of consecutive y-values is not constant, so you cannot write an exponential model $f(x) = ab^x$. But the difference in the values from term to term, 1, 0.5, 0.25, 0.125, 0.0625, shows exponential decay with a decay factor of 0.5. How can you use this fact to write a model of the data that contains an exponential expression of the form ab^x?

16. Challenge Suppose that you have two data points (x_1, y_1) and (x_2, y_2) that you know are fitted by an exponential model $f(x) = ab^x$. Can you always find an equation for the model? Explain.

Lesson Performance Task

According to data from the U.S. Department of Agriculture, the number of farms in the United States has been decreasing over the past several decades. During this time, however, the average size of each farm has increased.

Farms in the United States	
Year	Farms (Millions)
1940	6.35
1950	5.65
1960	3.96
1970	2.95
1980	2.44
1990	2.15
2000	2.17

a. From 1940 to 1980, the average size of a U.S. farm can be modeled by the function $A(t) = 174e^{0.022t}$ where t is the number of years since 1940 and A is the average farm size in acres. What was the average farm size in 1940? In 1980?

b. The table shows the number of farms in the United States from 1940 to 2000. Find an exponential model for the data using a calculator.

c. If you were to determine the exponential model without a calculator, would the value for *a* be the same as the value from the calculator? Explain your answer.

d. Based on the data in the table, predict what the number of farms in the United States in 2014.

e. Using a graphing calculator, determine how many years it takes for the number of farms to decrease by 50%.

f. Using a graphing calculator, determine when the number of farms in the United States will fall below 1 million.

g. Does an exponential model seem appropriate for all of the data listed in the table? Why or why not?

14.2 Choosing Among Linear, Quadratic, and Exponential Models

Essential Question: How do you choose among, linear, quadratic, and exponential models for a given set of data?

 TEKS **A2.8.A** Analyze data to select the appropriate model from among linear, quadratic, and exponential models. Also A2.8.B, A2.8.C

⊘ Explore   Developing Rules of Thumb for Visually Choosing a Model

Previously, you have found models for different function classes, including linear, quadratic, and exponential. In those cases, you were working with one kind of model. When you are working with data, you may not know ahead of time what kind of model may be appropriate. Sometimes, the choice may be relatively easy. For example, data lying along a curve that rises and then falls or falls and then rises will likely be well-fitted by a quadratic model. But sometimes it may not be as clear.

Use the scatter plots shown for the steps following.

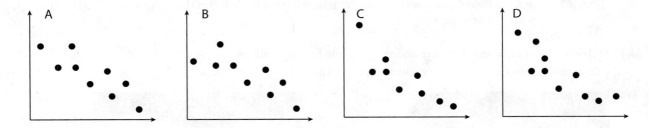

Ⓐ Look at scatter plot A. Do you think a linear model will be appropriate? Explain your reasoning. If you think a linear model is appropriate, what do you know about the lead coefficient?

Ⓑ Look at scatter plot B. What is different now that indicates that another kind of model might be appropriate? What characteristics would this model have?

Ⓒ Look at scatter plot C. What about this plot indicates that yet another kind of model might be appropriate? What characteristics would this model have?

Ⓓ Look at scatter plot D. This plot is very similar to plot C, but what indicates that a different model would be appropriate? What characteristics would this model have?

1. When can it be difficult to distinguish whether a quadratic or an exponential model is most appropriate?

2. Under what circumstances might it be difficult to tell exponential or quadratic data from linear data?

3. For data that do not lie tightly along a curve or line, what is different about the last data point that can make it potentially more misleading than other points?

⚙ Explain 1 Modeling with a Linear Function

As noted in the Explore, it is not always immediately clear what kind of model best represents a data set. With experience, your ability to recognize signs and reasons for choosing one model over another will increase.

Example 1 Make a scatter plot for each data set. Then complete the steps below.

> **Step 1:** Choose the data set that appears to be best modeled by a linear function. Explain your choice, whether you think a linear model will be a close fit, and whether any other model might possibly be appropriate. What characteristics do you expect the linear model will have?

> **Step 2:** Enter the data for your choice into your graphing calculator in two lists, and perform linear regression. Then give the model, defining your variables. What are the initial value and the rate of change of the model?

> **Step 3:** Graph the model along with the scatter plot using your calculator, then assess how well the model appears to fit the data.

(A) **Wildlife Conservation** Data sets and scatter plots for populations over time of four endangered, threatened, or scarce species are shown.

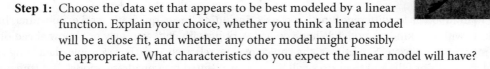

Whooping Crane, Texas Colony	
Year	**Population**
1940	22
1950	34
1960	33
1970	56
1980	76
1990	146
2000	177
2010	281

Florida Manatee	
Year	**Population**
2001	3300
2003	3127
2005	3143
2007	2817
2009	3802
2010	5077
2011	4834

Bald Eagle Pairs (Lower 48)	
Year	**Population**
1993	4015
1994	4449
1995	4712
1996	5094
1997	5295
1998	5748
1999	6104
2000	6471

California Least Terns, Breeding Pairs	
Year	**Population**
1998	4100
1999	3500
2000	4600
2001	4700
2002	3600
2003	6700
2004	6300
2005	6900

Step 1: The bald eagle population is clearly the one best modeled by a linear function, as the increase in the number of pairs is very steady, with no apparent curving or changes in the trend that might indicate a different model. The model will have a y-intercept of about 3 (in thousands) and will have a slope very close to 0.34, since the rate of change all along the graph remains close to the average rate of change from the first point to the last.

Step 2: A regression model is $y = 338.2x + 3042$ where x is the number of years after 1990 and y is the number of breeding pairs in thousands. The initial value is 3042, and the rate of change is about 338 pairs per year.

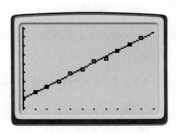

Step 3: The model is a very close fit to the data. It fits both the overall trend and the individual points very closely.

(B) **Automobiles** Data sets and scatter plots for various statistics about changes in automobiles of different model years are shown.

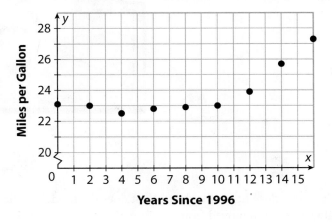

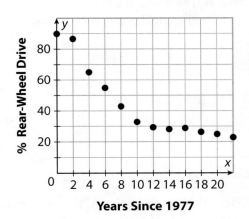

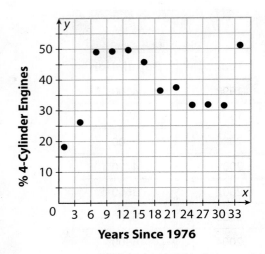

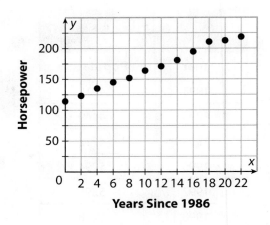

Step 1: The [horsepower data] are the data best modeled by a linear function, as the increase in [horsepower] over time is very steady, with the amount of increase never varying too much from the trend. All of the other data sets show clear variation in the rate of change. The model will have a *y*-intercept of about [114] and will have a positive slope that should be close to the overall average rate of change of [about 5], since the rate of change all along the graph remains close to the average rate of change from the first point to the last.

Step 2: A regression model is [$y = 4.967x + 113.9$] where x is the number of years after 1986 and y is the [114 horsepower] for the model year. The initial value is about 114 horsepower, and the rate of change is about [5 horsepower per year].

Step 3: The model is a very close fit to the data. It fits both the overall trend and the individual points very closely.

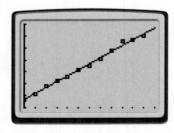

Reflect

4. **Discussion** In Example 1A, the linear model is a very close fit for the data. What does the model predict for the number of pairs in 2007, the year the bald eagle was removed from the Endangered Species list? Do you think that this was a good decision given the model and the fact that the actual 2007 number of pairs was 11,040? Explain.

5. What does the model in Example 1B predict for the horsepower in 2013? Given that the actual average horsepower for new vehicles in 2013 was about 230, observing your plot and model, and thinking about changes in passenger vehicles, do you think the trend in the model will continue, or change significantly? Explain.

6. **Demographics** Data sets and scatter plots for various changes in the United States population over time are shown. Using these data, complete the three steps described at the beginning of Example 1. Also, tell whether you would expect the trend indicated by your model to continue for a time after the data shown, or whether you expect that it would soon change, and explain your answer.

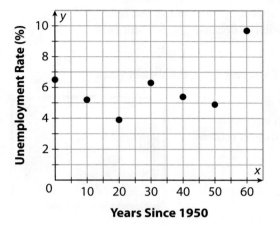

Year	Mean Full-time Wage ($)
1940	1315
1950	3180
1960	4816
1970	7501
1980	14,610
1990	25,236
2000	39,237

Year	Median Age (Years)
1950	30.2
1960	29.5
1970	28.1
1980	30.0
1990	32.9
2000	35.3
2010	37.2

🔑 Explain 2   Modeling With a Quadratic Function

Example 2   Using the groups of data sets and their scatter plots from Example 1:

Step 1: Choose the data set that appears to be best modeled by a quadratic function. Explain your choice, whether you think a quadratic model will be a close fit, and whether any other model might possibly be appropriate. What characteristics do you expect the quadratic model will have?

Step 2: Enter the data for your choice into your graphing calculator in two lists, and perform quadratic regression. Then give the model, defining your variables.

Step 3: Graph the model along with the scatter plot using your calculator, then assess how well the model appears to fit the data.

(A) Use the data about animal populations in Example 1 Part A.

Step 1: The Florida manatee population appears to be the one best modeled by a quadratic function, as its scatter plot is the only one with a clear change in direction, and it clearly would not be well represented by a linear or exponential model. The whooping crane data might also be fit fairly well on one side of a quadratic model, but it might also be exponential. The quadratic model for the manatee population will have a positive leading coefficient since it opens upward, but it is hard to predict what the y-intercept or the vertex will be. Because graph is not very symmetrical, the fit may not be very close.

Step 2: A regression model is $y = 48.50x^2 - 317.3x + 3411$ where x is the number of years after 2001 and y is the number of manatees

Step 3: The model is not a close fit, but it does look like an appropriate model for the overall trend during the time of the data. It misses the horizontal position for the vertex by a fairly wide margin, but otherwise is not too far from the data.

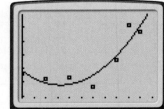

(B) Use the data about automobiles in Example 1 Part B.

Step 1: The miles per gallon data appear to be the data best modeled by a quadratic function, as its scatter plot seems to show a change of direction and a minimum point. The % Rear-Wheel Drive data looks approximately quadratic for a while, but the data continue to decline at the right, so a quadratic model would not be a good fit. Also, part of the percent 4-Cylinder data looks somewhat quadratic with a negative leading coefficient, but the graph changes direction again, indicating that a cubic model would be much more appropriate. The quadratic model for miles per gallon will have a positive leading coefficient since it opens upward. It appears that the vertex will not be too far from the minimum point on the plot, though it may be a little to the right.

Step 2: A regression model is $y = 0.0390x^2 - 0.3922x + 23.40$ where x is the number of years after 1996 and y is the average miles per gallon.

Step 3: The model is a fairly close fit to the data. Its minimum reflects the actual minimum miles per gallon closely, and the model reflects the trend at the right side of the data well.

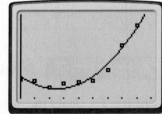

Reflect

7. Discussion The Florida manatee has been under consideration for being downgraded from endangered to threatened. Do you believe the graph and model of the manatee population in Part A of this Example support this concept or argue against it? Explain your reasoning.

8. How might the model for miles per gallon affect a decision on when to purchase a car?

9. Using the data in Your Turn Exercise 6, complete the three steps described at the beginning of Example 2. Also, tell whether you would expect the trend indicated by your model to continue for a time after the data shown, or whether you expect that it would soon change, and explain your answer.

⚙ Explain 3   Modeling with an Exponential Function

Example 3   **Using the groups of data sets and their scatter plots from Example 1:**

Step 1: Choose the data set that appears to be best modeled by an exponential function. Explain your choice, whether you think an exponential model will be a close fit, and whether any other model might possibly be appropriate. What characteristics do you expect the exponential model will have?

Step 2: Enter the data for your choice into your graphing calculator in two lists, and perform exponential regression. Then give the model, defining your variables. What are the initial value, growth or decay factor, and growth or decay rate of the model?

Step 3: Graph the model along with the scatter plot using your calculator, then assess how well the model appears to fit the data.

Ⓐ   Use the data about animal populations in Example 1 Part A.

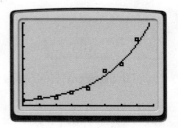

Step 1: The whooping crane population appears to be the one best modeled by an exponential function, as it rises increasingly quickly, but does not reflect a change in direction as a quadratic model can. Though the whooping crane plot is nearly linear in its midsection, the slow initial rise and fast later rise indicate that an exponential model is better. The California least tern data show a significant jump, but no clear pattern. An appropriate whooping crane model shows exponential growth, so the parameter b is greater than 1. Because the growth is not very large considering the time period of 70 years, however, the yearly growth factor will not be much above 1.

Step 2: A regression model is $y = 20.05(1.0374)^x$ where x is the number of years after 1940 and y is the population. The initial value for the model is 20 whooping cranes. The growth factor is 1.0374, and the growth rate is 0.0374, or about 3.74% per year.

Step 3: The model is very good fit for the data. Some data points are a little above the curve and some a little below, but the fit is close and reflects the trend very well.

Ⓑ   Use the data about automobiles in Example 1 Part B.

Step 1: The percent of cars with rear-wheel drive data appears to be the data best modeled by an exponential function (exponential decay), as overall, the graph drops less and less steeply with time. None of the other plots has this characteristic. Because the data indicate exponential decay instead of growth, the parameter b is less than 1. The model will likely not be a really close fit, as is appears that the ratio of y–values from term to term varies a fair amount.

Step 2: A regression model is $y = 80.45(0.9371)^x$ where x is the number of years after 1977 and y is the percent of cars with rear-wheel drive. The initial value for the model is 80.45%. The decay factor is 0.9371, and the decay rate is $1 - 0.9371 = 0.0629$, or about 6.3%.

Step 3: The model is a fairly good fit, but not a close fit. The model falls well below the first two data points, and does not represent the middle of the data well. It does match the trend better toward the end of the data, though the model's decay rate is a little too high for the actual data.

Reflect

10. Discussion What does the model for the whooping crane population predict for the population in 2040? Do you think it is possible that the whooping crane will be removed from the endangered species list any time in the next few decades? Explain.

Your Turn

11. Using the data in YourTurn Exercise 6, complete the three steps described at the beginning of Example 3. Also, tell whether you would expect the trend indicated by your model to continue for a time after the data shown, or whether you expect that it would soon change, and explain your answer.

💬 Elaborate

12. Discussion How does making a prediction from a model help make a decision or judgment based on a given set of data?

13. Describe the process for obtaining a regression model using a graphing calculator.

14. Essential Question Check-In How can a scatter plot of a data set help you determine the best type of model to choose for the data?

☆ Evaluate: Homework and Practice

- Online Homework
- Hints and Help
- Extra Practice

1. For scatter plots A–D, select the most appropriate model from the following. Do not use any choice more than once.

I. quadratic, $a > 0$ **II.** quadratic, $a < 0$ **III.** linear, $a < 0$

IV. exponential, $b > 1$ **V.** exponential, $b < 1$

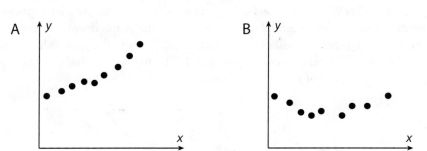

© Houghton Mifflin Harcourt Publishing Company

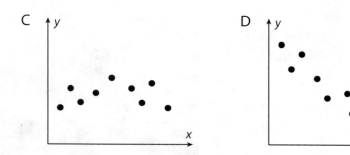

C

D

For the data set given in each of 2–5:

    a. Create a scatter plot of the data. What kind of model do you think is most appropriate? Why? What characteristics do you expect that this model will have?

    b. Use a graphing calculator to find an equation of the regression model. Then interpret the model, including the meaning of important parameters.

    c. Graph the regression model with its scatter plot using a graphing calculator. How well does the model fit?

    d. Answer the question following the data.

2. **Population Demographics** The data set shows the number of Americans living in multigenerational households.

Year	Number (in Millions)
1950	32
1960	27
1970	26
1980	28
1990	35
2000	42
2010	52

What does the model predict for the number in 2020? in 2040? Are these numbers reasonable? Explain.

3. Cycling The data set shows the inseam length for different frame sizes for road bicycles.

Frame Size (cm)	Inseam Length (cm)
46	69
48	71
49	74
51	76
53	79
54	81
58	86
60	89
61	91

Jarrell has an inseam of 84 cm, but the table does not give a frame size for him. He graphs the model on a graphing calculator and finds that a y-value of 84 is closest to an x-value of 56. He decides he needs a 56 cm frame. Do you think this is a reasonable conclusion. Explain.

4. Population Geography The data set shows the percent of the U.S. population living in central cities.

What does your model predict for the percent of the population living in central cities in 2010? How much confidence would you have in this prediction? Explain. Given that the actual number for 2010 was about 36.9%, does this support your judgment?

Year	% of Population
1910	21.2
1920	24.2
1930	30.8
1940	32.5
1950	32.8
1960	32.3
1970	31.4
1980	30.0

5. Animal Migration The data set shows the number of bald eagles counted passing a particular location on a migration route. Predict the number of bald eagles in 2033. How much confidence do you have in this prediction?

Year	Number of Eagles
1973	41
1978	79
1983	384
1988	261
1993	1725
1998	3289
2003	3356

6. **Smart Phones** The data set shows the percent of the world's population owning a smart phone.

   a. Create a scatter plot of the data.

   b. Use a graphing calculator to find equations for both exponential and quadratic regression models. Then interpret the models, including the meaning of important parameters.

   c. Graph both regression models with the scatter plot using a graphing calculator. Do both models fit the data well? Does one seem significantly better than the other?

   d. For how long after the data set do you think either model will be a good predictor? Explain your reasoning.

Year	% of Population
2006	1
2007	3
2008	4
2009	5
2010	7
2011	11
2012	16
2013	22

7. **Stock Market** The data set gives the U.S. stock market's average annual return rates by for each of the last 11 decades.

Decade Ending	Annual Return Rate (%)
1910	9.96
1920	4.20
1930	14.95
1940	−0.63
1950	8.72
1960	19.28
1970	7.78
1980	5.82
1990	17.57
2000	18.17
2010	3.1

   a. Make a scatter plot of the data.

   b. What kind of model do you think is most appropriate for the data? Explain your reasoning.

   c. Do the data give any kind of prediction about investing in the stock market for the future? Explain.

8. **Explain the Error** Out of curiosity, Julia enters the stock market data from Exercise 7 into her calculator and performs linear and quadratic regression. As she expected, there is almost no fit to the data at all. She then tries exponential regression, and get the message "ERR: DOMAIN." Why does she get this message?

9. **Critical Thinking** A student enters the road bicycle data from Exercise 3, accidentally performs quadratic regression instead of linear, and has the calculator graph the regression model with the scatter plot. The student sees the graph shown.

   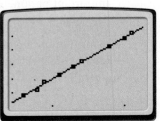

   The model graphed by the calculator is $y = -0.001241x^2 + 1.587x - 1.549$. It is obviously a very close fit to the data, and looks almost identical to the linear model. Explain how this can be true. (*Hint*: What happens when you zoom out?)

10. **Critical Thinking** A graphing calculator returns a linear regression equation $y = ax + b$, a quadratic regression equation $y = ax^2 + bx + c$, and an exponential regression equation $y = a \cdot b^x$. For exponential regression, a is always positive, which is not true of the other models. How does an exponential model differ from the other two models regarding translations of a parent function?

11. **Extension** In past work, you have used the correlation coefficient r, which indicates how well a line fits the data. The closer $|r|$ is to 1, the better the fit, and the closer to 0, the worse the fit. When you perform quadratic or exponential regression with a calculator, the *coefficient of determination* r^2 or R^2 serves a similar purpose. Return to the smart phone data in Exercise 6, and perform the quadratic and exponential regression again. (Make sure that "Diagnostics" is turned on in the Catalog menu of your calculator first.) Which model is the closer fit to the data, that is, for which model is R^2 closest to 1?

Lesson Performance Task

A student is given $50 to invest. The student chooses the investment very well. The following data shows the amount that the investment is worth over several years.

x (Years)	y (Dollars)
0	50
1	147
2	462
3	1411
4	4220
5	4431
6	4642

a. Determine an appropriate model for the data. If it is reasonable to break up the data so that you can use different models over different parts of the time, then do so. Explain the reasoning for choosing your model(s).

b. Write a situation that may reflect the given data.

Modeling with Exponential and Other Functions

Essential Question: How can modeling with exponential and other functions help you to solve real-world problems?

Key Vocabulary
exponential regression
(regresión exponencial)

KEY EXAMPLE (Lesson 14.1)

What type of function is illustrated in the table?

x	−1	0	1	2	3
f(x)	9	3	1	$\frac{1}{3}$	$\frac{1}{9}$

Whenever x increases by 1, $f(x)$ is multiplied by the common ratio of $\frac{1}{3}$. Since this ratio is less than 1, the table represents an exponential decay function.

KEY EXAMPLE (Lesson 14.2)

Create a scatter plot for the data in the table. Treat age as the independent variable x and median BMI as the dependent variable y. Then, use a graphing calculator to find an appropriate regression model of the data. Explain why you chose that particular type of function.

Age	2	3	4	5	6	7	8	9	10
Median BMI	16.5	16.0	15.2	15.2	15.6	15.6	15.8	16.0	16.3

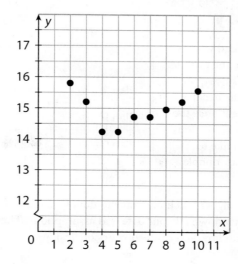

A quadratic regression of the data on a graphing calculator produces the equation $y = 0.0636x^2 - 0.7503x + 17.5867$. A quadratic function was chosen because the data points generally lie on a curve that approximates a parabola.

Choose the type of function (linear, quadratic, or exponential) you would use to model the data. *(Lesson 14.2)*

1.

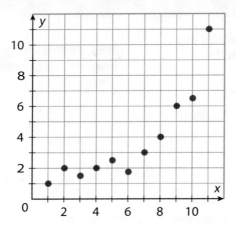

2.

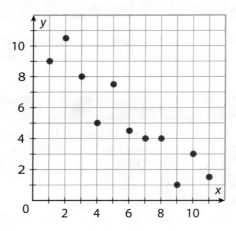

3. How does the Product of Powers Property of Exponents help you in deciding whether a given set of data is exponential? *(Lesson 14.1)*

MODULE PERFORMANCE TASK
Double Your Money

Jenna was a game show participant and won $10,000! She eventually wants to use the money as a down payment on a home but is not quite ready for such a big commitment. She decides to invest the money and plans to use it once the amount reaches $20,000. She researches various investment opportunities and would like to choose the one that will let her money double fastest.

Plan	Interest Rate	Compounding
Plan A	5.2%	Quarterly
Plan B	4.8%	Monthly
Plan C	4.25%	Continuously

To the nearest tenth of a year, how long will each plan take to double Jenna's money?. Which should Jenna choose? Be sure to write down all your data and assumptions. Then use graphs, numbers, words, or algebra to explain how you reached your conclusion.

Ready to Go On?

14.1–14.2 Modeling with Exponential an Other Functions

- Online Homework
- Hints and Help
- Extra Practice

The isotope X has a half-life of 10 days. Complete the table showing the decay of a sample of X. *(Lesson 14.1, 14.2)*

1.

Number of Half-Lives	Number of Days (t)	Percent of Isotope Remaining (p)
0	0	100
1	10	50
2	20	▮
3	▮	▮
4	▮	▮

2. Write the decay rate per half-life, r, as a fraction.

3. Write an expression for the number of half-lives in t days.

4. Write a function that models this situation. The function $p(t)$ should give the percent of the isotope remaining after t days.

ESSENTIAL QUESTION

5. What are two ways you can find an exponential function that models a given set of data?

Module 14   **575**   Study Guide Review

© Houghton Mifflin Harcourt Publishing Company

Assessment Readiness

1. Which exponential function has a graph that passes through $(1, 2)$ and $(3, 50)$?

   A. $y = \dfrac{3}{5} \cdot 5^x$

   B. $y = \dfrac{2}{5} \cdot 5^x$

   C. $y = \dfrac{1}{2} \cdot 5^x$

   D. $y = \dfrac{1}{3} \cdot 5^x$

2. What is the asymptote of the graph of the function $y = -2\left(\dfrac{1}{4}\right)^{x+1} + 7$?

   A. $y = 7$

   B. $y = \dfrac{1}{4}$

   C. $y = -2$

   D. $y = 2$

3. What are the real-number solutions of the equation $y^3 - 5y^2 = 0$?

   A. 0 and 5

   B. 5 and 10

   C. −5 and 0

   D. There are no real-number solutions.

4. What type of function is illustrated in the table?

x	4	5	6	7	8
f(y)	−4	−3	−4	−7	−12

   A. Exponential

   B. Quadratic

   C. Logarithmic

   D. Linear

5. How can you use the pattern formed by the points on a scatterplot to determine whether a linear, quadratic, or exponential function is most likely to be the best fit for the data?

Logarithmic Functions

TEKS

Essential Question: How can you use logarithmic functions to solve real-world problems?

REAL WORLD VIDEO
Check out some of the considerations that go into to determining the proper dosage of a medication and learn about the role of logarithmic functions in this process.

MODULE PERFORMANCE TASK PREVIEW
What's the Dosage?

Scientists working in the pharmaceutical industry discover, develop, and test drugs for everything from relieving a headache to controlling high blood pressure. One important question regarding a specific drug is how long the drug stays in a person's system. How can logarithmic functions be used to answer this question? Let's find out!

Are YOU Ready?

Complete these exercises to review skills you will need for this chapter.

Exponents

Example 1

Rewrite $x^{-3}y^2$ using only positive exponents.

$$x^{-3}y^2 = \frac{y^2}{x^3}$$

Rewrite each expression using only positive exponents.

1. $x^{-4}y^{-2}$

2. x^8y^{-5}

3. $\frac{x^{-1}}{y^{-2}}$

Rational and Radical Exponents

Example 2

Write $\sqrt[4]{a^6b^4}$ using rational exponents.

$$\sqrt[4]{a^6b^4} = \left(a^6b^4\right)^{\frac{1}{4}}$$

Remove the radical house.

$$= a^{\frac{3}{2}}b$$

Simplify.

Write the expression using rational exponents.

4. $\sqrt[6]{a^3b^{12}}$

5. $\sqrt[3]{ab^2}$

6. $\sqrt[4]{81a^{12}b^8}$

Graphing Linear Nonproportional Relationships

Example 3

Graph $y = -3x + 1$.

Graph the y–intercept of $(0, 1)$.

Use the slope $\frac{-3}{1}$ to plot a second point.

Draw a line through the two points.

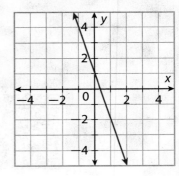

Graph each equation.

7. $y = \frac{2}{3}x - 4$

8. $y = 2x + 3$

15.1 Defining and Evaluating a Logarithmic Function

Essential Question: What is the inverse of the exponential function $f(x) = b^x$ where $b > 0$ and $b \neq 1$, and what is the value of $f^{-1}(b^m)$ for any real number m?

 TEKS A2.5.C Rewrite exponential equations as their corresponding logarithmic equations and logarithmic equations as their corresponding exponential equations. Also A2.2.A, A2.2.B, A2.2.C, A2.5.B, A2.7.I

Resource
Locker

⊘ Explore   Understanding Logarithmic Functions as Inverses of Exponential Functions

An exponential function such as $f(x) = 2^x$ accepts values of the exponent as inputs and delivers the corresponding power of 2 as the outputs. The inverse of an exponential function is called a **logarithmic function**. For $f(x) = 2^x$, the inverse function is written $f^{-1}(x) = \log_2 x$, which is read either as "the logarithm with base 2 of x" or simply as "log base 2 of x." It accepts powers of 2 as inputs and delivers the corresponding exponents as outputs.

Ⓐ Graph $f^{-1}(x) = \log_2 x$ by using a graph of $f(x) = 2^x$ as shown. Begin by reflecting the labeled points on the graph of $f(x) = 2^x$ across the line $y = x$ and labeling the reflected points with their coordinates. Then draw a smooth curve through the reflected points.

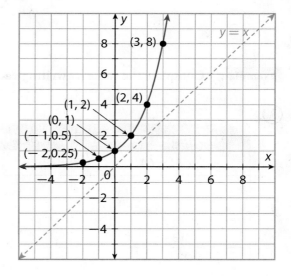

Ⓑ Using the labeled points on the graph of $f^{-1}(x)$, complete the following statements.

$f^{-1}(0.25) = \log_2 \boxed{} = \boxed{}$

$f^{-1}(0.5) = \log_2 \boxed{} = \boxed{}$

$f^{-1}(1) = \log_2 \boxed{} = \boxed{}$

$f^{-1}(2) = \log_2 \boxed{} = \boxed{}$

$f^{-1}(4) = \log_2 \boxed{} = \boxed{}$

$f^{-1}(8) = \log_2 \boxed{} = \boxed{}$

Reflect

1. Explain why the domain of $f(x) = 2^x$ doesn't need to be restricted in order for its inverse to be a function.

2. State the domain and range of $f^{-1}(x) = \log_2 x$ using set notation.

3. Identify any intercepts and asymptotes for the graph of $f^{-1}(x) = \log_2 x$.

4. Is $f^{-1}(x) = \log_2 x$ an increasing function or a decreasing function?

5. How does $f^{-1}(x) = \log_2 x$ behave as x increases without bound? As x decreases toward 0?

6. Based on the inverse relationship between $f(x) = 2^x$ and $f^{-1}(x) = \log_2 x$, complete this statement:

$$f^{-1}(16) = \log_2 \boxed{} = \boxed{} \quad \text{because } f\left(\boxed{}\right) = \boxed{}.$$

 Explain 1 ## Converting Between Exponential and Logarithmic Forms of Equations

In general, the exponential function $f(x) = b^x$, where $b > 0$ and $b \neq 1$, has the logarithmic function $f^{-1}(x) = \log_b x$ as its inverse. For instance, if $f(x) = 3^x$, then $f^{-1}(x) = \log_3 x$, and if $f(x) = \left(\frac{1}{4}\right)^x$, then $f^{-1}(x) = \log_{\frac{1}{4}} x$. The inverse relationship between exponential functions and logarithmic functions also means that you can write any exponential equation as a logarithmic equation and any logarithmic equation as an exponential equation.

Exponential Equation

$$b^x = a$$

Logarithmic Equation

$$\log_b a = x$$

$$b > 0, b \neq 1$$

Example 1 Complete the table by writing each given equation in its alternate form.

Ⓐ

Exponential Equation	Logarithmic Equation
$4^3 = 64$	?
?	$\log_5 \dfrac{1}{25} = -2$
$\left(\dfrac{2}{3}\right)^p = q$	?
?	$\log_{\frac{1}{2}} m = n$

Think of each equation as involving an exponential function or a logarithmic function. Identify the function's base, input, and output. For the inverse function, use the same base but switch the input and output.

Think of the equation $4^3 = 64$ as involving an exponential function with base 4. The input is 3, and the output is 64. So, the inverse function (a logarithmic function) also has base 4, but its input is 64, and its output is 3.

Think of the equation $\log_5 \frac{1}{25} = -2$ as involving a logarithmic function with base 5. The input is $\frac{1}{25}$, and the output is -2. So, the inverse function (an exponential function) also has base 5, but its input is -2, and its output is $\frac{1}{25}$.

Think of the equation $\left(\frac{2}{3}\right)^p = q$ as involving an exponential function with base $\frac{2}{3}$. The input is p, and the output is q. So, the inverse function (a logarithmic function) also has base $\frac{2}{3}$, but its input is q, and its output is p.

Think of the equation $\log_{\frac{1}{2}} m = -n$ as involving a logarithmic function with base $\frac{1}{2}$. The input is m, and the output is n. So, the inverse function (an exponential function) also has base $\frac{1}{2}$, but its input is n, and its output is m.

Exponential Equation	Logarithmic Equation
$4^3 = 64$	$\log_4 64 = 3$
$5^{-2} = \dfrac{1}{25}$	$\log_5 \dfrac{1}{25} = -2$
$\left(\dfrac{2}{3}\right)^p = q$	$\log_{\frac{2}{3}} q = p$
$\left(\dfrac{1}{2}\right)^n = m$	$\log_{\frac{1}{2}} m = n$

(B)

Exponential Equation	Logarithmic Equation
$3^5 = 243$	$\log_3 243 = 5$
$4^{-3} = \dfrac{1}{64}$	$\log_4 \dfrac{1}{64} = -3$
$\left(\dfrac{3}{4}\right)^r = s$	$\log_{\frac{3}{4}} s = r$
$\left(\dfrac{1}{5}\right)^w = v$	$\log_{\frac{1}{5}} v = w$

Think of the equation $3^5 = 243$ as involving an exponential function with base 3. The input is 5, and the output is 243. So, the inverse function (a logarithmic function) also has base 3, but its input is 243, and its output is 5.

Think of the equation $\log_4 \frac{1}{64} = -3$ as involving a logarithmic function with base 4. The input is $\frac{1}{64}$, and the output is -3. So, the inverse function (an exponential function) also has base 4, but its input is -3, and its output is $\frac{1}{64}$.

Think of the equation $\left(\frac{3}{4}\right)^r = s$ as involving an exponential function with base $\frac{3}{4}$. The input is r, and the output is s. So, the inverse function (a logarithmic function) also has base $\frac{3}{4}$, but its input is s, and its output is r.

Think of the equation $\log_{\frac{1}{5}} v = w$ as involving a logarithmic function with base $\frac{1}{5}$. The input is v, and the output is w. So, the inverse function (an exponential function) also has base $\frac{1}{5}$, but its input is w, and its output is v.

Reflect

7. A student wrote the logarithmic form of the exponential equation $5^0 = 1$ as $\log_5 0 = 1$. What did the student do wrong? What is the correct logarithmic equation?

8. Copy and complete the table. Write each given equation in its alternate form.

Exponential Equation	Logarithmic Equation
$10^4 = 10{,}000$	
	$\log_2 \frac{1}{16} = -4$
$\left(\frac{2}{5}\right)^c = d$	
	$\log_{\frac{1}{3}} x = y$

Explain 2 Evaluating Logarithmic Functions by Thinking in Terms of Exponents

The logarithmic function $f(x) = \log_b x$ accepts a power of b as an input and delivers an exponent as an output. In cases where the input of a logarithmic function is a recognizable power of b, you should be able to determine the function's output. You may find it helpful first to write a logarithmic equation by letting the output equal x and then to rewrite the equation in exponential form. Once the bases on each side of the exponential equation are equal, you can equate their exponents to find x.

Example 2

Ⓐ If $f(x) = \log_{10} x$, find $f(1000)$, $f(0.01)$, and $f(\sqrt{10})$.

$f(1000) = x$

$\log_{10} 1000 = x$

$10^x = 1000$

$10^x = 10^3$

$x = 3$

So, $f(1000) = 3$.

$f(0.01) = x$

$\log_{10} 0.01 = x$

$10^x = 0.01$

$10^x = 10^{-2}$

$x = -2$

So, $f(0.01) = -2$.

$f(\sqrt{10}) = x$

$\log_{10} \sqrt{10} = x$

$10^x = \sqrt{10}$

$10^x = 10^{\frac{1}{2}}$

$x = \frac{1}{2}$

So, $f(\sqrt{10}) = \frac{1}{2}$.

(B) If $f(x) = \log_{\frac{1}{2}} x$, find $f(4)$, $f\left(\frac{1}{32}\right)$ and $f(2\sqrt{2})$.

$$f(4) = x$$

$$\log_{\frac{1}{2}} 4 = x$$

$$\left(\frac{1}{2}\right)^x = 4$$

$$\left(\frac{1}{2}\right)^x = 2^{\boxed{2}}$$

$$\left(\frac{1}{2}\right)^x = \left(\frac{1}{2}\right)^{\boxed{-2}}$$

$$x = \boxed{-2}$$

So, $f(4) = \boxed{-2}$.

$$f\left(\frac{1}{32}\right) = x$$

$$\log_{\frac{1}{2}} \frac{1}{32} = x$$

$$\left(\frac{1}{2}\right)^x = \frac{1}{32}$$

$$\left(\frac{1}{2}\right)^x = \frac{1}{2^{\boxed{5}}}$$

$$\left(\frac{1}{2}\right)^x = \left(\frac{1}{2}\right)^{\boxed{5}}$$

$$x = \boxed{5}$$

So, $f\left(\frac{1}{32}\right) = \boxed{5}$.

$$f(2\sqrt{2}) = x$$

$$\log_{\frac{1}{2}} 2\sqrt{2} = x$$

$$\left(\frac{1}{2}\right)^x = 2\sqrt{2}$$

$$\left(\frac{1}{2}\right)^x = \sqrt{2^2 \cdot 2}$$

$$\left(\frac{1}{2}\right)^x = \sqrt{2^{\boxed{3}}}$$

$$\left(\frac{1}{2}\right)^x = 2^{\boxed{\frac{3}{2}}}$$

$$\left(\frac{1}{2}\right)^x = \left(\frac{1}{2}\right)^{\boxed{-\frac{3}{2}}}$$

$$x = \boxed{-\frac{3}{2}}$$

So $f(2\sqrt{2}) = \boxed{-\frac{3}{2}}$.

Your Turn

9. If $f(x) = \log_7 x$, find $f(343)$, $f\left(\frac{1}{49}\right)$, and $f(\sqrt{7})$.

10. If, $f(x) = \log_{\frac{1}{3}} x$, find $f(27)$, $f\left(\frac{1}{81}\right)$, and $f(9\sqrt{3})$.

⚙ Explain 3 Evaluating Logarithmic Functions Using a Scientific Calculator

You can use a scientific calculator to find the logarithm of any positive number x when the logarithm's base is either 10 or e. When the base is 10, you are finding what is called the *common logarithm* of x, and you use the calculator's `LOG` key because $\log_{10} x$ is also written as $\log x$ (where the base is understood to be 10). When the base is e, you are finding what is called the *natural logarithm* of x, and you use the calculator's `LN` key because $\log_e x$ is also written as $\ln x$.

Example 3 Use a scientific calculator to find the common logarithm and the natural logarithm of the given number. Verify each result by evaluating the appropriate exponential expression.

(A) 13

First, find the common logarithm of 13. Round the result to the thousandths place and raise 10 to that number to confirm that the power is close to 13.

Next, find the natural logarithm of 13. Round the result to the thousandths place and raise e to that number to confirm that the power is close to 13.

```
log(13)
        1.113943352
10^1.114
        13.00169578
```

```
ln(13)
        2.564949357
e^2.565
        13.00065837
```

So, log 13 ≈ 1.114.

So, ln 13 ≈ 2.565.

(B) 0.42

First, find the common logarithm of 0.42. Round the result to the thousandths place and raise 10 to that number to confirm that the power is close to 0.42.

log 0.42 ≈ $\boxed{-0.377}$

$10^{-0.377} \approx 0.42$

Next, find the natural logarithm of 0.42. Round the result to the thousandths place and raise e to that number to confirm that the power is close to 0.42.

ln 0.42 ≈ $\boxed{-0.868}$

$e^{-0.868} \approx 0.42$

Reflect

11. For any $x > 1$, why is log $x <$ ln x?

Your Turn

Use a scientific calculator to find the common logarithm and the natural logarithm of the given number. Verify each result by evaluating the appropriate exponential expression.

12. 0.25

13. 4

© Houghton Mifflin Harcourt Publishing Company

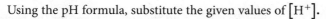

⚙ Explain 4 Evaluating a Logarithmic Model

There are standard scientific formulas that involve logarithms, such as the formulas for the acidity level (pH) of a liquid and the intensity level of a sound. It's also possible to develop your own models involving logarithms by finding the inverses of exponential growth and decay models.

Example 4

Ⓐ The acidity level, or pH, of a liquid is given by the formula $\text{pH} = \log \frac{1}{[\text{H}^+]}$ where $[\text{H}^+]$ is the concentration (in moles per liter) of hydrogen ions in the liquid. In a typical chlorinated swimming pool, the concentration of hydrogen ions ranges from 1.58×10^{-8} moles per liter to 6.31×10^{-8} moles per liter. What is the range of the pH for a typical swimming pool?

Using the pH formula, substitute the given values of $[\text{H}^+]$.

$$\text{pH} = \log\!\left(\frac{1}{6.31 \times 10^{-8}}\right)$$

$$\approx \log 15{,}800{,}000$$

$$\approx 7.2$$

$$\text{pH} = \log\!\left(\frac{1}{1.58 \times 10^{-8}}\right)$$

$$\approx \log 63{,}300{,}000$$

$$\approx 7.8$$

So, the pH of a swimming pool ranges from 7.2 to 7.8.

Ⓑ *Lactobacillus acidophilus* is one of the bacteria used to turn milk into yogurt. The population P of a colony of 3500 bacteria at time t (in minutes) can be modeled by the function $P(t) = 3500(2)^{\frac{t}{73}}$. How long does it take the population to reach 1,792,000?

Step 1 Solve $P = 3500(2)^{\frac{t}{73}}$ for t.

Write the model. $\qquad\qquad\qquad\qquad\qquad P = 3500(2)^{\frac{t}{73}}$

Divide both sides by 3500. $\qquad\qquad \dfrac{P}{\boxed{3500}} = (2)^{\frac{t}{73}}$

Rewrite in logarithmic form. $\quad \log_2 \dfrac{P}{\boxed{3500}} = \dfrac{t}{73}$

Multiply both sides by 73. $\quad 73 \log_2 \dfrac{P}{\boxed{3500}} = t$

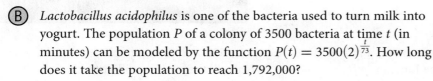

Step 2 Use the logarithmic model to find t when $P = 1{,}792{,}000$.

$$t = 73 \log_2 \dfrac{P}{\boxed{3500}}$$

$$= 73 \log_2 \dfrac{1{,}792{,}000}{\boxed{3500}}$$

$$= 73 \log_2 \boxed{512}$$

$$= 73 \left(\boxed{9} \right)$$

$$= \boxed{657}$$

So, the bacteria population will reach 1,792,000 in 657 minutes, or about 11 hours.

Reflect

14. Discussion Describe two ways you can use the solution in Part B to find the time it takes for the bacteria population to reach 3,584,000.

Your Turn

15. The intensity level L (in decibels, dB) of a sound is given by the formula $L = 10 \log \dfrac{I}{I_0}$ where I is the intensity (in watts per square meter, W/m^2) of the sound and I_0 is the intensity of the softest audible sound, about 10^{-12} W/m^2. What is the intensity level of a rock concert if the sound has an intensity of 3.2 W/m^2?

16. The mass (in milligrams) of beryllium-11, a radioactive isotope, in a 500-milligram sample at time t (in seconds) is given by the function $m(t) = 500e^{-0.05t}$. When will there be 90 milligrams of beryllium-11 remaining?

💬 Elaborate

17. What is a logarithmic function? Give an example.

18. How can you turn an exponential model that gives y as a function of x into a logarithmic model that gives x as a function of y?

19. Essential Question Check-In Write the inverse of the exponential function $f(x) = b^x$ where $b > 0$ and $b \neq 1$.

1. Copy and complete the input-output table for $f(x) = \log_2 x$. Plot and label the ordered pairs from the table. Then draw the complete graph of $f(x)$.

x	f(x)
0.25	
0.5	
1	
2	
4	
8	

2. Use the graph of $f(x) = \log_2 x$ to do the following.

   a. State the function's domain and range using set notation.

   b. Identify the function's end behavior.

   c. Identify the graph's x- and y-intercepts.

   d. Identify the graph's asymptotes.

   e. Identify the intervals where the function has positive values and where it has negative values.

   f. Identify the intervals where the function is increasing and where it is decreasing

3. Consider the exponential function $f(x) = 3^x$.

   a. State the function's domain and range using set notation.

   b. Describe any restriction you must place on the domain of the function so that its inverse is also a function.

   c. Write the rule for the inverse function.

   d. State the inverse function's domain and range using set notation.

4. Consider the logarithmic function $f(x) = \log_4 x$.

   a. State the function's domain and range using set notation.

   b. Describe any restriction you must place on the domain of the function so that its inverse is also a function.

   c. Write the rule for the inverse function.

   d. State the inverse function's domain and range using set notation.

Write the given exponential equation in logarithmic form.

5. $5^3 = 125$

6. $\left(\dfrac{1}{10}\right)^{-2} = 100$

7. $3^m = n$

8. $\left(\dfrac{1}{2}\right)^p = q$

Write the given logarithmic equation in exponential form.

9. $\log_6 1296 = 4$

10. $\log_{\frac{1}{4}} \dfrac{1}{64} = 3$

11. $\log_8 x = y$

12. $\log_{\frac{2}{3}} c = d$

13. If $f(x) = \log_3 x$, find $f(243)$, $f\left(\dfrac{1}{27}\right)$, and $f\left(\sqrt{27}\right)$.

14. If $f(x) = \log_6 x$, find $f(36)$, $f\left(\dfrac{1}{6}\right)$ and $f\left(6\sqrt[3]{6}\right)$.

15. If $f(x) = \log_{\frac{1}{4}} x$, find $f\left(\dfrac{1}{64}\right)$, $f(256)$, and $f\left(\sqrt[3]{16}\right)$.

Use a scientific calculator to find the common logarithm and the natural logarithm of the given number. Verify each result by evaluating the appropriate exponential expression.

16. 19

17. 9

18. 0.6

19. 0.31

20. The acidity level, or pH, of a liquid is given by the formula $\text{pH} = \log \dfrac{1}{[H^+]}$ where $[H^+]$ is the concentration (in moles per liter) of hydrogen ions in the liquid. What is the pH of iced tea with a hydrogen ion concentration of 0.000158 mole per liter?

21. The intensity level L (in decibels, dB) of a sound is given by the formula $L = 10 \log \dfrac{I}{I_0}$ where I is the intensity (in watts per square meter, W/m^2) of the sound and I_0 is the intensity of the softest audible sound, about 10^{-12} W/m^2. What is the intensity level of a lawn mower if the sound has an intensity of 0.00063 W/m^2?

22. *Bacillus megaterium* is one the largest bacteria known. The population P of a colony of 1000 bacteria at time t (in minutes) can be modeled by the function $P(t) = 1000e^{0.0277t}$. How long does it take the population to reach 1,000,000?

23. Thorium-230 is a radioactive isotope used in the dating of coral and some cave formations. The percentage of thorium-230 remaining in a sample after time t (in years) is modeled by the function $p(t) = 100(2)^{-\frac{t}{75,000}}$. How long has a coral reef been growing if the oldest portion has 1.5625% of its thorium-230 remaining?

24. For each pH, identify the correct liquid, given the concentration of hydrogen ions in the liquid.

	pH		Liquid	Hydrogen Ion Concentration
a.	3.5	A.	Cocoa	5.2×10^{-7}
b.	3.3	B.	Cider	7.9×10^{-4}
c.	2.4	C.	Ginger Ale	4.9×10^{-4}
d.	4.5	D.	Honey	1.3×10^{-4}
e.	6.3	E.	Buttermilk	3.2×10^{-5}
f.	6.4	F.	Cranberry juice	4.0×10^{-3}
g.	3.1	G.	Pinneapple juice	3.1×10^{-4}
h.	1.2	H.	Tomato juice	6.3×10^{-2}
i.	3.9	I.	Carrot juice	4.0×10^{-7}

H.O.T. Focus on Higher Order Thinking

25. Explain the Error Jade is taking a chemistry test and has to find the pH of a liquid given that its hydrogen ion concentration is 7.53×10^{-9} moles per liter. She writes the following.

$$\text{pH} = \ln \frac{1}{[\text{H}^+]}$$
$$= \ln \frac{1}{7.53 \times 10^9}$$
$$\approx 18.7$$

She knows that the pH scale ranges from 1 to 14, so her answer of 18.7 must be incorrect, but she runs out of time on the test. Explain her error and find the correct pH.

26. Multi-step Exponential functions have the general form $f(x) = ab^{x-h} + k$ where a, b, h, and k are constants, $a \neq 0$, $b > 0$, and $b \neq 1$.

a. State the domain and range of $f(x)$ using set notation.

b. Show how to find $f^{-1}(x)$. Give a description of each step you take.

c. State the domain and range of $f^{-1}(x)$ using set notation.

27. Justify Reasoning Evaluate each expression without using a calculator. Explain your reasoning.

    a. $\ln e^2$

    b. $10^{\log 7}$

    c. $4^{\log_2 5}$

Lesson Performance Task

Skydivers use an instrument called an altimeter to determine their height above Earth's surface. An altimeter measures atmospheric pressure and converts it to altitude based on the relationship between pressure and altitude. One model for atmospheric pressure P (in kilopascals, kPa) as a function of altitude a (in kilometers) is $P = 100e^{-a/8}$.

a. Since an altimeter measures pressure directly, pressure is the independent variable for an altimeter. Rewrite the model $P = 100e^{-a/8}$ so that it gives altitude as a function of pressure.

b. To check the function in part a, use the fact that atmospheric pressure at Earth's surface is about 100 kPa.

c. Suppose a skydiver deploys the parachute when the altimeter measures 87 kPa. Use the function in part a to determine the skydiver's altitude. Give your answer in both kilometers and feet. (1 kilometer $\approx$ 3281 feet)

15.2 Graphing Logarithmic Functions

Essential Question: How is the graph of $g(x) = a \log_b (x - h) + k$ where $b > 0$ and $b \neq 1$ related to the graph of $f(x) = \log_b x$?

 A2.5.A Determine the effects on the key attributes on the graphs of $f(x) = log_b (x)$ where b is 2, 10, and e when $f(x)$ is replaced by $af(x)$, $f(x) + d$, and $f(x - c)$ for specific positive and negative real values of a, c, and d. Also A2.2.A, A2.5.B, A2.7.I

Explore 1 Graphing and Analyzing Parent Logarithmic Functions

The graph of the logarithmic function $f(x) = \log_2 x$, which you analyzed in the previous lesson, is shown. In this Explore, you'll graph and analyze other basic logarithmic functions.

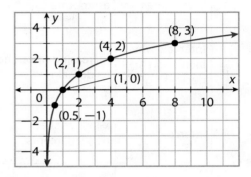

(A) Copy and complete the table for the function $f(x) = \log x$. (Remember that when the base of a logarithmic function is not specified, it is understood to be 10.) Then plot and label the ordered pairs from the table and draw a smooth curve through the points to obtain the graph of the function.

x	$f(x) = \log x$
0.1	
1	
10	

(B) Copy and complete the table for the function $f(x) = \ln x$. (Remember that the base of this function is e.) Then plot and label the ordered pairs from the table and draw a smooth curve through the points to obtain the graph of the function.

x	$f(x) = \ln x$
$\frac{1}{e} \approx 0.368$	
1	
$e \approx 2.72$	
$e^2 \approx 7.39$	

(C) Analyze the two graphs from Steps A and B. Then copy and complete the table.

Function	$f(x) = \log_2 (x)$	$f(x) = \log x$	$f(x) = \ln x$
Domain	$\{x \mid x > 0\}$		
Range	$\{y \mid 0 < y < \infty\}$		
End behavior	As $x \to +\infty$, $f(x) \to +\infty$. As $x \to 0^+$, $f(x) \to -\infty$.		
Vertical and horizontal asymptotes	Vertical asymptote at $x = 0$; no horizontal asymptote		
Intervals where increasing or decreasing	Increasing throughout its domain		
Intercepts	x-intercept at $(1, 0)$; no y-intercepts		
Intervals where positive or negative	Positive on $(1, +\infty)$; negative on $(0, 1)$		

Reflect

1. What similarities do you notice about all logarithmic functions of the form $f(x) = \log_b x$ where $b > 1$? What differences do you notice?

(⌖) Explore 2 Predicting Transformations of the Graphs of Parent Logarithmic Functions

You can graph the logarithmic function $f(x) = \log_b x$ where $b > 0$ and $b \neq 1$ on a graphing calculator by specifying the base when you enter the function's rule using the [LOG] key after pressing the [Y=] key. For instance, the first calculator screen shows how to enter the function $f(x) = \log_2 x$, and the second screen shows the function's graph. Notice that the graph passes through the point $(2, 1)$ as you would expect.

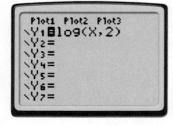

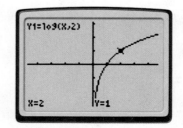

© Houghton Mifflin Harcourt Publishing Company

In this Explore, you will predict the effects of parameters on the graphs of logarithmic functions with bases 2, 10, and e. You will then confirm your predictions by graphing the transformed functions on a graphing calculator.

(A) Predict the effect of the parameter h on the graph of $g(x) = \log_b (x - h)$ for each function.

a. The graph of $g(x) = \log_2 (x - 2)$ is a ▮ of the graph of $f(x) = \log_2 x$ ▮ 2 units.

b. The graph of $g(x) = \log_2 (x + 2)$ is a ▮ of the graph of $f(x) = \log_2 x$ ▮ 2 units.

c. The graph of $g(x) = \log (x - 1)$ is a ▮ of the graph of $f(x) = \log x$ ▮ 1 unit.

d. The graph of $g(x) = \log (x + 1)$ is a ▮ of the graph of $f(x) = \log x$ ▮ 1 unit.

e. The graph of $g(x) = \ln (x - 3)$ is a ▮ of the graph of $f(x) = \ln x$ ▮ 3 units.

f. The graph of $g(x) = \ln (x + 3)$ is a ▮ of the graph of $f(x) = \ln x$ ▮ 3 units.

Check your predictions using a graphing calculator.

(B) Predict the effect of the parameter k on the graph of $g(x) = \log_b x + k$ for each function.

a. The graph of $g(x) = \log_2 x + 3$ is a ▮ of the graph of $f(x) = \log_2 x$ ▮ 3 units.

b. The graph of $g(x) = \log_2 x - 3$ is a ▮ of the graph of $f(x) = \log_2 x$ ▮ 3 units.

c. The graph of $g(x) = \log x + 2$ is a ▮ of the graph of $f(x) = \log x$ ▮ 2 units.

d. The graph of $g(x) = \log x - 2$ is a ▮ of the graph of $f(x) = \log x$ ▮ 2 units.

e. The graph of $g(x) = \ln x + 1$ is a ▮ of the graph of $f(x) = \ln x$ ▮ 1 unit.

f. The graph of $g(x) = \ln x - 1$ is a ▮ of the graph of $f(x) = \ln x$ ▮ 1 unit.

Check your predictions using a graphing calculator.

(C) Predict the effect of the parameter a on the graph of $g(x) = a\log_b x$ for each function.

a. The graph of $g(x) = 2 \log_2 x$ is a ▮ of the graph of $f(x) = \log_2 x$ by a factor of ▮ .

b. The graph of $g(x) = -\frac{1}{2} \log_2 x$ is a ▮ of the graph of

$f(x) = \log_2 x$ by a factor of ▮ as well as a ▮ across the ▮ .

c. The graph of $g(x) = -3 \log x$ is a ▮ of the graph of

$f(x) = \log x$ by a factor of ▮ as well as a ▮ across the ▮ .

d. The graph of $g(x) = \frac{1}{3} \log x$ is a ▮ of the graph of $f(x) = \log x$ by a factor of ▮ .

e. The graph of $g(x) = 4 \ln x$ is a ▮ of the graph of $f(x) = \ln x$ by a factor of ▮ .

f. The graph of $g(x) = -\dfrac{1}{4} \ln x$ is a [   ] of the graph of

$f(x) = \ln x$ by a factor of [   ] as well as a [   ] across the [   ].

Check your predictions using a graphing calculator.

Ⓓ Copy and complete the table. Identify which parameters $(a, h,$ and/or $k)$ affect the attributes of each logarithmic function listed in the table. When necessary, indicate specifically whether a positive or negative value of a parameter affects an attribute. (For end behavior, consider both x increasing without bound and x decreasing toward 0 from the right.)

Function	$g(x) = a \log_2 (x - h) + k$	$g(x) = a \log (x - h) + k$	$g(x) = a \ln (x - h) + k$
Parameters that affect the domain			
Parameters that affect the range			
Parameters that affect the end behavior			
Parameters that affect the vertical asymptote			
Parameters that affect whether the function is increasing or decreasing			
Parameters that affect the x-intercept			
Parameters that affect the intervals where the function is positive or negative			

Reflect

2. In Step D, do the effects of the parameters on the attributes of the logarithmic functions depend on the base of the function? Explain.

3. In Step D, would your answers change if the logarithmic functions had bases between 0 and 1 instead of bases greater than 1? Explain.

Graphing Combined Transformations of $f(x) = \log_b x$ Where $b > 1$

When graphing transformations of $f(x) = \log_b x$ where $b > 1$, it helps to consider the effect of the transformations on the following features of the graph of $f(x)$: the vertical asymptote, $x = 0$, and two reference points, $(1, 0)$ and $(b, 1)$. The table lists these features as well as the corresponding features of the graph of $g(x) = a \log_b (x - h) + k$.

Function	$f(x) = \log_b x$	$g(x) = a \log_b (x - h) + k$
Asymptote	$x = 0$	$x = h$
Reference point	$(1, 0)$	$(1 + h, k)$
Reference point	$(b, 1)$	$(b + h, a + k)$

Example 1 Identify the transformations of the graph of $f(x) = \log_b x$ that produce the graph of the given function $g(x)$. Then graph $g(x)$ on the same coordinate plane as the graph of $f(x)$ by applying the transformations to the asymptote $x = 0$ and to the reference points $(1, 0)$ and $(b, 1)$. Also state the domain and range of $g(x)$ using set notation.

Ⓐ $g(x) = -2 \log_2 (x - 1) - 2$

The transformations of the graph of $f(x) = \log_2 x$ that produce the graph of $g(x)$ are as follows:

- a vertical stretch by a factor of 2
- a reflection across the x-axis
- a translation of 1 unit to the right and 2 units down

Note that the translation of 1 unit to the right affects only the x-coordinates of points on the graph of $f(x)$, while the vertical stretch by a factor of 2, the reflection across the x-axis, and the translation of 2 units down affect only the y-coordinates.

Function	$f(x) = \log_2 x$	$g(x) = -2 \log_2 (x - 1) - 2$
Asymptote	$x = 0$	$x = 1$
Reference point	$(1, 0)$	$\left(1 + 1, -2(0) - 2\right) = (2, -2)$
Reference point	$(2, 1)$	$\left(2 + 1, -2(1) - 2\right) = (3, -4)$

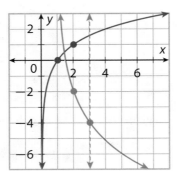

Domain: $\left\{ x \mid x > 1 \right\}$

Range: $\left\{ y \mid \infty < y < +\infty \right\}$

Ⓑ $g(x) = 2 \log (x + 2) + 4$

The transformations of the graph of $f(x) = \log x$ that produce the graph of $g(x)$ are as follows:

- a vertical stretch by a factor of 2
- a translation of 2 units to the left and 4 units up

Note that the translation of 2 units to the left affects only the x-coordinates of points on the graph of $f(x)$, while the vertical stretch by a factor of 2 and the translation of 4 units up affect only the y-coordinates.

Function	$f(x) = \log x$	$g(x) = 2 \log (x + 2) + 4$
Asymptote	$x = 0$	$x = \boxed{-2}$
Reference point	$(1, 0)$	$\left(\boxed{1} - 2, 2 \boxed{0} + 4 \right) = \left(\boxed{-1}, \boxed{4} \right)$
Reference point	$(10, 1)$	$\left(\boxed{10} - 2, 2 \boxed{1} + 4 \right) = \left(\boxed{8}, \boxed{6} \right)$

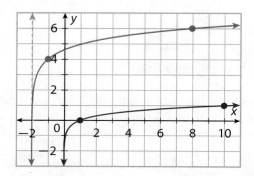

Domain: $\left\{ x \mid x > \boxed{-2} \right\}$

Range: $\left\{ y \mid -\infty < y < \boxed{+\infty} \right\}$

Identify the transformations of the graph of $f(x) = \log_b x$ that produce the graph of the given function $g(x)$. Then graph $g(x)$ on the same coordinate plane as the graph of $f(x)$ by applying the transformations to the asymptote $x = 0$ and to the reference points $(1, 0)$ and $(b, 1)$. Also state the domain and range of $g(x)$ using set notation.

4. $g(x) = 3 \ln (x + 4) + 2$

5. $g(x) = \frac{1}{2} \log_2 (x + 1) + 2$

6. $g(x) = -3 \log (x - 1) - 4$

🎸 Explain 2   Writing, Graphing, and Analyzing a Logarithmic Model

You can obtain a logarithmic model for real-world data either by performing logarithmic regression on the data or by finding the inverse of an exponential model if one is available.

Example 2   A biologist studied a population of foxes in a forest preserve over a period of time. The table gives the data that the biologist collected.

Years Since Study Began	Fox Population
0	55
2	72
3	99
5	123
8	151
12	234
15	336
18	475

From the data, the biologist obtained the exponential model $P = 62(1.12)^t$ where P is the fox population at time t (in years since the study began). The biologist is interested in having a model that gives the time it takes the fox population to reach a certain level.

Ⓐ One way to obtain the model that the biologist wants is to perform logarithmic regression on a graphing calculator using the data set but with the variables switched (that is, the fox population is the independent variable and time is the dependent variable). After obtaining the logarithmic regression model, graph it on a scatter plot of the data. Analyze the model in terms of whether it is increasing or decreasing as well as its average rate of change from $P = 100$ to $P = 200$, from $P = 200$ to $P = 300$, and from $P = 300$ to $P = 400$. Do the model's average rates of change increase, decrease, or stay the same? What does this mean for the fox population?

Using a graphing calculator, enter the population data into one list (L1) and the time data into another list (L2).

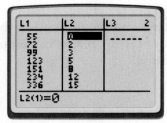

Perform logarithmic regression by pressing the [STAT] key, choosing the **CALC** menu, and selecting **9:LnReg**. Note that the calculator's regression model is a natural logarithmic function.

So, the model is $t = -35.6 + 8.66 \ln P$. Graphing this model on a scatter plot of the data visually confirms that the model is a good fit for the data.

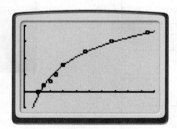

From the graph, you can see that the function is increasing. To find the model's average rates of change, divide the change in t (the dependent variable) by the change in P (the independent variable):

$$\text{Average rate of change} = \frac{t_2 - t_1}{P_2 - P_1}$$

Population	Number of Years to Reach That Population	Average Rate of Change
100	$t = -35.6 + 8.66 \ln 100 \approx 4.3$	
200	$t = -35.6 + 8.66 \ln 200 \approx 10.3$	$\frac{10.3 - 4.3}{200 - 100} = \frac{6.0}{100} = 0.060$
300	$t = -35.6 + 8.66 \ln 300 \approx 13.8$	$\frac{13.8 - 10.3}{300 - 200} = \frac{3.5}{100} = 0.035$
400	$t = -35.6 + 8.66 \ln 400 \approx 16.3$	$\frac{16.3 - 13.8}{400 - 300} = \frac{2.5}{100} = 0.025$

The model's average rates of change are decreasing. This means that as the fox population grows, it takes less time for the population to increase by another 100 foxes.

Ⓑ Another way to obtain the model that the biologist wants is to find the inverse of the exponential model. Find the inverse model and compare it with the logarithmic regression model.

In order to compare the inverse of the biologist's model, $P = 62(1.12)^t$, with the logarithmic regression model, you must rewrite the biologist's model with base e so that the inverse will involve a natural logarithm. This means that you want to find a constant c such that $e^c = 1.12$. Writing the exponential equation $e^c = 1.12$ in logarithmic form gives $c = \ln 1.12$, so $c = \boxed{0.113}$ to the nearest thousandth.

Replacing 1.12 with $e^{\boxed{0.113}}$ in the biologist's model gives $P = 62 \left(e^{\boxed{0.113}}\right)^t$, or $P = 62\, e^{\boxed{0.113}t}$. Now find the inverse of this function.

Write the equation. $P = 62e^{\boxed{0.113}t}$

Divide both sides by 62. $\dfrac{P}{62} = e^{\boxed{0.113}t}$

Write in logarithmic form. $\ln \dfrac{P}{62} = \boxed{0.113}\, t$

Divide both sides by $\boxed{0.113}$. $\boxed{8.85} \ln \dfrac{P}{62} = t$

So, the inverse of the exponential model is $t = \boxed{8.85} \ln \dfrac{P}{62}$. To compare this model with the logarithmic regression model, use a graphing calculator to graph both $y = \boxed{8.85} \ln \dfrac{x}{62}$ and $y = -35.6 + 8.66 \ln x$. You observe that the graphs roughly coincide, so the models are basically equivalent.

Reflect

7. **Discussion** In a later lesson, you will learn the quotient property of logarithms, which states that $\log_b \dfrac{m}{n} = \log_b m - \log_b n$ for any positive numbers m and n. Explain how you can use this property to compare the two models in Example 3.

Your Turn

8. Maria made a deposit in a bank account and left the money untouched for several years. The table lists her account balance at the end of each year.

Years Since the Deposit Was Made	Account Balance
0	$1000.00
1	$1020.00
2	$1040.40
3	$1061.21

a. Write an exponential model for the account balance as a function of time (in years since the deposit was made).

b. Find the inverse of the exponential model after rewriting it with a base of e. Describe what information the inverse gives.

c. Perform logarithmic regression on the data (using the account balance as the independent variable and time as the dependent variable). Compare this model with the inverse model from part b.

Elaborate

9. Which transformations of $f(x) = \log_b(x)$ change the function's end behavior (both as x increases without bound and as x decreases toward 0 from the right)? Which transformations change the location of the graph's x-intercept?

10. How are reference points helpful when graphing transformations of $f(x) = \log_b(x)$?

11. What are two ways to obtain a logarithmic model for a set of data?

12. **Essential Question Check-In** Describe the transformations you must perform on the graph of $f(x) = \log_b(x)$ to obtain the graph of $g(x) = a \log_b(x - h) + k$.

⭐ Evaluate: Homework and Practice

- Online Homework
- Hints and Help
- Extra Practice

1. Graph the logarithmic functions $f(x) = \log_2 x$, $f(x) = \log x$, and $f(x) = \ln x$ on the same coordinate plane. To distinguish the curves, label the point on each curve where the y-coordinate is 1.

2. Describe the attributes that the logarithmic functions $f(x) = \log_2 x$, $f(x) = \log x$, and $f(x) = \ln x$ have in common and the attributes that make them different. Attributes should include domain, range, end behavior, asymptotes, intercepts, intervals where the functions are positive and where they are negative, intervals where the functions are increasing and where they are decreasing, and the average rate of change on an interval.

3. For each of the six functions, describe how its graph is a transformation of the graph of $f(x) = \log_2 x$. Also identify what attributes of $f(x) = \log_2 x$ change as a result of the transformation. Attributes to consider are the domain, the range, the end behavior, the vertical asymptote, the x-intercept, the intervals where the function is positive and where it is negative, and whether the function increases or decreases throughout its domain.

a. $g(x) = \log_2 x - 5$

b. $g(x) = 4 \log_2 x$

c. $g(x) = \log_2 (x + 6)$

d. $g(x) = -\dfrac{3}{4} \log_2 x$

e. $g(x) = \log_2 x + 7$

f. $g(x) = \log_2 (x - 8)$

4. For each of the six functions, describe how its graph is a transformation of the graph of $f(x) = \log x$. Also identify what attributes of $f(x) = \log x$ change as a result of the transformation. Attributes to consider are the domain, the range, the end behavior, the vertical asymptote, the x-intercept, the intervals where the function is positive and where it is negative, and whether the function increases or decreases throughout its domain.

a. $g(x) = -3 \log x$

b. $g(x) = \log(x - 5)$

c. $g(x) = \log x + 1$

d. $g(x) = \log(x + 4)$

e. $g(x) = 0.5 \log x$

f. $g(x) = \log x - 2$

5. For each of the six functions, describe how the graph is a transformation of the graph of $f(x) = \ln x$. Also identify what attributes of $f(x) = \ln x$ change as a result of the transformation. Attributes to consider are the domain, the range, the end behavior, the vertical asymptote, the x-intercept, the intervals where the function is positive and where it is negative, and whether the function increases or decreases throughout its domain.

a. $g(x) = \ln(x + 6)$

b. $g(x) = \ln x - 1$

c. $g(x) = \frac{3}{2} \ln x$

d. $g(x) = \ln x + 8$

e. $g(x) = -\frac{2}{3} \ln x$

f. $g(x) = \ln(x - 4)$

Identify the transformations of the graph of $f(x) = \log_b x$ that produce the graph of the given function $g(x)$. Then copy the given graph of $f(x)$ and graph $g(x)$ on the same coordinate plane by applying the transformations to the asymptote $x = 0$ and to the reference points $(1, 0)$ and $(b, 1)$. Also state the domain and range of $g(x)$ using set notation.

6. $g(x) = -4 \log_2(x + 2) + 1$

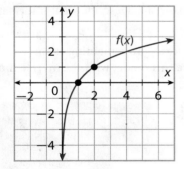

7. $g(x) = \frac{1}{2} \ln(x + 2) - 3$

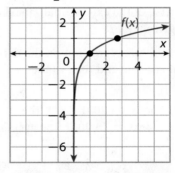

8. $g(x) = 3 \log(x - 1) - 1$

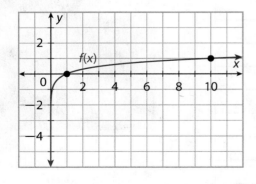

9. $g(x) = \frac{1}{2} \log_2(x - 1) - 2$

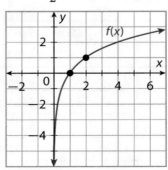

10. $g(x) = -4 \ln(x - 4) + 3$

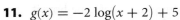

11. $g(x) = -2 \log(x + 2) + 5$

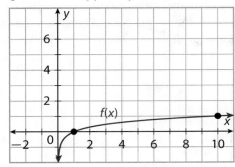

12. The radioactive isotope fluorine-18 is used in medicine to produce images of internal organs and detect cancer. It decays to the stable element oxygen-18. The table gives the percent of fluorine-18 that remains in a sample over a period of time.

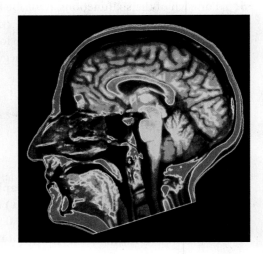

Time (hours)	Percent of Fluorine-18 Remaining
0	100
1	68.5
2	46.9
3	32.1

a. Write an exponential model for the percent of fluorine-18 remaining as a function of time (in hours).

b. Find the inverse of the exponential model after rewriting it with a base of e. Describe what information the inverse gives.

c. Perform logarithmic regression on the data (using the percent of fluorine-18 remaining as the independent variable and time as the dependent variable). Compare this model with the inverse model from part b.

13. During the period between 2001–2011, the average price of an ounce of gold doubled every 4 years. In 2001, the average price of gold was about $270 per ounce.

Year	Average Price of an Ounce of Gold
2001	$271.04
2002	$309.73
2003	$363.38
2004	$409.72
2005	$444.74
2006	$603.46
2007	$695.39
2008	$871.96
2009	$972.35
2010	$1224.53
2011	$1571.52

a. Write an exponential model for the average price of an ounce of gold as a function of time (in years since 2001).

b. Find the inverse of the exponential model after rewriting it with a base of *e*. Describe what information the inverse gives.

c. Perform logarithmic regression on the data in the table (using the average price of gold as the independent variable and time as the dependent variable). Compare this model with the inverse model from part b.

H.O.T. Focus on Higher Order Thinking

14. Multiple Representations For the function $g(x) = \log(x - h)$, what value of the parameter h will cause the function to pass through the point $(7, 1)$? Answer the question in two different ways: once by using the function's rule, and once by thinking in terms of the function's graph.

15. Explain the Error A student drew the graph of $g(x) = 2 \log_{\frac{1}{2}}(x - 2)$ as shown. Explain the error that the student made, and draw the correct graph.

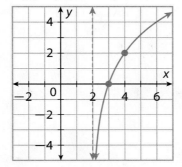

16. Construct Arguments Prove that $\log_{\frac{1}{b}} x = -\log_b x$ for any positive value of b not equal to 1. Begin the proof by setting $\log_{\frac{1}{b}} x$ equal to m and rewriting the equation in exponential form.

Lesson Performance Task

Given the following data about the heights of chair seats and table tops for children, make separate scatterplots of the ordered pairs (age of child, chair seat height) and the ordered pairs (age of child, table top height). Explain why a logarithmic model would be appropriate for each data set. Perform a logarithmic regression on each data set, and describe the transformations needed to obtain the graph of the model from the graph of the parent function $f(x) = \ln x$.

Age of Child (years)	Chair Seat Height (inches)	Table Top Height (inches)
1	5	12
1.5	6.5	14
2	8	16
3	10	18
5	12	20
7.5	14	22
11	16	25

Logarithmic Functions

Essential Question: How can you use logarithmic functions to solve real-world problems?

Key Vocabulary
asymptote
  (asíntota)
common logarithm
  (logaritmo común)
logarithm
  (logaritmo)
logarithmic function
  (función logarítmica)
natural logarithm
  (logaritmo natural)

KEY EXAMPLE (Lesson 15.1)

Evaluate $f(x) = \log_4 x$ when $x = 1024$.

$f(1024) = \log_4 1024$

$4^{f(1024)} = 1024$ by definition of logarithm.

$4^{f(1024)} = 4^5$ because $4^5 = 1024$.

$f(1024) = 5$

KEY EXAMPLE (Lesson 15.2)

Graph $f(x) = 3 \log_2 (x + 1) - 4$.

The parameters for $f(x) = a \log_b (x - h) + k$ are:

$a = 3$

$b = 2$

$h = -1$

$k = -4$

Find reference points:

$$(1 + h, k) = (0, -4)$$

$$(b + h, a + k) = (2 - 1, 3 - 4) = (1, -1)$$

The two reference points are $(0, -4)$ and $(1, -1)$.

Find the asymptote:

$x = h = -1$

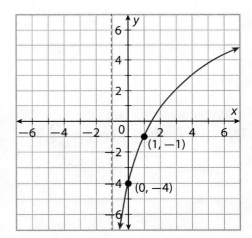

Plot the points and draw the asymptote. Connect the points with a curve that passes through the reference points and continually draws nearer the asymptote.

EXERCISES

Evaluate each logarithmic function for the given value. *(Lesson 15.1)*

1. $f(x) = \log_2 x$, for $f(256)$

2. $f(x) = \log_9 x$, for $f(6561)$

Graph each function. *(Lesson 15.2)*

3. $f(x) = 2 \log_3 (x - 2) + 1$

4. $f(x) = \log_5 (x + 1) - 1$

MODULE PERFORMANCE TASK

What's the Dosage?

Kira is a scientist working for a pharmaceutical lab and has developed a new drug. According to her research, 30% of the drug is eliminated from the bloodstream every 6 hours. Her initial dosage plan is to have the patient take a 1200 mg pill of the drug every 12 hours.

The patient needs to have at least 500 mg of the drug in the bloodstream at all times, but the total amount should never exceed 2500 mg. The drug should be taken for no more than 4 days. Does Kira's proposed dosage plan meet the medical requirements for the drug? Find a function that describes the amount of drug in the patient's bloodstream as a function of the number of doses.

Start by listing the information you will need to solve the problem. Be sure to write down all your data and assumptions. Then use graphs, numbers, words, or algebra to explain how you reached your conclusion.

Ready to Go On?

15.1–15.2 Logarithmic Functions

- Online Homework
- Hints and Help
- Extra Practice

Rewrite the given equation in exponential format. *(Lesson 15.1)*

1. $\log_6 x = r$

2. $\log_{\frac{3}{4}} 12x = 35y$

Evaluate each logarithmic function for the given value. *(Lesson 15.1)*

3. $f(x) = \log_5 x$ for $f(125)$

4. $f(x) = \log_3 x$ for $f(729)$

Graph each function. *(Lesson 15.2)*

5. $f(x) = -3 \log_e (x + 1) + 2$

6. $f(x) = 4 \log_{10} (x + 4) - 3$

ESSENTIAL QUESTION

7. How is the graph of the logarithmic function $f(x) = \log_4 x$ related to the graph of the exponential function $g(x) = 4^x$?

© Houghton Mifflin Harcourt Publishing Company

Assessment Readiness

1. What is the domain of the function $f(x) = \frac{1}{4}\log_5(x + 3) - 2$?
   A. $\{x \mid x > -3\}$
   B. $\{x \mid x > -2\}$
   C. $\{x \mid x > 2\}$
   D. $\{x \mid x > 3\}$

2. Let $f(x) = \log_4 x$. What is $f(8)$?
   A. $\frac{1}{2}$
   B. $\frac{2}{3}$
   C. $\frac{3}{2}$
   D. -2

3. Shelby is canoeing in a river. She travels 4 miles upstream and 4 miles downstream in a total of 5 hours. In still water, Shelby can travel at an average speed of 2 miles per hour. To the nearest tenth, what is the average speed of the river's current?
   A. 0.4 mi/h
   B. 0.6 mi/h
   C. 0.9 mi/h
   D. 1.6 mi/h

4. Which function shows exponential decay?
   A. $f(x) = \left(\frac{5}{4}\right)^x$
   B. $f(x) = 1.6\left(\frac{3}{4}\right)^x$
   C. $f(x) = \frac{3}{5}(1.1)^x$
   D. $f(x) = 0.2(1 + 0.03)^x$

5. Researchers have found that after 25 years of age, the average size of the pupil in a person's eye decreases. The relationship between pupil diameter d (in millimeters) and age a (in years) can be modeled by $d = -2.1158 \log_e a + 13.669$. What is the average diameter of a pupil for a person 25 years old? 50 years old? Explain how you got your answer.

Logarithmic Properties and Exponential and Logarithmic Equations

Essential Question: How do the properties of logarithms allow you to solve real-world problems?

REAL WORLD VIDEO
Scientists use radiocarbon dating and other techniques to study the fossils of mastodons and other extinct species found at the La Brea Tar Pits.

MODULE PERFORMANCE TASK PREVIEW
How Old Is That Bone?

All living organisms contain carbon. Carbon has two main isotopes, carbon-12 and carbon-14. C-14 is radioactive and decays at a steady rate. Living organisms continually replenish their stores of carbon, and the ratio between C-12 and C-14 stays relatively constant. When the organism dies, this ratio changes at a known rate as C-14 decays. How can we use a logarithmic equation and carbon dating to determine the age of a mastodon bone? Let's find out!

Are (YOU) Ready?

Complete these exercises to review skills you will need for this chapter.

• Online Homework
• Hints and Help
• Extra Practice

Exponents

Simplify $\dfrac{40 \cdot x^6 y}{5x^2 y^5}$.

$$\dfrac{40 \cdot x^6 y}{5x^2 y^5} = \dfrac{40}{5} \cdot x^{6-2} y^{1-5} \qquad \text{Subtract exponents.}$$

$$= \dfrac{8x^4}{y^4} \qquad \text{Simplify.}$$

Simplify each expression.

1. $\dfrac{xy^2}{x^3 y^2}$

2. $\dfrac{18x^3 y^7}{2y^5}$

3. $\dfrac{12x^4}{8x^9 y}$

Multi-Step Equations

Example 2

Solve $3(5 - 2x) = -x$ for x.

$$15 - 6x = -x \qquad \text{Distribute the 3.}$$

$$15 = 5x \qquad \text{Add } 6x \text{ to both sides.}$$

$$3 = x \qquad \text{Divide both sides by 5.}$$

The solution is $x = 3$.

Solve.

4. $5(4x + 9) = 2x$

5. $3(x + 12) = 2(4 - 2x)$

6. $(x - 2)^2 = 4(x + 1)$

Equations Involving Exponents

Example 3

Solve $2x^{\frac{1}{3}} - 1 = 3$ for x.

$$2x^{\frac{1}{3}} = 4 \qquad \text{Add 1 to both sides.}$$

$$x^{\frac{1}{3}} = 2 \qquad \text{Divide both sides by 2.}$$

$$\left(x^{\frac{1}{3}}\right)^3 = (2)^3 \qquad \text{Raise both sides to the power of 3.}$$

$$x = 8 \qquad \text{Simplify.}$$

Solve.

7. $3x^{\frac{1}{4}} + 2 = 11$

8. $8x^{\frac{1}{2}} + 20 = 100$

9. $4x^{\frac{1}{3}} + 15 = 35$

16.1 Properties of Logarithms

Essential Question: What are the properties of logarithms?

 TEKS **A2.5.C** Rewrite exponential equations as their corresponding logarithmic equations and logarithmic equations as their corresponding exponential equations. Also A2.5.B

Resource Locker

⊘ Explore 1 Investigating the Properties of Logarithms

You can use a scientific calculator to evaluate a logarithmic expression.

(A) Evaluate the expressions in each set using a scientific calculator.

Set A	Set B
$\log\dfrac{10}{e} \approx$ ⬛	$\dfrac{1}{\log e} \approx$ ⬛
$\ln 10 \approx$ ⬛	$1 + \log e \approx$ ⬛
$\log e^{10} \approx$ ⬛	$1 - \log e \approx$ ⬛
$\log 10e \approx$ ⬛	$10 \log e \approx$ ⬛

(B) Match the expressions in Set A to the equivalent expressions in Set B.

$\log\dfrac{10}{e} =$ ⬛

$\ln 10 =$ ⬛

$\log e^{10} =$ ⬛

$\log 10e =$ ⬛

Reflect

1. How can you check the results of evaluating the logarithmic expressions in Set A? Use this method to check each.

2. **Discussion** How do you know that $\log e$ and $\ln 10$ are reciprocals? Given that the expressions are reciprocals, show another way to represent each expression.

⊘ Explore 2 Proving the Properties of Logarithms

A logarithm is the exponent to which a base must be raised in order to obtain a given number. So $\log_b b^m = m$. It follows that $\log_b b^0 = 0$, so $\log_b 1 = 0$. Also, $\log_b b^1 = 1$, so $\log_b b = 1$. Additional properties of logarithms are the Product Property of Logarithms, the Quotient Property of Logarithms, the Power Property of Logarithms, and the Change of Base Property of Logarithms. Given positive numb ers m, n, and b $(b \neq 1)$, prove the Product Property of Logarithms.

Properties of Logarithms	
For any positive numbers a, m, n, b $\left(b \neq 1\right)$, and c $\left(c \neq 1\right)$, the following properties hold.	
Definition-Based Properties	$\log_b b^m = m$ $\qquad$ $\log_b 1 = 0$ $\qquad$ $\log_b b = 1$
Product Property of Logarithms	$\log_b mn = \log_b m + \log_b n$
Quotient Property of Logarithms	$\log_b \dfrac{m}{n} = \log_b m - \log_b n$
Power Property of Logarithms	$\log_b m^n = n\log_b m$
Change of Base Property of Logarithms	$\log_c a = \dfrac{\log_b a}{\log_b c}$

Ⓐ Let $x = \log_b m$ and $y = \log_b n$. Rewrite the expressions in exponential form.

$m = $ ▮

$n = $ ▮

Ⓑ Substitute for m and n.

$\text{Log}_b mn = \log_b \left(\text{▮} \right)$

Ⓒ Use the Product of Powers Property of Exponents to simplify.

$\log_b \left(b^x \cdot b^y \right) = \log_b b^{\text{▮}}$

Ⓓ Use the definition of a logarithm $\log_b b^m = m$ to simplify further.

$\log_b b^{x+y} = $ ▮

Ⓔ Substitute for x and y.

$x + y = $ ▮

Reflect

3. Prove the Power Property of Logarithms. Justify each step of your proof.

⚙ Explain 1   **Using the Properties of Logarithms**

Logarithmic expressions can be rewritten using one or more of the properties of logarithms.

> **Example 1**   **Express each expression as a single logarithm. Simplify if possible. Then check your results by converting to exponential form and evaluating.**

Ⓐ $\log_3 27 - \log_3 81$

$$\log_3 27 - \log_3 81 = \log_3\left(\frac{27}{81}\right) \qquad \text{Quotient Property of Logarithms}$$

$$= \log_3\left(\frac{1}{3}\right) \qquad \text{Simplify.}$$

$$= \frac{\log\left(\frac{1}{3}\right)}{\log 3} \qquad \text{Change of Base Property of Logarithms}$$

$$\approx \frac{-0.477}{0.477} \qquad \text{Evaluate the logarithms.}$$

$$= -1 \qquad \text{Simplify.}$$

Check:

$$\log_3\left(\frac{1}{3}\right) = -1$$

$$\frac{1}{3} = 3^{-1}$$

$$\frac{1}{3} = \frac{1}{3}$$

Ⓑ $\log_5\left(\frac{1}{25}\right) + \log_5 625$

$$\log_5\left(\frac{1}{25}\right) + \log_5 625 = \log_5\left(\frac{1}{25} \cdot \boxed{625}\right) \qquad \text{Product Property of Logarithms}$$

$$= \log_5 \boxed{25} \qquad \text{Simplify.}$$

$$= \frac{\log \boxed{25}}{\log \boxed{5}} \qquad \text{Change of Base Property of Logarithms}$$

$$\approx \frac{\boxed{1.398}}{\boxed{0.699}} \qquad \text{Evaluate the logarithms.}$$

$$= \boxed{2} \qquad \text{Simplify}$$

Check:

$$\log_5 25 = \boxed{2}$$

$$25 = 5^{\boxed{2}}$$

$$25 = \boxed{25}$$

Your Turn

Express each expression as a single logarithm. Simplify if possible.

4. $\log_4 64^3$

5. $\log_8 18 - \log_8 2$

⚙ Explain 2　Rewriting a Logarithmic Model

There are standard formulas that involve logarithms, such as the formula for measuring the loudness of sounds. The loudness of a sound $L(I)$, in decibels, is given by the function $L(I) = 10\log\left(\frac{I}{I_0}\right)$, where I is the sound's intensity in watts per square meter and I_0 is the intensity of a barely audible sound. It's also possible to develop logarithmic models from exponential growth or decay models of the form $f(t) = a(1 + r)^t$ or $f(t) = a(1 - r)^t$ by finding the inverse.

Example 2　Solve the problems using logarithmic models.

Ⓐ　During a concert, an orchestra plays a piece of music in which its volume increases from one measure to the next, tripling the sound's intensity. Find how many decibels the loudness of the sound increases between the two measures.

Let I be the intensity in the first measure. So $3I$ is the intensity in the second measure.

Increase in loudness $= L(3I) - L(I)$　　　Write the expression.

$\qquad = 10\log\left(\frac{3I}{I_0}\right) - 10\log\left(\frac{I}{I_0}\right)$　　　Substitute.

$\qquad = 10\left(\log\left(\frac{3I}{I_0}\right) - \log\left(\frac{I}{I_0}\right)\right)$　　　Distributive Property

$\qquad = 10\left(\log 3 + \log\left(\frac{I}{I_0}\right) - \log\left(\frac{I}{I_0}\right)\right)$　　　Product Property of Logarithms

$\qquad = 10\log 3$　　　Simplify.

$\qquad \approx 4.77$　　　Evaluate the logarithm.

So the loudness of sound increases by about 4.77 decibels.

B The population of the United States in 2012 was 313.9 million. If the population increases exponentially at an average rate of 1% each year, how long will it take for the population to double?

The exponential growth model is $P = P_0(1+r)^t$, where P is the population in millions after t years, P_0 is the population in 2012, and r is the average growth rate.

$P_0 = 313.9$

$P = 2P_0 = \boxed{627.8}$

$r = 0.01$

Find the inverse model of $P = P_0(1+r)^t$.

$$P = P_0(1+r)^t \qquad \text{Exponential model}$$

$$\frac{P}{P_0} = (1+r)^t \qquad \text{Divide both sides by } P_0.$$

$$\log_{1+r}\left(\frac{P}{P_0}\right) = \log_{\boxed{1+r}}(1+r)^t \qquad \text{Take the log of both sides.}$$

$$\log_{1+r}\left(\frac{\boxed{P}}{\boxed{P_0}}\right) = t \qquad \text{Definition of a logarithm}$$

$$\frac{\log\left(\dfrac{\boxed{P}}{\boxed{P_0}}\right)}{\log\left(\boxed{1+r}\right)} = t \qquad \text{Change of Base Property of Logarithms}$$

Substitute and solve for t.

$$t = \frac{\log\left(\dfrac{\boxed{627.8}}{313.9}\right)}{\log\left(1 + \boxed{0.01}\right)} \qquad \text{Substitute.}$$

$$= \frac{\log\boxed{2}}{\log\boxed{1.01}} \qquad \text{Simplify.}$$

$$= \frac{\boxed{0.301}}{\boxed{0.004}} \qquad \text{Evaluate the logarithms.}$$

$$= \boxed{75.25} \qquad \text{Simplify.}$$

The population of the United States will double in $\boxed{75.25}$ years from 2012, or in the year $\boxed{2087}$.

6. A bank account receives 0.06% annual interest compounded monthly. The balance B of the account after t months is given by the equation $B = B_0(1.06)^t$, where B_0 is the starting balance. If the account starts with a balance of $250, how long will it take to triple the balance of the account?

💬 Elaborate

7. On what other properties do the proofs of the properties of logarithms rely?

8. What properties of logarithms would you use to rewrite the expression $\log_7 x + \log_7 4x$ as a single logarithm?

9. Explain how the properties of logarithms are useful in finding the inverse of an exponential growth or decay model.

10. **Essential Question Check-In** State the Product, Quotient, and Power Properties of Logarithms in a simple sentence.

⭐ Evaluate: Homework and Practice

- Online Homework
- Hints and Help
- Extra Practice

Express each expression as a single logarithm. Simplify if possible.

1. $\log_9 12 + \log_9 546.75$

2. $\log_2 2.5 - \log_2 25.6$

3. $\log_{\frac{2}{5}} 0.0256^3$

4. $\log_{11} 11^{23}$

5. $\log_5 5^{x+1} + \log_4 256^2$

6. $\log(\log_7 98 - \log_7 2)^x$

7. $\log_{x+1}(x^2 + 2x + 1)^3$

8. $\log_4 5 + \log_4 12 - \log_4 3.75$

Solve the problems using logarithmic models.

9. **Geology** Seismologists use the Richter scale to express the energy, or magnitude, of an earthquake. The Richter magnitude of an earthquake M is related to the energy released in ergs E shown by the formula $M = \frac{2}{3}\log\left(\frac{E}{10^{11.8}}\right)$.

In 1964, an earthquake centered at Prince William Sound, Alaska registered a magnitude of 9.2 on the Richter scale. Find the energy released by the earthquake.

10. **Astronomy** The difference between the apparent magnitude (brightness) m of a star and its absolute magnitude M is given by the formula $m - M = 5\log\frac{d}{10}$, where d is the distance of the star from the Earth, measured in parsecs. Find the distance d of the star Rho Oph from Earth, where Rho Oph has an apparent magnitude of 5.0 and an absolute magnitude -0.4.

11. The intensity of the sound of a conversation ranges from 10^{-10} watts per square meter to 10^{-6} watts per square meter. What is the range in the loudness of the conversation? Use $I_0 = 10^{-12}$ watts per square meter.

12. The intensity of sound from the stands of a football game is 25 times as great when the home team scores a touchdown as it is when the away team scores. Find the difference in the loudness of the sound when the two teams score.

13. Finance A stock priced at $40 increases at a rate of 8% per year. Write and evaluate a logarithmic expression for the number of years that it will take for the value of the stock to reach $50.

14. Suppose that the population of one endangered species decreases at a rate of 4% per year. In one habitat, the current population of the species is 143. After how long will the population drop below 30?

15. The population P of bacteria in a culture after t minutes is given by the equation $P = P_0 (1.12)^t$, where P_0 is the initial population. If the number of bacteria starts at 200, how long will it take for the population to increase to 1000?

16. Chemistry Most swimming pool experts recommend a pH of between 7.0 and 7.6 for water in a swimming pool. Use $pH = -\log[H^+]$ and write an expression for the difference in hydrogen ion concentration over this pH range.

17. For each logarithmic expression, identify its equivalent expression.

a. $\log_2 4x$

A. $2x$

b. $\log_2 \frac{x}{4}$

B. $2 + \log_2 x$

c. $\log_2 4^x$

C. $\frac{\log x}{\log 2}$

d. $\log_2 x^4$

D. $4\log_2 x$

e. $\log_2 x$

E. $\log_2 x - 2$

18. Prove the Quotient Property of Logarithms. Justify each step of your proof.

19. Prove the Change of Base Property of Logarithms. Justify each step of your proof.

H.O.T. Focus on Higher Order Thinking

20. Multi-Step The radioactive isotope Carbon-14 decays exponentially at a rate of 0.0121% each year.

a. How long will it take 250 g of Carbon-14 to decay to 100 g?

b. The half-life for a radioactive isotope is the amount of time it takes for the isotope to reach half its initial value. What is the half-life of Carbon-14?

21. **Explain the Error** A student simplified the expression $\log_2 8 + \log_3 27$ as shown. Explain and correct the student's error.

$$\log_2 8 + \log_3 27 = \log(8 \cdot 27)$$

$$= \log(216)$$

$$\approx 2.33$$

22. **Communicate Mathematical Ideas** Explain why it is not necessary for a scientific calculator to have both a key for common logs and a key for natural logs.

23. **Analyze Relationships** Explain how to find the relationship between $\log_b a$ and $\log_{\frac{1}{b}} a$.

Lesson Performance Task

Given the population data for the state of Texas from 1920–2010, perform exponential regression to obtain an exponential growth model for population as a function of time (represent 1920 as 0).

Obtain a logarithmic model for time as a function of population two ways: (1) by finding the inverse of the exponential model, and (2) by performing logarithmic regression on the same set of data but using population as the independent variable and time as the dependent variable. Then confirm that the two expressions are equivalent by applying the properties of logarithms.

Year	U.S. Census Count
1920	4,663,228
1930	5,824,715
1940	6,414,824
1950	7,711,194
1960	9,579,677
1970	11,196,730
1980	14,229,191
1990	16,986,335
2000	20,851,820
2010	25,145,561

16.2 Solving Exponential Equations

Resource
Locker

Essential Question: What are some ways you can solve an equation of the form $ab^x = c$, where a and c are nonzero real numbers and b is greater than 0 and not equal to 1?

 TEKS **A2.5.D** Solve exponential equations of the form $y = ab^x$ where a is a nonzero real number and b is greater than zero and not equal to one…

⊘ Explore   Solving Exponential Equations Graphically

One way to solve exponential equations is graphically. First, graph each side of the equation separately. The point(s) at which the two graphs intersect are the solutions of the equation.

Ⓐ First, look at the equation $275e^{0.06x} = 1000$. To solve the equation graphically, split it into two separate equations.

$y_1 = $ ▢

$y_2 = $ ▢

Ⓑ What will the graphs of y_1 and y_2 look like?

Ⓒ Graph y_1 and y_2 using a graphing calculator.

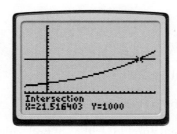

Intersection
X=21.516403 Y=1000

Ⓓ The x-coordinate of the point of intersection is approximately ▢ .

Ⓔ So, the solution of the equation is $x \approx$.

Ⓕ Now, look at the equation $10^{2x} = 10^4$. Split the equation into two separate equations.

$y_1 = $ ▢

$y_2 = $ ▢

Ⓖ What will the graphs of y_1 and y_2 look like?

(H) Graph y_1 and y_2 using a graphing calculator.

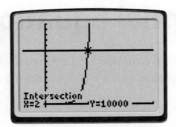

Intersection
X=2   Y=10000

(I) The x-coordinate of the point of intersection is [   ].

(J) So, the solution of the equation is $x \approx$ [   ].

Reflect

1. How can you check the solution of an exponential equation after it is found graphically?

⚙ Explain 1 Solving Exponential Equations Algebraically

In addition to solving exponential equations graphically, exponential equations can be solved algebraically. The Property of Equality for Logarithmic Equations states that for any positive number x, y, and b, $(b \neq 1)$, $\log_b x = \log_b y$ if and only if $w = y$.

Example 1 Solve the equations. Give the exact solution and an approximate solution to three decimal places.

(A) $10 = 5e^{4x}$

$10 = 5e^{4x}$	Original equation
$2 = e^{4x}$	Divide both sides by 5.
$\ln 2 = \ln e^{4x}$	Take the natural logarithm of both sides.
$\ln 2 = 4x \ln e$	Power Property of Logarithms
$\ln 2 = 4x$	Simplify $\ln e$.
$\dfrac{\ln 2}{4} = \dfrac{4x}{4}$	Divide both sides by 4.
$\dfrac{\ln 2}{4} = x$	Simplify.
$0.173 \approx x$	Evaluate. Round to three decimal palces.

Ⓑ $5^x - 4 = 7$

$$5^x - 4 = 7$$ Original equation

$$5^x - 4 + \boxed{4} = 7 + \boxed{4}$$ Add $\boxed{4}$ to both sides.

$$5^x = \boxed{11}$$ Simplify.

$$\log 5^x = \log \boxed{11}$$ Take the common logarithm of both sides.

$$\boxed{x\log 5} = \log 11$$ Power Property of Logarithms

$$x = \frac{\log \boxed{11}}{\log \boxed{5}}$$ Divide both sides by $\log 5$.

$$x \approx \boxed{1.490}$$ Evaluate. Round to three decimal palces.

Reflect

2. Consider the equation $2^{x-3} = 85$. How can you solve this equation using logarithm base 2?

3. **Discussion** When solving an exponential equation with base e, what is the benefit of taking the natural logarithm of both sides of the equation?

Your Turn

Solve the equations. Give the exact solution and an approximate solution to three decimal places.

4. $2e^{x-1} + 5 = 80$ **5.** $6^{3x} = 12$

⚙ Explain 2   Solve a Real-World Problem by Solving an Exponential Equation

Suppose that \$250 is deposited into an account that pays 4.5% compounded quarterly. The equation $A = P\left(1 + \frac{r}{4}\right)^n$ gives the amount A in the account after n quarters for an initial investment P that earns interest at a rate r. Solve for n to find how long it will take for the account to contain at least \$500.

🧩 Analyze Information

Identify the important information.

- The initial investment P is \$ $\boxed{250}$.

- The interest rate is $\boxed{4.5}$ %, so r is $\boxed{0.045}$.

- The amount A in the account after n quarters is \$ $\boxed{500}$.

🧩 Formulate a Plan

Solve the equation for $A = P\left(1 + \frac{r}{4}\right)^n$ for $\boxed{n}$ by substituting in the known information and using logarithms.

Solve

$$500 = 250 \left(1 + \frac{0.045}{4}\right)^n$$ Substitute.

$$2 = \left(1 + \frac{0.045}{4}\right)^n$$ Divide both sides by 250.

$$2 = 1.01125^{\,n}$$ Evaluate the expression in parentheses.

$$\log 2 = \log 1.01125^n$$ Take the common logarithm of both sides.

$$\log 2 = n \; \log 1.01125$$ Power Property of Logarithms

$$\frac{\log 2}{\log 1.01125} = n$$ Divide both sides by log 1.01125.

$$61.96 \approx n$$ Evaluate.

Justify and Evaluate

It will take about $\boxed{61.96}$ quarters, or about $\boxed{15.5}$ years, for the account to contain at least $500.

Check by substituting this value for n in the equation and solving for A.

$$A = 250 \left(1 + \frac{0.045}{4}\right)^{61.96}$$ Substitute.

$$= 250 \left(\boxed{1.01125}\right)^{61.96}$$ Evaluate the expression in parentheses.

$$\approx 250 \left(\boxed{2}\right)$$ Evaluate the exponent.

$$\approx \boxed{500}$$ Multiply.

So, the answer is reasonable.

Your Turn

6. Suppose that $250 is deposited into an account that pays 4.5% compounded quarterly. The equation $A = P\left(1 + \frac{r}{4}\right)^n$ gives the amount A in the account after n quarters for an initial investment P that earns interest at a rate r. Solve for n to find how long it will take for the account to contain at least $500.

    How long will it take to triple a $250 initial investment in an account that pays 4.5% compounded quarterly?

7. Describe how to solve an exponential equation graphically.

8. **Essential Question Check-In** Describe how to solve an exponential equation algebraically.

⭐ Evaluate: Homework and Practice

Solve the equations graphically.

1. $4e^{0.1x} = 60$

2. $120e^{2x} = 75e^{3x}$

3. $5 = 625e^{0.02x}$

Solve the equations graphically. Then check your solutions algebraically.

4. $10e^{6x} = 5e^{-3x}$

5. $450e^{0.4x} = 2000$

6. $500e^{\frac{1}{3}x} = 225e^{\frac{2}{3}x}$

Solve the equations. Give the exact solution and an approximate solution to three decimal places.

7. $6^{3x-9} - 10 = -3$

8. $7e^{3x} = 42$

9. $11^{6x+2} = 12$

10. $e^{\frac{2x-1}{3}} = 250$

11. $\left(10^x\right)^2 + 90 = 105$

12. $5^{\frac{x}{4}} = 30$

Solve.

13. The price P of a gallon of gas after t years is given by the equation $P = P_0(1 + r)^t$, where P_0 is the initial price of gas and r is the rate of inflation. If the price of a gallon of gas is currently $3.25, how long will it take for the price to rise to $4.00 if the rate of inflation is 10.5%?

14. Finance The amount A in a bank account after t years is given by the equation $A = A_0\left(1 + \frac{r}{6}\right)^{6t}$, where A_0 is the initial amount and r is the interest rate. Suppose there is $600 in the account. If the interest rate is 4%, after how many years will the amount triple?

15. A baseball player has a 25% chance of hitting a home run during a game. For how many games will the probability of hitting a home run in every game drop to 5%?

16. Meteorology In one part of the atmosphere where the temperature is a constant $-70\ °F$, pressure can be expressed as a function of altitude by the equation $P(h) = 128(10)^{-0.682h}$, where P is the atmospheric pressure in kilopascals (kPa) and h is the altitude in kilometers above sea level. The pressure ranges from 2.55 kPa to 22.9 kPa in this region. What is the range of altitudes?

17. You can choose a prize of either a $20,000 car or one penny on the first day, double that (2 cents) on the second day, and so on for a month. On what day would you receive at least the value of the car?

18. Population The population of a small coastal resort town, currently 3400, grows at a rate of 3% per year. This growth can be expressed by the exponential equation $P = 3400(1 + 0.03)^t$, where P is the population after t years. Find the number of years it will take for the population to reach 10,000.

19. A veterinarian has instructed Harrison to give his 75-lb dog one 325-mg aspirin tablet for arthritis. The amount of aspirin A remaining in the dog's body after t minutes can be expressed by $A = 325\left(\frac{1}{2}\right)^{\frac{t}{15}}$. How long will it take for the amount of aspirin to drop to 50 mg?

20. Agriculture The number of farms in Iowa (in thousands) can be modeled by $N(t) = 119(0.987)^t$, where t is the number of years since 1980. According to the model, when will the number of farms in Iowa be about 80,000?

21. For each exponential equation, identify its solution.

a. $9e^{3x} = 27$ A. $x \approx 1.099$

b. $9e^{x} = 27$ B. $x \approx 1.022$

c. $9e^{3x-4} = 27$ C. $x \approx 0.366$

d. $9e^{3x} + 2 = 27$ D. $x \approx 1.700$

22. **Explain the Error** A student solved the equation $e^{4x} - 6 = 10$ as shown. Find and correct the student's mistake. Is there an easier way to solve the problem? Verify that both methods result in the same answer.

$$e^{4x} - 6 = 10$$
$$e^{4x} = 16$$
$$\log e^{4x} = \log 16$$
$$4x \log e = \log 16$$
$$4x(1) = \log 16$$
$$x = \frac{\log 16}{4}$$
$$x \approx 0.301$$

23. **Multi-Step** The amount A in an account after t years is given by the equation $A = Pe\ rt$, where P is the initial amount and r is the interest rate.

   a. Find an equation that models approximately how long it will take for the initial amount P in the account to double with the interest rate r. Write the equation in terms of the interest rate expressed as a percent.

   b. The Rule of 72 states that you can find the approximate time it will take to double your money by dividing 72 by the interest rate. The rule uses 72 instead of 69 because 72 has more divisors, making it easier to calculate mentally. Use the Rule of 72 to find the approximate time it takes to double an initial investment of $300 with an interest rate of 3.75%. Determine that this result is reasonable by solving the equation $A = P_0(1.0375)^t$, where A is the amount after t years and P_0 is the initial investment.

24. **Represent Real-World Problems** Suppose you have an initial mass M_0 of a radioactive substance with a half-life of h. Then the mass of the parent isotopes at time t is $P(t) = M_0\left(\frac{1}{2}\right)^{\frac{t}{h}}$. Since the substance is decaying from the original parent isotopes into the new daughter isotopes while the mass of all the isotopes remains constant, the mass of the daughter isotopes at time t is $D(t) = M_0 - P(t)$. Find when the masses of the parent isotopes and daughter isotopes are equal. Explain the meaning of your answer and why it makes sense.

Lesson Performance Task

The frequency of a note on the piano, in Hz, is related to its position on the keyboard by the function $f(n) = 440 \cdot 2^{\frac{n}{12}}$, where n is the number of keys above or below the note concert A, concert A being the A key above middle C on the piano. Using this function, find the position n of the key that has a frequency of 110 Hz. Why is this number a negative value?

© Houghton Mifflin Harcourt Publishing Company • Image Credits: ©Ebby May/ Getty Images

16.3 Solving Logarithmic Equations

Resource
Locker

Essential Question: What are some ways you can solve logarithmic equations?

 TEKS **A2.5.D** Solve … single logarithmic equations having real solutions. Also A2.5.E

⊘ **Explore** **Solving Logarithmic Equations Graphically**

One way to solve logarithmic equations is graphically. First, graph each side of the equation separately. The point(s) at which the two graphs intersect are the solutions of the equation.

(A) Look at the equation $12.2 + 5.45 \ln x = 12.5 + 5.2 \ln x$. To solve the equation graphically, split it into two separate equations.

$y_1 = $ ▮

$y_2 = $ ▮

(B) What will the graphs of y_1 and y_2 look like?

(C) Graph y_1 and y_2 using a graphing calculator.

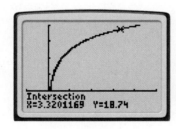

(D) The x-coordinate of the point of intersection is approximately ▮ .

(E) So, the solution of the equation is $x \approx$ ▮ .

Reflect

1. How can you check the solution of a logarithmic equation after it is found graphically?

2. How would you graph and solve a logarithmic equation where the base of the logarithmic function is not 10 or e if your calculator only graphed those bases?

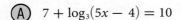

Explain 1   Solving Logarithmic Equations Algebraically

In addition to solving logarithmic equations graphically, logarithmic equations can be solved algebraically. The inverse relationship between logarithmic and exponential functions allows you to rewrite $\log_b x = a$ as $b^a = x$.

Example 1   **Solve the equations. Check for extraneous solutions.**

Ⓐ $7 + \log_3(5x - 4) = 10$

$7 + \log_3(5x - 4) = 10$	Original equation
$7 - 7 + \log_3(5x - 4) = 10 - 7$	Subtract 7 from both sides.
$\log_3(5x - 4) = 3$	Simplify.
$3^3 = 5x - 4$	Definition of a logarithm
$27 = 5x - 4$	Evaluate the exponent.
$31 = 5x$	Add 3 to both sides.
$6.2 = x$	Divied both sides by 5.

Check:

$$7 + \log_3\big(5(6.2) - 4\big) = 10$$

$$7 + \log_3(31 - 4) = 10$$

$$7 + \log_3(27) = 10$$

$$7 + \frac{\log 27}{\log 3} = 10$$

$$7 + 3 = 10$$

$$10 = 10$$

The solution is $x = 6.2$.

Ⓑ $\log x + \log(x + 9) = 1$

$$\log x + \log(x + 9) = 1$$ Original equation

$$\log\!\left(x \boxed{\;\cdot\;} (x + 9)\right) = 1$$ Production Property of Logarithms

$$\log\!\left(\boxed{x^2 + 9x}\right) = 1$$ Multiply.

$$\boxed{10}^{\,1} = x^2 + 9x$$ Definition of a logarithm

$$\boxed{10} = x^2 + 9x$$ Evaluate the exponent.

$$\boxed{0} = x^2 + 9x - \boxed{10}$$ Subtract 10 from both sides.

$$0 = \left(x + \boxed{10}\right)\!\left(x - \boxed{1}\right)$$ Factor.

$$\boxed{-10,\ 1} = x$$ Solve.

Check:

$$\log(-10) + \log(-10 + 9) = 1 \qquad\qquad \log 1 + \log(1 + 9) = 1$$

$$\log\!\left(\boxed{-10}\right) + \log\!\left(\boxed{-1}\right) = 1 \qquad\qquad \log 1 + \log \boxed{10} = 1$$

$$\boxed{\text{not defined}} = 1 \qquad\qquad\qquad \boxed{0} + \boxed{1} = 1$$

$$x = \boxed{-10}\ \text{is an extraneous solution.} \qquad\qquad \boxed{1} = 1$$

The solution is $x = \boxed{1}$.

Reflect

3. Explain how you would solve the equation $\log_5 45x = 1 + \log_5 3$. Then solve.

Your Turn

Solve the equations. Check for extraneous solutions.

4. $\log_4(2x + 12) + 5 = 8$

5. $\log_6(x - 5) = 2 - \log_6 x$

Given a logarithmic function $f(x)$ that models a real-world situation, find the value of x for which $f(x) = c$, where c is a constant. Check the reasonableness of the solution by graphing.

Example 2 Solve using properties of logarithms. Then check the reasonableness of the solution by graphing.

(A) The energy released by an earthquake can be a very large number, so a much smaller number is reported as the magnitude of the earthquake. The magnitude M of an earthquake with energy E (in ergs) is calculated using the formula $M = \frac{2}{3} \log E - 2.9$. The largest earthquake known to have occurred in Texas happened on August 16, 1931 and had a magnitude of 5.8. How much energy did the earthquake have?

Let $M = 5.8$. Substitute the value for M into the formula for the magnitude and solve for E.

$$5.8 = \frac{2}{3} \log E - 2.9 \qquad\qquad \text{Substitute.}$$

$$5.8 + 2.9 = \log E - 2.9 + 2.9 \qquad\qquad \text{Add 2.9 to both sides.}$$

$$8.7 = \frac{2}{3} \log E \qquad\qquad \text{Simplify.}$$

$$13.05 = \log E \qquad\qquad \text{Multiply both sides by } \frac{2}{3}.$$

$$E \approx 10^{13.05} \qquad\qquad \text{Definition of a logarithm}$$

$$E \approx 11{,}200{,}000{,}000{,}000 \qquad\qquad \text{Evaluate the exponent}$$

The earthquake had about 11,200,000,000,000 ergs of energy.

Check the reasonableness of the solution by graphing both sides of the equation on a graphing calculator.

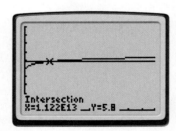

The two graphs intersect at approximately $x = 11{,}200{,}000{,}000{,}000$, so the answer is reasonable.

(B) An earthquake that occurred on December 7, 2013, near Volcano, Hawaii had a magnitude of 2.9. How much energy did the earthquake have?

Let $M = 2.9$. Substitute the value for M into the formula for the magnitude and solve for E.

$\boxed{2.9} = \frac{2}{3}\log E - 2.9$ Substitute.

$2.9 + \boxed{2.9} - \frac{2}{3}\log E - 2.9 + \boxed{2.9}$ Add 2.9 to both sides.

$\boxed{5.8} = \frac{2}{3}\log E$ Simplify.

$\boxed{8.7} = \log E$ Multiply both sides by $\frac{2}{3}$.

$E = \boxed{10}^{\;8.7}$ Definition of a logarithm

$E \approx \boxed{501{,}000{,}000}$ Evaluate the exponent.

The earthquake had about $\boxed{501{,}000{,}000}$ ergs of energy.

Check the reasonableness of the solution by graphing both sides of the equation on a graphing calculator.

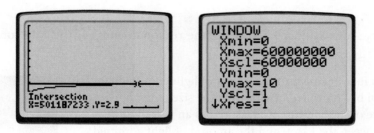

The two graphs intersect at approximately $x = \boxed{501{,}000{,}000}$, so the answer is reasonable.

Reflect

6. Compare the energies of the two earthquakes.

Your Turn

7. The difference between the apparent magnitude (brightness) m of a star and its absolute magnitude M is given by the formula $m - M = 5\log\frac{d}{10}$, where d is the distance of the star from Earth, measured in parsecs. The star Antares has an apparent magnitude of 1.0 and an absolute magnitude of -5.3. Find the distance d of Antares from Earth. Check the reasonableness of your answer by graphing.

💬 **Elaborate**

8. Explain why it's important to check the solutions of a logarithmic equation.

9. Describe how to solve an exponential equation graphically.

10. **Essential Question Check-In** Describe how to solve a logarithmic equation algebraically.

Solve the equations graphically.

1. $8 + \log x = 2\log x - 12$

2. $\log_6 2x = 2\log_6 x + 1$

3. $10 = 3\log_2 x$

4. $9.4 - \log_5 x = 4\log_5 x + 0.5$

5. $0.2\ln x + 5 = \ln x - 6$

6. $8\log_3 x - \dfrac{1}{4} = \dfrac{3}{4}\log_3 x + 2$

Solve the equations. Check for extraneous solutions.

7. $\log_9(4x + 5) = 2$

8. $\ln 8x = \ln 2 + 5$

9. $\log_2 x + \log_2(x - 4) = 5$

10. $\log_6 x = -\left(\log_6\left(x - \dfrac{1}{4}\right) + 2\right)$

11. $2.4\log_4 x = \log_4 3x + 1$

12. $\log 2x + \log(x - 5) = 2$

13. $\log_5(4x + 6) = \log_5(8x - 2)$

14. $2\ln x - 0.4 = 2.5 - 5\ln x$

Solve using properties of logarithms. Then check the reasonableness of the solution by graphing.

15. Photography On many cameras, the amount of light admitted through the lens can be controlled by changing the size of the opening, or aperture. The size of the aperture is measured as an f-stop setting. The relationship between the f-stop and the amount of light admitted can be represented by the equation $n = \log_2 \dfrac{1}{\ell}$, where n is the change in f-stop setting from the starting value, $\dfrac{f}{5.6}$. Solve the equation for ℓ when the f-stop setting is increased to $\dfrac{f}{16}$.

F–stop Setting	$\dfrac{f}{2}$	$\dfrac{f}{2.8}$	$\dfrac{f}{4}$	$\dfrac{f}{5.6}$	$\dfrac{f}{8}$	$\dfrac{f}{11}$	$\dfrac{f}{16}$
Change in F–stop Setting	−3	−2	−1	0	1	2	3

16. **Astronomy** A telescope's limiting magnitude m is the brightness of the faintest star that can be seen using the telescope. The limiting magnitude depends on the diameter d (in millimeters) of the telescope's objective lens. What diameter lens would be needed to view a faintest star with a brightness of 21?

Formulas for Determining Limiting Magnitude from Lens Diameter	
Standard formula	$m = 2.7 + 5\log d$

17. The equation for finding pH levels is $\text{pH} = -\log[\text{H}^+]$, where H^+ is the hydrogen ion concentration. Cow's milk has a pH level of 6.7 and goat's milk has a pH of 6.48. Find the difference in the hydrogen ion concentration between the two types of milk.

18. The sound level at a rock concert is 115 decibels. The loudness L of sound in decibels is given by the equation $L = 10\log\left(\frac{\ell}{\ell_0}\right)$, where I is the intensity of sound and ℓ_0 is the audible sound. If $\ell_0 = 10^{-12}$ decibels, what is the intensity of the sound at the rock concert?

19. The magnitude M of an earthquake with energy E (in ergs) is calculated using the formula $M = \frac{2}{3}\log E - 2.9$. How much energy does an earthquake with a magnitude of 3.8 have?

20. The brightness m of a star is given by the formula $m = 5\log\frac{d}{10} - 1.6$, where d is the distance of the star from Earth, measured in parsecs. Find the distance the star is from Earth if the brightness of the star is 3.2.

21. For each logarithmic equation, identify its solution.

    A. $2\log_5 x = 10$ a. $x = 390{,}625$

    B. $\log_5 2x = 10$ b. $x = 3125$

    C. $\log_5 x + 2 = 10$ c. $x = 1562.5$

    D. $2\log_5 2x = 10$ d. $x = 4{,}882{,}812.5$

22. **Multi-Step** Charles collected data on the atmospheric pressure (ranging from 4 to 15 pounds per square inch [psi]) and the corresponding altitude above the surface of Earth (ranging from 1 to 30,000 feet). He used regression to write two functions that give the altitude above the surface of the Earth given the atmospheric pressure.

$$f(x) = 66,990 - 24,747 \ln x$$

$$g(x) = -2870x + 40,393$$

     a. At what atmospheric pressure(s) do the equations give the same altitude?

     b. At what altitude(s) above Earth do these atmospheric pressures occur?

23. **Draw Conclusions** Solve the equation $\log_2(7x + 1) = \log_2(2 - x)$ by subtracting the logarithms. Is there an easier way to solve this equation? Explain.

24. **Explain the Error** A student found the solutions of the equation $\log_6 x + \log_6(x + 5) = 2$ to be $x = 4$ and $x = -9$. Explain the error in the student's reasoning.

Lesson Performance Task

A telescope's limiting magnitude m is the brightness of the faintest star that can be seen using the telescope. The limiting magnitude depends on the diameter d (in millimeters) of the telescope's objective lens. Limiting magnitude can be calculated in different ways. The table gives two formulas relating m to d. One is a standard formula used in astronomy. The other is a proposed new formula based on data gathered from users of telescopes of various lens diameters. For what lens diameter do the two formulas give the same limiting magnitude? Solve by graphing.

Formulas for Determining Limiting Magnitude from Lens Diameter	
Standard formula	$m = 2.7 + 5\log d$
Proposed formula	$m = 4.5 + 4.4\log d$

Logarithmic Properties and Exponential and Logarithmic Equations

Essential Question: How do the properties of logarithms allow you to solve real-world problems?

Key Vocabulary

exponential equation
(ecuación exponencial)
logarithmic equation
(ecuación logarítmica)

KEY EXAMPLE   (Lesson 16.1)

Simplify: $\log_5 5^{x+2} + \log_2 16^3$.

Apply properties of logarithms.

$$\log_5 5^{x+2} + \log_2 16^3 = (x+2)\log_5 5 + 3\log_2 16$$

$$= (x+2) + 3\left(\frac{\log 16}{\log 2}\right)$$

$$= x + 2 + 3\left(\frac{1.204}{0.301}\right)$$

$$= x + 2 + 3(4)$$

$$= x + 14$$

KEY EXAMPLE   (Lesson 16.2)

Solve the equation: $4^{3x+1} = 6$.

$$4^{3x+1} = 6$$

$$\log 4^{3x+1} = \log 6 \qquad \text{Take the log of both sides.}$$

$$(3x+1)\log 4 = \log 6 \qquad \text{Bring down the exponent.}$$

$$3x + 1 = \frac{\log 6}{\log 4} \qquad \text{Rearrange to isolate } x.$$

$$3x = \frac{\log 6}{\log 4} - 1$$

$$x = \frac{1}{3}\left(\frac{\log 6}{\log 4} - 1\right) \approx 0.0975$$

KEY EXAMPLE   (Lesson 16.3)

Solve the equation: $\log_2(3x - 7) = 5$.

$$\log_2(3x - 7) = 5$$

$$3x - 7 = 2^5$$

$$3x - 7 = 32 \qquad \text{Definition of logarithm.}$$

$$x = 13 \qquad \text{Evaluate.}$$

EXERCISES

Use properties of logarithms to simplify. *(Lesson 16.1)*

1. $\log_{\frac{3}{5}} 0.216^4$

2. $\log_4 4^{x-2} + \log_3 243^2$

3. $\log_8 0.15625^x$

4. $\log 10^{2x+1} + \log_3 9$

Solve each equation. *(Lesson 16.2, 16.3)*

5. $5^x = 50$

6. $6^{x+2} = 45$

7. $\log_3(2x - 5) = 2$

8. $\log_4 x + \log_4(x + 6) = 2$

MODULE PERFORMANCE TASK

How Old Is That Bone?

The La Brea Tar Pits in Los Angeles contain one of the best preserved collections of Pleistocene vertebrates, including over 660 species of organisms. An archeologist working at La Brea Tar Pits wants to assess the age of a mastodon bone fragment she discovered. She measures that the fragment has 22% as much carbon-14 as typical living tissue. Given that the half-life of carbon-14 is 5370 years, what is the bone fragment's age?

Start by listing the information you will need to solve the problem. Be sure to write down all your data and assumptions. Then use graphs, numbers, words, or algebra to explain how you reached your conclusion.

16.1–16.3 Logarithmic Properties and Exponential and Logarithmic Equations

- Online Homework
- Hints and Help
- Extra Practice

Use properties of logarithms to simplify. *(Lesson 16.1)*

1. $\log_{\frac{6}{5}} 2.0736^5$

2. $\log_2 3.2 - \log_2 0.025$

Solve each equation. Give the exact solution and an approximate solution to three decimal places. *(Lesson 16.2)*

3. $7^{2x} = 30$

4. $5^{2x-1} = 20$

Solve each equation. Check for extraneous solutions. *(Lesson 16.3)*

5. $3\log(x - 4) = 6$

6. $\log(6x^2) - \log 2x = 1$

ESSENTIAL QUESTION

7. How do you solve a logarithmic equation algebraically?

Assessment Readiness

1. What is the approximate solution of the equation $8^{x+1} = 12$?
   - **A.** 0.195
   - **B.** 0.837
   - **C.** 1.19
   - **D.** 2.19

2. What is the solution of the equation $\log_9 x^2 = 5$?
   - **A.** $\dfrac{5}{2}$
   - **B.** 9
   - **C.** 81
   - **D.** 243

3. Which function has an inverse that is **not** a function?
   - **A.** $f(x) = 4x^3 - 1$
   - **B.** $f(x) = \sqrt{3x} + 2$
   - **C.** $f(x) = 4x^2 + 2$
   - **D.** $f(x) = 2^x - 1$

4. At a constant temperature, the pressure, P, of an enclosed gas is inversely proportional to the volume, V, of the gas. If $P = 50$ pounds per square inch when $V = 30$ cubic inches, what is the pressure when the volume is 125 cubic inches?
   - **A.** 6 pounds per square inch
   - **B.** 12 pounds per square inch
   - **C.** 20 pounds per square inch
   - **D.** 75 pounds per square inch

5. $A = P(1 + r)^n$ gives amount A in an account after n years after an initial investment P that earns interest at an annual rate r. How long will it take for $250 to increase to $500 at 4% annual interest? Explain how you got your answer.

Assessment Readiness

1. What is the formula for the geometric sequence 5, 10, 20, 40, 80, ... ?

   A. $a_n = 5(2)^n$

   B. $a_n = 10(2n)$

   C. $a_n = 5(2)^{n-1}$

   D. $a_n = 5(2)^{n+1}$

2. What type of function would you use to model a population that doubles every 5 years?

   A. linear

   B. quadratic

   C. regression

   D. exponential

3. Let $f(x) = \log_6 x$. What is $f(216)$?

   A. 3

   B. 18

   C. 9

   D. 648

4. What is the inverse function of $f(x) = 8x^3 + 2$?

   A. $f^{-1}(x) = \dfrac{\sqrt[2]{x-2}}{2}$

   B. $f^{-1}(x) = \dfrac{\sqrt[3]{x-2}}{2}$

   C. $f^{-1}(x) = \dfrac{\sqrt[3]{x-2}}{8}$

   D. $f^{-1}(x) = \dfrac{\sqrt[3]{x+2}}{2}$

5. What is the solution of the equation $\log_3(4x + 1) = 4$?

   A. $x = \dfrac{11}{4}$

   B. $x = \dfrac{7}{12}$

   C. $x = 20$

   D. $x = 0$

6. A circular plot of land has a radius $3x - 1$. What is the polynomial representing the area of the land? *(Lesson 7.2)*

7. The number of bacteria growing in a petri dish after n hours can be modeled by $b(t) = b_0 r^n$, where b_0 is the initial number of bacteria and r is the rate at which the bacteria grow. If the number of bacteria quadruples after 1 hour, how many hours will it take to produce 51,200 bacteria if there are initially 50 bacteria? *(Lesson 16.2)*

Performance Tasks

★ **8.** The amount of freight transported by rail in the United States was about 580 billon *ton-miles* in 1960 and has been increasing at a rate of 2.32% per year since then.

  A. Write and graph a function representing the amount of freight, in billions of ton-miles, transported annually (1960 = year 0).

  B. In what year would you predict that the number of ton-miles would have exceeded or would exceed 1 trillion (1000 billion)?

★★ **9.** In one part of the atmosphere where the temperature is a constant $-70°F$ pressure can be expressed as a function of altitude by the equation $P(h) = 128(10)^{-0.0682h}$, where P is the atmospheric presser in kilopascals (kPa) and h is the altitude in kilometers above sea level. The pressure ranges from 2.55 kPa to 22.9 kPa in this region.

  A. What are the lowest and highest altitudes where this model is appropriate?

  B. A kilopascal is 0.145 psi. Would the model predict a sea-level pressure less than or greater than the actual sea-level pressure, 14.7 psi? Explain.

★★★**10.** The loudness of sound is measured on a logarithmic scale according to the formula $L = 10 \log\left(\frac{I}{I_0}\right)$, where L is the loudness of sound in decibels (dB), I is the intensity of sound, and I_0 is the intensity of the softest audible sound.

Sound	Intensity
Jet takeoff	$10^{15}I_0$
Jackhammer	$10^{12}I_0$
Hair dryer	$10^7 I_0$
Whisper	$10^3 I_0$
Leaves rustling	$10^2 I_0$
Softest audible sound	I_0

A. Find the loudness in decibels of each sound listed in the table.

B. The sound at a rock concert is found to have a loudness of 110 decibels. Find the intensity of this sound. Where should this sound be placed in the table in order to preserve the order from least to greatest intensity?

C. A decibel is $\frac{1}{10}$ of a bel. Is a jet plane louder than a sound that measures 20 bels? Explain.

Nuclear Medicine Technologist The radioactive properties of the isotope technetium-99m can be used in combination with a tin compound to map circulatory system disorders. Technetium-99m has a half-life of 6 hours.

a. Write an exponential decay function that models this situation. The function $p(t)$ should give the percent of the isotope remaining after t hours.

b. Describe domain, range, and the end behavior of $p(t)$ as t increases without bound for the function found in part a.

c. Write the inverse of the decay function. Use a common logarithm for your final function.

d. How long does it take until 5% of the technetium-99m remains? Round to the nearest tenth of an hour.

Glossary/Glosario

A

ENGLISH	SPANISH	EXAMPLES
absolute value of a complex number The absolute value of $a + bi$ is the distance from the origin to the point (a, b) in the complex plane and is denoted $\|a + bi\| = \sqrt{a^2 + b^2}$.	**valor absoluto de un número complejo** El valor absoluto de $a + bi$ es la distancia desde el origen hasta el punto (a, b) en el plano complejo y se expresa $\|a + bi\| = \sqrt{a^2 + b^2}$.	$\|2 + 3i\| = \sqrt{2^2 + 3^2} = \sqrt{13}$
absolute value of a real number The absolute value of x is the distance from zero to x on a number line, denoted $\|x\|$. $$\|x\| = \begin{cases} x & \text{if } x \geq 0 \\ -x & \text{if } x < 0 \end{cases}$$	**valor absoluto de un número real** El valor absoluto de x es la distancia desde cero hasta x en una recta numérica y se expresa $\|x\|$. $$\|x\| = \begin{cases} x & \text{si } x \geq 0 \\ -x & \text{si } x < 0 \end{cases}$$	$\|3\| = 3$ $\|-3\| = 3$
absolute-value function A function whose rule contains absolute-value expressions.	**función de valor absoluto** Función cuya regla contiene expresiones de valor absoluto.	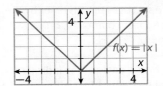
accuracy The closeness of a given measurement or value to the actual measurement or value.	**exactitud** Cercanía de una medida o un valor a la medida o el valor real.	
acute angle An angle that measures greater than 0° and less than 90°.	**ángulo agudo** Ángulo que mide más de 0° y menos de 90°.	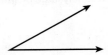
additive inverse of a matrix A matrix where each entry is the matrix. Two matrices are additive inverses if their sum is the zero matrix.	**inverso aditivo de una matriz** Matriz en la cual cada entrada es el opuesto de cada entrada en otra matriz. Dos matrices son inversos aditivos si su suma es la matriz cero.	$\begin{bmatrix} 1 & -2 \\ 0 & 4 \end{bmatrix}$ and $\begin{bmatrix} -1 & 0 \\ 2 & -4 \end{bmatrix}$ are additive inverses.
address The location of an entry in a matrix, given by the row and column in which the entry appears. In matrix A, the address of the entry in row i and column j is a_{1j}.	**dirección** Ubicación de una entrada en una matriz, indicada por la fila y la columna en las que aparece la entrada. En la matriz A, la dirección de la entrada de la fila i y la columna j es a_{1j}.	In the matrix $A = \begin{bmatrix} 2 & 3 \\ 4 & 1 \end{bmatrix}$, the address of the entry 2 is a_{11}, the address of the entry 3 is a_{12}.
amplitude The amplitude of a periodic function is half the difference of the maximum and minimum values (always positive).	**amplitud** La amplitud de una función periódica es la mitad de la diferencia entre los valores máximo y mínimo (siempre positivos).	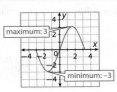 $$\text{amplitude} = \frac{1}{2}\left[3 - (-3)\right] = 3$$

Glossary/Glosario

Glossary/Glosario

angle of depression The angle formed by a horizontal line and a line of sight to a point below.

ángulo de depresión Ángulo formado por una recta horizontal y una línea visual a un punto inferior.

---

angle of elevation The angle formed by a horizontal line and a line of sight to a point above.

ángulo de elevación Ángulo formado por una recta horizontal y una línea visual a un punto superior.

---

angle of rotation An angle formed by a rotating ray, called the terminal side, and a stationary reference ray, called the initial side.

ángulo de rotación Ángulo formado por un rayo en rotación, denominado lado terminal, y un rayo de referencia estático, denominado lado inicial.

Terminal side   135°   45°   Initial side

---

arc An unbroken part of a circle consisting of two points on the circle, called the endpoints, and all the points on the circle between them.

arco Parte continua de un círculo formada por dos puntos del círculo denominados extremos y todos los puntos del círculo comprendidos entre éstos.

R S

---

arithmetic sequence A sequence whose successive terms differ by the same nonzero number d, called the *common difference*.

sucesión aritmética Sucesión cuyos términos sucesivos difieren en el mismo número distinto de cero d, denominado *diferencia común*.

$$4, 7, 10, 13, 16, \ldots$$
$$+ 3 + 3 + 3 + 3$$
$$d = 3$$

---

arithmetic series The indicated sum of the terms of an arithmetic sequence.

serie aritmética Suma indicada de los términos de una sucesión aritmética.

$$4 + 7 + 10 + 13 + 16 + \ldots$$

---

asymptote A line that a graph approaches as the value of a variable becomes extremely large or small.

asíntota Línea recta a la cual se aproxima una gráfica a medida que el valor de una variable se hace sumamente grande o pequeño.

Asymptote

---

augmented matrix A matrix that consists of the coefficients and the constant terms in a system of linear equations.

matriz aumentada Matriz formada por los coeficientes y los términos constantes de un sistema de ecuaciones lineales.

System of equations   Augmented matrix

$$3x + 2y = 5$$
$$2x - 3y = 1$$

$$\begin{bmatrix} 3 & 2 & | & 5 \\ 2 & -3 & | & 1 \end{bmatrix}$$

---

average rate of change The ratio of the change in the function values, $f(x_2) - f(x_1)$ to the change in the x-values, $x_2 - x_1$.

tasa de cambio promedio Razón entre el cambio en los valores de la función, $f(x_2) - f(x_1)$ y el cambio en los valores de x, $x_2 - x_1$.

---

axis of symmetry A line that divides a plane figure or a graph into two congruent reflected halves.

eje de simetría Línea que divide una figura plana o una gráfica en dos mitades reflejadas congruentes.

Axis of symmetry
$y = |x|$

B

base of an exponential function The value of b in a function of the form $f(x) = ab^x$, where a and b are real numbers with $a \neq 0$, $b > 0$, and $b \neq 1$.

base de una función exponencial Valor de b en una función del tipo $f(x) = ab^x$, donde a y b son números reales con $a \neq 0$, $b > 0$, y $b \neq 1$.

$f(x) = 5(2)^x$
$\uparrow$ base

---

biased sample A sample that does not fairly represent the population.

muestra no representativa Muestra que no representa adecuadamente una población.

---

binomial A polynomial with two terms.

binomio Polinomio con dos términos.

$x + y$
$2a^2 + 3$
$4m^3n^2 + 6mn^4$

---

binomial experiment A probability experiment consists of n identical and independent trials whose outcomes are either successes or failures, with a constant probability of success p and a constant probability of failure q, where $q = 1 - p$ or $p + q = 1$.

experimento binomial Experimento de probabilidades que comprende n pruebas idénticas e independientes cuyos resultados son éxitos o fracasos, con una probabilidad constante de éxito p y una probabilidad constante de fracaso q, donde $q = 1 - p$ o $p + q = 1$.

A multiple-choice quiz has 10 questions with 4 answer choices. The number of trials is 10. If each question is answered randomly, the probability of success for each trial is $\frac{1}{4} = 0.25$ and the probability of failure is $\frac{3}{4} = 0.75$.

---

binomial probability In a binomial experiment, the probability of r successes $(0 \leq r \leq n)$ is $P(r) = {}_nC_r \cdot p^r q^{n-r}$.

probabilidad binomial En un experimento binomial, la probabilidad de r éxitos $(0 \leq r \leq n)$ es $P(r) = {}_nC_r \cdot p^r q^{n-r}$.

In the binomial experiment above, the probability of randomly guessing 6 problems correctly is $P = {}_{10}C_6 (0.25)^6 (0.75)^4 \approx 0.016$.

Binomial Theorem For any positive integer n,
$(x + y)^n = {}_nC_0 x^n y^0 + {}_nC_1 x^{n-1} y^1 + {}_nC_2 x^{n-2} y^2 + ... + {}_nC_{n-1} x^1 y^{n-1} + {}_nC_n x^0 y^n$.

Teorema de los binomios Dado un entero positivo n,
$(x + y)^n = {}_nC_0 x^n y^0 + {}_nC_1 x^{n-1} y^1 + {}_nC_2 x^{n-2} y^2 + ... + {}_nC_{n-1} x^1 y^{n-1} + {}_nC_n x^0 y^n$.

$(x + 2)^4 = {}_4C_0 x^4 2^0 + {}_4C_1 x^3 2^1 + {}_4C_2 x^2 2^2 + {}_4C_1 x^1 2^3 + {}_4C_4 x^0 2^4 = x^4 + 8x^3 + 24x^2 + 32x + 16$

---

box-and-whisker plot A method of showing how data is distributed by using the median, quartiles, and minimum and maximum values; also called a *box plot*.

gráfica de mediana y rango Método para demostrar la distribución de datos utilizando la mediana, los cuartiles y los valores mínimos y máximos; también llamado *gráfica de caja*.

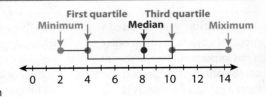

---

branch of a hyperbola One of the two symmetrical parts of the hyperbola.

rama de una hipérbola Una de las dos partes simétricas de la hipérbola.

Glossary/Glosario

C

census A survey of an entire population.

censo Estudio de una población entera.

---

circumference The distance around a circle.

circunferencia Distancia alrededor del círculo.

---

closure A set of numbers is said to be closed, or to have closure, under a given operation if the result of the operation on any two numbers in the set is also in the set.

cerradura Se dice que un conjunto de números es cerrado, o tiene cerradura, respecto de una operación determinada, si el resultado de la operación entre dos numerous cualesquiera del conjunto también está en el conjunto.

The natural numbers are closed under addition because the sum of two natural numbers is always a natural number.

---

cluster sample A sample in which the population is first divided into groups, a sample of the groups is randomly chosen, and all members of the chosen groups are surveyed.

muestra por grupos Muestra en la que la población se divide primeramente en grupos, se elige al azar una muestra de los grupos y se estudia a todos los miembros de los grupos elegidos.

---

coefficient matrix The matrix of the coefficients of the variables in a linear system of equations.

matriz de coeficientes Matriz de los coeficientes de las variables en un sistema lineal de ecuaciones.

System of equations	Coefficient matrix
$2x + 3y = 11$ $5x - 4y = 16$	$\begin{bmatrix} 2 & 3 \\ 5 & -4 \end{bmatrix}$

---

coefficient of determination The number R^2, with $0 \leq R^2 \leq 1$, that shows the fraction of the data that are close to the curve of best fit and, thus, how well the curve fits the data.

coeficiente de determinación El número R^2, con $0 \leq R^2 \leq 1$, que muestra la fracción de los datos cercanos a la línea de mejor ajuste y, por lo tanto, cuánto se ajusta la línea de mejor ajuste a los datos.

---

combination A selection of a group of objects in which order is *not* important. The number of combinations of r objects chosen from a group of n objects is denoted $_nC_r$.

combinación Selección de un grupo de objetos en la cual el orden *no* es importante. El número de combinaciones de r objetos elegidos de un grupo de n objetos se expresa así: $_nC_r$.

For 4 objects A, B, C, and D, there are $_4C_2 = 6$ different combinations of 2 objects: AB, AC, AD, BC, BD, CD.

---

combined variation A relationship containing both direct and inverse variation.

variación combinada Relación que contiene variaciones directas e inversas.

$y = \frac{kz}{x}$, where k is the constant of variation

---

common difference In an arithmetic sequence, the nonzero constant difference of any term and the previous term.

diferencia común En una sucesión aritmética, diferencia constante distinta de cero entre cualquier término y el término anterior.

In the arithmetic sequence 3, 5, 7, 9, 11, ..., the common difference is 2.

ENGLISH	SPANISH	EXAMPLES
common logarithm A logarithm whose base is 10, denoted $\log_{10}$ or just log.	**logaritmo común** Logaritmo de base 10, que se expresa $\log_{10}$ o simplemente log.	$\log 100 = \log_{10} 100 = 2$, since $10^2 = 100$.
common ratio In a geometric sequence, the constant ratio of any term and the previous term.	**razón común** En una sucesión geométrica, la razón constante r entre cualquier término y el término anterior.	In the geometric sequence 32, 16, 18, 4, 2 ..., the common ratio is $\frac{1}{2}$.
complement of an event All outcomes in the sample space that are not in an event E, denoted $\bar{E}$.	**complemento de un suceso** Todos los resultados en el espacio muestral que no están en el suceso E y se expresan $\bar{E}$.	In the experiment of rolling a number cube, the complement of rolling a 3 is rolling a 1, 2, 4, 5, or 6.
completing the square A process used to form a perfect-square trinomial. To complete the square of $x^2 + bx$, add $\left(\frac{b}{2}\right)^2$.	**completar el cuadrado** Proceso utilizado para formar un trinomio cuadrado perfecto. Para completar el cuadrado de $x^2 + bx$, hay que sumar $\left(\frac{b}{2}\right)^2$.	$x^2 + 6x + \blacksquare$ Add $\left(\frac{6}{2}\right)^2 = 9$. $x^2 + 6x + 9$ $(x + 3)^2$ is a perfect square.
complex conjugate The complex conjugate of any complex number $a + bi$, denoted $\overline{a + bi}$, is $a - bi$.	**conjugado complejo** El conjugado complejo de cualquier número complejo $a + bi$, expresado como $\overline{a + bi}$, es $a - bi$.	$\overline{4 + 3i} = 4 - 3i$ $\overline{4 - 3i} = 4 + 3i$
complex fraction A fraction that contains one or more fractions in the numerator, the denominator, or both.	**fracción compleja** Fracción que contiene una o más fracciones en el numerador, en el denominador, o en ambos.	$\dfrac{\frac{1}{2}}{1 + \frac{2}{3}}$
complex number Any number that can be written as $a + bi$, where a and b are real numbers and $i = \sqrt{-1}$.	**número complejo** Todo número que se puede expresar como $a + bi$, donde a y b son números reales e $i = \sqrt{-1}$.	$4 + 2i$ $5 + 0i = 5$ $0 - 7i = -7i$
complex plane A set of coordinate axes in which the horizontal axis is the real axis and the vertical axis is the imaginary axis; used to graph complex numbers.	**plano complejo** Conjunto de ejes cartesianos en el cual el eje horizontal es el eje real y el eje vertical es el eje imaginario; se utiliza para representar gráficamente números complejos.	
composite figure A plane figure made up of triangles, rectangles, trapezoids, circles, and other simple shapes, or a three-dimensional figure made up of prisms, cones, pyramids, cylinders, and other simple three-dimensional figures.	**figura compuesta** Figura plana compuesta por triángulos, rectángulos, trapecios, círculos y otras formas simples, o figura tridimensional compuesta por prismas, conos, pirámides, cilindros y otras figuras tridimensionales simples.	 18 in. 12 in.
composition of functions The composition of functions f and g, written as $(f \cdot g)(x)$ and defined as $f(g(x))$ uses the output of $g(x)$ as the input for $f(x)$.	**composición de funciones** La composición de las funciones f y g, expresada como $(f \cdot g)(x)$ y definida como $f(g(x))$ utiliza la salida de $g(x)$ como la entrada para $f(x)$.	If $f(x) = x^2$ and $g(x) = x + 1$, the composite function $(f \cdot g)(x) = (x + 1)^2$.

Glossary/Glosario

ENGLISH	SPANISH	EXAMPLES
compound event An event made up of two or more simple events.	**suceso compuesto** Suceso formado por dos o más sucesos simples.	In the experiment of tossing a coin and rolling a number cube, the event of the coin landing heads and the number cube landing on 3.
compression A transformation that pushes the points of a graph horizontally toward the *y*-axis or vertically toward the *x*-axis.	**compresión** Transformación que desplaza los puntos de una gráfica horizontalmente hacia el eje *y* o verticalmente hacia el eje *x*.	
conditional probability The probability of event *B*, given that event *A* has already occurred or is certain to occur, denoted $P(B \mid A)$; used to find probability of dependent events.	**probabilidad condicional** Probabilidad del suceso *B*, dado que el suceso *A* ya ha ocurrido o es seguro que ocurrirá, expresada como $P(B \mid A)$; se utiliza para calcular la probabilidad de sucesos dependientes.	
conditional relative frequency The ratio of a joint relative frequency to a related marginal relative frequency in a two-way table.	**frecuencia relativa condicional** Razón de una frecuencia relativa conjunta a una frecuencia relativa marginal en una tabla de doble entrada.	
congruent Having the same size and shape, denoted by ≅.	**congruente** Que tiene el mismo tamaño y forma, expresado por ≅.	$\overline{PQ} \cong \overline{RS}$
conic section A plane figure formed by the intersection of a double right cone and a plane. Examples include circles, ellipses, hyperbolas, and parabolas.	**sección cónica** Figura plana formada por la intersección de un cono regular doble y un plano. Algunos ejemplos son círculos, elipses, hipérbolas y parábolas.	Circle Ellipse Parabola Hyperbola
conjugate axis The axis of symmetry of a hyperbola that separates the two branches of the hyperbola.	**eje conjugado** Eje de simetría de una hipérbola que separa las dos ramas de la hipérbola.	Conjugate axis
constant function A function of the form $f(x) = c$, where *c* is a constant.	**función constante** Función del tipo $f(x) = c$, donde *c* es una constante.	$y = 3$
constant matrix The matrix of the constants in a linear system of equations.	**matriz de constantes** Matriz de las constantes de un sistema lineal de ecuaciones.	System of equations $\begin{cases} 2x + 3y = 11 \\ 5x - 4y = 16 \end{cases}$ Constant matrix $\begin{bmatrix} 11 \\ 16 \end{bmatrix}$
constant of variation The constant *k* in direct, inverse, joint, and combined variation equations.	**constante de variación** La constante *k* en ecuaciones de variación directa, inversa, conjunta y combinada.	$y = 5x$ ↑ constant of variation

ENGLISH	SPANISH	EXAMPLES
constraint One of the inequalities that define the feasible region in a linear-programming problem.	**restricción** Una de las desigualdades que definen la región factible en un problema de programación lineal.	Constraints: Feasible region $x > 0$ $y > 0$ $x + y \leq 8$ $3x + 5y \leq 30$ 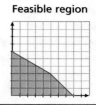
continuous data Data that can take on any real-value measurement within an interval.	**datos continuos** Datos obtenidos por medición que pueden asumir cualquier valor real dentro de un intervalo.	The quantity of water in a glass as the water evaporates is continuous data.
continuous function A function whose graph is an unbroken line or curve with no gaps or breaks.	**función continua** Función cuya gráfica es una línea recta o curva continua, sin espacios ni interrupciones.	
contradiction An equation that has no solutions.	**contradicción** Ecuación que no tiene soluciones.	$x + 1 = x$ $1 = 0x$
control group In a controlled experiment, the group that does not receive treatment. This group is used for comparison.	**grupo de control** En un experimento controlado, el grupo que no está expuesto a la manipulación; es el grupo que sirve como comparación.	
controlled experiment An experiment in which two groups are studied under conditions that are identical except for one variable.	**experimento controlado** Experimento en el que se estudia a dos grupos bajo condiciones que son idénticas, excepto por una variable.	
converge An infinite series converges when the partial sums approach a fixed number.	**convergir** Una sucesión o serie infinita converge cuando las sumas parciales se aproximan a un número fijo.	$\frac{1}{2} + \frac{1}{4} + \frac{1}{8} + \frac{1}{16} + \ldots$ converges to 1.
convenience sample A sample based on members of the population that are readily available.	**muestra de conveniencia** Una muestra basada en miembros de la población que están fácilmente disponibles.	A reporter surveys people he personally knows.
correlation A measure of the strength and direction of the relationship between two variables or data sets.	**correlación** Medida de la fuerza y dirección de la relación entre dos variables o conjuntos de datos.	 

© Houghton Mifflin Harcourt Publishing Company

ENGLISH	SPANISH	EXAMPLES
correlation coefficient A number *r*, where $-1 \leq r \leq 1$, that describes how closely the points in a scatter plot cluster around the least–squares line.	**coeficiente de correlación** Número *r*, donde $-1 \leq r \leq 1$, que describe a qué distancia de la recta de mínimos cuadrados se agrupan los puntos de un diagrama de dispersión.	An *r*–value close to 1 describes a strong positive correlation. An *r*–value close to 0 describes a weak correlation or no correlation. An *r*–value close to -1 describes a strong negative correlation.
cosecant In a right triangle, the cosecant of angle *A* is the ratio of the length of the hypotenuse to the length of the side opposite *A*. It is the reciprocal of the sine function.	**cosecante** En un triángulo rectángulo, la cosecante del ángulo *A* es la razón entre la longitud de la hipotenusa y la longitud del cateto opuesto a *A*. Es la inversa de la función seno.	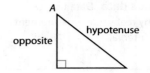 $$\csc A = \frac{\text{hypotenuse}}{\text{opposite}} = \frac{1}{\sin A}$$
cosine In a right triangle, the cosine of angle *A* is the ratio of the length of the side adjacent to angle *A* to the length of the hypotenuse. It is the reciprocal of the secant function.	**coseno** En un triángulo rectángulo, el coseno del ángulo *A* es la razón entre la longitud del cateto adyacente al ángulo *A* y la longitud de la hipotenusa. Es la inversa de la función secante.	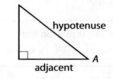 $$\cos A = \frac{\text{adjacent}}{\text{hypotenuse}} = \frac{1}{\sec A}$$
cotangent In a right triangle, the cotangent of angle *A* is the ratio of the length of the side adjacent to *A* to the length of the side opposite *A*. It is the reciprocal of the tangent function.	**cotangente** En un triángulo rectángulo, la cotangente del ángulo *A* es la razón entre la longitud del cateto adyacente a *A* y la longitud del cateto opuesto a *A*. Es la inversa de la función tangente.	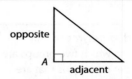 $$\cot A = \frac{\text{adjacent}}{\text{opposite}} = \frac{1}{\tan A}$$
coterminal angles Two angles in standard position with the same terminal side.	**ángulos coterminales** Dos ángulos en posición estándar con el mismo lado terminal.	
counterexample An example that proves that a conjecture or statement is false.	**contraejemplo** Ejemplo que demuestra que una conjetura o enunciado es falso.	
co-vertices of a hyperbola The endpoints of the conjugate axis.	**co-vértices de una hipérbola** Extremos de un eje conjugado.	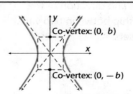
co-vertices of an ellipse The endpoints of the minor axis.	**co-vértices de una elipse** Extremos del eje menor.	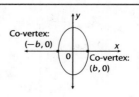

Glossary/Glosario

ENGLISH	SPANISH	EXAMPLES
critical values Values that separate the number line into intervals that either contain solutions or do not contain solutions.	**valores críticos** Valores que separan la recta numérica en intervalos que contienen o no contienen soluciones.	
cube-root function The function $f(x) = \sqrt[3]{x}$.	**función de raíz cúbica** La función $f(x) = \sqrt[3]{x}$.	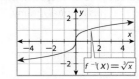
cubic function A polynomial function of degree 3.	**función cúbica** Función polinomial de grado 3.	
cycle of a periodic function The shortest repeating part of a periodic graph or function.	**ciclo de una función periódica** La parte repetida más corta de una gráfica o función periódica.	

D

ENGLISH	SPANISH	EXAMPLES
decay factor The base $1 - r$ in an exponential expression.	**factor decremental** Base $1 - r$ en una expresión exponencial.	$2(0.93)^t$ decay factor (representing $1 - 0.07$)
decay rate The constant percent decrease, in decimal form, in an exponential decay function.	**tasa de disminución** Disminución porcentual constante, en forma decimal, en una función de disminución exponencial.	In the function $f(t) = a(1 - 0.2)^t$, 0.2 is the decay rate.
decreasing A function is decreasing on an interval if $f(x_1) > f(x_2)$ when $x_1 > x_2$ for any x-values x_1 and x_2 from the interval.	**decreciente** Una función es decreciente en un intervalo si $f(x_1) > f(x_2)$ cuando $x_1 > x_2$ dados los valores de x, x_1 y x_2, pertenecientes al intervalo.	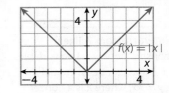 $f(x)$ is decreasing on the interval $x < 0$.
degenerate conic A degenerate conic is formed when a plane passes through the vertex of a hollow double cone. A point, a line, and a pair of intersecting lines are all degenerate conics.	**cónica degenerada** Una cónica degenerada se forma cuando un plano atraviesa el vértice de un cono doble hueco. Un punto, una línea y un par de líneas secantes son cónicas degeneradas.	A point is a circle with no radius.
degree of a monomial The sum of the exponents of the variables in the monomial.	**grado de un monomio** Suma de los exponentes de las variables del monomio.	$4x^2y^5z^3$ Degree: $2 + 5 + 3 = 10$ 5 Degree: $0 \; (5 = 5x^0)$
degree of a polynomial The degree of the term of the polynomial with the greatest degree.	**grado de un polinomio** Grado del término del polinomio con el grado máximo.	$3x^2y^2 + 4xy^5 - 12x^3y^2$ Degree 6 Degree 4 Degree 6 Degree 5

Glossary/Glosario

Glossary/Glosario

ENGLISH	SPANISH	EXAMPLES
dependent events Events for which the occurrence or nonoccurrence of one event affects the probability of the other event.	**sucesos dependientes** Dos sucesos son dependientes si el hecho de que uno de ellos se cumpla o no afecta la probabilidad del otro.	From a bag containing 3 red marbles and 2 blue marbles, drawing a red marble, and then drawing a blue marble without replacing the first marble.
dependent system A system of equations that has infinitely many solutions.	**sistema dependiente** Sistema de ecuaciones que tiene infinitamente muchas soluciones.	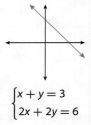 $$\begin{cases} x + y = 3 \\ 2x + 2y = 6 \end{cases}$$
dependent variable The output of a function; a variable whose value depends on the value of the input, or independent variable.	**variable dependiente** Salida de una función; variable cuyo valor depende del valor de la entrada, o variable independiente.	$y = 2x + 1$ $\uparrow$ dependent variable
determinant A real number associated with a square matrix. The determinant of $A = \begin{bmatrix} a & b \\ c & d \end{bmatrix}$ is $|A| = ad - bc$.	**determinante** Número real asociado con una matriz cuadrada. El determinante de $A = \begin{bmatrix} a & b \\ c & d \end{bmatrix}$ es $|A| = ad - bc$.	$\begin{vmatrix} 2 & -1 \\ 3 & 4 \end{vmatrix} = 2(4) - (-1)(3) = 11$
difference of two squares A polynomial of the form $a^2 - b^2$, which may be written as the product $(a + b)(a - b)$.	**diferencia de dos cuadrados** Polinomio del tipo $a^2 - b^2$, que se puede expresar como el producto $(a + b)(a - b)$.	$x^2 - 4 = (x + 2)(x - 2)$
dimensions of a matrix A matrix with m rows and n columns has dimensions $m \times n$, read "m by n."	**dimensiones de una matriz** Una matriz con m filas y n columnas tiene dimensiones $m \times n$, expresadas "m por n".	$\begin{bmatrix} -3 & 2 & 1 & -1 \\ 4 & 0 & -5 & 2 \end{bmatrix}$ Dimensions 2×4
direct variation A linear relationship between two variables, x and y, that can be written in the form $y = kx$, where k is a nonzero constant.	**variación directa** Relación lineal entre dos variables, x e y, que puede expresarse en la forma $y = kx$, donde k es una constante distinta de cero.	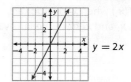 $y = 2x$
directrix A fixed line used to define a *parabola*. Every point on the parabola is equidistant from the directrix and a fixed point called the *focus*.	**directriz** Línea fija utilizada para definir una *parábola*. Cada punto de la parábola es equidistante de la directriz y de un punto fijo denominado *foco*.	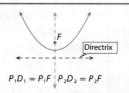 $P_1 D_1 = P_1 F$ $P_2 D_2 = P_2 F$
discontinuous function A function whose graph has one or more jumps, breaks, or holes.	**función discontinua** Función cuya gráfica tiene uno o más saltos, interrupciones u hoyos.	
discrete data Data that cannot take on any real-value measurement within an interval.	**datos discretos** Datos que no admiten cualquier medida de valores reales dentro de un intervalo.	the number of pennies in a jar over time

Glossary/Glosario

ENGLISH	SPANISH	EXAMPLES
discriminant The discriminant of the quadratic equation $ax^2 + bx + c = 0$ is $b^2 - 4ac$.	**discriminante** El discriminante de la ecuación cuadrática $ax^2 + bx + c = 0$ es $b^2 - 4ac$.	The discriminant of $2x^2 - 5x - 3$ is $(-5)^2 - 4(2)(-3) = 25 + 24 = 49$.
disjunction A compound statement that uses the word *or*.	**disyunción** Enunciado compuesto que contiene la palabra *o*.	John will walk to work OR he will stay home.
Distance Formula In a coordinate plane, the distance from (x_1, y_1) to (x_2, y_2) is $$d = \sqrt{(x_2 - x_1)^2 + (y_2 - y_1)^2}.$$	**Fórmula de distancia** En un plano cartesiano, la distancia desde (x_1, y_1) hasta (x_2, y_2) es $$d = \sqrt{(x_2 - x_1)^2 + (y_2 - y_1)^2}.$$	The distance from (2, 1) to (6, 4) is $$d = \sqrt{(6 - 2)^2 + (4 - 1)^2}$$ $$= \sqrt{4^2 + 3^2} = \sqrt{9 + 16} = 5.$$
diverge An infinite series diverges when the partial sums do not approach a fixed number.	**divergir** Una serie infinita diverge cuando las sumas parciales no se aproximan a un número fijo.	$1 + 2 + 4 + 8 + 16 + \ldots$ diverges.
domain The set of all possible input values of a relation or function.	**dominio** Conjunto de todos los posibles valores de entrada de una función o relación.	The domain of the function $f(x) = \sqrt{x}$ is $\{x \mid x \geq 0\}$.

E

ENGLISH	SPANISH	EXAMPLES
elementary row operations *See* row operations.	**operaciones elementales de fila** *Véase* operaciones de fila.	
elimination A method used to solve systems of equations in which one variable is eliminated by adding or subtracting two equations of the system.	**eliminación** Método utilizado para resolver sistemas de ecuaciones por el cual se elimina una variable sumando o restando dos ecuaciones del sistema.	
ellipse The set of all points P in a plane such that the sum of the distances from P to two fixed points F_1 and F_2, called the foci, is constant.	**elipse** Conjunto de todos los puntos P de un plano tal que la suma de las distancias desde P hasta los dos puntos fijos F_1 y F_2, denominados focos, es constante.	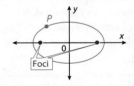
empty set A set with no elements.	**conjunto vacío** Conjunto sin elementos.	The solution set of $\lvert x \rvert < 0$ is the empty set, $\{\ \}$, or $\varnothing$.
end behavior The trends in the y-values of a function as the x-values approach positive and negative infinity.	**comportamiento extremo** Tendencia de los valores de y de una función a medida que los valores de x se aproximan al infinito positivo y negativo.	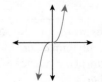 End behavior: $f(x) \rightarrow \infty$ as $x \rightarrow \infty$ $f(x) \rightarrow -\infty$ as $x \rightarrow -\infty$
entry Each value in a matrix; also called an element.	**entrada** Cada valor de una matriz; también denominado elemento.	3 is the entry in the first row and second column of $A = \begin{bmatrix} 2 & 3 \\ 0 & 1 \end{bmatrix}$, denoted a_{12}.

Glossary/Glosario

ENGLISH	SPANISH	EXAMPLES
equally likely outcomes Outcomes are equally likely if they have the same probability of occurring. If an experiment has n equally likely outcomes, then the probability of each outcome is $\frac{1}{n}$.	**resultados igualmente probables** Los resultados son igualmente probables si tienen la misma probabilidad de ocurrir. Si un experimento tiene n resultados igualmente probables, entonces la probabilidad de cada resultado es $\frac{1}{n}$.	If a coin is tossed, and heads and tails are equally likely, then $P(\text{heads}) = P(\text{tails}) = \frac{1}{2}$.
equation A mathematical statement that two expressions are equivalent.	**ecuación** Enunciado matemático que indica que dos expresiones son equivalentes.	$x + 4 = 7$ $2 + 3 = 6 - 1$ $(x - 1)^2 + (y + 2)^2 = 4$
even function A function in which $f(-x) = f(x)$ for all x in the domain of the function.	**función par** Función en la que para todos los valores de x dentro del dominio de la función.	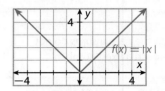 $f(x) = |x|$ is an even function.
event An outcome or set of outcomes in a probability experiment.	**suceso** Resultado o conjunto de resultados en un experimento de probabilidad.	In the experiment of rolling a number cube, the event "an odd number" consists of the outcomes 1, 3, and 5.
expected value The weighted average of the numerical outcomes of a probability experiment.	**valor esperado** Promedio ponderado de los resultados numéricos de un experimento de probabilidad.	The table shows the probability of getting a given score by guessing on a three-question quiz.

Score	0	1	2	3
Probability	0.42	0.42	0.14	0.02

The expected value is a score of $0\,(0.42) + 1\,(0.42) + 2\,(0.14) + 3\,(0.02) = 0.76$.

ENGLISH	SPANISH	EXAMPLES
experiment An operation, process, or activity in which outcomes can be used to estimate probability.	**experimento** Una operación, proceso o actividad cuyo resultado se puede usar para estimar la probabilidad.	Tossing a coin 10 times and noting the number of heads.
experimental probability The ratio of the number of times an event occurs to the number of trials, or times, that an activity is performed.	**probabilidad experimental** Razón entre la cantidad de veces que ocurre un suceso y la cantidad de pruebas, o veces, que se realiza una actividad.	Kendra made 6 of 10 free throws. The experimental probability that she will make her next free throw is $P(\text{free throw}) = \frac{\text{number made}}{\text{number attempted}} = \frac{6}{10}$.
explicit formula A formula that defines the nth term a_n, or general term, of a sequence as a function of n.	**fórmula explícita** Fórmula que define el enésimo término a_n, o término general, de una sucesión como una función de n.	Sequence: 4, 7, 10, 13, 16, 19, … Explicit formula: $a_n = 1 + 3n$
exponent The number that indicates how many times the base in a power is used as a factor.	**exponente** Número que indica la cantidad de veces que la base de una potencia se utiliza como factor.	$3^4 = 3 \cdot 3 \cdot 3 \cdot 3 = 81$ ↑ exponent

ENGLISH	SPANISH	EXAMPLES

exponential decay An exponential function of the form $f(x) = ab^x$ in which $0 < b < 1$. If r is the rate of decay, then the function can be written $y = a(1-r)^t$, where a is the initial amount and t is the time.

decremento exponencial Función exponencial del tipo $f(x) = ab^x$ en la cual $0 < b < 1$. Si r es la tasa decremental, entonces la función se puede expresar como $y = a(1-r)^t$, donde a es la cantidad inicial y t es el tiempo.

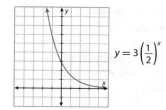
$y = 3\left(\dfrac{1}{2}\right)^x$

---

exponential equation An equation that contains one or more exponential expressions.

ecuación exponencial Ecuación que contiene una o más expresiones exponenciales.

$2^{x+1} = 8$

---

exponential function A function of the form $f(x) = ab^x$, where a and b are real numbers with $a \neq 0, b > 0$, and $b \neq 1$.

función exponencial Función del tipo $f(x) = ab^x$, donde a y b son números reales con $a \neq 0, b > 0$ y $b \neq 1$.

---

exponential growth An exponential function of the form $f(x) = ab^x$ in which $b > 1$. If r is the rate of growth, then the function can be written $y = a(1+r)^t$, where a is the initial amount and t is the time.

crecimiento exponencial Función exponencial del tipo $f(x) = ab^x$ en la que $b > 1$. Si r es la tasa de crecimiento, entonces la función se puede expresar como $y = a(1+r)^t$, donde a es la cantidad inicial y t es el tiempo.

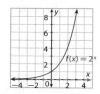

---

exponential regression A statistical method used to fit an exponential model to a given data set.

regresión exponencial Método estadístico utilizado para ajustar un modelo exponencial a un conjunto de datos determinado.

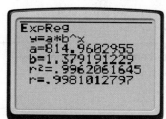

---

extraneous solution A solution of a derived equation that is not a solution of the original equation.

solución extraña Solución de una ecuación derivada que no es una solución de la ecuación original.

To solve $\sqrt{x} = -2$, square both sides; $x = 4$.
Check $\sqrt{4} = -2$ is false; so 4 is an extraneous solution.

F

Factor Theorem For any polynomial $P(x)$, $(x-a)$ is a factor of $P(x)$ if and only if $P(a) = 0$.

Teorema del factor Dado el polinomio $P(x)$, $(x-a)$ es un factor de $P(x)$ si y sólo si $P(a) = 0$.

$(x-1)$ is a factor of $P(x) = x^2 - 1$ because $P(1) = 1^2 - 1 = 0$.

---

factorial If n is a positive integer, then n factorial, written n!, is $n \cdot (n-1) \cdot (n-2) \cdot \ldots \cdot 2 \cdot 1$. The factorial of 0 is defined to be 1.

factorial Si n es un entero positivo, entonces el factorial de n, expresado como n!, es $n \cdot (n-1) \cdot (n-2) \cdot \ldots \cdot 2 \cdot 1$ Por definición, el factorial de 0 será 1.

$7! = 7 \cdot 6 \cdot 5 \cdot 4 \cdot 3 \cdot 2 \cdot 1 = 5040$
$0! = 1$

---

factoring The process of writing a number or algebraic expression as a product.

factorización Proceso por el que se expresa un número o expresión algebraica como un producto.

$x^2 - 4x - 21 = (x-7)(x+3)$

Glossary/Glosario

© Houghton Mifflin Harcourt Publishing Company

Glossary/Glosario

ENGLISH	SPANISH	EXAMPLES
family of functions A set of functions whose graphs have basic characteristics in common. Functions in the same family are transformations of their parent function.	**familia de funciones** Conjunto de funciones cuyas gráficas tienen características básicas en común. Las funciones de la misma familia son transformaciones de su función madre.	Some members of the family of quadratic functions with the parent function $f(x) = x^2$ are: $f(x) = 3x^2$ $f(x) = x^2 + 1$ $f(x) = (x - 2)^2$ 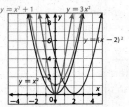
favorable outcome The occurrence of one of several possible outcomes of a specified event or probability experiment.	**resultado favorable** Cuando se produce uno de varios resultados posibles de un suceso específico o experimento de probabilidad.	In the experiment of rolling an odd number on a number cube, the favorable outcomes are 1, 3, and 5.
feasible region The set of points that satisfy the constraints in a linear-programming problem.	**región factible** Conjunto de puntos que cumplen con las restricciones de un problema de programación lineal.	Constraints: $x > 0$ $y > 0$ $x + y \leq 8$ $3x + 5y \leq 30$ Feasible region
Fibonacci sequence The infinite sequence of numbers beginning with 1, 1 such that each term is the sum of the two previous terms.	**sucesión de Fibonacci** Sucesión infinita de números que comienza con 1, 1 de forma tal que cada término es la suma de los dos términos anteriores.	1, 1, 2, 3, 5, 8, 13, 21, …
finite sequence A sequence with a finite number of terms.	**sucesión finita** Sucesión con un número finito de términos.	1, 2, 3, 4, 5
finite set A set with a definite, or finite, number of elements.	**conjunto finito** Conjunto con un número de elementos definido o finito.	$\{2, 4, 6, 8, 10\}$
first differences The differences between y-values of a function for evenly spaced x-values.	**primeras diferencias** Diferencias entre los valores de y de una función para valores de x espaciados uniformemente.	<table><tr><td>x</td><td>0</td><td>1</td><td>2</td><td>3</td></tr><tr><td>y</td><td>3</td><td>7</td><td>11</td><td>15</td></tr></table> first differences +4 +4 +4
first quartile The median of the lower half of a data set, denoted Q_1. Also called *lower quartile*.	**primer cuartil** Mediana de la mitad inferior de un conjunto de datos, expresada como Q_1. También se llama *cuartil inferior*.	Lower half Upper half 18, (23), 28, 36, 42, 49, First quartile
focus (pl. foci) of a hyperbola One of two fixed points F_1 and F_2 that are used to define a hyperbola. For every point P on the hyperbola, $PF_1 - PF_2$ is constant.	**foco de una hipérbola** Uno de los dos puntos fijos F_1 y F_2 utilizados para definir una hipérbola, Para cada punto P de la hipérbola, $PF_1 - PF_2$ es constante.	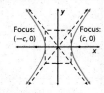 Focus: $(-c, 0)$ Focus: $(c, 0)$

Glossary/Glosario

ENGLISH	SPANISH	EXAMPLES
focus (pl. foci) of an ellipse One of two fixed points F_1 and F_2 that are used to define an ellipse. For every point P on the ellipse, $PF_1 + PF_2$ is constant.	**foco de una elipse** Uno de los dos puntos fijos F_1 y F_2 utilizados para definir una elipse. Para cada punto P de la elipse, $PF_1 + PF_2$ es constante.	y-axis diagram with ellipse, Focus: $(0, c)$ and Focus: $(0, -c)$
focus (pl. foci) of a parabola A fixed point F used with a *directrix* to define a *parabola*.	**foco de una parábola** Punto fijo F utilizado con una *directriz* para definir una *parábola*.	parabola diagram with Focus F
frequency of a data value The number of times the value appears in the data set.	**frecuencia de un valor de datos** Cantidad de veces que aparece el valor en un conjunto de datos.	In the data set 5, 6, 6, 6, 8, 9, the data value 6 has a frequency of 3.
frequency of a periodic function The number of cycles per unit of time. Also the reciprocal of the period.	**frecuencia de una función periódica** Cantidad de ciclos por unidad de tiempo. También es la inversa del periodo.	The function $y = \sin(2x)$ has a period of π and a frequency of $\frac{1}{\pi}$.
function A relation in which every input is paired with exactly one output.	**función** Una relación en la que cada entrada corresponde exactamente a una salida.	mapping diagram: 6, 5, 2, 1 to −4, −1, 0
function notation If x is the independent variable and y is the dependent variable, then the function notation for y is $f(x)$, read "f of x," where f names the function.	**notación de función** Si x es la variable independiente e y es la variable dependiente, entonces la notación de función para y es $f(x)$, que se lee "f de x", donde f nombra la función.	equation: $y = 2x$ function notation: $f(x) = 2x$
function rule An algebraic expression that defines a function.	**regla de función** Expresión algebraica que define una función.	$f(x) = 2x^2 + 3x - 7$ ↑ function rule
Fundamental Counting Principle For n items, if there are m_1 ways to choose a first item, m_2 ways to choose a second item after the first item has been chosen, and so on, then there are $m_1 \cdot m_2 \cdot \ldots \cdot m_n$ ways to choose n items.	**Principio fundamental de conteo** Dados n elementos, si existen m_1 formas de elegir un primer elemento, m_2 formas de elegir un segundo elemento después de haber elegido el primero, y así sucesivamente, entonces existen $m_1 \cdot m_2 \cdot \ldots \cdot m_n$ formas de elegir n elementos.	If there are 4 colors of shirts, 3 colors of pants, and 2 colors of shoes, then there are $4 \cdot 3 \cdot 2 = 24$ possible outfits.

G

Gaussian Elimination An algorithm for solving systems of equations using matrices and row operations to eliminate variables in each equation in the system.	**Eliminación Gaussiana** Algoritmo para resolver sistemas de ecuaciones mediante matrices y operaciones de fila con el fin de eliminar variables en cada ecuación del sistema.	

general form of a conic section $Ax^2 + Bxy + Cy^2 + Dx + Ey + F = 0$, where A and B are not both 0.

forma general de una sección cónica $Ax^2 + Bxy + Cy^2 + Dx + Ey + F = 0$, donde A y B no son los dos 0.

A circle with a vertex at $(1, 2)$ and radius 3 has the general form $x^2 + y^2 - 2x - 4y - 4 = 0$.

---

geometric mean In a geometric sequence, a term that comes between two given nonconsecutive terms of the sequence. For positive numbers a and b, the geometric mean is $\sqrt{ab}$.

media geométrica En una sucesión geométrica, un término que se encuentra entre dos términos no consecutivos dados de la sucesión. Dados los números positivos a y b, la media geométrica es $\sqrt{ab}$.

The geometric mean of 4 and 9 is $\sqrt{4(9)} = \sqrt{36} = 6$.

---

geometric probability A form of theoretical probability determined by a ratio of geometric measures such as lengths, areas, or volumes.

probabilidad geométrica Una forma de la probabilidad teórica determinada por una razón de medidas geométricas, como longitud, área o volumen.

The probability of the pointer landing on red is $\frac{2}{9}$.

---

geometric sequence A sequence in which the ratio of successive terms is a constant r, called the common ratio, where $r \neq 0$ and $r \neq 1$.

sucesión geométrica Sucesión en la que la razón de los términos sucesivos es una constante r, denominada razón común, donde $r \neq 0$ y $r \neq 1$.

---

geometric series The indicated sum of the terms of a geometric sequence.

serie geométrica Suma indicada de los términos de una sucesión geométrica.

$1 + 2 + 4 + 8 + 16 + \dots$

---

grade A measure of the steepness of surfaces, expressed as a percent.

grado Medida de la inclinación de las superficies, expresada como un porcentaje.

A ramp that rises 1 foot for every 5 feet of the horizontal distance has a grade of 20%.

---

greatest common factor (GCF) The product of the greatest integer and the greatest power of each variable that divides evenly into each term.

máximo común divisor (MCD) Dado Producto del entero mayor y la potencia mayor de cada variable que divide exactamente cada término.

The GCF of $4x^3y$ and $6x^2y$ is $2x^2y$.
The GCF of 27 and 45 is 9.

---

greatest-integer function A function denoted by $f(x) = [x]$ or $f(x) = \lfloor x \rfloor$ in which the number x is rounded down to the greatest integer that is less than or equal to x.

función de entero mayor Función expresada como $f(x) = [x]$ o $f(x) = \lfloor x \rfloor$ en la cual el número x se redondea hacia abajo hasta el entero mayor que sea menor que o igual a x.

$\lfloor 4.98 \rfloor = 4$
$\lfloor -2.1 \rfloor = -3$

---

growth factor The base $1 + r$ in an exponential expression.

factor de crecimiento La base $1 + r$ en una expresión exponencial.

$12,000(1 + 0.14)^t$

growth factor

---

growth rate The constant percent increase, in decimal form, in an exponential growth function.

tasa de crecimiento Aumento porcentual constante, en forma decimal, en una función de crecimiento exponencial.

In the function $f(t) = a(1 + 0.3)^t$, 0.3 is the growth rate.

Glossary/Glosario

H

half-life The half-life of a substance is the time it takes for one-half of the substance to decay into another substance.

vida media La vida media de una sustancia es el tiempo que tarda la mitad de la sustancia en desintegrarse y transformarse en otra sustancia.

Carbon-14 has a half-life of 5730 years, so 5 g of an initial amount of 10 g will remain after 5730 years.

---

half-plane The part of the coordinate plane on one side of a line, which may include the line.

semiplano Parte del plano cartesiano de un lado de una línea, que puede incluir la línea.

Heron's Formula A triangle with side lengths a, b, and c has area $A = \sqrt{s(s-a)(s-b)(s-c)}$, where s is one-half the perimeter, or $s = \frac{1}{2}(a+b+c)$.

fórmula de Herón Un triángulo con longitudes de lado a, b y c tiene un área $A = \sqrt{s(s-a)(s-b)(s-c)}$, donde s es la mitad del perímetro ó $s = \frac{1}{2}(a+b+c)$.

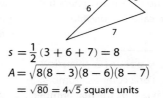

$$s = \frac{1}{2}(3 + 6 + 7) = 8$$
$$A = \sqrt{8(8-3)(8-6)(8-7)}$$
$$= \sqrt{80} = 4\sqrt{5} \text{ square units}$$

---

hole (in a graph) An omitted point on a graph. If a rational function has the same factor $x - b$ in both the numerator and the denominator, and the line $x = b$ is not a vertical asymptote, then there is a hole in the graph at the point where $x = b$.

hoyo (en una gráfica) Punto omitido en una gráfica. Si una función racional tiene el mismo factor $x - b$ tanto en el numerador como en el denominador, y la línea $x = b$ no es una asíntota vertical, entonces hay un hoyo en la gráfica en el punto donde $x = b$.

$f(x) = \frac{(x-2)(x+2)}{(x+2)}$ has a hole at $x = -2$.

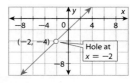

---

horizontal line A line described by the equation $y = b$, where b is the y-intercept.

línea horizontal Línea descrita por la ecuación $y = b$, donde b es la intersección con el eje y.

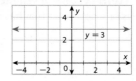

---

horizontal line test If a horizontal line crosses the graph of a function f at more than one point, then the inverse is not a function.

prueba de la línea horizontal Si una línea horizontal cruza la gráfica de una función f en más de un punto, entonces la inversa no es una función.

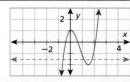

The inverse is not a function.

---

hyperbola The set of all points P in a plane such that the difference of the distances from P to two fixed points F_1 and F_2, called the foci, is a constant $d = |PF_1 - PF_2|$.

hipérbola Conjunto de todos los puntos P en un plano tal que la diferencia de las distancias de P a dos puntos fijos F_1 y F_2, llamados focos, es una constante $d = |PF_1 - PF_2|$.

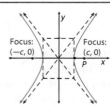

Glossary/Glosario

ENGLISH	SPANISH	EXAMPLES
hypothesis testing A type of testing used to determine whether the difference in two groups is likely to be caused by chance.	**comprobación de hipótesis** Tipo de comprobación que sirve para determinar si el azar es la causa probable de la diferencia entre dos grupos.	

I

ENGLISH	SPANISH	EXAMPLES
imaginary axis The vertical axis in the complex plane, it graphically represents the purely imaginary part of complex numbers.	**eje imaginario** Eje vertical de un plano complejo. Representa gráficamente la parte puramente imaginaria de los números complejos.	Imaginary axis diagram with $2i$, $0 + 0i$, $-2i$, and Real axis
imaginary number The square root of a negative number, written in the form bi, where b is a real number and i is the imaginary unit, $\sqrt{-1}$. Also called a *pure imaginary number*.	**número imaginario** Raíz cuadrada de un número negativo, expresado como bi, donde b es un número real e i es la unidad imaginaria, $\sqrt{-1}$. También se denomina *número imaginario puro*.	$\sqrt{-16} = \sqrt{16} \cdot \sqrt{-1} = 4i$
imaginary part of a complex number For a complex number of the form $a + bi$, the real number b is called the imaginary part, represented graphically as b units on the imaginary axis of a complex plane.	**parte imaginaria de un número complejo** Dado un número complejo del tipo $a + bi$, el número real b se denomina parte imaginaria y se representa gráficamente como b unidades en el eje imaginario de un plano complejo.	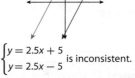 $5 + 6i$ real part imaginary part
imaginary unit The unit in the imaginary number system, $\sqrt{-1}$.	**unidad imaginaria** Unidad del sistema de números imaginarios, $\sqrt{-1}$.	$\sqrt{-1} = i$
inconsistent system A system of equations or inequalities that has no solution.	**sistema inconsistente** Sistema de ecuaciones o desigualdades que no tiene solución.	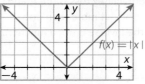 $\begin{cases} y = 2.5x + 5 \\ y = 2.5x - 5 \end{cases}$ is inconsistent.
Increasing A function is increasing on an interval if $f(x_1) < f(x_2)$ when $x_1 < x_2$ for any x-values x_1 and x_2 from the interval.	**creciente** Una función es creciente en un intervalo si $f(x_1) < f(x_2)$ cuando $x_1 < x_2$ dados los valores de x, x_1 y x_2, pertenecienlos al intervalo.	Graph showing $f(x) = |x|$ $f(x)$ is increasing on the interval $x > 0$.
independent events Events for which the occurrence or non-occurrence of one event does not affect the probability of the other event.	**sucesos independientes** Dos sucesos son independientes si el hecho de que se produzca o no uno de ellos no afecta la probabilidad del otro suceso.	From a bag containing 3 red marbles and 2 blue marbles, drawing a red marble, replacing it, and then drawing a blue marble.

ENGLISH	SPANISH	EXAMPLES

independent system A system of equations that has exactly one solution.

sistema independiente Sistema de ecuaciones que tiene exactamente una solución.

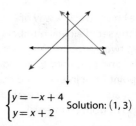

$$\begin{cases} y = -x + 4 \\ y = x + 2 \end{cases}$$ Solution: $(1, 3)$

---

independent variable The input of a function; a variable whose value determines the value of the output, or dependent variable.

variable independiente Entrada de una función; variable cuyo valor determina el valor de la salida, o variable dependiente.

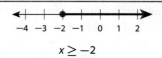

---

index In the radical $\sqrt[n]{x}$ which represents the nth root of x, n is the index. In the radical $\sqrt{x}$, the index is understood to be 2.`

index En el radical $\sqrt[n]{x}$, que representa la enésima raíz de x, n es el índice. En el radical $\sqrt{x}$, se da por sentado que el índice es 2.

The radical $\sqrt[3]{8}$ has an index of 3.

indirect measurement A method of measurement that uses formulas, similar figures, and/or proportions.

medición indirecta Método para medir objetos mediante fórmulas, figuras semejantes y/o proporciones.

---

inequality A statement that compares two expressions by using one of the following signs: $<, >, \leq, \geq$ or $\neq$.

desigualdad Enunciado que compara dos expresiones utilizando uno de los siguientes signos: $<, >, \leq, \geq$, ó, $\neq$.

$x \geq -2$

---

infinite geometric series A geometric series with infinitely many terms.

serie geométrica infinita Serie geométrica con una cantidad infinita de términos.

$$\frac{1}{10} + \frac{1}{100} + \frac{1}{1000} + \frac{1}{10,000} + \cdots$$

---

infinite sequence A sequence with infinitely many terms.

sucesión infinita Sucesión con infinitos términos.

$1, 3, 5, 7, 9, 11 \ldots$

---

infinite set A set with an unlimited, or infinite, number of elements.

conjunto infinito Conjunto con un número de elementos ilimitado o infinito.

The set of all integers is an infinite set.

---

initial side The ray that lies on the positive x-axis when an angle is drawn in standard position.

lado inicial El rayo que se encuentra en el eje positivo x cuando se traza un ángulo en la posición estándar.

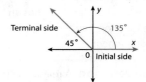

---

integer A member of the set of whole numbers and their opposites.

entero Miembro del conjunto de números cabales y sus opuestos.

$\ldots -3, -2, -1, 0, 1, 2, 3 \ldots$

---

interquartile range (IQR) The difference of the third (upper) and first (lower) quartiles in a data set, representing the middle half of the data.

rango entre cuartiles Diferencia entre el tercer cuartil (superior) y el primer cuartil (inferior) de un conjunto de datos, que representa la mitad central de los datos.

Lower half	Upper half
18, ㉓, 28,	29, ㊱, 42
First quartile	Third quartile

Interquartile range: $36 - 23 = 13$.

Glossary/Glosario

interval notation A way of writing the set of all real numbers between two endpoints. The symbols [and] are used to include an endpoint in an interval, and the symbols (and) are used to exclude an endpoint from an interval.

notación de intervalo Forma de expresar el conjunto de todos los números reales entre dos extremos. Los símbolos [y] se utilizan para incluir un extremo en un intervalo y los símbolos (y) se utilizan para excluir un extremo de un intervalo.

Interval notation	Set-builder notation
(a, b)	$\{x \mid a < x < b\}$
(a, b)	$\{x \mid a < x \leq b\}$
$[a, b]$	$\{x \mid a \leq x < b\}$
$[a, b]$	$\{x \mid a \leq x \leq b\}$

inverse cosine function If the domain of the cosine function is restricted to $[0, \pi]$, then the function $\cos \theta = a$ has an inverse function $\cos^{-1} a = \theta$, also called *arccosine*.

función coseno inverso Si el dominio de la función coseno se restringe a $[0, \pi]$, entonces la función Cos $\theta = a$ tiene una función inversa Cos$^{-1} a = \theta$, también llamada *arco coseno*.

$$\cos^{-1}\frac{1}{2} = \frac{\pi}{3}$$

inverse function The function that results from exchanging the input and output values of a one-to-one function. The inverse of $f(x)$ is denoted $f^{-1}(x)$.

función inversa Función que resulta de intercambiar los valores de entrada y salida de una función uno a uno. La función inversa de $f(x)$ se expresa $f^{-1}(x)$

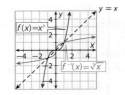

inverse relation The inverse of the relation consisting of all ordered pairs (x, y) is the set of all ordered pairs (y, x). The graph of an inverse relation is the reflection of the graph of the relation across the line $y = x$.

relación inversa La inversa de la relación que consta de todos los pares ordenados (x, y) es el conjunto de todos los pares ordenados (y, x). La gráfica de una relación inversa es el reflejo de la gráfica de la relación sobre la línea $y = x$.

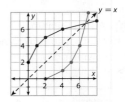

inverse sine function If the domain of the sine function is restricted to $\left[-\frac{\pi}{2}, \frac{\pi}{2}\right]$ then the 2 function $\sin \theta = a$ has an inverse function, $\sin^{-1} a = \theta$, also called *arcsine*.

función seno inverso Si el dominio de la función seno se restringe a $\left[-\frac{\pi}{2}, \frac{\pi}{2}\right]$, entonces la función Sen $\theta = a$ tiene una función inversa, Sen$^{-1} a = \theta\theta$, también llamada *arco seno*.

$$\sin^{-1}\frac{\sqrt{3}}{2} = \frac{\pi}{3}$$

inverse tangent function If the domain of the tangent function is restricted to $\left(-\frac{\pi}{2}, \frac{\pi}{2}\right)$, then the function $\tan\theta = a$ has an inverse function, $\tan^{-1} a = \theta$, also called *arctangent*.

función tangente inversa Si el dominio de la función tangente se restringe a $\left(-\frac{\pi}{2}, \frac{\pi}{2}\right)$ entonces la función Tan$\theta = a$ tiene una función inversa, Tan$^{-1} a = \theta$, también llamada *arco tangente*.

$$\tan^{-1}\sqrt{3} = \frac{\pi}{3}$$

inverse variation A relationship between two variables, x and y, that can be written in the form $y = \frac{k}{x}$, where k is a nonzero constant and $x \neq 0$.

variación inversa Relación entre dos x e y, que puede expresarse en la forma $y = \frac{k}{x}$ donde k es una constante distinta de cero y $x \neq 0$.

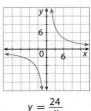

$$y = \frac{24}{x}$$

irrational number A real number that cannot be expressed as the ratio of two integers.

número irracional Número real que no se puede expresar como una razón de enteros.

$$\sqrt{2}, \pi, e$$

ENGLISH	SPANISH	EXAMPLES
irreducible factor A factor of degree 2 or greater that cannot be factored further.	**factor irreductible** Factor de grado 2 o mayor que no se puede seguir factorizando.	$x^2 + 7x + 1$
iteration The repetitive application of the same rule.	**iteración** Aplicación repetitiva de la misma regla.	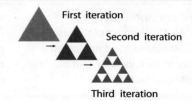First iteration Second iteration Third iteration

J

joint relative frequency The ratio of the frequency in a particular category divided by the total number of data values.	**frecuencia relativa conjunta** La razón de la frecuencia en una determinada categoría dividida entre el número total de valores.	
joint variation A relationship among three variables that can be written in the form $y = kxz$, where k is a nonzero constant.	**variación conjunta** Relación entre tres variables que se puede expresar de la forma $y = kxz$, donde k es una constante distinta de cero.	$y = 3xz$

L

Law of Cosines For $\triangle ABC$ with side lengths a, b, and c, $a^2 = b^2 + c^2 - 2bc \cos A$ $b^2 = a^2 + c^2 - 2ac \cos B$ $c^2 = a^2 + b^2 - 2ab \cos C$.	**Ley de cosenos** Dado $\triangle ABC$ con longitudes de lado a, b y c, $a^2 = b^2 + c^2 - 2bc \cos A$ $b^2 = a^2 + c^2 - 2ac \cos B$ $c^2 = a^2 + b^2 - 2ab \cos C$	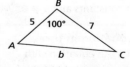$b^2 = 7^2 + 5^2 - 2(7)(5)\cos 100°$ $b^2 \approx 86.2$ $b \approx 9.3$
law of large numbers The tendency of experimental probability to approach theoretical probability as the number of trials gets very large.	**Ley de los números grandes** Tendencia de la probabilidad experimental a acercarse a la probabilidad teórica cuando el número de pruebas es muy grande.	The more times you toss a coin, the closer the experimental probability will be to $\frac{1}{2}$.
Law of Sines For $\triangle ABC$ with side lengths a, b, and c, $\frac{\sin A}{a} = \frac{\sin B}{b} = \frac{\sin C}{c}$.	**Ley de senos** Dado $\triangle ABC$ con longitudes de lado a, b y c, $\frac{sen A}{a} = \frac{sen B}{b} = \frac{sen C}{c}$.	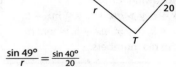$\frac{\sin 49°}{r} = \frac{\sin 40°}{20}$ $r = \frac{20 \sin 49°}{\sin 40°} \approx 23.5$
leading coefficient The coefficient of the first term of a polynomial in standard form.	**coeficiente principal** Coeficiente del primer termino de un polinomio en forma estandar	$3x^2 + 7x - 2$ ↑ Leading coefficient

Glossary/Glosario

© Houghton Mifflin Harcourt Publishing Company

Glossary/Glosario

least common denominator (LCD) The least common multiple of two or more given denominators.

mínimo común denominador (mcd) Mínimo común múltiplo de dos o más denominadores dados.

The LCD of $\frac{3}{4}$ and $\frac{5}{6}$ is 12.

---

least common multiple (LCM) The product of the smallest positive number and the lowest power of each variable that divides evenly into each term.

mínimo común múltiplo (mcm) El producto del número positivo más pequeño y la potencia más baja de cada variable que divide exactamente cada término.

The LCM of 10 and 18 is 90.
The LCM of $2x^2$ and $5x^3$ is $10x^3$.

---

least-squares line The line of fit for which the sum of the squares of the residuals is as small as possible.

recta de mínimos cuadrados Recta de ajuste para la cual la suma de los cuadrados de los residuos es la menor posible.

---

limit For an infinite arithmetic series that converges, the number that the partial sums approach.

límite Para un serie que coverge, el número que se aproximan las sumas.

The series $\frac{1}{2} + \frac{1}{4} + \frac{1}{8} + \frac{1}{16} + \cdots$ has a limit of 1.

---

line of best fit The line that comes closest to all of the points in a data set.

línea de mejor ajuste Línea que más se acerca a todos los puntos de un conjunto de datos.

---

linear equation in one variable An equation that can be written in the form $ax = b$, where a and b are constants and $a \neq 0$.

ecuación lineal en una variable Ecuación que puede expresarse en la forma $ax = b$, donde a y b son constantes y $a \neq 0$.

$x + 1 = 7$

---

linear equation in three variables An equation with three distinct variables, each of which is either first degree or has a coefficient of zero.

ecuación lineal en tres variables Ecuación con tres variables diferentes, sean de primer grado o tengan un coeficiente de cero.

$5 = 3x + 2y + 6z$

---

linear function A function that can be written in the form $f(x) = mx + b$, where x is the independent variable and m and b are real numbers. Its graph is a line.

función lineal Función que puede expresarse en la forma $f(x) = mx + b$, donde x es la variable independiente y m y b son números reales. Su gráfica es una línea.

---

linear inequality in two variables An inequality that can be written in one of the following forms: $y < mx + b$, $y > mx + b$, $y \leq mx + b$, $y \geq mx + b$, or $y \neq mx + b$, where m and b are real numbers.

desigualdad lineal en dos variables Desigualdad que puede expresarse de una de las siguientes formas: $y < mx + b$, $y > mx + b$, $y \leq mx + b$, $y \geq mx + b$, o $y \neq mx + b$, donde m y b son números reales.

$2x + 3y \leq 6$
$y > \frac{1}{2}x - 7$

---

linear regression A statistical method used to fit a linear model to a given data set.

regresión lineal Método estadístico utilizado para ajustar un modelo lineal a un conjunto de datos determinado.

ENGLISH	SPANISH	EXAMPLES
linear system A system of equations containing only linear equations.	**sistema lineal** Sistema de ecuaciones que contiene sólo ecuaciones lineales.	$$\begin{cases} y = 2x + 1 \\ x + y = 8 \end{cases}$$
local maximum For a function f, $f(a)$ is a local maximum if there is an interval around a such that $f(x) < f(a)$ for every x-value in the interval except a.	**máximo local** Dada una función f, $f(a)$ es el máximo local si hay un intervalo en a tal que $f(x) < f(a)$ para cada valor de x en el intervalo excepto a.	Local maximum
local minimum For a function f, $f(a)$ is a local minimum if there is an interval around a such that $f(x) > f(a)$ for every x-value in the interval except a.	**mínimo local** Dada una función f, $f(a)$ es el mínimo local si hay un intervalo en a tal que $f(x) > f(a)$ para cada valor de x en el intervalo excepto a.	Local minimum
logarithm The exponent that a specified base must be raised to in order to get a certain value.	**logaritmo** Exponente al cual debe elevarse una base determinada a fin de obtener cierto valor.	$\log_2 8 = 3$, because 3 is the power that 2 is raised to in order to get 8; or $2^3 = 8$.
logarithmic equation An equation that contains a logarithm of a variable.	**ecuación logarítmica** Ecuación que contiene un logaritmo de una variable.	$\log x + 3 = 7$
logarithmic function A function of the form $f(x) = \log_b x$, where $b \neq 1$ and $b > 0$, which is the inverse of the exponential function $f(x) = b^x$.	**función logarítmica** Función del tipo $f(x) = \log_b x$, donde $b \neq 1$ y $b > 0$, que es la inversa de la función exponencial $f(x) = b^x$.	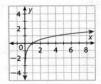 $f(x) = \log_4 x$
logarithmic regression A statistical method used to fit a logarithmic model to a given data set.	**regresión logarítmica** Método estadístico utilizado para ajustar un modelo logarítmico a un conjunto de datos determinado.	
logistic function An exponential growth function that tapers off at an asymptote.	**función logística** Función de crecimiento exponencial que disminuye en una asíntota.	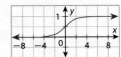

M

major axis The longer axis of an ellipse. The foci of the ellipse are located on the major axis, and its endpoints are the *vertices of the ellipse*.	**eje mayor** El eje más largo de una elipse. Los focos de la elipse se encuentran sobre el eje mayor y sus extremos son los *vértices de la elipse*.	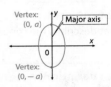
margin of error In a random sample, it defines an interval, centered on the sample percent, in which the population percent is most likely to lie.	**margen de error** En una muestra aleatoria, define un intervalo, centrado en el porcentaje de muestra, en el que es más probable que se encuentre el porcentaje de población.	

Glossary/Glosario

ENGLISH	SPANISH	EXAMPLES
marginal relative frequency The sum of the joint relative frequencies in a row or column of a two-way table.	**frecuencia relativa marginal** La suma de las frecuencias relativas conjuntas en una fila o columna de una tabla de doble entrada.	
mathematical induction A type of mathematical proof. To prove that a statement is true for all natural numbers n, first show that the statement is true for $n = 1$; then assume it is true for some number k and prove that it is true for $k + 1$. It follows that the statement is true for all values of n.	**inducción matemática** Tipo de demostración matemática. Para demostrar que un enunciado se cumple para todos los números naturales n, primero se demuestra que el enunciado se cumple para $n = 1$; luego se supone que se cumple para un número k y se demuestra que se cumple para $k + 1$. Por lo tanto, el enunciado se cumplirá para todos los valores de n.	
matrix A rectangular array of numbers.	**matriz** Arreglo rectangular de números.	$\begin{bmatrix} 1 & 0 & 3 \\ -2 & 2 & -5 \\ 7 & -6 & 3 \end{bmatrix}$
matrix equation An equation of the form $AX = B$, where A is the coefficient matrix, X is the variable matrix, and B is the constant matrix of a system of equations.	**ecuación matricial** Ecuación del tipo $AX = B$, donde A es la matrizde coeficientes, X es la matriz de variables y B es la matriz de constantes de un sistema de ecuaciones.	System of equations: $\begin{aligned} 2x + 3y &= 7 \\ 4x - 6y &= 5 \end{aligned}$ Matrix equation: $\begin{bmatrix} 2 & 3 \\ 4 & -6 \end{bmatrix} \begin{bmatrix} x \\ y \end{bmatrix} = \begin{bmatrix} 7 \\ 5 \end{bmatrix}$
matrix product The product of two matrices, where each entry in P_{ij} is the sum of the products of consecutive entries in row i in matrix A and column j in matrix B.	**producto matricial** Producto de dos matrices, donde cada entrada de P_{ij} es la suma de los productos de las entradas consecutivas de la fila i de la matriz A y de la columna j de la matriz B.	$\begin{bmatrix} 1 & 2 \\ 3 & 4 \end{bmatrix} \begin{bmatrix} 5 & 6 \\ 7 & 8 \end{bmatrix}$ $= \begin{bmatrix} 1(5) + 2(7) & 1(6) + 2(8) \\ 3(5) + 4(7) & 3(6) + 4(8) \end{bmatrix}$ $= \begin{bmatrix} 19 & 22 \\ 43 & 50 \end{bmatrix}$
maximum value of a function The y-value of the highest point on the graph of the function.	**máximo de una función** Valor de y del punto más alto en la gráfica de la función.	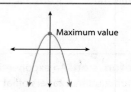 Maximum value
mean The sum of all the values in a data set divided by the number of data values. Also called the *average*.	**media** Suma de todos los valores de un conjunto de datos dividida entre el número de valores de datos. También llamada *promedio*.	Data set: 4, 6, 7, 8, 10 Mean: $\frac{4 + 6 + 7 + 8 + 10}{5} = \frac{35}{5} = 7$
measure of central tendency A measure that describes the center of a data set.	**medida de tendencia dominante** Medida que describe el centro de un conjunto de datos.	the mean, median, or mode
measure of variation A measure that describes the spread of a data set.	**medida de variación** Medida que describe la amplitud de un conjunto de datos.	the range, variance, standard deviation, or interquartile range

ENGLISH	SPANISH	EXAMPLES
median of a data set For an ordered data set with an odd number of values, the median is the middle value. For an ordered data set with an even number of values, the median is the average of the two middle values.	**mediana de un conjunto de datos** Dado un conjunto de datos ordenados con un número impar de valores, la mediana es el valor del medio. Dado un conjunto de datos ordenados con un número par de valores, la mediana es el promedio de los dos valores del medio	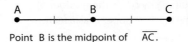 8, 9, ⑨, 12, 15 median: 9 4, 6, ⑦, 10, 10, 12 median: $\frac{7+10}{2} = 8.5$
midpoint The point that divides a segment into two congruent segments.	**punto medio** Punto que divide un segmento en dos segmentos congruentes.	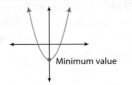 Point B is the midpoint of $\overline{AC}$.
minimum value of a function The y-value of the lowest point on the graph of the function.	**mínimo de una función** Valor de y del punto más bajo en la gráfica de la función.	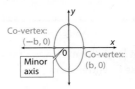
minor axis The shorter axis of an ellipse. Its endpoints are the *co-vertices of the ellipse.*	**eje menor** El eje más corto de una elipse. Sus extremos son los *co-vértices de la elipse.*	Co-vertex: $(-b, 0)$ Co-vertex: $(b, 0)$ Minor axis
mode The value or values that occur most frequently in a data set; if all values occur only once, the data set is said to have no mode.	**moda** El valor o los valores que se presentan con mayor frecuencia en un conjunto de datos. Si todos los valores se presentan con la misma frecuencia, se dice que el conjunto de datos no tiene moda.	Data set: 3, 6, ⑧, ⑧, 10 mode: 8 Data set: 2, ⑤, ⑤, ⑦, 7 Mode: 5 and 7 Data set: 2, 3, 6, 9, 11 No mode
monomial A number or a product of numbers and variables with whole-number exponents, or a polynomial with one term.	**monomio** Número o producto de números y variables con exponentes de números cabales, o polinomio con un término.	$8x, 9, 3x^2y^4$
multiple root A root r is a multiple root when the factor $(x - r)$ appears in the equation more than once.	**raíz múltiple** Una raíz r es una raíz múltiple cuando el factor $(x - r)$ aparece en la ecuación más de una vez.	 3 is a multiple root of $P(x) = (x - 3)^2$.
multiplicative identity matrix A square matrix with 1 in every entry of the main diagonal and 0 in every other entry.	**matriz de identidad multiplicativa** Una matriz cuadrada que contiene 1 en cada entrada de la diagonal principal y 0 en las demás entradas.	$\begin{bmatrix} 1 & 0 \\ 0 & 1 \end{bmatrix}, \begin{bmatrix} 1 & 0 & 0 \\ 0 & 1 & 0 \\ 0 & 0 & 1 \end{bmatrix}$

ENGLISH	SPANISH	EXAMPLES
multiplicative inverse of a square matrix The multiplicative inverse of square matrix A, if it exists, is notated A^{-1}, where the product of A and A^{-1} is the identity matrix.	**inverso multiplicativo de una matriz cuadrada** El inverso multiplicativo de una matriz cuadrada A, si existe, se escribe A^{-1}, donde el producto de A y A^{-1} es la matriz de identidad.	The multiplicative inverse of $$A = \begin{bmatrix} -2 & 5 \\ 1 & -3 \end{bmatrix} \text{ is } A^{-1} = \begin{bmatrix} -3 & -5 \\ -1 & -2 \end{bmatrix}$$ because $AA^{-1} = A^{-1}A = \begin{bmatrix} 1 & 0 \\ 0 & 1 \end{bmatrix}$.
multiplicity If a polynomial $P(x)$ has a multiple root at r, the multiplicity of r is the number of times $(x - r)$ appears as a factor in $P(x)$.	**multiplicidad** Si un polinomio $P(x)$ tiene una raíz múltiple en r, la multiplicidad de r es la cantidad de veces que $(x - r)$ aparece como factor en $P(x)$.	For $P(x) = (x - 3)^2$, the root 3 has a municipality of 2.
mutually exclusive events Two events are mutually exclusive if they cannot both occur in the same trial of an experiment.	**sucesos mutuamente excluyentes** Dos sucesos son mutuamente excluyentes si ambos no pueden ocurrir en la misma prueba de un experimento.	In the experiment of rolling a number cube, rolling a 3 and rolling an even number are mutually exclusive events.

N

ENGLISH	SPANISH	EXAMPLES
natural logarithm A logarithm with base e, written as ln.	**logaritmo natural** Logaritmo con base e, que se escribe ln.	$\ln 5 = \log_e 5 \approx 1.6$
natural logarithmic function The function $f(x) = \ln x$, which is the inverse of the natural exponential function $f(x) = e^x$. Domain is $\{x \mid x > 0\}$; range is all real numbers	**función logarítmica natural** Función $f(x) = \ln x$, que es la inversa de la función exponencial natural $f(x) = e^x$. El dominio es $\{x \mid x > 0\}$; el rango es todos los números reales.	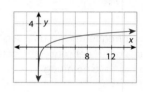
natural number A counting number.	**número natural** Número que sirve para contar.	1, 2, 3, 4, 5, 6, . . .
negative exponent A base raised to a negative exponent is equal to the reciprocal of that base raised to the opposite exponent: $b^{-n} = \frac{1}{b^n}$.	**exponente negativo** Una base elevada a un exponente negativo es igual al recíproco de dicha base elevado al exponente opuesto: $b^{-n} = \frac{1}{b^n}$.	$5^3 = \frac{1}{5^3} = \frac{1}{125}$
net A diagram of the faces of a three-dimensional figure arranged in such a way that the diagram can be folded to form the three-dimensional figure.	**plantilla** Diagrama de las caras de una figura tridimensional que se puede plegar para formar la figura tridimensional.	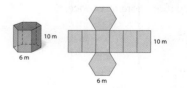
nonlinear system of equations A system in which at least one of the equations is not linear.	**sistema no lineal de ecuaciones** Sistema en el cual por lo menos una de las ecuaciones no es lineal.	$$\begin{cases} y = 2x^2 \\ y = -3^2 + 5 \end{cases}$$

nth root The *n*th root of a number *a*, written as $\sqrt[n]{a}$ or $a^{\frac{1}{n}}$, is a number that is equal to *a* when it is raised to the *n*th power.

enésima raíz La enésima raíz de un número *a*, que se escribe como $\sqrt[n]{a}$ o $a^{\frac{1}{n}}$, es un número igual a *a* cuando se eleva a la enésima potencia.

$\sqrt[5]{32} = 2$, because $2^5 = 32$.

O

objective function The function to be maximized or minimized in a linear programming problem.

función objetiva Función que se debe maximizar o minimizar en un problema de programación lineal.

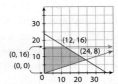

The objective function $P = 18x + 25y$ is maximized at (24, 8).

observational study A study that observes individuals and measures variables without controlling the individuals or their environment in any way.

estudio de observación Estudio que permite observar a individuos y medir variables sin controlar a los individuos ni su ambiente.

odd function A function in which $f(-x) = -f(x)$ for all *x* in the domain of the function.

función impar Función en la que $f(-x) = -f(x)$ para todos los valores de *x* dentro del dominio de la función

$f(x) = x^3$ is an odd function.

one-to-one function A function in which each *y*-value corresponds to only one *x*-value. The inverse of a one-to-one function is also a function.

función uno a uno Función en la que cada valor de *y* corresponde a sólo un valor de *x*. La inversa de una función uno a uno es también una función.

order of operations A process for evaluating expressions:
First, perform operations in parentheses or other grouping symbols.
Second, evaluate powers and roots.
Third, perform all multiplication and division from left to right.
Fourth, perform all addition and subtraction from left to right.

orden de las operaciones
Proceso para evaluar las expresiones:
Primero, realizar las operaciones entre paréntesis u otros símbolos de agrupación.
Segundo, evaluar las potencias y las raíces.
Tercero, realizar todas las multiplicaciones y divisiones de izquierda a derecha.
Cuarto, realizar todas las sumas y restas de izquierda a derecha.

$2 + 3^2 - (7 + 5) \div 4 \cdot 3$
$2 + 3^2 - 12 \div 4 \cdot 3$ Add inside parentheses.
$2 + 9 - 12 \div 4 \cdot 3$ Evaluate the power.
$2 + 9 - 3 \cdot 3$ Divide.
$2 + 9 - 9$ Multiply.
$11 - 9$ Add.
2 Subtract.

ordered triple A set of three numbers that can be used to locate a point (x, y, z) in a three-dimensional coordinate system.

tripleta ordenada Conjunto de tres números que se pueden utilizar para ubicar un punto (x, y, z) en un sistema de coordenadas tridimensional.

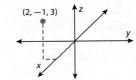

Glossary/Glosario

origin The intersection of the x- and y-axes in a coordinate plane. The coordinates of the origin are $(0, 0)$.

origen Intersección de los ejes x e y en un plano cartesiano. Las coordenadas de origen son $(0, 0)$.

P

parabola The shape of the graph of a quadratic function. Also, the set of points equidistant from a point F, called the focus, and a line d, called the *directrix*.

parábola Forma de la gráfica de una función cuadrática. También, conjunto de puntos equidistantes de un punto F, denominado *foco*, y una línea d, denominada *directriz*.

parameter One of the constants in a function or equation that may be changed. Also the third variable in a set of parametric equations.

parámetro Una de las constantes en una función o ecuación que se puede cambiar. También es la tercera variable en un conjunto de ecuaciones paramétricas.

$$y = (x - h)^2 + k$$
parameters

parametric equations A pair of equations that define the x- and y-coordinates of a point in terms of a third variable called a parameter.

ecuaciones paramétricas Par de ecuaciones que definen las coordenadas x e y de un punto en función de una tercera variable denominada parámetro.

$$x(t) = t + 1$$
$$y(t) = -2t$$

parent cube root function The function $f(x) = \sqrt[3]{x}$.

función madre de la raíz cúbica Función del tipo $f(x) = \sqrt[3]{x}$.

$$f(x) = \sqrt[3]{x}$$

parent function The simplest function with the defining characteristics of the family. Functions in the same family are transformations of their parent function.

función madre La función más básica con las características de la familia. Las funciones de la misma familia son transformaciones de su función madre.

$f(x) = x^2$ is the parent function for $g(x) = x^2 + 4$ and $h(x) = 5(x + 2)^2 - 3$.

parent square root function The function $f(x) = \sqrt{x}$, where $x \geq 0$.

función madre de la raíz cuadrada Función del tipo $f(x) = \sqrt{x}$, donde $x \geq 0$.

$$f(x) = \sqrt{x}$$

partial sum Indicated by $S_n = \sum_{i=1}^{n} a_i$, the sum of a specified number of terms n of a sequence whose total number of terms is greater than n.

suma parcial Expresada por $S_n = \sum_{i=1}^{n} a_i$, la suma de un número específico n de términos de una sucesión cuyo número total de términos es mayor que n.

For the sequence $a_n = n^2$, the fourth partial sum of the infinite series $\sum_{k=1}^{\infty} k^2$ is $\sum_{k=1}^{4} k^2 = 1^2 + 2^2 + 3^2 + 4^2 = 30$.

Pascal's triangle A triangular arrangement of numbers in which every row starts and ends with 1 and each other number is the sum of the two numbers above it.

triángulo de Pascal Arreglo triangular de números en el cual cada fila comienza y termina con 1 y cada uno de los demás números es la suma de los dos números que están encima de él.

```
      1
     1 1
    1 2 1
   1 3 3 1
  1 4 6 4 1
```

Glossary/Glosario

perfect square A number whose positive square root is a whole number.

cuadrado perfecto Número cuya raíz cuadrada positiva es un número cabal.

36 is a perfect square because $\sqrt{36} = 6$.

---

perfect-square trinomial A trinomial whose factored form is the square of a binomial. A perfect-square trinomial has the form $a^2 - 2ab + b^2 = (a - b)^2$ or $a^2 + 2ab + b^2 = (a + b)^2$.

trinomio cuadrado perfecto Trinomio cuya forma factorizada es el cuadrado de un binomio. Un trinomio cuadrado perfecto tiene la forma $a^2 - 2ab + b^2 = (a - b)^2$ o $a^2 + 2ab + b^2 = (a + b)^2$.

$x^2 + 6x + 9$ is a perfectsquare trinomial, because $x^2 + 6x + 9 = (x + 3)^2$.

---

period of a periodic function The length of a cycle measured in units of the independent variable (usually time in seconds). Also the reciprocal of the frequency.

periodo de una función periódica Longitud de un ciclo medido en unidades de la variable independiente (generalmente el tiempo en segundos). También es la inversa de la frecuencia.

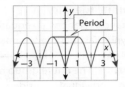

---

periodic function A function that repeats exactly in regular intervals, called *periods*.

función periódica Función que se repite exactamente a intervalos regulares denominados *periodos*.

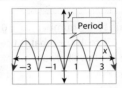

---

permutation An arrangement of a group of objects in which order is important. The number of permutations of r objects from a group of n objects is denoted $_nP_r$.

permutación Arreglo de un grupo de objetos en el cual el orden es importante. El número de permutaciones de r objetos de un grupo de n objetos se expresa $_nP_r$.

For 4 objects A, B, C, and D, there are $_4P_2 = 12$ different permutations of 2 objects: AB, AC, AD, BC, BD, CD, BA, CA, DA, CB, DB, and DC.

---

phase shift A horizontal translation of a periodic function.

cambio de fase Traslación horizontal de una función periódica.

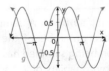

g is a phase shift of f $\frac{\pi}{2}$ units left.

---

piecewise function A function that is a combination of one or more functions.

función a trozos Función que es una combinación de una o más funciones.

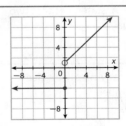

$$f(x) = \begin{cases} -4 & \text{if } x \leq 0 \\ x + 1 & \text{if } x > 0 \end{cases}$$

---

point-slope form The point-slope form of a linear equation is $y - y_1 = m(x - x_1)$, where m is the slope and (x_1, y_1) is a point on the line.

forma de punto y pendiente La forma de punto y pendiente de una ecuación lineal es $y - y_1 = m(x - x_1)$, donde m es la pendiente y (x_1, y_1) es un punto en la línea.

The equation of the line through $(2, 1)$ with slope 3 is $y - 1 = 3(x - 2)$.

polynomial A monomial or a sum or difference of monomials.

polinomio Monomio o suma o diferencia de monomios.

$2x^2 + 3x - 7$

---

polynomial function A function whose rule is a polynomial.

función polinomial Función cuya regla es un polinomio.

$f(x) = x^3 - 8x^2 + 19x - 12$

---

polynomial identity A mathematical relationship equating one polynomial quantity to another.

identidad de polinomios Relación matemática que iguala una cantidad polinomial con otra.

$\left(x^4 - y^4\right) = \left(x^2 + y^2\right)\left(x^2 - y^2\right)$

---

population The entire group of objects or individuals considered for a survey.

población Grupo completo de objetos o individuos que se desea estudiar.

In a survey about the study habits of high school students, the population is all high school students.

---

probability A number from 0 to 1 (or 0% to 100%) that is the measure of how likely an event is to occur.

probabilidad Número entre 0 y 1 (o entre 0% y 100%) que describe cuán probable es que ocurra un suceso.

A bag contains 3 red marbles and 4 blue marbles. The probability of choosing a red marble is $\frac{3}{7}$.

---

probability distribution for an experiment The function that pairs each outcome with its probability.

distribución de probabilidad para un experimento Función que asigna a cada resultado su probabilidad.

A number cube is rolled 10 times. The results are shown in the table.

Outcome	1	2	3	4	5	6
Probability	$\frac{1}{10}$	$\frac{1}{5}$	$\frac{1}{5}$	0	$\frac{3}{10}$	$\frac{1}{5}$

---

probability sample A sample in which every member of the population being sampled has a nonzero probability of being selected.

muestra de probabilidad Muestra en la que cada miembro de la población que se estudia tiene una probabilidad distinta de cero de ser elegido.

---

proportion A statement that two ratios are equal; $\frac{a}{b} = \frac{c}{d}$.

proporción Enunciado que establece que dos razones son iguales; $\frac{a}{b} = \frac{c}{d}$.

$\frac{2}{3} = \frac{4}{6}$

---

pure imaginary number *See* imaginary number.

número imaginario puro Ver número imaginario.

$3i$

Q

quadratic equation An equation that can be written in the form $ax^2 + bx + c = 0$, where a, b, and c are real numbers and $a \neq 0$.

ecuación cuadrática Ecuación que se puede expresar como $ax^2 + bx + c = 0$, donde a, b y c son números reales y $a \neq 0$.

$x^2 + 3x - 4 = 0$
$x^2 - 9 = 0$

© Houghton Mifflin Harcourt Publishing Company

Glossary/Glosario

ENGLISH	SPANISH	EXAMPLES
Quadratic Formula The formula $x = \frac{-b \pm \sqrt{b^2 - 4ac}}{2a}$, which gives solutions, or roots, of equations in the form $ax^2 + bx + c = 0$, where $a \neq 0$.	**fórmula cuadrática** La fórmula $x = \frac{-b \pm \sqrt{b^2 - 4ac}}{2a}$, que da soluciones, o raíces, para las ecuaciones del tipo $ax^2 + bx + c = 0$, donde $a \neq 0$.	The solutions of $2x^2 - 5x - 3 = 0$ are given by $$x = \frac{-(-5) \pm \sqrt{(-5)^2 - 4(2)(-3)}}{2(2)}$$ $$= \frac{5 \pm \sqrt{25 + 24}}{4} = \frac{5 \pm 7}{4};$$ $x = 3$ or $x = -\frac{1}{2}$.
quadratic function A function that can be written in the form $f(x) = ax^2 + bx + c$, where a, b, and c are real numbers and $a \neq 0$, or in the form $f(x) = a(x - h)^2 + k$, where a, h, and k are real numbers and $a \neq 0$.	**función cuadrática** Función que se puede expresar como $f(x) = ax^2 + bx + c$, donde a, b y c son números reales y $a \neq 0$, o como $f(x) = a(x - h)^2 + k$, donde a, h y k son números reales y $a \neq 0$.	$f(x) = x^2 - 6x + 8$
quadratic inequality in two variables An inequality that can be written in one of the following forms: $y < ax^2 + bx + c$, $y > ax^2 + bx + c$, $y \leq ax^2 + bx + c$, $y \geq ax^2 + bx + c$, or $y \neq ax^2 + bx + c$, where a, b, and c are real numbers and $a \neq 0$.	**desigualdad cuadrática en dos variables** Desigualdad que puede expresarse de una de las siguientes formas: $y < ax^2 + bx + c$, $y > ax^2 + bx + c$, $y \leq ax^2 + bx + c$, $y \geq ax^2 + bx + c$, o $y \neq ax^2 + bx + c$, donde a, b y c son números reales y $a \neq 0$.	 $y > -x^2 - 2x + 3$
quadratic model A quadratic function used to represent a set of data.	**modelo cuadrático** Función cuadrática que se utiliza para representar un conjunto de datos.	<table><tr><td>x</td><td>4</td><td>6</td><td>8</td><td>10</td></tr><tr><td>$f(x)$</td><td>27</td><td>52</td><td>89</td><td>130</td></tr></table> A quadratic model for the data is $f(x) = x^2 + 3.3x - 2.6$.
quadratic regression A statistical method used to fit a quadratic model to a given data set.	**regresión cuadrática** Método estadístico utilizado para ajustar un modelo cuadrático a un conjunto de datos determinado.	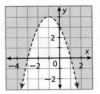

R

radian A unit of angle measure based on arc length. In a circle of radius r, if a central angle has a measure of 1 radian, then the length of the intercepted arc is r units. 2π radians $= 360°$ 1 radian $\approx 57°$	**radián** Unidad de medida de un ángulo basada en la longitud del arco. En un círculo de radio r, si un ángulo central mide 1 radián, entonces la longitud del arco abarcado es r unidades. 2π radianes $= 360°$ 1 radián $\approx 57°$	
radical An indicated root of a quantity.	**radical** Raíz indicada de una cantidad.	$\sqrt{36} = 6$, $\sqrt[3]{27} = 3$

Glossary/Glosario

ENGLISH	SPANISH	EXAMPLES
radical equation An equation that contains a variable within a radical.	**ecuación radical** Ecuación que contiene una variable dentro de un radical.	$\sqrt{x+3} + 4 = 7$
radical function A function whose rule contains a variable within a radical.	**función radical** Función cuya regla contiene una variable dentro de un radical.	$f(x) = \sqrt{x}$
radical inequality An inequality that contains a variable within a radical.	**desigualdad radical** Desigualdad que contiene una variable dentro de un radical.	$\sqrt{x+3} \leq 7$
radical symbol The symbol $\sqrt{}$ used to denote a root. The symbol is used alone to indicate a square root or with an index, $\sqrt[n]{}$, to indicate the nth root.	**símbolo de radical** Símbolo $\sqrt{}$ que se utiliza para expresar una raíz. Puede utilizarse solo para indicar una raíz cuadrada, o con uníndice, $\sqrt[n]{}$, para indicar la enésima raíz.	$\sqrt{36} = 6, \sqrt[2]{27} = 3$
radicand The expression under a radical sign.	**radicando** Número o expresión debajo del signo de radical.	$\underset{\text{Radicand}}{\underbrace{\sqrt{x+3}}} - 2$
randomized comparative experiment An experiment in which the individuals are assigned to the control group or the treatment group at random, in order to minimize bias.	**experimento comparativo aleatorizado** Experimento en el que se elige al azar a los individuos para el grupo de control o para el grupo experimental, a fin de minimizar el sesgo.	
range of a data set The difference of the greatest and least values in the data set.	**rango de un conjunto de datos** La diferencia del mayor y menor valor en un conjunto de datos.	The data set $\left\{3, 3, 5, 7, 8, 10, 11, 11, 12\right\}$ has a range of $12 - 3 = 9$.
range of a function or relation The set of output values of a function or relation.	**rango de una función o relación** Conjunto de los valores desalida de una función o relación.	The range of $y = x^2$ is $\left\{y \mid y \geq 0\right\}$.
rate A ratio that compares two quantities measured in different units.	**tasa** Razón que compara doscantidades medidas en diferentes unidades.	$\frac{55 \text{ miles}}{1 \text{ hour}} = 55\text{mi/hr}$
ratio A comparison of two quantities by division.	**razón** Comparación de dos cantidades mediante una división.	$\frac{1}{2}$ or $1{:}2$
rational equation An equation that contains one or more rational expressions.	**ecuación racional** Ecuación que contiene una o más expresiones racionales.	$\frac{x+2}{x^2+3x-1} = 6$

ENGLISH	SPANISH	EXAMPLES
rational exponent An exponent that can be expressed as $\frac{m}{n}$ such that if m and n are integers, then $b^{\frac{m}{n}} = \sqrt[n]{b^m} = \left(\sqrt[n]{b}\right)^m$.	**exponente racional** Exponente quese puede expresar como $\frac{m}{n}$ tal que, si m y n son números enteros, entonces $b^{\frac{m}{n}} = \sqrt[n]{b^m} = \left(\sqrt[n]{b}\right)^m$	$4^{\frac{2}{3}} = \sqrt[3]{4^3} = \sqrt[3]{64} = 8$ $4^{\frac{2}{3}} = \left(\sqrt[3]{4}\right)^3 = 2^3 = 8$
rational expression An algebraic expression whose numerator and denominator are polynomials and whose denominator has a degree ≥ 1.	**expresión racional** Expresión algebraica cuyo numerador y denominador son polinomios y cuyo denominador tiene un grado ≥ 1.	$\dfrac{x+2}{x^2+3x-1}$
rational function A function whose rule can be written as a rational expression.	**función racional** Función cuya regla se puede expresar como una expresión racional.	$f(x) = \dfrac{x+2}{x^2+3x-1}$
rational inequality An inequality that contains one or more rational expressions.	**desigualdad racional** Desigualdad que contiene una o más expresiones racionales.	$\dfrac{x+2}{x^2+3x-1} \geq 6$
rational number A number that can be written in the form $\frac{a}{b}$, where a and b are integers and $b \neq 0$.	**número racional** Número que se puede expresar como $\frac{a}{b}$, donde a y b son números enteros y $b \neq 0$.	$3, 1.75, 0.\overline{3}, -\frac{2}{3}, 0$
rationalizing the denominator A method of rewriting a fraction by multiplying by another fraction that is equivalent to 1 in order to remove radical terms from the denominator.	**racionalizar el denominador** Método que consiste en escribir nuevamente una fracción multiplicándola por otra fracción equivalente a 1 a fin de eliminar los términos radicales del denominador.	$\dfrac{1}{\sqrt{2}}\left(\dfrac{\sqrt{2}}{\sqrt{2}}\right) = \dfrac{\sqrt{2}}{2}$
real axis The horizontal axis in the complex plane; it graphically represents the real part of complex numbers.	**eje real** Eje horizontal de un plano complejo. Representa gráficamente la parte real de los números complejos.	
real number A rational or irrational number. Every point on the number line represents a real number.	**número real** Número racional o irracional. Cada punto de la recta numérica representa un número real.	$-5, 0, \frac{2}{3}, \sqrt{2}, 3.1, \pi$
real part of a complex number For a complex number of the form $a + bi$, a is the real part.	**parte real de un número complejo** Dado un número complejo del tipo $a + bi$, a es la parte real.	$5 + 6i$ Real part Imaginary part
reciprocal For a real number $a \neq 0$, the reciprocal of a is $\frac{1}{a}$. The product of reciprocals is 1.	**recíproco** Dado el número real $a \neq 0$, el recíproco de a es $\frac{1}{a}$. El producto de los recíprocos es 1.	$\frac{1}{2}$ is the reciprocal of 2. $\frac{5}{3}$ is the reciprocal of $\frac{3}{5}$.
recursive rule A rule for a sequence in which one or more previous terms are used to generate the next term.	**Regla recurrente** Regla para una sucesión en la cual uno o más términos anteriores se utilizan para generar el término siguiente.	For the sequence 5, 7, 9, 11, ..., a recursive rule is $a_1 = 5$ and $a_n = a_{n-1} + 2$

Glossary/Glosario

reduced row-echelon form A form of an augmented matrix in which the coefficient columns form an identity matrix.

forma escalonada reducida por filas Forma de matriz aumentada en la que las columnas de coeficientes forman una matriz de identidad.

$$\begin{bmatrix} 1 & 0 & \vdots & -1 \\ 0 & 1 & \vdots & 3 \end{bmatrix}$$

---

reference angle For an angle in standard position, the reference angle is the positive acute angle formed by the terminal side of the angle and the *x*-axis.

ángulo de referencia Dado un ángulo en posición estándar, el ángulo de referencia es el ángulo agudo positivo formado por el lado terminal del ángulo y el eje *x*.

---

reflection A transformation that reflects, or "flips," a graph or figure across a line, called the line of reflection, such that each reflected point is the same distance from the line of reflection but is on the opposite side of the line.

reflexión Transformación que refleja, o invierte, una gráfica o figura sobre una línea, llamada la línea de reflexión, de manera tal que cada punto reflejado esté a la misma distancia de la línea de reflexión pero que se encuentre en el lado opuesto de la línea.

---

regression The statistical study of the relationship between variables.

regresión Estudio estadístico de la relación entre variables.

---

relation A set of ordered pairs.

relación Conjunto de pares ordenados.

$$\{(0, 5), (0, 4), (2, 3), (4, 0)\}$$

Remainder Theorem If the polynomial function $P(x)$ is divided by $x - a$, then the remainder r is $P(a)$.

Teorema del resto Si la función polinomial $P(x)$ se divide entre $x - a$, entonces, el residuo r será $P(a)$.

---

replacement set A set of numbers that can be substituted for a variable.

conjunto de reemplazo Conjunto de números que pueden sustituir una variable.

The solution set of $y = x + 3$ for the replacement set $\{1, 2, 3\}$ is $\{4, 5, 6\}$.

---

right angle An angle that measures 90°.

ángulo recto Ángulo que mide 90°.

---

right triangle A triangle with one right angle.

triángulo rectángulo Triángulo con un ángulo recto.

---

rigid transformation A transformation that does not change the size or shape of a figure.

transformación rígida Transformación que no cambia el tamaño o la forma de una figura.

Reflection, rotations, and translations are rigid transformations.

---

root of an equation Any value of the variable that makes the equation true.

raíz de una ecuación Cualquier valor de la variable que transforme la ecuación en verdadera.

The roots of $(x - 2)(x + 1) = 0$ are 2 and -1.

Glossary/Glosario

ENGLISH	SPANISH	EXAMPLES
roster notation A way of representing a set by listing the elements between braces, { }.	**notación de lista** Forma de representar un conjunto enumerando los elementos entre llaves, { }.	The first 5 positive odd numbers are $\left\{1, 3, 5, 7, 9\right\}$.
rotation A transformation that rotates or turns a figure about a point called the center of rotation.	**rotación** Transformación que hace rotar o girar una figura sobre un punto llamado centro de rotación.	
rotation transformation graph A transformation used to rotate a figure about the origin.	**Transformatión de rotación** transformatión utilizada para rotar una figura sobre el origen.	The system $\begin{cases} x^1 = x\cos90 - y\sin90 \\ y^1 = x\sin90 + y\cos90 \end{cases}$ was used to rotate the 90° clockwise.
row operation An operation performed on a row of an augmented matrix that creates an equivalent matrix.	**operación por filas** Operación realizada en una fila de una matriz aumentada que crea una matriz equivalente.	$\begin{bmatrix} 2 & 0 & \vdots & -2 \\ 0 & 1 & \vdots & 3 \end{bmatrix} = \begin{bmatrix} \frac{1}{2}(2) & \frac{1}{2}(0) & \vdots & \frac{1}{2}(-1) \\ 0 & 1 & \vdots & 3 \end{bmatrix}$ $= \begin{bmatrix} 1 & 0 & \vdots & -1 \\ 0 & 1 & \vdots & 3 \end{bmatrix}$
row-reduction method The process of performing elementary row operations on an augmented matrix to transform the matrix to reduced row echelon form.	**método de reducción por filas** Proceso por el cual se realizan operaciones elementales de filas en una matriz aumentada para transformar la matriz en una forma reducida de filas escalonadas.	$\begin{bmatrix} 2 & 0 & \vdots & -2 \\ 0 & 1 & \vdots & 3 \end{bmatrix} = \begin{bmatrix} \frac{1}{2}(2) & \frac{1}{2}(0) & \vdots & \frac{1}{2}(-1) \\ 0 & 1 & \vdots & 3 \end{bmatrix}$ $= \begin{bmatrix} 1 & 0 & \vdots & -1 \\ 0 & 1 & \vdots & 3 \end{bmatrix}$

S

sample A part of the population.	**muestra** Una parte de la población.	In a survey about the stud habits of the high school students, a sample is a survey of 100 students.
sample space The set of all possible outcomes of a probability experiment.	**espacio muestral** Conjunto de todos los resultados posibles en un experimento de probabilidades.	In the experiment of rolling a number cube, the sample space is 1, 2. 3, 4, 5, 6.
scalar A number that is multiplied by a matrix.	**escalar** Número que se multiplica por una matriz.	$3\underset{\underset{\text{scalar}}{\uparrow}}{\begin{bmatrix} 1 & -2 \\ 2 & 3 \end{bmatrix}} = \begin{bmatrix} 3 & -6 \\ 6 & 9 \end{bmatrix}$
scatter plot A graph with points plotted to show a possible relationship between two sets of data.	**diagrama de dispersión** Gráfica con puntos que se usa para demostrar una relación posible entre dos conjuntos de datos.	

Glossary/Glosario

Glossary/Glosario

second-degree equation in two variables An equation constructed by adding terms in two variables with powers no higher than 2.

ecuación de segundo grado en dos variables Ecuación compuesta por la suma de términos en dos variables con potencias no mayores a 2.

$$ax^2 + by^2 + cx + dy + e = 0$$

---

second differences Differences between first differences of a function.

segundas diferencias Diferencias entre las primerasdiferencias de una función.

x	0	1	2	3
y	1	4	9	16

first differences   +3   +5   +7
second differences   +2   +2

---

self-selected sample A sample in which members volunteer to participate.

muestra de voluntarios Muestra en la que los miembros se ofrecen voluntariamente para participar.

---

sequence A list of numbers that often form a pattern.

sucesión Lista de números que generalmente forman un patrón.

1, 2, 4, 8, 16, …

---

series The indicated sum of the terms of a sequence.

serie Suma indicada de los términos de una sucesión.

1 + 2 + 4 + 8 + 16 + …

---

set A collection of items called elements.

conjunto Grupo de componentes denominados elementos.

$$\{1, 2, 3\}$$

---

set-builder notation A notation for a set that uses a rule to describe the properties of the elements of the set.

notación de conjuntos Notación para un conjunto que se vale de una regla para describir las propiedades de los elementos del conjunto.

$\{x | x > 3\}$ read, "The set of all x such that x is greater than 3. "

Sierpinski triangle A fractal formed from a triangle by removing triangles with vertices at the midpoints of the sides of each remaining triangle.

triángulo de Sierpinski Fractal formado a partir de un triángulo al cual se le recortan triángulos cuyos vértices se encuentran en los puntos medios de los lados de cada triángulo restante.

---

simple event An event consisting of only one outcome.

suceso simple Suceso que contiene sólo un resultado.

In the experiment of rolling a number cube, the event consisting of the outcome 3 is a simple event.

---

simple random sample A sample selected from a population so that each member of the population has an equal chance of being selected.

muestra aleatoria simple Muestra seleccionada de una población tal que cada miembro de ésta tenga igual probabilidad de ser seleccionada.

Mr. Hansen chose a random sample of the class by writing each student's name on a slip of paper, mixing up the slips, and drawing five slips without looking.

ENGLISH	SPANISH	EXAMPLES
simulation A model of an experiment, often one that would be too difficult or time-consuming to actually perform.	**simulación** Modelo de un experimento; generalmente se recurre a la simulación cuando realizar dicho experimento sería demasiado difícil o llevaría mucho tiempo.	A random number generator is used to simulate the roll of a number cube.
sine In a right triangle, the ratio of the length of the side opposite $\angle A$ to the length of the hypotenuse.	**seno** En un triángulo rectángulo, razón entre la longitud del cateto opuesto a $\angle A$ y la longitud de la hipotenusa.	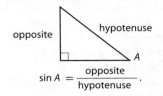 $$\sin A = \frac{\text{opposite}}{\text{hypotenuse}}.$$
slope A measure of the steepness of a line. If (x_1, y_1) and (x_2, y_2) are any two points on the line, the slope of the line, known as m, is represented by the equation $m = \frac{y_2 - y_1}{x_2 - x_1}$.	**pendiente** Medida de la inclinación de una línea. Dados dos puntos (x_1, y_1) y (x_2, y_2) en una línea, la pendiente de la línea, denominada m, se representa con la ecuación $m = \frac{y_2 - y_1}{x_2 - x_1}$.	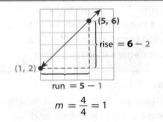 $$m = \frac{4}{4} = 1$$
slope-intercept form The slope intercept form of a linear equation is $y = mx + b$, where m is the slope and b is the y-intercept.	**forma de pendiente-intersección** La forma de pendiente-intersección de una ecuación lineal es $y = mx + b$, donde m es la pendiente y b es la intersección y.	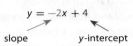
solution set of an equation The set of values that make an equation true.	**conjunto solución de una ecuación** Conjunto de valores que hacen verdadero un enunciado.	The solution set of $x^2 = 9$ is $\left\{-3, 3\right\}$.
solving a triangle Using given measures to find unknown angle measures or side lengths of a triangle.	**resolución de un triángulo** Utilizar medidas dadas para hallar las medidas desconocidas de los ángulos o las longitudes de los lados de un triángulo.	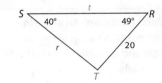 $$49° + 40° + m\angle T = 180°$$ $$m\angle T = 91°$$ $$\frac{\sin 49°}{r} = \frac{\sin 40°}{20} \quad \frac{\sin 91°}{t} = \frac{\sin 40°}{20}$$ $$r \approx 23.5 \qquad t \approx 31.1$$
special right triangle A 45° −45°−90° triangle or a 30°−60°−90° triangle.	**triángulo rectángulo especial** Triángulo de 45°−45°−90° o triángulo de 30°−60°−90°.	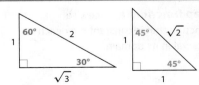
square matrix A matrix with the same number of rows as columns.	**matriz cuadrada** Matriz con el mismo número de filas y columnas.	$\begin{bmatrix} 1 & 2 \\ 0 & -3 \end{bmatrix}, \begin{bmatrix} 1 & -3 & 1 \\ 2 & 0 & -2 \\ 0 & 1 & 3 \end{bmatrix}$

ENGLISH	SPANISH	EXAMPLES
square-root function A function whose rule contains a variable under a square-root sign.	**función de raíz cuadrada** Función cuya regla contiene una variable bajo un signo de raíz cuadrada.	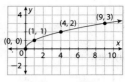 $f(x) = \sqrt{x}$
standard deviation A measure of dispersion of a data set. The standard deviation σ is the square root of the variance	**desviación estándar** Medida de dispersión de un conjunto de datos. La desviación estándar σ es la raíz cuadrada de la varianza	Data set: $\{6, 7, 7, 9, 11\}$ Mean: $\frac{6+7+7+9+11}{5} = 8$ Variance: $\frac{1}{5}(4+1+1+1+9) = 3.2$ Standard deviation: $\sigma = \sqrt{3.2} \approx 1.8$
standard form of a polynomial A polynomial in one variable is written in standard form when the terms are in order from greatest degree to least degree.	**forma estándar de un polinomio** Un polinomio de una variable se expresa en forma estándar cuando los términos se ordenan de mayor a menor grado.	$3x^3 - 5x^2 + 6x - 7$
standard form of a quadratic equation $ax^2 + bx + c = 0$, where a, b, and c are real numbers and $a \neq 0$.	**forma estándar de una ecuación** cuadrática $ax^2 + bx + c = 0$, donde a, b y c son números reales y $a \neq 0$.	$2x^2 + 3x - 1 = 0$
standard normal value A value that indicates how many standard deviations above or below the mean a particular value falls, given by the formula $z = \frac{x - \mu}{\sigma}$, where z is the standard normal value, x is the given value, μ is the mean, and σ is the standard deviation of a standard normal distribution.	**valor normal estándar** Valor que indica a cuántas desviaciones estándar por encima o por debajo de la media se encuentra un determinado valor, dado por la fórmula $z = \frac{x - \mu}{\sigma}$, donde z es el valor normal estándar, x es el valor dado, μ es la media y σ es la desviación estándar de una distribución normal estándar.	
standard position An angle in standard position has its vertex at the origin and its initial side on the positive x–axis.	**osición estándar** Ángulo cuyo vértice se encuentra en el origen y cuyo lado inicial se encuentra sobre el eje x.	
statistic A number that describes a sample.	**estadística** Número que describe una muestra.	
step function A piecewise function that is constant over each interval in its domain.	**función escalón** Función a trozos que es constante en cada intervalo en su dominio.	
stratified sample A sample in which a population is divided into distinct groups and members are selected at random from each group.	**muestra estratificada** Muestra en la que población está dividida en grupos diferenciados y los miembros de cada grupo se seleccionan al azar.	Ms. Carter chose a stratified sample of her school's student population by randomly selecting 30 students from each grade level.

ENGLISH	SPANISH	EXAMPLES
stretch A transformation that pulls the points of a graph horizontally away from the y–axis or vertically away from the x–axis.	**estiramiento** Transformación que desplaza los puntos de una gráfica en forma horizontal alejándolos del eje y o en forma vertical alejándolos del eje x.	
substitution A method used to solve systems of equations by solving an equation for one variable and substituting the resulting expression into the other equation(s).	**sustitución** Método utilizado para resolver sistemas de ecuaciones resolviendo una ecuación para una variable y sustituyendo la expresión resultante en las demás ecuaciones.	$$\begin{cases} 2x + 3y = -1 \\ x - 3y = 4 \end{cases}$$ Solve for x. $x = 4 + 3y$ Substitute into the first equation and solve. $2(4 + 3y) + 3y = -1$ $y = -1$ Then solve for x. $x = 4 + 3(-1) = 1$
summation notation A method of notating the sum of a series using the Greek letter $\sum$ (capital *sigma*).	**notación de sumatoria** Método de notación de la suma de una serie que utiliza la letra griega $\sum$ (SIGMA mayúscula).	$$\sum_{n=1}^{5} 3k = 3 + 6 + 9 + 12 + 15 = 45$$
synthetic division A shorthand method of dividing by a linear binomial of the form $(x - a)$ by writing only the coefficients of the polynomials.	**división sintética** Método abreviado de división que consiste en dividir por un binomio lineal del tipo $(x - a)$ escribiendo sólo los coeficientes de los polinomios.	$(x^3 - 7x + 6) \div (x - 2)$ $\underline{2}\rfloor\quad 1\quad 0\quad -7\quad 6$ $\quad 2\quad 4\quad 6$ $\overline{\quad 1\quad 2\quad -3\ \lfloor 0}$ $(x^3 - 7x + 6) \div (x - 2) = x^2 + 2x - 3$
synthetic substitution The process of using synthetic division to evaluate a polynomial $p(x)$ when $x = c$.	**sustitución sintética** Proceso que consiste en usar la división sintética para evaluar un polinomio $p(x)$ cuando $x = c$.	
system of equations A set of two or more equations that have two or more variables.	**sistema de ecuaciones** Conjunto de dos o más ecuaciones que contienen dos o más variables.	$$\begin{cases} 2x + 3y = -1 \\ x^2 = 4 \end{cases}$$
system of linear inequalities A system of inequalities in two or more variables in which all of the inequalities are linear.	**sistema de desigualdades lineales** Sistema de desigualdades en dos o más variables en el que todas las desigualdades son lineales.	$$\begin{cases} 2x + 3y \geq -1 \\ x - 3y < 4 \end{cases}$$
systematic sample A sample based on selecting one member of the population at random and then selecting other members by using a pattern.	**muestra sistemática** Muestra en la que se elige a un miembro de la población al azar y luego se elige a otros miembros mediante un patrón.	Mr. Martin chose a systematic sample of customers visiting a store by selecting one customer at random and then selecting every tenth customer after that.

T

ENGLISH	SPANISH	EXAMPLES
tangent line A line that is in the same plane as a circle and intersects the circle at exactly one point.	**línea tangente** Línea que está en el mismo plano que un círculo y corta al círculo en exactamente un punto.	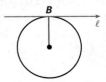

Glossary/Glosario

Glossary/Glosario

ENGLISH	SPANISH	EXAMPLES
term of a sequence An element or number in the sequence.	**término de una sucesión** Elemento o número de una sucesión.	5 is the third term in the sequence 1, 3, 5, 7, . . .
terminal side For an angle in standard position, the ray that is rotated relative to the positive *x*–axis.	**lado terminal** Dado un ángulo en una posición estándar, el rayo que rota en relación con el eje positivo *x*.	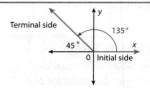
theoretical probability The ratio of the number of equally likely outcomes in an event to the total number of possible outcomes.	**probabilidad teórica** Razón entre el número de resultados igualmente probables de un suceso y el número total de resultados posibles.	The theoretical probability of rolling an odd number on a number cube is $\frac{3}{6} = \frac{1}{2}$.
third quartile The median of the upper half of a data set. Also called *upper quartile*.	**tercer cuartil** La mediana de la mitad superior de un conjunto de datos. También se llama *cuartil superior*.	
three-dimensional coordinate system A space that is divided into eight regions by an *x*–axis, a *y*–axis, and a *z*–axis. The locations, or coordinates, of points are given by ordered triples.	**sistema de coordenadas tridimensional** Espacio dividido en ocho regiones por un eje *x*, un eje *y* y un eje *z*. Las ubicaciones, o coordenadas, de los puntos son dadas por tripletas ordenadas.	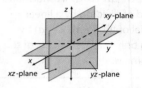
transformation A change in the position, size, or shape of a figure or graph.	**transformación** Cambio en la posición, tamaño o forma de una figura o gráfica.	
translation A transformation that shifts or slides every point of a figure or graph the same distance in the same direction.	**traslación** Transformación en la que todos los puntos de una figura se mueven la misma distancia en la misma dirección.	
translation matrix A matrix used to translate points on the coordinate plane.	**matriz de traslación** Matriz utilizada para trasladar puntos en el plano cartesiano.	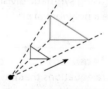 Matrix $\begin{bmatrix} -2 & -2 & -2 \\ 3 & 3 & 3 \end{bmatrix}$ is used to translate the figure 2 units left and 3 units up.
transpose A matrix that reverses the rows and columns of a matrix.	**transposición** Matriz que invierte las filas y columnas de una matriz.	$\begin{bmatrix} 1 & 2 \\ 3 & 4 \\ 5 & 6 \end{bmatrix}$ is the transpose of $\begin{bmatrix} 1 & 3 & 5 \\ 2 & 4 & 6 \end{bmatrix}$.

transverse axis The axis of symmetry of a hyperbola that contains the vertices and foci.

eje transversal Eje de simetría de una hipérbola que contiene los vértices y focos.

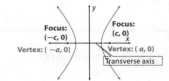

treatment group In a controlled experiment, the group that receives treatment.

grupo experimental En un experimento controlado, el grupo que está expuesto a la manipulación.

trial In probability, a single repetition or observation of an experiment.

prueba En probabilidad, una sola repetición u observación de un experimento.

In the experiment of rolling a number cube, each roll is one trial.

trigonometric function A function whose rule is given by a trigonometric ratio.

función trigonométrica Función cuya regla es dada por una razón trigonométrica.

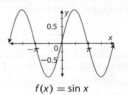

$f(x) = \sin x$

trigonometric ratio Ratio of the lengths of two sides of a right triangle.

razón trigonométrica Razón entre dos lados de un triángulo rectángulo.

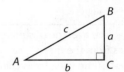

$\sin A = \frac{a}{c}, \cos A = \frac{b}{c}, \tan A = \frac{a}{b}$

trigonometry The study of the measurement of triangles and of trigonometric functions and their applications.

trigonometría Estudio de la medición de los triángulos y de las funciones trigonométricas y sus aplicaciones.

trinomial A polynomial with three terms.

trinomio Polinomio con tres términos.

$4x^2 + 3xy - 5y^2$

turning point A point on the graph of a function that corresponds to a local maximum (or minimum) where the graph changes from increasing to decreasing (or vice versa).

punto de inflexión Punto de la gráfica de una función que corresponde a un máximo (o mínimo) local donde la gráfica pasa de ser creciente a decreciente (o viceversa).

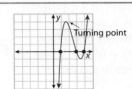

U

unit circle A circle with a radius of 1, centered at the origin.

círculo unitario Círculo con un radio de 1, centrado en el origen.

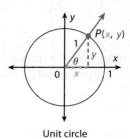

Unit circle

V

variable A symbol used to represent a quantity that can change.

variable Símbolo utilizado para representar una cantidad que puede cambiar.

$$2x + 3$$
↑
variable

variable matrix The matrix of the variables in a linear system of equations.

matriz de variables Matriz de las variables de un sistema lineal de ecuaciones.

System of equations

$$\begin{cases} 2x + 3y = -1 \\ x - 3y = 4 \end{cases}$$

Variable matrix

$$\begin{bmatrix} x \\ y \end{bmatrix}$$

variance The average of squared differences from the mean. The square root of the variance is called the *standard deviation*.

varianza Promedio de las diferencias cuadráticas en relación con la media. La raíz cuadrada de la varianza se denomina *desviación estándar*.

Data set: is $\{6, 7, 7, 9, 11\}$

Mean: $\dfrac{6 + 7 + 7 + 9 + 11}{5} = 8$

Variance: $\frac{1}{5}(4 + 1 + 1 + 1 + 9) = 3.2$

Venn diagram A diagram used to show relationships between sets.

diagrama de Venn Diagrama utilizado para mostrar la relación entre conjuntos.

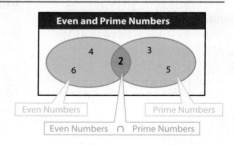

vertex form of a quadratic function A quadratic function written in the form $f(x) = a(x - h)^2 + k$, where a, h, and k are constants and (h, k) is the vertex.

forma en vértice de una función cuadrática Una función cuadrática expresada en la forma $f(x) = a(x - h)^2 + k$, donde a, h y k son constantes y (h, k) es el vértice.

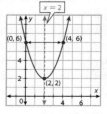

$$f(x) = (x - 2)^2 + 2$$

ENGLISH	SPANISH	EXAMPLES
vertex of a hyperbola (vertices) The endpoints of the transverse axis of the hyperbola.	**vértice de una hipérbola** Extremos del eje transversal de la hipérbola.	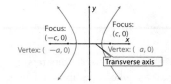
vertex of an absolute-value graph The point where the axis of symmetry intersects the graph.	**vértice de una gráfica de valor absoluto** Punto donde en el eje de simetría interseca la gráfica.	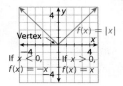
vertex of an ellipse (vertices) The endpoints of the major axis of the ellipse.	**vértice de una elipse** Extremos del eje mayor de la elipse.	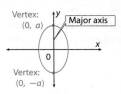
vertex of a parabola The highest or lowest point on the parabola.	**vértice de una parábola** Punto más alto o más bajo de una parábola.	
vertical line A line whose equation is $x = a$, where a is the x-intercept. The slope of a vertical line is undefined.	**línea vertical** Línea cuya ecuación es $x = a$, donde a es la intersección con el eje x. La pendiente de una línea vertical es indefinida.	
vertical-line test A test used to determine whether a relation is a function. If any vertical line crosses the graph of a relation more than once, the relation is not a function.	**prueba de la línea vertical** Prueba utilizada para determinar si una relación es una función. Si una línea vertical corta la gráfica de una relación más de una vez, la relación no es una función.	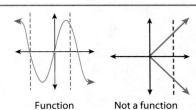

W

whole number The set of natural numbers and zero.	**número cabal** Conjunto de los números naturales y cero.	0, 1, 2, 3, 4, 5, …

X

x-intercept The x-coordinate(s) of the point(s) where a graph intersects the x-axis.	**intersección con el eje x** Coordenada(s) x de uno o más puntos donde una gráfica corta el eje x.	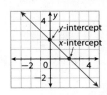

© Houghton Mifflin Harcourt Publishing Company

Glossary/Glosario

Glossary/Glosario

Y

y-intercept The y-coordinate(s) of the point(s) where a graph intersects the y-axis.

intersección con el eje y Coordenada(s) de uno o más puntos donde una gráfica corta el eje y.

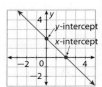

Z

z-axis The third axis in a three-dimensional coordinate system.

eje z Tercer eje en un sistema de coordenadas tridimensional.

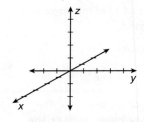

zero exponent For any nonzero real number x, $x^0 = 1$.

exponente cero Dado un número real distinto de cero x, $x^0 = 1$.

$5^0 = 1$

zero of a function For the function f, any number x such that $f(x) = 0$.

cero de una función Dada la función f, todo número x tal que $f(x) = 0$.

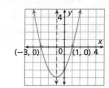

The zeros of $f(x) = x^2 + 2x - 3$ are -3 and 1.

Index

Index locator numbers are in Module. Lesson form. For example, 2.1 indicates Module 2, Lesson 1 as listed in the Table of Contents.

Index

Table of Measures

LENGTH

1 inch = 2.54 centimeters

1 meter = 39.37 inches

1 mile = 5,280 feet

1 mile = 1760 yards

1 mile = 1.609 kilometers

1 kilometer = 0.62 mile

MASS/WEIGHT

1 pound = 16 ounces

1 pound = 0.454 kilograms

1 kilogram = 2.2 pounds

1 ton = 2000 pounds

CAPACITY

1 cup = 8 fluid ounces

1 pint = 2 cups

1 quart = 2 pints

1 gallon = 4 quarts

1 gallon = 3.785 liters

1 liter = 0.264 gallons

1 liter = 1000 cubic centimeters

Symbols

≠	is not equal to	π	pi: (about 3.14)
≈	is approximately equal to	⊥	is perpendicular to
10^2	ten squared; ten to the second power	∥	is parallel to
		$\overleftrightarrow{AB}$	line AB
$2.\overline{6}$	repeating decimal 2.66666...	$\overrightarrow{AB}$	ray AB
$\lvert -4 \rvert$	the absolute value of negative 4	$\overline{AB}$	line segment AB
$\sqrt{}$	square root	m∠A	measure of ∠A

Formulas

FACTORING

Perfect square trinomials	$a^2 + 2ab + b^2 = (a+b)^2$
	$a^2 - 2ab + b^2 = (a-b)^2$
Difference of squares	$a^2 - b^2 = (a-b)(a+b)$
Sum of cubes	$a^3 + b^3 = (a+b)(a^2 - ab + b^2)$
Difference of cubes	$a^3 - b^3 = (a-b)(a^2 + ab + b^2)$

PROPERTIES OF EXPONENTS

Product of powers	$a^m a^n = a^{(m+n)}$
Quotient of powers	$\dfrac{a^m}{a^n} = a^{(m-n)}$
Power of a power	$(a^m)^n = a^{mn}$
Rational exponent	$a^{\frac{m}{n}} = \sqrt[n]{a^m}$
Negative exponent	$a^{-n} = \dfrac{1}{a^n}$

QUADRATIC EQUATIONS

Standard form	$f(x) = ax^2 + bx + c$
Vertex form	$f(x) = a(x-h)^2 + k$
Parabola	$(x-h)^2 = 4p(y-k)$ $(y-k)^2 = 4p(x-h)$
Quadratic formula	$x = \dfrac{-b \pm \sqrt{b^2 - 4ac}}{2a}$
Axis of symmetry	$x = \dfrac{-b}{2a}$